TOUCHED BY THE MOTHER

TOUCHED BY THE MOTHER

BLACK MEN, AMERICAN ART, FEMINIST HORIZONS

HUEY COPELAND

The University of Chicago Press
Chicago and London

The University of Chicago Press, Chicago 60637
The University of Chicago Press, Ltd., London

Published 2026

Printed in China

35 34 33 32 31 30 29 28 27 26   1 2 3 4 5

ISBN-13: 978-0-226-58125-5 (cloth)
ISBN-13: 978-0-226-58139-2 (paper)
ISBN-13: 978-0-226-58142-2 (ebook)

DOI: https://doi.org/10.7208/chicago/9780226581422.001.0001

Library of Congress Cataloging-in-Publication Data

Names: Copeland, Huey, author.

Title: Touched by the mother : Black men, American art, feminist horizons / Huey Copeland.
Other titles: Black men, American art, feminist horizons
Description: Chicago ; London : The University of Chicago Press, 2026. | Includes bibliographical references and index.
Identifiers: LCCN 2025035936 | ISBN 9780226581255 (cloth) | ISBN 9780226581392 (paperback) | ISBN 9780226581422 (ebook)
Subjects: LCSH: African American art. | African American artists. | Women, Black, in art. | Mothers in art. | Feminism and art.
Classification: LCC N6538.B53 C66 2026
LC record available at https://lccn.loc.gov/2025035936

⊚This paper meets the requirements of ANSI/NISO Z39.48-1992 (Permanence of Paper).

Authorized Representative for EU General Product Safety Regulation (GPSR) queries: **Easy Access System Europe**–Mustamäe tee 50, 10621 Tallinn, Estonia, gpsr.requests@easproject.com
Any other queries: https://press.uchicago.edu/press/contact.html

CONTENTS

PART III: REFRACTING MEMORY

PART IV: ART HISTORY AFTER INTERSECTIONALITY

Introduction

INCIDENTS IN THE LIFE OF A CORRECTING MIRROR

This book brings together twenty-five of my articles, essays, interviews, and reviews of the past twenty-odd years (2003–25), a period whose shifting antiblack logics once welcomed Obama's hope and now license Trump's revenge. In the main, the writings focus on black men's cultural production as well as a range of artistic practices that refract mainstream visual representations of black masculinity in the United States, from the assemblages of Noah Purifoy, constructed from the refuse of the Watts rebellion in 1966, to the opening of the National Museum of African American History and Culture in Washington, DC, in 2016. Taken together, the texts assembled in *Touched by the Mother* provide a multifaceted perspective on the means and methods of American art and discourse of the past fifty years; a collation of and farewell to the art historical methods in which I was trained; and an account of one black gay scholar's journey from graduate school to tenured professor, from a modernist art historian preoccupied with radical interventions to an interdisciplinary visual thinker oriented to black feminist horizons.

Most straightforwardly, *Touched by the Mother* offers an art-centered exploration of those pernicious dynamics that continue to frame African diasporic men as sites of violence, creativity, and contestation. For me—a public school–educated Gen Xer born and raised in the American Midwest—such concerns always felt particularly pressing in Chicago, where I was based for nearly twenty years, especially as the city struggled to stem ongoing gun violence and continues to wrestle with the spectacular murders of black males at the hands of police officers who usually go unpunished by the state or anyone else. While at times more visible than ever, the deaths of these men and boys are often immune to the consolations of justice, however conceived, because they are part and parcel of an infernal American tradition predicated on the waste and exploitation of ungendered black life that has its roots in the transatlantic slave trade and that is hardwired into the modern world's libidinal circuitry. In taking seriously the ongoing implications of these lethal economies, particularly for narratives of racial progress, the contributions in this book aim to extend the work of black male thinkers such as Ta-Nehisi Coates, Ralph Ellison, David Marriott, Kobena Mercer, and especially Frantz Fanon, the renowned Martinican theorist, psychiatrist, playwright, and activist whose writings of the 1950s transformed the cultural field.[1] His classic *Black Skin, White Masks* has consistently provided languages for articulating aspects of my embodied experience and has indelibly shaped my intellectual and professional life almost since my first days as an undergraduate at the University of Michigan in the mid-1990s.

"I came into the world imbued with the will to find a meaning in things, my spirit filled with the desire to attain to the source of the world, and then I found that I was an object in the midst of other objects."[2] These lines, drawn from the opening pages of Fanon's chapter "The Fact of Blackness," better translated as "The Lived Experience of the Black," provided the epigraph to the very first article I published, the coauthored introduction to "History, Representation, and the Impossible Subject of Race," a special dossier of the journal *Qui Parle* that I organized with Jared Sexton ("Raw Life," 2003).[3] Alongside Frank B. Wilderson III, Sexton was a comrade-in-arms in the struggle for black intellectual freedom during our graduate training in critical theory at the University of California, Berkeley; in an era that was ostensibly "postracial" and in which subjectivity itself was constantly "troubled," in the queer theorist Judith Butler's sense, Fanon was our lodestar.[4] While his work is notoriously limited when it comes to questions of gender and sexual difference—by Fanon's lights, the black woman has only one preoccupation, "to whiten the race"—his theorizations of objecthood, the effects of the white gaze, and the genitalization of the black male figure proved fundamental to my and so many other approaches to understanding the construction of black being in the visual field.[5]

Just as important, Fanon's often-neglected comments on artistic production in the subsequent chapter of *Black Skin, White Masks*, "The Negro and Psychopathology," have often buoyed my sense of what might be possible if the discipline of art history were ethically reconceptualized from blackness up. For Fanon:

> The *eye* is not merely a mirror, but a correcting mirror. The *eye* should make it possible for us to correct cultural errors. I do not say the *eyes*, I say the *eye*, and there is no mystery about what that *eye* refers to; not to the crevice in the skull but to that very uniform light that wells out of the reds of Van Gogh, that glides through a concerto of Tchaikovsky, that fastens itself desperately to Schiller's *Ode to Joy*, that allows itself to be conveyed by the worm-ridden bawling of Césaire.[6]

In these lines, which resonate deeply with the celebrated approaches to the visual elaborated by white French theorists—particularly those of the psychoanalyst Jacques Lacan, whose pathbreaking work continues to inform my thinking—Fanon attributes to art the power to correct our racialized and, I would add, gendered and sexuated modes of seeing. In practice, of course, this is easier said than done.[7] As we all know now, far from a site of black feminist liberation, visual art in the West has often travestied or erased those forms of difference that are, in fact, constitutive of its appearance before us.

For my part, since 2009, I have been preoccupied with a project—first imagined as an article, then as a book, now as a film treatment and exhibition, but ultimately best understood as a heuristic—that aims to apprehend the structural significance of the "black-fem," to borrow the ecocritic Chelsea Frazier's apt descriptor, for the making of the modern world and its visual regimes.[8] My work on that endeavor, *In the Shadow of the Negress: A Brief History of Modern Artistic Practice in the Transatlantic World*, has provided an implicit conceptual framework that crystallizes the concerns and ambitions of almost all of my writing since, so a few words on it are in order. In the project, I interrogate the ways in which race intersects with gender in artistic depictions of black womanhood typified by representations of the "negress." This recurring figure within European and American art takes us from Marie-Guillemine Benoist's *Portrait d'une négresse* (1800) to the silhouettes of the contemporary artist Kara Walker, who reimagines slavery from the perspective of, in her words, "an Emancipated Negress."

In exploring how the imaging and imagining of black female bodies actively constitutes artistic practice in the West, the *Shadow* has had transformative consequences for my thinking. An early iteration of it, focused on the Museum of Modern Art's checkered history with regard to racial justice and gender equality, is included in this volume as the introduction to the final section, "Art History After Intersectionality"; the text was shaped foremost by the pioneering scholarship of the African American art historian Judith Wilson, which has, since the 1980s, consistently centered the work and thought of black women ("In the Wake of the Negress," 2007/2010). Indeed, while questions of race and gender have long enjoyed central places in other areas of humanistic inquiry, most art historical discourse has been comparatively slow on the uptake. In the past three decades, however, the mainstream art world has afforded black women practitioners greater critical attention; scholars such as Barbara Thompson have begun to explore the visual history of black womanhood; and an increasing number of art historians, from Griselda Pollock to Darcy Grimaldo Grigsby, have pointed out the significance of black female figures in canonical eighteenth- and nineteenth-century European paintings.[9]

My research on and teaching with the *Negress* have convinced me of the absolute centrality of black women's figures and resistive practices to the history of modern art, spurring me to consider further ways in which the art historical script might be turned inside out in expanding and redrawing its key subjects, sites, and modes of material engagement. This was the impetus behind my critical return to and re-elaboration of Renée Ater's groundbreaking essay on the work of Meta Vaux Warrick Fuller, whose sculptures continue to serve as models of liberatory conscientization among African American art historians ("Making Black Feminist Art Histories," 2017). Around the same time, amid increasingly spectacularized murders of black men on US streets, I found myself thinking, "Well, what about the brothers? What would an art history from a black male perspective look like, particularly if we place black women at the heart of the Paris–to–New York narrative of modern art's evolution in the West?" I realized that in my occasional writings and conversations, many of which focused on the work of African diasporic male artists of my generation, I had already begun to formulate answers to these questions that might be collated and reframed to bring out their animating condition of possibility: namely, their necessary imbrication with and distance from the black maternal.

In this respect, *Touched by the Mother* takes its bearings from the field-turning scholarship of the black cultural theorist Hortense Spillers. I have been wrestling with and learning from Spillers since first reading her work in Saidiya Hartman's 1999 graduate seminar, "Histories of Slavery." In "Mama's Baby, Papa's Maybe: An American Grammar Book," her influential 1987 essay exploring the effects of slavery on African American constructions of gender and family, Spillers comes to an astonishing conclusion: because of the black father's inability to claim, protect, or even know his children in the context of bondage, she argues,

> the African-American male has been touched, therefore, by the *mother*, *handed by* her in ways that he cannot escape. . . . The black American male embodies the *only* community of males handed the specific occasion to learn *who* the female is within itself, the infant child who beats the life against the could-be fateful gamble, against the odds of pulverization and murder, including her own. It is the heritage of the *mother* that the African-American male must regain as an aspect of his own personhood—the power of "yes" to the "female" within.[10]

Now, the first thing that must be attended to is Spillers's use of quotation marks around "yes" and "female" in that last clause—rightly so, given that her effort in the foregoing pages is to demonstrate the radical *un*gendering of the black body, its reduction to mere flesh, within the conditions of enslavement. Thus, to respond affirmatively to the "'female' within" is, despite the odds, to recover gender as a meaningful space of embodiment for black folks *and* to embrace those aspects of the self that typical gender categories would foreclose.

Such a gambit, of course, is neither without risks nor a guarantor of a liberatory ethos. First, we must contend with the ambivalence of touch itself, which can nurture and harm, sometimes both at once; this is underscored by how quickly Spillers slides from "touched" to "handed," which can suggest a slap to the face as much as a gift given.[11] As Rizvana Bradley explains, in "Spillers's account, touch emerges in the first instance as a singularly violent immediacy to which the black is always already subject. Touch cuts two ways; it might be understood as the gateway to the most intimate experience of exchange and mutuality between subjects, or taken as the fundamental element of the absence of self-ownership."[12] And to be sure, the maternal touch is equally charged, as shown by Hartman in *Lose Your Mother: A Journey Along the Atlantic Slave Route*, in which she adamantly refuses the romantic and particularly African American vision of Africa as a lost motherland, a site of wholeness and Edenic fantasy. Instead, she comes to embrace her structural inheritance as the issue of slaves, a stranger in search of strangers who together might *make* community rather than having it *handed* to them.[13] For me, then, to be "touched by the mother" is to sit with such ambivalences in reaching toward a black feminist approach to life and work that the strictures of art history would all too often foreclose.

This orientation has several implications for *Touched by the Mother*'s content and structure. It must be said, for one, that the book does not aim to provide an exhaustive survey of mother-and-child imagery within the twentieth-century African American visual tradition. Such works, including, say, Sargent Johnson's play on the dyadic theme, *Forever Free*, are surely of interest, yet they risk forwarding a normative assumption of familial suturing that, as Spillers makes clear, African Americans have never been able to rely on given our structural vulnerability to violence and the always already attenuated status of kinship ties (Fig. I.1). Like later works in this tradition, such as Romare Bearden's 1974 collage *Morning*, with its enigmatic central pairing, the pieces in *Touched by the Mother* at once index and undermine fantasies of unified, repaired, and riven mother-child relations, sometimes all at once, engaging closeness and distance, presence and absence, to argue that the touch of the mother can be felt and must be considered even when she is not literally represented. In this way, the book, like the Bearden, lingers with and gradually homes in on the formative influence of the black maternal, providing a retrospective protocol for reading both my own work and that of the practitioners whose art, exhibitions, and writings I have engaged.

Many of the African American gay cultural figures featured in these pages—whether the writer and curator Hilton Als or the artist Glenn Ligon—are

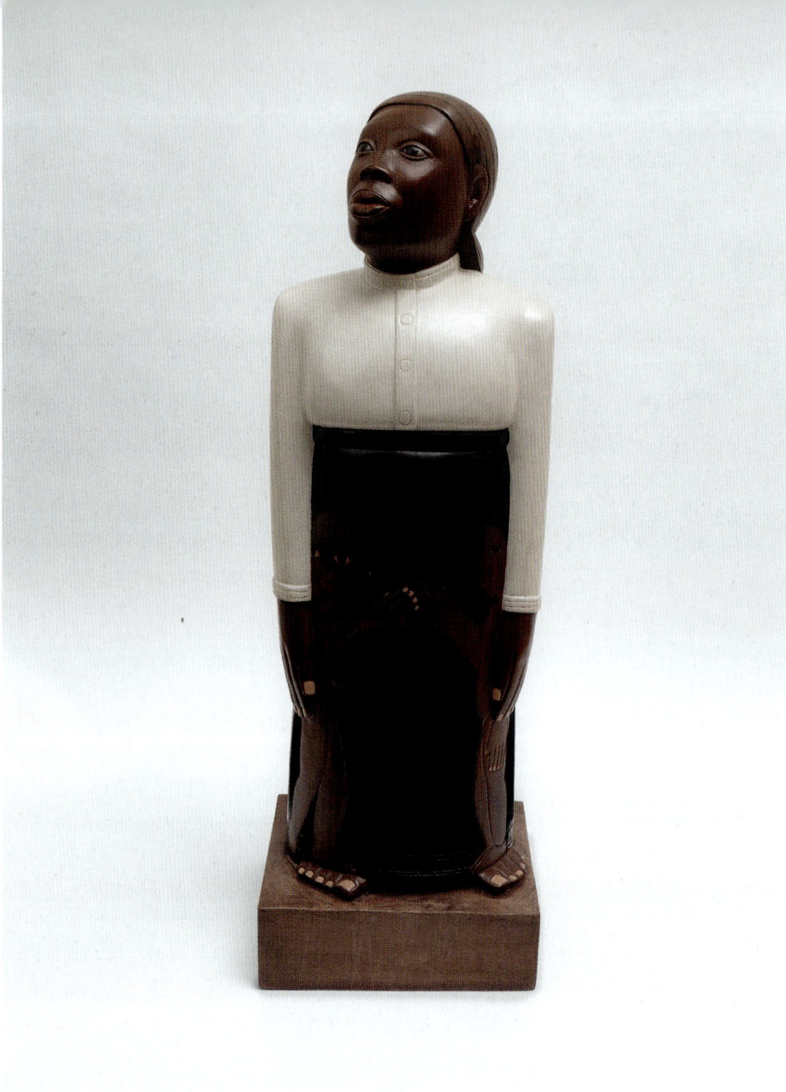

Figure I.1

Sargent Johnson, *Forever Free*, 1933. Paint and wood, 36 × 11½ × 9½ in. (91.44 cm × 29.21 cm × 24.13 cm). San Francisco Museum of Modern Art; gift of Mrs. E. D. Lederman. © Estate of Sargent Johnson. Photo: Don Ross.

also of a similar cast of mind. I think, on this score, of Mark Bradford, the Los Angeles–based MacArthur "Genius" Fellowship–winning artist initially acclaimed for his quasi-abstract paintings, such as *Enter and Exit the New Negro* [2000; see fig. 7.2 on p. 99], made from perming endpapers sourced from his mother's beauty shop where he used to work. His art, I argue, stages an experience of vision that is not only at odds with the way in which racialized or gendered perception often operates, but is also actively invested in expanding the visual to embrace the tactile, the haptic, and the sonic, which must always be juxtaposed with one another given how often they are despotically mobilized against black-fem bodies. This feminist perspective animates Bradford's life and work, particularly Art+Practice, the cultural hub he launched in L.A.'s Leimert Park neighborhood with his partner, the activist Alan DiCastro, and the philanthropist Eileen Harris Norton, in order to provide exposure to contemporary art and on-the-ground training for foster kids in the historically underserved African American community.

Touched by the Mother includes my early writing on Bradford ("A Range of Convergences," 2011), as well as a conversation in which the artist explains that, for him, black women, regardless of their orientation to "properly" feminist frameworks, have always served as role models "who have demanded life on their own terms" ("Painting After All," 2014). Both the artist and his elders have learned to negotiate what the theorist Joy James would call their status as "captive maternals"—those who, regardless of biological sex or social gender, are "tied to the state's violence through their non-transferable agency they have to care for another."[14] At the same time, Bradford's words, and the interview format itself, speak well to the importance of dialogical engagements with the contemporary artists I have had the privilege of working with, on, and alongside. The book features a conversation with Als and the museum director Thelma Golden ("'Looking Back at *Black Male*,'" 2014), as well as an interview with Wilderson ("Red, Black, and Blue," 2017), so as to highlight the centrality of collaboration to ethical research on contemporary art and culture. The same impetus animates my dialogue with the white queer artist Zoe Leonard about her work's reframing of archives intent on black-fem disappearance ("Photography, the Archive, and the Question of Feminist Form," 2013) and my interview with the curator Allison Glenn, whose praxis—emblematized by the exhibition she mounted in remembrance of Breonna Taylor, an African American woman senselessly murdered by the police—so generatively models black feminist care and convening ("Taking Care," 2021).

In this sense, the book is also indebted to the work of Fred Moten, particularly his and Stefano Harney's notion of "black study," that communal, informal mode of thinking and being together that is just as important to knowledge formation as experiences within institutional structures—and doubtless more affirming for black-fems invested in carving out spaces of nonhierarchical joy and engagement.[15] Though not always named as such, a similar impulse can, I think, be felt percolating within the practices of African American men who take their cues from black women's traditions of self-fashioning and cultural repair, such as the Chicago social practice artist Theaster Gates, the subject of an *Artforum* feature ("Dark Mirrors," 2013). In forwarding such an approach, my aim is neither to impose an essentializing frame on Gates nor to make the case that all these black men's works are feminist. Rather, in bringing together black feminist lines of inquiry alongside my work with, by, and about men of African descent—including artistic and curatorial projects by David Hammons ("Already-made," 2021; unpublished), Barkley Hendricks ("Figures and Grounds,"

2009), and Hamza Walker ("The Blackness of Blackness," 2008)—I hope to accent the radical multiplicity and particularity of their engagements; at the same time, I point toward the horizons opened up within artistic practices by and about black men that are necessarily, if differentially, touched by the mother. Thus shaped by Hartman's, Moten's, and Spillers's critical approaches to black culture, *Touched by the Mother* addresses the wide range of forms—assemblage, exhibition, painting, performance, photography, social practice, sculpture, video, and writing—that have shaped the aesthetic field over the past half century, thereby providing an overview similar in spirit to that offered by *A House Divided: American Art Since 1955*, an essay collection penned by my PhD adviser, the feminist art historian Anne M. Wagner.[16]

The pieces selected here from over seventy-five publications tend to move from monographic foci to dialogic exchanges—as emblematized by my repeated engagements with the art of Glenn Ligon ("Untitled [Jackpot!]," 2005; "I AM A MAN and the Writing of Afrotropic Art Histories," 2025)—and eventually to more symptomatic accounts of aesthetic eras, tendencies, and conceptual trajectories ("Unfinished Business as Usual," 2014). With the exception of those gathered in Part III, the contributions are, for the most part, ordered chronologically by date of completion rather than publication, with both dates noted in the text and in the table of contents when there is a discrepancy between the two. This tack allows the consistency of certain investments across writerly modes to come to the fore and indexes the varying time lags that shape academic publishing as well as the historiographic record. The collection's variety of modes for advancing knowledge of artistic practices is, I hope, one of its strengths.

In bringing together essays from exhibition catalogs with limited initial runs that are now out of print, articles and interviews from journals usually only accessible to academics, and reviews in commercial magazines occasioned by an exhibition but aimed at intervening in broader artistic discourses, the volume not only gathers disparate forms and audiences but also underlines the ongoing necessity of on-site library and archival research—above and beyond digital scraping—for deep understandings of contemporary art and artists. With that in mind, I have added relevant citations to reviews that originally ran without them and also author's notes at the outset of certain essays to further frame the pieces' original contexts and my contemporaneous research on them. Otherwise, I have not substantively altered or updated the texts in order to maintain their writerly texture and to accentuate their historical resonances. However, the entire manuscript has been edited to fall in line with Chicago style conventions and to correct factual or grammatical errors that appeared in the original publications. While the writings can and should be read together, particularly by section, each stands on its own.[17]

The book's first part, "Post Black Male," begins to engage black radical thought, especially that of Fanon, across a range of writerly modes and in relation to the work of specific practitioners—Ligon, Walker, Kori Newkirk ("A Family Resemblance," 2007), and Lorna Simpson ("Outtakes," 2008)—as I first gained a professional footing in the art and academic worlds after earning my PhD and landing my first full-time position at Northwestern University just outside Chicago. In these years, the beating of Rodney King, the lapses of multiculturalism, and Golden's curatorial interventions—particularly her exhibitions *Black Male* (1994) and *Freestyle* (2001), which introduced the notion of post-blackness—provided vital frames of reference for identifying the temporal specificity and historical continuity of recent African diasporic critical praxis.[18] The title of Part II, "The Signifier's Work," is inspired by a rather different if no less telling source, the post-structuralist art historian Rosalind Krauss. She once defined the critic's responsibility as honoring artists' *work* on the signifier, that at once semiotic and material manipulation, which determines "what sorts of meanings can arise," whether in tension with or in opposition to the artwork's signified or ostensible content.[19] Accordingly, this section, comprised primarily of features written for mainstream publications, finds a young assistant professor not only thinking blackness as an artistic material, but further developing it as an analytical framework that enables us to see how African American male artists, from Clifford Owens ("*Mal d'Anthologie*," 2012) to Dave McKenzie ("*Babel* Screened," 2011/2013), at once carefully engage their chosen media and open up angles that radically disrupt the unspoken white supremacy of the aesthetic fields in which they operate and the anti-black metaphysics that subtend them.

Part III, "Refracting Memory"—a play on the title of the Algerian French artist Kader Attia's 2016 film essay, *Reflecting Memory*, in which I was a featured commentator—contains the bulk of the interviews, foregrounding my increased interest in dialogical modes and my increasingly explicit self-positioning as a student of black culture. At the same time, I sought to make interventions that mattered beyond art history and engaged more broadly with current discourses in Africana studies that I hoped to revise and contest, such as the then-emerging critical momentum surrounding "Afrofuturism" ("Solar Ethics," 2018; unpublished). "Art History After Intersectionality," the book's fourth and final part, tracks the development of my black feminist conscientization, autocitational tactics, and narrative voicing: while "Flow and Arrest" (2015) offers a reflection on method after the publication of my first book, *Bound to Appear*, the newer essays "Necessary Abstractions" (2019/2023) and "Alreadymade" (2021) see that method mobilized to theorize, respectively, nonobjective painting of the second half of the twentieth century and the Western readymade sculptural tradition in relationship to black women's structural position in the modern world.[20] That ambition also characterizes my self-reflective return to Ligon's early work in the collection's penultimate essay, which is followed by the conversation with Allison Glenn; it seems only fitting that a black woman at the leading edge of artistic and curatorial practice should have the book's final word.

Like Kellie Jones's *EyeMinded*, *Touched by the Mother* is not shy, when needed, about revealing its author's implication in the processes through which knowledge of black culture is circulated and produced.[21] Over the two decades that the book encompasses, I have had the opportunity to sit for several artists—as myself for Attia and LaMont Hamilton, as Tina Turner alongside Anika Burt's Ike for Derek Jackson in the 2003 photograph *Ike and Tina with Their Genders and Roles Reversed* (Fig. I.2), and as a generic black male type for Lorna Simpson. Writing about my experience as the New York conceptualist's model for the 2003 series, *Cameos and Appearances*, became a spur for my art historical investigation of how men signify within her practice. This tack characterizes several pieces reprinted here, including my affective account of an Alicia Hall Moran *soirée musicale* in Cambridge, Massachusetts, that I took in with the artists Adam Pendleton and Hank Willis Thomas ("Northern Soul," 2011).

In each of these instances, a personal reflection serves as the motor for art historical narration and underlines the various roles—audience, collaborator, critic, curator, friend, model, and scholar—that many of us working in the contemporary visual field now play, particularly as the distinctions between such positions have continued to blur over the past fifty years. This focus on the "I" in my work has been licensed in equal parts by black feminist scholars like bell hooks as well as by art historians such as Krauss and my dissertation's second reader, T. J. Clark, who have served as touchstones, interlocutors, and agonists throughout my career. The emphasis on the "I" is also, perhaps, as the French curator Caroline Honorien suggested to me, demanded by the African American slave narrative tradition, with its continual refrain, "I was born."[22] As in those texts, the "I" in my writing, like Fanon's eye, is a kind of correcting mirror: a device intended to locate myself and my limitations within the field of knowledge, as well as a performative utterance meant to intervene in the constitution of that field, which too often sacrifices the personal for the proper, the ambivalent for the authoritative.

When all is said and done, I want to position myself less in relation to the spectacular visualization of black masculinity in the public sphere and more in the context of those personal, familial, and professional relationships that have had such a profound impact on my approach to the writing of black feminist art histories. As such, *Touched by the Mother* is also an homage to the many maternals who have—like Als, Golden, Hartman, Ligon, and Spillers—touched me deeply as mentors and cultural practitioners. This list could easily go on, but it would not be complete without

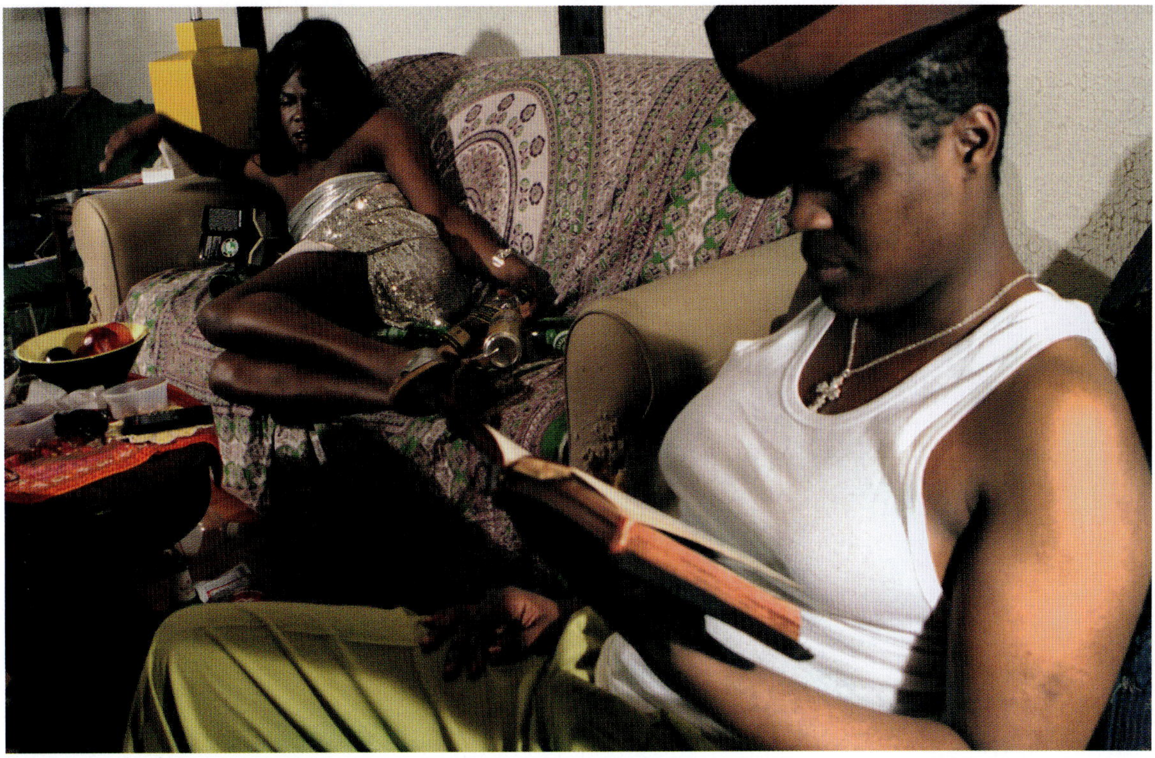

Figure I.2
Derek Jackson, *Ike and Tina with Their Genders and Roles Reversed*, 2003.
Courtesy of the artist.

my father, Huey Copeland I, who more than once appears as a character in my work, or my own black radical mother, Mary Towns Copeland, a "firebrand," social worker, and organic intellectual born and raised in the segregated South.[23] Mrs. Copeland nourished me in every sense, providing a model of ethical engagement with the world and of ruthless critical judgment through her ceaseless advocacy on behalf of black youth, her cutting critiques of the American sociopolitical order, and a sprawling library filled with the writing of folks like Maya Angelou, Stokely Carmichael, and Ivan Van Sertima. My hope is that *Touched by the Mother* will sit well on her shelf and alongside the work of Jones and other queer and feminist art writers such as Richard Meyer and Renée Green, whose work also acknowledges rather than suppresses the complexities generated by lived entanglements with art and culture.[24]

Despite such black feminist role models throughout my life, my path toward a truly intersectional scholarly praxis—in Kimberlé Crenshaw's original sense of attending to "the various ways in which race and gender interact to shape the multiple dimensions of Black women's . . . experiences"—has been a halting, uneven, and recursive journey, not unlike those of many of the practitioners engaged in this book.[25] At times hopeful but united even in despair, we are each differentially touched by and responsive to the mother, who provides the very precondition for our being in the world. It is that maternal pulse or beat, at times submerged, that I have come to tend toward in my art historical work and that the final pieces in the volume aim to make sensible. However, the fraught relation between black masculinity and the maternal has been a long-standing intellectual preoccupation, first crystallized for me in writing about the nineteenth-century abolitionist, former slave, and orator Frederick Douglass in Hartman's seminar.

In Douglass's three autobiographies, I discovered, it is both reason and remembrance that allow him to chart the movement from slave to free, to remake his life as a story to tell himself. As much as he downplays his literary achievements, emphasizing instead his physical battles with and arduous travails against white male mastery, it is the practice of writing that lies at the core of his project. The effects of this rewriting are nowhere more apparent than in the shift between the first two books in his description of his mother. In his initial 1845 *Narrative of the Life of Frederick Douglass*, she is a specter with whom he has little or no relation, simply a memory he can hardly make visible on the page, always displaced by the inescapable presence of Douglass's master and father.[26] Yet in his second life story, published ten years later, she assumes greater importance: a woman who can read and write, who rallies to her son's defense and makes the best she can of motherhood. She begins, in other words, to attain all those characteristics that Douglass might aspire to himself, yet "the image is mute, and I have no striking words of hers treasured up."[27] Because she cannot be recalled as a speaking subject, Douglass's mother must always remain a fantasy conjured from elsewhere, yet her silence allows her to remain a site of projective desire and identification, a place of ideality created by the irrepressible logic of forgetting. The persistence of this woman in his memory underlines the constructive and indeed constitutive work that she and his aunt Hester do for Douglass, as well as for the many black male practitioners who would follow in their wake.

Subsequently, I have found myself turning less to Douglass and more to Harriet Jacobs's *Incidents in the Life of a Slave Girl, Written by Herself* [1861], which details how she spent seven years hiding from and surveilling her master in a tiny garret above her grandmother's attic. Her text, while autobiographical, declares its allegiance to fictive devices right from the beginning, posing "Linda Brent" rather than Jacobs herself as the subject of the harrowing events that follow. This allows Jacobs to create a psychic and textual distance between herself and her avatar that imbues the work with the turns and twists of a more novelistic treatment, a fiction more real than life. For her, writing itself is a tool for subterfuge, especially given the layering of subjects and speaking positions that populate the textual and historical record. Numerous incidents in the book posit the written word as a vehicle of seduction: the amorous notes sent by her master "Flint," on the one hand, and, on the other, her own letters, written in self-imposed imprisonment, smuggled out of hiding, and then sent to her grandmother to make it appear as if she had indeed escaped north. Here, language is a subversive measure of defense that is not backed up by violence as it must be for Douglass, yet because it *is* so staged, so capacious in scope, Jacobs's story somehow has a greater ring of truth.[28]

I think this difference is a manifestation of a larger divergence between the two writers and their concepts of subjection. By Jacobs's lights, subjectivity and recognition are not "achieved" through attempting to accede to some externally imposed ideal of womanhood; rather, they are *approached* through a process of becoming only glanced asymptotically within the intersubjective relation. Like Douglass, she becomes subject to and receives recognition within the crucible of slavery but also through the extensibility of pain, for in explaining her travails to the reader, she creates a space in language for us to dwell. She helps us understand, in the words of the philosopher Veena Das, "how one should inhabit a world that has been made strange through the desolating experience of violence and loss."[29]

To center such concerns in working toward an art history PhD circa 2003 was not impossible to imagine but difficult to undertake given my experience of the discipline. Art history, to borrow a phrase from the poet and theorist Dionne Brand, is the mode of coloniality that made me.[30] To find a voice within that foundationally antiblack field was necessarily to engage in a process of queer reading and active disidentification as I was interpellated by text, image, and discourse, pressing me to question traditional habits of looking, to push against the tyranny of visual evidence in search of black cultural intelligence, and to explore the economies of power that produce artworks themselves as much as the relations that pertain within a given aesthetic formation. Thankfully, I had the model of Jacobs and her progeny at hand, groundbreaking black-fem rethinkings of the aesthetic that would license, orient, and inspire my writing at the intersection of modern art and black study. My work has dwelled within this gap, but now it reaches toward a black feminist horizon and to different modes of engagement, whatever form they might take.

Philadelphia, May 2025

Notes

1. Ta-Nehisi Coates, *Between the World and Me* (Spiegel & Grau, 2015); Ralph Ellison, *Shadow and Act* (1953) (Vintage Books, 1995); David Marriott, *On Black Men* (Columbia University Press, 2001); Kobena Mercer, "Reading Racial Fetishism: The Photographs of Robert Mapplethorpe," in

Welcome to the Jungle: New Positions in Black Cultural Studies (Routledge, 1994), 171–219; Frantz Fanon, *Black Skin, White Masks*, trans. Charles Lam Markmann (1952; Grove Press, 1967). For important rejoinders, see bell hooks, *We Real Cool: Black Men and Masculinity* (Routledge, 2003); Jared Sexton, *Black Men, Black Feminism: Lucifer's Nocturne* (Palgrave, 2018).

2. Fanon, *Black Skin, White Masks*, 109.

3. For a useful summary of the implications of these two different English translations of Fanon's title for black cultural study, see Sampada Aranke, *Death's Futurity: The Visual Life of Black Power* (Duke University Press), 78–80. For a far-reaching engagement with and revision of "Raw Life"'s key terms of articulation from which I continue to learn, see Fred Moten, "The Case of Blackness," *Criticism* 50, no. 2 (Spring 2008): 177–218.

4. See Judith Butler, *Gender Trouble: Feminism and the Subversion of Identity* (Routledge, 1990).

5. Fanon, *Black Skin, White Masks*, 47.

6. Fanon, *Black Skin, White Masks*, 202; emphases original.

7. I think here of Jacques Lacan, "The Line and Light," in *The Seminar of Jacques Lacan, Book XI: The Four Fundamental Concepts of Psychoanalysis*, trans. Alan Sheridan, ed. Jacques-Alain Miller (W. W. Norton, 1981); and Maurice Merleau-Ponty, "Cézanne's Doubt," in *Sense and Non-Sense*, trans. Hubert L. Dreyfus and Patricia Allen Dreyfus (Northwestern University Press, 1964), 9–25.

8. A note on terminology: In general, unless I am quoting another writer or heeding the style conventions of a given publication, "black" is not capitalized in this book even when referring to people of African descent, so as to maintain and accentuate the storied multivalence of blackness in the visual field. Similarly, I have maintained originally gendered language in addressing the reader or viewer. Although my work variously, if not always interchangeably, uses several terms for beings positioned at the intersection of blackness and femininity, I am inspired by Chelsea Frazier's theorization of "black-fem," which offers a capacious framework for thinking the gendered and racialized violence of white, capitalist cisheteropatriarchy and a specific call to identify the liminal spaces that connect cis and trans black women, black females, and black (queer) femmes. See Chelsea Frazier, "Thinking Red, Wounds and Fungi in Wangechi Mutu's EcoArt," in *Ecologies, Agents, Terrains*, ed. Christopher P. Heuer and Rebecca Zorach (Yale University Press, 2018), 167–94.

9. Barbara Thompson, ed., *Black Womanhood: Images, Icons, and Ideologies of the African Body* (Hood Museum of Art, Dartmouth College; and University of Washington Press, 2008); Griselda Pollock, "A Tale of Three Women," in *Differencing the Canon: Feminist Desire and the Writing of Art's Histories* (Routledge, 1999), 246–315; Darcy Grimaldo Grigsby, "Still Thinking about *Olympia*'s Maid," *Art Bulletin* 97, no. 4 (December 2015): 430–51.

10. Hortense J. Spillers, "Mama's Baby, Papa's Maybe: An American Grammar Book," *Diacritics* 17, no. 2 (Summer 1987): 80; emphases original.

11. Spillers, "Mama's Baby, Papa's Maybe," 80. See also Hortense J. Spillers, "To the Bone: Some Speculations on the Problem of Touch," November 19, 2018, https://gendersexuality.northwestern.edu/about/news/video-hortense-spillers-to-the-bone-some-speculations-on-the-problem-of-touch.html; Rizvana Bradley, "The Vicissitudes of Touch," *boundary 2*,

November 21, 2020, https://www.boundary2.org/2020/11/rizvana-bradley-the-vicissitudes-of-touch-annotations-on-the-haptic/.

12. Rizvana Bradley, *Anteaesthetics: Black Aesthesis and the Critique of Form* (Stanford University Press, 2023), 96.

13. Saidiya Hartman, *Lose Your Mother: A Journey Along the Atlantic Slave Route* (Farrar, Straus & Giroux, 2007).

14. Joy James, https://sites.williams.edu/jjames/captive-maternals/. Also see Joy James, "The Womb of Western Theory: Trauma, Time Theft, and the Captive Maternal," *Carceral Notebooks* 12 (2016): 253–95.

15. Stefano Harney and Fred Moten, *The Undercommons: Fugitive Planning and Black Study* (Minor Compositions, 2013), 110.

16. Anne Middleton Wagner, *A House Divided: American Art Since 1955* (University of California Press, 2011).

17. For a general discussion of my art historical method, see my remarks in Jarrett Earnest, "Huey Copeland," in *What It Means to Write About Art: Interviews with Art Critics* (David Zwirner Books and DAP, 2018), 68–82.

18. See Thelma Golden, *Black Male: Representations of Masculinity in Contemporary American Art*, exh. cat. (Whitney Museum of American Art; distributed by Harry N. Abrams, 1994; and Golden, "Introduction: Post . . . ," in *Freestyle*, exh. cat. (Studio Museum in Harlem, 2001), 14.

19. See Krauss's comments on Cindy Sherman in Hal Foster, Rosalind Krauss, Silvia Kolbowski, Miwon Kwon, and Benjamin Buchloh, "The Politics of the Signifier: A Conversation on the Whitney Biennial," *October* 66 (Fall 1993): 21.

20. See Huey Copeland, *Bound to Appear: Art, Slavery, and the Site of Blackness in Multicultural America* (University of Chicago Press, 2013).

21. Kellie Jones, *EyeMinded: Living and Writing Contemporary Art* (Duke University Press, 2011).

22. See, respectively, T. J. Clark, *The Sight of Death: An Experiment in Art Writing* (Yale University Press, 2008); Rosalind Krauss, *The Optical Unconscious* (MIT Press, 1994); James Olney, "'I was Born': Slave Narratives, Their Status as Autobiography and as Literature," in *The Slave's Narrative*, ed. Charles T. Davis and Henry Louis Gates Jr. (Oxford University Press, 1985), 155.

23. As a college student, Towns earned a reputation as a firebrand—in the words of the white history professor Don Baldridge—thanks to her advocacy of social integration and her demand for black faculty at Southern State College, located in her hometown, Magnolia, Arkansas. For a more expansive treatment of this episode and its significance within civil rights history, see Paula Killian Agee, "Pickings v. Bruce: Students United for Rights and Equality," *First Amendment Studies in Arkansas: The Richard S. Arnold Essays*, ed. Stephen A. Smith (University of Arkansas Press, 2016), 1-21.

24. Here I have in mind Kellie Jones, "In the Thick of It: David Hammons and Hair Culture in the 1970s," *Third Text* 44 (Autumn 1998): 17-24; Richard Meyer, "'Artists sometimes have feelings,'" *Art Journal* 67, no. 4 (Winter 2008): 38–55; Renée Green, *Other Planes of There: Selected Writings* (Duke University Press, 2014).

25. See Kimberlé Williams Crenshaw, "Mapping the Margins: Intersectionality, Identity, and Violence Against Women of Color," *Stanford Law Review* 43, no. 6 (July 1991): 1244; Kimberlé Williams Crenshaw, "Demarginalizing the Intersection of Race and Sex: A Black Feminist Critique of Antidiscrim-

ination Doctrine, Feminist Theory, and Antiracist Politics," *University of Chicago Legal Forum* 1 (1989): 139-67.

26. Frederick Douglass, *Narrative of the Life of Frederick Douglass* (1845; Dover Publications, 1995), 20.

27. Frederick Douglass, *My Bondage and My Freedom* (1855; Dover Publications, 1969), 57. Douglass's third and final biography, *The Life and Times*, first published in 1881 and then revised in 1892, extends this process of fabulating a fleshly maternal presence from the shreds of memory.

28. Harriet Jacobs, *Incidents in the Life of a Slave Girl, Written by Herself* [1861], ed. Jean Fagin Yellin (Harvard University Press, 1987).

29. Veena Das, "Language and Body: Transactions in the Construction of Pain," in *Social Suffering*, ed. Arthur Kleinman, Veena Das, and Margaret Lock (University of California Press, 1997), 67.

30. Dionne Brand, *An Autobiography of the Autobiography of Reading* (University of Alberta Press, 2020), 13.

PART I

POST BLACK MALE

1

RAW LIFE with Jared Sexton

I came into the world imbued with the will to find a meaning in things, my spirit filled with the desire to attain to the source of the world, and then I found that I was an object in the midst of other objects.

Frantz Fanon, *Black Skin, White Masks*, 1967[1]

What does it mean to be that object "in the midst of other objects," the thing against which all other subjects take their bearing? What is it to live in the domain of nonexistence, to inhabit an impossible time between life and death, when one simply cannot be sure whether one is here or there, alive or dead? "In other words, how is it possible to live while going to death, while being somehow already dead"?[2]

To speak in such terms, of "a fatal way of being alive,"[3] is not philosophical concision. It is, rather, the signature of the unthought position,[4] that which can only be imagined through its affective dimension. How might it feel to be that sort of problem,[5] a scandal to ontology, an outrage to every marker of the human? What, in the final analysis, does it mean to suffer? This question, which underwrites the opening of the New World and the making of the modern one, is, quite literally, unapproachable; one cannot get near to it, approximate an answer, or fabricate a just response. Not without erasing the enigma that is race, not without annihilating the dreaded presence of that other whose radical eccentricity to the life of society generates such fundamental anxiety—here and now, back then, for the foreseeable future. Everyone encounters it, lives it, indelibly preceded by "a constellation of postulates, a series of propositions."[6]

It is at this impasse and with such questions that the essays collected here begin: with the notion derived from Fanon, of the impossibility of representing race, either for the slave or for the master, outside of an

This article first appeared in *Qui Parle* 13, no. 2 (Spring-Summer 2003): 53-62. *Qui Parle* is currently published by Duke University Press.

entrenched visual schema predicated on the fungibility of the black body. That this reckoning comes to the fore at this moment and that it connects cultural practitioners working across a range of disciplines—art, history, literature, film, critical theory—not only suggests the longevity of Fanon's insight but also underlines the pressing need to think the structural and structuring function of racial difference for our symbolic economies.

For it is that very function which contemporary racial theory more often than not seeks to leap over, in the process revealing its own ineffectuality, a kind of willful blindness that cannot be overstated. In its single-minded capacity to concentrate on everything except that which matters most in the restructuring of white supremacy, such theory is undoubtedly more egregious than intellectual faux pas or public disservice. It is a modality of complicity, or better, fraud. But the fraudulence of this diverse intellectual project is not only analytic; it is also ethical. Besieged by the conservative restoration, the Left finds itself today enamored of political pragmatism and in thrall to the lures of counterhegemonic populism. From the emergent networks of anti-globalization to the reinvigorated peace movement, from the embattled environmentalist campaigns to the desperate efforts at urban police reform, the official rhetoric is multiracial and the organizational logic is coalition. Yet, for whatever energies are dispensed in elaborating the new complexity of race in the age of globality, the radical imagination inexorably comes to rest on the assumption of horizontality, that is to say, a progressive community-in-struggle, even if only a possible one.

Indeed, it has become commonplace in the United States to call for a paradigm shift with respect to racial theory and the politics of antiracism. This clarion call resonates in the ivory towers of academe, in the pages of the most useless print media outlets, certainly in the alternative press, and in the policy papers and strategic deliberations of progressive non-profit institutes and community-based organizations. What we are told, in a variety of tones and tenors, is that race matters are no longer—if they ever were—"simply black and white." At the least, the focus of such a Manichean lens is deemed inadequate to apprehend the current and historical reality of US racial formation (to say nothing of the Americas more generally or other regions of the world). At its worst, this dichotomous view is rendered as politically stunting and, moreover, as effectively excluding "discussion of the colors in the middle, now inexorable parts of the Black/white spectrum."[7] We now enjoy a vast literature in the social sciences and humanities detailing the vexed position (or positions) between the black and the white. "Neither black nor white" thus indicates not only the articulation of multiracial (or mixed-race) identity claims in the post–civil rights era[8] but also the contemporary reformulations of critique and political mobilization among Asian Americans, Pacific Islanders, Chicana/os, Latina/as, and Native American peoples.[9]

Of course, racial discourse in what would become the United States, from the colonial era onward, has always been multipolar, so to speak, and the psychodynamics of race have always been quite complex; the lines of force and the relations of racial power have been reconfigured regularly across a multiplicity of times and spaces. In fact, the notion of a black/white paradigm is something of a theoretical fiction, deployed for a wide range of purposes. In our attempts to displace it, then, we do well to recognize it as a recent emergence, involved in an imaginary lure that says more about the historical preoccupations of white supremacy than it does about, say, the blind insistence of black scholars, activists, or communities.[10] When perusing the critical literature on the "explanatory difficulty"[11] of present-day racial politics, one frequently wonders exactly to whom the demand to go "beyond black and white" is being addressed. Also puzzling is the singularly incoherent nature of the reasoning demonstrated in current race talk, a failure, that is, to offer cogent accounts of the implications of this newfound (or, more precisely, rediscovered) complexity.[12] Taken together, these twin ambiguities beg a key question: what economies of enunciation are involved in this broadly patterned discursive gesture to put an end to "biracial theorizing"?

The legal scholar Mari Matsuda offers a provocative thought on this score. During a symposium on critical race theory at the Yale Law School in 1997, she claimed:

> We when say we need to move beyond Black and white, this is what a whole lot of people say or feel or think: "Thank goodness we can get off that paradigm, because those Black people made me feel so uncomfortable. I know all about Blacks, but I really don't know anything about Asians, and while we're deconstructing that Black-white paradigm, we also need to reconsider the category of race altogether, since race, as you know, is a constructed category, and thank god I don't have to take those angry black people seriously anymore."[13]

Importantly, the comment is drawn from an otherwise sympathetic meditation on a particular danger attendant to the desire for new analyses, and the often anxious drive for multiracial coalition, namely, the persistent risk of forgetting the centrality of antiblackness to global white supremacy.[14] Fanon, again, is prescient: "Wherever he goes, the Negro remains a Negro."[15] Wherever; there is no outside. Too often we forget, here in the United States especially, that there are blacks everywhere. When so many speak of the peculiarity of race as a North American obsession (one hears of the odd rigidity of the Anglo-Saxon racial formation), it is important to think about black people as situated in those myriad locales supposedly outside of or alternate to the black-white binary. Lewis Gordon, philosopher and leading contemporary commentator on Fanon, writes:

> Although there are people who function as "the blacks" of particular contexts, there is a group of people who function as the blacks everywhere. They are called, in now-archaic language—Negroes. Negroes are the blacks of everywhere, the black blacks, the blackest blacks. Blackness functions as the prime racial signifier. It is the element that enters a room and frightens Reason out. The historical specificity of blackness as a point from which the greatest distance must be forged entails its status as metaphor.[16]

It is from firmly within this global context—what Gordon aptly calls *the antiblack world*—that we might begin to think beyond black and white, if by that we mean to think about those who are "neither black nor white" (or those who are "black and . . .") in their concrete, and not analogical, relations to blackness and whiteness. The diverse practices of racialization and the shifting race rules that characterize the long career of white supremacy gather overarching consistency at the site of the black body. If whiteness constructs itself as "raceless,"[17] then blackness becomes the depository of the most concentrated racialized essence, a matrix of value organized, in large part, by ratios or gradients of color.[18] "In the antiblack world there is but one race, and that race is black. Thus, to be racialized is to be pushed 'down' toward blackness, and to be deracialized is to be pushed 'up' toward whiteness."[19] This does not mean, of course, that there are only blacks and whites in some anthropological sense. It does not mean that political reality with regard to race simply reduces to two positions, two histories, or two struggles. Rather, it is to say that the vectors of the "international racial hierarchy"[20]—with its black and white extremities—can and should be brought to bear on every discussion. In this light, one might productively read both the resonance and divergence among the articles that follow, a strategy that may highlight and contemplate (perhaps by proxy) a tension often left unremarked in Fanon between the specificity of his analysis of Negrophobia and the generality of his comments on the dehumanization of the native, the colonized, "the wretched of the earth." The challenge, of course, is to think both at once, and it is a challenge that the pieces collected in this dossier take as their own.

In refusing the flattening of racial hierarchy into a rainbow-colored affair—whether multiculturalism's celebratory play of difference or postmodernism's often apolitical de-essentialization of the subject—the thinkers assembled here work to put a kind of historical density into their analyses of race, even if the theorization of hierarchy isn't always explicit to their terms. In so doing, they aim to make visible the continuity of white supremacy's modes of subjection, tactics of coercion, and rhetorics of representation, attesting to a fact of terrible if unassailable consequence: it is the black/the slave, in what Fanon terms its "absolute dereliction," that provides the linchpin of whiteness, that marks the horizon of its thought, and that is burdened with the cipher of negativity so central to Western metaphysics.[21] What's more, this "fact of blackness" suggests the possibility that the color line as such marks out not only a division between white and nonwhite, but, as becomes increasingly clear, one between black and nonblack as well.[22]

It is perhaps fitting, then, that these texts should appear together in a journal such as *Qui Parle*, which has placed poststructuralist and psychoanalytic theory at the heart of its enterprise, yet has failed (or refused) to consistently and critically examine race, that "impermissible origin,"[23] which would most radically complicate recent critical thinking apropos of the aporias of the subject. We have accordingly titled this dossier, "History, Representation, and the Impossible Subject of Race," to indicate not only the limits of any politics of representation[24] and the inescapability of entanglement with an insane and absolute violence, but to also suggest the foreclosure of race—embodied most forcefully in the figure of the black body—from the cultural milieu of white institutionality. The touchstones of cohesion that allow for that magical translation of an unannounced white filiation into an equally unremarked white affiliation are put into crisis whenever the conundrum of race is explicitly broached.[25] "There is a quest for the Negro, the Negro is in demand, one cannot get along without him, he is needed, but only if he is made palatable in a certain way. Unfortunately, the Negro knocks down the system and breaks the treaties."[26] Beneath this black shadow, "things fall apart," in print and in life.

As this issue goes to press, the editorial board of *Qui Parle* is internally riven by the recent and contentious resignation of one of its members, an act of solidarity and protest over the questionable interview process for a black woman candidate to the editorial board. This principled departure was matched by detailed public criticism from that candidate herself, who chose ultimately not to accept a belabored invitation to join the ranks. As a result of this clash (not to mention the occasionally rancorous nature of the board's movement toward consensus regarding the articles that follow), the journal now finds itself at a crucial juncture, one precipitated by the fleshy figuration of blackness both within and beyond these pages. The appearance of this dossier—whose contents represent some of the brightest and most challenging thinking around race available in recent years—marks an opening in the history of the journal but an opening whose future is already in doubt. Whether this event and the conversations it has spawned will become an opportunity for questioning or a moment of irrevocable finitude will suggest not only a stance vis-à-vis the (now-reconfigured) politics of blackness-whiteness, but will again test the scope and ambition of this journal's poignantly eponymous question: Who speaks?

Notes

The essays included in the dossier were David Marriott, "The Love of Neither-Either–Racial Integration in *Pressure Point*"; Kara Keeling, "'In the Interval': Frantz Fanon and the 'Problems' of Visual Representation"; Hank Willis Thomas, *Frames*; Huey Copeland, "Being in the Picture: Hank Willis Thomas' *Frames* Series"; Neferti X. M. Tadiar, "In the Face of Whiteness as Value: Fall-Outs of Metropolitan Humanness"; and Frank B. Wilderson III, "The Position of the Unthought: An Interview with Saidiya V. Hartman."

The essay title is taken from the following quotation: "We must firmly place ourselves in another space to describe our age, the age and space of *raw life*. . . . It is a place where life and death are so entangled that it is no longer possible to distinguish them, or to say what is on the side of the shadow or its obverse." See Achille Mbembe, *On the Postcolony*, trans. A. M. Berrett, Janet Roitman, Murray Last, and Steven Rendall (University of California Press, 2001), 197.

1 Frantz Fanon, *Black Skin, White Masks*, trans. Charles Lam Markmann (Grove Press, 1967), 109.

2 Mbembe, *On the Postcolony*, 201.

3 This phrase is taken from David Marriott, *On Black Men* (Columbia University Press, 2000), 15.

4 See Saidiya V. Hartman, *Scenes of Subjection: Terror, Slavery, and Self-Making in Nineteenth-Century America* (Oxford University Press, 1997); also see Wilderson's interview with Hartman, "The Position of the Unthought.'"

6 From Fanon's discussion of "Negro-phobogenesis": the construction of "the Negro" as "a phobic object, a stimulus to anxiety," in *Black Skin, White Masks*, 151-52.

7 Sumi Cho, "Korean Americans vs. African Americans," in *Reading Rodney King / Reading Urban Uprising*, ed. Robert Gooding-Williams (Routledge, 1993), 205.

8 See G. Reginald Daniel, *More Than Black* (Temple University Press, 2002); Rainier Spencer, *Spurious Issues* (Westview, 1999); Jon Michael Spencer, *The New Colored People* (New York University Press, 1997).

9 For an example of such a reformulation from within Asian American studies, see Frank Wu, *Yellow* (Basic Books, 2001).

10 The casting of racial politics in predominantly black/white terms is largely an effect of the postwar race relations industry in the United States, developing as it did around the emergence of the modern black civil rights movement, and its radicalization as Black Power. Perhaps the most well-known document in that vein remains the *Report of the National Advisory Commission on Civil Disorders* (Bantam Books, 1968), a.k.a. the Kerner Commission, where the infamous phrase "two societies, one black, one white–separate and unequal" was first introduced (1). The black civil rights struggle–dating back to at least 1787–has, however, consistently been understood not in and of itself but in relation to the struggles of other oppressed peoples around the world, in and beyond the Americas. See Jonathan Birnbaum and Clarence Taylor, eds., *Civil Rights Since 1787* (New York University Press, 2000).

11 This phrase is taken from Michael Omi and Howard Winant, "The Los Angeles 'Race Riot' and Contemporary U.S. Politics," in Gooding-Williams, *Reading Rodney King*.

12 The 1992 multiracial conflagration in Los Angeles following the acquittal of four white LAPD officers for the videotaped beating of a black motorist, Rodney King, has spurred a good deal of confusion in this regard. See, for instance, the articles by Cho and Omi and Winant, as well as Elaine Kim, in Gooding-Williams, *Reading Rodney King.*

13 Mari Matsuda, "Beyond, and Not Beyond, Black and White: Deconstruction Has a Politics," in *Crossroads, Directions, and a New Critical Race Theory*, ed. Angela Harris (Temple University Press, 2002), 395.

14 For an extended discussion of global white supremacy, see Charles Mills, *Blackness Visible* (Cornell University Press, 1998).

15 Fanon, *Black Skin, White Masks*, 173.

16 Lewis Gordon, *Her Majesty's Other Children* (Rowman & Littlefield, 1997), 53. Gordon states things even more clearly: "Blackness, in the end, functions as a constant, underlying mark of racialization as does no other racial designation. Its persistence suggests that the fluidity of racial identities points upward in continuing spirals of potential whiteness" (57).

17 Richard Dyer, "White," in *The Matter of Images: Essays on Representations* (Routledge, 1993), 141–63.

18 This is not to say that color and racial hierarchies are identical, however. There are instances in which one may be "darker" than some blacks but nonetheless closer to whiteness along the matrices of value. One need only explore the vagaries and fluidity of the racial category of whiteness across the history of the US Census. South Asians, for instance, were long classed as white (and this debate continues currently at the public policy level) despite being frequently read as more "colored" than so many light-skinned blacks, whether the latter were designated "mixed race" (e.g., mulatto, quadroon) or not. On colorism vs. racism, see Trina Jones, "Shades of Brown," 49 *Duke Law Journal* 1487 (April 2000). On the racialization of South Asians in the United States, see Vijay Prashad, *The Karma of Brown Folk* (University of Minnesota Press, 2000).

19 Gordon, *Her Majesty's Other Children*, 53.

20 Cho, "Korean Americans vs. African Americans," 209.

21 Mbembe, *On the Postcolony*, 1–9. As noted above, the analytic centering of blackness in examinations of race in no way precludes the treatment of subjects (in both senses of the word) that are not black (in the common sense). In fact, it enables and enriches such treatments. Neferti X. M. Tadiar's powerful examination of race, gender, and sexuality within the political economic restructuring of Metropolitan Manila considers the Philippines as a postcolony in the throes of globalizing capital, supplementing the topical focus of the other works collected here. Consider the following comment: "Race begins to stand in for that *which must be eschewed in order to approach value* [emphasis ours], and in this way retroactively determines the meaning of value as that which is not raced. . . . Since race comes to signify precisely this appropriable corporeal nature as a consequence of the histories of slavery and colonization, value itself, as the invisible content of an object or person distinguishable from its outward form, becomes aligned with that which is not raced." Since it is established elsewhere that blackness and whiteness signify most firmly these respectively reified positions of raced/not-raced or corporeal/incorporeal, we can better determine the precise locus in which the discussion of the Filipino subject(s) unfolds. Tadiar, "In the Face of Whiteness as Value."

22 In this vein, we might usefully revisit W. E. B. Du Bois's famous pronouncement on the color line. In his words, "The problem of the twentieth century is the problem of the color line." Typically, this is as far as most get in their citation of Du Bois's prophetic observation. However, let us read further: "the relation of the darker to the lighter races of men in Asia and Africa, in America and the islands of the sea." What do we make of this allusion to darkness/lightness in the current context? Think also of Du Bois's positioning of the Negro in direct relation–historically, culturally, and politically–to all the "civilized" peoples of the earth: Europeans, Arabs, and Asians. In his words, "After the Egyptian and Indian, the Greek and Roman, the Teuton and Mongolian, the Negro is a sort of seventh son." See W. E. B. Du Bois, *The Souls of Black Folk* (Gramercy Books, 1994), 12, 5.

23 A phrase borrowed from Hortense J. Spillers, "Interstices: A Small Drama of Words," in *Pleasure and Danger: Exploring Female Sexuality*, ed. Carole Vance (Routledge & Kegan Paul, 1984), 88.

24 See Hank Willis Thomas's photo-essay, *Frames*; and Huey Copeland's commentary, "Being in the Picture."

25 This notion of ideological and affective movement from filiation to affiliation (and experiencing a crisis of the latter whenever difficulty emerges in the former) is taken from Edward Said, *The World, the Text, and the Critic* (Harvard University Press, 1989).

26 Fanon, *Black Skin, White Masks*, 176.

2

UNTITLED (JACKPOT!)

The black man insists, by whatever means he finds at his disposal, that the white man cease to regard him as an exotic rarity and recognize him as a human being.
James Baldwin, "Stranger in the Village," 1953[1]

"I AM A MAN" (Fig. 2.1). In Ernest C. Withers's 1968 photograph of striking Memphis sanitation workers, that assertion of identity is repeatedly materialized, printed on placards held up by a multitude of invisible hands; the black men pictured here signal to us forthrightly and for themselves. Yet that they do so en masse, in such a spectacularly choreographed way, indicates that the truth their statement holds to be self-evident remains in doubt and must again be spelled out for the imagined audiences they would address: "I AM / A MAN." In this instance, for these men, those four little words are haunted by the antithetical identifications they work hard to disavow, and Baldwin's "exotic rarity" is surely the least stinging among them: for if not a man, then "boy"; if not a man, then "'Dirty nigger!' Or simply, 'Look, a Negro!'"[2]

It is with these words that the Martinican theorist Frantz Fanon begins his unforgettable essay "The Fact of Blackness," which appeared in English the year before Withers snapped his indelible portrait. Like Fanon, we might say, the photographer's subjects know what it feels like to fade away beneath the most venomous of racial signifiers and so to be eviscerated of particularity, subjectivity, and manhood by an utterance that is as brute and instrumental in its force as they are presumed to be in their very being: "Nigger!" These men know the "vicious pantomime" of reification and projection that word encapsulates: they know what it is to be "intimately dispossessed" by the white look, "how white fears and desires slice like a knife through the eyes of petrified black men."[3] They know that "it is by

This essay first appeared in *Glenn Ligon: Some Changes*, exh. cat. (Power Plant, 2005), 119–32.

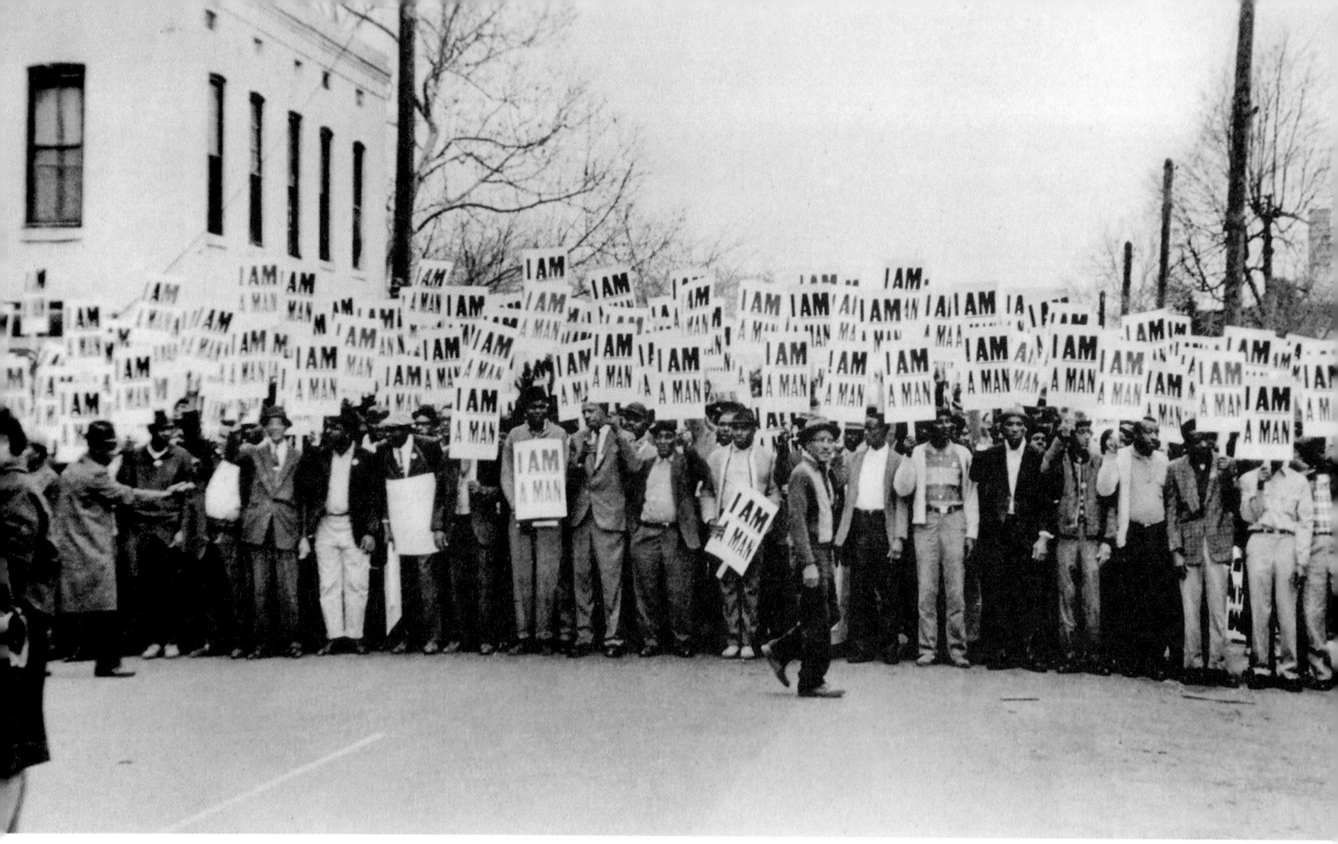

Figure 2.1
Ernest Withers, *I AM A MAN*, Sanitation Workers' Strike, Memphis, Tennessee, March 28, 1968. © Dr. Ernest C. Withers, Sr. Courtesy of the Withers Family Trust.

an abiding bankruptcy of vision that black male bodies in public spheres go phantasmatically misrecognized,"[4] a seemingly immutable fact of blackness that always threatens to overdetermine their appearance.

Even knowing all of this, the men at once captured and obscured in the photograph would not be spooked. They assembled in front of Clayborn Temple on March 28; they insistently appeared to make their case and to contest social inequality despite the white sneers and sharpened bayonets aimed their way. Clearly, they were not unprepared.[5] The posters held above heads, before faces and torsos, function almost like shields meant to deflect "scopic malice,"[6] and consequently, the locus of speech, of perceptual interest, is displaced from those whose dark skins render them virtual signs onto the literal ones they carry. What Withers's picture records, then, is black men embracing the disappearance that is an effect of language in the hope that different words might somehow differently give them back to themselves.[7]

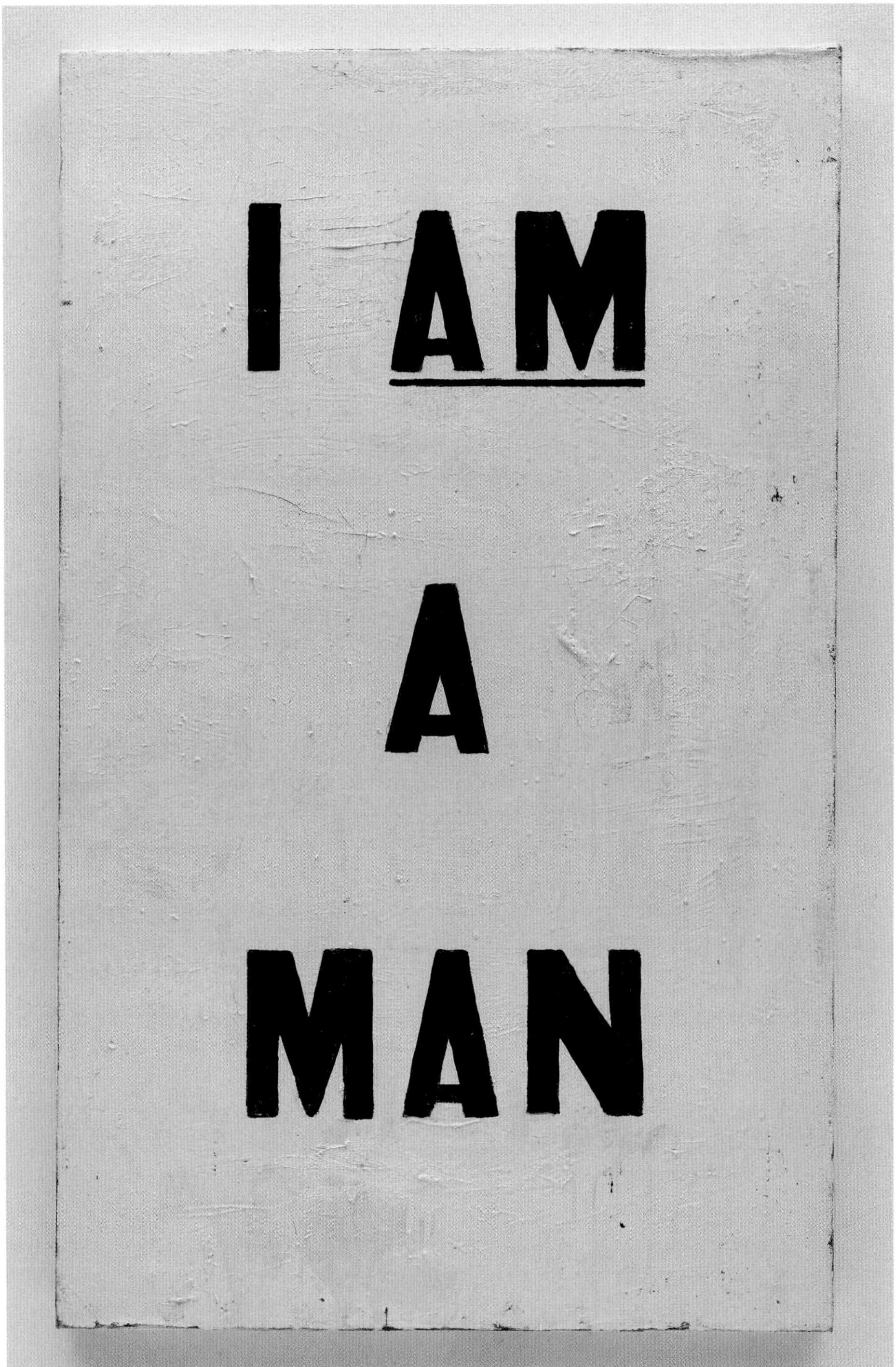

Figure 2.2

Glenn Ligon, *Untitled (I Am a Man)*, 1988. Oil and enamel on canvas, 40 × 25 in. (101.6 × 63.5 cm). Collection of the National Gallery of Art. Photography credit: Ronald Amstutz. © Glenn Ligon; Courtesy of the artist, Hauser & Wirth, and Thomas Dane Gallery.

His survival depended, and his development depends, on his ability to turn his peculiar status in the Western world to his own advantage and, it may be, to the very great advantage of that world. It remains for him to fashion out of his experience that which will give him sustenance, and a voice.[8]

When he turned to Withers's iconic image exactly twenty years after it was taken, the artist Glenn Ligon chose as his subject the sign. The resulting painting, his first to depend exclusively on text for its means, seems to tell us everything and nothing about its maker, many things and the only thing: "I AM / A / MAN" (Fig. 2.2). In this revision, Ligon has subtly altered the Memphis poster's line breaks, so rather than reading as a compact two-tiered mass that proposes an indisputable link between subject and object—"I" and "MAN"—in this untitled work, that lonesome central "A" becomes the thread that holds the sentence and the composition together.[9] It is as if in momentarily staving off the final word, the artist wants to emphasize that manhood, whatever it might be, is necessarily unstable and never assured.

As this painting suggests, Ligon has time and again looked to signal episodes in African American history, poaching words, images, and attitudes from the modern cultural lexicon in order to explore his own ambivalent relationship to the depiction of black bodies within the Western aesthetic tradition. For if the specular economies of white supremacy have denigrated black subjects in life, then they might also be said to have persistently complicated black self-representation in art. To such an extent that in 1990 the cultural critic Michele Wallace famously proclaimed that visuality itself marks a certain limit within black culture, constituting a "negative scene of instruction," which stands in stark contrast to "what is now triumphantly called the 'tradition' of Afro-American music."[10]

There is more than a grain of truth in Wallace's sweeping assessment. Getting a grip on its implications for black artists on the ground or in the studio, however, requires greater attention to the irreducible specificity of individual objects and practices. What Ligon himself insists, and what the variety of work gathered in the present exhibition makes clear, is that "we need to go to the fine point."[11] For this African American artist, I want to argue, "the problem of the visual"[12] is not so much a barrier to be crossed as a set of productive constraints that he beautifully, succinctly, makes over into form.

In the late 1980s, Ligon, at the time a properly agonized abstract painter, came to realize that language could provide the basis for such form: it offered "a very simple way" to approach "a whole body of things,"[13] a whole body of blackness, which could not otherwise be registered. Words mattered, then, because they compulsively referred, and as the protesters of '68 so ably demonstrated, they also rerouted. Language could bracket the metonymic chain of associations—"tomtoms, cannibalism, intellectual deficiency"—that, Fanon teaches us, are set off by the sight of black skin and doggedly pursue the black subject wherever he appears.[14] Language could address the demonization of black masculinity prevalent within American culture,[15] allowing the black body to be disentangled from the graphic "scenes of subjection" in which it is continually emplotted.[16] The curator Thelma Golden aptly diagnosed this state of affairs in the brochure accompanying Ligon's 1992 exhibition, *Good Mirrors Are Not Cheap*: among critically engaged black artistic practices "it is the written word that has become the oppositional voice which replaces visual representation."[17]

Cast in this light, it makes sense that the paintings, which have come to emblematize Ligon's oeuvre, should sidestep the image of the black body and instead evoke it with a cascade of words let fall on a canvas of

Figure 2.3
Glenn Ligon, *Untitled (I Feel Most Colored When I Am Thrown Against a Sharp White Background)*, 1990. Oil stick, gesso, and graphite on wood, 80 × 30 in. (203.2 × 76.2 cm). © Glenn Ligon.

pointedly corporeal dimensions (Fig. 2.3). Here was an apotropaic double, a surrogate self that could speak of and for him in a voice not his own. "I feel most colored when I am thrown against a sharp white background. I feel most colored when I am thrown against a sharp white background. I feel most colored . . ." Appropriating a line from Zora Neale Hurston's "How It Feels to Be Colored Me," Ligon rewrites it with black oil stick, dragging his stencil across the surface of the painting to produce smears and smudges, the idiosyncratic residue of a deductive procedure that transmutes figure into ground, protective mantra into sentient blur. This untitled work takes Hurston at and as her word, elucidating the contextual character of racial identity in no uncertain terms.[18] But despite Ligon's fidelity to his source and her now-anachronistic use of "colored"—with its connotations of the infinite variety of African American skin tones and lived experiences—in seizing upon the material and metaphorical properties of language, he sticks to that timeless dyad: "the black" and "the white."

The one is literally illegible without the other. Or as Fanon stated about the making of men in modernity, "The Negro is not. Any more than the white man,"[19] both caught up in an antagonistic bind that disallows mutual recognition and therefore the attainment of the human on either side of the color line. In performing this impossibility and its perpetual recurrence within representation, Ligon's painting runs headlong into the quandary and the solution thrown up by Fanon's negative ontology of race. As the scholar Kara Keeling argues, "The ontological interrogation into the Black's being can be answered only via a description of the Black's affective constitution; how does it feel to be Black?"[20] Thus, it is the plenitude, contingency, and symbolic import of black feeling that open onto those complex states of being that the image of the black body, in its tendency toward stereotypical reduction, would seem to foreclose.[21]

In Ligon's *Untitled (I Feel Most Colored When I Am Thrown Against a Sharp White Background)*, as in the other works from 1990 that likewise cull phrases from Hurston's 1928 meditation, affect is all: "I Am Not Tragically Colored," "I Do Not Always Feel Colored," "I Remember the Very Day That I Became Colored." Yet it is James Baldwin's "Stranger in the Village" of 1953—the writer's wide-ranging reflection prompted by being the first black man ever to set foot in a tiny snowbound Swiss hamlet—that most vividly describes what it feels like to be colored when thrown against a sharp white background. When the artist set out to put these words into paint, the results were stunningly and resolutely dark.

Figure 2.4
Glenn Ligon, *Untitled*, 2002. Coal dust, printing ink, oil stick and acrylic on canvas, 74.88 × 118.13 in. (190.2 × 300.1 cm). Collection of Dallas Museum of Art. Photographer credit: Dallas Museum of Art. © Glenn Ligon; Courtesy of the artist, Hauser & Wirth, and Thomas Dane Gallery.

> When, beneath the black mask, a human being begins to make himself felt one cannot escape a certain awful wonder as to what kind of human being it is.[22]

What kind of blackness is this? To stand before Ligon's *Untitled* (2002) is to encounter a rectangular canvas, roughly ten feet wide and six feet high, neither truly abstract nor altogether representational, somehow inscrutable, and so all the more seductive (Fig. 2.4). Its surface, covered with a glimmering exhalation of coal dust, has an uneven, crumbling texture, and the overall effect is of a mottled veil, which in some patches opacifies and in others lifts to reveal fragments of the first five paragraphs of Baldwin's essay in their orderly horizontal spread.

The painterly technique employed throughout the "Stranger in the Village" series—begun around 1997 and now numbering over twenty pieces of varying size, shape, darkness, and citation—obviously revisits Ligon's signature strategy of stenciled inscription. Indeed, the 2002 picture seems to get going where *Untitled (I Feel Most Colored When I Am Thrown Against a Sharp White Background)* left off, again tarrying in the gap between legibility and illegibility to achieve a sensuous image and now metastasizing the linguistic morass that accumulated at the foot of the earlier work until it comprises a total field. But unlike its "Colored" cousin, this "Stranger" is replete in its strangeness. It does not propose a structural affinity between our bodies and itself; it does not ask that we lend a sympathetic ear to its uncanny voicing; and it resists open flirtation with the conceit of self-portraiture, particularly when compared to the artist's previous engagements with Baldwin.

In his 1992 exhibition at the Wadsworth Atheneum (*Matrix 120*), for example, Ligon selected the following lines from one of the writer's last interviews and printed them directly onto the wall in a corner of the gallery (Fig. 2.5).

> You see, whites want black artists to mostly deliver something as if it were an official version of the black experience. But the vocabulary won't hold it, simply. No true account really of black life can be held, can be contained, in the American vocabulary. As it is, the only way that you can deal with it is by doing great violence to the assumptions on which the vocabulary is based. But they won't let you do that. And when you go along, you find yourself very quickly painted into a corner; you've written yourself into a corner.[23]

As we might expect, any attempt to read this text required the viewer to go along with it, to walk into that corner and so physically experience the situation figuratively described in Baldwin's account of black discursive constraint. For his part, in enacting that speech, the artist was doubly cast as the "I" and the "you," both the author and his ideal reader, conjuring forth only to put under pressure the historical and structural continuities that might lead one black gay man to feign identity with another in negotiating the scene of American cultural production.

Given the similar flow of their lives, Ligon's sense of subjective alignment with Baldwin is perhaps—among all his identifications with literary avatars, from Ralph Ellison to Jean Genet—the most resonantly felt.[24] But if in the wall drawing he projected himself into the writer's place, then in the canvas executed ten years later, he made a picture out of it.[25] This untitled painting, I want to say, does not so much stage as it effectively materializes Baldwin's "peculiar status," and it is the breadth, density, and enabling alienation of his perspective that guided its facture at every turn. "I remember an interview," the artist tells us, "where Baldwin is asked if he didn't, at some point, think his life was hopeless being poor, black, and gay and Baldwin says, 'No, I thought I'd hit the jackpot.' It is his contention that the place of the marginal, of the disesteemed, of the left behind, is a productive place to speak from."[26]

And for Ligon to work *after*: as Baldwin's presumed lack affords an embarrassment of riches, so in every *Stranger*, coal dust sprinkled onto wet canvas generates inexhaustible visual incident in a further recalibration of "blackness." It too is a kind of excess, the by-product of a racializing apparatus, which aimed to naturalize "white" superiority and justify the violent transformation of African subjects into American objects with no content save the historicity of their abjection. "Fetichism, racial defects, slave-ships":[27] such, we know, were the phantasms that plagued Fanon. Yet as Baldwin reminds us near the close of his essay, the dereliction of blackness also limns the transatlantic origins of the African American subject and uniquely positions him at the nexus of the modern world.[28]

> The history of the American Negro problem is not merely shameful, it is also something of an achievement. For even when the worst has been said, it must also be added that the perpetual challenge posed by this problem was always, somehow, perpetually met. It is precisely this black-white experience which may prove of indispensable value to us in the world we face today.[29]

It is Baldwin's self-imposed exile—amid folk who regard him as a dark abstraction suddenly made flesh—that allows him to perceive that the particular tortures and deep intimacies of the US black-white relation have at least made necessary the attempt to differently imagine what manhood might be, and whom it might encompass.[30]

In its interrogation of the limits of the human and their complex imbrication with definitions of blackness, Baldwin's "Stranger in the Village" has itself proven to be indispensable. As Ligon attests, "Almost fifty years after its publication, it continues to open up a space in which to comprehend debates in Europe around immigration and xenophobia and the failure of the dream in post–Civil Rights America."[31] With his *Untitled* (2002), then, the artist marked that space in what he eloquently calls a "melancholy echo"[32] of the expatriate's world-historical vision: the painting is a darkened screen of panoramic scale that masks and archives the writer's voice. And it is not by chance that the work also rehearses a familiar modernist form—the black painting—which is equally international in its appearance, and notorious for its concatenative signification, playing at absolution though radically dependent on historical circumstance for its meaning.[33]

Like its dark antecedents—say, Malevich's *Black Square* of 1915, or Ad Reinhardt's black paintings of the early '60s—Ligon's *Untitled* (2002) summons up death, matter, and the obliterative beyond; it seduces with a certain sleight of hand; it narrativizes perception.[34] Yet, in so doing, the work revises these earlier practices with the overlaying scrim of a blackness that is not merely rhetorical, but lived and *felt*.[35] Blackness as negation is here redoubled: we must look and look again, attentive to word and image,

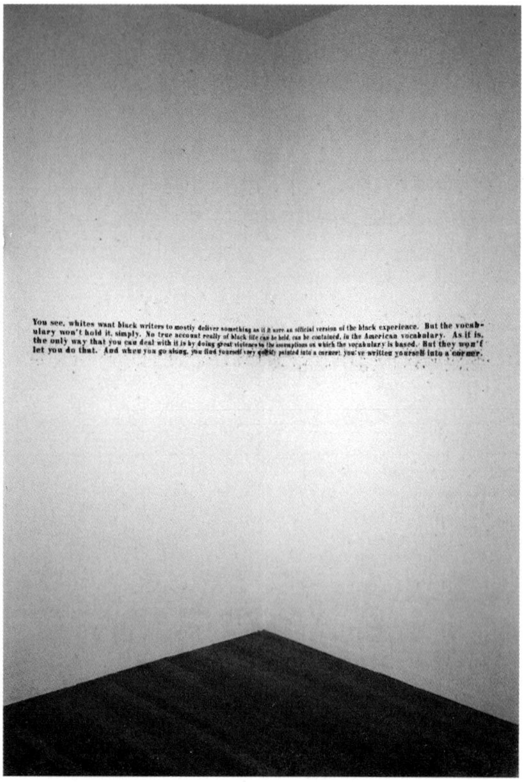

Figure 2.5

Glenn Ligon, *Untitled (James Baldwin)*, 1992. Acrylic, oil, and pencil on wall, 123 × 10 in. (312.4 × 25.4 cm). © Glenn Ligon.

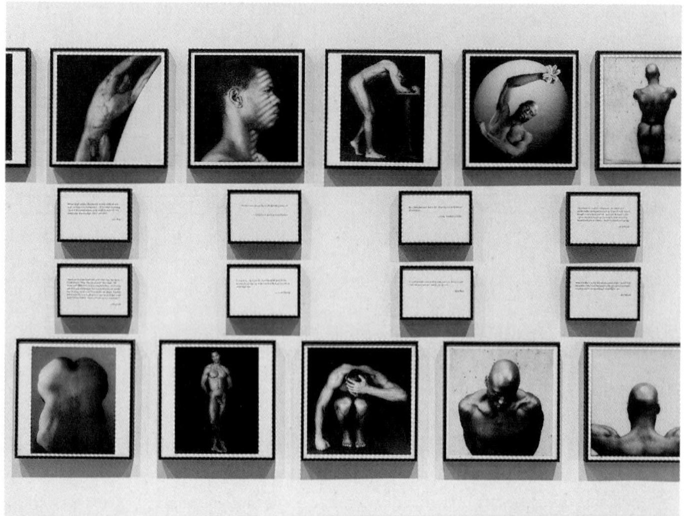

Figure 2.6

Glenn Ligon, *Notes on the Margin of the Black Book*, detail, 1991-93. 91 offset prints, 78 text pages, Each Framed: Prints 11.5 × 11.5 in. (29.2 × 29.2 cm); text pages 5.25 × 7.25 in. (13.3 × 18.4 cm). Collection of Solomon R. Guggenheim Museum, New York; gift of the Bohen Foundation. Photographer credit: Ronald Amstutz. © Glenn Ligon.

self and other as they come in and out of focus, giving us glimpses into an impenetrable whole that refuses to lie transparent beneath our gaze.

This painting, I think, might be thought of as a monochrome that spooks itself, and from its retrospect we can perhaps best perceive how the artist's practice takes up the "limits of visibility"[36] imposed on blackness within representation, soliciting the scopic energies aimed at the black body only to deform them into aesthetic attention. Think back to his *Notes on the Margin of the Black Book* of 1991–93, which directs us from Robert Mapplethorpe's fetishizing images of black men to the cultural frameworks in which they were hotly contested (Fig. 2.6); or recall the crates in his installation *To Disembark*, which wittily conflate the Minimalist cube with the box in which an enslaved Henry Brown shipped himself to freedom (Fig. 2.7). What each of these instances testifies to is how Ligon has consistently seized upon previous artistic modes, oeuvres, no, *languages*, which already suggest a certain kind of visual exhaustion—in order to press them

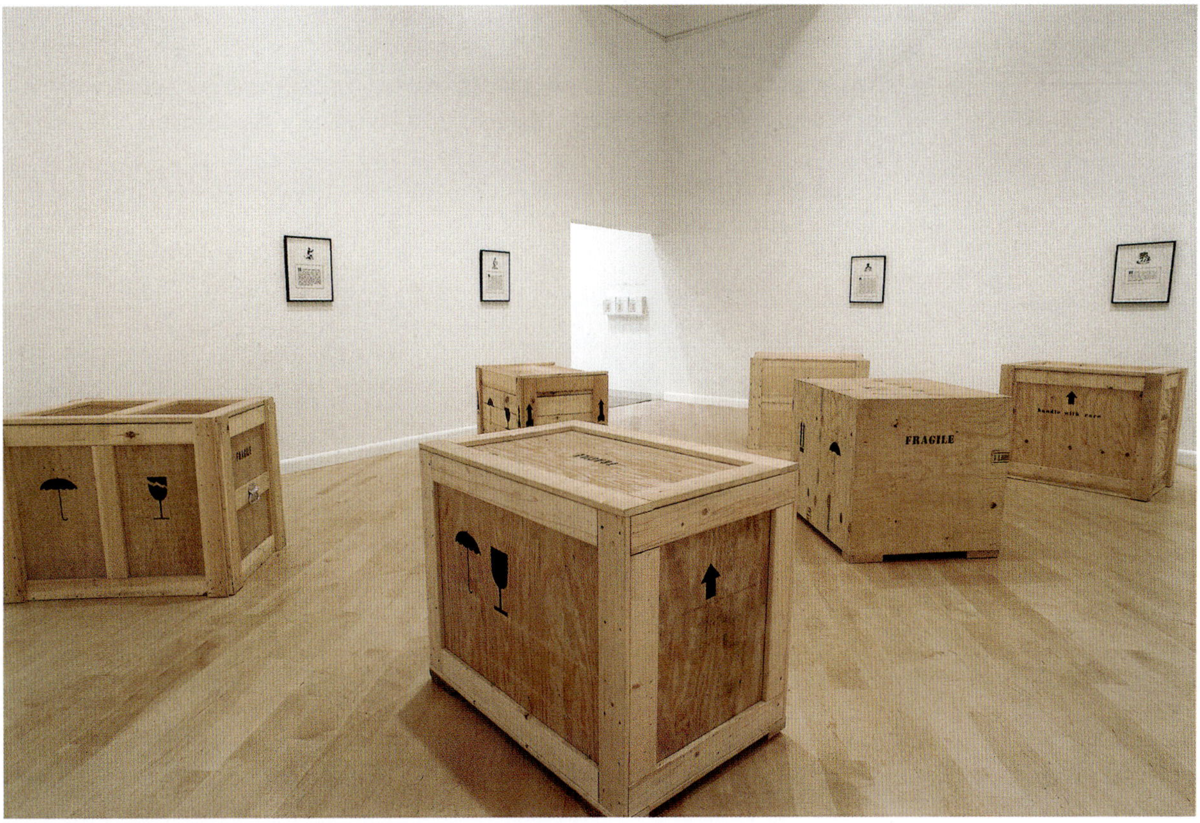

Figure 2.7

Glenn Ligon, *Untitled (To Disembark)*, detail, 1993. Nine wood crates with synthetic polymer, acrylic paint, and nine audio recordings, 31.25 × 38.25 × 25.25 in. (79.4 × 97.2 × 64.1 cm). © Glenn Ligon.

Figure 2.8

Glenn Ligon, *Untitled (Contact)*, 2002. Coal dust, printing ink, oil stick, glue, acrylic paint and gesso on canvas. 74.88 × 118.13 in (190.2 × 300.1 cm). The Latner Family Art Collection, Toronto, © Glenn Ligon.

up against the capricious negativity of blackness.

As the artist's *Untitled (Contact)* of 2002 makes clear, in the aftermath of that encounter, both are transformed. In this work, Ligon has rubbed a blank canvas on the still wet *Untitled* (2002) to produce a mirror image that is again treated with fine soot. The result is a white shadow of a dark echo that seems lightly touched, yet indelibly altered (Fig. 2.8). If, as Michele Wallace instructs, the problem of the visual "remains the unilateral unwillingness of Euro-American culture to admit and acknowledge its debt, or even its relationship, to African and Afro-American culture,"[37] then in Ligon's hands, our understanding of modernism, of masculinity, of vision itself cannot help but come undone, everywhere traversed by a dark recursive force. To quote Baldwin: "The world is white no longer, and it will never be white again."[38] While it remains to be seen whether the world can make good on his fortune, it is evident that Ligon already has, and in the gloaming shadow cast by his art, we might begin to envision ourselves darkly.

Notes

1 James Baldwin, "Stranger in the Village," *Harper's Magazine*, October 1953, 45.

2 Frantz Fanon, *Black Skin, White Masks*, trans. Charles Lam Markmann (Grove Press, 1967), 109.

3 The phrases quoted here are taken from David Marriott's brilliant examination of the role played by black men within the Western cultural imaginary and the deleterious consequences for the psychic lives of black male subjects. See *On Black Men* (Columbia University Press, 2000), xiv.

4 Maurice O. Wallace, *Constructing the Black Masculine: Identity and Ideality in African-American Men's Literature and Culture, 1775-1995* (Duke University Press, 2002), 33. Like Marriot, Wallace combines poststructuralist and psychoanalytic perspectives to produce a compelling description of the specular predication of the black male subject that expands on and deepens our understanding of Fanon.

5 In fact, according to Richard Lentz, the "heavy sticks" to which the signs were attached "became weapons when trouble broke out." See his *Symbols, the News Magazines, and Martin Luther King* (Louisiana State University Press, 1990), 273, for an account of the demonstration, the ensuing violence, and its bearing on King's final days.

6 Wallace, *Constructing the Black Masculine*, 50.

7 On the subject's fading before the signifier, see Jacques Lacan, *The Four Fundamental Concepts of Psychoanalysis*, ed. Jacques-Alain Miller, trans. Alan Sheridan (W. W. Norton, 1981), 216-20.

8 Baldwin, "Stranger in the Village," 47-48.

9 Though several civil rights-era posters featuring the "I Am a Man" slogan deployed line breaks identical to Ligon's [see Fig. 24.5 on p. 362]—as illustrated, for instance, on p. 138 of Flip Schulke's *He Had A Dream: Martin Luther King, Jr., and the Civil Rights Movement* (W. W. Norton,

1995)—when the artist executed his *Untitled (I Am A Man)* painting, he was unaware of these versions. Glenn Ligon, telephone conversation with the author, March 6, 2005.

10 Michele Wallace, "Modernism, Postmodernism, and the Problem of the Visual in Afro-American Culture," in *Marginalization and Contemporary Cultures*, ed. Russell Ferguson et al. (MIT Press, 1990), 40–41.

11 See Glenn Ligon, "Black Light: David Hammons and the Poetics of Emptiness," *Artforum*, September 2004, 242–49, which considers how blackness functions as a site of aesthetic construction. In its original context the sentence quoted calls for greater specificity in thinking about the various practices grouped under the rubric "African American Art" (243).

12 Wallace, "Modernism, Postmodernism, and the Problem of the Visual in Afro-American Culture," 39.

13 Ligon, quoted in *Matrix 120*, Wadsworth Atheneum, August 1992, 6.

14 Fanon, *Black Skin, White Masks*, 112.

15 For a signal instance of Ligon's work on the production of black masculinity as menace, see his series of paintings focusing on the accused in the Central Park Jogger case: "Profiles," *Third Text* (Spring 1991): 53–61.

16 A reference to Saidiya V. Hartman's *Scenes of Subjection: Terror, Slavery and Self-Making in Nineteenth-Century America* (Oxford University Press, 1997), which offers a thorough assessment of the physical and phantasmatic labor compulsively extracted from black bodies.

17 Thelma Golden, *Good Mirrors Are Not Cheap* (Whitney Museum of American Art at Philip Morris, 1992), n.p. Golden's comments in this vein apply equally well to the work of a Lorna Simpson, a Gary Simmons, or any number of black neoconceptual practitioners who had recourse to language in the late '80s and early '90s.

18 See Zora Neale Hurston, "How It Feels to be Colored Me," in *I Love Myself When I Am Laughing . . . And Then Again When I Am Looking Mean and Impressive: A Zora Neale Hurston Reader*, ed. Alice Walker (Feminist Press at the City University of New York, 1979), 152–55.

19 Fanon, *Black Skin, White Masks*, 231. The reading that follows is deeply informed by Kara Keeling's "'In the Interval': Frantz Fanon and the 'Problems' of Visual Representation," *Qui Parle* 13, no. 2 (Spring-Summer 2003): 91–117.

20 Keeling, "'In the Interval,'" 101.

21 For an incisive account of racializing discourses that might be brought to bear on the way Ligon's paintings invert the logic of stereotype, see Homi K. Bhabha, "The Other Question: Stereotype, Discrimination, and the Discourse of Colonialism," in *The Location of Culture* (Routledge, 1994), 66–84.

22 Baldwin, "Stranger in the Village," 45.

23 As quoted in Quincy Troupe, "Last Testament: An Interview with James Baldwin," in *Conversations with James Baldwin*, ed. Fred L. Standley and Louis H. Pratt (University of Mississippi Press, 1989), 285.

24 For relevant comments on this score, see "A Conversation," in *Glenn Ligon: Stranger*, ed. Christine Y. Kim (Studio Museum in Harlem, 2001), 10, 23.

25 One well might argue for a distinction between the painting and the wall drawing in terms of "absorption" and "theatricality," as elaborated by Michael Fried in "Art and Objecthood," in *Minimal Art: A Critical Anthology*, ed. Gregory Battcock (University of California Press, 1995),

116-47–though Ligon's practice interestingly complicates such a scheme of perceptual differentiation.

26 As quoted in an interview with Malik Gaines featured in *Glenn Ligon: Text Paintings 1990-2004* (Regen Projects, 2004), n.p.

27 Frantz Fanon, quoted (and glossed) in Keeling, "'In the Interval,'" 101.

28 Michelle M. Wright, "'Alas, Poor Richard!': Transatlantic Baldwin, the Politics of Forgetting, and the Project of Modernity," in *James Baldwin Now*, ed. Dwight A. McBride (New York University Press, 1999), 230.

29 Baldwin, "Stranger in the Village," 48.

30 Baldwin, "Stranger in the Village," 46.

31 Glenn Ligon, "Stranger," in *Documenta XI: Platform 5 Catalog*, ed. documanta und Museum Fridericanum, VeranstaltungsGmbH, Kassel (Hatje Cantz Publishers, 2002), 576. It is worth noting that although the New York-based artist began the *Stranger* series in the United States, he executed the painting in question while on a DAAD fellowship in Berlin, a brief expatriation that further underlines Ligon's dissonant similarity to Baldwin.

32 Ligon, "Stranger." For more on the import of belatedness within contemporary African American art, see my "'Bye, Bye Black Girl': Lorna Simpson's Figurative Retreat," *Art Journal* 64, no. 2 (Summer 2005): 62-77.

33 See Benjamin H. D. Buchloh's excellent if not exhaustive account of the changes rung on the monochromatic canvas, "The Primary Colors for the Second Time: A Paradigm Repetition of the Neo-Avant-Garde," *October* 37 (Summer 1986): 41-52.

34 On Malevich, see T. J. Clark, "God Is Not Cast Down," in *Farewell to an Idea: Episodes from a History of Modernism* (Yale University Press, 1999), 225-97. On Reinhardt, see Yve-Alain Bois, "The Limit of Almost," in *Ad Reinhardt* (Rizzoli, 1991), 29.

35 On this point, I have taken my cue from Thelma Golden: "Visually, Glenn's work has asked the viewer alternately to look, to see, to read, to think, and now, in the expansive glow of these paintings, to feel." Golden, "Every Night," in *Glenn Ligon: Un/becoming*, ed. Judith Tannenbaum (Institute of Contemporary Art, University of Pennsylvania, 1997), 48.

36 Richard Meyer, "Borrowed Voices: Glenn Ligon and the Force of Language," in Tannenbaum, *Glenn Ligon: Un/becoming*, 13-35.

37 Wallace, "Modernism, Postmodernism, and the Problem of the Visual in Afro-American Culture," 43.

38 Baldwin, "Stranger in the Village," 48.

3

A FAMILY RESEMBLANCE

This is an essay about Kori Newkirk, his art and the steps both take toward disidentifying with the presumed coordinates of African American male subjectivity. It is a modest attempt to map out the critical postures that Newkirk's varied body of work enables and to consider how he has refashioned dominant cultural models for himself and his viewers over the past dozen years. Given the artist's complex relationship to identity politics, the calculated opacity of his signature pieces, and my own interest in such positions, this is a reasonable tale for me to tell. I want to begin, however, with a subject even closer to home.

My father was obsessed with Oldsmobile Cutlass Supremes. Maybe he loved them because they seemed like the most stylish carriage a self-respecting black father could still justify as a family car, maybe he simply had a taste for their sharklike contours, or maybe they seemed like just compensation for days spent managing the floor of an automotive plant in a white midwestern town. Whatever its roots, the attraction was strong if in no way unique. Although my mother was generally content to drive whatever hatchback was put in her path, she too was "touched," and together my parents purchased a series of Cutlasses beginning in the early 1980s.

The first one I can remember was black with thin, elegant red stripes running along either side. I'm not certain of this cruiser's eventual fate, though I imagine it went the way of the next two Supremes that rolled up our driveway. The second was light blue with a dark blue hard top. To me as a child, it seemed impossibly long, and the only thing more striking than its presence was its sudden disappearance one Saturday morning. Thieves were blamed, and the police dutifully did their work. But in the case of our third Cutlass—a silky gray vehicle that began to smoke one July afternoon—the culprit would be more difficult to pin down.

This essay first appeared in *Kori Newkirk: 1997-2007* (Studio Museum in Harlem, 2007), 48-77.

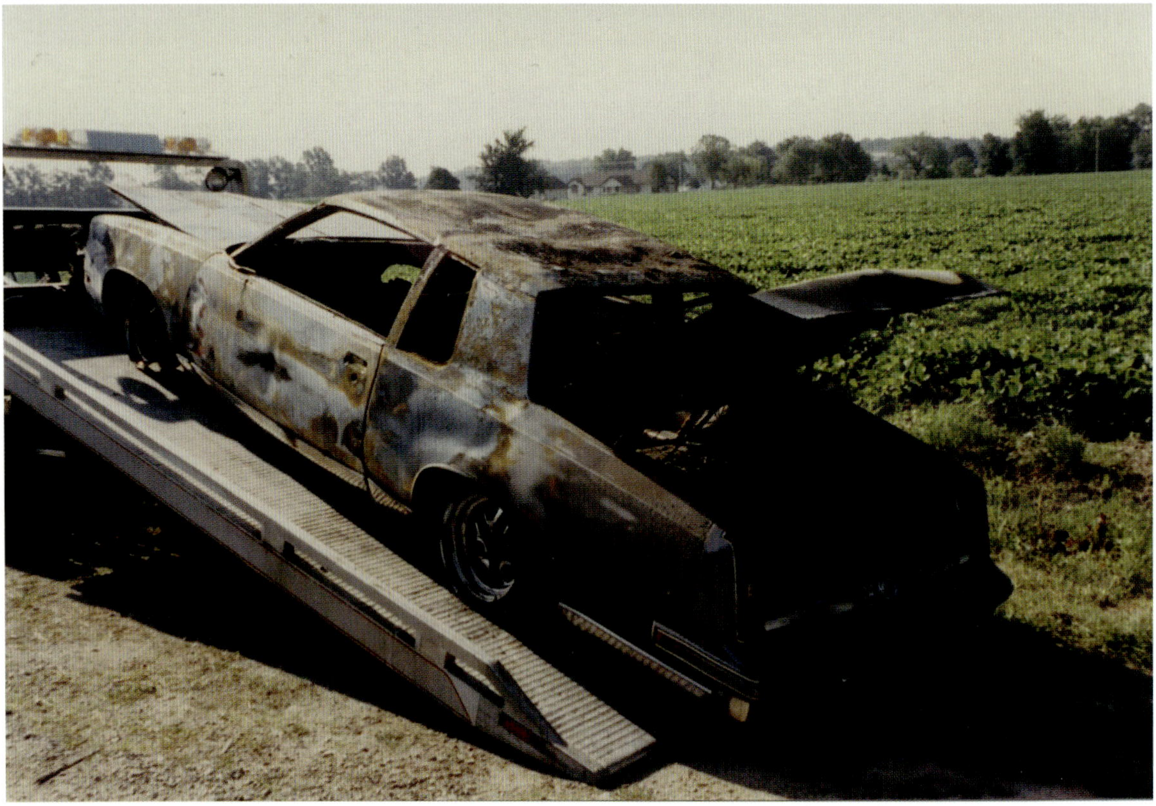

Figure 3.1
Huey Copeland I, *Cutlass Supreme*, 1987.

I was eleven at the time, maybe twelve, and we were all comfortably situated in the car—father, mother, sister, and me—en route to visit relatives in Arkansas. Soon after the smoldering began, my father pulled over onto the shoulder of the interstate. In the five minutes that elapsed after his feet hit the pavement, he opened the hood, failed to extinguish the engine, and calmly hustled us a hundred yards down the highway, where, astonished, we watched as the Cutlass burst into flames. The next time we saw it was at the insurer's office. Propped up on a tow truck and backed by a verdant landscape, the thing looked like an ashen wreck, a cartoonish shell of its former self, yet my father's allegiance to the make would end only when a design overhaul rendered the new models altogether unrecognizable (Fig. 3.1).

In recounting this story, I like to imagine that Kori, more than almost anyone else, knows where I'm coming from and gets where I'm at,[1] not just because our blackness and gayness and middle-class angst led us to analogous pathways out of suburbia and into the art world, but because he too is still trying to make sense of what it means to come from a clan of auto-

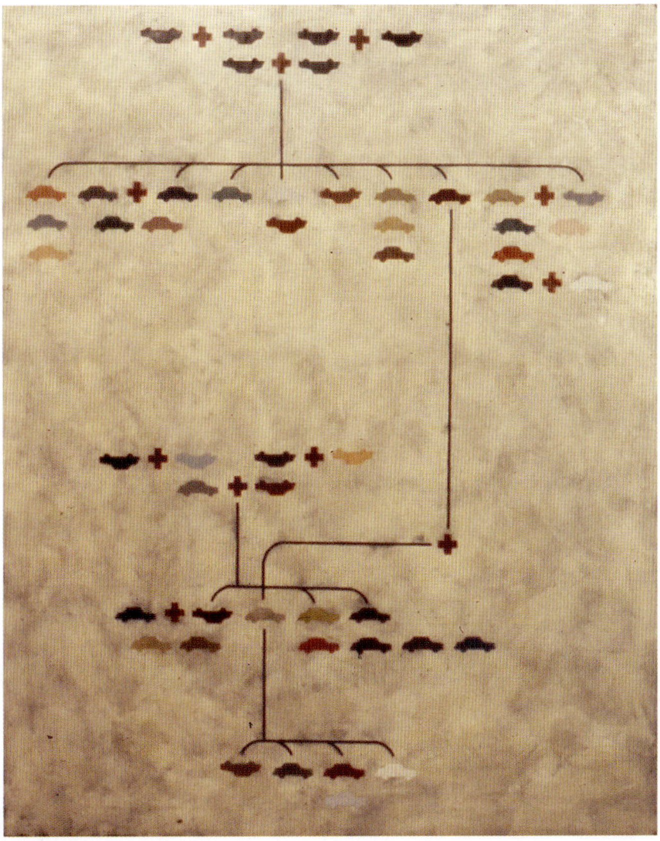

Figure 3.2
Kori Newkirk, *I Come from a Long Line of Cadillacs*, 1995.
Courtesy Studio Museum in Harlem Archives.

motive obsessives. Kori is descended from a long line of Cadillacs, men and women who take after, have taken up with, or have been taken over by that iconic American brand. This, at least, is what the title of one of his earliest works straightforwardly declares. Executed in 1995 and measuring 4 by 3 feet, *I Come from a Long Line of Cadillacs* is an encaustic on wood panel that represents the artist's forebears with mutely colored silhouettes: upright cars for living relatives, overturned ones for the deceased (Fig. 3.2).[2] In its diagrammatic tidiness, this work eschews names, dates, and genders, retaining the conceit of the family tree while effectively abandoning its logic; here, affinity, not filiation, is the name of the game. Couples are few and far between, roots are easily confused with branches, and rather than flow from top to bottom in unbroken lines of descent, this genealogy seems to move in several directions at once, embedding the Cadillac name in Newkirk blood in forms as emptied out as my father's final Cutlass.

These days Kori does not drive a Caddy—they no longer suit his taste, perhaps they never did—but the reference resonates sufficiently within the culture at large and in the artist's imagination to occur with some regular-

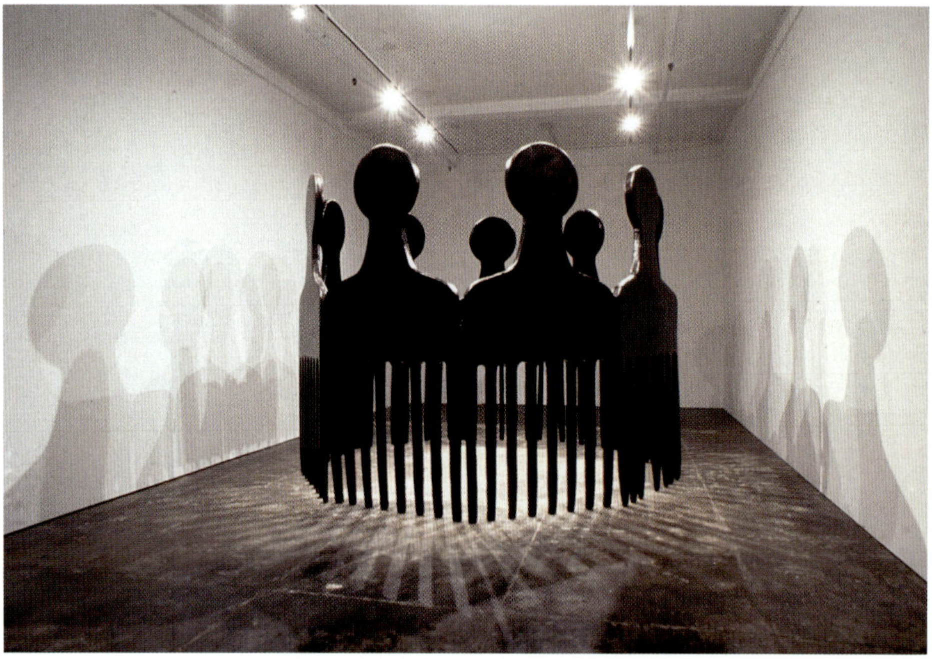

Figure 3.3
Kori Newkirk, *Legacy*, 1999. Courtesy Studio Museum in Harlem Archives.

ity in his early work of the late 1990s. Newkirk profiled the vehicle's outline with red Lite-Brites and silver gelatin prints, multiplied and dispersed it in fragrant black pomade on sheets of white paper, and even sprawled the Cadillac logo across a gallery wall, its metallic cursive stenciled in fluffy black hair. These cars are funky, no doubt, but their facture takes a distance from the pimped-out rides that populate blaxploitation classics like *The Mack* or crop up in MTV tours of rap stars' cribs. Instead, these artworks function as spurs to memory for a generation of mothers, fathers, sisters, and brothers who found themselves on the run from the black wreck and wondering what to do with the ashes falling on their skin.

Newkirk's art holds out a series of responses to this quandary, seizing on the centrality of imaginative self-fashioning to the historical production of black identity. In his practice, especially in the pony bead curtains for which he remains best known, the vernacular styles and materials of the post–civil rights inheritance are time and again unmoored from the figures they adorned, edited to generalities and tweaked in scale to stunning effect. *Legacy* (1999) is a case in point: in it, polyurethane afro picks, each precisely the height of the artist's body, form a circle that simultaneously reads as an outsized crown and a discomfiting enclosure (Fig. 3.3).[3] In thus riffing on the cultural nationalist hairstyling tool of choice, Newkirk puffs up, parodies, and pays homage to the ambitions of black pride, registering the limits of that ethos as well as its subsequent commodification.

Off of the street and into the gallery: this is a well-trodden road within the annals of modern art that handily takes us from one end of the twentieth century to the other, from Dada Duchamp to Brother Basquiat.[4] Like his precursors', Newkirk's turn to everyday objects plays to the art world's predilection for urban grit as shocking museum display. But just as importantly, his choices reflect on the peculiar bond between black bodies and the other shiny things with which they have been conflated and exchanged. That storied relation, so the psychiatrists tell us, is one marked by love, loss, and every kind of disaffection. According to William H. Grier and Price M. Cobbs, authors of the 1968 classic *Black Rage*, "For black people the ability to divorce oneself emotionally from an object is necessary for survival."[5] Yet in the face of dispossession and dire circumstance, colored folks go on embracing whatever objects they can, either carried on the body or serving as its stunning conveyance: Caddies and gold chains, picks and pomade, beads and basketballs, even fake floss. This is the stuff of selfhood and solace in the West, and on this score, it is worth recalling the words of the critic Kobena Mercer, who wrote, "The question of style can be seen as a medium for expressing the aspirations of black people historically excluded from access to official social institutions of representation and legitimation in urban, industrialized societies of the capitalist First World."[6]

As Mercer intimates, this is very much a modern narrative, but while the romance is Kori's, the substance is not. The artist—himself well represented and officially sanctioned—willingly concedes the point; while he has lived in downtown Los Angeles for over a decade and even taught at an inner-city high school, back in the day he had other questions to answer:[7] "I always knew that Black was beautiful in the 60s and powerful in the 70s, but growing up in central New York State in the 80s and 90s, I didn't know what Black was supposed to be for me."[8] In these lines, race comes across as a historically contingent signifier capable of qualifying experiences constructed at a remove from the city and in the aftermath of hails aimed at redefining African American identity. But race in what terms? To hear Newkirk tell it, blackness is up for grabs, ready to be made up and turned out, but he is all too aware that the meaning of the black image produced by spectacle can be as constraining as it is ubiquitous.[9]

We needn't look far for proof. In 1999 the artist executed a pair of self-portraits: *Channel 9*, a photograph, and *Channel 11*, another encaustic on wood (Figs. 3.4, 3.5). In each instance, the face of the subject, or, rather, the suspect, is distorted beyond recognition, as if to literalize and so reveal how reality television programs such as *LAPD: Life on the Beat* and *COPS* render "the black male" a dark menace who is always already culpable.[10]

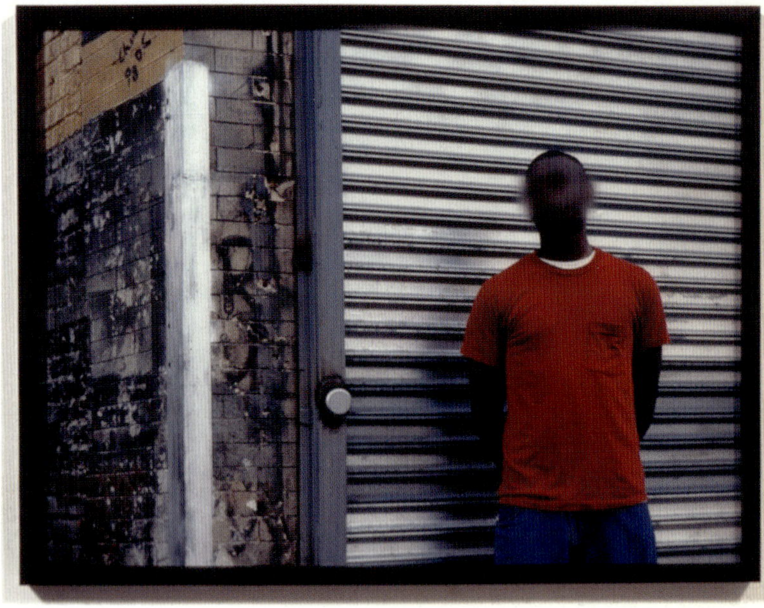

Figure 3.4
Kori Newkirk, *Channel 9*, 1999. C-print mounted on Plexiglas, framed 30 × 40 in. Courtesy the artist. Photo courtesy Studio Museum in Harlem Archives.

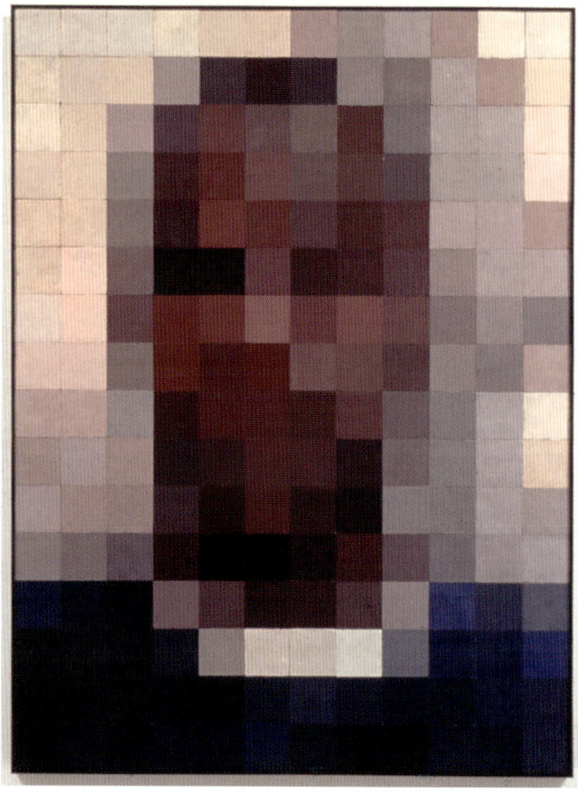

Figure 3.5
Kori Newkirk, *Channel 11*, 1999. Encaustic on wood panels, framed 64 × 49 in. Collection of Barry Sloane, Los Angeles. Courtesy Studio Museum in Harlem Archives.

Taken together, Newkirk's words and works evince an attitude toward the visual predication of blackness familiar to students of contemporary art; in adding his two cents to the great catalog of Negro life, he can afford to skip the soliloquies and the suffering, the triumph and the tragedy, to head straight for an ironic inversion of those mythical attributes figured as endemic to the black male body, particularly his own.

For an artist who came of age in the era of Air Jordan, what better location to enact such inversion than the basketball court?[11] If you've met Kori, sidled up to *Legacy*, or seen him in *Patter* (2007), you know he's about 6 feet 2: not Shaquille O'Neal tall, but tall enough and lithe enough and black enough to be pegged as a baller, despite the fact that his sport of choice growing up was competitive figure skating.[12] Even now, the game clings to him like so much other residue, material that he recoups in works such as *Black Top* (2002), *Assumption-Full Court* (2002) and *Pool* (2007), a trio as consistent in their shared target as they are promiscuous in their tactics. In *Black Top*, the artist's shorn hair, patiently glued to paper, diagrams a court; the body's cast-offs construct an image of the place from which it is absent. Inkjet prints of basketballs are linked by chains of acrylic paint in *Assumption-Full Court*, wittily replicating the structure of a DNA sequence while dispelling any assumptions about the artist's inherent athletic gifts. Last but not least, *Pool* presents the objects of the game sliced into sections like so many oranges, then placed in a neat circular arrangement, a gesture that is almost as precious as it is aggressive (Fig. 3.6).

Precious and aggressive. Just what kind of moves do these works make? And what really is the artist's game? Is he going "ghetto" to get over? I don't think so. The tone of Newkirk's practice hardly smacks of "the rage of a privileged class."[13] It feels, rather, like a funny kind of loving otherwise, something akin to that mixture of anxiety and admiration you might have for your "crazy" aunt who prefers her cigarettes mentholated and her pants stretchy, the sort of figure ripe for institutionalization, be it in the madhouse or the museum.[14] As in the Cadillac pieces, in his plays on basketball, Newkirk stages his own alienation from an archetypal site associated with African American men, registering his interest in and distance from those modes of representation—family trees, blueprints, and genetic codes—that would presume to locate his position in the world before he has arrived within it.[15]

In recasting racial fictions in styles more befitting his taste, he engages in what the cultural theorist José Muñoz calls "the process of disidentification," which

> scrambles and reconstructs the encoded message of a cultural text in a fashion that both exposes the encoded message's universalizing and exclusionary machinations and recruits its workings to account for, include, and empower minority identities and identifications. Thus, disidentifi-

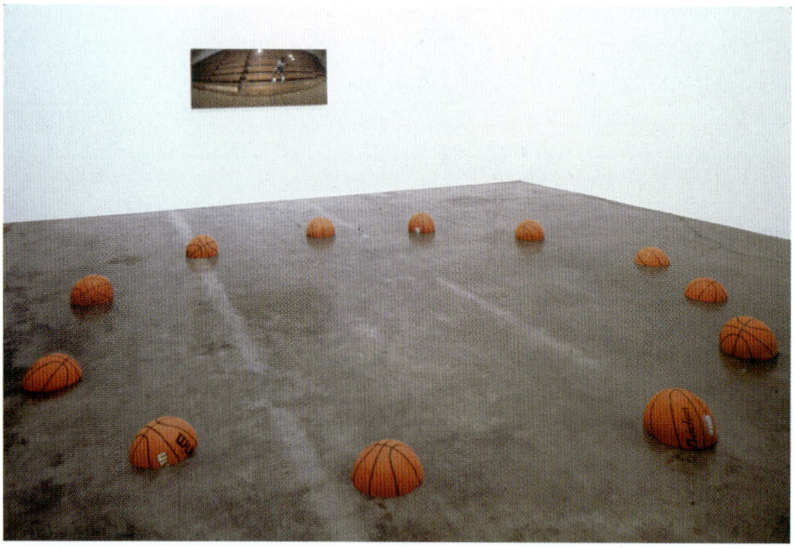

Figure 3.6
Kori Newkirk, *Pool*, 2001. Courtesy Studio Museum in Harlem Archives.

> cation is a step further than cracking open the code of the majority: it proceeds to use this code as raw material for representing a disempowered politics or positionality that has been rendered unthinkable by the "dominant culture."[16]

Pool, I would argue, offers one possible outcome of this process. In cutting and then dispersing basketballs, Newkirk disrupts one metric by which the black male is measured, and with his punning title, he begins to suggest other arenas in which that subject might be imagined, even if still phantasmatically connected to the court. Although he hates basketball, Kori can't let it go.[17] Or, as Muñoz puts it in psychoanalytic terms, "like a melancholic subject holding on to a lost object, a disidentifying subject works to hold on to this object and invest it with new life."[18] For Newkirk, as for so many queers of color who have felt themselves alien and invisible within the American cultural landscape, the figuration of unthinkable positions through familiar means becomes not only a mode of survival, but a method of worldmaking.[19]

Although he rarely points up his sexuality in his practice, several of Newkirk's basketball works—in particular hoop pieces such as *Net Gains* (2000), *Suggett* (2002), and *Huddle* (2002)—are fabulously queer, which is to say that they deform and misappropriate the game, "spawning a different order of values"[20] and begging the question of gay visibility within the overdetermined arena of black male athleticism. In *Huddle*, for example, a white cotton net has been traded for long strands of false hair covered with silver beads, the whole ensemble tapering to a narrow opening before

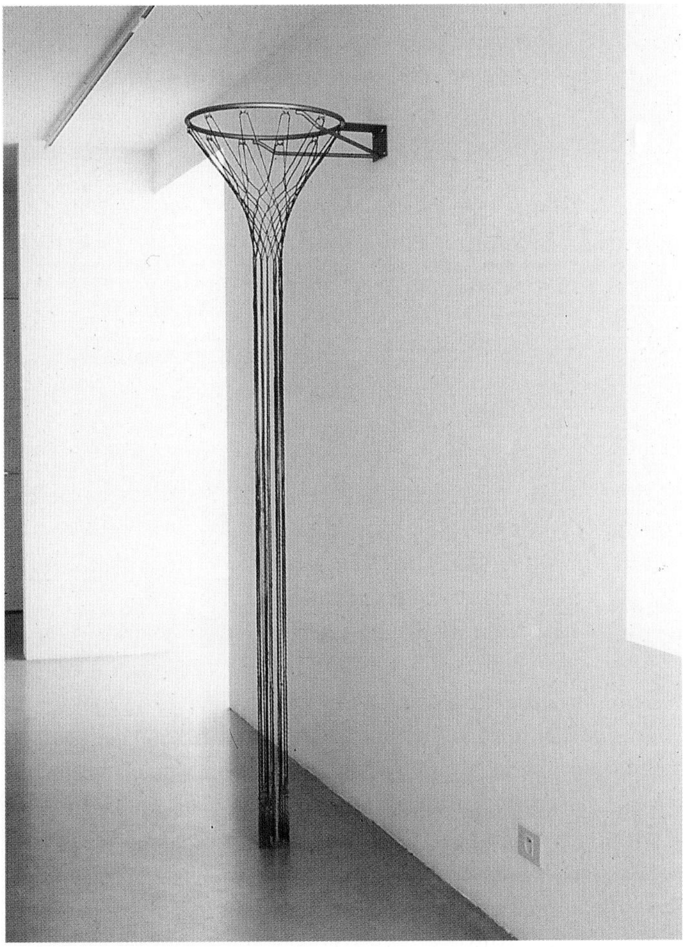

Figure 3.7
Kori Newkirk, *Huddle*, 2002. Courtesy Studio Museum in Harlem Archives.

cascading to the floor (Fig. 3.7). The artist has siphoned energy from the court in favor of the gallery's hieratic cool, displacing visual attention from the movement of sweating black bodies to static shimmering baskets and imbuing a tired "masculine" figure with freshly "feminized" meaning. You might call it "subversive": I would say it's fierce.

Transformed from a functional to a queered object, *Huddle* signifies wildly, calling up hairnets and chain mail and jockstraps and jellyfish of the most glamorous and unnatural orders. But this work and its fellows refer most pointedly, I think, to David Hammons's over-the-top basketball goals, produced in and around New York in the mid-1980s. Hyperbolically tall, decorously patterned with bottle caps and razor-sharp in their critique of the game's viability as a way out of black dereliction, these works set the standard that Newkirk looks toward.[21] Indeed, his affinity with Hammons and a whole host of more established black male practitioners is unmistakable, particularly in the case of Glenn Ligon, whose art plumbs the visual construction of black masculinity through reflexive iterations of a "self" that differentially opens onto the social and spectatorial fields.[22]

All three of these brothers know how to make a picture. They do so by letting their materials—whether paint, body, or wax—accede both to their internal logic and to the weight of history, an economy of means that imbricates "black culture" and conceptual stratagem. Note how Ligon traced Ralph Ellison's words onto panels of bodily dimensions. Consider one of the prints in which Hammons forced his face into the contours of a spade to enact physically the constriction of racial stereotypes [see Fig. 18.7 on p. 240]. Now picture these works alongside *Channel 11*. Together they comprise a suite of improvisations on the facts of blackness so famously noted by the philosopher Frantz Fanon more than fifty years ago: "I came into the world imbued with the will to find a meaning in things, my spirit filled with the desire to attain to the source of the world, and then I found that I was an object in the midst of other objects."[23] Like their not-so-distant relation, these artists play on the dissonance engendered when black men literally or metaphorically run up against the sites, tropes, and visual techniques that give racial phantasms their grounding in the real.[24]

But how do we get at the historical specificity of Newkirk's tactics? What does his art suggest about how racialized reference operates now? Is it enough to call his work "post-black" and leave it at that? Coined by Ligon in conjunction with the curator Thelma Golden, that term was meant to encapsulate the outlook of artists, such as Newkirk, Dave McKenzie, and Mark Bradford, who were included in the 2001 Studio Museum exhibition *Freestyle* and "who were adamant about not being labeled as 'black' artists, though their work was steeped, in fact deeply interested, in redefining complex notions of blackness."[25] The attitude described here certainly speaks to Kori's statements in interviews and articles, and it also offers an opening onto his approach to the disarticulation of race.

The artist and critic Kianga Ford takes us one step further. To her mind, what is new about Newkirk's practice and that of his peers is that while previous strands of artistic production also emphasize the material signifiers associated with blackness, in the work of the younger set, those signifiers are no longer pressed first and foremost into deconstructive service but are primarily accumulated for pictorial gain without ever positing a racialized subject. Of course, such a distinction does not cut cleanly along temporal or generational lines, but it does highlight a posture toward blackness, which, while evident in past artistic discourses, comes hurtling to the fore in the present.[26] As my father might say, it's all about the contours; as Kori himself will tell you, "the first thing is the aesthetics," and as his work makes manifest, that aesthetic entails neither a repudiation of identity politics nor a simple return to earlier canons of beauty.[27] I would contend, rather, that Newkirk doubly disidentifies—on the one hand, from the conventions of Modernist painting and, on the other, from the consti-

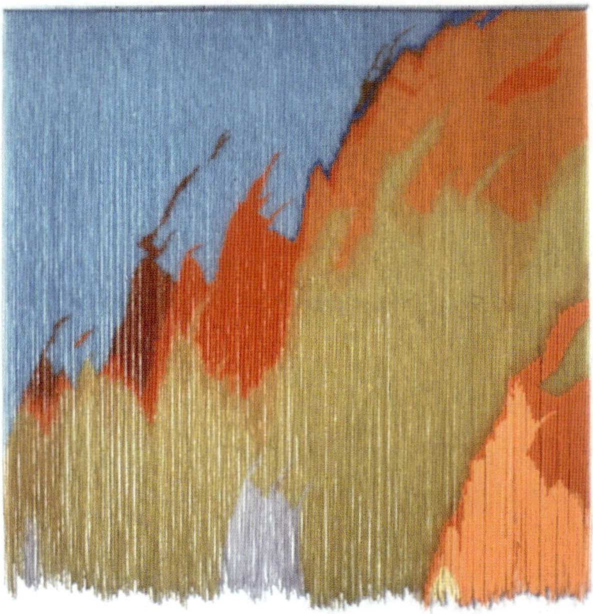

Figure 3.8
Kori Newkirk, *Jubilee*, 1999. Plastic pony beads, micro braids, aluminum, 96 × 96 in. Collection of Dean Valentine. Courtesy Studio Museum in Harlem Archives.

tutive vectors of black visibility—to string together pictures of the world as if remade from memory.

Jubilee (1999), the artist's very first curtain, is one such picture (Fig. 3.8). A brilliantly hued 8-foot square, the work is composed of braided strands of synthetic hair threaded through plastic pony beads and hung from an aluminum frame. The media attention focused on the tennis stars Venus and Serena Williams's beaded braids inspired Newkirk's choice of materials, and a mélange of memories and photographs, including ones of Los Angeles aflame during the 1992 uprising, provided the basis of an image.[28] Like the Color Field paintings to which it bears more than a passing resemblance, this work depicts no bodies—no crouching Rodney King, no angry rioters—but its virtual abstraction is as much about optical transcendence as it is about black eschatology.[29] Among the more than sixty curtains Newkirk has executed to date, *Jubilee* is exceptional for its topical and identifiable referent. Yet it shares with the others a haunting figural emptiness and a "black" materiality, the better with which to undermine fixed ideas of the African American subject's "proper" place and allow both the artist and the viewer to plot themselves imaginatively in the locations pictured, as belonging among the trees, along the skyline, in the city or in the suburbs.[30]

To many eyes, the homes nestled just over the fence in *Younger* (2004) do, in fact, appear welcoming (Fig. 3.9). The image itself is quaint, but the

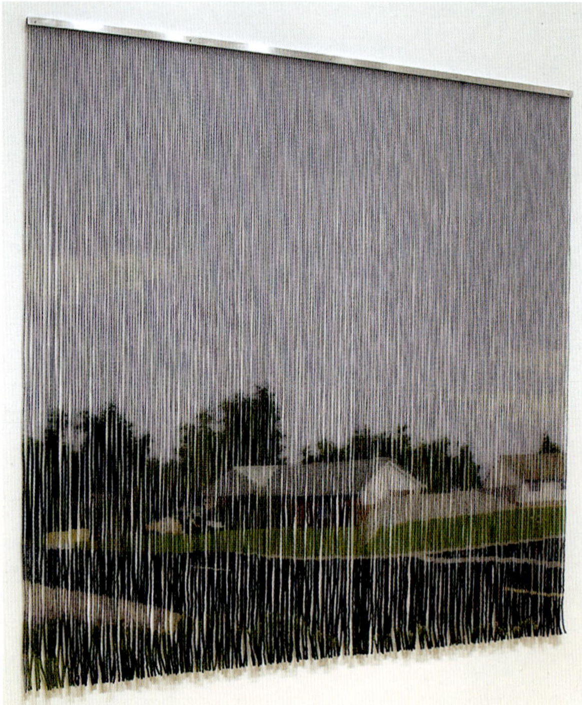

Figure 3.9
Kori Newkirk, *Younger*, 2004. Courtesy Studio Museum in Harlem Archives.

interest of the work derives from its massive scale and its ability to lure us closer, not to seek out traces of the artist's hand, but to inspect more closely the curtain's pixelated facture and to assess its capacity for breath, movement, and blackness. The title is key. "Younger" is the name of the working-class African American family immortalized in Lorraine Hansberry's 1959 play, *A Raisin in the Sun*. Set in a cramped apartment in Chicago's south side, the drama takes place after the death of Mr. Younger and principally revolves around the tension between his widow, Mama, and their son, Walter Lee, who have conflicting ideas about what to do with the $10,000 insurance payout. Ultimately the family decides to proceed with Mama's initial dream, so despite the expense and the veiled threats, the Youngers prepare to move into white suburban Clybourne Park.[31]

For Newkirk, that neighborhood might have been his own, and in conceiving the curtain he recalled Hansberry's cast: "I thought of myself as the son in the family, or maybe the son of the son, and maybe this is the house they moved into."[32] More than a fanciful projection, the artist's account of *Younger* alters the valence of the work, uncovering the invisible presence of black subjects and the realities of segregation within a seemingly innocuous scene. For all its divergent representational modes and swings in mood and emphasis, Newkirk's practice consistently explores the coordinates of life lived black by working with and against the grain of African American popular iconicity. "Universally," he tells us, "I am engaged with the idea of the black body, in all these different permutations and situations—and not necessarily 'the black male body,' but the idea of the body as fact not as spectacle."[33] To this we might add, the body as produced by spectacle, caught in the grip of stereotype, moved by queer notions, and awash in representations of itself: these are Newkirk's facts of blackness. Yet his Fanon is less the man who feels "sealed into [a] crushing objecthood" and more the spirit who continues to "attain to the source of the world."[34]

When I interviewed Kori in his studio several months ago, he was at work on a curtain. The beading went slowly, but our conversation flowed easily, so much so that I neglected to check my parking meter. When I reached the street, it became clear that my rental car—a nondescript white bubbly thing—had been towed by the city. Kori came to my rescue, and the curtain is now complete. While the events of that afternoon will doubtless fade in time, the work still connects us, a site that opens onto recollections to which we both might lay claim. Kinship is where you find it, and the art of Kori Newkirk shows us how we might remake our relations in the world one object at a time.

Notes

Several friends and colleagues have lent their time, thoughts, and words to this essay. Thanks to Hannah Feldman, Kianga Ford, Bibiana K. Obler, Krista A. Thompson, and the editors at the Studio Museum in Harlem for their incisive comments on previous drafts of this text. I have also benefited from conversations with Blake Bradford and Darby English, as well as from the research assistance of Melissa Daniels at Northwestern University; Penelope Santana at The Project; my father, Huey Copeland I; and, of course, Kori Newkirk.

1 My words here are meant to echo those of the hip-hop artist Rakim or more accurately with the critic Paul Gilroy's use of them in his essay "It's a Family Affair." The germane quote reads, "I am excited, for example, by Rakim's repeated suggestion that 'it ain't where you're from, it's where you're at.' It grants a priority to the present, emphasizing a view of identity as an ongoing process of self-making at a time when myths of origins hold so much appeal." Gilroy's essay offers a moving critique of the patriarchal family as the ground of solidarity among black subjects, which speaks productively to the development of Newkirk's practice and my approach to it. See Paul Gilroy, "It's a Family Affair," in *Black Popular Culture: A Project by Michele Wallace*, ed. Gina Dent (Bay Press, 1998), 311.

2 Newkirk, as redacted in Alice Thorson, "Drawing a Bead on Art: Kori Newkirk Raises Consciousness–and His Prices," *Kansas City Star*, May 26, 2002.

3 My description of this work is informed by Thorson, "Drawing a Bead on Art."

4 See, for example, the important account of this trajectory in Thomas Crow, "Modernism and Mass Culture in the Visual Arts," in *Modern Art in the Common Culture* (Yale University Press, 1996), 3-37.

5 William H. Grier and Price M. Cobbs, *Black Rage* (1968; repr. Wipf and Stock, 2000), 107.

6 Kobena Mercer, "Black Hair/Style Politics," in *Welcome to the Jungle: New Positions in Black Cultural Studies* (Routledge, 1994), 100.

7 Gina Kaufman, "Hair Apparent," *Pitch Weekly*, May 9, 2002.

8 Newkirk, quoted in Christine Y. Kim, "Color Blind," *V*, March-April 2003, 142.

9 Maurice O. Wallace theorizes these determining conditions in "Spectagraphia," the first part of his book, *Constructing the Black Masculine: Identity and Ideality in African-American Men's Literature and Culture, 1775-1995* (Duke University Press, 2002), 19-50.

10 Newkirk kindly pointed out each of these references to me in an email on August 30, 2007. It should also be noted that his work on the modes of violence directed at black men extends beyond the symbolic realm. I think in particular of *Swinging on the Family Tree* (1997) and *Always* (1999), which formally recalibrate lynching ropes and handguns, respectively.

11 Indeed, several black male practitioners roughly of Newkirk's generation, such as Hank Willis Thomas and Dave McKenzie, have made use of Michael Jordan as an icon in their art. See Hank Willis Thomas, "Swoosh: Looking Back at Nike, Moses and Jordan in the '80s" (master's thesis, California College of the Arts, 2004); and Glenn Ligon, "Dave McKenzie," *Artforum*, September 2005, 291.

12 See Newkirk's comments in Rujeko Hockley, "Kori Newkirk," *Studio*, Fall-Winter 2006-7, 25.

13 A passing reference to *The Rage of a Privileged Class*, which attempts to explore the "excruciating pain" of America's successful black middle class. Ellis Cose, *The Rage of a Privileged Class* (HarperCollins, 1993), 1.

14 I tip my hat here to Glenn Ligon, "Black Light: David Hammons and the Poetics of Emptiness," *Artforum*, September 2004, 242-49, particularly the opening gambit in which the artist describes his relationship to that "Crazy Nigger," his uncle Tossy, to begin charting the discursive and affective space occupied by several contemporary African American artists.

15 The curator Elizabeth A. Brown makes an analogous point in her *Kori Newkirk: To See It All*, exh. brochure (Henry Art Gallery, 2003).

16 José Ésteban Muñoz, *Disidentifications, Queers of Color, and the Performance of Politics* (University of Minnesota Press, 1999), 31. Not only does Muñoz's book brilliantly theorize disidentification, but it also examines a family of cultural practitioners whose work might be usefully compared with Newkirk's. Of particular interest are the essays treating Jean-Michel Basquiat, Issac Julien, Vaginal Creme Davis, and "the *reconstructed* identity politics" of Felix Gonzalez-Torres (164; emphasis original).

17 Newkirk makes this claim in Peter Goddard, "Beads Speak of Suburban Dreams and Delusions," *Toronto Star*, January 29, 2005.

18 Muñoz, *Disidentifications*, 12.

19 Here I redact Newkirk's comments from his conversation with me on April 20, 2007. In my use of the term "worldmaking," I again follow Muñoz's lead (Muñoz, *Disidentifications*, 195-200).

20 My language here is borrowed from Judith Butler, "Critically Queer," in *Bodies That Matter: On the Discursive Limits of Sex* (Routledge, 1993,) 229, 231.

21 For one take on Newkirk's debt to Hammons from which I have profited, see Christopher Knight, "Ideas Are Being Bounced Around in These Basketball Puns," *Los Angeles Times*, June 22, 2001. For incisive readings of the older artist's practice, see *David Hammons: Rousing the Rubble*, exh. cat. (MIT Press and Institute for Contemporary Art, P.S. 1, 1991).

22 I outline Ligon's relationship to the specular articulation of blackness in Huey Copeland, "Untitled (Jackpot!)," in *Glenn Ligon: Some Changes*, exh. cat. (Power Plant, 2005), 119-32 [reprinted in this volume, 27-40]. That argument is fleshed out in my chapter on the artist in Huey Copeland, "Bound to Appear: Figures of Slavery in the Art of Glenn Ligon, Lorna Simpson, and Fred Wilson" (PhD diss., University of California, Berkeley, 2006).

23 Frantz Fanon, "The Fact of Blackness," in *Black Skin, White Masks*, trans. Charles Lam Markmann (Grove Press, 1967), 109.

24 Newkirk's African American artistic "relations"—those practitioners invested in radically deconstructive approaches to the figuration of blackness—might also be said to include Leonardo Drew, Ellen Gallagher, Lorna Simpson, and, of course, Mark Bradford, the Los Angeles-based artist whose well-documented interest in black hair and basketball as materials have often earned him comparisons to Newkirk. Here, however, I want both to clarify and muddy the lines of descent linking three "generations" of black male artists. For an analogous effort that examines Hammons, Gallagher, and Newkirk, see Ines Gebetsroither, "Moves, Cracks, Hair," *Spike*, Summer 2006, 60-68.

25 Thelma Golden, "Introduction: Post . . . ," in *Freestyle*, exh. cat. (Studio Museum in Harlem, 2001), 14.

26 Kianga Ford, "Matters of Race: Medium, Material, and Post-Identity" (paper presented at the Ninety-second Annual Conference of the College Art Association, Seattle, February 19, 2004).

27 Newkirk, quoted in an insightful article by Malik Gaines, which, along with Ford's essay, has directed my thinking in this paragraph. See Malik Gaines, "Young, Gifted and Confused: Four Emerging Artists Talk Politics," *X-Tra* (Fall 1998): 13-14. In that article, Newkirk underlines the importance of the "politicized" art of the early 1990s for his own practice, both in terms of what he might freshly articulate and what could possibly be heard in a post-identarian art world. On this score, also see Bruce Hainley, "Kori Newkirk," *Artforum*, February 2000, 124.

28 Newkirk described his image choices in an email to me on August 22, 2007. On the significance of the Williams sisters for his art, see Goddard, "Beads Speak of Suburban Dreams and Delusions"; Rachel Teagle, *Cerca Series: Kori Newkirk*, exh. brochure (Museum of Contemporary Art, San Diego, 2005).

29 The curator Olukemi Ilesanmi points to *Jubilee*'s kinship "with the color-fielded world of Clyfford Still and Barnett Newman." See Olukemi Ilesanmi, "Ease on Down Newkirk Road," in *Kori Newkirk*, exh. brochure (Johnson County Community College Gallery of Art, 2002), n.p.

30 Newkirk's comments on the projective relationship to the sites he pictures can be found in Ilesanmi, "Ease on Down Newkirk Road."

31 Lorraine Hansberry, *A Raisin in the Sun* (Samuel French, Inc., 1959).

32 Newkirk, quoted in Goddard, "Beads Speak of Suburban Dreams and Delusions."

33 Newkirk, quoted in Rujeko Hockley, "Kori Newkirk," *Studio*, 25.

34 Fanon, "The Fact of Blackness," 109.

4

OUTTAKES

In the fall of 2002, while in New York City researching my dissertation on contemporary African American artists' engagements with the slave past, I modeled for Lorna Simpson, a practitioner whose work has figured largely in my own.[1] In this essay, I want to consider the liabilities posed and the possibilities engendered by my positioning on both sides of the camera and to reexamine the significance of masculinity in the oeuvre of an artist who has been lauded by numerous writers for her visual deconstruction of "the black woman."[2]

Before I posed for Simpson I had never formally met her, though we had several friends in common. It was one of those friends who made the connection. I was at IKEA, browsing for bookshelves with my roommate, when she rang and told me that Lorna needed a model. None of the artist's more obvious choices were available. Was I free? "Uh . . . yeah!" I immediately agreed, in part because I was honored, in part because I needed the money—and despite a vague concern that such collusion with one of "my artists" might undermine the integrity of my critical work. My confidants and colleagues were unequivocally thrilled. Posing for Simpson, they told me—as I soon came to tell myself—would be an excellent way for me to gain insight into her process. Thanks to this entrée, I developed a social and professional rapport with the artist, who generously invited me into her home, answered my research questions, allowed me to consult her personal archives, and even entertained me at her wedding.

But I'm getting ahead of myself. About a week after the call, Lorna showed up at my stoop in Bed-Stuy, picked me up in her SUV, and whisked

This article was first published by the College Art Association (CAA) in *Art Journal* 67, no. 4 (Winter 2008): 20-32. It began as a paper, subtitled "Picturing Masculinity in the Work of Lorna Simpson," that I presented on February 22, 2008, at the 96th Annual CAA Conference in Dallas, Texas, at the panel "I'll Be Your Mirror, or Why and How do We Work on Living Artists," chaired by Suzanne Hudson and Anne Byrd. The other papers—presented by Ágnes Berecz, Johanna Burton, Richard Meyer, and Phyllis Tuchman—were published in an *Art Journal* "Forum" alongside my own.

me off. The shoot itself, done in the back of her cluttered Brooklyn studio over the course of a few hours, was at once relatively unremarkable and utterly unforgettable. Having never sat for an artist, I somehow imagined a scene not unlike the one played out in Lynda Benglis's 1973 video, *Now*, with me squirming as I tried to live up to and cannily outdo the artist's expectations. "Do you wish to direct me? Do you wish to direct me, Lorna?" Thankfully, there was no such aphasic frenzy. Simpson did direct, patiently, almost offhandedly, requesting that I turn my head or torso this way or that, occasionally snaping her Polaroid instant camera, then pulling off the black-and-white image and glancing at it briefly, as if to make a quick decision about its future before she set it down to dry.

All the while, we chatted about the work, the weather, and the people we knew in common as the radio played a procession of smooth soul hits. Knowing the coolly explosive visual effect of her work, I did my best to be equally cool. I wanted to seem laid-back, though I kept worrying that I had worn the wrong T-shirt, I couldn't help thinking that I should have shaved, and I found myself hoping that Lorna would use what I considered to be the more flattering takes. Like Roland Barthes writing in *Camera Lucida*, I hoped "that my (mobile) image, buffeted among a thousand shifting photographs," would seamlessly "coincide with my (profound) 'self.'" Yet as the theorist is quick to remind us, "It is the contrary that must be said: 'myself' never coincides with my image; for it is the image which is heavy, motionless, stubborn (which is why society sustains it), and 'myself' which is light, divided, dispersed."[3] I was similarly preoccupied. Although I well knew the ability of Simpson's work to index and undo precisely those means by which society sustains its images of black subjects, I could not help but wonder, "What of my 'self' would I find in Simpson's photographs once they were matted, paired with text, and arranged in grids?"

The less existential questions came later as my accounts of the experience entered into circulation. "Are you nude?" one friend asked. Another immediately wanted to know how much I had been paid for my services and only half-jokingly inquired if I could "hook a sister up." The more surreal queries arose once the works were completed and installed at the Whitney Museum of American Art for Simpson's exhibition that year, *Cameos and Appearances*. One day as I sat in the gallery engaged in the queer act of taking notes on art featuring my own image, a not unattractive man in his early forties approached me. I thought he was cruising, but no: he just wondered if my presence in the gallery was part of the work. The memory of that encounter evokes a heady triangulation of gaze, desire, and misrecognition, a structure of looking and being looked at whose impossible conjugation—I see myself seeing my "self" being seen—seems straight out of a psychoanalytic tract by Jacques Lacan.[4]

When I recounted the anecdote to Richard Meyer, he said, "That's so interesting! You need to write about that!" But what to write and how? In so doing, is it possible to avoid pandering to a nearly universal interest in gossip, of appearing to trade on a certain kind of intimacy for name-dropping kicks? What is to be gained in telling this tale, especially given my previous writing on Simpson, which appeared in the pages of this very journal and in which my sympathy with the artist's critical enterprise was first articulated in print?[5] Does publishing this additional account constitute a breach of the rules of decorum that govern "serious" art writing and professionalized art relations? To be sure, decorum has its uses—some things are productively left unsaid—and, to be honest, any account I could provide would give little away about Lorna. In describing my varied investments and anxieties as Simpson's model, colleague, and critic, I want to move among and perhaps put pressure on the modes of speaking associated with each of those roles. But the real difficulty lies in crafting a narrative that at once respects the trust she has placed in me and attends vigilantly to the tone of her work in its sociohistorical and phenomenological unfolding.

It is easier by far to say just what Simpson did with my image. The works in the exhibition ranged from the winglike expanse of *Men* to the regulated sprawl of *Film*, in which my visage plays an elegant game of hide-and-seek with that of the artist Wangechi Mutu (Figs. 4.1, 4.2). Of the group, *Study* has most fired my imagination, because its very title seems to solicit the historian's discourse and because it so neatly, even presciently, thematizes the relations that might pertain when the conventional flow of meaning between artist and critic is rerouted (Fig. 4.3). I, a student of Lorna Simpson, here become the object of her study, or better, an avatar of black masculinity in the visual field. For despite the familiarity of the face that looks back, this is a work with its sights set on a whole class of representations, and in attempting to confront it, my first impulse is to make recourse to the conceit of impersonalized description.

The piece is composed of three photographs placed under frosted Plexiglas that depict their subject within slightly divergent optics—in profile and in three-quarters, in cameo and squared-off frames, blurred and focused, crisply defined and entirely covered over. The logic governing the combination of these modalities is unclear, though the photographer's aim is surely to secure the opacity of her sitter while invoking an entire history of visual strategies intended to render a particular black male subject a transparent text. The words running between the first and second images in a single column suggest as much: "portrait of a boy," "michael," "african youth," "a negro prince," "janitor paints a picture." The list goes on, but as always in Simpson's art, such designations are complicated by the specificity of the images: these photographs—like the paintings in American

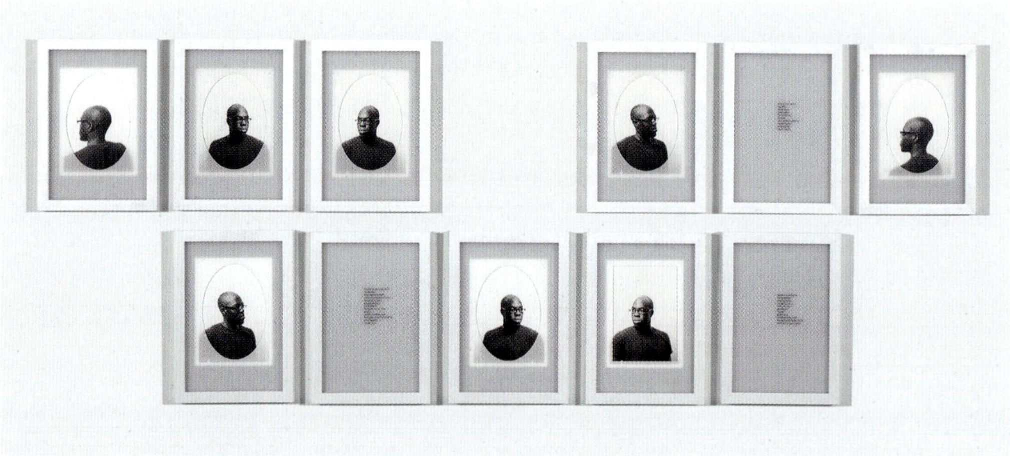

Figure 4.1

Lorna Simpson, *Men*, 2002. Archival silver gelatin prints with black vinyl lettering. Overall: 25 × 65.5 in. (63.5 × 166.4 cm), Each framed print: 12 × 8½ in. (30.5 × 21.6 cm). © Lorna Simpson. Courtesy the artist and Hauser & Wirth.

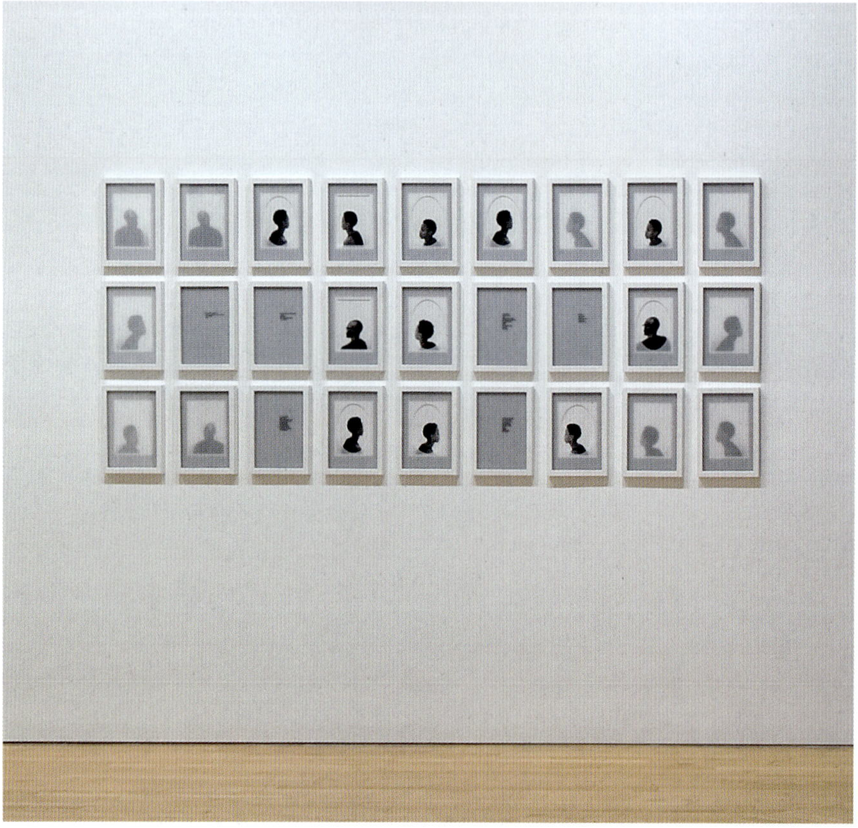

Figure 4.2

Lorna Simpson, *Film*, 2002. Archival silver gelatin prints under semitransparent plexiglass with black vinyl lettering in 27 wooden frames. Overall: 38 × 84½ in. (96.5 × 214.6 cm), Each framed print: 12 × 8½ in. (30.5 × 21.6 cm). © Lorna Simpson. Courtesy the artist and Hauser & Wirth.

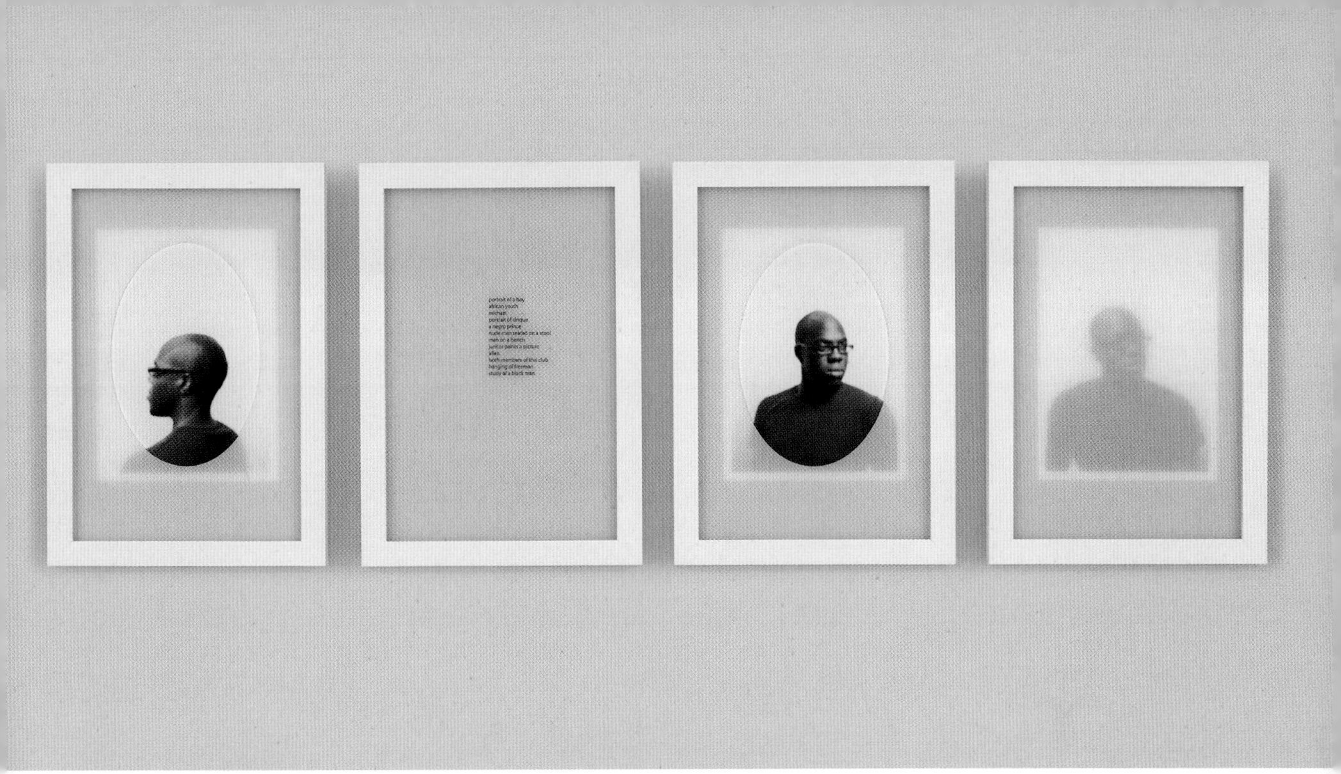

Figure 4.3
Lorna Simpson, *Study*, 2002. Archival silver gelatin prints under semitransparent plexiglass with black vinyl lettering in 4 wooden frames. Overall: 12⅛ × 37½ × ¾ in. (30.8 × 95.3 × 1.9 cm), each framed print: 12 × 8½ in. (30.5 × 21.6 cm). © Lorna Simpson. Courtesy the artist and Hauser & Wirth.

museums that they are meant to recall and so refigure—partially depend on our estrangement from the people pictured for their rhetorical force.

Such a reading falls in line with other productive approaches to Simpson's work, which might be furthered by a consideration of the sitter's corporeal disposition.[6] This, in fact, is what I argue in my previous article "'Bye, Bye Black Girl.'" The experience of modeling for Simpson brought home to me the importance of thinking about the tension between the specular and haptic predication of the black bodies in her art, whether depicted or only evoked.[7] *Study* is no exception. In the photograph on the left, a shift in the angling of the head deflects our vision; in the next one, I can almost bodily remember the odd tension of an unnaturally held pose. The last image holds out something more consonant with what I feel to be myself, to be in my body, but it of course has been covered over: it is a self present yet lost, rendered sculptural, thinglike, obscure.

As if in compensation, Simpson gave me three of the photographs from the shoot, souvenirs of our session together. I am grateful, to say the least. Yet I wonder whether it is mere accident that of that trio, the image I consider to most resemble myself, the one that has become my public

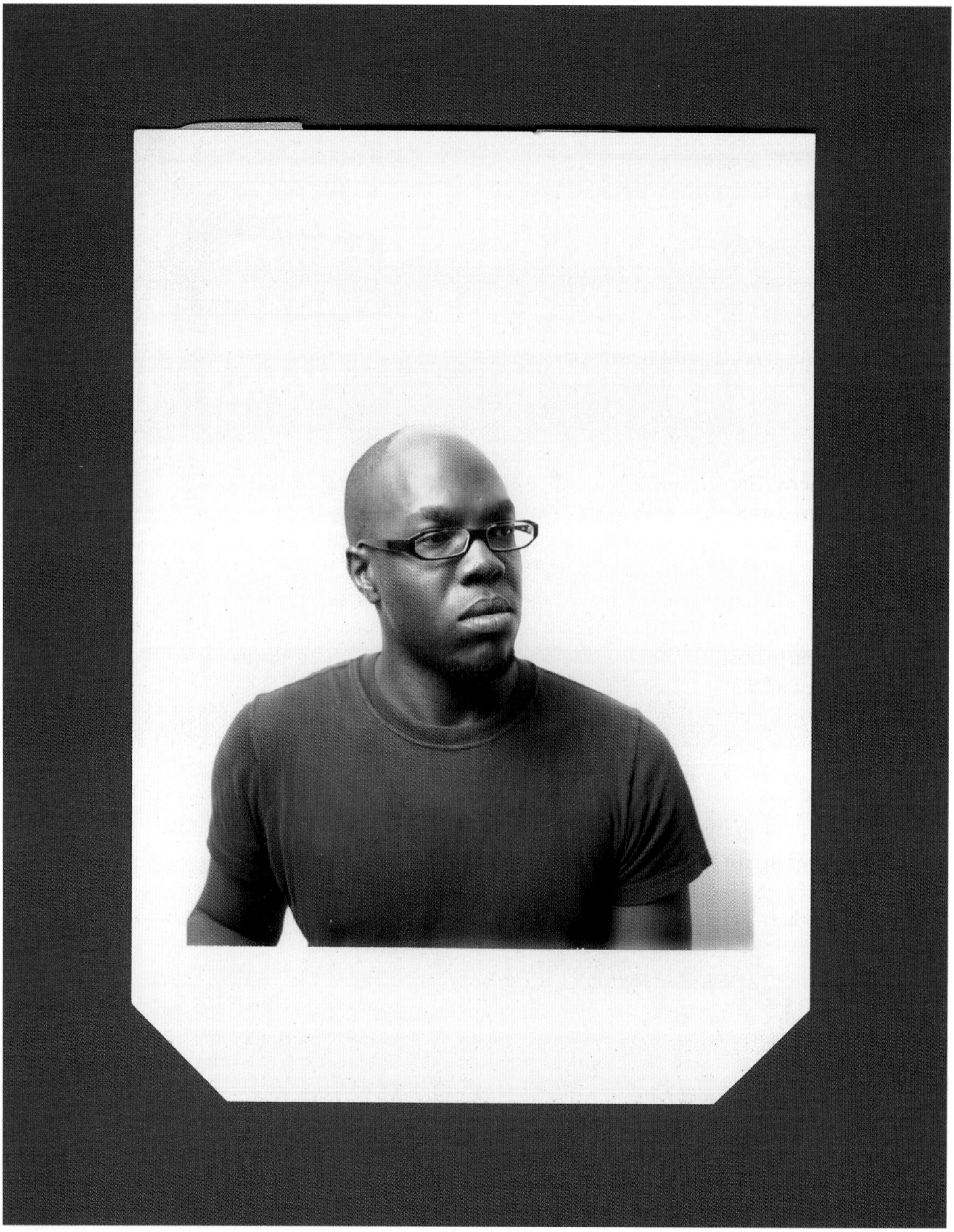

Figure 4.4

Lorna Simpson, *Untitled*, 2002. Black-and-white Polaroid print, 5¾ × 4¼ in. (14.6 × 10.8 cm). © Lorna Simpson. Courtesy the artist and Hauser & Wirth. Photograph provided by the author.

face on the internet and elsewhere, is also a dead ringer for the picture that the artist dramatically occludes (Fig. 4.4). The logic of Simpson's work, its emphasis on the antiportrait and all of its expansive semantic potentiality for both viewer and sitter, has never seemed clearer to me.[8]

Estrangement, not anonymity, I think, is the key to that expansiveness, a distancing effected by the photographic that is complicated and intensified by my experience before the lens. Since the pieces from *Cameos and Appearances* were first exhibited, several folks have sought me out to say that they have seen "me." No matter how many times I hear this locution, I still find it disorienting: not only because it confirms that my image has a life that outstrips and qualifies my own, but also because of the way it performatively conflates my "self" and the work, throwing me back onto a triply confounded position. From what place do I speak back?

I imagine that I am not alone in posing this question. Although I may be the first of her models to press my studio session into critical service, the artist's sitters can often be recognized from their appearances elsewhere. The lips of Alva Rogers—the composer and vocalist who often served as Simpson's visual surrogate—were featured in *Hypothetical?* [see Fig. 13.2 on p. 179] not long after Rogers's turn in the 1991 film, *Daughters of the Dust*; the curator Claire Tancons's every move was assiduously tracked in the 2002 video installation *31*; Mutu would go on to star in *Corridor* of 2003 as her own career was taking off. Simpson's models might be said, then, to hint at the contours of the artist's social world at a given moment, even as they are mobilized to conjure the regimes of violence that persistently impinge on the subject, who, in her work, is usually black and most often female.

As is well known, men are strangely missing from much of Simpson's photographic oeuvre, despite the fact that her first mature photo-text was the all-male *Gestures/Reenactments* of 1985 (Fig. 4.5). The fellow pictured in that work, so the captions tell us, is also a surrogate of sorts—for Larry when he found out, for Buck being himself, for Sam standing like his mother, for Cecile, and Calvin, for Mr. Johnson, a runnin' buddy—holding out fragments of the emotional lives of so many nameless others still somehow in evidence. When *Gestures* made its debut in April 1985, it was the standout of Simpson's solo show at the Fifth Street Market Alternative Gallery in San Diego. Since then, it has come to occupy a privileged place within critical debates on the deconstruction of black masculinity, serving, for instance, as a key point of articulation in Thelma Golden's landmark 1994 exhibition, *Black Male: Representations of Masculinity in Contemporary American Art* at the Whitney Museum.

More recently, the curator Okwui Enwezor has argued that what we witness in this work is the "appearance of the castration complex." In *Gestures*, he suggests, Simpson points up the aporetic social condition of a subject, "who is simultaneously feminized . . . and menacing," "completely

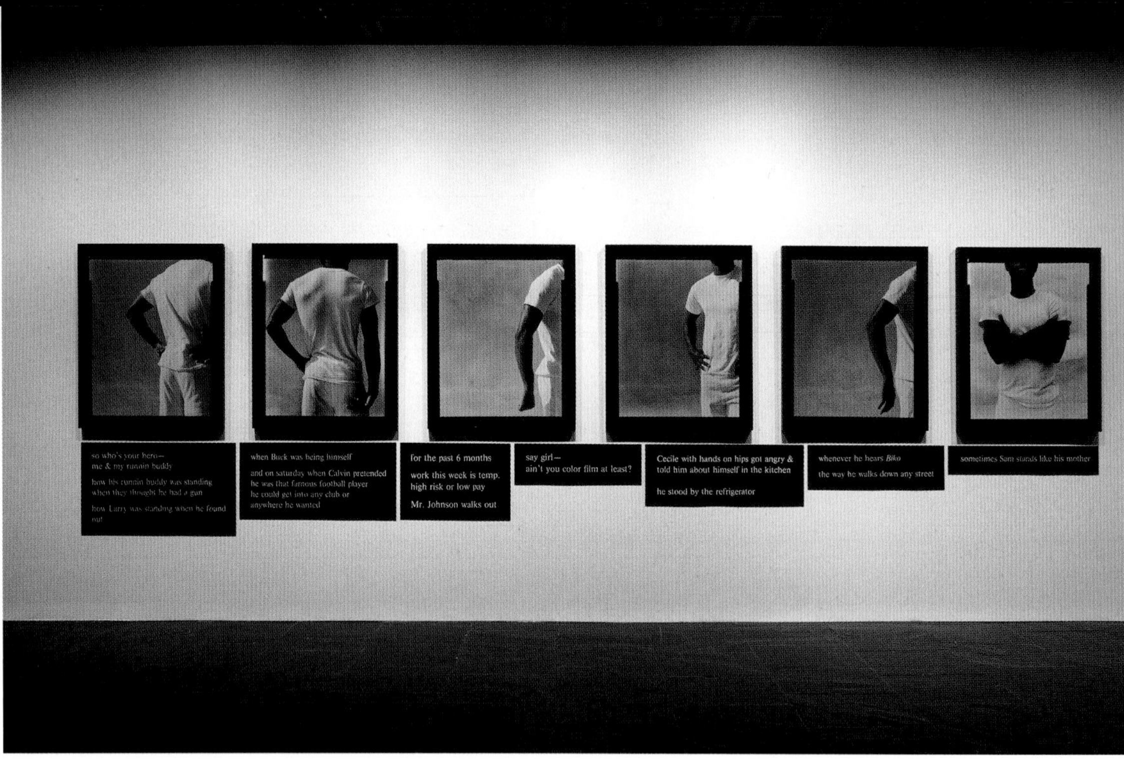

Figure 4.5
Lorna Simpson, *Gestures / Reenactments*, 1985. 6 silver gelatin prints, 7 engraved text plaques. Overall: 57⅛ × 278¾ in. (145.1 x 708 cm), Each framed print: 48¼ × 39¼ in. (122.6 × 99.7 cm). © Lorna Simpson. Courtesy the artist and Hauser & Wirth.

devoid of the armors of masculine toughness yet exorbitantly endowed with such masculinity" within the cultural imaginary.[9] In her 2002 survey of Simpson's practice, the art historian Kellie Jones follows the lead of the theorist Jack Halberstam in arguing that the work denaturalizes black masculinity and opens a space to reenvision it as a kind of performance. By Jones's lights, *Gestures/Reenactments* serves as a "prototype" for Simpson's subsequent work with "masculinized" women, as in *She* and in pieces like *You're Fine* that revivify in order to dissect "feminized" visual paradigms such as the odalisque (Figs. 4.6, 4.7).[10]

Points well taken. When I initially read these accounts, however, I will admit to feeling a desire to defend my positions both as a critic and as a fellow photographic subject. (We are all cut off by language, but who wants to be a poster child for castration writ large?) In further engaging with Jones's and Enwezor's productive commentaries, such sentiments have ceded to an investment in getting Simpson's art right and in getting a grip on my place within it. Indeed, the first draft of my dissertation chapter on her work—ostensibly focused on *Five Rooms*, a 1991 collaborative project with Rogers that explored the legacies of "the peculiar institution" in Charleston, South Carolina—was overly preoccupied with questions that I still find pressing: Why is it the male figure that inaugurated Simpson's now-

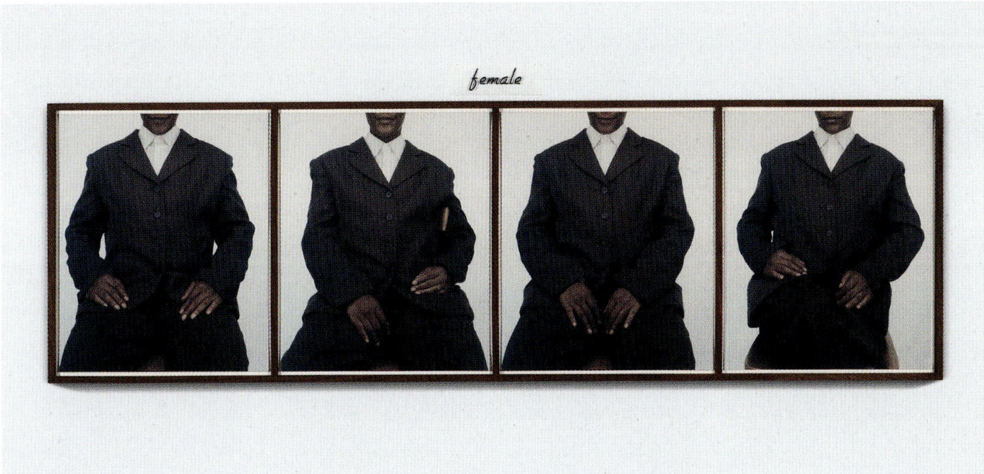

Figure 4.6

Lorna Simpson, *She*, 1992. 4 dye diffusion color Polaroid prints, 1 engraved plastic plaque. Overall: 29½ × 85⅛ × 2 in. (75 × 216.2 × 5.1 cm). Each panel: 25 × 85⅛ × 2 in. (65.7 × 216.2 × 5.1 cm), Plaque: 3 × 8¾ × ⅛ in. (7.6 × 22.2 × 0.3 cm). © Lorna Simpson. Courtesy the artist and Hauser & Wirth. Photo: Nathan Keay.

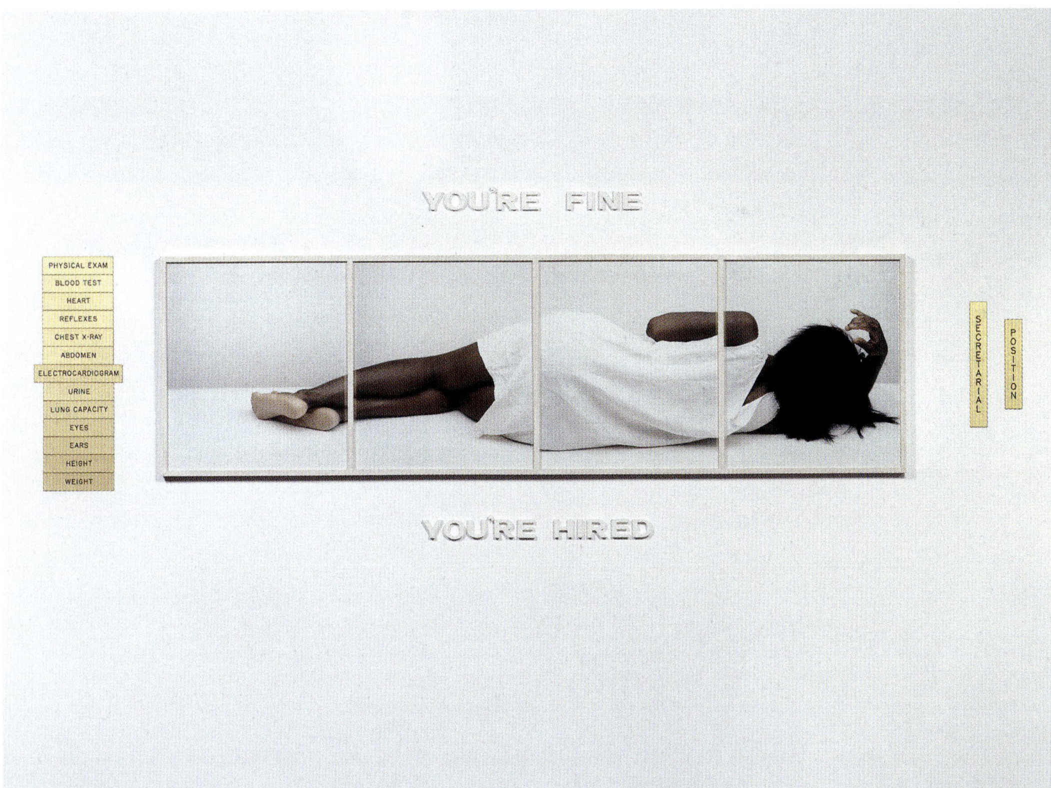

Figure 4.7

Lorna Simpson, *You're Fine*, 1988. 4 dye diffusion color Polaroid prints, 15 engraved plastic plaques, ceramic letters. Overall: 37¾ × 114 × 1⅝ in. (95.9 × 289.6 × 4.1 cm). © Lorna Simpson. Courtesy the artist and Hauser & Wirth.

trademark mode of production? In what terms is he couched in her art? What, in other words, do the pictured men allow her practice to articulate that it could not otherwise?

For answers, we might look back to a 1988 interview that Trevor Fairbrother conducted with the artist. Here is Simpson's reading of *Gestures*:

> The photographs might be taken as a set of very defensive, very masculine poses, as, for instance, in the first one, in which a man is seen with his hands on his hip and his back. If a cop were to look at this, he might see a black man who is assumed to be "dangerous," one who is a suspect and a threat. Without even seeing his face, anyone, black or white, might imagine it to be a confrontational or defiant pose. The other photos suggest other emotions.[11]

"Emotions," to say the least. As Simpson's comments bear out, the black male image—at once dreaded and desired, transparent and inscrutable, marked by and in the excess of the law—poses a formidable challenge for any critical practice. *Gestures/Reenactments* reinvests the figure as a locus of differential signification, depicting momentarily held poses that imbue its particular subject with a depth and recalcitrance, a sense of affinity and opacity that fly in the face of stereotype. Through the slightly overblown scale of its individual pictorial elements, the work materializes the larger-than-life public career of the black male image only to undermine the viewer's anxious cathection to a specter that is as dangerous as endangered.[12]

Even when African American men do not appear within Simpson's oeuvre, their absence is often marked textually by violent threat or its implication: consider the final line of *The Service* of 1991, "he jumped from the / empire state building"; or recall the text that accompanies *Waterbearer* of 1986: "SHE SAW HIM DISAPPEAR BY THE RIVER / THEY ASKED HER TO TELL WHAT HAPPENED / ONLY TO DISCOUNT HER MEMORY." In considering these lines, it is worth remembering that Simpson emerged in a moment when images of disfigured and disappeared black men were commonplace within the nation's networks of media production. As the cultural theorist Kobena Mercer then noted, "Black masculinity is not merely a social identity in crisis. It is also a key site of ideological representation upon which the nation's crisis comes to be dramatized, demonized, and dealt with—enter Willie Horton as apogee of the most *un*American Otherness imaginable."[13] Awash in that stream of images, so charged and intransigent, it makes sense that Simpson—much like her contemporaries—should attempt to redirect the flow or refuse to contribute to it altogether, particularly after what happened on March 3, 1991.

Anyone who has seen George Holliday's videotape from that day is not likely to forget it. For eighty-one excruciating seconds, Rodney King is viciously beaten, every attempt he makes to rise answered with another kick of the foot, another whack of the baton. In a 1992 canvas, the artist Danny Tisdale freezes a singular moment from that visual narrative, repeating the image in which the white officers' feet come into contact with the black man's back and distilling the very structure of American racial violence.[14] As Elizabeth Alexander notes in "'Can you be BLACK and look at this?,'" her brilliant 1994 essay on the beating, such terrifying moments are the meat and drink of American culture, satisfying white fantasies of the black body in pieces. More important, she argues, such moments forge untold links between and among black subjects, who relive King's pain and Michael Griffith's and Emmett Till's and Yusef Hawkins's and Amadou Diallo's, feeling in their lives and in their bodies the kind of disintegration that might be arbitrarily visited on them by the officers of the state supposedly sworn to serve and protect.[15]

Simpson's *Figure* of 1991 might be thought of as a response to such depredation, though it seems a world away from the blurry man crawling along the ground in Holliday's tape or on Tisdale's canvas (Fig. 4.8). Standing erect with left knee bent and arms hanging loosely at her sides, the woman pictured here is whole rather than riven, standing guard, not under attack. Yet the slight turn of her body to the left and the tension in her shoulders seem to telegraph an alertness to the unheard call that might solicit her at any moment. If, as the theorists Steve Martinot and Jared Sexton argue, the police are the avant-garde of white supremacy, then the black body, particularly the black male body, is its medium par excellence.[16] It is this relation of subordination and terror that *Figure* succinctly figures on: "figured the worst," "figured on all the times there / was no camera," "he was disfigured," "figured there / would be no reaction," "figured legality had nothing / to do with it," "figured she was suspect," "figured he was suspect."

In these lines, taken from text panels flanking either side of the photograph, Simpson articulates the redundancy, the complacency, and the sense of inevitability that made the Rodney King beating at once extraordinary because it was recorded and yet rather banal within the context of American history.[17] Invoked here with the lightest of allusive touches, the black male body is purposefully absented from view in order to point up the gendering of racial violence and to differently figure racial visibility. *Figure* is all about figuring, in both its literal and metaphorical senses, and the work makes vivid how African American men matter to Simpson's art.[18] Despite our rarity within her practice, we serve to index the state of a nation and the possibilities for representation itself, opening onto the series of female icons, structures, and phantoms that have come to emblematize her art.[19]

Seen in this light, Simpson might be said to follow the lead of Adrian Piper in her *Mythic Being* series (Fig. 4.9). In this seminal body of work, begun in 1973, Piper posed as her seeming visual Other, in her words, "a third world, working class, overtly hostile male."[20] Decked out in Afro wig,

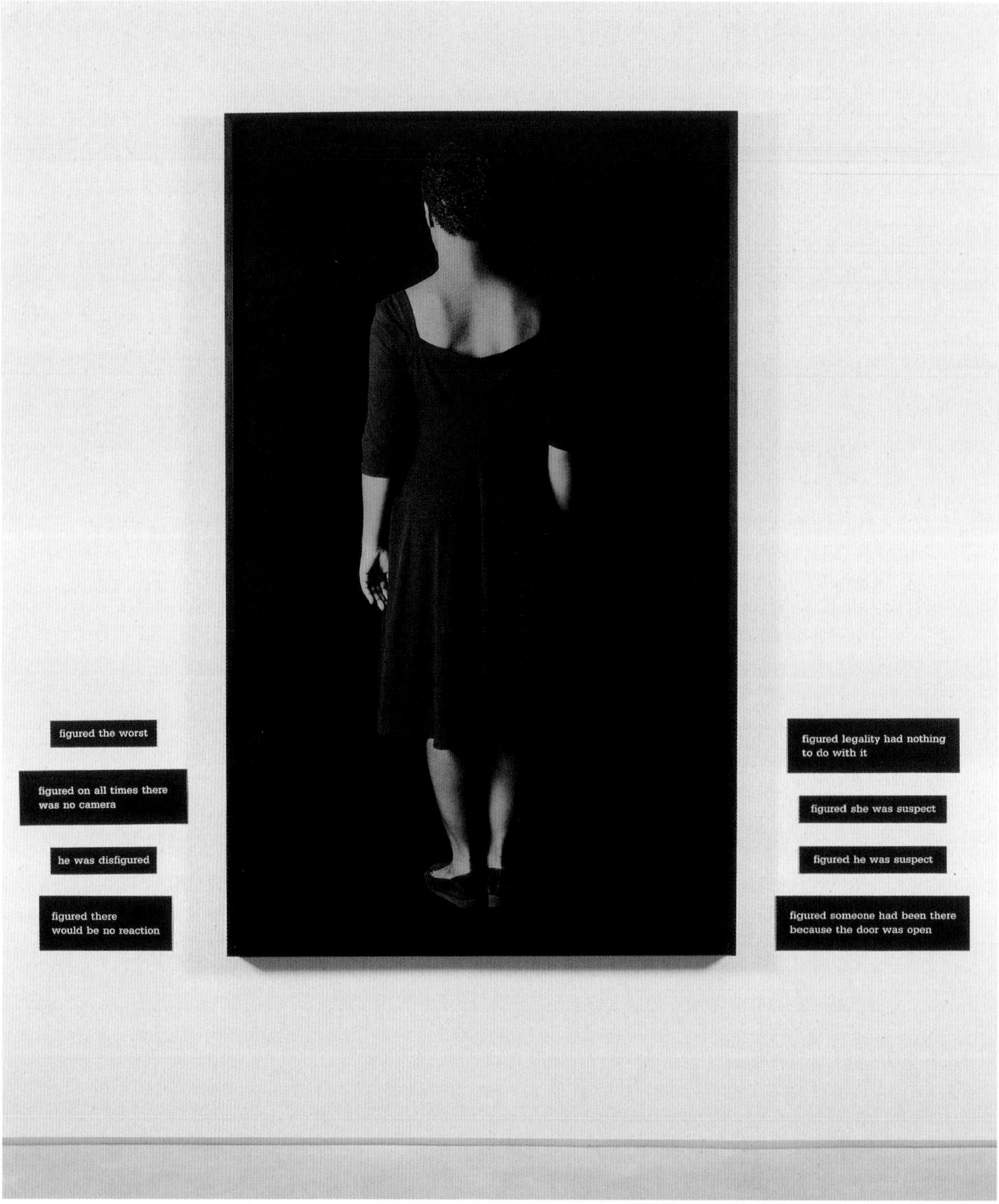

Figure 4.8

Lorna Simpson, *Figure*, 1991. 1 silver gelatin print, 8 engraved plastic plaques. Overall: 73 × 82½ in. (185.4 × 209.6 cm), Framed print: 42 × 74 in. (106.7 × 188 cm). © Lorna Simpson. Courtesy the artist and Hauser & Wirth.

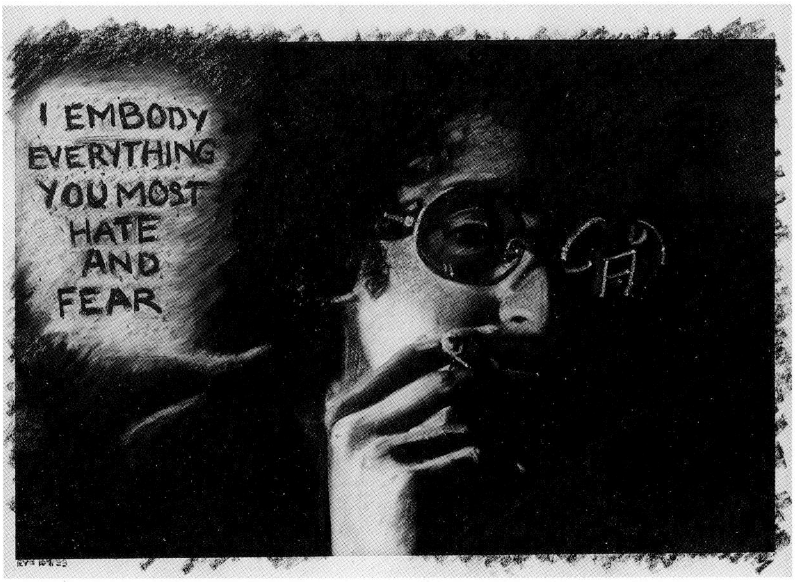

Figure 4.9
Adrian Piper, *The Mythic Being: I Embody Everything You Most Hate and Fear,* 1975. Oil crayon on silver gelatin print, 8 × 10 in. (20.3 × 25.4 cm). Collection of the Art Institute of Chicago. © Adrian Piper Research Archive Foundation.

mustache, and dark sunglasses and puffing on the occasional cigar, Piper's evocation of masculinity in its most clichéd if mediagenic guise could not have been more timely given the recent explosion of "baadasssss" brothers onto the silver screen and the continued persecution of black nationalist icons in the street.[21] For Piper, the impersonation of America's nightmare would prove crucial in the articulation of a self, an art, and a politics that critically explore the phantasms required to keep racial and gender hierarchies in place. The analogy with Simpson should be clear. In order to understand and critique the visual logic of white supremacy, she too mobilized the specter of black masculinity, which would provide the grounds for the formal transformation of her practice and its engagement with circumstances on the ground.[22]

In the end, this line of inquiry fell beyond the frame of my dissertation; in fact, this article, like the photographs of me that now reside with my father and godson, constitutes another kind of outtake from my session with Simpson. Yet charting the trajectory of the black male figure within her work has productively oriented my writing to the sexualized economies of terror and dispossession that have troubled the constitution of the African American image from slavery to the present and toward the resources that artists have turned to in reconfiguring its contours. As I modeled for Simpson, her practice has modeled for me what might be called "a tending-toward-blackness"—in the senses of leaning toward and caring for—that not only embraces those figures closest to home and forges an implausible community from the artist's photographic subjects but also proposes a new understanding of how our corporeal being expansively links us to one another in political and aesthetic terms.

Of course, every critic's writing is a reflection of his investments in the artist's work and often, with a living practitioner, in her person. It might he argued that my interpretive approach to Simpson too neatly mirrors her sensibility and my fantasies as revealed in her aesthetic deployment of my image. Yet to make that case is to accept a seamless concept of identification rather than to plumb those sites of disjuncture from which the subject emerges in time, always glancing back at what he has been in relation to another in the attempt to assess the meaning of the various roles he has assumed.[23] My encounters with *Study*, the artist, Lorna, and the man in the museum are reminders of this necessary and productive temporal estrangement: they are calls to engage critically with the leftovers of narration, to prioritize what lies outside the established purview of Simpson's practice, and to recognize the enabling limits of my own position within it—all of which are part of the ongoing challenge of seeing one's best and least familiar self from one place at a time.

Notes

Thanks to Johanna Burton, Anne Byrd, Suzanne Hudson, Steve Reinke, and Krista A. Thompson for their helpful comments on previous drafts of this text, and to the artists for kindly allowing me to reproduce their work.

1 Huey Copeland, "Bound to Appear: Figures of Slavery in the Art of Glenn Ligon, Lorna Simpson, and Fred Wilson" (PhD diss., University of California, Berkeley, 2006).

2 See, for example, bell hooks, "Facing Difference: The Black Female Body," in *Art on My Mind: Visual Politics* (New Press, 1995), 94-100; Deborah Willis, "Eyes in the Back of Your Head: The Works of Lorna Simpson," in *Lorna Simpson* (Friends of Photography, 1992); Coco Fusco, "Uncanny Dissonance: The Work of Lorna Simpson," in *Lorna Simpson*, exh. cat. (Colgate University, Dana Arts Center, 1991), n.p.; repr. in Coco Fusco, *English Is Broken Here: Notes on Cultural Fusion in the Americas* (New Press, 1995), 97-102.

3 Roland Barthes, *Camera Lucida: Reflections on Photography*, trans. Richard Howard (Hill and Wang, 1981), 12.

4 I refer here to Lacan's critique of Cartesian vision and of the mode of consciousness that imagines "seeing oneself seeing oneself," in *The Seminar of Jacques Lacan*, vol. 11, *The Four Fundamental Concepts of Psychoanalysis*, ed. Jacques-Alain Miller, trans. Alan Sheridan (W. W. Norton, 1981), 74.

5 Huey Copeland, "'Bye, Bye Black Girl': Lorna Simpson's Figurative Retreat," *Art Journal* 64, no. 2 (Summer 2005): 62-77.

6 The reading I have in mind is Okwui Enwezor's compelling analysis of *Study* as a form of counter-ethnography in his essay "Archive Fever:

Photography between History and the Monument," in *Archive Fever: Uses of the Document in Contemporary Art*, exh. cat. (International Center of Photography and Steidl Publishers, 2008), 42.

7 For different perspectives on the relation between figural absence and presence in Simpson's work, see Nicole De Armendi, "Lorna Simpson's *Public Sex* Series: The Voyeuristic Presence and the Embodied Figure's Absence," *Athanor* 19 (2001): 67-71, as well as the postscript to Okwui Enwezor's article "Social Grace: The Work of Lorna Simpson," *Third Text* 35 (Summer 1996): 43-58.

8 In all likelihood, the image with which I most identify and the one covered over in *Study* are identical. Simpson produced the entirety of *Cameos and Appearances* using Polaroid positive/negative film, "which means that there is a positive image that peels off of a negative film, all in one" (email from the artist, November 6, 2008). The negatives served as the bases for the gelatin silver prints used in the final work, and the positives were quite literally outtakes. For further remarks on Simpson's work as antiportraiture, see Lauri Firstenberg, "Autonomy and the Archive in America: Reexamining the Intersection of Photography and Stereotype," in *Only Skin Deep: Changing Visions of the American Self*, exh. cat., ed. Coco Fusco and Brian Wallis (International Center for Photography and Harry N. Abrams, 2003), 317-20.

9 Okwui Enwezor, "Repetition and Differentiation—Lorna Simpson's Iconography of the Racial Sublime," in *Lorna Simpson*, exh. cat. (Harry N. Abrams and American Federation of Arts, 2006), 110, 111.

10 On this score, see Kellie Jones, "(Un)Seen & Overheard: Pictures by Lorna Simpson," in *Lorna Simpson* (Phaidon, 2002), 58.

11 The artist, quoted in Trevor Fairbrother, "Lorna Simpson," in *The BiNational: American Art of the Late 80s*, exh. cat. (DuMont Buchverlag, with Institute of Contemporary Art and Museum of Fine Arts Boston, 1988), 175-76.

12 For further analysis in this vein, see Maurice O. Wallace. "On Dangers Seen and Unseen: Identity Politics and the Burden of Black Male Specularity," in *Constructing the Black Masculine: Identity and Ideality in African American Men's Literature and Culture, 1775-1995* (Duke University Press, 2002), 19-50.

13 Kobena Mercer, "Black Masculinity and the Sexual Politics of Race," in *Welcome to the Jungle: New Positions in Black Cultural Studies* (Routledge, 1994), 160; emphasis original. The portion of the text I cite here was originally published as the essay "Engendered Species: Danny Tisdale and Keith Piper," *Artforum*, Summer 1992, 74-77.

14 Tisdale's visual strategy is of course indebted to Andy Warhol's, and *Rodney King Police Beating* is meant to resonate with the Pop artist's *Race Riot* silkscreens of the early 1960s. See Kobena Mercer and Anne M. Wagner, "Warhol Paints History, or Race in America," *Representations* 55 (Summer 1996): 98-119.

15 Elizabeth Alexander, "'Can you be black and look at this?': Reading the Rodney King Video(s)," in the useful compendium *Black Male: Representations of Masculinity in Contemporary American Art*, exh. cat. (Whitney Museum of American Art; distributed by Harry N. Abrams, 1994), 91-110. Alexander takes her title from a line in Pat Ward Williams's 1986 phototext, *Accused/Blowtorch/Padlock*, another black female artist's response to the history of racialized violence as it is acted out on the black male body.

16 Steve Martinot and Jared Sexton, "The Avant Garde of White Supremacy," *Social Identities* 9, no. 2 (2003): 175. In describing how the black subject becomes a "fictional channel, a medium for the realization of police impunity," Martinot and Sexton refer to the police murder of a young black woman named Tyisha Miller, underlining how state violence disarticulates gender even as the spectacle endlessly reproduces racial conflict as a battle among men.

17 See Alexander, "'Can you be black and look at this?,'" 99-101. Also see the essays collected in *Reading Rodney King / Reading Urban Uprising*, ed. Robert Gooding-Williams (Routledge, 1993). Simpson's 1992 *Hypothetical?* can likewise be thought of as a response to the rebellion that raged in Los Angeles following the acquittal of King's assailants. For an instructive reading of this work, see Jones, "(Un)Seen & Overheard," 58-63.

18 For analyses of Simpson's work that take up the question of figural discourse, particularly in relation to the concept of signifyin' as theorized by Henry Louis Gates Jr., see Fusco, "Uncanny Dissonance"; Yasmin Ramirez-Harwood, *Centric 38, Lorna Simpson*, exh. brochure (University Art Museum, California State University, Long Beach, 1990), n.p.

19 Of related interest is Simpson's 2004 video, *Cloudscope*, which features the artist Terry Adkins whistling in a gallery. In the course of three minutes a fog slowly fills the room, entirely obscures the man, and then dissipates, leaving emptiness in its wake until Adkins emerges and the cycle begins again. This work, like *Study* and *Gestures*, offers a meditation on the contingencies governing appearance as such through the disfiguration of black masculinity.

20 Adrian Piper, "The Mythic Being: Getting Back," in *Out of Order, Out of Sight*, vol. 1, *Selected Writings in Meta-Art, 1968-1992* (MIT Press, 1996), 147.

21 I refer, of course, to Melvin Van Peebles's *Sweet Sweetback's Badasssss Song*, 35mm, 97 min. (Yeah, Inc., 1971, dist. Xenon Pictures) and to the fates of figures such as Fred Hampton and Huey Newton. My thinking rhymes with that of John Bowles in "Adrian Piper as African American Artist," *American Art* 20, no. 3 (Fall 2006): 108-17, which also features a brief yet incisive overview of the Piper scholarship. In this respect, Cherise Smith reminds us that Piper has often engaged with the mainstream media's production of racial difference: in 1992. she executed *Black Box, White Box*, her own take on the King beating. See Cherise Smith, "Remember the Audience: Adrian Piper's Mythic Being Advertisements." *Art Journal* 66, no. 1 (Spring 2007): 46-58.

22 Jennifer Drake offers an alternative framework for thinking about Simpson's and Piper's practices together in "Variations on Negation: Breaking the Frame with Lorna Simpson and Adrian Piper," in *Interfaces: Women, Autobiography, Image, Performance*, ed. Sidonie Smith and Julia Watson (University of Michigan Press, 2002), 211-39.

23 My argument here is informed by Lacan's theorization of how the subject may develop a critical relation to his structuring *imagos* through the agency of language. See "The Mirror Stage as Formative of the Function of the I," in *Écrits: A Selection*, trans. Alan Sheridan (W. W. Norton, 1977), 1-7; and "The Concept of Analysis," in *The Seminar of Jacques Lacan*, vol. 1, *Freud's Papers on Technique, 1953-1953*, ed. Jacques-Alain Miller, trans. John Forrester (W. W. Norton, 1991), 273-87.

5

THE BLACKNESS OF BLACKNESS

As ever in Chicago, there is no dearth of tragedy where racial politics are concerned: ongoing revelations about city hall's involvement in covering up police torture of black suspects; a recent 18 percent increase in the homicide rate that disproportionately affects black youth; and the threat of further black disenfranchisement for the sake of the 2016 Olympics bid. For the past several months, however, conversations about race in the Black Metropolis, as elsewhere in the United States, have turned to Democratic presidential nominee, Barack Obama. He too is a marked man, at once targeted for castration by Jesse Jackson and hailed by Ted Kennedy as a leader of messianic proportions. As I write, it seems inevitable that in the weeks to come, the hopes, epithets, and ire heaped on him—whether in "celebrity" commercials or on "satirical" magazine covers—will only increase. Because for all of Obama's best efforts to be reasonable, the schizoid discourse around his candidacy gives further legs to an old adage of Frantz Fanon's: when blacks walk through the door, Reason walks out. (And, we might add, the palpable phantasms of race, sex, and violence that are the legacy of slavery swoop in to take its place.)[1] For some folks, the responses to the Illinois senator's exceptional rise have underscored the continuing grip of antiblack sentiment on the organizing structures of American life. For others, his nomination sums up a shift, however provisional and symbolic, in previously held attitudes toward race within the culture at large.

As the *New York Times* critic Holland Cotter argued this past March in a reflection on the past few decades of African American art seen through the lens of Obama's "color-blind, or color-embracing," dream, the art world is also of several minds.[2] Race has become a productive if persistently problematic subject for artists of various inclinations, raising questions that come thick and fast. What does blackness mean now, in the wake of multiculturalism? Are there particular formal vocabularies and

This "Slant" column first appeared in *Artforum* 47, no. 2 (October 2008): 151-54.

stylistic antecedents that currently matter to its articulation in the visual field? Is it possible to make sense of the radically divergent discourses of race evoked by, say, Martin Puryear's recent retrospective at the Museum of Modern Art in New York and the concurrent run of the late artist Jason Rhoades's final installation, *Black Pussy*, 2006, at David Zwirner's Chelsea gallery? Given the exhibition spaces from Watts to Warsaw that make some claim on, or at least some use of, black visual culture, how might we begin to analyze the competing investments that currently inform the imaging of blackness on either side of the color line? What is the critical purchase of any racial signifier in an age when a white politician from Tennessee spearheads a congressional apology for slavery and when Bill Cosby has made it clear that for many class has trumped race as the prime site of social schism?

A much-needed map of this uncertain terrain was on view this past summer right in Obama's backyard. Borrowing its title from the famous sermon in the prologue to Ralph Ellison's 1952 novel, *Invisible Man*, the exhibition *Black Is, Black Ain't*—elegantly mounted at the Renaissance Society at the University of Chicago and traveling to the Museum of Contemporary Art in Detroit next spring and to the H&R Block Artspace at the Kansas City Art Institute, Missouri, in the summer of 2009—is intended to survey, in the words of the curator Hamza Walker, "a moment in which race is retained yet is simultaneously rejected."[3] To trace the contours of that moment, Walker called upon a multiracial roster of twenty-seven artists, whose individual contributions are by turns sly, disturbing, melancholic, and humorous, sometimes all at once. They range from Andres Serrano's *Woman with Infant* of 1996, a photograph that signifies on the role of black women in the nourishment of white children, to Sze Lin Pang's *Fétichito* of 2006, a dark, lumpy mass decked out with charms, peacock feathers, and Afro picks for extra talismanic punch. The different histories of blackness and relations of power summoned up in each instance make clear that the works gathered in *Black Is, Black Ain't* resist any singular program, thereby affirming the willingness of contemporary practitioners to imagine how what Fanon called "the fact of blackness" might open onto a wild array of aesthetic conceits. It was fitting, then, that in Chicago Glenn Ligon's 2005 neon sculpture *Warm Broad Glow* graced the entrance to the gallery, for in its rendition of the words NEGRO SUNSHINE—culled from Gertrude Stein's 1909 novella, *Melanctha*—the work models a wry attitude toward the historicity of blackness as well as a complex imbrication of artistic discourse, racial politics, and cultural memory that *Black Is, Black Ain't* makes its own (Fig. 5.1).

Such an ambition for art is, of course, at least as old as Ellison's text, though in this case we need not go back so far: the earliest work in the exhibition, a video of Shannon Jackson's autocritical performance *White Noises* (1993), gives us a clear date of departure. Not unlike several exhi-

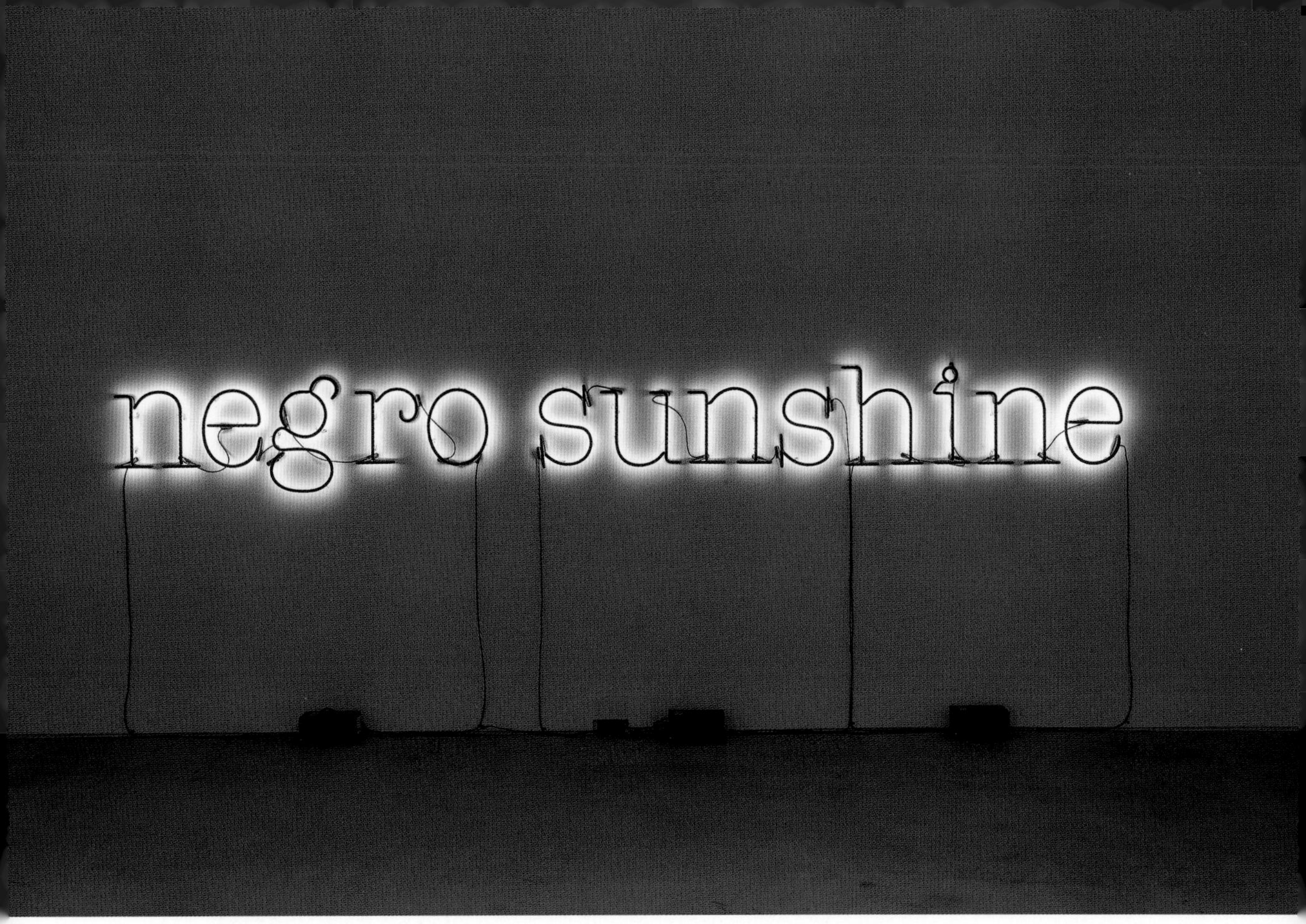

Figure 5.1
Glenn Ligon, *Warm Broad Glow*, 2005. Neon and paint, 36 × 192 in. (91.4 × 487.7 cm). Collection of Museum of Modern Art, New York. Photographer Credit: Thomas Barratt.

bitions from that moment which took up related thematics, such as *Black Male: Representations of Masculinity in Contemporary American Art* in New York in 1994, at the Whitney, and *Mirage: Enigmas of Race, Difference, and Desire* at the Institute of Contemporary Arts and Iniva in London in 1995, *Black Is, Black Ain't* takes the ambivalent play of the sign as central to the visual articulation of race, perhaps the most intransigent of social constructions. In the "post-black" present, the game seems to have loosened up:[4] for artists today, blackness is not only globally commodified and affectively charged but also an always already deconstructed and culturally networked cipher, providing the basis for a lingua franca that anyone can mobilize, whether to "capsiz[e] the niggerati" (as in the title of Deborah Grant's witty collages on view here) or "to think things you don't want to" about black men, which, in a sense, is precisely what happens in Joanna Rytel's thus-titled 2005 video, whose Swedish narrator appears caught up in the web of fantasies that structures her interracial relations.

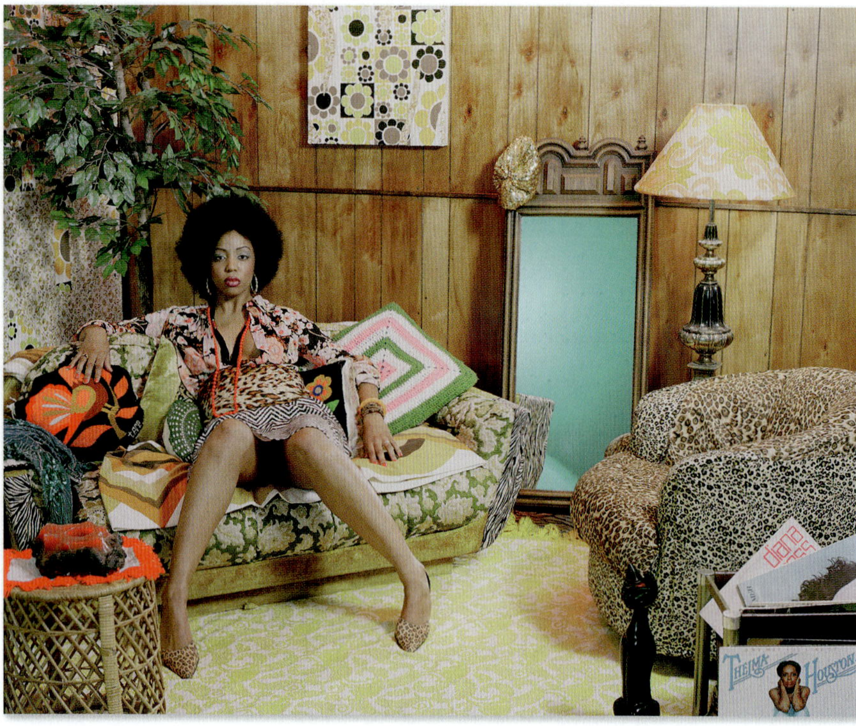

Figure 5.2

Mickalene Thomas, *Lovely Six Foota*, 2007. C-print, 20 × 30 in. Nasher Museum of Art at Duke University. © 2025 Mickalene Thomas / Artists Rights Society (ARS), New York.

The shifts within artistic discourse that have recently taken place are made clearer by comparing *Black Is, Black Ain't* with two older works that were crucial to the 1990s redefinition of black identity and that took Ellison's same words for their titles: Marlon Riggs's semiautobiographical 1995 film and Isaac Julien's 1992 essay, subtitled "Notes on De-Essentializing Black Identities."[5] Both works invoked the eponymous phrase to debunk stereotypes of black masculinity, to pointedly critique the homophobia of contemporary popular culture, and to carve out an expansive terrain for the imagining of queer African diasporic subjectivities. In Riggs's film, embracing the diversity within blackness is cast as the only way to forward "our progress as a people." In Walker's exhibition, there is no such heartfelt sentiment, less faith in a communitarian ethos, and little overt figuration of queer subjectivity—though illicit difference still matters: indeed, it seems to be taken for granted or taken in another direction. Consider the kind of desiring gaze directed at a seated and retro-clad woman in Mickalene Thomas's 2007 photograph *Lovely Six Foota* (Fig. 5.2), or the variations evident between thirteen street artists' renderings of one woman in Virginia Nimarkoh's *Nubian Queen*, 1999.

Nimarkoh's artistic strategy—the accumulation of images in order to emphasize the differential visual production of a single black subject—is also one of Walker's key curatorial moves, perhaps most strikingly in the juxtaposition of two photographs centered around Emmett Till, a fourteen-year-old black Chicagoan on summer vacation in Mississippi who was brutally murdered by white racists in 1955, ostensibly for whistling at a white woman. The criminal investigation of this notorious case has sputtered along for a half century, but the photographs of Till's disfigured body that circulated in *Jet* magazine not only spurred on the civil rights movement but also supplied a lasting image of racial violence in all of its caprice and ubiquity that has been internalized by countless black boys born after his death. In *Till*, 2004, Demetrius Oliver—black—at once reenacts and exorcises that image by capturing his own face slathered with chocolate frosting. Jason Lazarus—white—seems to say it all in the title of his photograph: *Standing at the Grave of Emmett Till, Day of Exhumation, June 1, 2005 (Alsip, IL)* (Fig. 5.3).

This pairing would appear—despite calls by some thinkers for African American politics to move beyond black and white—to assert the relevance of the binary that continues to structure the racial imaginary. While the

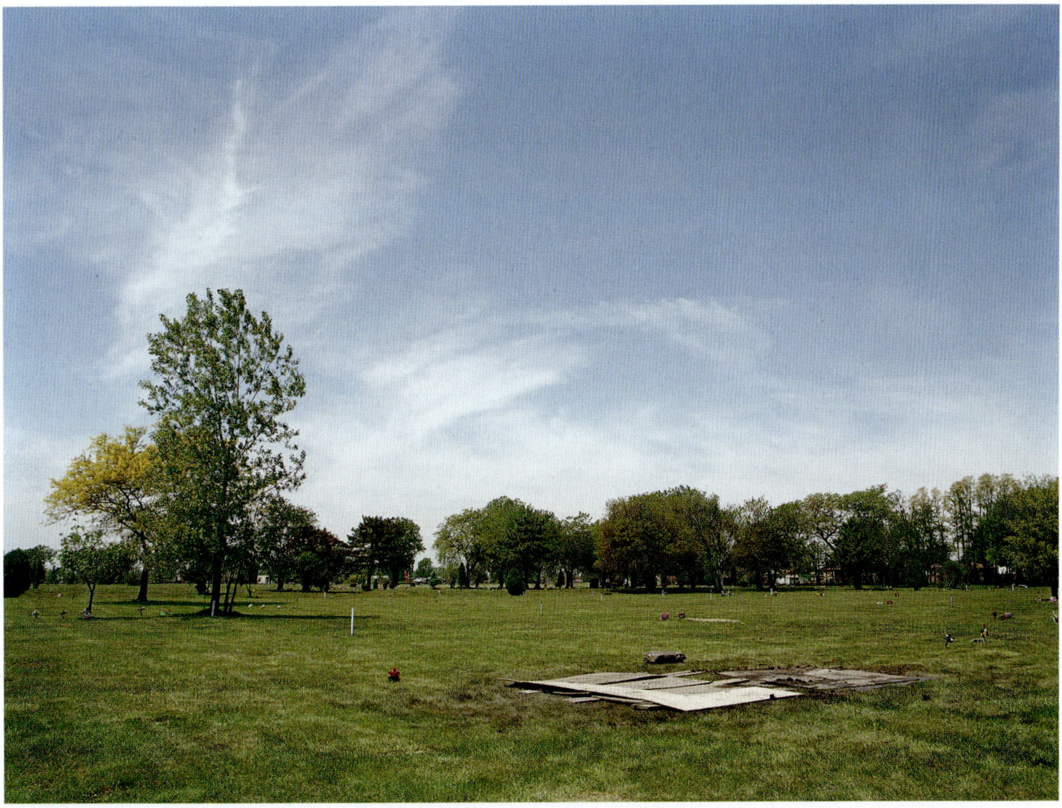

Figure 5.3
Jason Lazarus, *Standing at the Grave of Emmett Till, Day of Exhumation, June 1, 2005 (Alsip, IL)*, 2005.

formal and affective differences that separate Lazarus's work from Oliver's might be partially attributed to the artists' respective identities, in working through Till's legacy, they each underline the ongoing necessity of artistic attempts to find a language capable of describing individual investments that acknowledge—without capitulating to—a racial endgame. This concern is particularly prominent in the exhibition's video program, which models a host of possibilities for engagement. You might give in to what Rosalind Krauss long ago called video's "aesthetics of narcissism," repetitively confessing your white straight male obsession with "what a black man feels like," as in Thomas Johnson's 2004 piece of that name.[6] You might follow Elizabeth Axtman's lead in *American Classics*, 2005, performing a hilarious "re-speaking" of the words Hollywood cinema has put into the mouths of its "tragic mulattoes" [see Fig. 9.8. on p. 121]. Or you could try Dave McKenzie's tack, in *Babel*, 2000, using sign language to communicate your attempt at communicating, with a microphone in your mouth and (in the version on display here) its cord snaking around your throat [see Fig. 9.1 on p. 116].

For these practitioners, the issue is less, What does it mean to be black?, and more, What can I make out of blackness? As their works attest, in *Black Is, Black Ain't* the logic of race and the terms of recent artistic production are mutually undone, recasting the look of blackness if not its enduring political, cultural, and ontological coordinates. The transatlantic slave trade, the commodification of black bodies, the persistence of racial stereotypes, the loss and failure of black leadership, the collapse of public housing: all of these topoi are figured here, in compelling works by Edgar Arceneaux, Terry Adkins, Paul D'Amato, Todd Gray, David Levinthal, Jerome Mosley, Carl Pope, Robert A. Pruitt, Randy Regier, Daniel Roth, and Hank Willis Thomas. Other realities that also matter to the evolving contours of race in America—music as a site of resistance, the black presence within suburban milieus, and the growing visibility of African immigrant populations, for example—have a more muted presence in the exhibition. This no doubt speaks to the near-impossibility of canvassing the long reach of blackness, yet it also clarifies the thrust of the exhibition's brilliantly orchestrated sight lines, such as the juxtaposition of Rodney McMillian's sculpture *Chair*, 2003, and Jonathan Calm's 2008 photographs of apartment buildings reflected in pools of water, which created a rhyming of the run-down and runoff that left race somewhere up in the air between them. As Walker's loosely defined organizing categories—disfiguration, whiteness, stereotype, class, gendered performance, soul, history—indicate, *Black Is, Black Ain't* brings forward those sites of institutional and ideological formation that are most reiterated, most legible, and, thus, paradoxically, most readily made over into varied aesthetic forms that hold out the possibility that we might, to quote another Ellison text, "change the joke and slip the yoke."

Numerous works in the exhibition pursue this time-tested strategy, though perhaps none more trenchantly than those of William Pope.L, who

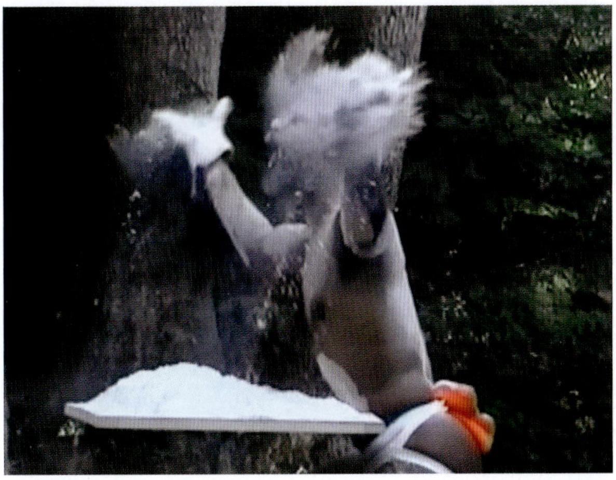

Figure 5.4
Pope.L, Still from *A Negro Sleeps Beneath the Susquehanna*, 1998. Video of performance, Cowan Compound, Bucknell College, Lewisburg, PA, 12 minutes. © The Estate of Pope.L. Courtesy of the Estate of Pope.L.

is represented by a set of eight flour-cone sculptures and twenty of his *Skin Set Drawings*, 2003–6, which parody the tautology of racial reasoning with phrases such as BLACK PEOPLE ARE CROSSOVER. Most mesmerizing is his twelve-minute video titled *A Negro Sleeps Beneath the Susquehanna (son version)*, 1998–2008 (Fig. 5.4). Playing the part of the eponymous Negro, Pope.L sits on a stool near a riverbank, his face immersed in a flour-covered table before he raises his head and begins to speak. It appears he has been having trouble sleeping. "I wish I could—dream stuff," he goes on to remark, "like that guy—what's his name? Martin—Luther—King . . . Fisher! I wish I could love something that much—I wish I could love something—But all I got—is the crawfish and the minnow. I wish I could love something that much, but—I'm too black—too naked." After concluding his pronouncement, he throws a cracked mirror on his back and wanders into the river, presumably in a renewed attempt to sleep—a gesture that brings to mind another line from Ellison's prologue to *Invisible Man*: "A hibernation is a covert preparation for a more overt action."[7]

Like Pope.L's video piece, *Black Is, Black Ain't* plumbs the possibilities for thinking *with* rather than *beyond* race—its figures, tropes, and trademark forms—possibilities that all too rarely emerge in the realm of politics proper. For if only as a free-floating trace unmoored from individual subjects, an index of the economies that continue to conflate persons and things, or the corroded linchpin of a modern metaphysics, blackness continues to tell us something about what T. J. Clark has termed the "true *structure* of dream-visualization,"[8] as well as the forms of despotism on which it relies—not to mention the terms in which it might be contested. Walker's deft curating encourages us to wonder what we might make of blackness if we took it to be a social formation given over to the marginal, the object, the fugitive, or the socially dead. What would it mean to imagine a utopian future other than a postracial one? The challenge, here as elsewhere, remains how to hold on to what the cultural historian Robin D. G. Kelley calls "freedom dreams," which allow us to rethink the world from blackness up.[9] For the time being, it seems that Obama is the closest we will get—and change, no matter how much you believe in it, is obviously worthwhile given the current regime—but he should not prevent us from having other dreams or even from making the most of a fitful sleep.

Notes

1 On this score, see Lewis Gordon, *Her Majesty's Other Children* (Rowman & Littlefield, 1997), 53.

2 Holland Cotter, "The Topic Is Race; the Art Is Fearless," *New York Times*, March 30, 2008, https://www.nytimes.com/2008/03/30/arts/design/30cott.html.

3 Hamza Walker, "Domino Effect," exh. brochure, Renaissance Society of Chicago, n.p., 2008.

4 The curator Thelma Golden coined the quoted word with the artist Glenn Ligon "as a clarifying term that had ideological and chronological dimensions and repercussions. It was characterized by [a new generation of] artists who were adamant about not being labeled as 'black' artists, though their work was steeped, in fact deeply interested, in redefining complex notions of blackness." Thelma Golden, "Introduction: Post . . . ," in *Freestyle*, exh. cat. (Studio Museum in Harlem, 2001), 14.

5 Isaac Julien, "Black Is, Black Ain't: Notes on De-Essentializing Black Identities," in *Black Popular Culture*, ed. Gina Dent (Bay Press, 1992), 255-63.

6 Rosalind Krauss, "Video: The Aesthetics of Narcissism," *October* 1 (Spring 1976): 50-64.

7 Ralph Ellison, *Invisible Man* (Vintage International [1952] 1990), 13.

8 T. J. Clark, "Modernism, Postmodernism, and Steam," *October* 100 (Spring 2002): 173; emphasis original.

9 Robin D. G. Kelley, *Freedom Dreams: The Black Radical Imagination* (Beacon Press, 2003).

PART II

THE SIGNIFIER'S WORK

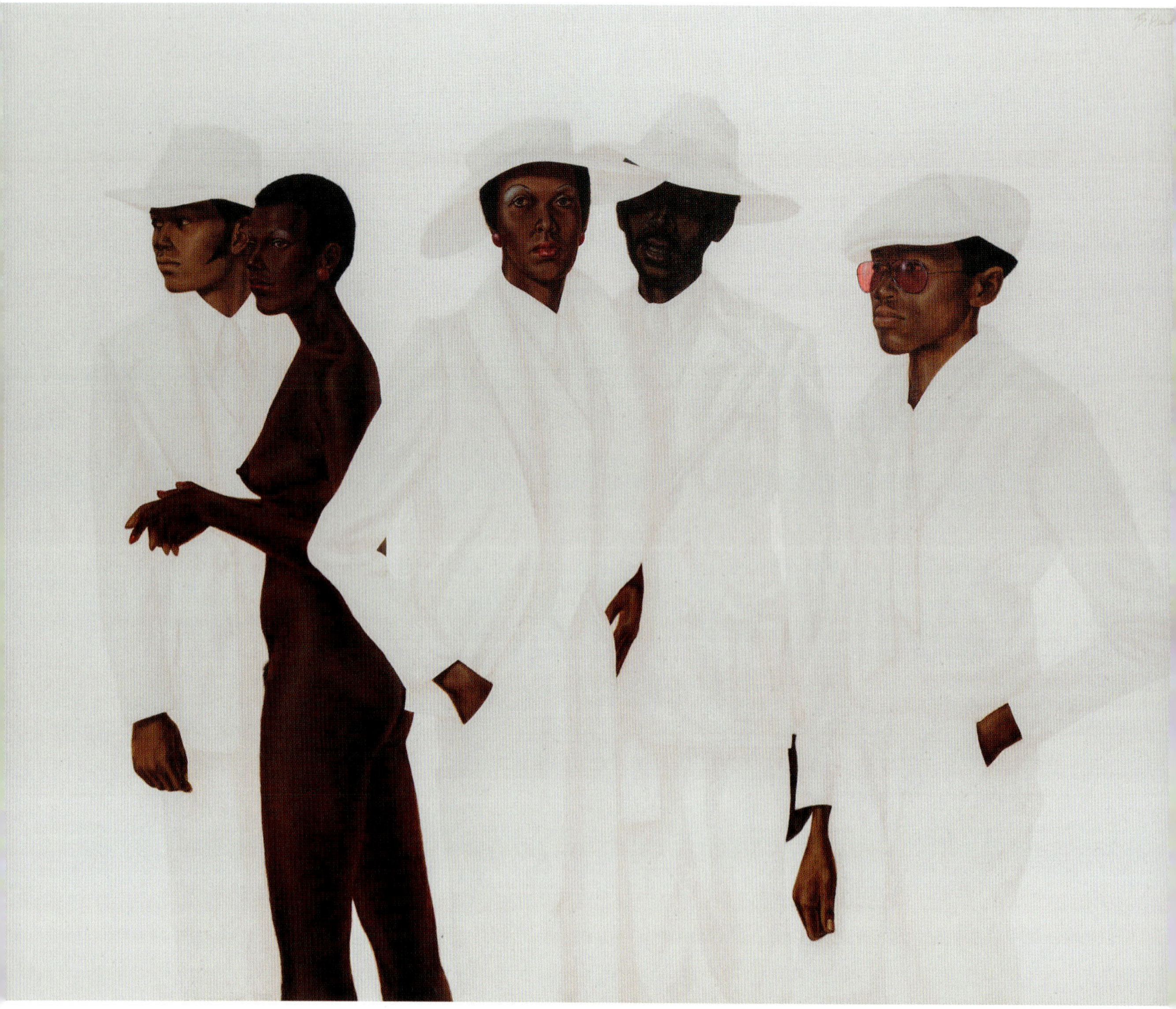

Figure 6.1

Barkley L. Hendricks, *What's Going On*, 1974. Oil, acrylic, and Magna paint on cotton canvas, 65¾ × 83¾ in. © Barkley L. Hendricks. Courtesy of the Estate of Barkley L. Hendricks and Jack Shainman Gallery, New York.

6

FIGURES AND GROUNDS

The Art of Barkley L. Hendricks

By turns extravagant and direct, the portraits Barkley L. Hendricks has made of his African American friends and neighbors since the late 1960s variously recall the indolent nudes of Philip Pearlstein and the deadpan chic of David Hockney. But in these canvases and in other works—such as his series of landscapes freighted with Barbizon-school scrupulousness—the artist has sought modes of representing that go beyond the pursuit of likeness, gesturing toward abstraction, anamorphosis, and anachronism. On the occasion of a major traveling exhibition centered on these two bodies of work (organized by Trevor Schoonmaker for the Nasher Museum of Art at Duke University in Durham, North Carolina, recently shown at the Studio Museum in Harlem, New York, and appearing this summer at the Santa Monica Museum of Art in California), *Artforum* asked art historian Huey Copeland to engage Hendricks's alternate realisms.
The Editors, *Artforum*, 2009

The white-suited black subjects are rendered with varying degrees of realism (Fig. 6.1): there is the chalky brown man at left, who possesses all the charm of a department store mannequin; the androgynous youth at right, with unfurled scarf and ghostly tinted glasses; and, of course, the woman at the center of the work, whose adjacent nude double seems to both teasingly recede into and forcefully protrude beyond the group. Barkley L. Hendricks executed this large-scale canvas, *What's Going On*, in 1974, and it is perhaps the most striking of what the artist calls his "limited palette" works, with its fractured modes of depiction and hue. Indeed, for all their matching *Ebony* elegance, the figures might as well inhabit separate pictures, appearing less a community than a cast of characters layered into the same phantasmic envelope. Cool, aloof, and ethereal, these men and women are packaged together, in an assembly that evokes at once the rhetoric of *grande peinture* and that of the Pictures generation—one part *Le Déjeuner sur l'herbe*, one part deconstructed album cover.

This cover story first appeared in *Artforum* 47, no. 8 (April 2009): 142-49.

Like the Manet it recollects, Hendricks's painting is decidedly inconclusive, its personages inscrutable and its narrative indecipherable; yet it is rendered in terms that resonate with the visual production of African American culture as consumer spectacle. The work's life-size figures in oil, shimmering against a monochromatic acrylic ground, illuminate the crisis of blackness within representation—a crisis everywhere shaped by an engagement with and an opposition to those persistent forms of reification, high and low, that transform liberatory self-fashioning into co-opted cliché. Not incidentally, Hendricks painted *What's Going On* just three years after Marvin Gaye's eponymous record was released, recalling the way in which, as the scholar Mark Anthony Neal reminds us, Gaye's album became the "quintessential black protest recording" even as the black protest genre was being successfully commodified.[1] At the same time, advances in recording technology had allowed Gaye to layer multiple vocal registers in new ways, thus echoing the sound of black resistive communities and traditions threatened, as ever, with violence, rupture, and dissolution—a threshold that Hendricks has limned for more than forty years with inimitable virtuosity.

In the 1960s and 1970s, such pressures were acutely felt and sharply reflected across African American culture, particularly among its panoply of black nationalisms. In a series of insightful essays addressing Hendricks and this moment from which he emerged, the art historian Richard J. Powell has shown how the artist's pictures participated in this transformation of racial imaginaries, which not only valorized blackness, but gave rise to emphatic displays of a new, self-conscious "to-be-looked-at-ness."[2] These surfaced across the visual spectrum, from Huey Newton posters to films like *Shaft* to the 1976 Dewar's Scotch ad in which Hendricks himself appeared. Take the figure in *Tequila* (1978), who stands in a familiar pose, cigarette in hand (Fig. 6.2). The work, however, is no ad for Virginia Slims: the woman's idiosyncratic chic, probing glance, and stilled self-possession are a far cry from the smiling insouciance of the typical magazine model. Hendricks is interested not so much in the look of mass culture as in the individuated appearance of the mass subject; he tests the fragile boundaries between subcultural experience and middlebrow consumption, between avant-garde tactics and kitsch genres. The artist's sitters present themselves with an attitude and a sartorial flair that, as the critic Kobena Mercer has argued, attract the gaze yet also defend against primitivist projection, carving out a space where the self and its aesthetic construction can take center stage.[3]

Many of Hendricks's subjects are, in fact, people he saw in his local neighborhoods: New London, Connecticut, where he has been a professor of art at Connecticut College since 1972; New Haven, where he went to graduate school at Yale in the early '70s; and the hoods of North Philadelphia, where he grew up in the '50s and '60s. When recently seen together at

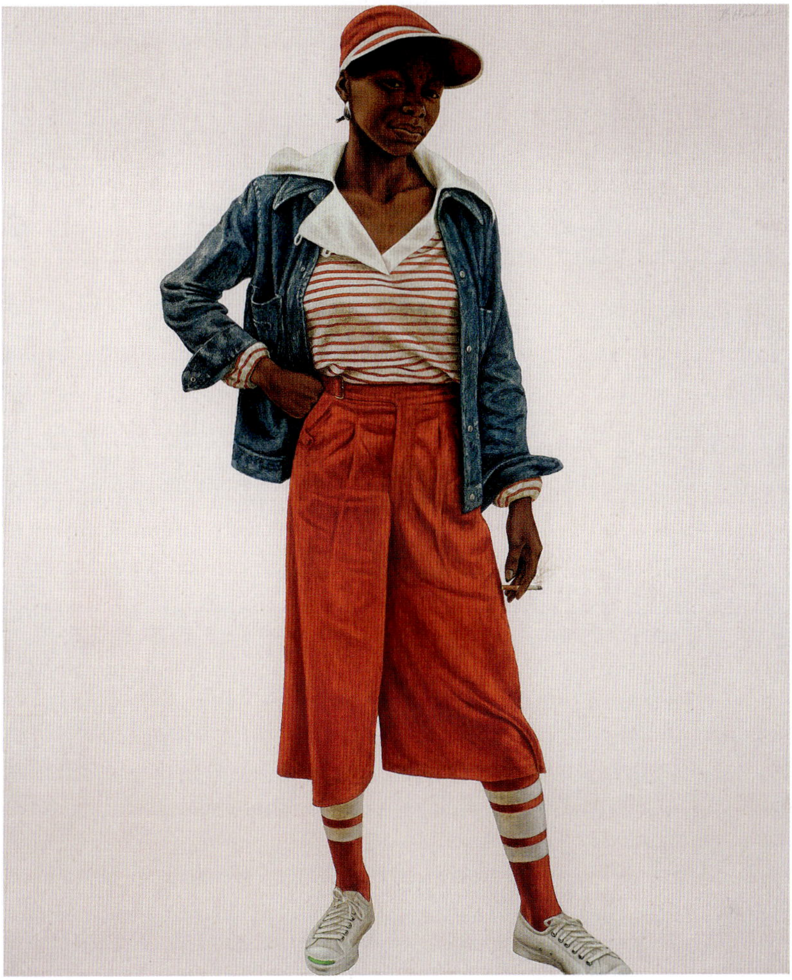

Figure 6.2
Barkley L. Hendricks, *Tequila*, 1978. Oil and acrylic on linen canvas, 60¾ × 50¼ in. © Barkley L. Hendricks. Courtesy of the Estate of Barkley L. Hendricks and Jack Shainman Gallery, New York.

the Studio Museum in Harlem in *Birth of the Cool*, the traveling retrospective of Hendricks's work—a rhyming and rhythmic layout of individuals and groups, dark paintings and light ones, men and women—the artist's compositions suggested a series of contrapuntal relations between various forms of cultural alterity and vernacular style. For example, in the second-floor gallery of the museum, a fiercely styled woman of color in skintight yellow capris smiled out from a gold ground, calling to the orange-clad, crotch-grabbing superstar Fela Kuti to her left, while between them the protagonist of *North Philly Niggah (William Corbett)* (1975), luxuriated in his peach coat and beige surround, casting a wary eye on the whole scene. Hung close to the floor and brightly lit, the paintings evoked religious icons

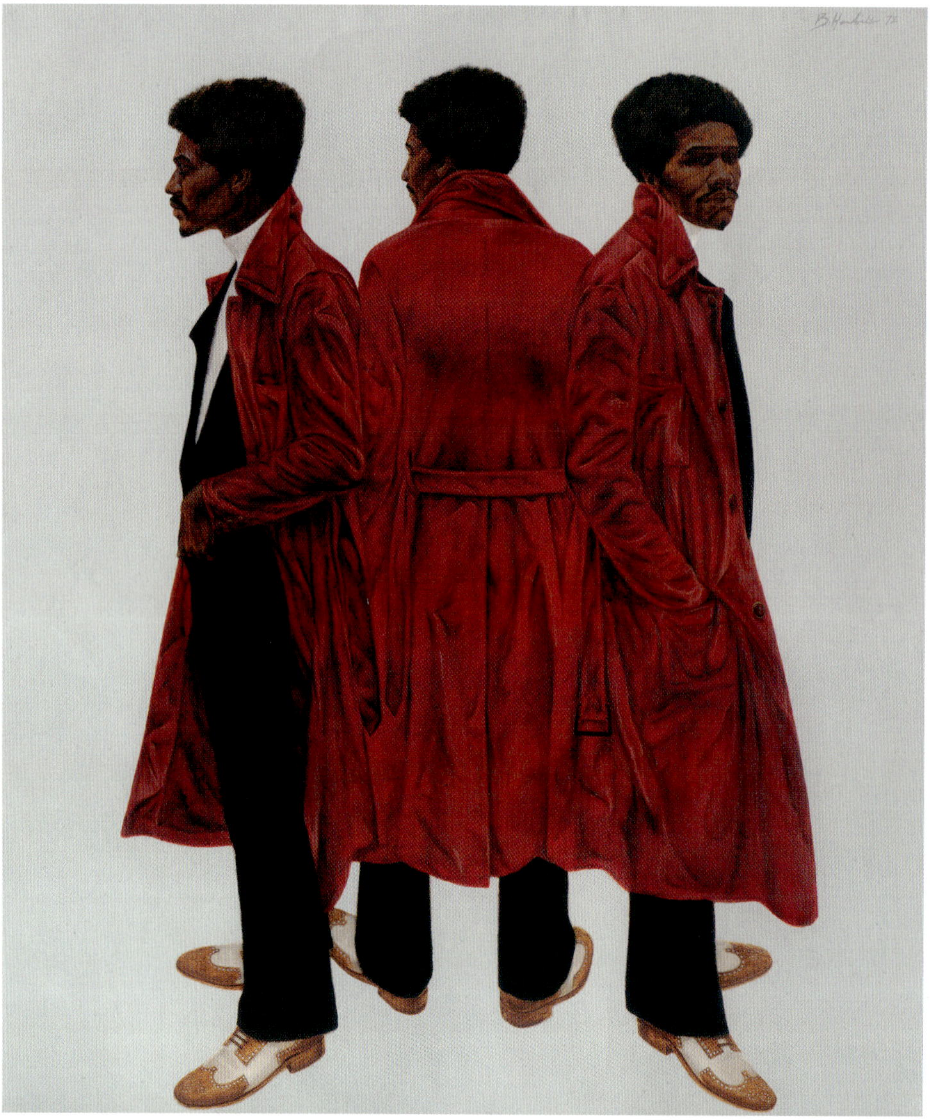

Figure 6.3
Barkley L. Hendricks, *Sir Charles, Alias Willie Harris*, 1972. Oil and acrylic on linen canvas, 84⅛ × 72 in. Courtesy of the Estate of Barkley L. Hendricks and Jack Shainman Gallery, New York.

in both their format and their sumptuous adornment—even as the figures within them seemed liable to emerge from the frame, doubly restructuring our understanding of the social arenas in which they moved and the museal space of the viewer.

As the exhibition curator, Trevor Schoonmaker, has noted, when Hendricks's canvases first appeared, they proposed a figural confrontation that disrupted the art world's racial status quo.[4] The artist often represented

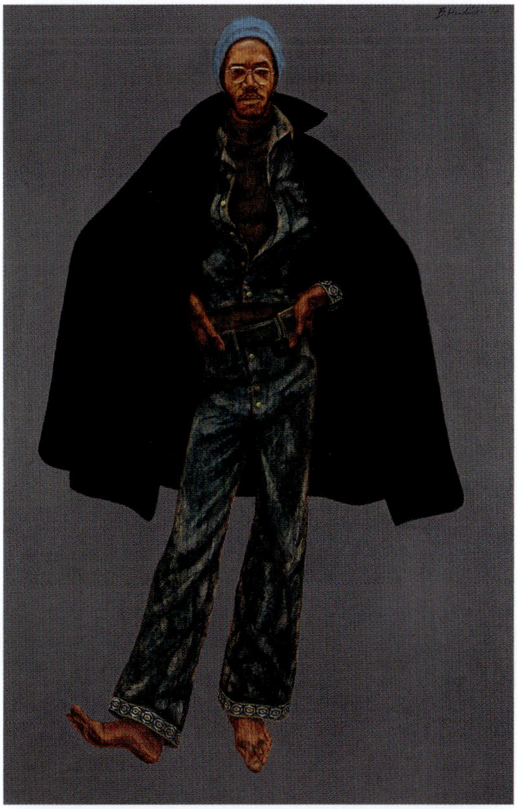

Figure 6.4
Barkley L. Hendricks, *George Jules Taylor*, 1972. Oil and acrylic on cotton canvas, 91½ × 60¼ in. © Barkley L. Hendricks. Courtesy of the Estate of Barkley L. Hendricks and Jack Shainman Gallery, New York.

those groups whose protests for rights and recognition had splintered the social field in the '60s and '70s and paradoxically opened new vistas of commodification. Yet Hendricks does not pose his subjects as protesters or victims or celebrities. They are, rather, avatars of themselves who model (to borrow from the art historian Thomas Crow) a range of imaginary relations to dominant culture, from the merely dandyish to the queerly transgressive, from what Powell identifies as the "player chic" of the small-time drug dealer depicted in *Sir Charles, Alias Willie Harris* to the gay intellectual swing of Hendricks's Yale student who is the subject of *George Jules Taylor*, both 1972 (Figs. 6.3, 6.4).[5] The latter two figures take up and twist black masculine style conventions, just as African American gay, working-class, and women's groups were beginning to critique the bourgeois and heterosexist tendencies of certain black liberationist politics. This proliferation of perspectives is key to Hendricks's figurative painting and its central unit, the personage: he would paint Taylor in different moods and poses at least four times over the course of as many years. But, as the artist insisted in a 1976 interview, "I want to create a total painting rather than just a portrait."[6] Thus Sir Charles is trebled within a single canvas to arrive at a distinctive brand of totality—one that flirts with the conventional treatment

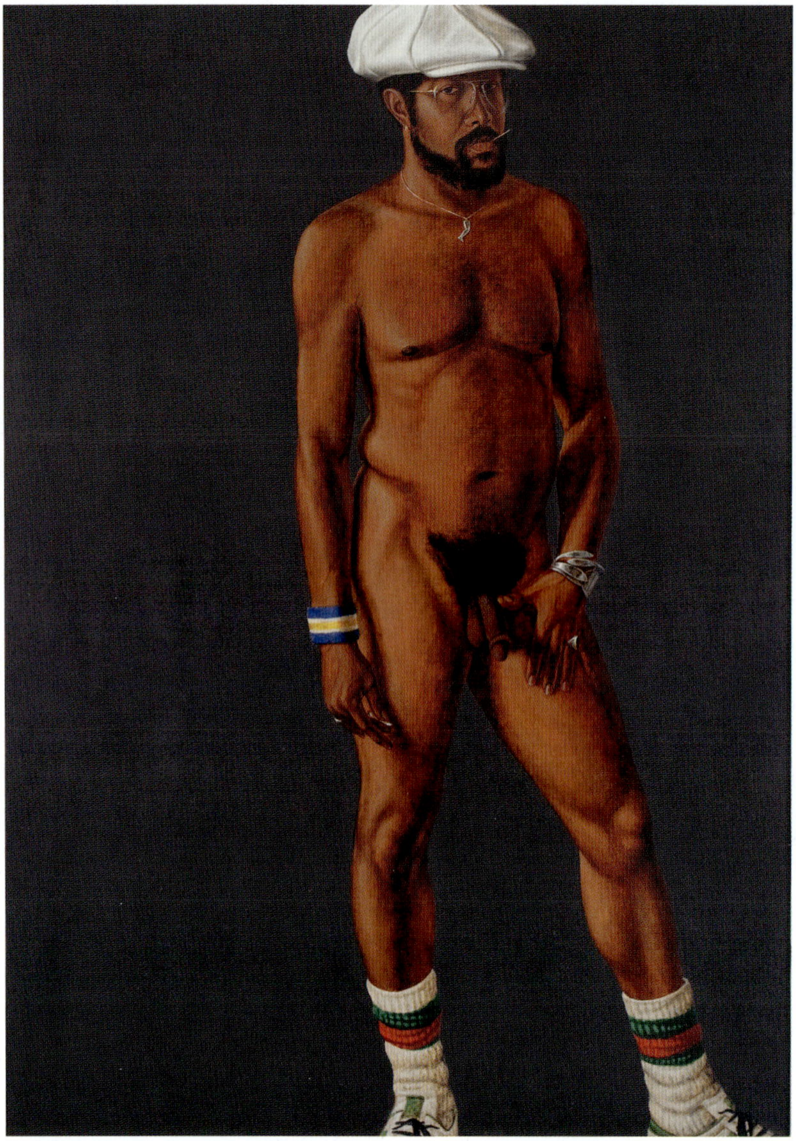

Figure 6.5
Barkley L. Hendricks, *Brilliantly Endowed (Self-Portrait)*, 1977. Oil and acrylic on linen canvas, 66 × 48 in., 72 × 53¾ × 2 in. (framed). © Barkley L. Hendricks. Courtesy of the Estate of Barkley L. Hendricks and Jack Shainman Gallery, New York.

of the Three Graces only to displace it and that destabilizes modernist tactics meant to secure the "facingness" (to use the art historian Michael Fried's term) of the picture as a whole.[7]

Throughout his career, Hendricks has stood alongside the subjects featured in his series, as in *Slick (Self-Portrait)* (1977), a limited-palette painting whose title winkingly refers to a common characterization of his work by critics. One such writer was Hilton Kramer, who also notoriously described the artist as "brilliantly endowed";[8] Hendricks adopted this designation as the title for his nude 1977 self-portrait, at once appropriating and fulfilling the language of critical appraisal: *Brilliantly Endowed (Self-Portrait)* depicts the artist as an embarrassment of riches—his body, his adornments, and his skill in rendering both—as he adopts a knowing and confident pose (Fig. 6.5). At the Studio Museum, this painting took its place next to several self-portraits that depict the artist similarly undressed, including the charmingly vulnerable *Brown Sugar Vine* (1970), and the deadpan *Icon for My Man Superman (Superman never saved any black people—Bobby Seale)* (1969). In each of these works, he wears not only an array of vaguely fetishistic accents—a toothpick, a joint, a "third leg" around his neck—but also his own poise, which renders his nudity a kind of performative suiting-up. In so doing, Hendricks contravenes the modernist pictorial injunction against ornament and intervenes in an African American tradition that has often shied away from the unclothed body, owing to the violent and anxious stereotypes with which black male sexuality has been burdened from slavery to the present.[9]

For Hendricks, reckoning with such realities means painting against historical stereotype and humanist essence. He therefore undertakes abstraction as well as figuration, in order to activate a multiplicity of visual and cognitive experiences that define and dislodge the contours of blackness. In *Vertical Hold*, 1967, for instance, a basketball and backboard become the basis for an urban take on the shaped canvas, as if to reply to Fried's declaration that painting circa 1966 needed to hold its shape to compel conviction (Fig. 6.6).[10] Here, shape is modeled not on the abstract geometry of a pictorial image but on a tabular field crisscrossed by black subjects. This is,

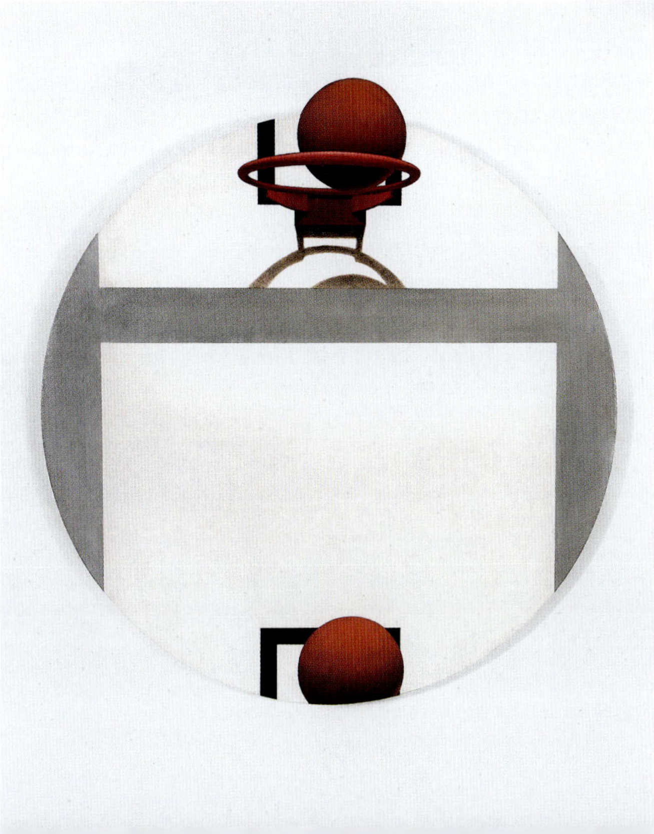

Figure 6.6
Barkley L. Hendricks, *Vertical Hold*, 1967. Oil, acrylic, and metallic silver on cotton canvas, 47 × 44 in. © Barkley L. Hendricks. Courtesy of the Estate of Barkley L. Hendricks and Jack Shainman Gallery, New York.

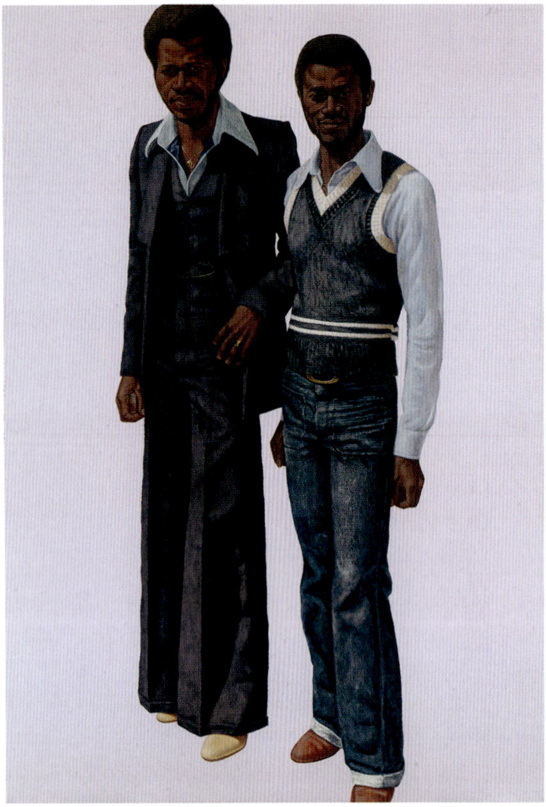

Figure 6.7
Barkley L. Hendricks, *APB's (Afro-Parisian Brothers)*, 1978. Oil and acrylic on linen canvas, 72 × 50 in. © Barkley L. Hendricks. Courtesy of the Estate of Barkley L. Hendricks and Jack Shainman Gallery, New York.

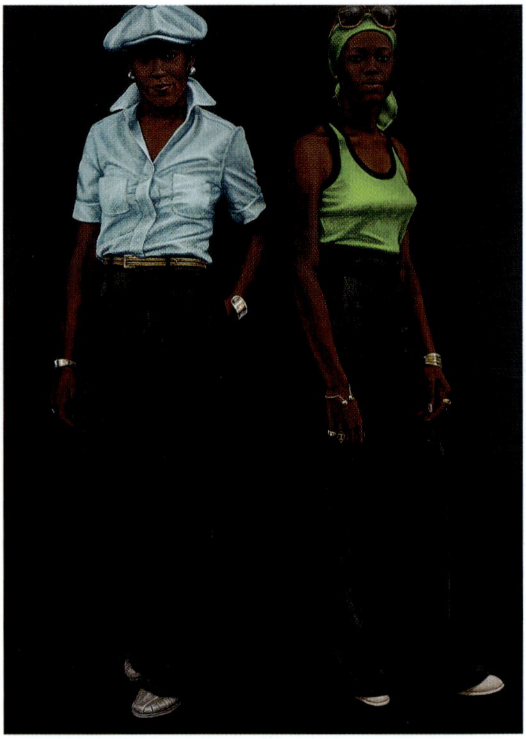

Figure 6.8
Barkley L. Hendricks, *Sisters (Susan and Toni)*, 1977. Oil and acrylic on linen canvas, 66 × 48 in. © Barkley L. Hendricks. Courtesy of the Estate of Barkley L. Hendricks and Jack Shainman Gallery, New York.

then, a reorientation of the modernist picture in the art historian Leo Steinberg's sense, a move from vertical plane to horizontal site.[11] Such a shift differentially inflects our notion of location—whether on the canvas-as-basketball-court of *Granada*, 1970, or before the chessboard motif in *Buck*, 1967, both emblematic traversals of black diasporic culture.

Hendricks is no stranger to this terrain, having visited Europe, Africa, and the Caribbean on trips that bolstered the sense of Pan-African connection revealed in his work. Consider his *APB's (Afro-Parisian Brothers)* of 1978, which depicts smartly dressed figures who look like they might easily commune with the fabulously laid-back *Sisters (Susan and Toni)*, 1977, hung next to them at the Studio Museum, and who could seem equally at home staring out of a photograph taken by Malick Sidibe before a concrete wall in Bamako or by Sanford Sawyer before an ornate gold curtain in Nassau (Figs. 6.7, 6.8). By placing his subjects against grounds that appear to stand in for such surfaces—but that hold out no such spatial or architectural

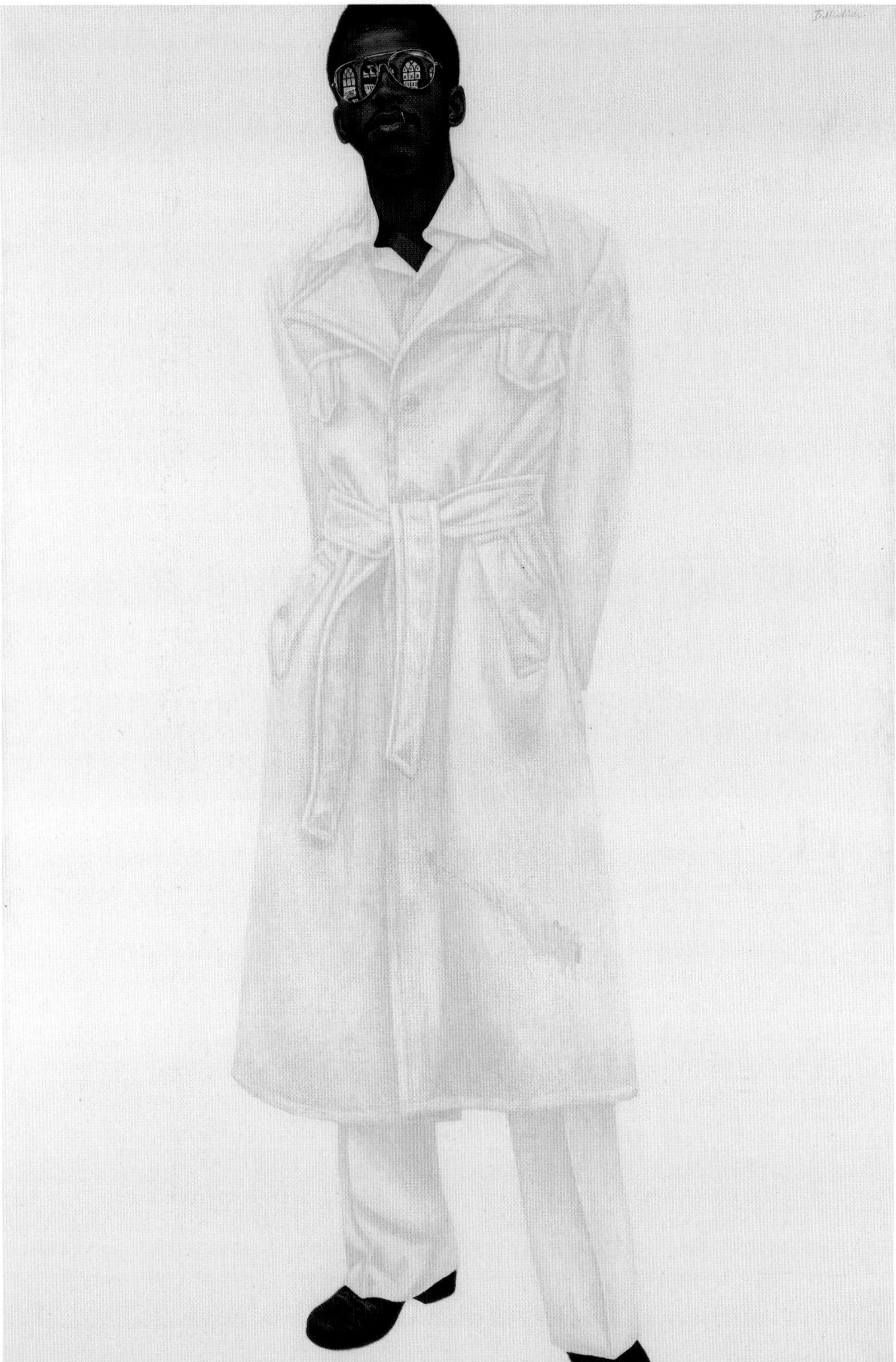

Figure 6.9

Barkley L. Hendricks, *Steve*, 1976. Oil, acrylic, and Magna paint on linen canvas, 72 × 48 in. © Barkley L. Hendricks. Courtesy of the Estate of Barkley L. Hendricks and Jack Shainman Gallery, New York.

purchase—Hendricks suggests the differences and affinities among modes of self-visualization across the black world in the '70s, when, as the art historian Krista Thompson has written, blackness appeared as if it could be "dislodged from a particular space and time and . . . embodied anywhere."[12] While Hendricks has stated that he prefers to work with live models, his paintings are often produced after photographs.[13] Indeed, because his backdrops tend to rhyme with the coloration of the subjects themselves, his figures might be said to metaphorically develop from the grounds on which they sit, a kind of perverse photographic effect that commingles the real and the virtual. Hendricks's settings are suggestive of the studio, the screen, and monochrome painting, as well as the flat permutations of what Steinberg has called "design technology,"[14] against which transnational and diasporic blackness could startlingly become visible.

In painting a subject like the one in *Steve*, 1976, a youth decked out in a downy white coat, Hendricks probes these conditions of visibility: he renders the white ground as a flat halation from which the figure's textural edges emerge (Fig. 6.9). While the reflections in Steve's sunglasses position him within Hendricks's studio, this is the only clue that situates him before the painter. He is both present and absent, flattened and in depth, unmoored from the sites to which black subjects are presumed to belong. In such paintings, we must engage with the figures on the grounds they offer rather than those that we supply: ostensibly frontal, Hendricks's paintings slyly induct us into a hall of mirrors and subjects who cast no shadows. They suggest, in the words of the scholar Richard Iton, a whole host of "black fantastic sensibilities" that outstrip the limitations imposed by the modern, the aesthetic, and the political as rationally understood.[15]

The paintings of Jamaica that Hendricks began making in the early 1990s—such as the characteristically gold-framed *New Year's Marl Hole* (2007) (Fig. 6.10)—manifest another itinerant optic. Instead of picturing human subjects, the artist gives us views of the island in oval and tondo frames, formats that have been compared to the porthole of a tourist ship, though they might as easily conjure fifteenth-century Florentine painting. The works thereby reproduce—and then disarticulate—spectatorial expectations of religious allegory and of what Thompson has called the Caribbean picturesque, the island landscape imagined as a site of verdant exoticism structured by dreams of tourist, imperialist, and colonial consumption.[16] Bypassing such tropical hallucinations, Hendricks depicts a quarry: Jamaica as a literal and figurative mine for the extraction of resources, whether limestone, bauxite, or the image of the place itself.

The exhibition at the Studio Museum featured several of these canvases, a few basketball works, and a number of figurative portraits, numbering nearly forty in all. Taken together, Hendricks's oil paintings describe both the expansive possibilities and the storied limitations of those key sites of blackness that have presented themselves to his gaze. By

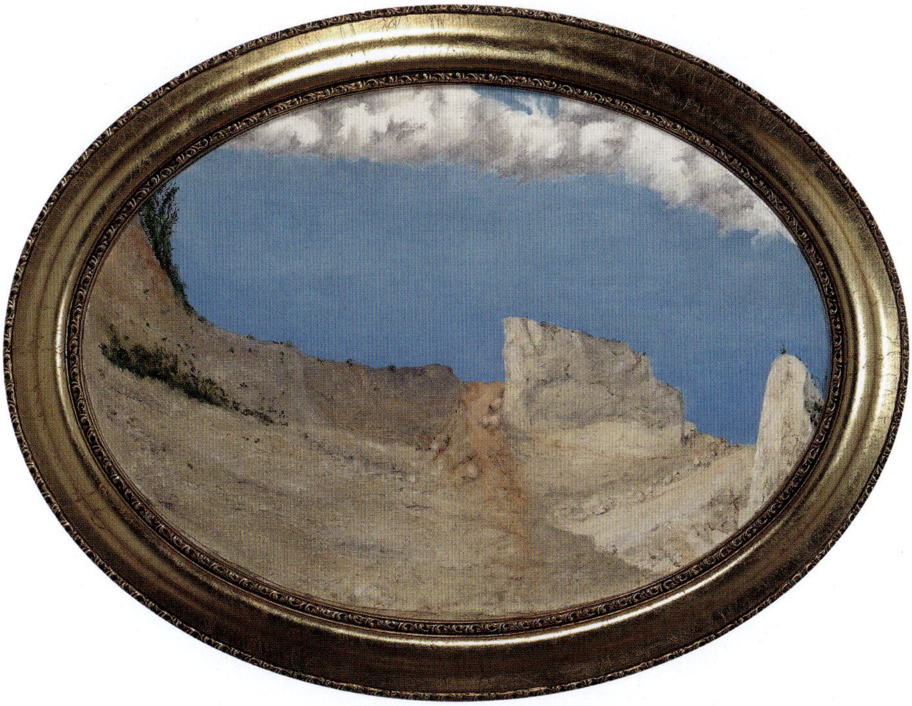

Figure 6.10
Barkley L. Hendricks, *New Year's Marl Hole,* 2007. Oil on linen canvas, 23½ × 31¼ in. (framed). © Barkley L. Hendricks. Courtesy of the Estate of Barkley L. Hendricks and Jack Shainman Gallery, New York.

seizing upon the ambivalence of various painterly systems—portraiture, landscape, icons, shaped canvases, monochromes—that can be read as either transcendent or commercial or both, Hendricks is able to perform a conversion of his own, adapting modes of representation that have historically occluded or instrumentalized black subjects into vehicles that cut through the dross of racial phantasm.

Not surprisingly, then, Hendricks's work has been positioned in relation to Pop, hard-edged abstraction, photorealism, and old master painting and has garnered comparisons to a dizzying array of figures (Rembrandt, Malevich, Ellsworth Kelly, Alex Katz, Chuck Close, David Hammons, and Corot, among them). The term *cool realism*, which originated in the '70s to describe Hendricks's work, seems inadequate, as does any single categorization:[17] his practice is as revelatory as it is materialist, drawing on any aesthetic means necessary. When Hendricks's paintings were shown in the 1994 exhibition *Black Male* at the Whitney Museum of American Art in New York, they stood out not only against the other work in the show, much of which took a deconstructionist approach to race, but also against images of black masculinity such as O. J. Simpson's, then seemingly omnipresent within the public sphere. In fact, from 1984 to 2002, during what Hendricks

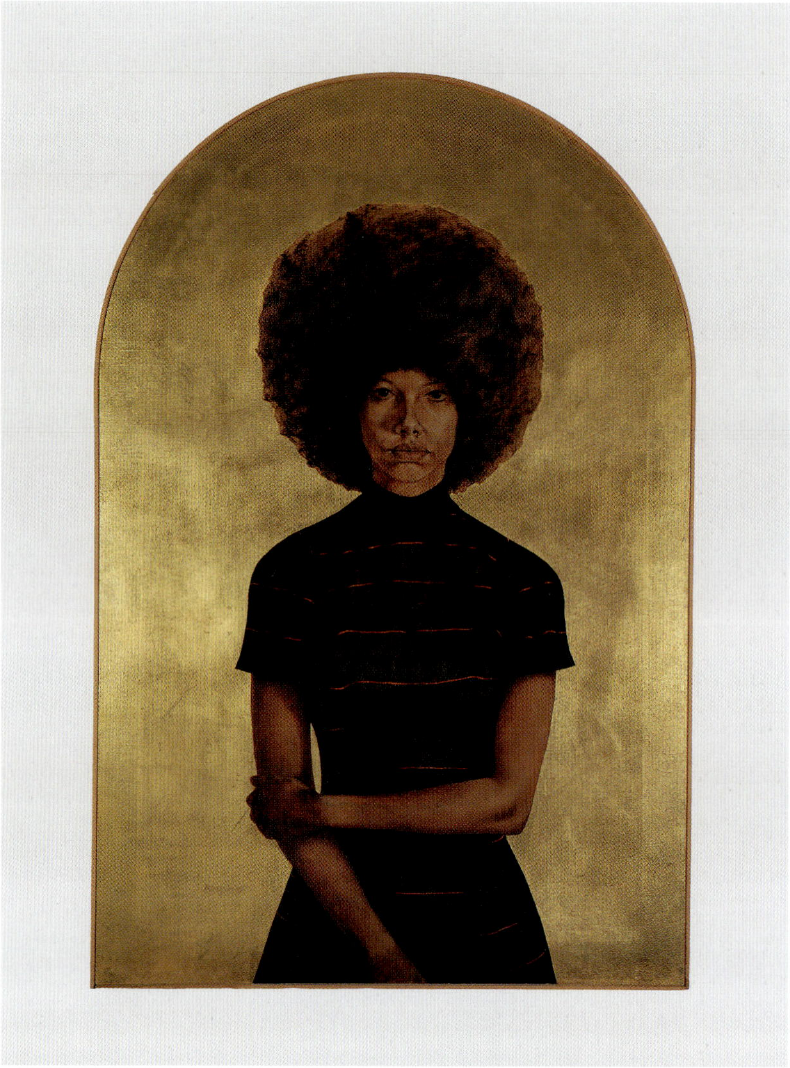

Figure 6.11
Barkley L. Hendricks, *Lawdy Mama*, 1969. Oil and gold leaf on canvas, 53¾ × 36¼ in. © Barkley L. Hendricks. Courtesy of the Estate of Barkley L. Hendricks and Jack Shainman Gallery, New York.

calls the "'Ronaissance' (the age of Ronald Reagan),"[18] he produced little figurative painting, as if that era's provisions for possibility, range, and depth within the visual field could no longer sustain a meditation on the facts of the black image.

During this time, however, Hendricks continued to produce prints, photographs, watercolors, drawings, and collages, such as *I've Known Rivers*, 1987—a schematic outline of the female figure that is suggested with the merest of means: a shock of human hair denoting "head" and what appears to be a grommeted belt for "spine" connected to a hand-drawn pelvis. These engagements allowed for an exploration of symbol and index at the very moment that the black icon seemed saturated yet again with the historicity of its dereliction. Hendricks avows that different media are integral to his practice, allowing him "to get a different perspective" both on his painting and on his subjects.[19] Although they have been featured in his retrospectives in 1980 at the Studio Museum and in 2001 at the Lyman Allyn Art Museum in New London, Connecticut, such works are not included in *Birth of the Cool*. In time, a retrospective is due that accounts for a fuller range of Hendricks's practice, including his figurative oil paintings of white subjects.

Today, amid younger artists concerned with the black figure and its effects, such as Mickalene Thomas, Jeff Sonhouse, and Kehinde Wiley—whose exhibition *The World Stage: Africa, Lagos ~ Dakar* immediately preceded *Birth of the Cool* at the Studio Museum—Hendricks's practice seems all the more relevant for its desire to depict actual black subjects in all of their fullness and particularity. If practitioners of the "post-black" generation have, as the curator Thelma Golden noted in 2001, emerged in a moment when "their particular cultural specificity is marketed to the planet and sold back to them,"[20] then Hendricks's canvases might be seen as the *Nachträglich* anticipation of and answer to this condition. His art considers what is possible within representation given the dialectic of commodification, co-optation, and resistive self-fashioning that has shaped the black image in modernity. Hendricks's paintings thus offer not so much transcendent portraits as temporal disruptions. In *Lawdy Mama* (1969) (Fig. 6.11), the layering of postponement and projection reaches a fever pitch: a young black woman is centered on a gold background, the shape of her Afro echoed by the round frame of the canvas, a double halo that suggests Black Power's enshrinement of the female figure, so many Madonnas lost to history, and black subjectivity's never-ending iteration as shining spectacle, the optical effect par excellence. Hendricks launches a deferred action that allows us to see how the black past, present, and future continue to manifest themselves in the image.

Notes

Barkley L. Hendricks passed away on April 18, 2017, in New London, CT. My *Artforum* feature subsequently provided both structure and content for the obituaries that would follow, in some cases both. For one example, see Kriston Capps, "Remembering Barkley L. Hendricks: Master of Black Postmodern Portraiture," April 19, 2017, *The Atlantic*, https://www.theatlantic.com/entertainment/archive/2017/04/remembering-barkley-l-hendricks-a-master-of-black-postmodern-portraiture/523518/.

1 Mark Anthony Neal, *What the Music Said: Black Popular Music and Black Public Culture* (Routledge, 2013), 66.

2 Richard J. Powell, "Racial Imaginaries, from Charles White's Preacher to Jean-Paul Goude & Grace Jones' Nigger Arabesque," in *Back to Black: Art, Cinema & the Racial Imaginary*, ed. Richard J. Powell, David A. Bailey, and Petrine Archer Straw (Whitechapel Gallery, 2005), 21. I borrow the phrase, "to-be-looked-at-ness," of course, from Laura Mulvey, "Visual Pleasure and Narrative Cinema," in *Issues in Feminist Film Criticism*, ed. Patricia Erens (Indiana University Press, 1990), 38.

3 Kobena Mercer, Introduction to *Pop Art and Vernacular Cultures*, ed. Kobena Mercer (MIT Press, 2007), 31-32.

4 Trevor Schoonmaker, "Birth of the Cool," *Nka: Journal of Contemporary African Art*, no. 24 (2009): 23.

5 Thomas Crow, "Modernism and Mass Culture in the Visual Arts," in *Modern Art and the Common Culture* (Yale University Press, 1996), 3-38; Richard J. Powell, "Sartor Africanus," in *Dandies: Fashion and Finesse in Art and Culture*, ed. Susan Fillin-Yeh (New York University Press, 2001), 228-29.

6 Hendricks, quoted in Doreen Mangan, "Barkley Hendricks and His Figurative Drama," *American Artist* 40, no. 408 (July 1976): 37.

7 See Michael Fried, *Manet's Modernism: Or, The Face of Painting in the 1860s* (University of Chicago Press, 1998).

8 Hilton Kramer, "Art: To the Last Detail," *New York Times*, June 17, 1977, C21.

9 On this score, see Judith Wilson, "Getting Down to Get Over: Romare Bearden's Use of Pornography and the Problem of the Black Female Body in Afro-U.S. Art," in *Black Popular Culture: A Project by Michele Wallace*, ed. Gina Dent (Bay Press, 1992), 112-22.

10 Michael Fried, "Shape as Form: Frank Stella's Irregular Polygons," in *Art and Objecthood: Essays and Reviews* (University of Chicago Press, 1998).

11 See Leo Steinberg, "Other Criteria," in *Other Criteria: Confrontations with Twentieth-Century Art* (Oxford University Press, 1972), 66-91.

12 Krista A. Thompson, *Developing Blackness: Studio Photographs of "Over the Hill" Nassau in the Independence Era* (National Art Gallery of the Bahamas, 2008), 13.

13 Hendricks, quoted in Benjamin Genocchio, "Pop Art Meets Photorealism," *New York Times*, January 27, 2008.

14 Steinberg, "Other Criteria," 79.

15 Richard Iton, *In Search of the Black Fantastic: Politics and Popular Culture in the Post-Civil Rights Era* (Oxford: Oxford University Press, 2008).

16 Krista Thompson, *An Eye for the Tropics: Tourism, Photography, and Framing the Caribbean Picturesque* (Duke University Press, 2006).

17 See, for example, Edith DeShazo, "Hendrick's Cool Realism on View," *Sunday News Journal* (Wilmington, DE), February 11, 1979, 26.

18 Barkley L. Hendricks, "Selected Artist Chronology," in *Birth of the Cool*, ed. Trevor Schoonmaker (Nasher Museum of Art at Duke University, 2008), 120.

19 Thelma Golden and Barkley L. Hendricks, "Conversation with Barkley Hendricks," in Schoonmaker, *Birth of the Cool*, 59.

20 Thelma Golden, Introduction to the catalog of the exhibition *Freestyle*, (Studio Museum in Harlem, 2001), 14.

7

A RANGE OF CONVERGENCES

I

Like any number of successful contemporary artists, Mark Bradford works in a range of media that includes sculpture, photography, video, and installation. But to hear him tell it, he is, at heart, a "paper chaser," most often these days of posters lifted from the fences of South Central Los Angeles where he works.[1] He hauls these finds back to his studio and stores them until he is ready: to cut paper, soak, cover or singe it, to adhere it to canvas, and then to paint, sand, or rip it further. In this essay, it is to Bradford's operative dislocations that I ultimately want to attend as they are vital to understanding the convergences that have shaped his public profile, the historical field in which he moves, and the spatial logic of his trademark pieces (Fig. 7.1).

Consider, for one, the propulsive fractured energy of *Los Moscos* (2004), a nearly sixteen-foot collage of urban detritus that has become emblematic of his art due to its vertiginous spatial perspective and punning title, which translates as "flies," a derogatory term for Mexican day laborers that gather outside Home Depot, one of the artist's favorite haunts.[2] Faced with such pictorial and discursive complexity, writers have trotted out a long list of assignations aimed at describing Bradford and his procedures ever since he emerged with canvases like *Enter and Exit the New Negro* (2000) (Fig. 7.2), covered in a loosely arranged grid of the endpapers used to style African American hair. With these works in view and the artist's identities in mind—black, gay, L.A. bred, and CalArts educated—critics have labeled him a beauty operator, a cultural historian, a postmodern flaneur, a hustler, an urban geographer, an anti-cartographer, an archaeologist, and, no less contentiously, a painter, often at Bradford's prompting.[3]

All of these metaphors ring more or less true, especially given the complex circuit between "an institutional inside and outside" that Malik Gaines has rightly noted "is the scene of Bradford's most triumphant con-

This article first appeared in *Parkett* 89 (Fall 2011): 152–69.

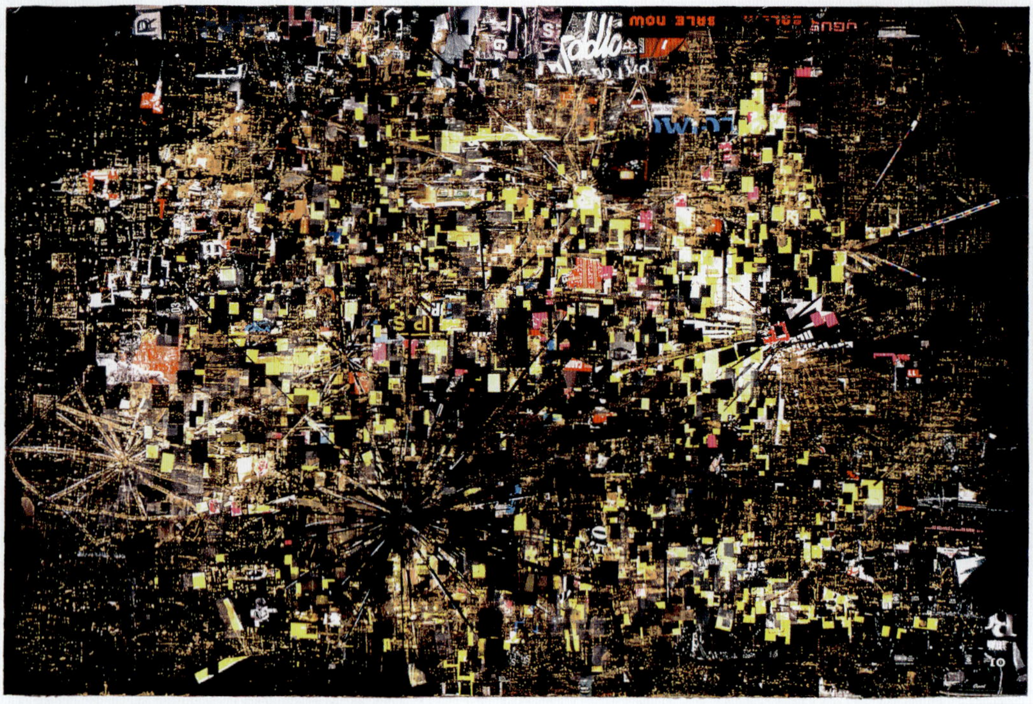

Figure 7.1
Mark Bradford, *Los Moscos*, 2004. Mixed media on canvas, 317.5 × 483.9 cm / 125 × 190½ in. © Mark Bradford. Courtesy the artist and Hauser & Wirth.

tradictory syntheses."[4] Yet as the artist well knows, the ambitions behind those shifting monikers are part and parcel of the art historical game, which often entails peculiar risks for African American practitioners.[5] On the one hand, while attempts at categorization abet the visibility and marketing of his work, they also threaten to moor it within always already prescribed cultural narratives that occlude the art itself. On the other hand, without the specifying frame such narratives provide, the work may well be written off as merely a tired redux of the once-radical aesthetic forms—the grid, the minimal, the assemblage—that it so pointedly recollects.[6]

II

Steven Nelson, one of the artist's most astute commentators, offers us one way out of this false dichotomy by focusing on what the work and its maker enact. He argues that Bradford's practice cross-wires the metaphorical and the metonymic, thereby undoing stable attributions of meaning and indexing both hidden and overt social relationships. As such, the work is animated by what he identifies, with a nod to Craig Owens, as an "allegor-

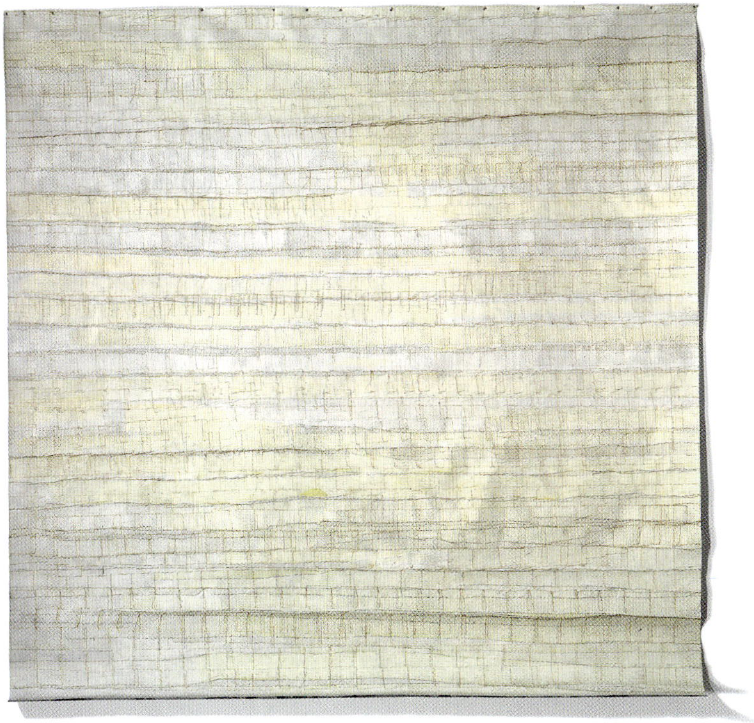

Figure 7.2
Mark Bradford, *Enter and Exit the New Negro*, 2000. Mixed media, 274 × 244 cm / 108 × 95 in. © Mark Bradford. Courtesy the artist and Hauser & Wirth.

ical impulse": by his lights, a canvas such as *Los Moscos* "constitutes a site from which the artist collapses lived experience and formal structure."[7] For Nelson and many others, that structure takes its primary cue from the method of *décollage* pioneered by Jacques Villeglé and Raymond Hains, who, in 1949, began ripping layers of posters—already lacerated by passersby—straight from the fences erected around postwar Paris's many construction sites and affixing them to canvas.[8]

As Hannah Feldman has shown, however, it would be some years before this aesthetic conceit would materialize into a "historically determined critical practice," and perhaps nowhere more strikingly than in the Hains-orchestrated exhibition *La France déchirée* of 1961.[9] The *décollages* assembled for this occasion literally and metaphorically figured a France torn by political imperatives that were inextricably bound up with the nation's colonial enterprises in Algeria and elsewhere. In her account, Feldman contends that the titles of and posters comprising these works not only brought struggles for decolonization into the space of the gallery but also made visible, however obliquely and fleetingly, those "faceless populations," who, in defacing the signage of the street, gave visual form to publics otherwise excluded from representation.[10]

III

Within Bradford's oeuvre, few works register the retooling of Hains' procedures as directly as his two iterations of *James Brown Is Dead* (2007) (Fig. 7.3), sprawling banners on unstretched canvas each measuring more than twenty feet in length. Though possessed of dissimilar factures as a result of variations in weathering, public engagement, and the artist's means of attack, the two pieces were actually pulled from a single billboard, which at the time sported a smartphone advertisement whose trademark images still emerge through abraded surfaces.[11]

Now owned by separate museums in New York and Los Angeles, these works share a matrix and a mark: Bradford has irrevocably conjoined his *décollages* by excising the same eponymous phrase from their upper layers. Not long after the passing of the "Godfather of Soul," he noticed the announcement in a local paper, whose font, blown up hundreds of times, provided him with a textual template that was at once suitably deadpan and wildly referential.[12] More than marking the end of an iconic performer's tumultuous life on Christmas 2006 and giving a shout-out to the Dutch duo L.A. Style's 1991 techno hit, the phrase "James Brown Is Dead" and its laborious double inscription allegorize the forms of cultural crisis that provide the grounds for Bradford's work with what he calls the "ghost economies" of South Central.[13]

Figure 7.3

Mark Bradford, *James Brown Is Dead*, 2007. Mixed media on paper, 122 × 681 cm / 48 × 268 in. © Mark Bradford. Courtesy the artist and Hauser & Wirth.

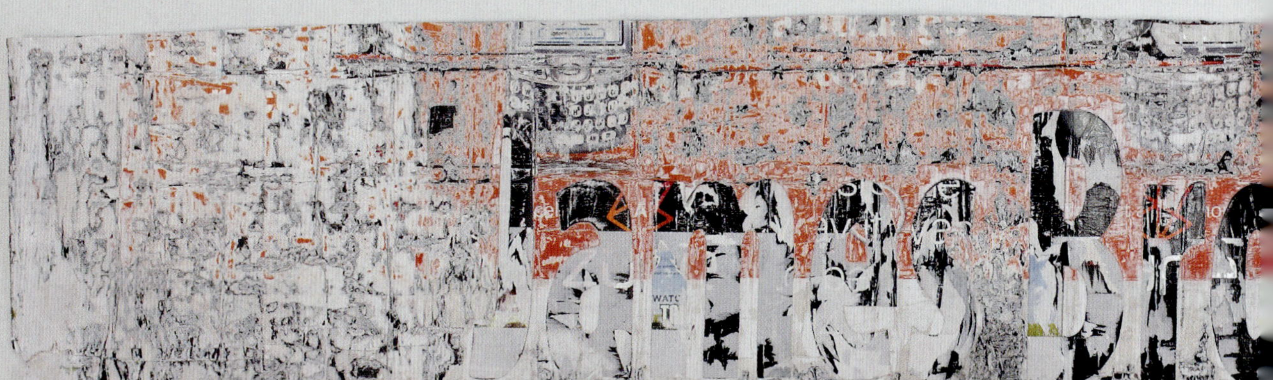

In the mid-seventies, around the same time that Brown's career was on the wane, the manufacturing jobs that enabled a modicum of economic stability for the area's black middle class began to disappear, leading to higher rates of poverty and unemployment. These conditions, which were only exacerbated in the ensuing decade by the ravages of the AIDS crisis, the crack cocaine epidemic, and the rise of violent gang cultures, would reach a culmination of sorts in 1992. One year after L.A. Style released their track—itself a tongue-in-cheek critique of the ubiquitous sampling of Brown's music—South Central erupted in rage and fire in response to the acquittal of the four police officers who had brutally beaten Rodney King. In the wake of the uprisings, the area was spatially reconfigured and rendered more bereft than ever of crucial businesses, the ruins of which were frequently marked off with the cyclone fencing that has become a defining feature of the cityscape. It was on these ostensibly temporary structures that local merchants began to advertise their wares with brightly colored posters, which Bradford has increasingly made the substrate of his art, whether sundered and repurposed or largely covered over, their declamations left legible: Gun show! DNA testing! Cheap auto parts! (Fig. 7.4).[14]

Bradford's *décollages*, then, both converge with and importantly diverge from those of his midcentury, European antecedents. Rather than interrupt the sanctity of the gallery with evidence of publics and conflicts not otherwise seen within it, he conjures visions of an elsewhere created from the material life-world of those on our own shores who are often rendered

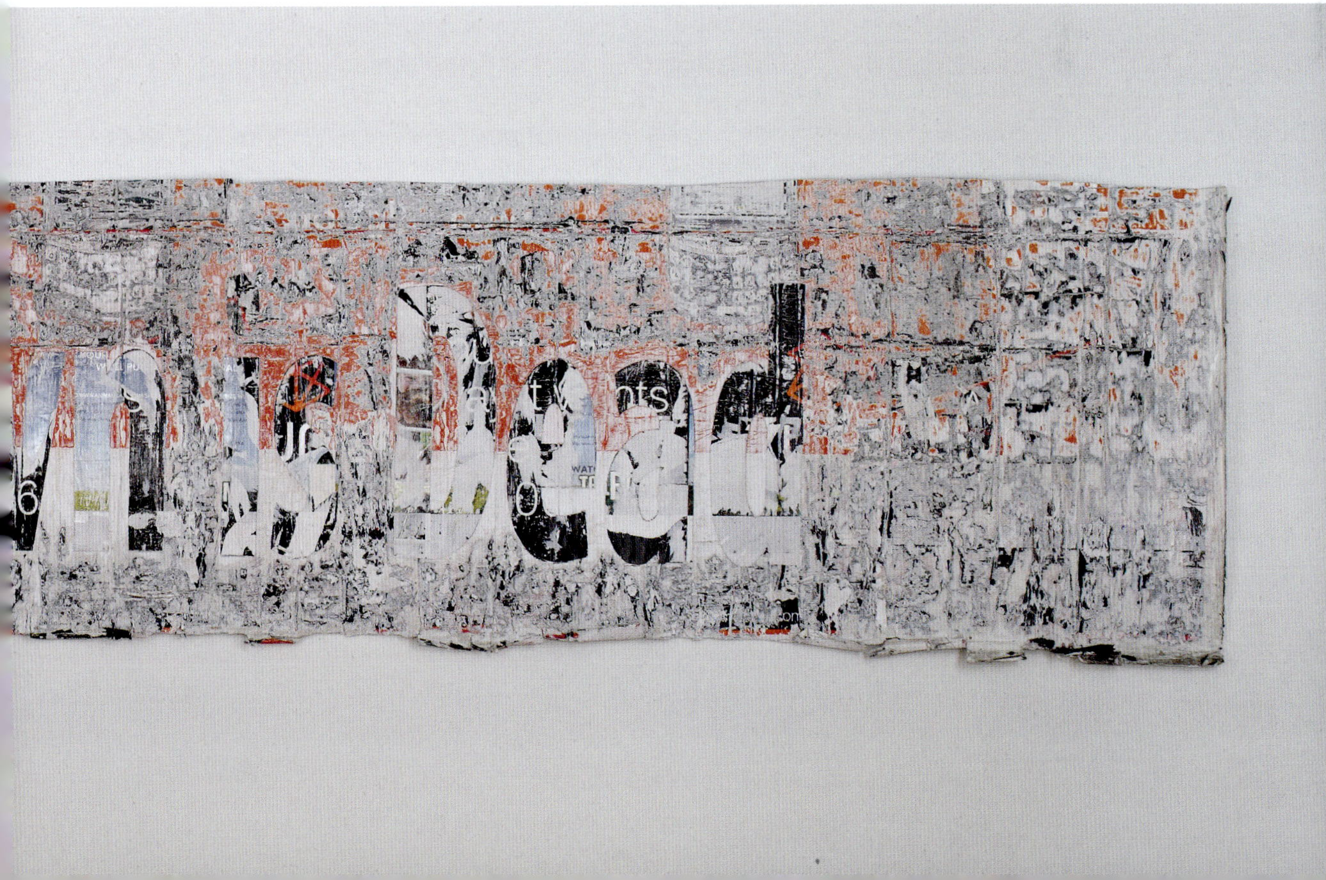

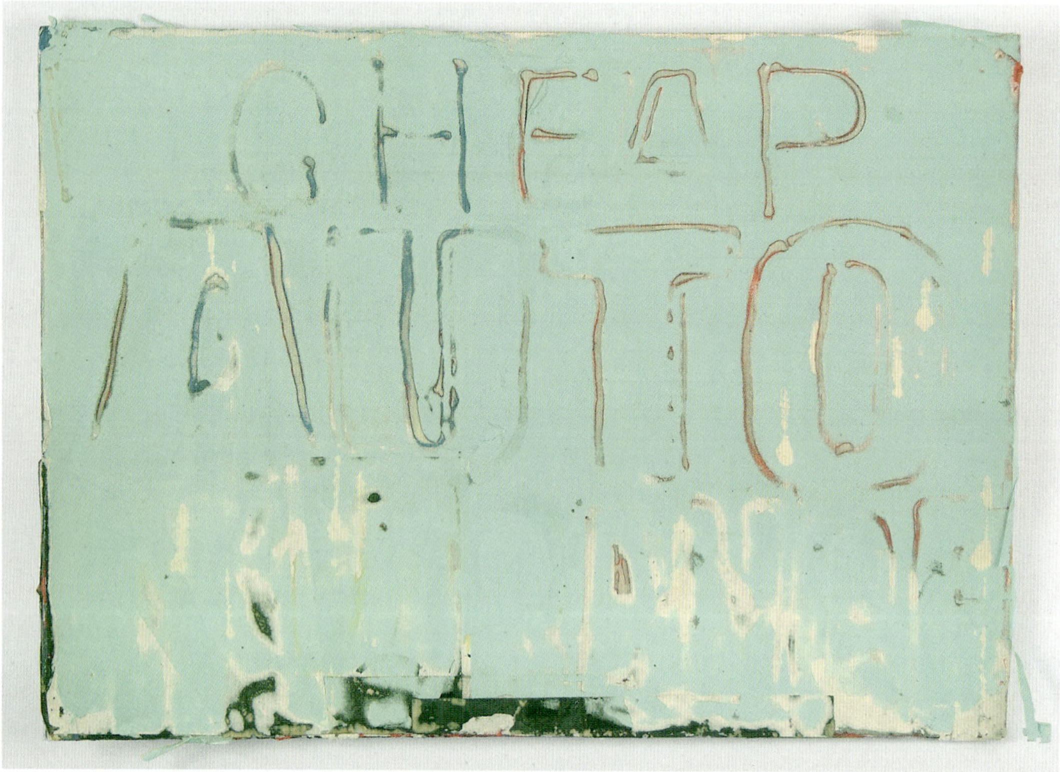

Figure 7.4
Mark Bradford, *Untitled (CHEAP AUTO INSURANCE)*, 2006. Mixed media on paper, 37 × 52 cm / 14⅝ × 20½ in. © Mark Bradford. Courtesy the artist and Hauser & Wirth.

socially dead, politically disenfranchised, and at times subject to both low-grade harassment and spectacular catastrophe.[15] In this ambition, Los Angeles is not Bradford's only site and paper is far from his sole medium: he designed carts given away free to the *maleteros* who help border crossers transport their goods from Mexico to the United States (2005); he executed twin homages to the prosperous black community of Tulsa, Oklahoma, which was completely razed in 1924 during a spree of white violence (*Black Wall Street*, 2006, and *Scorched Earth*, 2006) (Fig. 7.5); and on the roof of a gallery, he painted a sign reading "HELP US," only visible from above, that was meant to echo the impassioned utterance and the conditional visibility of a woman trapped at the New Orleans Convention Center in the wake of Hurricane Katrina (2008) (Fig. 7.6).[16] By making such gestures, Bradford secures attention for the *Nonsite* of his work, allowing scopic investment to shuttle back to the *Site* from whence it emerges.

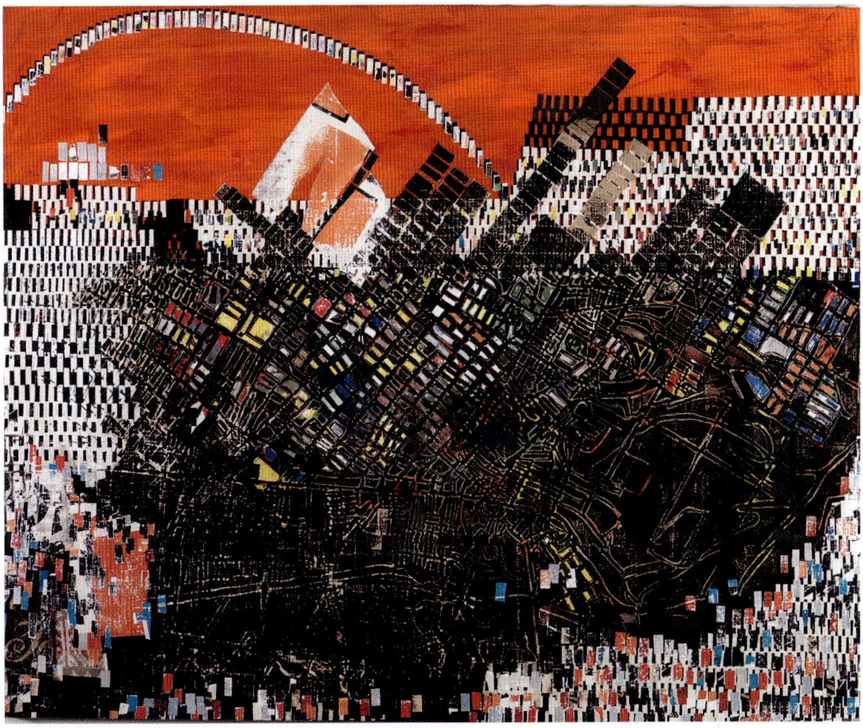

Figure 7.5
Mark Bradford, *Scorched Earth*, 2006. Mixed media on canvas, 240 × 299.7 cm / 94½ × 118 in. © Mark Bradford. Courtesy the artist and Hauser & Wirth.

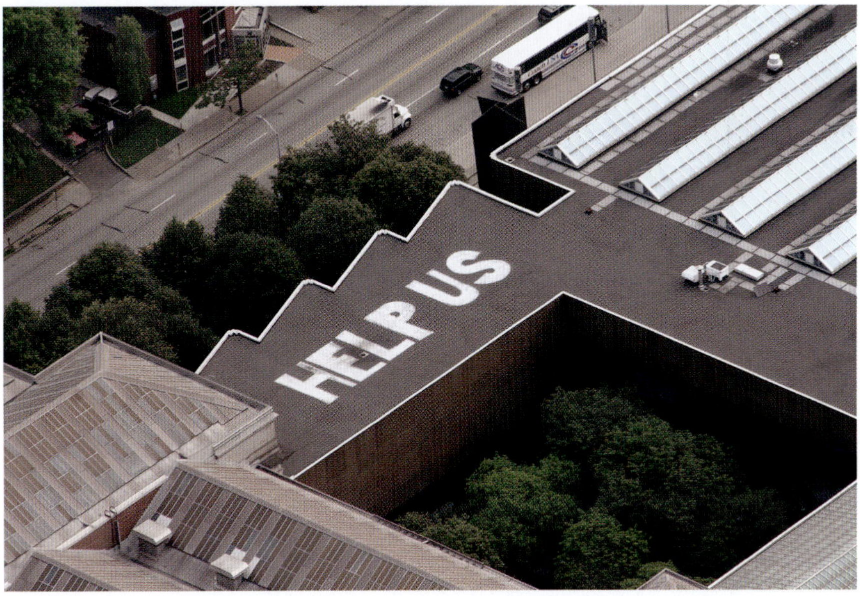

Figure 7.6
Mark Bradford, *Help Us*, 2008. Text on roof, with signed certificate. Photo: Bob Enos. © Mark Bradford. Courtesy the artist and Hauser & Wirth.

IV

I borrow the italicized terms as well as the title of my essay from Robert Smithson. A student of ruin and, for Owens, the allegorist par excellence, Smithson paired Site and Nonsite to produce artworks that brought earth from afar into the realm of appearance, at once marking out and collapsing spatial distance.[17] Doing so was no simple feat.

> The range of convergence between Site and Nonsite consists of a course of hazards, a double path made up of signs, photographs, and maps that belong to both sides of the dialectic at once. Both sides are present and absent at the same time. The land or ground from the Site is placed in the art (Nonsite) rather than the art placed on the ground. The Nonsite is a container within another container—the room. The plot or yard outside is yet another container. Two-dimensional and three-dimensional things trade places with each other in the range of convergence. Large scale becomes small. Small scale becomes large. A point on a map expands to the size of the land mass. A land mass contracts into a point. Is the Site a reflection of the Nonsite (mirror), or is it the other way around? The rules of this network of signs are discovered as you go along uncertain trails both mental and physical.[18]

Smithson's almost dizzying account of the shifts in scale, location, and dimensionality involved in negotiating the Site/Nonsite dialectic speaks aptly, I think, to the visual experience held out by *Los Moscos* and its fellows, to the ties that connect *James Brown Is Dead*s across a continent, and to Bradford's practice tout court. For if his art can be described as animated by an allegorical impulse, then he might be said to operate in and on the range of convergence engendered by the disjunction between the Site of a subaltern public whose image is effaced and the Nonsite of his collages whose facticity is undeniable.

This goes some way toward explaining the array of names that Bradford has been called, which tend to root his activity in the locations he inhabits rather than in the contingent linkages he establishes between them.[19] Indeed, his art and persona seem to require the traversal and production of spatial distance to maintain their integrity: in gathering the carpenter's tools he uses to assemble his fine art, he zips off to Home Depot; in attaching a network of strings to canvas, he runs in and out of his studio to gauge his lines' look against the patterning of telephone wires; and in reflecting on his trajectory, he regards his decision to re-create his mother's salon at the 2002 Art Basel Miami Beach fair as a misstep, since it brought the marketplace too close to and effectively overdetermined the narration of his practice in relation to a particular site.[20]

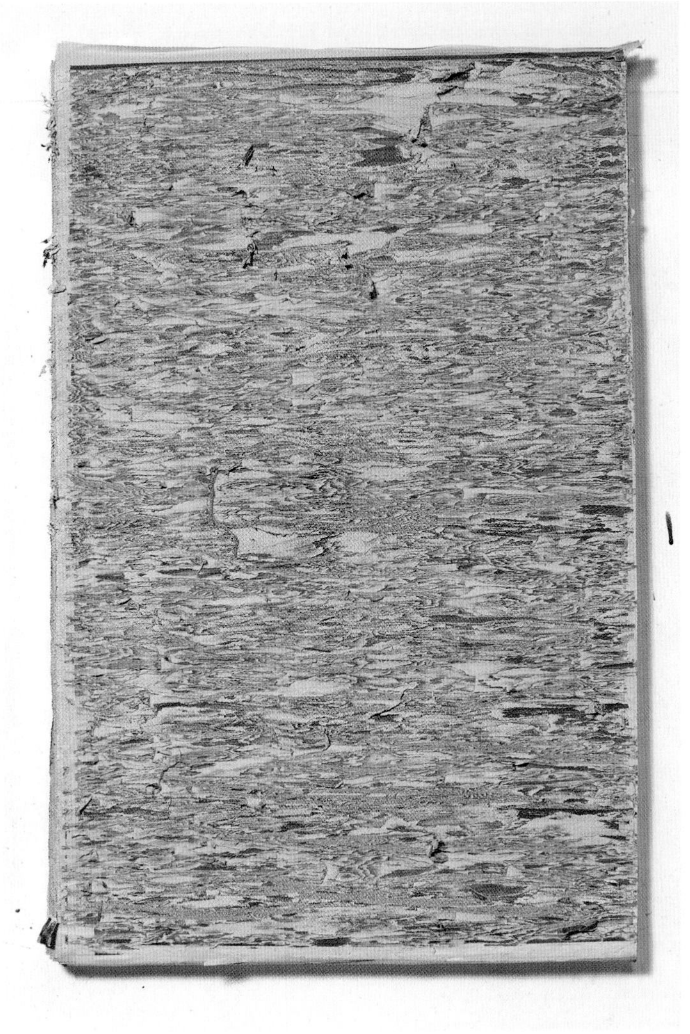

Figure 7.7
Mark Bradford, *NTSC*, 2010. Mixed media on panel, 86 × 56 cm / 34 × 22 in. © Mark Bradford. Courtesy the artist and Hauser & Wirth.

Viewed in this light, one might argue that the components of Bradford's successive bodies of work index the milieus he finds himself negotiating at any given moment, from his beginnings in the beauty shop to his current ubiquity in those mainstream media—print and video—that have made him an art world star. To wit, in *NTSC* (2010), the artist glued together sheets of newspaper printed with slightly different shades of gray and mounted them on board before beginning one of his improvisational sanding assaults (Fig. 7.7). The resulting work, named for the dominant analog television system used in the United States, thus unites two obsolescent technologies in its suggestion of a frothily blurred screen, emptying out the Site of dazed visual consumption so that the rigorous optical demands of the Nonsite that is the work may occupy its place.[21]

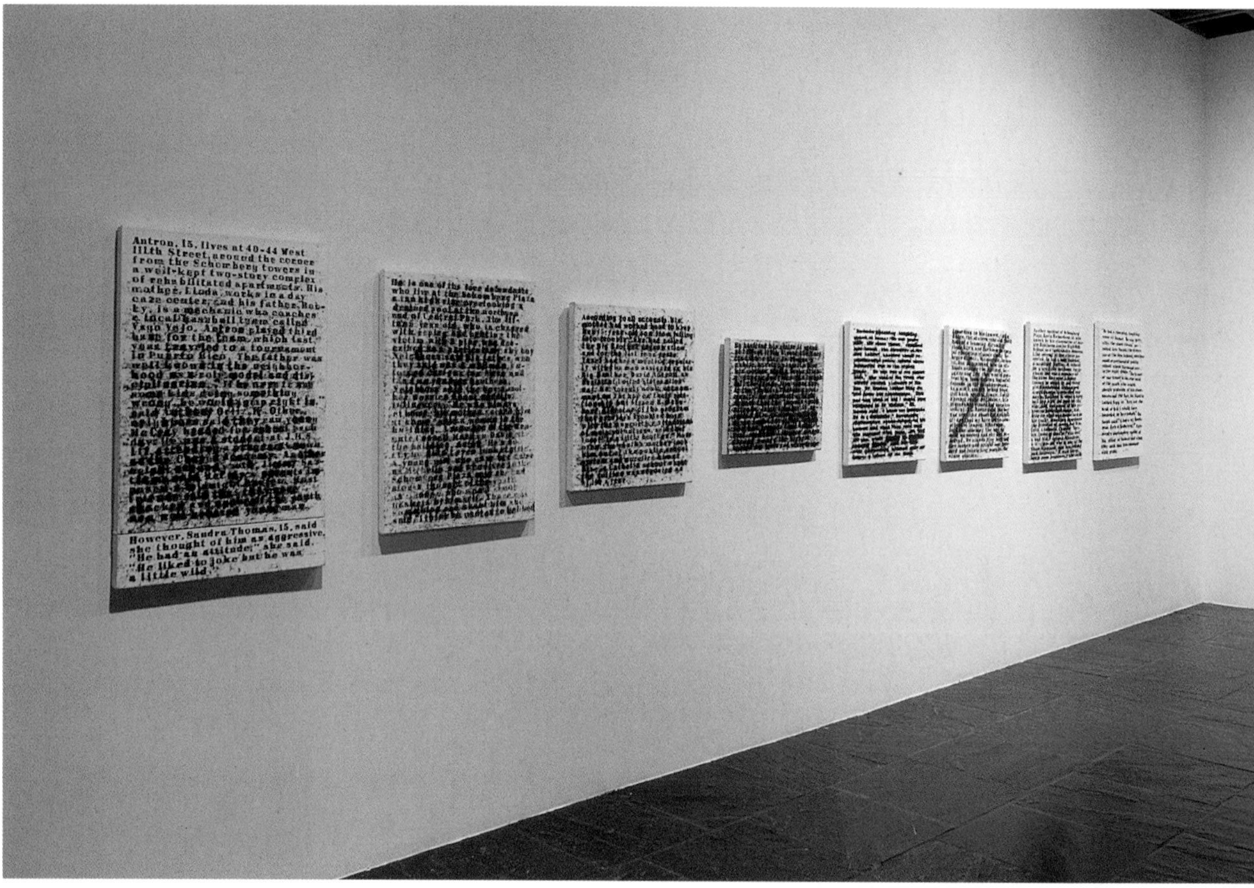

Figure 7.8
Glenn Ligon, *Profile Series*, 1990–91, installation view. Collection of Whitney Museum of American Art, New York; gift from the Emily Fisher Landau Collection. © Glenn Ligon.

In this practice as in Smithson's text, the terms of the dialectic slide uneasily back and forth, rendering the zones from which materials were culled no-places and the finished objects that they enable as loci of meaning adrift from, though still redolent of, their original contexts. In this way, Bradford's art resonates with attempts by practitioners working through the context of American struggles for decolonization, such as Andy Warhol, David Hammons, and Theaster Gates, to transpose figures of black dereliction into the realm of art. This mode of painting by other means, forever haunted by the economies of racialization that deform its subjects and sources, is exemplified by Glenn Ligon's *Profile Series* (1990–91) (Fig. 7.8), in which shadowy figurative outlines emerge from oil renderings of *The New York Times*' write-ups on the youths unjustly accused and convicted in the Central Park Jogger case.

While analogous in their performative dislocation, Bradford's works usually eschew the figure, approximating the look of abstraction the better to smuggle their material histories into the museum. The inverse can be said of the artist himself, who dresses up in an official-looking jumpsuit so that he can proceed unmolested through his poaching grounds, where he not-quite-legally removes the illicit posters that populate his canvases.[22] In both cases, a locational camouflage is assumed in order to produce a picture and to register its elisions, so that the subject, in the words of Jacques Lacan, may "be inserted in a function whose exercise grasps it," a longed-for belonging that shapes individual desires and pursuits regardless of identarian position, though especially for those historically cast out of the *socius* itself.[23]

V

With a view to an end, let us ring one more change on the subject in question, the range of convergence in which Bradford plies his trade. For his part, the artist—a paper chaser 'til the end—allies himself with the merchant class: "As a merchant, you service the sub-class, the working class, and the professional class, but you really don't belong to any of them."[24] To pay heed to this statement is not to privilege one of Bradford's descriptions above all others but to look toward situating his practice, structurally and operationally, within the terrain of the artwork, the commodity, and the psyche, which is to say, of the fetish.

As William Pietz so convincingly argues, that far-reaching historical field—of the object's territorialization, historicization, reification, and personalization—was constituted some four hundred years ago when Portuguese merchants first encountered their counterparts on African soil.[25] At issue in such moments of cross-cultural exchange, then and since, is the question of how valuation proceeds when discrepant material economies intersect. Are beads worth their weight in gold? Can gods be compared? How might different kinds of paper be rendered equivalent? Attuned to the constitutive differences in perception that attend every form of commerce, Bradford has seized upon the flow of capital that connects artists to their clients—a tie that Clement Greenberg famously likened to "an umbilical cord of gold"—so that it might be productively rerouted.[26]

Perhaps most notable in this regard—and as a model of "historically determined critical practice"—is his collaboration with the New Orleans Lower Ninth Ward community association L9 Center for the Arts with whom he organized a benefit auction of work by himself and a cast of renowned practitioners as part of his contribution to the 2008 exhibition *Prospect.1 New Orleans*. Taking advantage of the international biennial

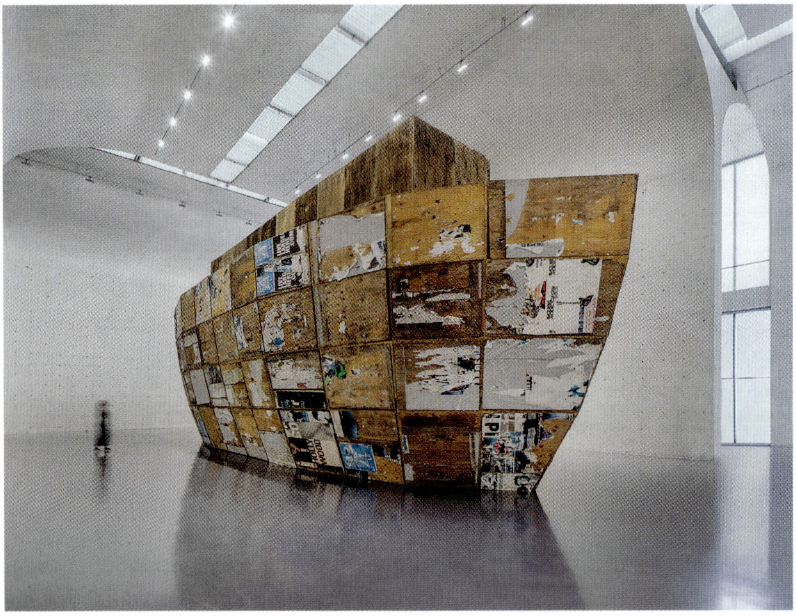

Figure 7.9
Mark Bradford, *Mithra*, 2008. Mixed media, 726.4 × 1963.4 × 635 cm / 286 × 773 × 250 in. Installation view, Prospect.1 New Orleans, 2008. © Mark Bradford. Courtesy the artist and Hauser & Wirth.

circuit's publicity and patronage, Bradford was able to direct funds to the predominantly black working-class neighborhood devastated by Hurricane Katrina and its aftermath (Fig. 7.9).[27] Converting paper into "painting" and back again into money, the artist roams the United States and beyond, replaying and articulating his distance from the displaced subject's predication as belonging everywhere and nowhere. Much the same can be said of his works, which, though stilled, continue to make moves: hovering between Site and Nonsite, fact and fetish, they model an alchemy that, while all their own, is as old as the modern world itself.[28]

Notes

1 Bradford, quoted in Carol S. Eliel, "Dynamism and Quiet Whispers: Conversations with Mark Bradford," in *Mark Bradford*, ed. Christopher Bedford (Wexner Center for the Arts and Yale University Press, 2010), 57.

2 Steven Nelson, "Mark Bradford's Allegorical Impulse," in *Mark Bradford* (Sikkema Jenkins & Co., 2006), 8.

3 I refer, respectively, to Hilton Als, "Darkness Visible," http://www.newyorker.com/online/blogs/hiltonals/2008/02/darkness-visibl.html, February 5, 2008; Carolee Thea, "Profile: Mark Bradford," *Art Asia Pacific*, no. 40 (Spring 2004): 28-29; Doryun Chong, "Mark Bradford," in *Brave New*

Worlds, by Doryun Chong and Yasmil Raymond (Walker Art Center, 2007), 53; Trevor Schoonmaker, "Hot Comb," *One World* 7, no. 4 (September 2002), 122; Kathryn Brown, "The Artist as Urban Geographer: Mark Bradford and Julie Mehretu," *American Art*, no. 24 (Fall 2010): 100-113; Carter E. Foster, *Neither New Nor Correct* (Whitney Museum of American Art, 2007); Mark Bradford, phone conversation with the author, April 27, 2011; Christopher Bedford, "Against Abstraction," in Bedford, *Mark Bradford*, 7-29.

4 Malik Gaines, "The Artist Formerly Known as Mark Bradford," in *Mark Bradford: Merchant Posters* (Gregory R. Miller & Co. and Aspen Art Museum, 2010), 27-28.

5 See Bradford's comments in Charmaine Picard, "It's a Complex Conversation and There's No Closure," *The Art Newspaper*, no. 213 (May 2010): 48.

6 For examples of this tendency, see Jaleh Mansoor, "Mark Bradford: Wexner Center for the Arts, Columbus, Ohio," *Artforum* 60, no. 3 (November 2010): 258; Morgan Falconer, "Morgan Falconer on Mark Bradford at Sikkema Jenkins, New York," http://magazine.saatchionline.com/culture/reports-from/liechtenstein/morgan_falconer_on_mark_bradfo, January 24, 2008. For a critique of both approaches to African American art, see Huey Copeland, "'Bye, Bye Black Girl': Lorna Simpson's Figurative Retreat," *Art Journal* 64, no. 2 (Summer 2005): 62-77.

7 Nelson, "Mark Bradford's Allegorical Impulse," 10; Craig Owens, "The Allegorical Impulse: Toward a Theory of Postmodernism," in *Beyond Recognition: Representation, Power, and Culture*, ed. Scott Bryson et al. (University of California Press, 1992), 52-69.

8 Nelson, "Mark Bradford's Allegorical Impulse," 10. On Hains and Villeglé's achievement, see Hannah Feldman, "Of the Public Born: Raymond Hains and *La France déchirée*," *October*, no. 108 (Spring 2004): 73.

9 Feldman, "Of the Public Born," 75.

10 Feldman, "Of the Public Born," 93-94. The discourse on Bradford remains somewhat reticent on this aspect of the history of *décollage*. One notable exception is Philippe Vergne, "No More Fire, the Paper Next Time," in *Mark Bradford: Merchant Posters*, 20.

11 Mark Bradford, phone conversation with the author, April 27, 2011.

12 Mark Bradford, phone conversation with the author, April 27, 2011.

13 The artist, quoted in Ernest Hardy, "The Eye of L.A.: Mark Bradford," http://articles.latimes com/2006/jun/11/magazine/tm-bradford24. For an instructive reading of these works in relation to Jacques Derrida's notion of hauntology, see Michael Wilson, "Mark Bradford Sikkema Jenkins & Co.," *Artforum* 46, no. 8 (April 2008): 369-70.

14 In crafting this narrative, I have drawn on the indispensable Robert Gooding-Williams, *Reading Rodney King/Reading Urban Uprising* (Routledge, 1993), as well as my April 27, 2011, conversation with the artist.

15 Orlando Patterson, *Slavery and Social Death: A Comparative Study* (Harvard University Press, 1982), 1-14.

16 On these works, see, respectively, Jennie Klein, "Performance, Post-Border Art, and Urban Geography," *PAJ* 86 (2007): 35; Thelma Golden, "Interview with Mark Bradford," http://www.worldclassboxing.org/exhibit_mbradford.php, October 23, 2006; Christopher Knight, "Mark Bradford Examines Life Viewed Through Today's Technology," *Los Angeles Times*, April 2, 2008.

17 Craig Owens, "Earthwords," in Bryson et al., *Beyond Recognition*, 40-51.

18 Robert Smithson, "The Spiral Jetty," in *Robert Smithson: The Collected Writings*, ed. Jack Flam (University of California Press, 1996), 153.

19 The most trenchant analysis of the relation between identity and place in contemporary art remains Miwon Kwon, *One Place After Another: Site-Specific Art and Locational Identity* (MIT Press, 2002).

20 See the artist's comments in *Bedford*, 23-24; Brian Keith Jackson, "How I Made It: Mark Bradford," *New York Magazine*, http://nymag.com/arts/art/features/37954/, September 24, 2007.

21 For an in-depth discussion of these "graphite" collages, see Richard Shiff, "Move with Chance," in Bedford, *Mark Bradford*, 89-91.

22 See the artist's comments in Picard, "It's a Complex Conversation and There's No Closure," 48.

23 Jacques Lacan, "The Line and Light," in *The Seminar of Jacques Lacan, Book XI: The Four Fundamental Concepts of Psychoanalysis*, trans. Alan Sheridan, ed. Jacques-Alain Miller (W. W. Norton, 1981), 100. For another engagement with Bradford's work along these lines, see Katy Siegel, "Somebody and Nobody," in Bedford, *Mark Bradford*, 103-20.

24 The artist, quoted in Hardy, "The Eye of L.A.: Mark Bradford."

25 William Pietz, "The Problem of the Fetish, I," *Res* 9 (Spring 1985): 5-17.

26 Clement Greenberg, "Avant-Garde, and Kitsch," in *The Collected Essays and Criticism*, vol. 1, *Perceptions and Judgments, 1939-1944*, ed. John O'Brian (University of Chicago Press, 1988), 11.

27 Irie Jones, http://cultureserve.net/blog/2008/06/01/artculture-diaries-prospectl-new-orleans/, June 1, 2008.

28 For an account of the relation between blackness, fugitivity, and fetishism, see Huey Copeland, "Glenn Ligon and Other Runaway Subjects," *Representations*, no. 113 (Winter 2011): 73-110.

8

NORTHERN SOUL

As the arrest of Henry Louis Gates Jr. on the steps of his own house made clear, the dynamics of racialized subjection are particularly vexed in ivory-tower towns like Cambridge, Massachusetts.[1] On the one hand, black bodies are continuously surveyed and assessed as either "hood," "Harvard," or "homeless"; on the other, the city and its environs play host to a range of the most visible African diasporic cultural institutions and practitioners anywhere. Yet there are, of course, much-needed escapes from these specular extremes of life lived black.

It was just this kind of phenomenal experience—of solace and sublimity, communion and catharsis—that Alicia Hall Moran conjured into being for an intimate crowd in February at Cambridge's Regattabar, a jazz venue in the upscale Charles Hotel. A classically trained soprano, Hall Moran has increasingly come to work within the spaces of the art world, collaborating with the conceptualist Adam Pendleton on his 2007 performance *The Revival* and unfurling one of her song installations—a series of site-sensitive vocal interventions—at a *soirée musicale*, curated by the artist Whitfield Lovell. Migration across locales and audiences also undergirds her *Motown Project*, reprised here after first being presented in December 2009 at the Kitchen in New York. Aptly described by the musicologist Guthrie Ramsey as a kind of "Schubertian song cycle," the *Motown Project* primarily mixes 1960s Motor City classics with eighteenth- and nineteenth-century operatic hits.[2]

In the age of the mash-up, Hall Moran's conceit might sound jejune, but what her arrangements achieved was less a conjoining of opposites than an embodied recombination of musical traditions that somehow yearn for each other across lines of race, class, and nation. Accompanied by an equally brilliant and worldly ensemble—operatic baritone Steven Herring, guitarist Thomas Flippin, bassist Tarus Mateen, *taiko* drummer

This essay first appeared in *Artforum* 49, no. 9 (May 2011): 103 © *Artforum*.

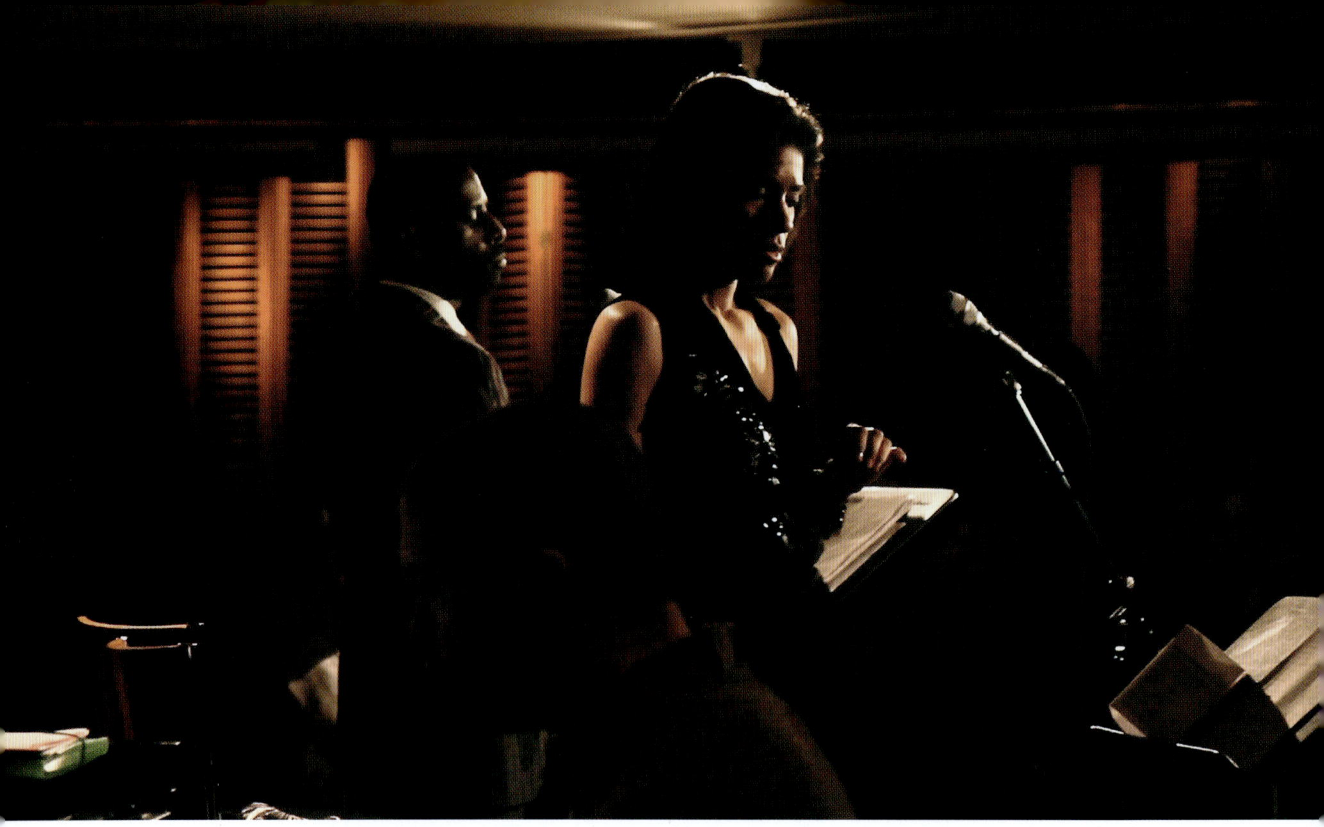

Figure 8.1
Steven Herring and Alicia Hall Moran performing at the Regattabar, Cambridge, MA, February 15, 2001. Photo © Gregg Conde.

Kaoru Watanabe, and Hall Moran's husband, jazz musician Jason Moran, stepping in for harpist Adan Vasquez, on piano—she wended her way through an hour-long set that moved effortlessly among affective registers while pursuing the shared motifs of desire and infatuation that unite the genres: Mozart meets Marvin Gaye (Fig. 8.1).

Hall Moran's navigation of these traditions was as striking as it was clever. After singing the refrain from the Four Tops's "I Can't Help Myself (Sugar Pie Honey Bunch)," which was then taken up by Herring, she launched into "Non So Più Cosa Son," an aria from *The Marriage of Figaro* about male helplessness in the face of womanly charms. While the rendition of the former tune initially brought appreciative chuckles from the audience, Hall Moran performed both classical levity and pop sweetness with fierce vocal commitment, inexorably pulling in her listeners. In the process, she not only united the two songs and alluded to their unspoken trajectories—the Four Tops later recorded a version of their single in Italian—she also deftly turned them out: the irrationality of opera transformed the clean mechanical sensibility of Berry Gordy, even as Motown's sure melodic pleasures were inflected to fit opera's demands for hyperbolic feeling.

These fissures created space for both tenderness and signification. Sitting at the piano, Hall Moran began to sing an English translation of "Sono Andati?" from Puccini's *La Bohème*, a declaration of a love more expansive than the sea, before segueing into "Ain't No Mountain High Enough," first recorded by Marvin Gaye and Tammi Terrell. At that moment, Jason Moran began to shadow her movements and then assumed her position at the instrument, allowing the artist to rise and face Herring as she resolved the chorus of the duet. Through such performative recastings of Motown, an especially familiar and commercialized form of black musical expression—remember the *Big Chill* sound track—Hall Moran restored the style's affective potential through her stunning operatic range.

Savvy stagecraft and intertextual play, however, only begin to describe the corporeal impact of her performance, which variously elicited laughter, tears, hoots of joy, and the occasional "Amen," reactions infrequently encountered together within the provinces of "high" culture, regardless of hue. She brought down the house with her piercing renditions of "I Heard It Through the Grapevine" and "(Love Is like a) Heat Wave," in the latter case starting slowly, her phrases crisp, then building to a medium tempo until she was swaying in place and owning the stage. Hall Moran's ability to command should come as no surprise: she received degrees from Columbia University and the Manhattan School of Music and trained with the late Betty Allen, among other luminaries. Indeed, the diva who appeared at the Regattabar that night—toned arms, elegant gown—brought to mind the composure of Michelle Obama, while her occasional interjections of haute girlfriend banter suggested the mien of Sandra Bernhard.

Ultimately, however, the term "diva" does not quite say enough, for Hall Moran is an artist who plays on rather than accedes to such gendered conventions. In remixing what might otherwise be the canned expressiveness of opera, she elicited an intensely felt response that swept through and revivified the bodies in her thrall. At the same time, she maintained a perfect inscrutability, evoking a long lineage of cultural practitioners bound by social injunction to hide their compulsions and critiques yet nonetheless able to telegraph their dissent. As the theorist Fred Moten has argued, "the history of Afro-diasporic art" is "the history of the keeping of this secret even in the midst of its intensely public and highly commodified dissemination. These secrets are relayed and miscommunicated, misheard, and overheard, often all at once, in words and in the bending of words . . . in the names of people you'll never know."[3] These lines speak eloquently to Hall Moran's name and work and revelatory voice: I, for one, left her performance feeling newly comfortable in Cambridge and in my own skin, however the gaze might fall.

Notes

1 Abby Goodnough, "Harvard Professor Jailed; Office Is Accused of Bias," *New York Times*, July 20, 2009; https://www.nytimes.com/2009/07/21/us/21gates.html.

2 Dr. Guy [Ramsey], "From Mozart to Motown: Alicia Hall Moran's Motor City Musings," January 8, 2011, https://musiqology.com/blog/2011/01/08/from-mozart-to-motown-alicia-hall-morans-motor-city-musings/.

3 Fred Moten, quoted in Charles Rowell, "'Words Don't Go There': An Interview with Fred Moten," *Callaloo* 27, no. 4 (Autumn 2004): 960.

9

BABEL SCREENED

On Race, Narcissism, and the Predication of American Video Art

You hear the artist before you see him sitting before a white wall (Fig. 9.1). His eyes are closed, his expression focused, and for almost the entirety of the video's thirteen minutes, his mouth is full, stuffed with a microphone whose cord loops tautly around his neck. Every now and then—around minutes four, six, nine, and eleven—he pauses to clear his airways and to wipe away the spit pooling on his gray T-shirt. In the process, he removes the microphone that so amply registers his breathing, choking, and yelping even as its physical presence and burps of feedback occlude his speech. Except in these intervals, for the duration of the performance the artist signs with exasperated hands, "I am talking to you," a deictic utterance that points up the conditions of enunciation as much as anything else. Repeatedly confronted with such a straightforward yet obfuscated declaration, enjoined to witness such a disturbing but mesmeric image, you can hardly help but wonder: Just what is being said here by not saying, and why must it be said in this particular way?

A few things are for sure: Dave McKenzie is the artist in question and this work, *Babel*, first enacted in 2000, has since become a touchstone of his conceptually based practice. Although he has formatted the piece as a single-channel DVD that sutures one viewer at a time into its heart-stopping circuitry, he continues to enact it in front of live audiences, who must work hard to maintain an emotional distance from the sight of a spastic black man who comes close to falling apart before their very eyes and seems to risk electrocution at every moment.[1] Like much of the Jamaican-born US artist's work, the digitally recorded version of *Babel* considered here models a view of history in which the differential effects of subjection position his body not as a marginalized object but as vital locus through which to chart the networks of desire and consumption, liberation and disenfranchisement, violence and filiation that shape the modern social field.

This essay first appeared in *Black Is, Black Ain't*, ed. Hamza Walker and Karen Reimer (Renaissance Society at the University of Chicago, 2013), 44-55.

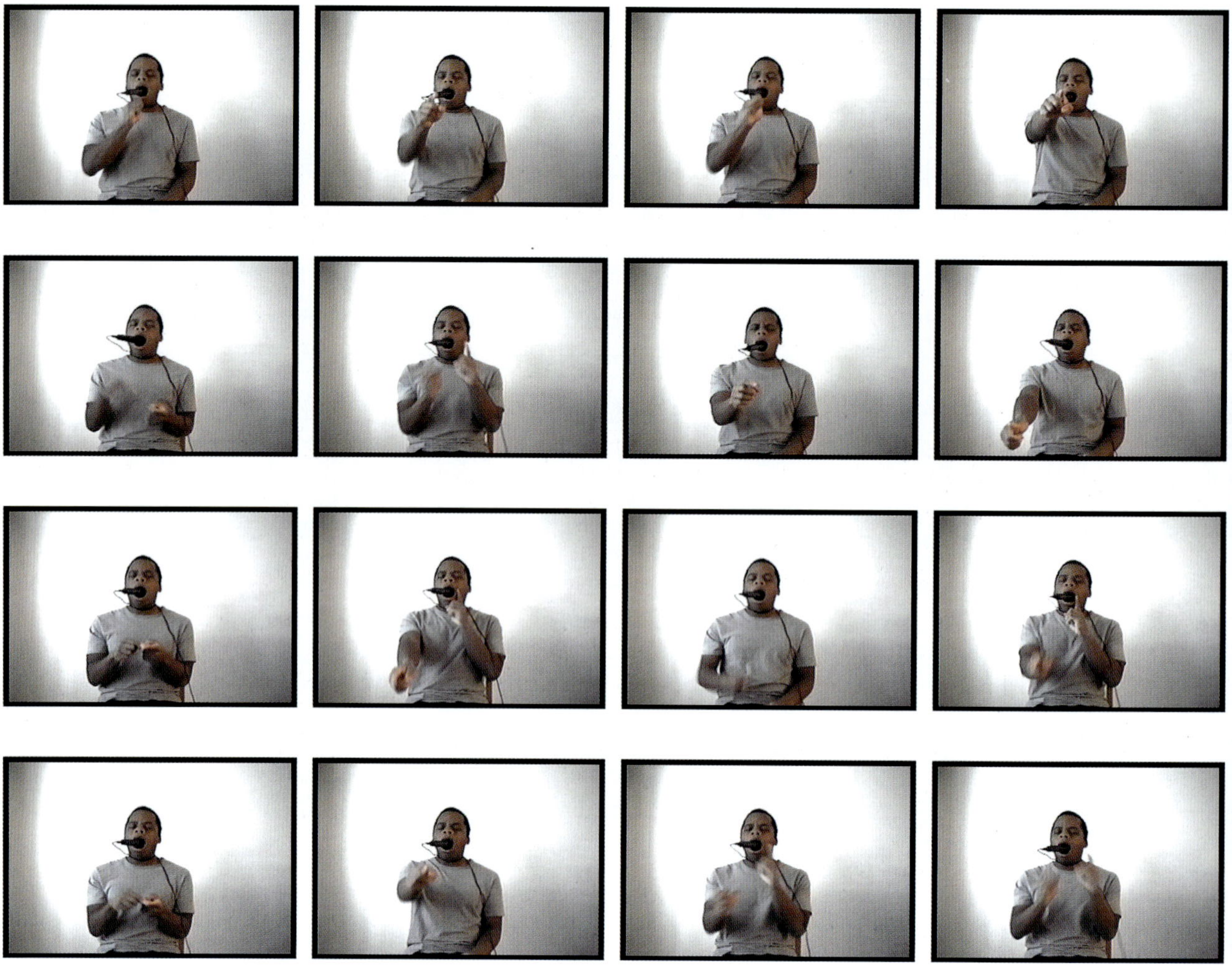

Figure 9.1
Dave McKenzie, *Babel*, stills, 2000. Video, 13 min, 47 sec. © Dave McKenzie.

It is just such concerns that animate this essay, which aims to articulate how the vicissitudes of racial terror have shaped the production and reception of American art, above all, work in performance and video. McKenzie's practice offers a fitting vehicle for this endeavor thanks to its rare wedding of discursive complexity and kindhearted solicitousness. For regardless of the form his work takes or the site in which you encounter it, Dave wants somehow to be with you: in your wallet as a card for noting enemies in the case of his *Shit List* (2004) (Fig. 9.2); on your mantel as a bobble head cast in his own image as demonstrated by *While Supplies Last* (2002) (Fig. 9.3); or as a *Self-Portrait Piñata* replete with candy (2003) (Fig. 9.4), hanging in the gallery and awaiting the instant when your taste for

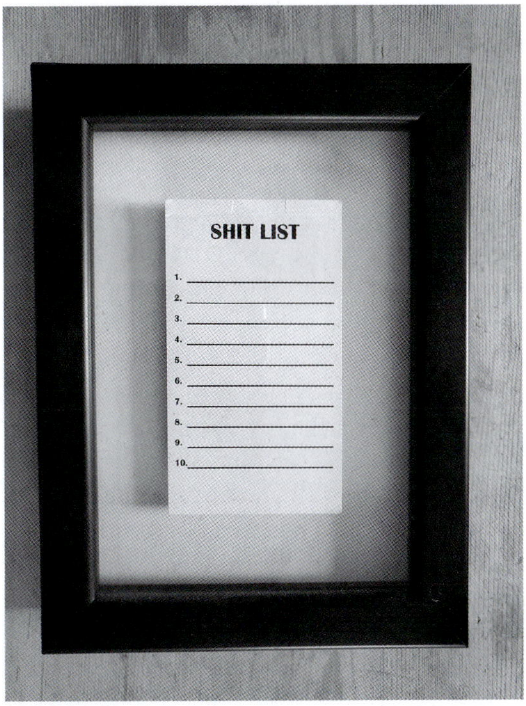

Figure 9.2
Dave McKenzie, *Shit List*, 2004. Printed cards, 2 × 3½ in. each. © Dave McKenzie.

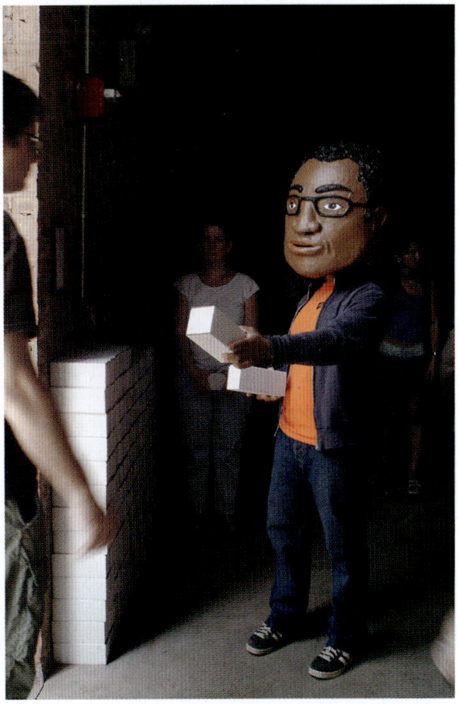

Figure 9.3
Dave McKenzie, *While Supplies Last*, 2003. Sculpture and event. © Dave McKenzie.

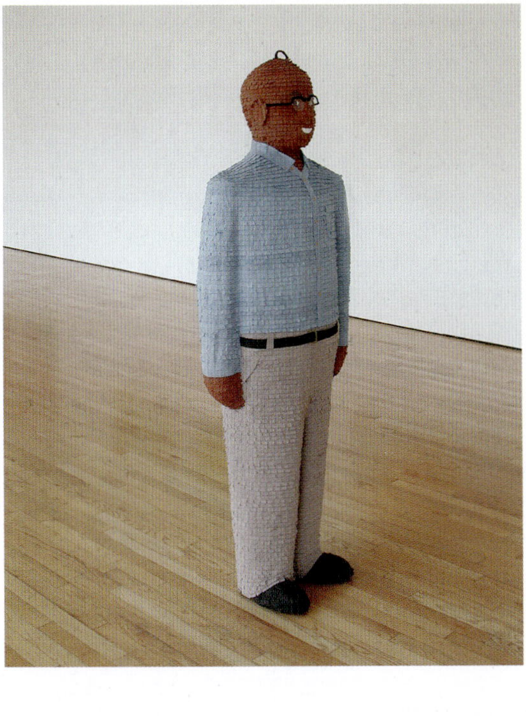

Figure 9.4
Dave McKenzie, *Self-Portrait Piñata*, 2002. Papier-mâché and crepe paper. © Dave McKenzie.

sweets gets the better of your political pieties. Each of these darkly humorous interventions is characterized by an extreme generosity as well as a lightness of touch that, in taking its measure from the artist's body, serves to make visible otherwise unremarkable occurrences by cross-wiring them with the libidinal economies of black death and their inextricable relationship to the production of white pleasure.[2]

In so doing, McKenzie engages and recasts what Jacqueline Goldsby calls "the cultural logic of lynching," which "can be understood as an articulation of the social world's organization at any given point in time," whether the victim in question is a very real Henry Smith, murdered in 1893 by a white mob numbering in the thousands, or a televisual Clarence Thomas, persecuted almost one hundred years later in the course of his Supreme Court appointment.[3] Unlike these men, the artist has not, to my knowledge, ever been accused of sexual impropriety, yet his *Shit List*, *While Supplies Last*, and *Self-Portrait Piñata* variously bear the imprint of an infernal American tradition as well as its modes of identifying targets, procuring souvenirs from victims, and gathering an expectant crowd eager for the delectation of riven black flesh. In every instance, forms of contemporary kitsch are shadowed by darker narratives of capitalist consumption.

Babel is doubtless the most pointed of the artist's works to date to court the specter of torture, summoning images of lynched black male bodies whose mouths have been crammed with their own castrated genitals. The video does not, of course, precisely replay these scenarios: as the artist himself is quick to emphasize, the cable around his neck is far from a noose and at the end of the piece, he removes the microphone, unwraps the cord, and covers his eyes, as if to shield himself both from the trauma of his own actions and the fact that he must live to almost die another day.[4] Like Demetrius Oliver's 2004 self-portrait in a lather of ketchup and chocolate frosting—modeled after *Jet* magazine's 1955 photographs of Emmett Till's horrifically disfigured face—*Babel* makes clear the extent to which lynching has been internalized as the future death toward which African American masculinity necessarily tends. The black male body, both practitioners know, is always already available for public consumption, perennially haunted by the threat of murder, policing, and dismemberment even within the safe confines of the studio.[5]

Cast in this light, McKenzie's performance can be situated within a long lineage of artistic responses to the spectacular dereliction of African diasporic subjectivity, from Meta Vaux Warrick Fuller's sculptural homage to a pregnant *Mary Turner: Silent Protest Against Mob Violence* (1919) [see Fig. 15.1 on. p. 199] to Pat Ward Williams's emotional analysis of torture images published in *Life* magazine, *Accused/Blowtorch/Padlock* (1986). Arguably more to the point is *Babel*'s rhyming with a range of post–civil rights performative works intent on figuring the discursive and corporeal dispossession of black male being, perhaps best emblematized by the 1970s body

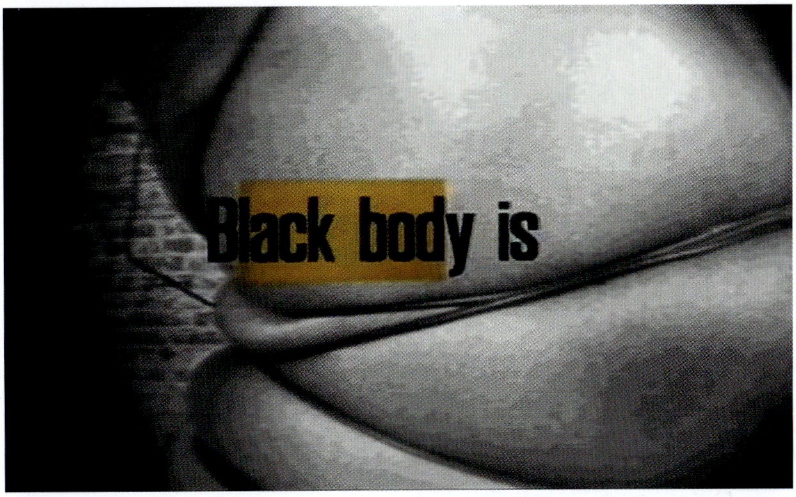

Figure 9.5
Thomas Allen Harris, *Black Body (A Work in Progress)*, still, 1992. © Thomas Allen Harris.

prints of David Hammons [see Fig. 18.7 on p. 240], the 1980s street crawls of William Pope.L, and, more recently, Thomas Allen Harris's 1992 video, *Black Body (A Work in Progress)* (Fig. 9.5). In this five-minute tape—shot in black and white with a fish-eye lens and set to an avant-jazz soundtrack—Harris depicts the gyrations of a nude figure trussed up with wire while a female narrator recounts incidents of sexualized abuse and a litany of brightly colored words defining the black body flashes across the screen.

In each of these cases, an artist stages African American men's exposure to acts of violence issuing from within and beyond the frame. I would argue, however, that McKenzie's aesthetic means resonate just as strongly with the many strands of endurance performativity that marked the emergence of video art as a genre. Of particular import is the practice of Vito Acconci, whose 1970 work, *Hand to Mouth*, records the artist's repeated attempts to swallow his fist until halted by his gag reflex.[6] Like such early pieces, *Babel* tightly trains its lens on a lone actor in a neutralized space, capturing failures of communication, stunts gone awry, bodies at their wits' ends. These characteristics, along with video's ability to trap its subjects between camera and monitor in a closed loop of self-regard, have done much to shore up Rosalind Krauss's contention that the medium is undergirded by an "aesthetics of narcissism," which effectively centralizes the artist while aggressively recruiting viewers presumed to be otherwise in thrall to television's surer pleasures.[7]

For Krauss and her most astute critics, Acconci's videos provide the case in point, and none better than *Centers* (1971): in this work, the artist unwaveringly points his finger at the camera, and by extension his audi-

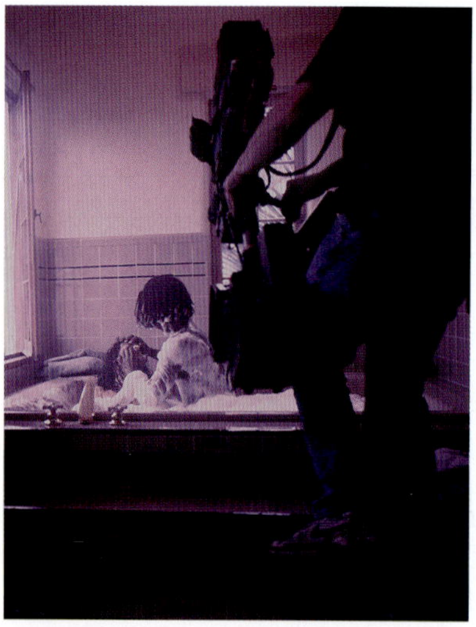

Figure 9.6
Mike Kelley and Paul McCarthy, *Fresh Acconci*, detail, 1995. 15 color photos with video, 11½ × 14½ × 2¾ in. Edition of 30 (5 APSs). Courtesy the artist and Hauser & Wirth.

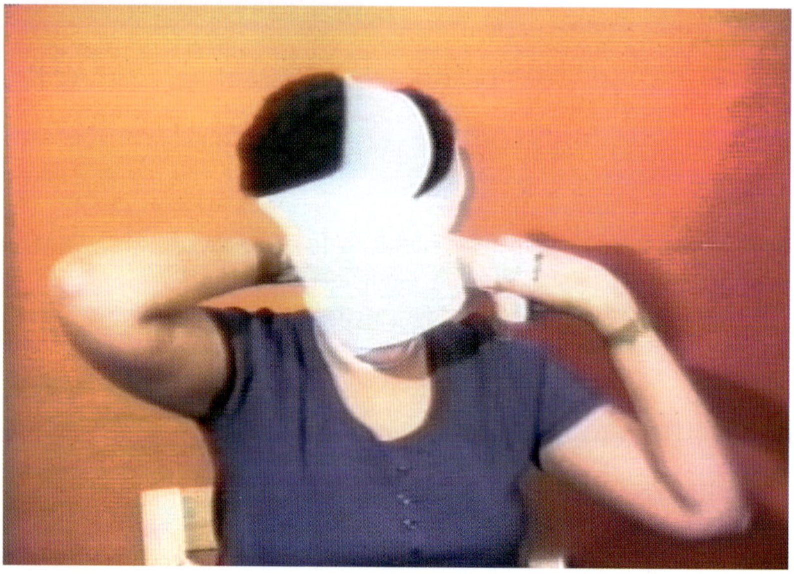

Figure 9.7
Howardena Pindell, *Free, White and 21*, still, 1980.

ence, for twenty-three long minutes. Yet few commentators have reckoned with how deeply the rhetoric and economy of Acconci's narcissism and of video art itself rely on whiteness as a lingua franca to do their work. This observation holds true even within later performance documentation that is critically attuned to the visual production of race. Whether the footage features the erstwhile masseur Thomas Johnson neurotically confessing his preoccupation with *What a Black Man Feels Like* (2004) or the theorist Shannon Jackson coming to grips with the ironic privileges and perils of her own *White Noises* (1993), it would seem that the vision of nonblack skin

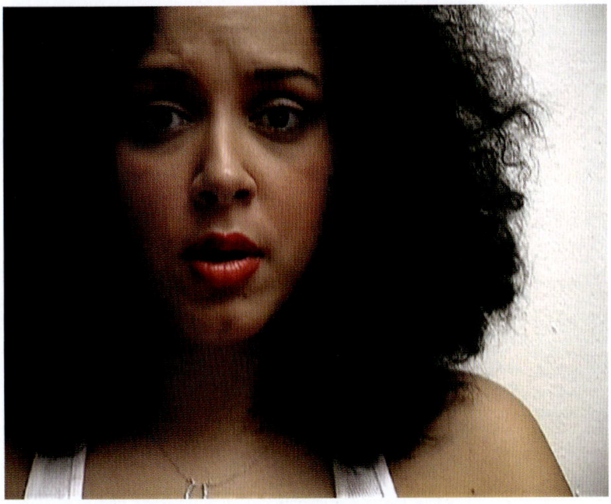

Figure 9.8
Elizabeth Axtman, *American Classics*, still, 2006. © Elizabeth Axtman.

remains central to video's ability to secure the authority of its practitioners and the attention, if not the composition, of its publics.[8]

Consider, then, the changes rung upon Acconci's oeuvre by the artists Mike Kelley and Paul McCarthy, who remade several of his seminal pieces in 1995—not, however, in New York art spaces, but in a Los Angeles mansion, and starring smooth, gym-toned models rather than the hirsute aging body of the artist himself. The resulting tape, *Fresh Acconci*, features a black man in several reperformances and in two iterations of the 1972 work, *Pryings*, their source's attempt to open the tightly shut eyes of his collaborator Kathy Dillon. In Kelley and McCarthy's first interracial restaging of this Acconci work, the black male is the actor, wrestling in a hot tub with a white man; in the second, he is acted upon, laid out in bed next to a white woman (Fig. 9.6).[9] In each instance, the psychic, sexual, and political valences of the scene and of the original tape shift drastically: once straightforward performances about the mechanics of intersubjectivity become scrims on which the phantasms of race and the predication of what the theorist Frank B. Wilderson III titles "the structure of U.S. antagonisms" are forcefully projected.[10]

Taken together, Acconci's originals and the remakes of them begin to suggest the constitutive realities and discursive structures that African American video artists have for decades indicted to biting and hilarious effect. In Howardena Pindell's foundational 1980 account of the everyday mechanics of racial prejudice, *Free, White and 21* (Fig. 9.7), for example, the artist plays both her earnest black self and her blithely dismissive white counterpart. In her 2006 work, *American Classics* (Fig. 9.8), Elizabeth Axtman further multiplies such voicings, lip-synching speech fragments that Hollywood cinema has placed in the mouths of its "tragic mulattoes." Through their ventriloquizations of whitened subjectivity, Pindell's and

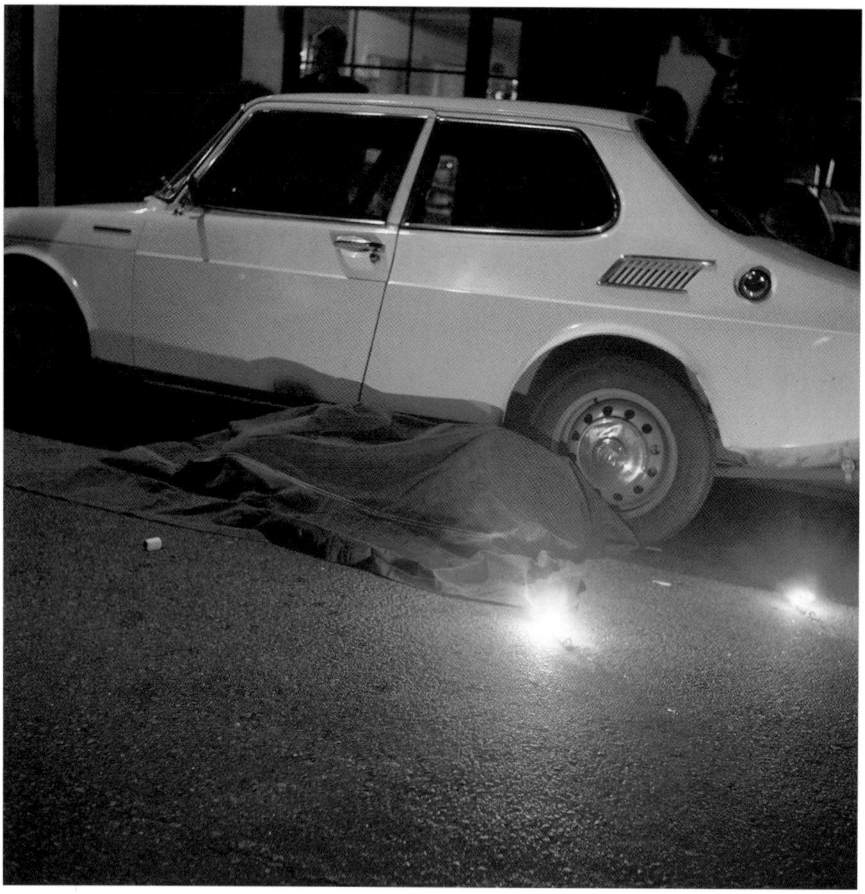

Figure 9.9
Chris Burden, *Deadman*, 1972 (still). Video, black and white, 2 min. 53 sec, edition of 5 + 2AP. © 2024 Chris Burden / licensed by The Chris Burden Estate and Artists Rights Society (ARS), New York.

Axtman's performances index the ways in which video art has time and again figured forms of narcissism, coupling, and relation that can be imagined only within the embrace of a society from which dark citizens have been summarily ejected.

This makes a certain sense, especially if we delve deeper into Wilderson's groundbreaking work. He argues that relationality is impossible for the black subject given his political ontology as the corpse on which white civilization unfolds.[11] Thus, when McKenzie turns the camera on himself, the gesture is one caught up not in the dialectic of narcissism and aggressivity, but of being dead in the world and being cast out of it altogether. In recording his attempt to speak, the artist provides a metacommentary on his own structural location and insists on differentiating between actual corporeal exposure and its aestheticized impersonation in the work of

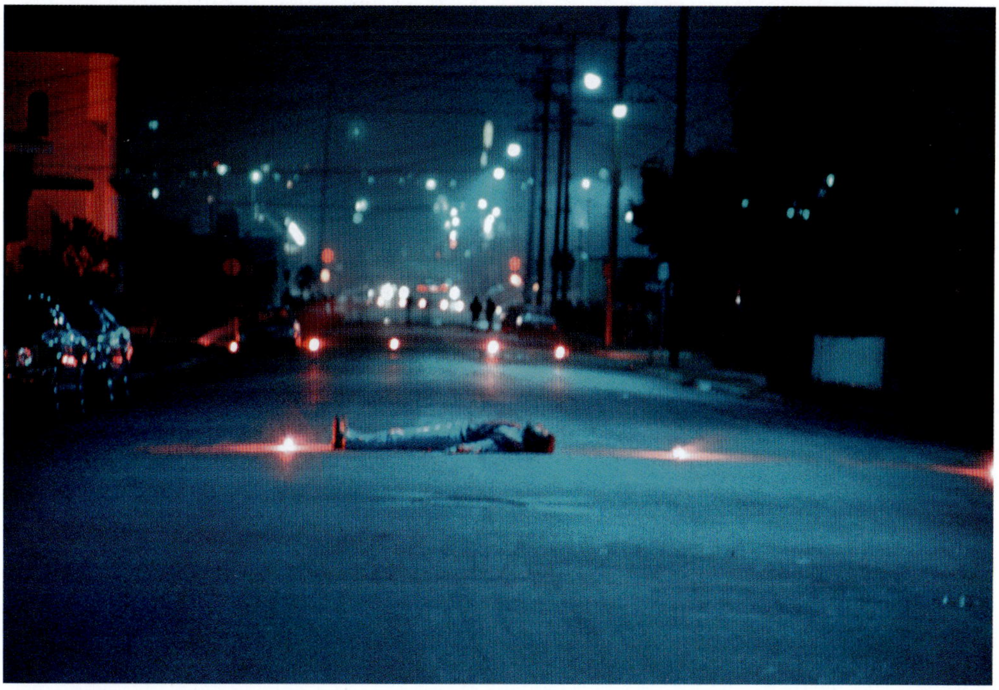

Figure 9.10
Harry Gamboa Jr., *Decoy Gang War Victim*, 1974, from the Asco era. © 1974, Harry Gamboa Jr. Chromogenic print, 12⅝ × 19 in. (32.1 × 48.3 cm), sheet: 16 × 20 in. (40.6 × 50.8 cm). Smithsonian American Art Museum; museum purchase through the Luisita L. and Franz H. Denghausen Endowment. 2013.44.1. Photo: Smithsonian American Art Museum, Washington, DC / Art Resource, NY.

1960s and 1970s body artists. On this score, the performances of Chris Burden provide the most salient examples, since they time and again asymptotically approached the conditions faced by black subjects on the ground—perhaps nowhere more poignantly than in his 1973 work, *Deadman* (Fig. 9.9). To execute the piece, the artist lay on a Los Angeles street under a tarp, looking like nothing so much as a young man of color, the demographic category then, as ever, at greatest risk of homicide.

In fact, the murder rate in Los Angeles increased 84 percent during the 1970s, in part due to the escalation of gang violence in black and Latino communities, which was luridly described and perniciously stoked by local media coverage.[12] In response, the Chicano collective ASCO would offer their own staged corpse in *Decoy Gang War Victim*—a performance captured in a sumptuous color slide delivered to and broadcast by local television stations in 1974 (Fig. 9.10)—which was meant to "generate a pause in the violence" and "to rob newspapers of their daily list of victims."[13] The aim and end of Burden's performance one year earlier were markedly different: according to the artist, when the police arrived on the scene of *Deadman*, he was promptly arrested and eventually charged with "false emergency."[14] In the end, his greatest fear in confronting the LAPD was of juridical persecution rather than of continued bloodshed or of corporeal disintegration, worries a world apart from those of the average black man. Over the course of the decade, African Americans in Los Angeles were 5.6 times more likely than whites and 2.4 times more likely than Hispanics to be the victims of murder, statistics that would receive harrowing visual affirmation some twenty years later in George Holliday's videotape of the Rodney King beating.[15]

Connecting these episodes in a single gesture, McKenzie's video articulates the gulf separating the nonblack subject's performance of vulnerability and the black body's constitutive grounding within it, much as it interrogates the fabric of racialization that tints every African American speech act.[16] As such, *Babel* both points to the stifling of black voices in dominant accounts of recent artistic practice and parodies our nation's incessant demand for black faces that offer much in the way of sound and fury but little direction for resistive struggle. In contrast to contemporary politicians, preachers, and emcees, McKenzie stops himself up, illuminating how technologies of transmission, always liable to reduce their subjects to aphasic disorder, can easily become weaponized obstacles when trained on black sights.[17] What his performance reveals, in other words, are the limits of the sayable within American political and artistic discourse, which are always underpinned by the silence of its most violently negated class of citizens, dark figures fixed in their bodies and denied access to the performative at almost every turn.[18] To cite Wilderson, the transhistorical condition of the Black is not only one of "absolute captivity" but also constitutes a "state of virtual noncommunication within official culture."[19]

All of which makes McKenzie's desperate attempts to talk to you that much more incisive—since he does, in fact, speak: his performance indexes only to undo what Michael Hatt has termed "the substitution of the gestural for the verbal" that undergirds acts of racialized violence.[20] By using American Sign Language, the artist refigures black folks' storied attempts to make themselves visibly legible as conscious subjects, even as the perception of their bodies and the cries that issue from them vituperate against such agency.[21] Indeed, his muffled sounds are in and of themselves a means of communication if understood in light of Édouard Glissant's theorization of black utterance: "Since speech was forbidden, slaves camouflaged the word under the provocative intensity of the scream. No one could translate the meaning of what seemed to be nothing but a shout. It was taken to be nothing but the call of a wild animal. This is how the dispossessed man organized his speech by weaving it into the apparently meaningless texture of extreme sound."[22] For the black subject, Glissant would say, "din is discourse."[23] McKenzie's noise and body can therefore be

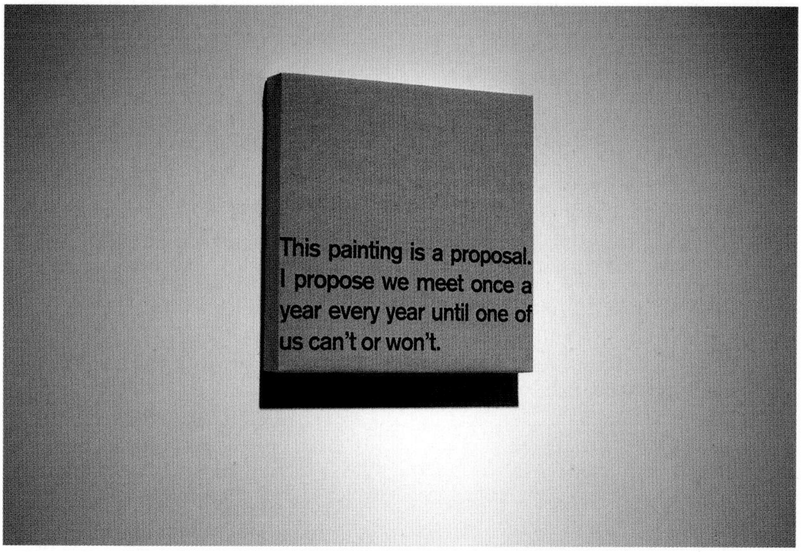

Figure 9.11
Dave McKenzie, *Proposal*, 2007. Acrylic on canvas, 16 × 16 in. © Dave McKenzie.

read as the metaphorical grounds on which the Tower of Babel, the oppression of Babylon, and the human itself have been erected in the modern West.[24]

For his part, the artist performs what Wilderson maintains is vital to any black radical practice of the image, a coupling of "real violence" "with representational 'monstrosity,'" which would allow "Blacks [to] move from the status of things to the status of . . . of what, we'll just have to wait and see."[25] As intimated by his painting *Proposal* (2007) (Fig. 9.11), in which he asks that you meet him for a date, McKenzie is content to see what unfolds at a later time, even as his work models a transformation of representational orders and effects a shake-up of the all-too-white historiography of mainstream video art, which, for forty years, has refused to properly countenance the presence, or even the image, of African American subjects.[26] Like ontological violence, such haunted expectations of a future that may never arrive are part and parcel of what it means to be a black subject in the modern world, ever suspended in the interstices of representation and always slowed down by the impositions of racial time.[27] Luckily, Dave is still happy to wait for you.

Notes

I thank Emilie Boone and Rashida Bumbray for their assistance in researching this essay and Janet Dees, Eve Meltzer, Karen Reimer, Steve Reinke, and Krista Thompson for their helpful comments on previous drafts of it.

1 See Aaron Moulton, "Chicago: 40000," *Flash Art*, June 2006, 72, for one audience's attempt to "feign an unaffected cool" in the face of McKenzie's performance.

2 See David Marriott, "'I'm gonna borer me a Kodak': Photography and Lynching," in *On Black Men* (Columbia University Press, 2000), 1-22, for a thoroughgoing analysis of these dynamics.

3 Jacqueline Goldsby, *A Spectacular Secret: Lynching in American Life and Literature* (University of Chicago Press, 2006), 26-27.

4 Dave McKenzie, in discussion with the author, September 30, 2004.

5 Maurice O. Wallace, *Constructing the Black Masculine: Identity and Ideality in African-American Men's Literature and Culture, 1775-1995* (Duke University Press, 2002), 33. See also *Without Sanctuary: Lynching Photography in America* (Twin Palms Publishers, 2000), an important book and exhibition that featured nearly one hundred images, which brought the history of racialized violence freshly into view for a broad swath of audiences.

6 While the late artist approved publication of his work in the original essay, unfortunately the Acconci estate never responded to requests to reproduce the work in the present volume.

7 Rosalind Krauss, "Video: The Aesthetics of Narcissism," *October* 1 (Spring 1976): 50-64. See Anne M. Wagner, "Performance, Video, and the Rhetoric of Presence," *October* 91 (Winter 2000): 59-80, for a brilliant reframing of Krauss's essay in light of the politics of aggressivity, viewership, and artistic reception circa 1970. See David Joselit, *Feedback: Television Against Democra*cy (MIT Press, 2007), 188-89, for an even more pointed critique that aims to debunk Krauss's theoretical framework altogether. Although I concur with both of these assessments, particularly their desire to bracket the reach of narcissism as an aesthetic condition, as I hope to show, actively working through the limitations of the concept still has much to teach us about the production of difference within the visual field and the historiography of video as a cultural discourse. See Ewa Lajer-Burcharth, "Real Bodies: Video in the 1990s," *Art History* 20, no. 2 (June 1997): 185-213, for a like-minded effort.

8 See Bryant Keith Alexander, "Black Skin/White Masks: The Performative Sustainability of Whiteness (with Apologies to Frantz Fanon)," *Qualitative Inquiry* 10, no. 5 (October 2004): 647-72, for a compelling account of how racial privilege is enacted and reproduced.

9 Such recastings, it is worth noting, have continued apace: in his 2006 video *Studio Visits: Patty Chang*, for instance, the African American performance artist Clifford Owens enjoined the Asian American practitioner named in the work's title to assume Acconci's role in a twenty-eight-second send-up of *Pryings*.

10 Frank B. Wilderson III, *Red, White & Black: Cinema and the Structure of U.S. Antagonisms* (Duke University Press, 2010).

11 Wilderson, *Red, White & Black*, 56-57.

12 Centers for Disease Control and Prevention, "Homicide–Los Angeles, 1970-1979," *Morbidity and Mortality Weekly Report* 35, no. 5 (February 7, 1986): 61.

13 Harry Gamboa Jr., "L.A. Stories: A Roundtable Discussion," *Artforum*, October 2011, 246. Also see C. Ondine Chavoya, "No-Movies: The Art of False Documents," in *Only Skin Deep: Changing Visions of the American Self*, ed. Coco Fusco and Brian Wallis (International Center of Photogra-

phy; distributed by Harry N. Abrams, 2003), 199-200. For a more recent engagement with the figure of the artist as corpse, see Jonathan Monk's 2007 hyperrealist sculpture, *Deadman*, which wears Burden's face but transposes his figure from '70s L.A. to present-day Iraq.

14 See Chris Burden, *Documentation of Selected Works 1971-1974*, video transferred to DVD (Electronic Arts Intermix), for the artist's commentary. Also see Frazer Ward, "Gray Zone: Watching *Shoot*," *October* 95 (Winter 2001): 114-30. My reading of *Deadman* is meant to rhyme with and ultimately depart from Ward's analysis of the most seminal Burden performance, *Shoot* (1971), in which the artist took a bullet fired by a friend. Although Ward importantly places this work in the context of the Vietnam War and its media representation, in so doing, he casts the primal scene of American violence as occurring elsewhere rather than at home and again leaves the white artist's body racially unmarked.

15 Centers for Disease Control and Prevention, "Homicide–Los Angeles, 1970-1979," 61. See Elizabeth Alexander, "'Can you be black and look at this?': Reading the Rodney King Video(s)," in *Black Male: Representations of Masculinity in Contemporary American Art*, ed. Thelma Golden, 90-110 (Whitney Museum of American Art; distributed by Harry N. Abrams, 1994), 90-110; as well as Huey Copeland, "Outtakes," *Art Journal* 67, no. 4 (Winter 2008): 20-32, for accounts of artistic and vernacular responses to King's assault [reprinted in this volume, 57-72].

16 Wilderson, *Red, White & Black*, 49-50.

17 Two artworks seem especially relevant on this score: Richard Serra's video *Boomerang* (1974), in which the artist Nancy Holt's speech into a microphone almost immediately returns to her via headset, resulting in considerable disorientation; and Mel Chin's *Night Rap* (1994), a sculpture in the form of a police nightstick whose handle the artist transformed into a black dildo and whose tip he replaced with a microphone.

18 Michael Hatt, "Race, Ritual, and Responsibility: Performativity and the Southern Lynching," in *Performing the Body/Performing the Text*, ed. Amelia Jones and Andrew Stephenson (Routledge, 1999), 83.

19 Wilderson, *Red, White & Black*, 64.

20 Hatt, "Race, Ritual, and Responsibility," 80.

21 Henry Louis Gates Jr., "The Face and Voice of Blackness," in Guy C. McElroy, *Facing History: The Black Image in American Art 1710-1940*, ed. Christopher C. French (Bedford Arts Publishers in association with the Corcoran Gallery of Art, 1990), xxix-xliv.

22 Édouard Glissant, "Cross-Cultural Poetics" (1973), in *Caribbean Discourse: Selected Essays*, trans. J. Michael Dash (University of Virginia Press, 1989), 124.

23 Glissant, "Cross-Cultural Poetics," 123.

24 Barry Chevannes, *Rastafari: Roots and Ideology* (Syracuse University Press, 1994), 208. "Babylon" refers to the Rastafarian moniker for the unjust social order as currently constituted.

25 Wilderson, *Red, White & Black*, 66.

26 To take two texts virtually at random from the chronological endpoints of the discourse, neither *Video Art: An Anthology*, ed. Ira Schneider and Beryl Korot (Harcourt Brace Jovanovich, 1976), nor *100 Video Artists*, ed. Rosa Olivares (Fundación ICO, 2010), make mention of a single African American practitioner. There are, of course, exceptions, as well as a compelling discourse on black video practice, though the latter exhibitions, texts, and artworks are rarely addressed in analyses of the genre as such. In particular I think of Jacqueline Bobo, *Black Women Film and Video Artists* (Routledge, 1998); Leslie King-Hammond and Lowery S. Sims, *Art as a Verb: The Evolving Continuum: Installations, Performances, and Videos by 13 Afro-American Artists* (Maryland Institute, College of Art, 1989); Erika D. Muhammad, *Race in Digital Space: Artists' Video, Audio, CD-ROM, Internet and Sound Projects* (MIT List Visual Arts Center, 2001); Patrick Ogle, *Facets African-American Video Guide* (Facets Multimedia, 1994); Valerie C. Oliver and Andrea B. Brownlee, *Cinema Remixed & Reloaded: Black Women Artists and the Moving Image Since 1970* (Contemporary Arts Museum Houston, 2008); Reginald Woolery and Deirdre Scott, *Too Black, Too Strong! An Exhibition of Video and Works on Paper Organized by Reginald Woolery* (Artists Space, 1988); Philip Mallory Jones, *Icono Negro: The Black Aesthetic in Video Art* (Long Beach Museum of Art, 1989).

27 See Kara Keeling, "In the Interval," in *The Witch's Flight: The Cinematic, the Black Femme, and the Image of Common Sense* (Duke University Press, 2007), 27-44; Michael Hanchard, "Afro-Modernity: Temporality, Politics, and the African Diaspora," *Public Culture* 11, no. 1 (1999): 245-68.

10

MAL D'ANTHOLOGIE

Clifford Owens and the Crises of African American Performance Art

Clifford Owens's 2011 MoMA PS1 exhibition, *Anthology*, compiles a selection of the twenty-six performance scores that he solicited from an intergenerational cast of African American artists, ranging from the elder statesmen Terry Adkins to emerging figures such as Saya Woolfalk. As Owens recounts, *Anthology* began as a frustrated response to the inadequate representation, the near-invisibility, of black practitioners within dominant accounts of performance art history in the United States.[1] His point is baldly put but nonetheless well taken: a casual flip through the pages of RoseLee Goldberg's 1996 survey of the genre reveals an enormous black absence—only highlighted, in this instance, by the inclusion of an Adrian Piper illustration—and underlines the value of a reparative historical project.[2]

Such projects are, by definition, belated.[3] Yet in many ways, Owens's timing and that of his sponsoring institution could hardly be better: *Anthology* records the sites and aims of African American performance art at a moment when US imperialism sports a brown face and when few aesthetic postures, no matter how radical their pedigrees, seem capable of gaining much political traction. Recent art world phenomena provide ample testament to these contradictions. In the past decade, black artists of various stripes have benefited from increasing representation within mainstream venues, thanks, in part, to discourses around globalization and postracial identity that have rendered "black work" both commercially viable and discursively intelligible, if no less constrained.[4] At the same time, performance art has been institutionally embraced, advanced, and spectacularized like never before, effectively roped into the high-end "experience" industry, as evidenced by the successes of Goldberg's Performa Biennial, launched in 2005, and Marina Abramović's star turns at blue-chip New York museums, first the Guggenheim in that same year and subsequently at the Museum of Modern Art in 2010.[5] These twin developments have helped open a dis-

This essay first appeared in *Clifford Owens: Anthology*, ed. Christopher Y. Lew (MoMA PS1, 2012), 15–30.

cursive space between them in which black performative interventions and their political possibilities might be said to properly reside. Owens's project thus aims to both temporarily occupy and actively construct this long-neglected terrain, and in a format that makes deep historical sense: as the cultural theorist Brent Hayes Edwards argues, the black anthology most often serves not to confirm an existing canon but to found the very tradition that it ostensibly records.[6]

These considerations provide one basis for approaching Owens's *Anthology*, but they cannot explain the peculiar form his intervention has come to take or its multiple ramifications, which is my ultimate aim in the pages that follow. Rather than create an archive, write a history, or mount an exhibition focused on extant traces of black US performance, Owens solicited his collaborators to write brand-new scores, usually textual instructions for him and him alone. A few of these he has yet to enact; some others he has only performed; the majority, however, have been originated by Owens and compulsively documented in the photographs and videos that comprise the exhibition and make the artist their star. This framing conceit is, I think, both more coherent and less narcissistic than it might sound: in forwarding his own image as a threshold through which future histories of performance might pass, Owens aims to spectacularly undo the visual effacement of black bodies within those narratives while referring back to the work of practitioners whose contributions, both storied and forgotten, can now be freshly reckoned with on their own terms.

Of course, the exhibition's drive toward the accumulation of a totality of black artistic production risks abetting continued complacency where the subject of African American performance is concerned, satiating a taste for racial difference and quelling voices of racialized dissent. This is a particular pitfall of the anthological, which, Edwards argues, "delimits the borders of an expressive mode or field, determining its beginning and end points, its local or global resonance, its communities of participants and audiences."[7] Yet I would contend that Owens's *Anthology* also functions as a spur to further historical investigation precisely because its order and its inconsistencies internalize the status of black performance art within the archive and because the artist offers himself up as a site of articulation that expands who and what might be encompassed within its scope.

Anthology's roster of participants begins to tell the tale. It registers the new vistas for practitioners of color that have opened up over the past twenty years, as well as a calculated orientation toward the brighter lights within the black artistic firmament circa 2011, the category "performance artist" be damned.[8] Owens's repertoire includes a diagrammatic dance score from the recently "rediscovered" Fluxus mastermind, musician, and performer Ben Patterson; a "controversial" INSTRUCTION from the infamous Kara

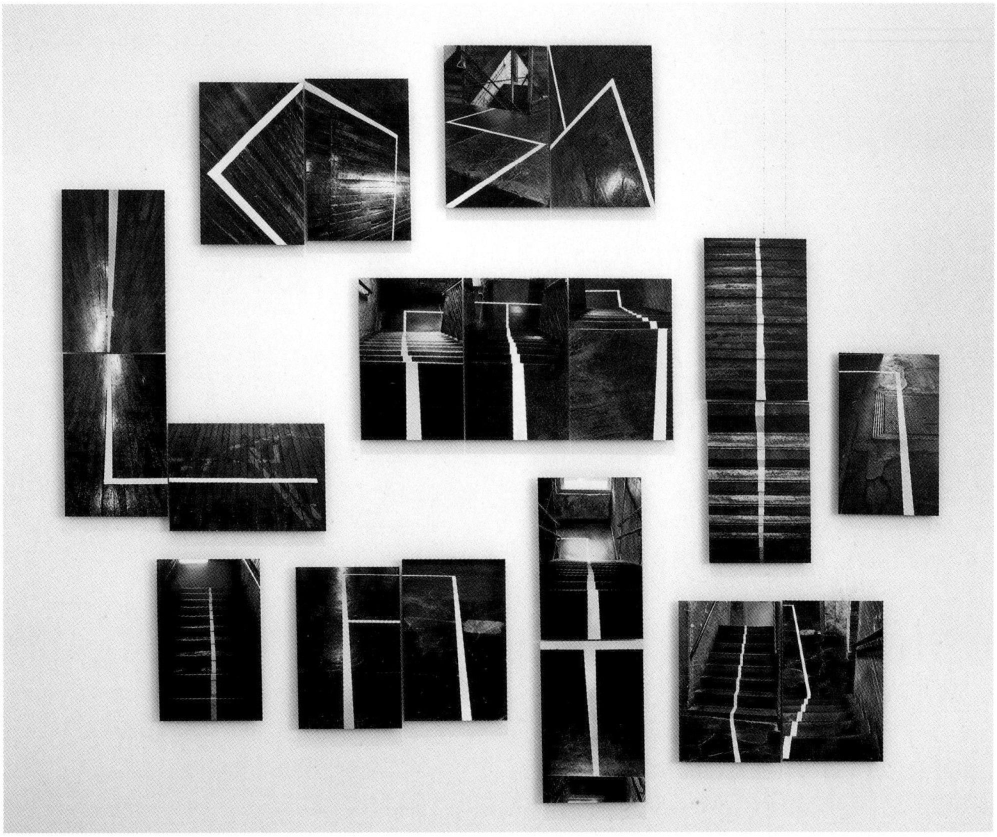

Figure 10.1
Clifford Owens, *Anthology (William Pope.L)*, detail, 2011. © Clifford Owens.

Walker, whose work is deeply performative even when not literally so;[9] and a piece from Glenn Ligon, who is somebody, to be sure, but no performer at all: he usually eschews the visualization of the black body by introducing a host of material surrogates for it.[10]

Perhaps because of this, Ligon's script for Owens is arguably the most capacious and the most revelatory. Unlike the majority of the scores, his prompt does not enjoin the younger practitioner to perform a clearly delineated series of physical actions. Nor does it leave interpretation almost entirely up to the performer, as in the case of William Pope.L's coy yet ideologically charged imperative, "Be African-American. Be very African American," which Owens could not help but render in contrary terms. Instead of picturing the black actor he hired to execute the score—who was instructed to walk through the museum while sharing personal confessions with his trailing audience—the artist presents a grid-like arrangement of photographs documenting the line of white tape running through MoMA PS1 that determined the performer's course (Fig. 10.1).[11]

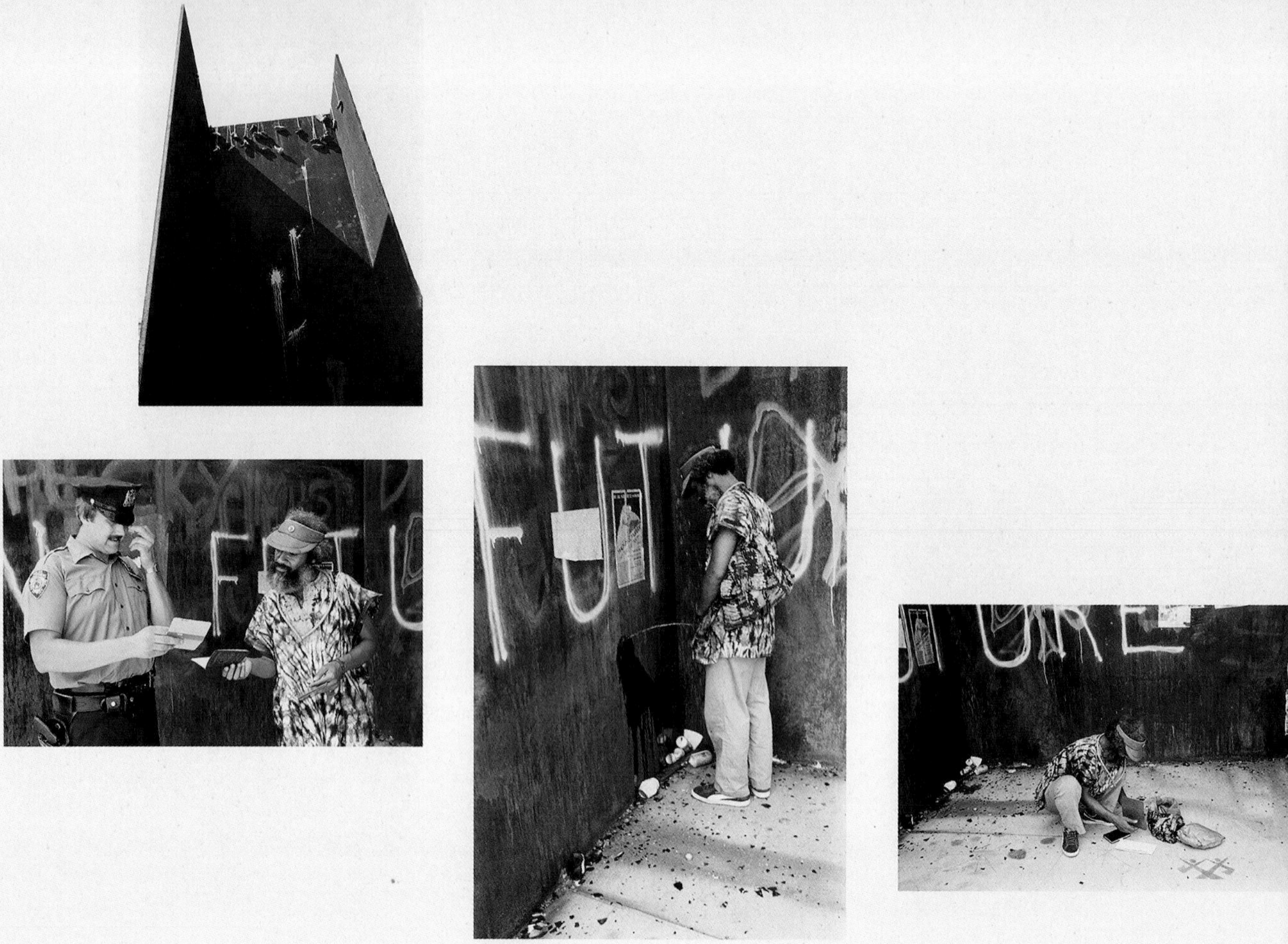

Figure 10.2

Dawoud Bey, *David Hammons, Pissed Off*, 1981. Photographs. Sheet a: 33 × 23 in. (83.8 × 58.4 cm); Sheet b: 23½ × 33 in. (59.7 × 83.8 cm); Sheet c: 44 × 30½ in. (111.8 × 77.5 cm); Sheet d: 23 × 33 in. (58.4 × 83.8 cm). © Dawoud Bey.

Sidestepping such physical and philosophical temptations, Ligon asked Owens to "annotate an existing performance/score" of his choosing and then to "perform that performance annotated." These are directives that go straight to the heart of *Anthology*'s ambition to serve as a repository of black aesthetic interventions; they solicit the work's author to lay his own cards on the table, to fully disclose his particular investments within the history of black performance art, and to enter into the discursive fray around the ethics of reperformance within the museum.[12] As so often in Ligon's practice, which takes annotation as one of its central procedures, in this score, an artist is called upon to select, inhabit, and thereby revivify earlier material whose discursive coordinates enable a reckoning with the ongoing structural conditions of the past and the liabilities of the present for African American artists at work in the performative field.[13]

Owens's choice does not disappoint. Although he did not take on Yvonne Rainer's *Trio A*, to which Ligon refers in describing what an annotation might entail, he also did not veer too far from the beaten path, selecting a work by David Hammons, who helped legitimate performance as a site of inquiry for the generations of artists who followed in his wake.[14] Owens specifically lighted upon Hammons's 1981 intervention, *Pissed Off*, in which the renowned artist—photographed all the while by his friend Dawoud Bey—urinated into a trash-filled corner of Richard Serra's 1980 sculpture, *T.W.U.*, a work temporarily sited at the intersection of Franklin and Broadway in then-still-gentrifying Lower Manhattan (Fig. 10.2).[15] For his annotation, Owens climbed from his MoMA PS1 studio to the institution's roof where, with a hired photographer primed to capture every dribble and splash, he pissed on another Serra work, a 1976 site-specific sculpture created for the inaugural exhibition, *ROOMS*, back when P.S.1 was a crumbling schoolhouse under the aegis of the pioneering alternative space the Institute for Art and Urban Resources (Fig. 10.3).[16]

While the basic headline remains the same—black male artist bodily defaces work of the sculptor Richard Serra—the multiple registers of difference separating these actions are worth spelling out. Hammons's target was a monumental public work, always meant to be relocated, whose imposing structure created a quasi-private space that fostered graffiti, postings, and his own alternate use.[17] In irreverently vandalizing the sculpture, he both contested SoHo's transformation into an art world hub and marked the presence of those "undesirable" publics soon to be absented from its streets in consequence.[18] Owens, by contrast, let loose his stream on an unobtrusive steel trough sunken into the building that both hosted Hammons's 1991 retrospective and incorporated Serra's sculpture into its very structure. In so marking this territory, Owens at once perversely honored his "Daddies" and inscribed himself within the institutional framework supporting their practices and his own.

The images depicting each performance serve to exacerbate these positional, historical, and spatial discrepancies, which highlight, to borrow Rebecca Schneider's apt formulation, the "*theatricality* of time."[19] Bey's black-and-white photographs document a clandestine action—in one shot, the tie-dyed-dashiki-wearing Hammons is seen explaining himself to a white police officer—while the images of Owens's work, carefully staged by the artist himself, expertly mime the lingua franca of contemporary large-format color photography.[20] Unlike Hammons, he is situated safe within the confines of MoMA PS1, dressed in the artist's uniform of black shirt and jeans, openly displaying his penis and unfurling his stream. In the central image his piss creates a golden arc that harks back to the S/M photographs of Robert Mapplethorpe; in another, the liquid forms a wet iridescent mark that recalls the oxidation paintings of Andy Warhol. Daddies, indeed.

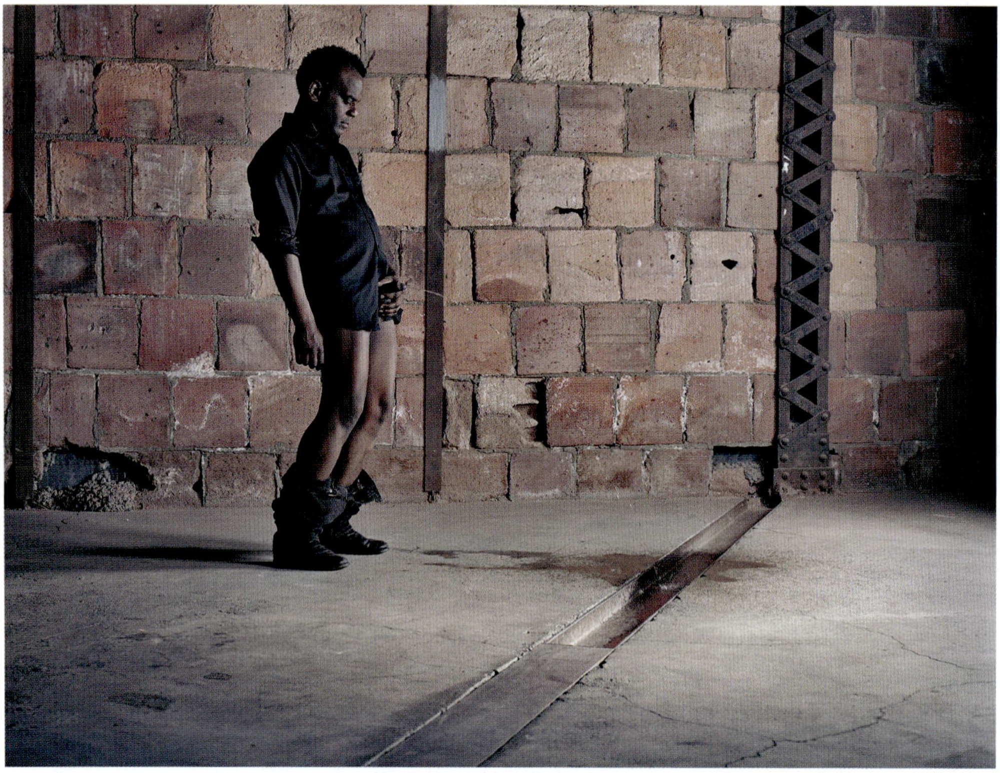

Figure 10.3
Clifford Owens, *Anthology (Glenn Ligon)*, detail, 2011. © Clifford Owens.

At stake here is more than mere one-upmanship. Taken together, Ligon's score, Hammons's performance, and Owens's highly mediated queering of both gesture toward the questions underpinning, in the anthologist's words, the "crisis of meaning" confronted by "black U.S. artists working in the medium of performance," who "often find themselves farther at the bounds" of any notion of community, African American, aesthetic, or otherwise.[21] Where, how, and for whom should black performance unfold? What, if any, is its relationship to the art world and its economies of promotion, displacement, and canonization? Must African American performative interventions necessarily address the racialized exclusions of the public sphere to achieve sufficient critical weight and "colored" content? What is the valence of such actions when they unfold within and are in fact supported by institutions that have historically turned a blind eye to African American artists?

MoMA, which has been affiliated with P.S.1 since 2000, is well practiced in institutionalized blindness, as testified by its uneven collection and exhibition of work by African Americans.[22] According to Owens, black practitioners fare even worse in the institution's publicly offered seminars on the history of performance art and even the anthological can only provisionally disturb the operative presumptions on which these narratives are predicated.[23] The implications are as much practical as theoretical. On the one hand, *Anthology* constitutes a response to a legacy of exclusions and holds out the rich array of performative interventions of which black artists are capable; on the other, the project carefully stage manages a cacophony of voices whose imperatives the artist embodies, travesties, and recasts, sometimes all at once.

Hammons again provides the most telling example. Appearances to the contrary, he was not a willing participant in *Anthology*. In fact, relatively early on in the project's production, Owens attempted to secure a score from the famously elusive artist to no avail. As luck would have it, Christopher Y. Lew, *Anthology*'s curator, found himself seated next to Hammons at another artist's birthday party. Lew reiterated Owens's request, which Hammons declined repeatedly over the course of the night, each time recasting the grounds of his refusal without any further prompting on the curator's part and thereby providing additional fodder for the younger artist's annotations. Hammons's first, dismissive response, "This is high school," licensed Owens's pissing contest and reframed his own; his second, more considered critique, "There's no tension," laid down a challenge for what the reenactment should aim to produce. His final parting shot? The verbal equivalent of a pat on the back: "I'm just not feeling it."[24]

In the completed work on view at the museum, *Anthology (Glenn Ligon)*, these three lines, printed in red, surmount a blown-up black-and-white Bey photograph of Hammons's *Pissed Off*, which is sandwiched between Owens's color images of his own performance. So positioned, Hammons's refusal is both indexed and contained through a selective rendition of the work's coming into being that highlights the interpersonal dynamics so crucial to the art world's functioning yet so rarely countenanced in its histories.[25] More important to Owens's problematic appropriation of Hammons is the evidence offered by the photograph itself, which provides a clear point of visual reference and so clarifies the logic behind *Anthology* as a whole. All too aware of the lapses of memory that plague even recorded black performances, Owens has produced a series of photographs and videos, complete as artworks in and of themselves, that tend to reproduce the look and logic of canonical performance art with its singular focus on the artist's body but with little of performance theory's worries about "live"-ness, loss, and commodification: these are market-ready objects targeted at History.[26]

To create them, Owens meticulously records each performance, enacting every score multiple times and producing a sea of documentation—never intended for public circulation—from which he carefully selects the footage or photographs that, to his mind, best capture the conceptual tension animating the work.[27] For evidence of this process and its range of

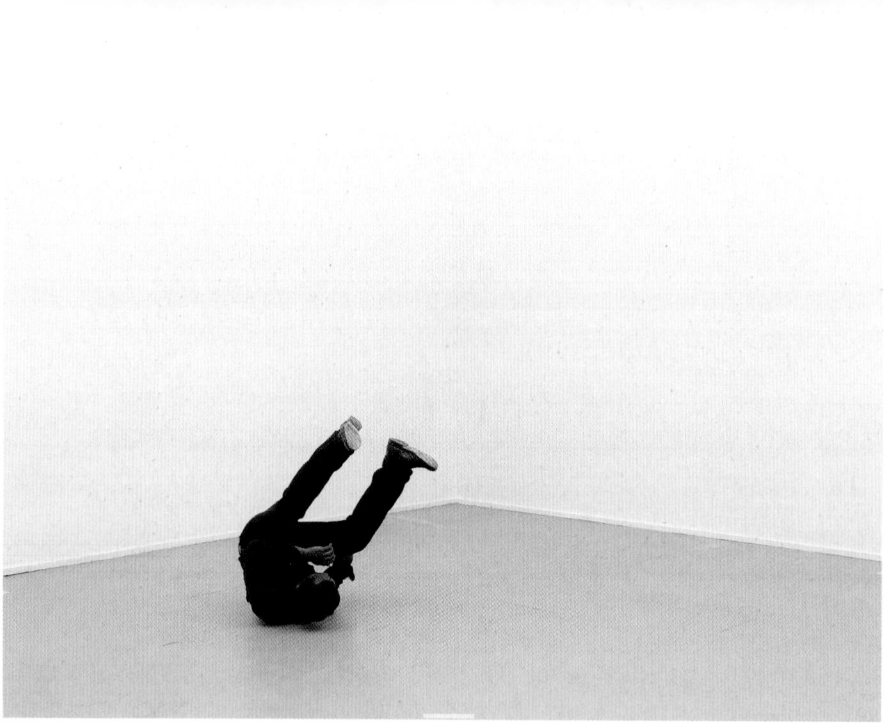

Figure 10.4
Clifford Owens, *Anthology (Dave McKenzie)*, detail, 2011. © Clifford Owens.

outcomes, compare the dramatic stills of Owens performing Dave McKenzie's score (Fig. 10.4), which begins, "Pick a corner of the room and place yourself in it and against it," with that of him enacting Senga Nengudi's *Sweep* (Fig. 10.5), a piece that requires the artist to sully the floor with sand before completing the titular action.[28] The "McKenzie" work consists of a suite of pictures, unframed and hung in a corner, that recapitulate the direction and sequencing of Owens's Vito Acconci–style antics in one of MoMA PS1's galleries; the "Nengudi" is a large-format diptych featuring two photographs taken in the institution's basement: one depicts the aftermath of Owens's action, and the other shows the artist standing in a pool of light, emptying a sandbag, and channeling the shamanistic energy of a Joseph Beuys.

If the exhibition evokes tried and true roles from the performance art playbook, then it also smuggles its collaborators, their sensibilities, and a whole host of formal and site-specific antecedents into the frame so that the official record might be rearticulated in light of black artistic practices. In sum, to secure a measure of visibility, the anthologist narrows the range of his own imagistic production and that of the African American performative tradition he is at pains to unearth, putting his faith in the documentary apparatus of the canon and the allure of his carefully conceived pictures. His live renditions, however, open onto other economies—of affect, desire, and bodily engagement—that can only be hinted at by the surface of an image.

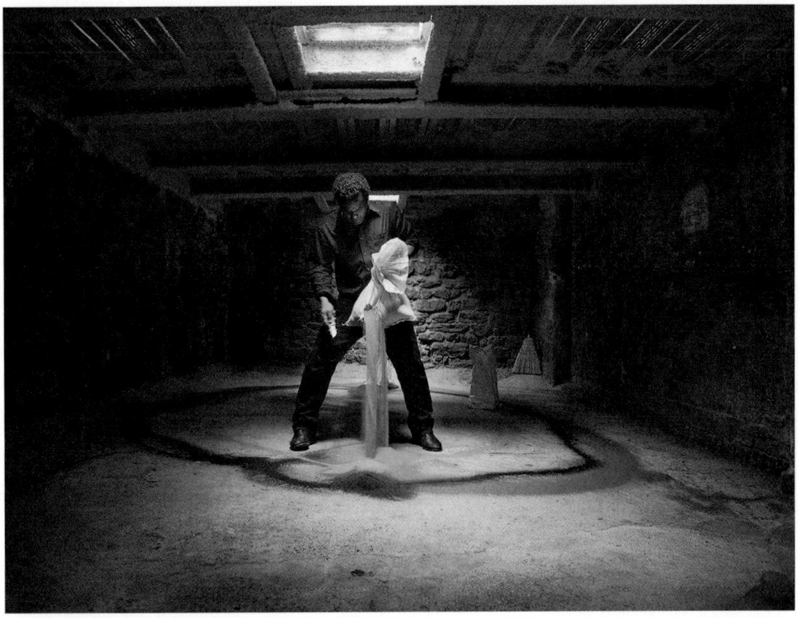

Figure 10.5
Clifford Owens, *Anthology (Senga Nengudi)*, detail, 2011. © Clifford Owens.

Owens's December 17, 2011, performance of *Restating the Image: Construct #10, 1989, Lyle Ashton Harris* provides a case in point. The preparatory staging of the score—set up in the interior entranceway of MoMA PS1—presented its own kind of spectacle, a ceaseless to and fro of lighting adjustments, last-minute errands, and quiet joking with the gathering crowd. Once the audience of thirty or so had settled into place and Owens had fortified himself with a beer, he called upon Lew, in his role as the organizer of the exhibition's hanging and performances, to read the score.[29]

"Requirement: Performance is to be performed by Clifford Owens. Once image is shot, Owens is to recite memorized paragraph of scholarly text on the image by Kobena Mercer in front of back drop."[30] Following the beat of his own drummer, Owens began by posing questions about Harris's work and offhandedly tossing out 11 × 17 inch color copies of the eponymous black-and-white photograph. In it, the older artist sports a black bobbed wig, a rolled-up tank top, and a white tutu as he stares directly out at the viewer, his arms akimbo, his genitals exposed, and his legs twisted into an elegant *contrapposto* (Fig. 10.6). In line with Harris's original picture, the focal point of Owens's mise-en-scène was a simple studio setup comprised of tungsten lamps and a long backdrop—now deep pink rather than velvety black—hung from above and extending onto the floor. Rather than insert himself into this scenario, at the outset Owens put his audience to work: each individual who responded to one of his queries—What is this photograph about? Do you identify as a gay man?—was asked to step

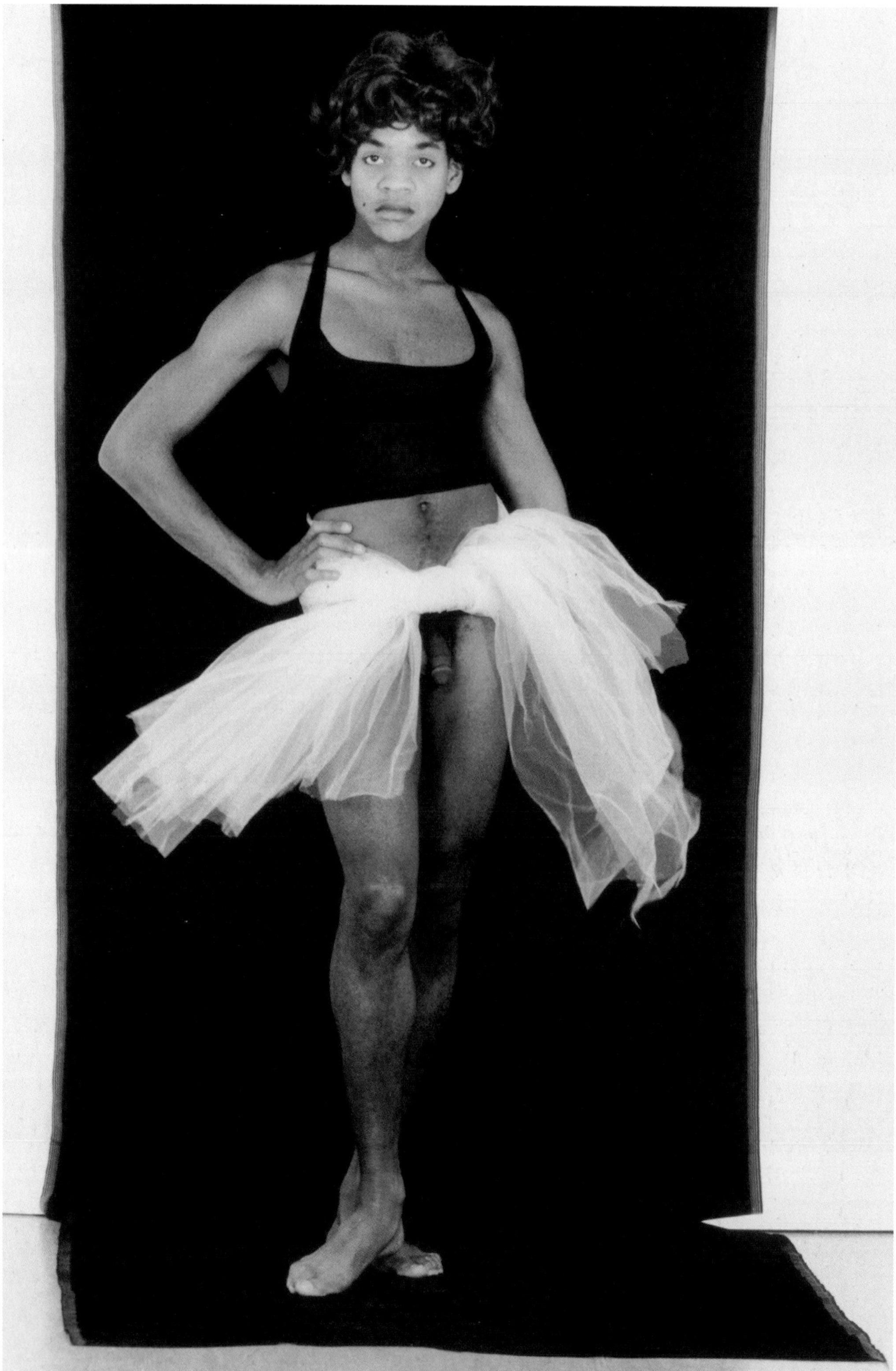

Figure 10.6

Lyle Ashton Harris, *Construct #10*, 1989. © Lyle Ashton Harris.

onto the backdrop and to assume the pose so that Owens might remake the picture. In this way, the artist contravened Harris's instructions and the conventions of his private studio self-portrait session in order to produce a dialogic theater for the assumption of an image, the revelation and affirmation of gay male identities, and a running commentary on the public unfolding of both.

Throughout this initial phase, Owens's tone was undeniably charming and vaguely coercive. His banter became more critical as the performance wore on, leading him to question the assumptions undergirding Harris's work and his reenactment of it. "What happened to the critical moment of the 1990s of identity politics? What's changed other than there being an asshole black President?" Soon enough, half-serious quips morphed into solicitous confessions: "I can't make images about representation anymore, it just doesn't matter. . . . I love to fail publicly. . . . Tell me what I need to do to re-stage this image."

Through such signifyin' asides, Owens at once parodied and ventriloquized a presumed art world common sense about the limitations of Harris's art, which can read as earnestly confrontational when compared to the messy evasions of a younger black queer practitioner like Kalup Linzy.[31] While Harris has been one of a handful of black figures included in widely read volumes on performance art, his work, and that of many artists who emerged in the context of late 1980s multiculturalism, has usually been positioned in terms of "identity," rendering it vulnerable to charges of formal underdevelopment and social overdetermination despite assertions to the contrary by scholars like Mercer.[32] What the score demanded, then, and what the performance allowed was not so much Harris's inclusion within an anthology but a rescripting of the terms of his work's discursive appearance.

Enter the artist in question. Harris, seated in the audience for the duration of the performance, took the opportunity afforded by a break in Owens's monologue to vocally rearticulate his directive: "Just do the score!" Despite his apparent resistances—he never did recite those paragraphs—Owens handed over the camera to Harris and quickly got naked, joking that the audience had no need to be terrified of him, since this was one black man whose penis was neither gargantuan nor tantalizingly hidden from view. With contributions from the audience, he began to suit himself up, donning lipstick, face powder, a black bra, and an array of scarves around his waist (Fig. 10.7). His props in place, Owens announced, "I feel it now," and began striking the imaged stance, which, he admitted, was far from a physically easy or emotionally neutral feat: Harris's photograph demands a measured admixture of mimicry and disarticulation, defiance and seduction.[33] As he aimed to perfect the pose with the guidance of the audience—now quite familiar with Harris and his *Construct*—Owens, holding back tears, commented on how such a bodily disposition recalled

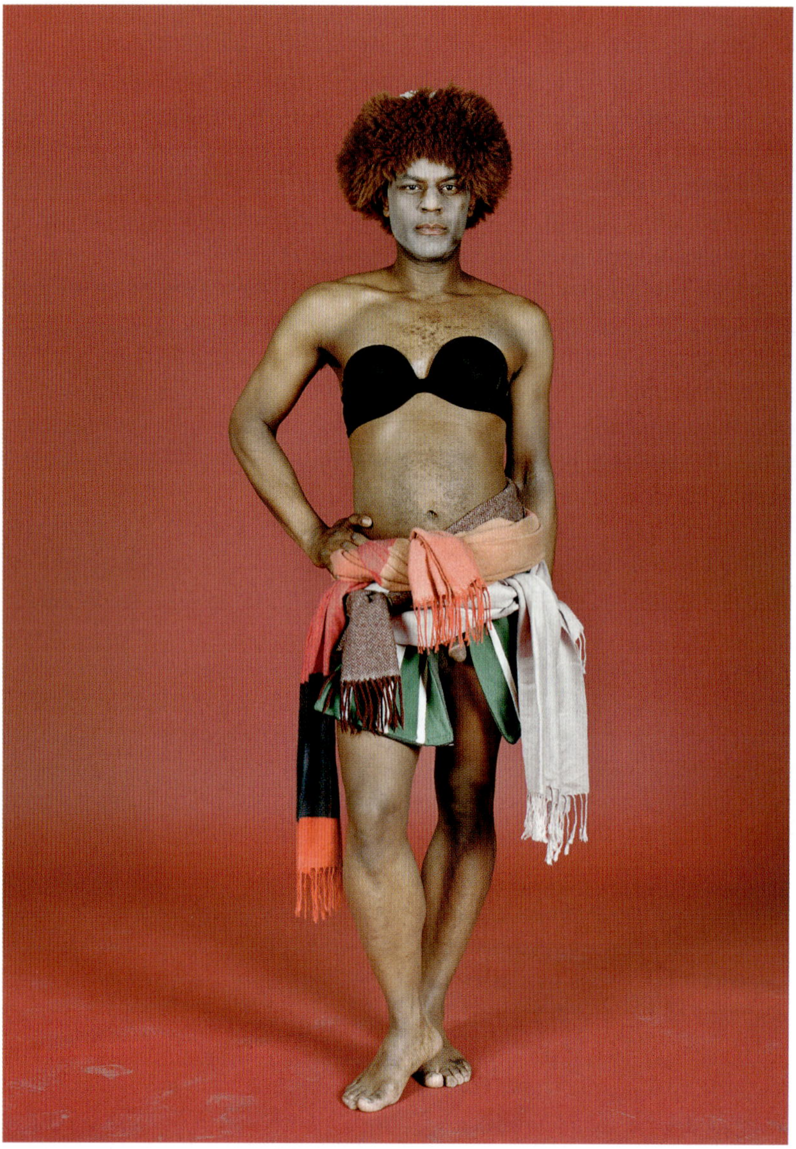

Figure 10.7
Clifford Owens, *Anthology (Lyle Ashton Harris)*, detail, 2011. © Clifford Owens.

that of his own queer family members, uncles and cousins, who died of AIDS-related complications.

These reflections, in their turn, led to another affective shift and a further solicitation of the audience: having framed Harris's work as a bodily performance of black gay subjectivities under threat of extinction, Owens asked that everyone present who knew someone who had died of AIDS join him before the backdrop, creating a portrait of individuals left standing

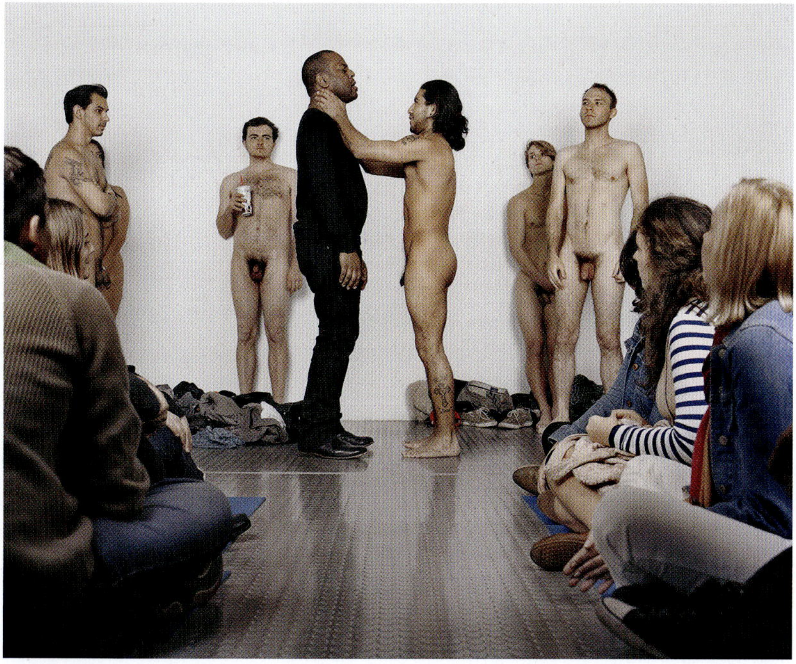

Figure 10.8
Clifford Owens, *Photographs with an Audience (Houston) (Choke)*, performance still, 2011. © Clifford Owens.

in the wake of the epidemic's first brutal wave in the United States. In its participatory structure and emotional ambition, the performance resonated with Owens's ongoing series *Photographs with an Audience*—variously enacted in New York (2008); Chapel Hill, North Carolina (2009); Houston, Texas (2011); and Miami, Florida (2011)—in which the audience, at times nude along with the artist, becomes the subject of the performance and its imaging (Fig. 10.8).[34] In these works and in the live version of *Anthology (Lyle Ashton Harris)*, the artist enjoins his spectators in the construction of a public in a move away from what Kathy O'Dell defines as the social contract of performance and toward what Ariella Azoulay terms the "civil contract of photography," each represented body made visible as the author of claims to history and citizenship and their mutually constitutive boundaries in the imagistic field.[35]

With my eyewitness account of this performance in view—itself a trace that might otherwise fall out of the anthologist's scope—the ends of this essay are now in sight.[36] For if Owens's differing engagements with Hammons (by way of Ligon) and Harris (by way of the audience) emphasize the centrality of the image to histories of black performance art, then they also provide further insight into the particular problems faced by African

American practitioners in the present, which are hyperbolized, even exacerbated, by *Anthology*'s structure. Meaning, to recall Owens's declaration, is in crisis, particularly for contemporary black artists intent on making critical interventions without a political field or a discursive framework to call their own.

Arguably, this was not always the case. Coco Fusco contends that, historically, the medium of photography and the genre of performance art, which so often privilege the nude body, have posed inherent difficulties to African American artists given the production of black subjects as the loci of the camera's often-violent, criminalizing gaze and of slavery's infernal processes of corporeal objectification.[37] In *Pissed Off* and *Construct #10*, Hammons and Harris scandalously repudiate such impositions, the former with his clandestine urination and the latter with his confrontational stare. By contrast, when Owens stripped down at MoMA PS1, there was little of the anxiety that has long accompanied the sight of the nude black male body: this was simply an artist in an institution putting on the standard performative suit.[38]

The same might be said of the photograph that records Owens's performance—in dark shades and an actual black suit—of Rico Gatson's score *Five Minutes*, which calls for a rehearsal of the Black Power salute raised by John Carlos and Tommie Smith at the 1968 Mexico City Olympics.[39] The resulting work, however, gains its charge less from the current political relevance of the gesture and more from its restaging within the frame of James Turrell's permanent 1986 MoMA PS1 installation, *Meeting* (Fig. 10.9). Like Serra's trough, this work is a cut into the building's roof, yet rather than orienting viewers toward the ground, its precisely delineated opening turns them toward the heavens, thereby allowing *Anthology (Rico Gatson)* to read as a new model of transcendence. Here and elsewhere, *Anthology* suggests that there are no longer any radical moves to be made, injunctions to be refused, or criteria to be rejected other than the poses provided by a host of antecedents, whose performances, when masterfully or halfheartedly restaged, just might manage to make some claim on the present and its grounds of articulation. In Owens's work, these grounds can only be fleetingly located, if not secured, by the photographic image and the subjects who appear within it.

This is not, I think, merely a symptom of his art or of its emergence within a post-black, post-Obama, post-Performa world. Rather, it is an effect of a larger transformation in the Western public sphere occasioned by the expansion of the neoliberal capitalist enterprise and its attendant destabilization of meaning since the 1980s. As the critical theorist Lauren Berlant has argued, in this milieu, neither citizenship nor its emotional valences are surely intelligible, leading subjects to delegate affects and ideologies to others so that their impact might be viewed, evaluated, and assimilated at a subjective remove, strategies entirely in line with the logic

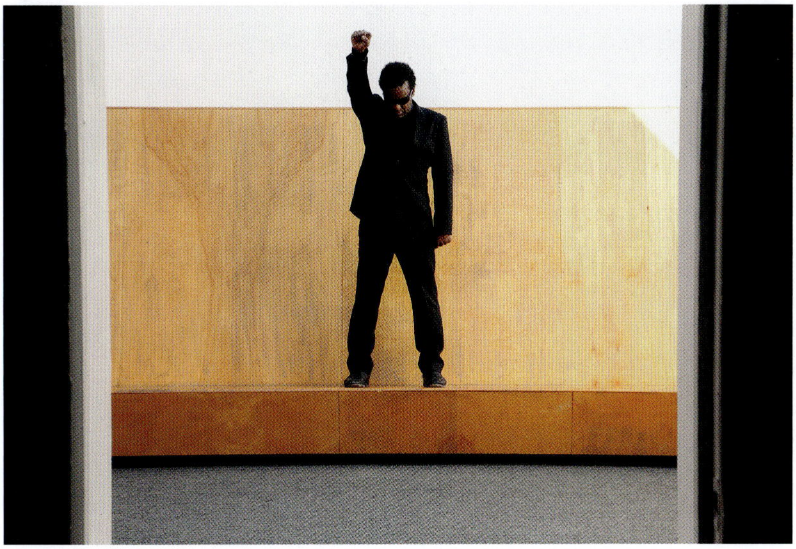

Figure 10.9
Clifford Owens, *Anthology (Rico Gatson)*, detail, 2011. © Clifford Owens.

of outsourcing that drives the contemporary service economy.[40] This set of conditions speaks well both to *Anthology*'s rampant contradictions and its provisional achievement: nowadays, it would seem, the best bet is to photograph everything and to mount the most resonant images on the wall in the hopes that some histories will stick, some feeling will come through.

Notes

My title is, of course, meant to rhyme with that of Jacques Derrida's *Mal d'Archive*, published in English as *Archive Fever: A Freudian Impression*, trans. Eric Prenowitz (University of Chicago Press, 1995). Not so clear are the debts that this essay owes to the guidance of Christopher Y. Lew, the vision of Clifford Owens, the research assistance of Luke Fidler, and the incisive commentaries of Janet Dees, Hannah Feldman, Ramón Rivera-Servera, Lorna Simpson, and Krista Thompson. As ever, they have my thanks.

1 Clifford Owens, in Nick Stillman, "Clifford Owens," *Bomb* 117 (Fall 2011): 55.

2 RoseLee Goldberg, *Performance Art: From Futurism to the Present* (Harry N. Abrams, 1996), 173. Of course, there have been more racially inclusive attempts to frame the history of performance art of late—subsequent editions to Goldberg's text among them—as well as vital interventions within African American art history. See, for example, John Bowles, *African American Performance Art Archive*, 2010, http://aapaa.org/; Paul Schimmel, *Out of Actions: Between Performance and the Object, 1949-1979* (Museum of Contemporary Art and Thames and Hudson, 1998);

Cherise Smith, *Enacting Others: Politics of Identity in Eleanor Antin, Nikki S. Lee, Adrian Piper, and Anna Deavere Smith* (Duke University Press, 2011); *Radical Presence: Black Performance in Contemporary Art* (Contemporary Arts Museum Houston, 2012); Lowery Stokes Sims, "Aspects of Performance in the Work of Black American Women Artists," in *Feminist Art Criticism: An Anthology*, ed. Arlene Raven, Cassandra L. Langer, and Joanna Frueh (UMI Research Press, 1988), 207-25. However, a thoroughgoing scholarly examination of black contributions to performance art from an explicitly art historical perspective has yet to appear.

3 Michael Hanchard, "Afro-Modernity: Temporality, Politics, and the African Diaspora" *Public Culture* 11, no. 1 (1999): 245-68.

4 One touchstone for these discourses, especially within discussions of the postracial, is Thelma Golden's introduction of the term "post-black" in the exhibition catalog *Freestyle* (Studio Museum in Harlem, 2001), 14-15. I take my critical stance toward the notion of "black work" from Darby English, "Black Artists, Black Work? Regarding Difference in Three Dimensions" (PhD diss., University of Rochester, 2002).

5 For a valuable consideration of the conditions of performance art now, see Amelia Jones, "Introduction: Performance, Live or Dead," *Art Journal* 70, no. 3 (Fall 2011): 33-38.

6 Brent Hayes Edwards, *The Practice of Diaspora: Literature, Translation, and the Rise of Black Internationalism* (Harvard University Press, 2003), 44. Edwards's discussion and my own are informed by Theodore O. Mason Jr., "The African-American Anthology: Mapping the Territory, Taking the National Census, Building the Museum," *American Literary History* 10, no. 1 (Spring 1998): 185-98.

7 Edwards, *The Practice of Diaspora*, 44.

8 Judith Butler's emphasis on notions of performativity in *Gender Trouble: Feminism and the Subversion of Identity* (Routledge, 1990) has had profound ramifications across the arts and humanities, notably among interdisciplinary practitioners invested in black performance in its various guises—music, speech, photography, film—who are less bound by art historical conventions when engaging works defined as performance art. Here, I have foremost in mind Fred Moten's radical reframing of black performativity, *In the Break: The Aesthetics of the Black Radical Tradition* (University of Minnesota Press, 2003), as well as texts such as Nicole Fleetwood, *Troubling Vision: Performance, Visuality, and Blackness* (University of Chicago Press, 2011); E. Patrick Johnson, *Appropriating Blackness: Performance and the Politics of Authenticity* (Duke University Press, 2003); Catherine Ugwu, ed., *Let's Get It On: The Politics of Black Performance* (Institute of Contemporary Arts and Bay Press, 1995).

9 Walker's score trades in the same economies of sexualized violence pictured in the silhouettes for which she is most renowned. See Kara Walker, INSTRUCTION, in Lew, *Clifford Owens: Anthology*, R.

10 Huey Copeland, "Glenn Ligon and Other Runaway Subjects," *Representations* 113 (Winter 2011): 78.

11 Clifford Owens, conversation with the author, December 16, 2011.

12 In regard to questions of reperformance, see Rebecca Schneider, *Performing Remains: Art and War in Times of Theatrical Reenactment* (Routledge, 2011).

13 On the importance of annotation in Ligon's work, see Huey Copeland, "Feasting on Scraps," *Small Axe: A Caribbean Journal of Criticism* 38 (July 2012): 198-201.

14 The relevant passage from Ligon's score is, "For example: Yvonne Rainer dancing 'Trio A' while telling the audience what she is feeling as she is doing it, what moves she can't do because she is older, etc." Glenn Ligon, "Untitled," in Lew, *Clifford Owens: Anthology*, N.

15 Harriet F. Senie, *The* Tilted Arc *Controversy: Dangerous Precedent?* (University of Minnesota Press, 2002), 14-17.

16 Alanna Heiss, *ROOMS P.S.1* (Institute for Art and Urban Resources, 1977). The most influential account of the works in this exhibition—several of which bear a striking affinity to Owens's *Anthology (William Pope.L)*—remains Rosalind Krauss, "Notes on the Index: Seventies Art in America, Part 2," *October* 4 (Autumn 1977): 58-67. As will become clear, Krauss's emphasis on the photographic in that text is equally pertinent here.

17 Senie, *The* Tilted Arc *Controversy*, 17.

18 For an account of *Pissed Off* and Hammons's other engagements with *T.W.U.*, see Tom Finkelpearl, "On the Ideology of Dirt," in *David Hammons: Rousing the Rubble* (Institute for Contemporary Art, P.S.1 Museum; and MIT Press, 1991), 85-88. On the spatial transformation of Lower Manhattan and its attendant displacements in the 1970s and 1980s, see Rosalyn Deutsche, *Evictions: Art and Spatial Politics* (MIT Press, 1996).

19 Schneider, *Performing Remains*, 6; emphasis in original.

20 Finkelpearl, "On the Ideology of Dirt," 85-88.

21 Clifford Owens, "Notes on Critical Black U.S. Performance Art and Artists," *HZ* 3 (October 2003), http://www.hz-journal. org/n3/owens.html.

22 For a critique of the museum's attitude toward black artists, specifically women, see Huey Copeland, "In the Wake of the Negress," in *Modern Women: Women Artists at The Museum of Modern Art*, ed. Cornelia Butler and Alexandra Schwartz (Museum of Modern Art, 2010), 480-97 [reprinted in this volume, 265-85].

23 Owens, in Stillman, "Clifford Owens," 55.

24 Christopher Y. Lew, conversation with the author, December 16, 2011.

25 Owens is not alone in devising tactical end runs around Hammons's resistance. I think foremost of the exhibition of the artist's work mounted without his permission by the gallery Triple Candie, a show that featured nothing but printouts and photocopies. See "David Hammons: The Unauthorized Retrospective," January 8, 2006, http://www.triplecandie.org/Archive%202006%20Hammons.html.

26 On the artist's body as the privileged site of performance, see Coco Fusco, "The Bodies That Were Not Ours: Black Performers, Black Performance," *Nka: Journal of Contemporary African Art* 5 (Fall-Winter 1996): 28. On the importance of live rendition to the genre, see Peggy Phelan, "The Ontology of Performance: Representation without Reproduction," in *Unmarked: The Politics of Performance* (Routledge, 2003), 146-66.

27 Clifford Owens, conversation with the author, December 16, 2011.

28 For the complete scores of the McKenzie and Nengudi works, see Dave McKenzie, "Untitled," and Senga Nengudi, "Sweep," in Lew, *Clifford Owens: Anthology*, I and P, respectively.

29 Christopher Y. Lew, email to the author, April 18, 2012.

30 The Mercer excerpts were to be derived from the essays "Black Masculinity and the Sexual Politics of Race" and "Dark & Lovely: Black Gay Image-Making," in *Welcome to the Jungle: New Positions in Black Cultural Studies* (Routledge, 1994), 131, 222, 230-32.

31 Tavia Nyong'o, "Brown Punk: Kalup Linzy's Musical Anticipations," *TDR: The Drama Review* 54, no. 3 (Fall 2010): 71-86.

32 For the relevant discussions of Harris's work, see Amelia Jones, *Body Art: Performing the Subject* (University of Minnesota Press, 1998), 215-20; Tracey Warr, ed., *The Artist's Body* (Phaidon Press, 2000), 155. For a key example of the critical dissensus around so-called multicultural practices, see Hal Foster, Rosalind Krauss, Silvia Kolbowski, Miwon Kwon, and Benjamin Buchloh, "The Politics of the Signifier: A Conversation on the Whitney Biennial," *October* 66 (Fall 1993): 3-27.

33 On the psychosexual and sociohistorical implications of the pose, see Craig Owens, "Posing," in *Beyond Recognition: Representation, Power, and Culture*, ed. Scott Bryson, Barbara Kruger, Lynne Tillmann, and Jane Weinstock (University of California Press, 1994), 201-17.

34 Valerie Cassel Oliver, "Clifford Owens: Some Questions," in *Perspectives 173: Clifford Owens* (Contemporary Arts Museum Houston, 2011), 6. For a particularly compelling account of the Houston performance, see Hank Hancock, "Getting Naked with Clifford Owens at CAMH," *Houston Press*, January 7, 2011, http://blogs.houstonpress.com/artattack/2011/01/clifford_owens.php/.

35 Kathy O'Dell, *Contract with the Skin: Masochism, Performance Art, and the 1970s* (University of Minnesota Press, 1998); Ariella Azoulay, *The Civil Contract of Photography* (Zone Books, 2008).

36 While Owens executed a photographic work based on this performance not long before this essay went to press—see Lew, *Clifford Owens: Anthology*, z—he effectively blocked any documentation of the live rendition other than his own, whether personal or institutional. According to Lew, at present, "there are no plans for the project to enter the MoMA collection," a fact that again raises the question of *Anthology*'s eventual fate within the archive, a concern anticipated by the artist Lorraine O'Grady. Her score *Xenosphere*—printed in full in Lew, *Clifford Owens: Anthology*, AA—ends with the following request: "Send a (low-res, lowtech, low-value) copy of this record of interaction to Lorraine O'Grady for her archive." Christopher Y. Lew, email to the author, April 3, 2012.

37 Fusco, "The Bodies That Were Not Ours," 28-33.

38 Fusco, "The Bodies That Were Not Ours," offers a useful genealogy of these dynamics (29)—particularly in her discussion of the furor generated by Robbie McCauley's 1990 nude performance at the Studio Museum in Harlem—which might be extended to construct a genealogy of nude African American performance that includes the work of less well-known artists such as Sherman Fleming in addition to those practitioners discussed here.

39 The full score reads: "Is inspired by the 1968 Olympics medal ceremony where Tommie Smith and John Carlos accept the gold and bronze medal in the 200 meters while giving the black power salute. My score is for Cliff to interpret the scene / moment as he sees fit dressed or not also according to his desires. The desired duration of the piece would be five minutes." Rico Gatson, "Five Minutes," in Lew, *Clifford Owens: Anthology*, T. For a snapshot of contemporary artists' deployment of such figures, see

11

DARK MIRRORS

Theaster Gates and *Ebony*

Since the middle of the past century, the magazines produced by the Chicago-based Johnson Publishing Company (JPC)—most famously *Ebony* and *Jet*—have visualized models of black aspiration and petit bourgeois achievement. At the same time, they have directed their readers' sights toward texts and photographs of transformative import, from Larry Neal's writings on black aesthetics to images of the brutalized body of Emmett Till. These periodicals, along with the company's cosmetics and hair-care lines, provided sources of employment as well as safe havens for black cultural producers forced to navigate a segregated world in an even more segregated city. For decades, visiting dignitaries who would have been turned away from white establishments regardless of their fame knew that they could find a welcome place of respite at the corporation's headquarters.

With his wife, Eunice Johnson, JPC founder John H. Johnson audaciously imagined and financially supported a modern black world that would become a tendentious model of commercialized uplift, a bulwark against racialized oppression, and an inspiring *Gesamtkunstwerk*. As such, JPC stands as a peculiar mirror to another Chicago-based corporate enterprise: namely, the practice of Theaster Gates. An ensemblic concatenation that includes performance, painting, sculpture, and video, as well as a series of urban renewal projects, Gates's work has at times specifically evoked or cited the images and infrastructure of JPC. But, more broadly and significantly, Gates's art is animated by the same tensions between social imperatives and economic exigencies that have shaped JPC's shifting fortunes. To consider his practice alongside the company's history is, then, to illuminate the contradictions that mark the lives of black institutions and to underscore the ongoing necessity of such formations in our own neoliberal moment, in which white supremacy's hold still seems secure even as its means of reproduction take on ever subtler guises.

This feature first appeared in *Artforum* 52, no. 2 (October 2013): 222-29.

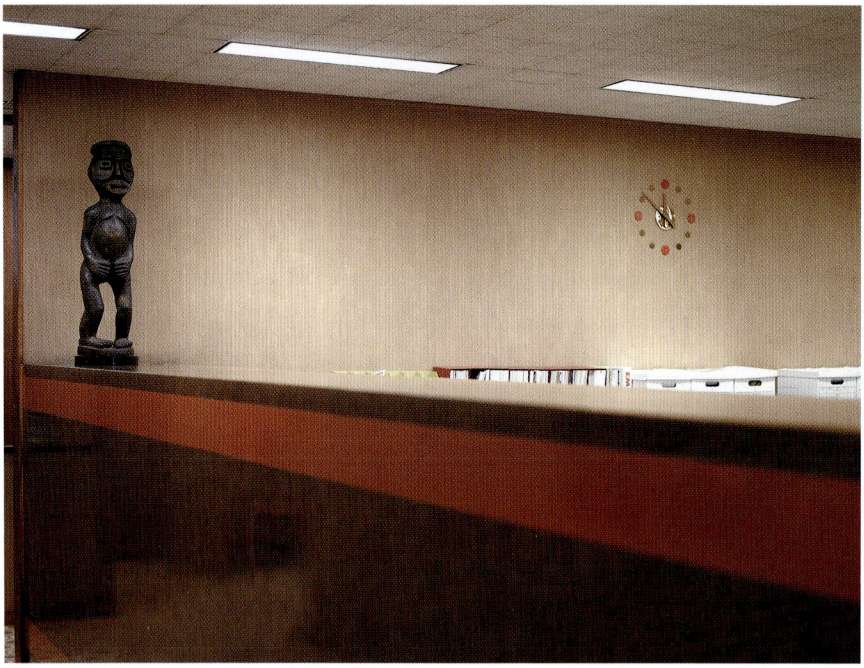

Figure 11.1a

David Hartt, *Archive at The Johnson Publishing Company Headquarters, Chicago, Illinois*, 2011. From *Stray Light*, 2011. Archival pigment print mounted to Dibond and framed, 60 × 80 in. Edition of Six. Courtesy the artist and Corbett vs. Dempsey, Chicago.

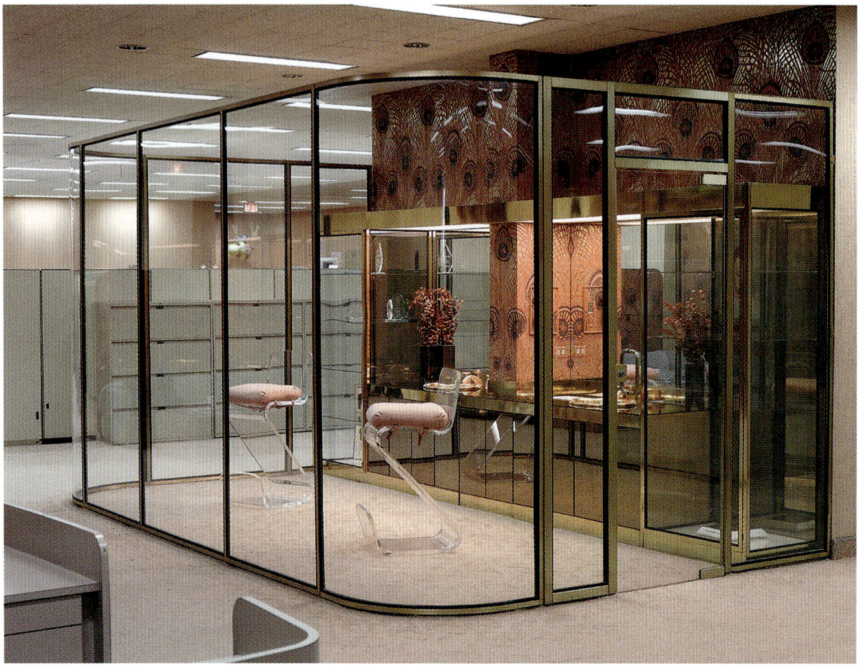

Figure 11.1b

David Hartt, *Kiosk at The Johnson Publishing Company Headquarters, Chicago, Illinois*, 2011. From *Stray Light*, 2011. Archival pigment print mounted to Dibond, 48 × 60 in. Edition of Six. Courtesy the artist and Corbett vs. Dempsey, Chicago.

Certainly, Gates is not the only artist for whom JPC and its magazines have functioned as generative sites. Ellen Gallagher, for example, has been exhibiting modified pages from the company's publications for over a decade, and in a 2010 painting by Hank Willis Thomas, the titles *Ebony* and *Life* are neatly conjoined, underlining the shared visual logic of the two magazines' branding as well as the distance between their coverage and constituencies. In David Hartt's multimedia project *Stray Light* (2011), the sumptuous William Raiser and Arthur Elrod–designed interiors of the JPC's 1972 John Moutoussamy skyscraper on Michigan Avenue become the ethereal stuff of late modernist fantasia (Figs. 11.1a, 11.1b). And in a 2012 collage by Lorna Simpson, a female figure taken from the pages of *Ebony* is crowned with a cutout halo of ink that reads as both stylized coiffure and Rorschach test, its mixed gray color calling attention to and confounding the black/white binary that continues to structure racialization in America. Each of these works insists on the iconicity of its sources—the magazine logos, the company's building, or advertisements that helped fund JPC's operations—and their lasting affective punch.

Gates's own connection to the Johnson brand is considerably more material and far more synergistic. For his 2012 exhibition at London's White Cube gallery, alongside other items redolent of African American progress and protest, the artist displayed John H. Johnson's sprawling office library, which was given to Gates by Linda Johnson Rice, current chair of JPC's board (Fig. 11.2). Wheeled ladders and reading tables installed in the gallery made the library accessible, establishing it not as a monument to be mourned or a cipher to be commoditized but as a capacious resource to be engaged. Other works on view, though, were available for sale; in one of several nods to JPC's array of brands, there was even a Fashion Fair Cosmetics booth open for makeover consultations. The exhibition as a whole, titled *My Labor Is My Protest*, brought into focus Gates's characteristic confusion of those boundaries—between work and resistance, art and commerce, radicalism and reform, politics and policy—that black practitioners working within hegemonic frames have sought to at once master and disarticulate in reimagining history and tracking the past's unfolding in the present.

Like Gates's eclectic London installation, *Ebony* and *Jet* have consistently played with and against hegemonic assumptions about the realities of life lived black. But this tack has not always guaranteed financial success. As hardly needs saying, the past ten years have not been easy for the publishing industry, especially for companies that market to "niche" groups, and JPC has weathered its fair share of storms: layoffs, restructuring, and declining subscription rates for its flagship magazine, *Ebony*, which is synonymous in many minds with an older generation's Cosbyesque dreams of black success. Of late, the company has regained its footing through outsourcing its circulation department, forging relationships with the likes of

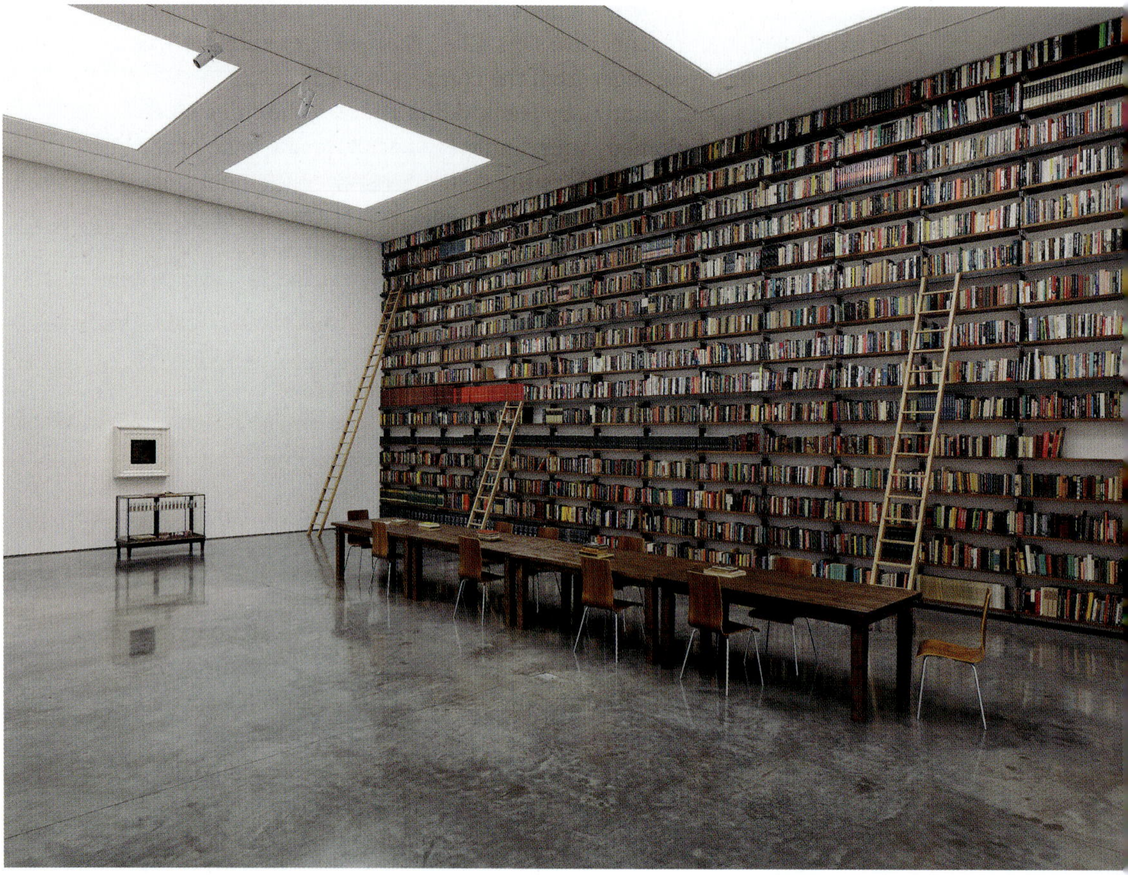

Figure 11.2

Theaster Gates, *Johnson Editorial Library*, 2012. Books, wood, metal. Installation view, White Cube Bermondsey, London. Photo: Ben Westoby. Johnson Publishing Company Archive and Theaster Gates Studio, courtesy Ford Foundation, J. Paul Getty Trust, John D. and Catherine T. MacArthur Foundation, Andrew W. Mellon Foundation, and Smithsonian Institution.

JPMorgan Chase, and updating its profile as a lifestyle brand.[1] In addition to magazines and cosmetics, JPC now sells framed historical photographs printed from its negatives, and it plans to develop a line of Hermès-inspired accessories, including bangles and handbags.[2] These ventures have not, however, obviated the need for austerity measures: JPC recently sold its chic headquarters and has quietly dispersed items from its stunning collection of African American art. Of course, it also handed over those books that have now found a home with Gates, who intends to house them in a cultural center to be constructed in a once-condemned bank building on Chicago's South Side.[3]

The irony here is worth lingering over. In order to survive in the digital economy, JPC is expanding its brand by hawking a greater range of lifestyle wares and representations while selectively unburdening itself of physical stuff. By contrast, Gates's acquisition of those very same materials crowns his triumphant emergence within and recasting of contemporary financial economies. By now, the story of Gates's meteoric rise within the art world and in the pages of the *Wall Street Journal* (which selected him as one of its 2012 Innovator of the Year Award winners) is almost as familiar as *Ebony*'s successes in the corporate media, though the basic lineaments bear repeating. Born on the West Side of Chicago in 1973, Gates received a master's degree in ceramics, urban planning, and religious studies from Iowa State University in 2006 before embarking in earnest on a practice that reflected his trio of academic interests. In 2008, for example, he produced the video *The Yamaguchi Story*, which explores the relationship between black and Japanese arts and centers on a fictional meeting between Gates and the ceramicist Shoji Yamaguchi; that same year, he staged a performance at Eindhoven's Van Abbemuseum that constituted the international debut of a musical ensemble he founded, the Black Monks of Mississippi, whose members include Chicago-based musicians and monks from various traditions around the world. He participated in the 2010 Whitney Biennial and in last year's Documenta 13 and has had a number of high-profile solo exhibitions that have been reviewed in the pages of this magazine and seemingly everywhere else.

Gates's best-known work, *Dorchester Projects* (2009–), is a suite of beautifully restored South Side buildings that collectively function as a hybrid art center, gathering place, and residence; almost from the start its development was intertwined with the economic downturn that affected JPC so adversely. Searching for a house within his means in 2006, Gates selected a property located on South Dorchester Avenue in Chicago's Grand Crossing neighborhood, a predominantly black area whose neglect by the city abetted both the house's decay and its affordability. Within a few years, thanks to the subprime mortgage crisis, he was able to acquire the adjacent building and another property across the street.[4] He used the structures to house his growing collections of cast-off cultural artifacts, many of them—such as the University of Chicago's glass lantern slides and a cache of vinyl records from a neighborhood music store that had gone out of business—casualties of the digital revolution (Fig. 11.3).[5] As the economy fell, Gates rose up to meet it, at once satisfying and exceeding sociocultural demand with a vision to rival the Johnsons', albeit one that materially foregrounded rather than wished away the precarious circumstances in which blackness often unfolds.

Since then, Gates's production has only grown more expansive and complex, constantly shifting to meet his own outsize ambition as well as the demands and criticisms of the communities within which he operates. Indeed, his practice can be said to work with and against a particular admixture of aesthetics, theories, contexts, and attitudes: white guilt, the archival

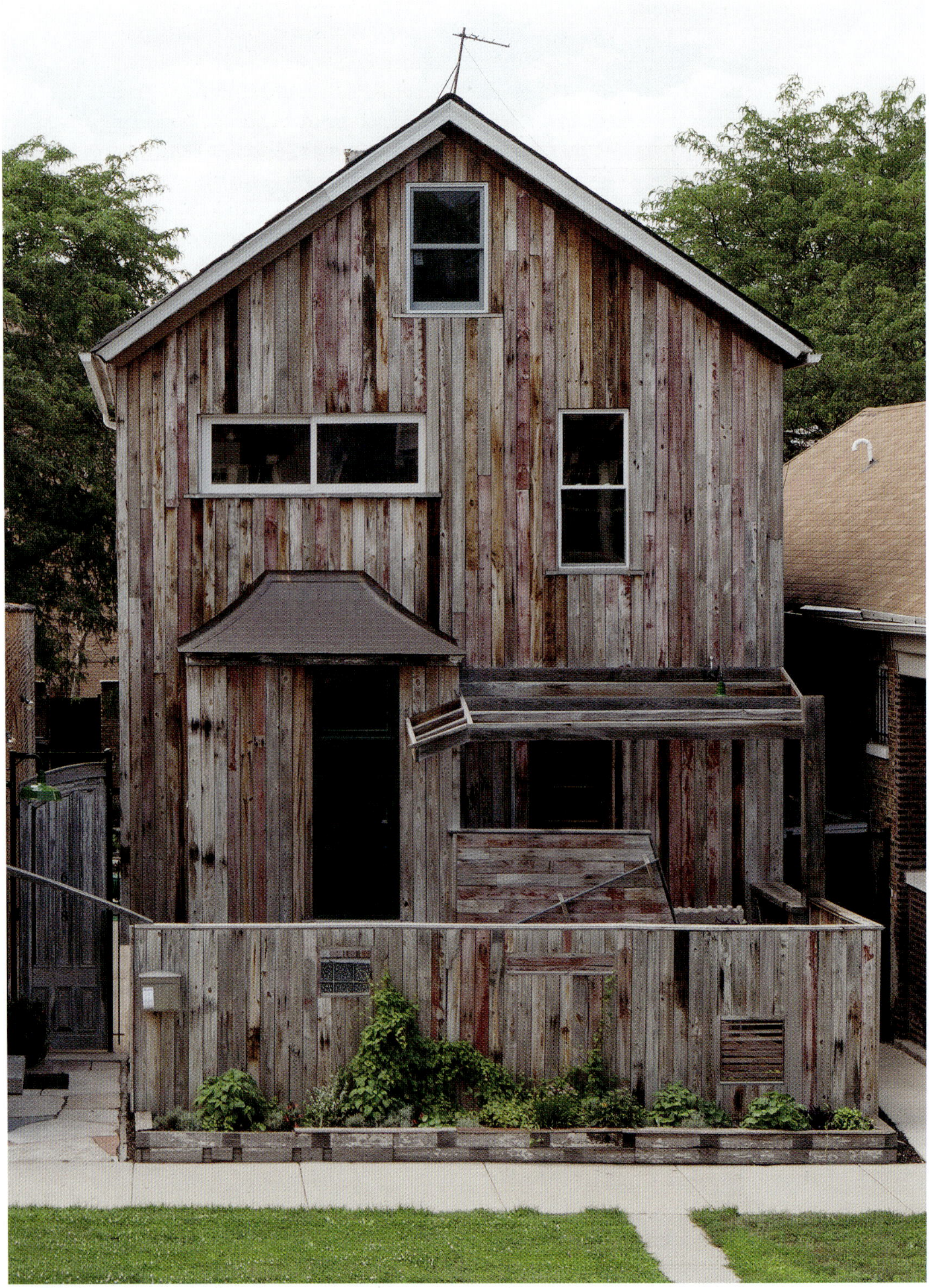

Figure 11.3
Archive House at Theaster Gates's *Dorchester Projects*, 2009- . Chicago, 2012. Photo: Sara Pooley. Johnson Publishing Company Archive and Theaster Gates Studio, courtesy Ford Foundation, J. Paul Getty Trust, John D. and Catherine T. MacArthur Foundation, Andrew W. Mellon Foundation, and Smithsonian Institution.

turn, DIY aesthetics, the uplift impulse, parafiction, actor-network theory, and, perhaps unavoidably, privatization and the concomitant proliferation of nonprofits and nongovernmental organizations. His endeavors reflect the extent to which nonprofits, rather than government agencies, are now viewed as providers of crucial services and as "agents of change," a term favored by postmillennial plutocrats and policy wonks alike. At Dorchester, such transformation works something like this: Under the aegis of his Rebuild Foundation, Gates and his collaborators hire and train local laborers to refurbish buildings that then serve as cultural hubs—so far there is a Black Cinema House, a Listening House, and an Archive House—all of which are funded by granting organizations and by the transformation of detritus from the sites into salable art objects. These works, which may be derived from floors, sinks, or walls, are squared off and positioned in the gallery as Afro-modernist ripostes to the white past masters of abstract art and civil society.

It is this process, which the artist terms a "circular ecosystem,"[6] that energizes some of his most historically resonant bodies of work, such as the *Civil Tapestries* (2011–) (Fig. 11.4). The *Tapestries*, comprising decommissioned 1960s fire hoses carefully layered to create subtly hued striped patterns, do not merely unite wrapping procedures evocative of Eva Hesse's sculptures with the deflated weapons used against black civil rights protesters; they also insist on their belonging together as emanations of the same fractured yet continuous cultural field. This kind of approach to and revision of the recent past is one that art historical scholarship on the '60s and '70s, however "expanded," has frequently failed to countenance, no matter how clear the connections between art and racial politics (whether bluntly spelled out by a text like Alex Gross's 1970 essay "The Artist as Nigger" or brilliantly conjured up as in the Museum of Modern Art's 1970 *Information* exhibition catalog, where photographs of the Black Panthers and a work by Marcel Duchamp were conjoined in a single spread).[7]

In comparison with JPC, which the art historian Darby English once cast as "a kind of black Fort Knox,"[8] Gates is disarmingly open in interviews and lectures about his own manipulation of such apparently discrepant histories, roles, and economies of value as well as the ambition that undergirds them: "I think I'm a full-time artist, a full-time urban planner, and a full-time preacher with an aspiration of no longer needing any of those titles. Rather, I'm trying to do what for some seems a very messy work or a complicated work. I feel we have to give more time and more consideration to the disparity between wealth and poverty in our country."[9] Viewed from one angle, such transparency would seem to jibe with the vaunted aims of the "new international financial architecture."[10] That term, popularized by economists in the wake of the '90s Asian financial crisis, was coined to describe the International Monetary Fund's woefully inadequate program of structural readjustments aimed at staving off yet

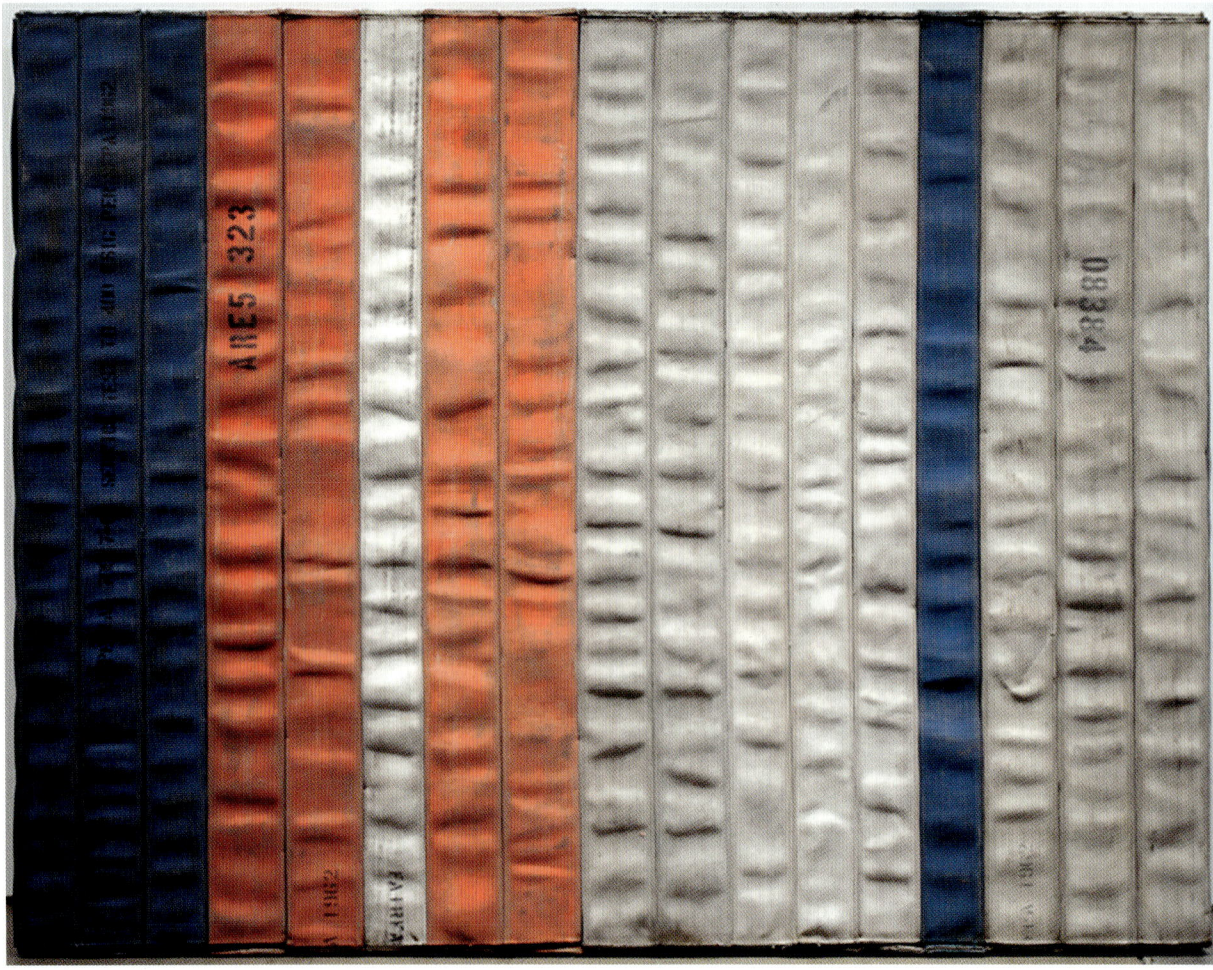

Figure 11.4
Theaster Gates, *Civil Tapestry, Flag Series*, 2012. Decommissioned fire hoses, wood, 66 × 84 × 4½ in. From the series "Civil Tapestries," 2011– . Johnson Publishing Company Archive and Theaster Gates Studio, courtesy Ford Foundation, J. Paul Getty Trust, John D. and Catherine T. MacArthur Foundation, Andrew W. Mellon Foundation, and Smithsonian Institution.

another global economic downturn. It has since been critically recast by the Los Angeles–based artist Edgar Arceneaux, cofounder of the Watts House Project, a nonprofit that gathers artists, designers, and residents of the eponymous neighborhood to renovate homes as well as the fabric of the community itself. For Arceneaux, "new financial architecture" serves to connote the types of arrangements that artists now ought to seek out with institutions in making their works and livings.[11]

But even more than Arceneaux, Rick Lowe (founder of Houston's nonprofit art center–cum–artwork, Project Row Houses), or Mark Bradford (in his fundraising work with the New Orleans neighborhood association L9),

Gates has made his name by both perverting and making good on Andy Warhol's desire to be a "business artist."[12] He is, in this sense, a business artist for the new millennium, which is to say, a development artist: an entrepreneurial creator of "public-private partnerships" who not only invests in his own community but also exports his model to satellites in cities across the Midwest, including Omaha and Saint Louis. Like his predecessors, Gates aims to grab hold of what Clement Greenberg once famously called "the umbilical cord of gold" connecting artists and their patrons[13] and redirect it in the service of creating new communities, discursive platforms, and networks that have a tentacular reach (and in which I too have been caught up, not unwillingly: Gates was an intellectual and financial contributor to "Black Collectivities," a conference I coorganized with the Museum of Contemporary Art Chicago curator Naomi Beckwith that productively charted many of the questions posed in these lines).

As the cultural critic Romi Crawford has noted, Gates has effectively mobilized and generously shared both his practice and his properties, creating unique spaces for black cultural exchange, arts education, and youth outreach.[14] These spaces in turn resonate with previous models of African American institutionality in Chicago, from the collectors' association Diasporal Rhythms to the South Side Community Art Center. As the historically attuned artist knows well, such institutions exist in spite of and in opposition to hegemonic models that would deny their necessity or promise to "integrate" their constituents. In many ways, these organizations are utopian enterprises, counterfactual propositions whose success at dreaming a world without racist injunctions has made them susceptible to obsolescence precisely because those barriers may appear to have been removed, though the work these organizations perform is definitively unfinished.

Unlike *Ebony* and other black cultural formations that grew from and catered to a once relatively captive market, Gates's practice has garnered support from "mainstream" audiences, institutions, and discourses. The latter have relatively little to say about the actual works of art he puts on display, those linchpins of his circular ecosystem. When seen in a gallery setting, these objects by themselves can be uneven in quality and effect. *Theaster Gates: 13th Ballad*, the artist's summer 2013 exhibition at the MCA Chicago, for instance, featured an array of sculptures, videos, and performances derived from his 2012 Documenta installation, *12 Ballads for Huguenot House*. In that work, the aforementioned building in downtown Kassel served as a residence, yoga studio, and music hall for performances by the Monks and others, while the artist and a team of collaborators from Chicago made over the interiors with materials shipped from another Dorchester house (Fig. 11.5). The videos on view at the MCA tantalizingly documented the affective dimensions of these activities, including Gates's own charismatic singing and signing presence, while the sculptural constructions registered his Kassel sojourn literally and figuratively, as in the

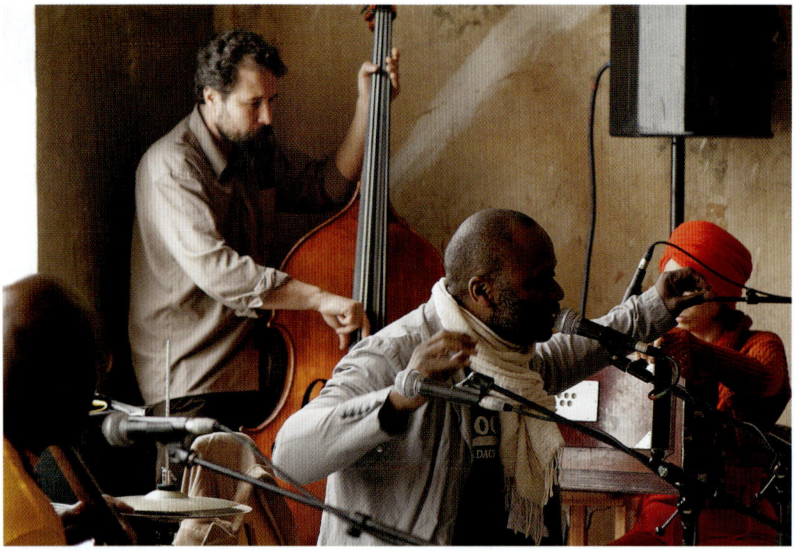

Figure 11.5
Theaster Gates, *12 Ballads for Huguenot House*, 2012. Performance view, Huguenot House, Kassel, June 7, 2012. From *Documenta 13*. Johnson Publishing Company Archive and Theaster Gates Studio, courtesy Ford Foundation, J. Paul Getty Trust, John D. and Catherine T. MacArthur Foundation, Andrew W. Mellon Foundation, and Smithsonian Institution.

case of wheeled carts that evoked both the artist's peripatetic status and larger histories of migration on both sides of the Atlantic.

A few of these sculptures functioned convincingly as discrete objects as well as in the larger context into which they were conscripted. Take *Huguenot Lightbox with Throne Maquette* (2012), a rough-hewn white cabinet of surrealist pedigree that houses a chair with impossibly long legs reminiscent of the throne sculptures of Wangechi Mutu (Fig. 11.6). The work was illuminated by a spare, unshaded bulb that cut through the darkness, pointedly drawing attention to a sculpture installed not in the white cube but in the black box. While *Huguenot Lightbox* deftly inflected its own conditions of display, other works seemed dead by comparison. The facture of a roof fragment paired with a truncated shoeshine stand, for example, fit neatly into Gates's overall aesthetic, but it was not clear why it belonged to this particular exhibition. For all their historical weight, without the additional charge of Gates's performative presence or a specifying self-reflexive frame à la Robert Smithson, Gordon Matta-Clark, or Renée Green, the sculptures risk appearing as commodities cynically extruded by the circuitry of the artist's practice, as opposed to activated participants in his ongoing spatial transformations.

Surely, this apparent commodification is part of Gates's point, as implied by the literary theorist Bill Brown, who has praised the artist's

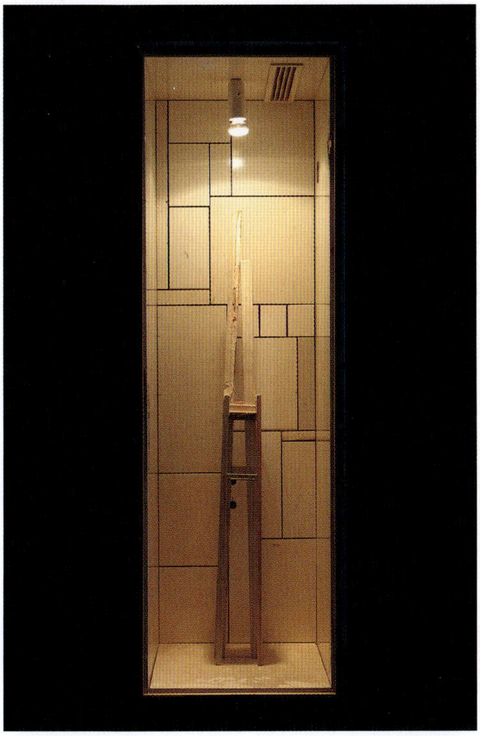

Figure 11.6
Theaster Gates, *Huguenot Lightbox with Throne Maquette*, 2012. Wood, Plexiglas, 68 × 22½ × 26 in. From *Theaster Gates: 13th Ballad*, Museum of Contemporary Art Chicago, 2013. Johnson Publishing Company Archive and Theaster Gates Studio, courtesy Ford Foundation, J. Paul Getty Trust, John D. and Catherine T. MacArthur Foundation, Andrew W. Mellon Foundation, and Smithsonian Institution.

practice as a mode of "redemptive reification."[15] Collectors and museums are eager to get their hands on manifestations of what the artist has called his "shine" and on the larger social interventions that they represent. But as *Ebony*'s fate makes clear, such luster is as fugitive as it is speculative.[16] The exhibition strategy modeled by the *13th Ballad* tends to position the museum as a mere repository or an occasional staging area, just as JPC's buildings, art, and library have been left out of the loop of its attempted reinvention. In both instances, the object is set adrift from the economies that produced it in order that black life might thrive elsewhere. For the scholar Fred Moten, this is a key aspect of Gates's sculptural works, since they ask for—even if they do not enact—a reconfiguration of the gallery as the kind of "open institution" that blackness itself is and that the artist has materialized "nowhere, everywhere."[17]

Nowhere, everywhere: This, I think, is an apt characterization of Gates's decentered practice and of JPC's transnational brand, both of which differently pose questions about what constitutes an aesthetic enterprise, where it ought to reside, and how it ought to be considered in light of the deformations of race. It is tempting and perhaps productive to subject both efforts to the trenchant critiques of corporate culture and of socially engaged practice issuing from the left—to lambaste JPC's collusion with American cultural imperialism and to take issue with Gates's art for its alignment with

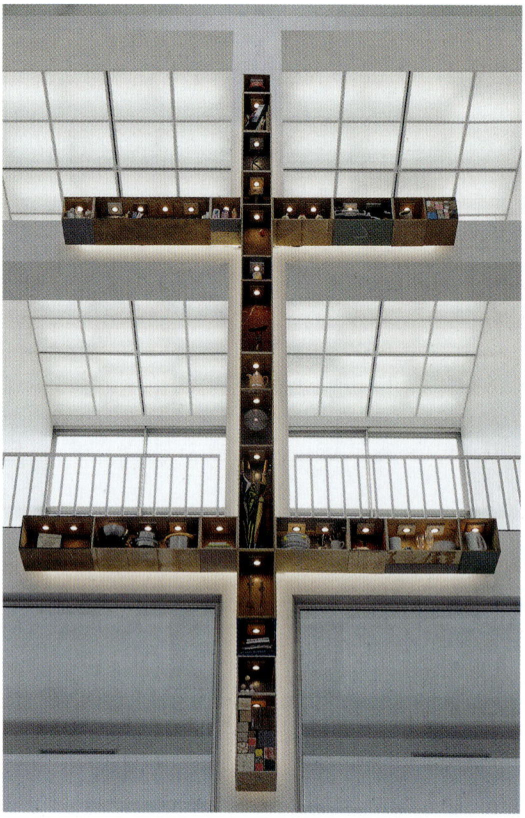

Figure 11.7

Theaster Gates, *Double Cross*, 2013. Wood, neon, objects from Huguenot House. Installation view, Museum of Contemporary Art Chicago, 2013. Johnson Publishing Company Archive and Theaster Gates Studio, courtesy Ford Foundation, J. Paul Getty Trust, John D. and Catherine T. MacArthur Foundation, Andrew W. Mellon Foundation, and Smithsonian Institution.

what Beckwith has termed "late-latest capital's capitulations."[18] For unlike other black collaborative projects that assume public faces, such as South Africa's Chimurenga and Keleketla! libraries, the American outfits under discussion here have taken as models those forms of private property—the house, the corporation—whose construction within the Western bourgeois public sphere might seem antithetical to the principles undergirding black liberation.

Yet despite their considerable liabilities, such structures are, by definition, also capable of securing opacity, dissemblance, and multiplicity—precisely those qualities historically denied black subjects, whose abjection has been central to the construction of whiteness and its institutions. Any critic seeking to fathom Gates's work would do well to remember that he has said, in regard to his exhibitions, "I am a bit of a trickster. . . . I want to seduce with an object, and I don't even want you to know of my social agenda."[19] While Gates's strategies may read as very much of their moment, they should also be understood as feints and tactics grounded in opposition to a racialized social order that has much deeper roots than our current socioeconomic condition and that must be battled on all fronts, within and beyond artistic discourse. Like two sides of the same coin,

Gates and JPC are for-profit purveyors of goods with divergent aims and attitudes—one aesthetically down-home, the other committedly aspirational. But both are also invested, whether primarily or incidentally, in the construction of spaces of black autonomy. Such operations must be seen as transpiring within a world in which blackness is already in the red, inhabiting an economy that is always in recession and that requires the constant retooling of time-tested cultural practices and ways of making do.

Given the centrality of the church as a model of collective formation within black communities, it should perhaps come as no surprise that Gates's MCA show also featured a makeshift sanctuary in the museum's atrium, complete with pews and surmounted by *Double Cross* (2013), a large wooden cabinet bisected twice and filled with items brought back from Kassel (Fig. 11.7). The work's punning title and the economies of exchange, belief, treachery, and freedom it evoked call up the multiple meanings of the word *recessional*, which, as the artist Paul Chan has pointed out, both suggests an economic condition and describes the hymn sung when the congregation takes its leave, when the service ends and something else begins.[20] It is this spirit that sparks Gates's practice, which calls us in so that we might eventually go out again, with our own entanglements in other histories, practices, and economies in mind, a necessary first step toward transformation, however conceived. Can I get an "Amen"?

Notes

The original version of this essay illustrated the August 1949 cover of *Ebony* featuring Lionel Hampton as well as the June 5, 1958, cover of *Jet* featuring Lynn Jordan. Currently these and other publications from the Johnson Publishing Company can be accessed here: https://getty.libguides.com/jpcarchive/magazines. However, Wrights Media, which now controls the licenses, charges $2,250 per cover for permission to reprint, a price that is more than twice the fee of any other image published in this book. I have elected not to reproduce original images but urge readers to look at back issues available gratis in their local libraries.

1 "'Ebony,' 'Jet' Parent Takes a Bold New Tack," *NPR News*, September 22, 2011.

2 Matt Haber, "Ebony Looks to Its Past as It Moves Forward," *New York Times*, December 9, 2012.

3 Greg Scruggs, "Making All the Things: The Theaster Gates Approach to Improving Space," *Next City*, March 4, 2013, http://nextcity.org/daily/entry/making-all-the-things-the-theaster-gates-approach-to-improving-space.

4 Cassie Walker Burke and Elly Fishman, "Theaster Gates: The Rise of an Unconventional Art Star," *Chicago Magazine*, May 7, 2013, http://www.chicagomag.com/Chicago-Magazine/June-2013/Theaster-Gates-The-Rise-of-an-Unconventional-Art-Star/.

5 Bomi Odufunade and Lloyd Degrane, "The Artist: Theaster Gates,"

Arise Live, 2013, http://www.ariselive.com/articles/the-artist-theaster-gates/126847/.

6 Theaster Gates, "Visual Thoughts," in *12 Ballads for Huguenot House* (Museum of Contemporary Art and Walther König, 2012), 25.

7 Alex Gross, "The Artist as Nigger," *East Village Other*, December 22, 1970; Kynaston McShine, *Information*, exh. cat. (Museum of Modern Art, 1970), 148–49.

8 Darby English, email message to author, May 8, 2013.

9 Jessica Mlinaric, "Interview: Artist Theaster Gates Discusses His New MCA Exhibit," *Chicagoist*, May 23, 2013. http://chicagoist.com/2013/05/23/interview_theaster_gates_13th_balla.php#photo-1.

10 See Barry J. Eichengreen, *Toward a New International Financial Architecture: A Practical Post-Asia Agenda* (Institute for International Economics, 1999).

11 Edgar Arceneaux, "New Financial Architectures for Creative Communities (NFACC)," Independent Curators International, August 10, 2013, http://curatorsintl.org/posts/new-financial-architectures-for-creative-communities-nfacc.

12 Andy Warhol, *The Philosophy of Andy Warhol: From A to B and Back Again* (Harcourt Brace and Company, 1975).

13 Clement Greenberg, "The Plight of Culture," in *Art and Culture* (Beacon Press, 1961), 32.

14 Romi Crawford, "Yours in Blackness: Blocks, Corners, and Other Desire Settings," *Nka: Journal of Contemporary African Art*, no. 34 (2014): 80–89.

15 Bill Brown, "Redemptive Reification (Theaster Gates, Gathering)," in *Theaster Gates: My Labor Is My Protest*, exh. cat. (*White Cube*, 2012), 36–40.

16 See Elly Fishman, "The Space Between: Artist Theaster Gates Bridges the Gap between Culture and Community," *Chicago Weekly*, January 22, 2009, http://chicagoweekly.net/2009/01/22/the-space-between-artist-theaster-gates-bridges-the-gap-between-culture-and-community/.

17 Fred Moten, "Nowhere, everywhere," in *Theaster Gates: My Labor Is My Protest*, 76.

18 Naomi Beckwith, email message to the author, May 13, 2013.

19 "Theaster Gates: Inner City Blues," *ArtMag*, 2013, http://db-artmag.com/en/76/feature/theaster-gates-inner-city-blues/.

20 Paul Chan, "The Spirit of Recession," *October* 129 (2009): 10–11.

12

PHOTOGRAPHY, THE ARCHIVE, AND THE QUESTION OF FEMINIST FORM

A Conversation with Zoe Leonard

Over the past two decades, the American artist Zoe Leonard (b. 1961) has emerged as one of the most visually attuned photographers of her generation, using images as a means of documentation, invention, remembrance, and critique. Regardless of the sites and objects on which she trains her lens—from piles of shoes to tangled tree branches—Leonard works from an implicitly queer and feminist perspective that puts pressure on both hegemonic modes of seeing and our ways of narrating them. Such concerns have similarly animated my own work as a historian and critic of modern and contemporary art invested in understanding how forms of cultural difference productively deform Western conceptualizations of the aesthetic. On February 12, 2011, I spoke with Leonard about her practice and its implications for feminist approaches to vision, history, and the archive. Our conversation took place at the College Art Association annual conference in New York as part of a daylong series of events sponsored by the Feminist Art Project and organized by art historians Julia Bryan-Wilson and Johanna Burton. Leonard and I took two of her works as touchstones for our exchange: The Fae Richards Photo Archive *(1993–1996), originally conceived as part of Cheryl Dunye's film* Watermelon Woman *(1996), and* You see I am here after all *(2008), a gridded concatenation of vintage postcards depicting views of Niagara Falls.[1] Our conversation began with the latter work.*

Copeland: I'd like to start by asking how your approach to photography in general and in *You see I am here after all* in particular might be said to pose and answer the question of feminist form (Figs. 12.1a, 12.1b).

Leonard: I am looking at how the world is ordered and thinking about how we organize our experience of it. In this work, the postcards are arranged by vantage point. The work is installed in a long space that is fairly narrow, so as the viewer, you walk past the work, rather than having a frontal

This interview first appeared in *Camera Obscura: Feminism, Culture, and Media Studies* 28, no. 2 (83) (Fall 2013): 177-89.

Jeffrey D. Grove, *After 1968: Contemporary Artists and the Civil Rights Legacy* (High Museum of Art, 2008).

40 Lauren Berlant, "Structures of Unfeeling: *Mysterious Skin*," public lecture, George Washington University, March 30, 2012. Berlant's analysis relies on Slavoj Žižek, "The Interpassive Subject," *Traverses* (1998), http://www.egs.edu/faculty/zizek/zizek-the-interpassive-subject.html/. For analyses of the relation between contemporary performance art and the larger service economy, see Schneider, *Performing Remains*, 137; Claire Bishop, "Outsourcing Authenticity? Delegated Performance in Contemporary Art," in *Double Agent*, ed. Claire Bishop and Silvia Tramontana (Institute of Contemporary Arts, 2008), 110-25.

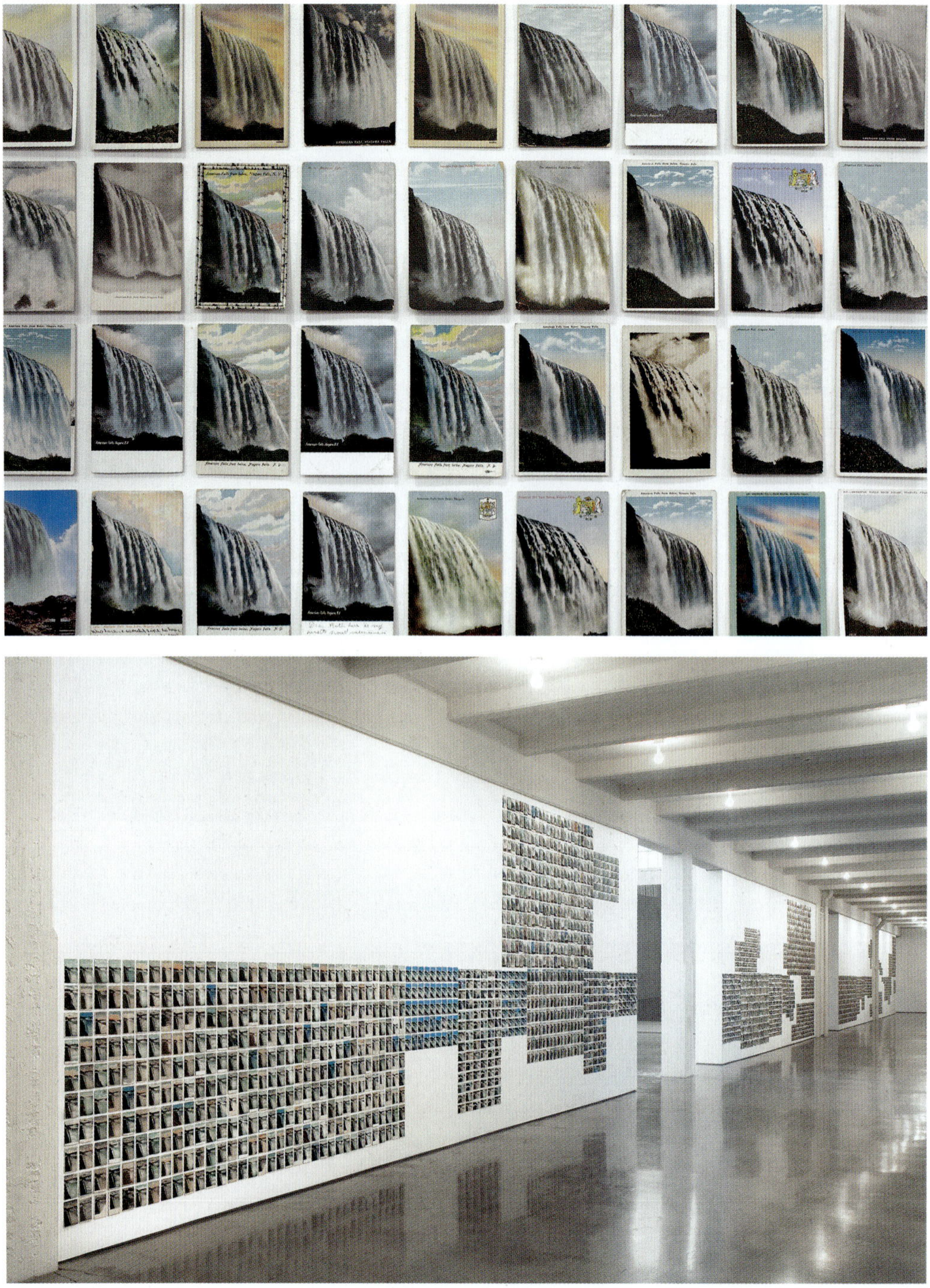

Figure 12.1

Zoe Leonard, *You see I am here after all*, details, 2008. Vintage postcards, 3,851 parts, 3 m 62 cm × 44 m 80.6 cm / 11 ft. 10.5 in. × 147 ft. Installation view, Dia:Beacon, New York, 2008. © Zoe Leonard. Courtesy the artist, Galerie Gisela Capitain, Cologne and Hauser & Wirth. Photo: Bill Jacobson Studio, New York.

experience of the installation. As you look up and down, your perspective is reflected back to you. Your perspective keeps changing, but your eyes are always in line with the original vantage point of the photographer. For me, this piece is a lot about deconstructing our process of looking—each of us individually from our personal points of view, and also collectively, how our looking is constructed historically, socially, politically. A number of questions arise: How is something recorded? What's the frame? How does the frame and the process of recording something determine its meaning? When I use a term like "vantage point" or "point of view," I don't just mean the physical space that I occupy, but also my whole conceptual frame that I bring into the room along with my camera. Photography is such an immediate way of showing you my point of view: "This is how I saw it, I took this picture, and what I'm showing you is literally my perspective on something." For me, these questions—"Where do you look from? What's your process of looking?"—are inherently political. They are feminist questions because they are about power and agency, about where you stand in the world, and what you can see from where you stand. I think this is a contemporary concern. Although I understand the relevance of the critique of the male gaze, I'm more interested in *my own* gaze, in considering the potential of the feminist gaze, the individual gaze, the queer gaze. It's not that I don't think it is important to deconstruct the male gaze, but I also think that continuing to focus on it gives it a lot of power, a lot of space. Maybe for women artists, the challenge is to ask, "What do I see? Where do I see from?," to recognize our own viewpoints, to engage with our desires, with our interests, and to examine the things that cloud or affect or determine how and what we see. That's where I think the conversation can really start: when you are clear on what you see, then you can talk to someone else about their different viewpoint. For me, these questions are always in my work regardless of what the "subject matter" is.

Copeland: I wonder if you could say a bit more about how you came to Niagara Falls as the site around which you would accumulate this set of images? Although it isn't a "feminine" subject or site, Niagara Falls has, of course, become loaded with all of these highly gendered, heteronormative connotations about nuptials and honeymooning. How did those connotations filter into—or fall out of—your thinking?

Leonard: This piece started out very differently in my studio. I was collecting postcards of many different waterfalls with the idea that I would put them all on the wall to create one visual mass. I had this idea about working with representation and abstraction at the same time: Could I use an image as both an image and a mark? Could a group of images take up space in an abstract way but simultaneously remain images and have meaning on that level? Around this time, Lynne Cooke invited me to make a site-specific commission for Dia:Beacon and I said, "Well, I'm kicking this thing around in my studio and it wouldn't really be site-specific, but maybe it could rhyme with the site in some way." She came to the studio and thought that it could work, so I began thinking of the work in relation to the spaces at Dia:Beacon. I went on a number of site visits and each time I brought a bunch of postcards. A thousand wasn't enough. I came back with two thousand, that wasn't enough. I came back with three thousand, and so on. The first visit I brought all the cards I had in the studio, from various different waterfalls, but when I put them up, it just didn't work on the wall, it wasn't holding. I actually hadn't intended to use the Niagara Falls images at all. I thought they were too cliché, and they were so different from all of the other waterfalls—they always stood out. But I didn't have enough of the other cards, so I brought the Niagara cards as "filler," just to try out the idea in the space. Anyway, I was up on the ladder with a group of Niagara Falls cards and I realized that in the scale of the space, they were the only images that really held the wall. Up on this ladder, looking down the length of the room, I thought, "I'm doing this backwards. Instead of taking multiple places and trying to make them into one experience, I need to take one site and deconstruct it. Take one place apart and map it out on this wall." It was one of those moments: I said to myself, "Okay, change course and get on eBay and start buying those Niagara Falls postcards!" This turned out to be the right decision for many reasons. As you say, as a society we have projected many different meanings onto the Falls over time. At different moments in history, the Falls have stood for power, the sublime, God, territory, the mystical. Later on they came to signify tourism and adventure, and still later, they became a symbol for romance and the honeymoon—the honeymoon being the place and time that you were supposed to be discovering sex. When you read some of the text on these postcards, when people write about viewing the Falls from every angle and every vantage point—"Oh this marvelous experience and we're going here and we're going there and we're seeing this and it's more magnificent than I thought it would be, or it's less magnificent than I thought it would be"—there's another kind of subtext. In the 1950s, the power of Niagara Falls also came to stand for the power of female desire. There is an amazing movie called *Niagara*. It stars Marilyn Monroe, and it's about—what is the line from the poster?—"Marilyn Monroe and Niagara: A raging torrent of emotion that even nature can't control." The film reveals an incredible fear of the power of female desire, which could be beautiful, certainly, but the implication is that the nature of female desire is so inherently destructive that if it is unleashed everyone is going to die!

Copeland: And that gets visually enacted in the poster for the movie, which features an astonishing image of Monroe wearing a dress that looks like a thin sheet but is actually the Falls thundering over her. The image is supposed to lure you in through a complete conflation of femininity and the sublime that is, as you say, both alluring and terrifying.[2]

Leonard: Yes, exactly, that was the cultural mind-set in the 1950s and early 1960s: that any kind of overpowering visual or physical experience was bad and terrifying. So, the more I worked on the project, I realized that Niagara Falls was the ideal subject. It was the perfect site for taking apart how a place is photographed, how we look at it, and what we project on to it. It's also a place that was photographed a great deal from the earliest days of photography, so these postcards also track the history of photography. From very early on, the Falls were photographed from a number of specific vantage points, and they have been photographed repeatedly from these same positions over the last 150 years. The cards inventory a small history of printed matter, printing technology and photographic approaches. For me, the project was a way to bring together a history of documentation and to think about the hierarchy of viewpoints and the idea of an ideal viewpoint. The title, *You see I am here after all*, is taken from one of the postcards, it's a single line written on the front of a postcard, signed by someone named Lulu. Something about that line struck me as sort of amazing; I think Lynne used the word *defiant* to describe it (and when I first showed her the card, she said, "Only a woman would say that"). For me, the sentence is also uncomfortable; I was embarrassed to say it at first, but I think that's ok. I also loved that almost every word in the sentence is a deictic: "you," "I," "here," and "after all." Depending on who says the sentence, it means something completely different. Who's the "you"? Who's the "I"? Where's the "here"? If you read it aloud it means something different, if you just read it yourself it means something different. For me, that phrase does two important things for the work. It implies or indicates the many different voices on the cards, bringing the history of this writing into the picture, all of these people communicating with each other. It also calls attention to the fact that looking is always an agreement between two people, it's a correspondence. Much as a postcard is a correspondence between two people, looking is an interaction. It's not a one-way thing, it's an interaction between subject and object, between viewed and viewer. I liked the way that the title opens that up and complicates the meaning of the work.

Copeland: I think it's interesting that there's this figure called Lulu who is clearly present in the work but somehow not there visually, all of which brings me to how this piece represents a shift, in a certain sense, from some of your earlier projects, particularly *The Fae Richards Photo Archive* project (Fig. 12.2). In contrast to *You see*, that work was about trying to fabulate a photographic history that actively pictured a subject lost to the archive. Despite these differences, scholars like Johanna have written, I

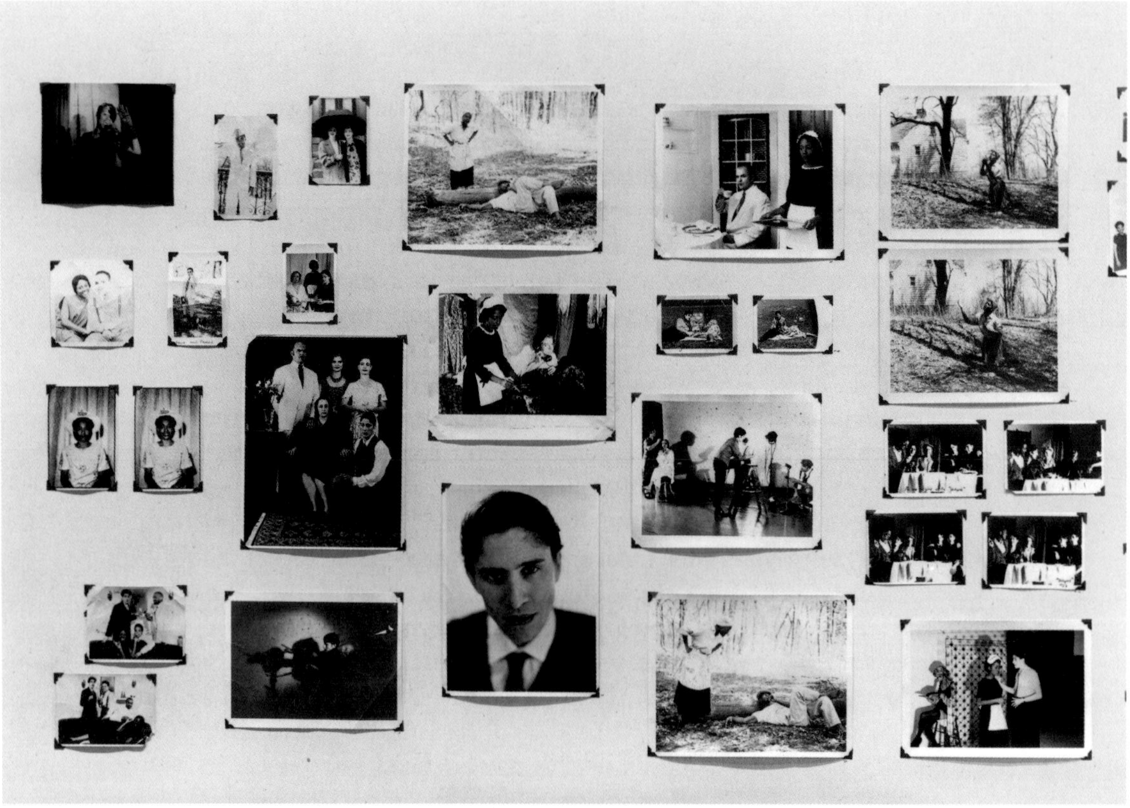

Figure 12.2
Zoe Leonard, *The Fae Richards Photo Archive*, detail, 1993-96. 78 black and white photographs, 4 color photographs, 6 pages of typed text on typewriter paper, dimensions variable. Installation view, 1997 Whitney Biennial, Whitney Museum of American Art, New York.

think rightly, about the reparative urge that seems to animate your practice.[3] I was wondering if you could speak, then, about the shift from a work like the *Fae Richards Photo Archive* to *You see I am here after all*? It seems as if there's still that reparative urge in the newer piece, an attempt to give voice to those perspectives excluded from the archive, but now those voices don't have to be announced in the same way. What I'm trying to get at is how you understand the differences between the earlier and later works, which seem to diverge on the level of "content" and speak to different exigencies in terms of what counts as a feminist artistic engagement.

Leonard: I guess for me there are ways in which these works are very different, yet there are also certain things that keep cropping up in my work, like the idea of the archive or the fact that I often use multiple images to make one work. *The Fae Richards Photo Archive*—like a lot of my work—started on a very instinctive level, and then I slowly found a form for it. The work began when Cheryl Dunye, the filmmaker, approached me. She wanted to make a documentary film about a woman who never actually existed, a character named Fae Richards. She asked me if I could make evidence of her life, an archive of her life. I said, "Yes, let's do that," so it really started from that problem: to figure out how to fill out that form. Perhaps most interesting for me about that piece—and most radical about it when I look back, is that we were interested in the ways that Fae Richards is real. Fae Richards is fictional, but her life is historically possible. It's a number of photographs that would have been taken over the course of this woman's life. She was a singer and an actress and then later did some political work with the NAACP. She was queer, and she had a relationship with a white film director, a woman. So, her life has a very lively trajectory. First, we wrote a timeline of her life, and then I staged and photographed a number of different events from it. The first step was to imagine when this person might have been photographed, and then to decide how many of those images might have survived. It's an archive full of holes and absences, it's not complete, in the way that no "real" archive would be complete. There might be a lot of pictures of one birthday party and then nothing for five years. So that's the form of the piece. What was exciting for me was the decision to make her a complex character. In many ways her life was determined by the political realities of her day—she was hampered by racism, sexism, and homophobia—and yet she had a great life. She was beautiful, she had love, she had a lot of joy, a lot of pleasure. She had intelligence and she had agency, she made choices. In the photographs, you see someone who maybe didn't get to be as big of a star as some of her white contemporaries in Hollywood—she always had to play the maid—but at the same time you see someone who is having a full life. You don't feel sorry for her, you feel pissed off that her talent couldn't be fully recognized in a larger forum, but this isn't the story of a downtrodden person. We made this character someone inventive who found ways to enjoy her life. And *that* feels radical and important.

Copeland: One of the things that I find so compelling about this work, and your work in general, is the attempt to ethically fabulate a history, to get at some reality that is otherwise occluded. The effect is something that I aim to do in my writing in some small way: to enter into a space that allows for an engagement with the facticity of racism and sexism and homophobia as they exist on the ground but that also opens up something else and gets us to a different set of possibilities that we wouldn't have come upon if we were just hemmed in by what was available to us.

Leonard: Yes, the way you described that is interesting. And it brings up the other interest, or challenge, in making these photographs for Cheryl.

Certain histories are so vastly, wildly, crazily underrepresented that there's this kind of wide-open field. So much is unknown. But, by looking at certain real histories, factual, documented histories, it was possible to imagine and create a historically possible person, someone who could have lived: fragments of Richards's story were taken from the lives of Dorothy Arzner, Butterfly McQueen, Josephine Baker, and many others. I loved the challenge of imagining a person who's fictional but who is also kind of real in a way. That is, she could have lived, though even if she had we probably wouldn't have known about her. This work points to invisibility. It points to all of the people we don't get to know about because we're really busy knowing about Jackson Pollock, which is not to say that he's not great, but to call attention to the fact that there's this incredible yawning, continuing, exhausting invisibility of all the other kinds of makers and artists that are women, that are black, that are poor, that live in countries that don't have the kind of art market that we have here. It felt so amazing to just go in and imagine this person. Fae Richards is a star. This work started out as material for Cheryl's film *Watermelon Woman*, but the project became an artwork unto itself. I think partly because the project got so big but also because the photographs have their own kind of logic and completeness independent from the film. Cheryl ended up only using the photographs briefly in the film, but it became clear to me that they constituted something on their own. I worked hard to develop Cheryl's initial idea and make the *Archive* believable. It was a technically challenging work to make; every decision about how I photographed it and how everything was printed was made so that the project could be read as work from that time; it's a facsimile, and we knew it would only work if it could "pass."

Copeland: For me, what you've said has resonances with Hilton Als's book *The Women* and with the work of scholars like Saidiya Hartman who are trying to come up with different ways of narrating the past.[4] I also think that your work is an incredible spur for us as historians and critics to do the work of finding these subjects, bringing those different narratives into the frame.

Leonard: I think a lot of what we experience in the world does get constructed for us. There are habits, and there are forms or places where the money gets spent, where the energy gets put, and those things get a lot of attention. But we don't have to comply with that. You can look at whatever you want to look at. That's what we can do as artists and thinkers and historians—just as people! And we can also look at the artists we really want to look at. We can ask to see more of their work and push for those shows to be curated. Of course, we live in a certain kind of society and capitalism determines a lot of what gets seen. But we're us and we can come here and look at each other, and that's a good thing. Do you want to add to that, Huey?

Copeland: "YES! Preach, sister!" The only thing I would add is that it's by looking to other sites that are not privileged that you begin to develop a different kind of optic. So even things that are omnipresent can start to appear differently and we can begin to understand something about the deep structure of how those appearances are administered and produced for us. I think that awareness of one's own desires and how they're shaped and produced opens onto other libidinal economies to work with and against.

Leonard: Actually, we made a book of *You see* that provides several other "different optics" or potential readings. I made a work after it, a text composed of messages from a number of Niagara Falls postcards. The text engages with the possibilities of multiple voices.[5] But, visually, in that space? I mean, God, I don't even know how to describe the level of optical lunacy that was involved in getting that piece up on the wall. I mean, it's 4,000 postcards spread over 147 feet of wall and you can't really be wrong by a millimeter because that will travel . . .

Copeland: The idea of multiple optics and voices might lead us back to the topic of thinking about Niagara Falls as a feminist form and also trying to think about the archive as a kind of feminist form.

Leonard: I think the archive is a form we can take on and make feminist. The *Fae Richards* project was about taking on the preexisting form of the archive, and by extension, the whole idea of the academy, of how history is ordered and who gets the last word—what gets saved, what gets collected, how it gets presented and what disappears—and what gets lost in that process. So the work was about taking on the form of the archive and making it work for us. I love the idea of the guerrilla academy, of being able to take on the forms that are preexisting in the world and to make them work for us. In a way, that relates to what Gertrude Stein does with form. Stein asks about the world and our ever-changing individual experiences of it, yet it's always the same experience of living. The form in which she poses the question is in itself radical.

Copeland: This reminds me of conversations I've had with Gregg Bordowitz about Stein: he argues that she "writes with the drives." There's something about that description that resonates with *You see I am here after all.* There are words that recur in Stein's writing in a kind of circulatory movement, as in "a rose is a rose is a rose," a phrase that's getting at a particular object but that loops around it, denaturalizing the thing through its linguistic repetition.[6] It's not so much the object of the drive, but the completion of its circuit that propels the writing and desire along. I think the same thing is true of your work: the accretion of all these images in *You see I am here* is about trying to understand not just the images in their singularity, but the imperative to construct the same image over and over again. In bringing them together as a kind of archive, we can think about what that kind of ocular drive, in fact, is.

Leonard: Absolutely. I think the other thing I would add is that Stein never lets you get past the writing to just the story. You're always kept in the act of her writing, the act of your reading. That's something I'm interested in doing in my work: I constantly re-present the frame to ask you to look at the act of looking. That's what's interesting to me. Yes, there is a subject, a story, or a narrative, but there's also a consciousness of the frame and of language. And the fact that language can never quite jump over and substitute for experience. There's always a gap, the difference between my experience and yours. And that gap, it's a problem, but it's an interesting problem, it's where a lot of life happens: you and I trying to explain, to describe, that gap to each other.

Notes

1 Zoe Leonard and Cheryl Dunye, *The Fae Richards Photo Archive* (Artspace Books, 1997); Cheryl Dunye, *Watermelon Woman*, 16mm, 90 min. (Dancing Girl Productions, 1996); Zoe Leonard, *You see I am here after all* (Dia Art Foundation and Yale University Press, 2010).

2 On this score, see Ann Reynolds, "Curving into a Straight Line," in *You see I am here after all*, 154-74.

3 Johanna Burton, "In Your Eyes," *Parkett* 84 (2008): 60-65.

4 Hilton Als, *The Women* (Noonday Press, 1996); Saidiya Hartman, "Venus in Two Acts," *Small Axe: A Caribbean Journal of Criticism* 12, no. 2 (June 2008): 1-14. Two theatrical projects that are equally relevant to a discussion of *The Fae Richards Photo Archive* are Eleanor Antin, *Eleanora Antinova Plays* (Sun and Moon, 1994); and Lynn Nottage, *By the Way, Meet Vera Stark* (Theater Communications Group, 2013).

5 Zoe Leonard, "This is where I was," in Leonard, *You see I am here after all*, 8-21.

6 Gertrude Stein, "Sacred Emily" (1913), in *Geography and Plays* (University of Wisconsin Press, 1993), 187.

PART III

REFRACTING MEMORY

13

UNFINISHED BUSINESS AS USUAL

African American Artists, New York Museums, and the 1990s

On December 17, 2011, at New York's MoMA PS1, Clifford Owens staged one of the twenty-six performances whose documentary traces comprise *Anthology*, an ongoing project that at once aims to highlight and repair the historical record's elision of black performance art. On the day in question, his brief was to "restat[e]" a photograph by Lyle Ashton Harris, *Construct #10* of 1989, and then to recite a "memorized scholarly text on the image by Kobena Mercer" [see Fig. 10.6 on p. 138].[1] Such a restaging would seem straightforward enough, especially for a performer as fearless as Owens, simply requiring him to mimic the *contrapposto* stance, confrontational stare, dragged-out attire, and partial nudity of Harris's original photograph. During the performance, however, Owens found himself both resistant to assuming the pose and nostalgic for the era with which his predecessor's work has become synonymous. "What," he asked, "happened to the critical moment of the 1990s of identity politics? What's changed other than there being an asshole black President?"[2] More than one artist's frustrated aside, Owens's comments begin to suggest the ambitions of African American art in the 1990s, the promise of art world transformation it represented, and the many ways in which that "critical moment" has been forgotten, travestied, or indefinitely deferred.

The acclaim that greeted Ashton Harris's adamantly queer performative deconstructions of black masculinity, which coincided with the rise of multiculturalist and identarian discourses, provides a telling snapshot of the concerns of the day and the terms in which they were articulated. In his images, Mercer argues, "Harris not only parodies the existential anguish of inauthenticity that remains unsaid, and unspeakable, in the discourse of black cultural nationalism[,] . . . but camps up the categories of race and gender identity by positing a version of black masculine identity that mimics Judy Garland and a hundred other (white) feminine icons of met-

This essay first appeared in *Come as You Are: Art of the 1990s*, ed. Alexandra Schwartz (University of California Press and Montclair Art Museum, 2014), 24-32.

ropolitan gay sensibility."[3] At the same time, practitioners without such a fine ear for the visual exigencies of difference quickly found themselves called to account for their ostensible transgressions. The white male duo of Rob Pruitt and Jack Early, for example, were critically excoriated for their 1992 exhibition, *Red Black Green Red White Blue Project*, an eclectic mash-up of black artistic, vernacular, and historical posters formatted in interlocking geometric frames that lined a gallery space done up in shiny reflective metallics.[4] In the 1990s, such punning plays were deadly serious: gender was to be "troubled," patriarchy was to be unveiled, and subjects at the "margins" were poised not merely to contest, but to occupy the "center" of the art world.[5] Indeed, in the year that Ashton Harris made his *Constructs*, the *New York Times* critic Michael Brenson proclaimed that black artists were now finally taking their "place in the sun."[6]

Brenson's forecast accurately predicted one representational drift of the long decade from 1989 to 2001, when black artists and curators enjoyed unprecedented access to and visibility within mainstream US exhibition venues and discourses.[7] Consider the benchmarks that have come to define the critical fates and fortunes of black artists in New York during the period. In 1990, three "alternative" institutions—the Museum of Contemporary Hispanic Art, the New Museum of Contemporary Art, and the Studio Museum in Harlem—launched *The Decade Show: Frameworks of Identity in the 1980s*, which aimed both to right the wrongs of the past ten years and to set the standard of inclusion for omnibus exhibitions in the decade to come. Few institutions embraced this agenda more fiercely than the Whitney Museum of American Art as evidenced by changes in the racial composition of the artists featured in the museum's influential biennials. In contrast to the 1989 exhibition, which featured a sole black participant, the abstract sculptor Martin Puryear, the 1991 iteration included contributions by Nayland Blake, Glenn Ligon, Lorna Simpson, and Carrie Mae Weems, all artists, like Ashton Harris, associated with a semiotic approach to the black image.[8]

Even this gathering would pale in comparison to the hotly debated 1993 Whitney Biennial, which featured more than a dozen artists of African descent—about 15 percent of the total practitioners tapped for the exhibition—who worked in an even more expansive array of modes, from the wooden figurative sculptures of Alison Saar to the site-sensitive installations of Renée Green.[9] One of that biennial's co-curators, Thelma Golden, would go on to mount *Black Male: Representations of Masculinity in American Art* at the Whitney in 1994, the same year that *Time* magazine triumphantly announced the emergence of a "Black Renaissance" across the cultural field.[10] From one vantage, *Time*'s coverage represented a high-water mark in the general awareness of African American visual practice, one that was only matched sporadically during the rest of the decade. To be sure, black artists of various aesthetic proclivities were featured in subsequent Whitney biennials: Ellen Gallagher in 1995; MacArthur Genius Fellows Kerry James Marshall and Kara Walker in 1997; and Dawoud Bey, Thornton Dial, and Arthur Jafa in 2000, to name only those figures who come foremost to mind.[11] Arguably, however, it would not be until Golden's 2001 exhibition *Freestyle* at the Studio Museum in Harlem, which notoriously introduced the notion of "post-blackness," that a New York exhibition highlighting artists of color would again seize the mainstream imagination.[12]

A few things can be gleaned from this admittedly partial and partisan narrative that are of both sociological and artistic import. Many of the artists who garnered attention at the outset of the decade were championed because their work rhymed with and seemed to extend the concerns of white feminists such as Eleanor Antin, Mary Kelly, and Martha Rosler, whose poststructuralist approaches to the image had placed them at the forefront of advanced critical practice.[13] Of course, practitioners in the 1990s could also look back to the examples provided by at least two strands of influential African American art that had emerged in the 1970s: on the one hand, to the black conceptualism of Adrian Piper, David Hammons, and Charles Gaines; and on the other, to the irreverent formalism of Robert Colescott, Barkley Hendricks, and Howardena Pindell, whose work in painting and sculpture worked with and against the racialized biases of the most traditional of aesthetic media. Taken together, these tendencies opened up an "expanded field" of blackness that would enable subsequent artists to fully exploit the dialectical constitution of the racial sign.[14]

To mobilize the notion of the expanded field in a discussion of black artistic practices is to turn to an unlikely source: the art historian Rosalind Krauss's highly influential essay on a generation of European American sculptors whose three-dimensional work of the 1970s led her to generate a new grammar for the examination of aesthetic transformation.[15] By her lights, accounting for, say, Robert Smithson's *Spiral Jetty*, required an analysis of the ways that the "historically bounded" term "sculpture" and the antimonies on which it depends—architecture, landscape, and most salient, the structural negation of both—might be logically expanded, thereby generating a new set of relations between forms and establishing a gridded order over the site of what modernist sculpture had become, a "black hole in the space of consciousness" (Fig. 13.1).[16] The phrase is worth remembering: it speaks to the ways in which Krauss's essay casts the unintelligible, the ontologically absent, and the products of radical negativity in shadow so that they may be better brought to light. Now, in all likelihood, Krauss did not have the metaphorics of race in mind when she penned those words; she is, after all, the critic who, as the theorist Fred Moten reminds us, "once said something to the effect that there must not be any important black artists because, if there were, they would have brought themselves to her attention."[17]

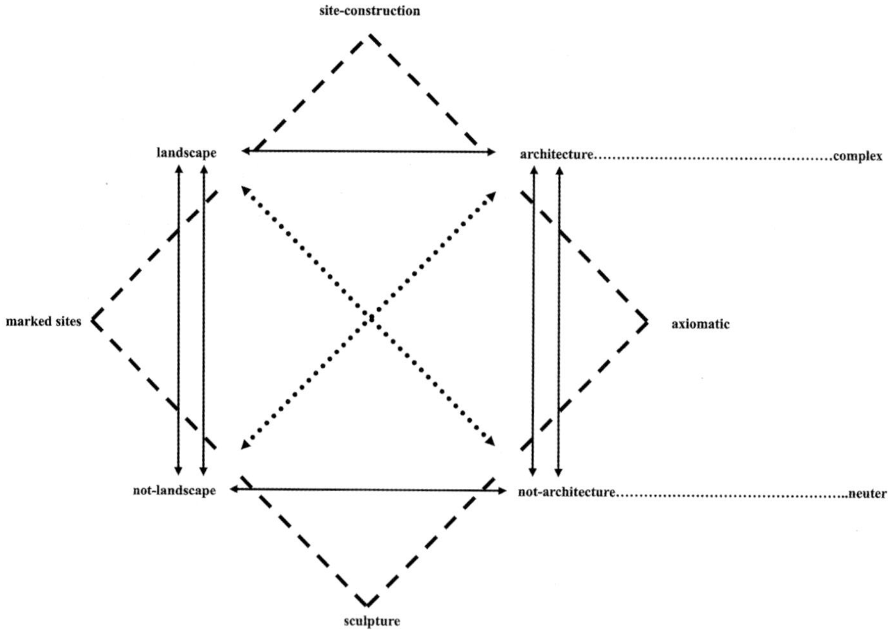

Figure 13.1
Diagram originally published in Rosalind Krauss, "Sculpture in the Expanded Field," *October* 8 (Spring 1979): 30–44.

Even more to the point is Krauss's actual engagement with the work of an African American artist, which was featured in a roundtable discussion on the 1993 Whitney Biennial published in the journal *October*. In that conversation, Krauss takes issue with the exhibition catalog's tendency—emblematized, for her, by Golden's essay, "What's White"—to rush to the signified of denotative social meaning rather than to pay heed to each artist's work on the material constitution of the signifier. Krauss's prime example is Lorna Simpson's installation *Hypothetical?*, in which a black-and-white photograph of a woman's lips faces off against an orderly array of brass instrument mouthpieces (Fig. 13.2). As the art historian notes, "On the wall bridging between the two 'grids,' there was a newspaper clipping about Tom Bradley being asked whether, were he not mayor of Los Angeles, would he, as a black man, be afraid after the Rodney King verdict. And he said, 'No, I wouldn't be afraid; I'd be angry.' I thought that was irrelevant to the piece, and not particularly interesting."[18] In these lines, as in "Sculpture in the Expanded Field," Krauss consigns everything outside of a recognizable order—meaning, affect, race—to a space of unintelligibility, the very site that African American artists have often been summarily consigned to or purposefully sought to occupy within visual representation.[19]

Krauss's dismissal, however, is more than merely indicative of the racialized lapses of the structuralist imaginary that has everywhere shaped art historical and critical discourse since the 1970s. Through its very

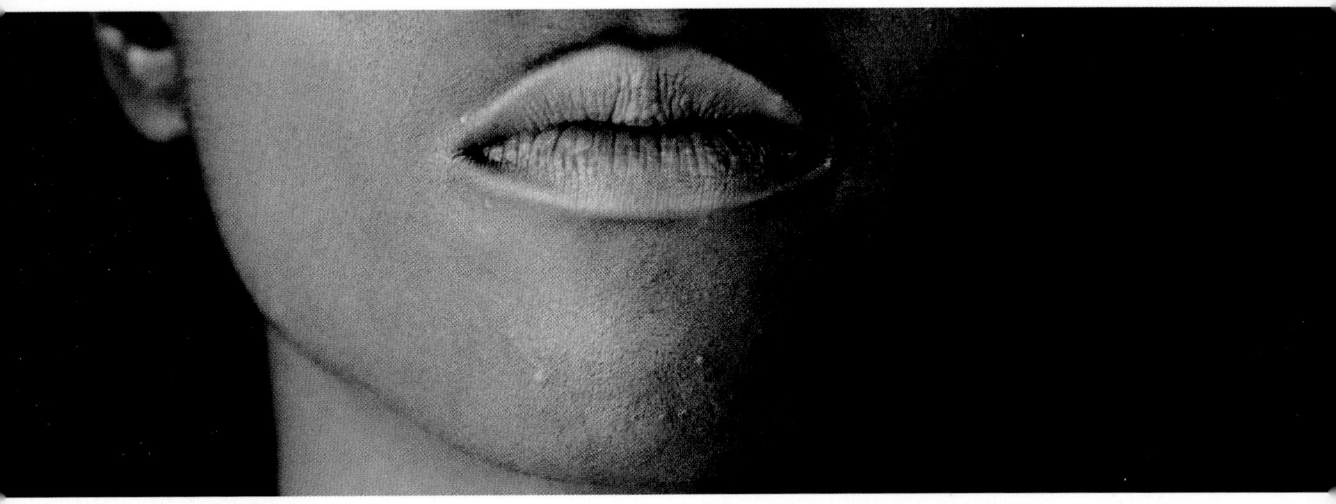

Figure 13.2
Lorna Simpson, *Hypothetical?*, detail, 1992. Photograph, newspaper clipping, instrument mouth pieces, sound, installation dimensions variable. © Lorna Simpson. Courtesy the artist and Hauser & Wirth.

blindness, her generative rhetoric brings into focus the historical production of blackness as a kind of negative space, which, as the philosopher Frantz Fanon teaches us, has no ontological resistance and so figures the ground over which the symbolic economies of white institutionality stretch their meaning.[20] In negotiating these discursive and structural conditions, African American artists have undertaken their own expansions of the visual field but with other sets of antimonies in mind: abstraction and figuration, stereotype and portraiture. Such pairings tack between a cryptic figuration of blackness—"a mastery of form [that] conceals, disguises, floats like a trickster butterfly in order to sting like a bee"—and its obverse strategy, the phaneric—defined as clearly visible to the naked eye—which entails "the deformation of mastery . . . a go(ue)rilla action in the face of acknowledged adversaries."[21] I borrow these terms from the literary theorist Houston Baker because they provide a set of coordinates—predicated on the play between concealment and advertisement, masking and revelation—that would come to shape possibilities for engagement with the matter of blackness in the 1990s. By working the intermediary spaces opened up between the cryptic and phaneric, artists found a way out of what the art historian Darby English has called the trap of "black representational space"—the cul-de-sac of "positive imagery," defined as not-cryptic and not-phaneric—and entered into a new regime of critical image making.[22]

The signal works of the 1990s, many gathered in this exhibition, make the case. In the art of Vik Muniz and Kerry James Marshall, the black fig-

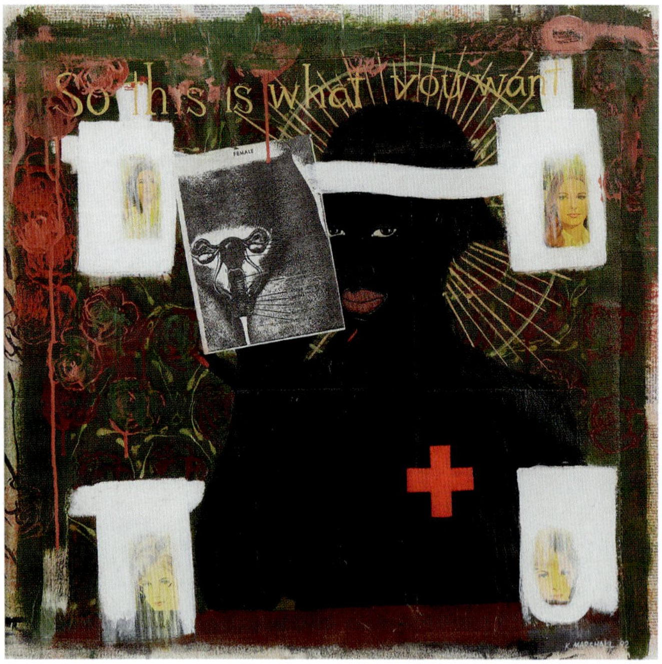

Figure 13.3
Kerry James Marshall, *So This Is What You Want?*, 1992. Acrylic and collage on canvas, 28 × 28½ in., 31¾ × 32¾ × 1⅝ in. framed. © Kerry James Marshall. Courtesy of the artist and Jack Shainman Gallery, New York.

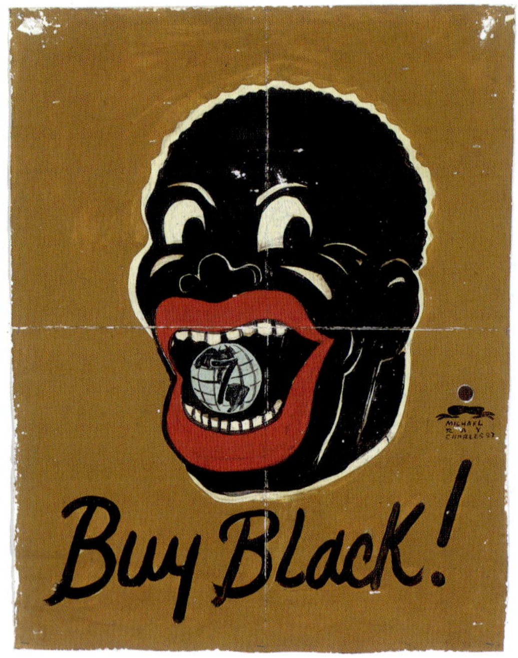

Figure 13.4
Michael Ray Charles, *(Forever Free) Buy Black!*, 1996. © Michael Ray Charles.

ure is given a revivified opacity and raised to the level of history painting, while in the works of Michael Ray Charles and Nikki S. Lee, the residues of racist stereotype are given fresh legs that are immediately undercut (Figs. 13.3, 13.4). Charles and Marshall, for instance, share an emphasis on dark painterly tonalities in the depiction of black skin, but the former artist unabashedly accedes to the logic of cliché in order to bring out the particularity of the stereotype's visual construction, whereas the latter produces individuated presences that nevertheless conform to a generic type. Other artists, such as Glenn Ligon, Julie Mehretu, Jason Rhoades, Ellen Gallagher, and Mendi + Keith Obadike would seek to downplay the figure, searching for alternative means—words, signs, and symbols—to invoke less the body of blackness than the material histories that continue to produce it as a site for the extraction of value [see Fig 2.3 on p. 31]. Emblematic in this regard is the Obadikes' 2001 sale of Keith's own "blackness" through the online retailer eBay, an absurd gesture that simultaneously underlines the intransigence of racial identity and the fungibility of those products emerging from it (Fig. 13.5). These modes of working, positioned between the phaneric, the cryptic, and their constitutive negations, effectively disarticulate the logics that have long defined the black image. In the Greenhead paintings of Laylah Ali (Fig. 13.6) and the cuts of Kara Walker [see Fig. 20.6 on p. 271], these antinomies are uncannily wed to occupy the complex axis, pointing us in the direction of African American art now: thoroughly deconstructed, cloaked yet aggressive, and still on the hunt for a promise of life in which difference might thrive.

Of course, the very success of these practitioners underlines how opportunities for black artists often depend upon tastemakers such as Golden who are positioned within powerful mainstream institutions and who can therefore create momentary openings for alternative voices that make freshly visible African American art's capacious range of procedures and positions. Such opportunities, however, are all too contingent and always under threat of reverting to business as usual. To wit, Harris, despite his initial acclaim, has yet to receive a mid-career retrospective at a major New York museum, while Pruitt has been critically resuscitated, thanks in part to his own clever rebranding and to the support of curators at Tate Modern who have insisted on restaging the very exhibition that once promised to consign him to the dustbin of history.[23] We might say, then, in response to Clifford Owens's second, searching question, that what has changed between the "critical moment" of the early 1990s and our post-everything present is not merely the discrediting of identity politics, but the recession of race as a vital organizing front or even a sociopolitical reality worth naming now that an illusion of black representation has been installed in art and politics.

Ironically, this all-too-familiar narrative was foretold before the 1990s even properly began. In her essay for *The Decade Show* catalog, curator Eunice Lipton succinctly diagnosed the modes of forgetting that continue to structure marginalized histories.

> Endlessly we—women, Asians, Latins, gays, blacks, Native Americans—search the public record for our histories and for the wholeness we felt—wasn't it just a minute ago? That wholeness that comes from satisfying work, good friends, a fortifying home. Or to put it another way, from seeing and being seen, speaking to and being responded to, feeling hungry and being fed. Just as the satisfaction accompanying that visibility begins to warm us, it vanishes. The timing of denial is always exquisite.[24]

We needn't look far to find confirmation not only of the erasure of black artists from official narratives but also of the continuing ghettoization of the aesthetic, discursive, and political implications of their work. For while the explosion of African American artistic practices in the 1990s can no longer be ignored, in the reigning surveys of modern and contemporary art, they are still couched as late arrivals relative to the defining artistic achievements of the past two hundred years, despite the fact that black

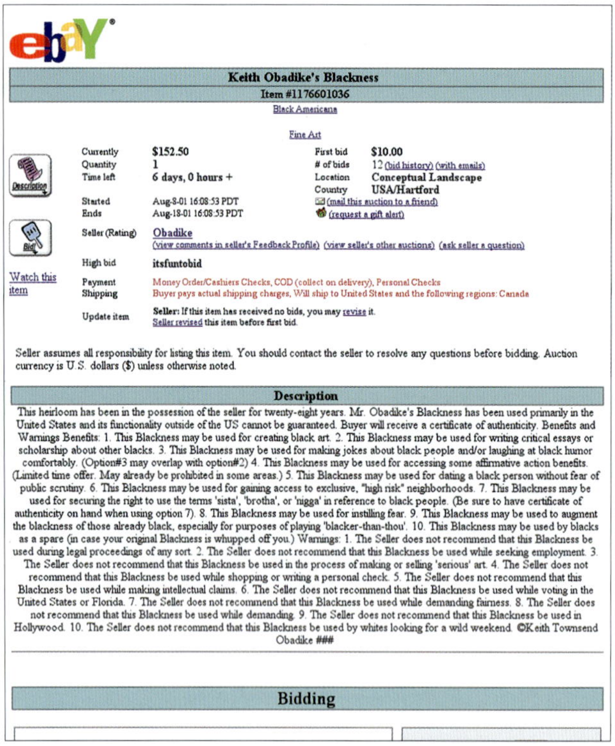

ebay

Keith Obadike's Blackness

Item #1176601036

Black Americana

Fine Art

Currently	$152.50	First bid	$10.00
Quantity	1	# of bids	12 (bid history) (with emails)
Time left	6 days, 0 hours +	Location	Conceptual Landscape
		Country	USA/Hartford
Started	Aug-8-01 16:08:53 PDT		(mail this auction to a friend)
Ends	Aug-18-01 16:08:53 PDT		(request a gift alert)

Description

Bid!

Watch this item

Seller (Rating) Obadike
(view comments in seller's Feedback Profile) (view seller's other auctions) (ask seller a question)

High bid itsfuntobid

Payment Money Order/Cashiers Checks, COD (collect on delivery), Personal Checks
Shipping Buyer pays actual shipping charges, Will ship to United States and the following regions: Canada

Update item **Seller:** If this item has received no bids, you may revise it.
Seller revised this item before first bid.

Seller assumes all responsibility for listing this item. You should contact the seller to resolve any questions before bidding. Auction currency is U.S. dollars ($) unless otherwise noted.

Description

This heirloom has been in the possession of the seller for twenty-eight years. Mr. Obadike's Blackness has been used primarily in the United States and its functionality outside of the US cannot be guaranteed. Buyer will receive a certificate of authenticity. Benefits and Warnings Benefits: 1. This Blackness may be used for creating black art. 2. This Blackness may be used for writing critical essays or scholarship about other blacks. 3. This Blackness may be used for making jokes about black people and/or laughing at black humor comfortably. (Option#3 may overlap with option#2) 4. This Blackness may be used for accessing some affirmative action benefits. (Limited time offer. May already be prohibited in some areas.) 5. This Blackness may be used for dating a black person without fear of public scrutiny. 6. This Blackness may be used for gaining access to exclusive, "high risk" neighborhoods. 7. This Blackness may be used for securing the right to use the terms 'sista', 'brotha', or 'nigga' in reference to black people. (Be sure to have certificate of authenticity on hand when using option 7). 8. This Blackness may be used for instilling fear. 9. This Blackness may be used to augment the blackness of those already black, especially for purposes of playing 'blacker-than-thou'. 10. This Blackness may be used by blacks as a spare (in case your original Blackness is whupped off you.) Warnings: 1. The Seller does not recommend that this Blackness be used during legal proceedings of any sort. 2. The Seller does not recommend that this Blackness be used while seeking employment. 3. The Seller does not recommend that this Blackness be used in the process of making or selling 'serious' art. 4. The Seller does not recommend that this Blackness be used while shopping or writing a personal check. 5. The Seller does not recommend that this Blackness be used while making intellectual claims. 6. The Seller does not recommend that this Blackness be used while voting in the United States or Florida. 7. The Seller does not recommend that this Blackness be used while demanding fairness. 8. The Seller does not recommend that this Blackness be used while demanding. 9. The Seller does not recommend that this Blackness be used in Hollywood. 10. The Seller does not recommend that this Blackness be used by whites looking for a wild weekend. ©Keith Townsend Obadike ###

Bidding

Figure 13.5

Mendi + Keith Obadike, *Blackness for Sale*, 2001. © Mendi + Keith Obadike.

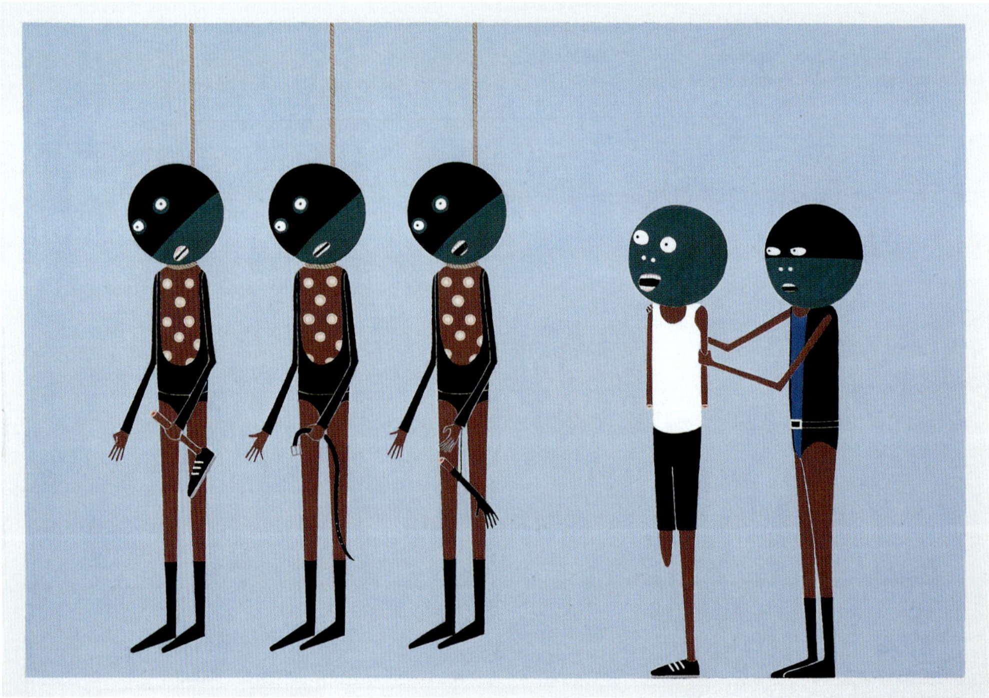

Figure 13.6

Laylah Ali, *Untitled (Greenheads)*, 2000. Gouache and pencil on paper. © Laylah Ali.

practitioners' work over this *longue durée* demands a radical recasting of what constitutes the aesthetic itself.[25] Indeed, the entire history of modern and contemporary art can be narrated as a story of engagement with and retreat from the vicissitudes of race and gender as manifested in the visual field, from Marie-Guillemine Benoist's *Portrait d'une négresse* (1800) up through Kara Walker's psychosexually charged silhouettes.[26]

There have been numerous terms to describe this yawning critical failure: Golden has called it "exclusion by self-imposed amnesia"; the cultural critic Michele Wallace has gone as far as to deem the visual itself a "negative scene of instruction" within black culture; and Howardena Pindell, ever forthright, has documented the evidence of "art world racism" in meticulous and damning detail.[27] Placed alongside Lipton's account, each of these ascriptions suggests the economies of denial and forgetting that are part and parcel of artistic discourse's fantasy of itself as a liberal space of gamesmanship. I would contend, however, that the structural underpinnings of the art world and its institutions must be seen as coterminous with the modern era's varied techniques for the "social reproduction" of "white supremacy." A few words on each of these phrases is in order. According to Barbara Laslett and Johanna Brenner, social reproduction "refers to the activities and attitudes, behaviors and emotions, responsibilities and relationships directly involved in the maintenance of life on a daily basis"; for Eduardo Bonilla-Silva, white supremacy encompasses "the racially based political regimes that emerged post-fifteenth-century" and that are now maintained "through institutional, subtle, and apparently nonracial means."[28]

The work of these adamantly feminist and antiracist sociologists provides a powerful explanatory framework. On the one hand, they allow us to understand how, despite substantive gains over the past five decades, black incomes in the 1990s remained well below those of any other ethnic group. Black populations continue to be produced as abject classes, both visually and materially, phenomena that continue to be confirmed, whether by the beating of Rodney King in '91 or the murder of yet another unarmed black male, Trayvon Martin, more than twenty years later. These episodes and accounts ask us to consider the insidious day-to-day personal and institutional biases that black subjects within the "racialized social system" of the art world aim to negotiate and make visible.[29] For if, as the artist and critic Lorraine O'Grady has argued, the rise of poststructuralist and feminist artistic discourses in the 1980s represented the consolidation of white supremacy, then our task now, as ever, must be to question all cultural formations that make use of blackness as a mode or a material.[30] It is with these imperatives in mind that we might revisit the art of the 1990s—asshole presidents aside—so that the endless task of imagining its future can properly, even joyfully, begin.

Notes

1 Huey Copeland, "*Mal d'Anthologie*: Clifford Owens and the Crises of African American Performance Art," in *Clifford Owens: Anthology*, ed. Christopher Y. Lew (MoMA PS1, 2012), 24 [reprinted in this volume, 129–47].

2 Copeland, "*Mal d'Anthologie*," 26.

3 Kobena Mercer, "Dark & Lovely: Black Gay Image-Making," in *Welcome to the Jungle: New Positions in Black Cultural Studies* (Routledge, 1994), 230.

4 For just one example of the almost globally damning response to the exhibition, see David Rimanelli, "Pruitt and Early: Leo Castelli Gallery," *Artforum* 30, no. 7 (March 1992): 101–3.

5 I refer here, of course, to Judith Butler, *Gender Trouble: Feminism and the Subversion of Identity* (Routledge, 1990); and less obviously to Amei Wallach's proclamation—in the context of a profile on Lorna Simpson—"The Outsider Is In," *New York Newsday*, September 19, 1990, which is entirely emblematic in its rhetorical framing of the rise of artists of color.

6 Michael Brenson, "Black Artists: A Place in the Sun," *New York Times*, March 12, 1989, http://www.nytimes.com/1989/03/12/arts/art-view-black-artists-a-place-inthe-sun.html.

7 For a thoroughgoing account of the first half of this period, on which the present essay implicitly depends, see Huey Copeland, *Bound to Appear: Art, Slavery. and the Site of Blackness in Multicultural America* (University of Chicago Press, 2013).

8 *1989 Biennial Exhibition* (Whitney Museum of American Art, 1989); *1991 Biennial Exhibition* (Whitney Museum of American Art, 1991).

9 *1993 Biennial Exhibition* (Whitney Museum of American Art, 1993).

10 See, respectively, *Black Male: Representations of Masculinity in Contemporary American Art* (Whitney Museum of American Art, 1994); Jack E. White, "The Beauty of Black Art," *Time*, October 10, 1994, 66–73.

11 *1995 Biennial Exhibition* (Whitney Museum of American Art, 1995); *1997 Biennial Exhibition* (Whitney Museum of American Art, 1997); *2000 Biennial Exhibition* (Whitney Museum of American Art, 2000).

12 For Golden, "post-black" was "a clarifying term that had ideological and chronological dimensions and repercussions. It was characterized by [a new generation of] artists who were adamant about not being labeled as 'black' artists, though their work was steeped, in fact deeply interested, in redefining complex notions of blackness." Thelma Golden, "Introduction: Post . . . ," in *Freestyle*, exh. cat. (New York: Studio Museum in Harlem, 2001), 14.

13 See Huey Copeland, "Lorna Simpson's Figurative Transitions," in *Bound to Appear*, 72–73.

14 See Kobena Mercer, "Tropes of the Grotesque in the Black Avant-Garde," in *Pop Art and Vernacular Cultures*, ed. Kobena Mercer (MIT Press, 2007), 139.

15 Rosalind Krauss, "Sculpture in the Expanded Field," in *The Originality of the Avant-Garde and Other Modernist Myths* (MIT Press, 1985), 276–90.

16 Krauss, "Sculpture in the Expanded Field," 279–80.

17 Fred Moten, *In the Break: The Aesthetics of the Black Radical Tradition* (University of Minnesota Press, 2003), 233.

18 See Krauss's comments in Hal Foster et al., "The Politics of the Signifier: A Conversation on the Whitney Biennial," *October* 66 (Fall 1993): 6.

19 For two thoroughgoing critiques of Krauss's essay that have directed my own, see Anne M. Wagner, "Splitting and Doubling: Gordon Matta-Clark and the Body of Sculpture," *Grey Room* 14 (Winter 2004): 30-32; Eve Meltzer, "The Expanded Field and Other, More Fragile States of Mind," in *Systems We Have Loved: Conceptual Art, Affect, and the Antihumanist Turn* (University of Chicago Press, 2013), 117-52.

20 Frantz Fanon, "By Way of Conclusion," in *Black Skin, White Masks*, trans. Charles Lam Markmann (Grove Press, 1967), 231.

21 Houston A. Baker Jr., *Modernism and the Harlem Renaissance* (University of Chicago Press, 1987), 50. Baker, in turn, derives his terms from the zoologist Hugh B. Cott's work on "allaesthetic" masking in the animal kingdom. See Hugh B. Cott, "Animal Form in Relation to Appearance," in *Aspects of Form: A Symposium on Form in Nature and Art*, ed. Lancelot Law Whyte (Pellegrini & Cudahy Publishers, 1951), 121-42.

22 Darby English, *How To See a Work of Art in Total Darkness* (MIT Press, 2007), 27-70.

23 On Harris's critical fortunes and the restaging of *Red Black Green*, see, respectively, Copeland, "*Mal d'Anthologie*," 26; and "Tate Modern to Stage 'Racist' Exhibition," *Independent*, September 26, 2009, http://www.independent.co.uk/arts-entertainrnent/art/news/tate-modern-to-stageracist-exhibition-1793497.html.

24 Eunice Lipton, "Here Today. Gone Tomorrow? Some Plots for a Dismantling," in *The Decade Show: Frameworks of Identity in the 1980s* (Museum of Contemporary Hispanic Art, New Museum of Contemporary Art, and the Studio Museum in Harlem, 1990), 19-20.

25 For just a few examples of this phenomenon, see Irving Sandler, *Art of the Postmodern Era* (Westview Press, 1996); Hal Foster, Rosalind Krauss, Yve-Alain Bois, and Benjamin H. D. Buchloh, *Art Since 1900: Modernism, Antimodernism, Postmodemism*, vol. 2, *1945 to the Present* (Thames and Hudson, 2005); Frances K. Pohl, *Framing America: A Social History of American Art* (Thames and Hudson, 2008).

26 See Huey Copeland, "In the Wake of the Negress," in *Modern Women: Women Artists at the Museum of Modem Art*, ed. Cornelia Buller and Alexandra Schwartz (Museum of Modern Art, 2010), 480-97 [reprinted in this volume, 265-85].

27 I refer, respectively, to Golden's comments in Huey Copeland, "Post/Black/Atlantic: A Conversation with Thelma Golden and Glenn Ligon," in *Afro Modern: Journeys in the Black Atlantic*, ed. Tanya Barson and Peter Gorschluter (Tate, 2010), 81; Michele Wallace, "Modernism, Postmodernism, and the Problem of the Visual in Afro-American Culture," in *Out There: Marginalization and Contemporary Cultures*, ed. Russell Ferguson et al. (MIT Press, 1990), 41; Howardena Pindell, "Art World Racism: A Documentation," *New Art Examiner* 16 (March 1989): 32-36.

28 Barbara Laslett and Johanna Brenner, "Gender and Social Reproduction: Historical Perspectives," *Annual Review of Sociology* 15 (1989): 382-404; Eduardo Bonilla-Silva, *White Supremacy and Racism in the Post-Civil Rights Era* (Lynne Rienner, 2001), 11, 12.

29 Bonilla-Silva, *White Supremacy and Racism in the Post-Civil Rights Era*, 12.

30 Lorraine O'Grady, "This Will Have Been: My 1980s," Public Lecture, Museum of Contemporary Art Chicago, March 15, 2012.

14

"LOOKING BACK AT *BLACK MALE*"

In Conversation with Thelma Golden and Hilton Als

Huey Copeland: As we're all well aware, the nationwide protests of the unpunished murders of two unarmed black men, Michael Brown and Eric Garner, have again brought into vivid focus how the black male is a perennial sight of fear and projection, policing and pathology, contestation and coalition. To look back at the exhibition *Black Male*, then, is in part to reconsider how those logics took shape at a particular moment in our history and how one institution and one visionary curator understood the ways that artists were trying to engage with or bypass the visual effects of those conditions in making innovative aesthetic forms (Fig. 14.1). So I thought we would start by trying to home in on that moment of the early '90s. Thelma, I wonder if you could speak about the circumstances and histories—personal, artistic, institutional—that led you to the exhibition as well as how Hilton became involved with it?

Thelma Golden: It would be completely disingenuous of me not to admit how much trepidation I had about this conversation tonight. And part of it has to do with the fact that you were going to ask me that question and many more which in many ways I have yet to fully myself understand and be able to answer, because, really, how did *Black Male* come to be? Well, through the great privilege but also the great challenge of understanding who I would be as a curator at the Whitney Museum in 1993 or 1994, it became clear to me that I could chart a path to open up some broader conversations. I knew that that's really what my work had to be, and so *Black Male* really started as very episodic conversations with artists about their work, with the backdrop of all that was happening in that period. It happened as a result of my own relationship to cultural specificity and exhibition making in museums. I know that there will be a time when I'll be able to have a much more direct sense of how this exhibition really happened,

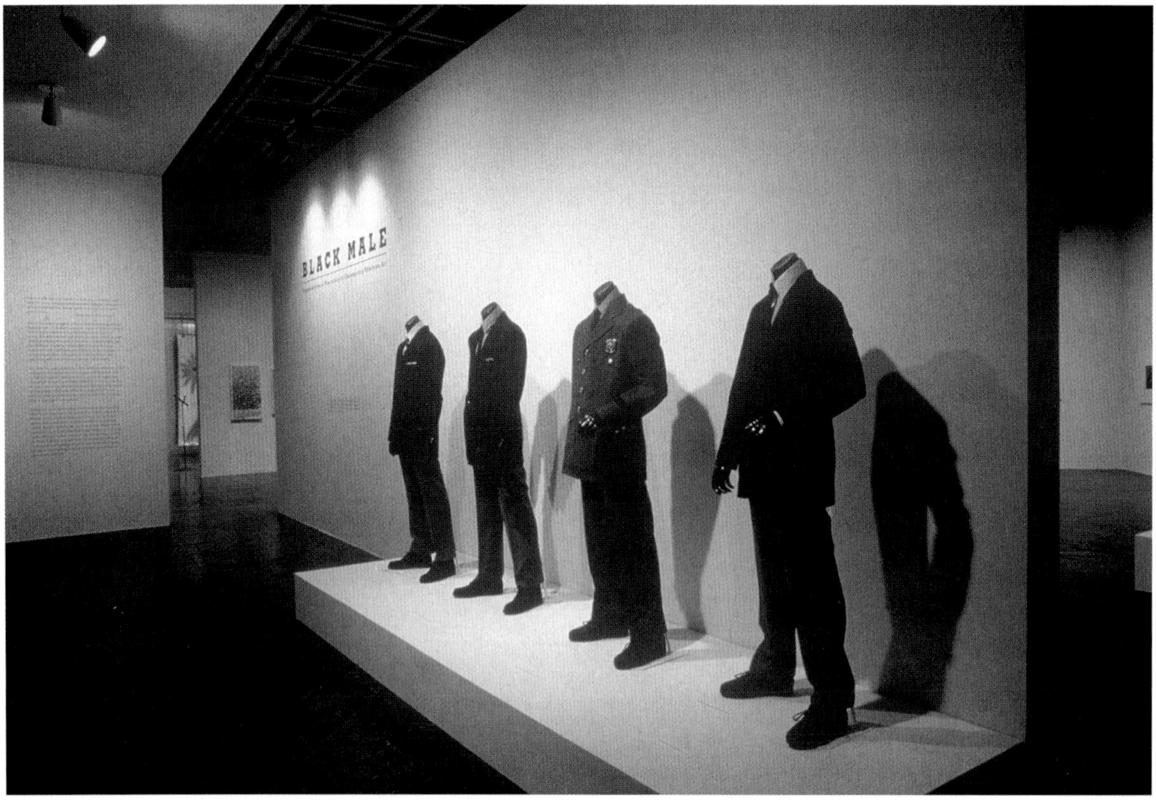

Figure 14.1
Installation view of *Guarded View*, 1991 by Fred Wilson in *Black Male: Representations of Masculinity in Contemporary American Art* (November 10, 1994–March 5, 1995). Wood, paint, steel and fabric. Whitney Museum of American Art, New York; gift of the Peter Norton Family Foundation, 97.84a-d. © Fred Wilson, courtesy Pace Gallery. Photograph by Geoffrey Clements. Digital image © Whitney Museum of American Art / Licensed by Scala / Art Resource, NY.

but now it still continues to feel like the collision of a million different ways in which art works, artists, and ideas came together in an exhibition. How Hilton got involved is that then, like now, my only way to understand a lot of what I'm doing is to hear the echo of my voice in Hilton's projection back to me. So I say something, and Hilton, the great writer, editor, usually says it back better than I said it myself.

Hilton Als: You might see me sort of start crying during this conversation, because I'm remembering one of the first times we ever met. Thelma saw what I was writing, not just in *Artforum*, but in the [*Village*] *Voice*. She knew that I spent many evenings at the Odeon misbehaving, and she had me meet her at the Odeon. The first thing she said was this idea about *Black Male*, and I said, "Oh, you should just paint the galleries red, black, and green." And it was the first thing that we said.

Golden: Exactly.

Als: She laughed and said, "I don't know if they'll do that, but let's go!" And that's how it started.

Golden: It is, exactly, exactly. Hilton had written really powerfully about many of the artists who would form the base of the work in *Black Male*. Actually, a lot of my understanding of those artists came from reading Hilton's writing about them in the *Village Voice*. In the late '80s as a student in Northampton, Massachusetts, waiting for the *Voice* to come, Hilton's writing provided my sense of the terrain that really did become what *Black Male* was.[1] But really, in the very beginning, it felt like in those nights at the Odeon with you—and your socks and your Birkenstocks and your coat over your pajamas—I began to work out not just the ideas for *Black Male*, but many of the ideas that have informed my work since. We were talking through the possibility of what it could mean to make an exhibition like this, to present artists in this way, to look at the complicated spaces and say, "Is there a way in a museum context that this could happen?"

Als: We have to tell the children that the language didn't exist. I mean, I was writing stuff, but there really was no core curriculum. There was no discussion. All I could do was describe what I was seeing and responding to. What Thelma was doing was completely profound and radical, because she was doing it in an institution, in an art institution, and in New York. I mean, these were three levels of experience that I had not encountered before. How do you make the institution work with radicalism, and also, how do you make the institution new when the institution is asking for a new image of itself? So that's a three-tiered wedding cake that she gave New York. Thelma knew how the institution worked and, within the institution, how to make various conversations happen with permission.

Golden: Well, I was actually looking at how I could begin to contribute to an art history that was slightly different from the art history I was given or taught. In many ways for me *Black Male* really was an exhibition that began and centered around Adrian Piper, David Hammons, and Robert Colescott. That was sort of the holy trinity for me, and I wanted to imagine that if I started there, I was going to possibly create a new pathway for thinking about black artists and their work through a conceptual lens. And so really, that was a beginning, but it was a beginning that was made necessary by the fact that there were actual works of art being made by my peers: the artists of our generation that really made this show seem completely necessary and possible.

Als: One of the things that I remember, now, is that so much of it was pointing toward the future. When you go to a large exhibition or survey—when they say from 1987 to 2014—they mean that, and it stops there. One of the things that I remember so well about *Black Male* was that it was like looking at a vista, at something that was opening, as opposed to something that was closing. That was the first time I'd ever really felt that in a museum.

Copeland: That's absolutely amazing. I think for someone like me who was eighteen when the show opened; I mean, to have that catalog . . . *this* was the future. It was constructing a discourse to which I would belong and really marked a shift in terms of what would be possible for me. A whole generation of scholars and thinkers would emerge with *Black Male* as our bible. And I think that's one of the things that's so fascinating about the exhibition and how it unfolded—that it also resulted in this book, which is a landmark anthology that people return to endlessly. I wonder if you could talk a little bit more about that kind of fantasized audience. Were there specific constituencies that you were hoping to bring to the Whitney and somehow change the culture of the institution?

Golden: Here's the truth of it, and this is why it's so complicated to talk about this now, because it's so hard for me to really touch and feel how it felt then, but here's the reality: I was twenty-seven when I made that exhibition. This could have been my first and last curatorial project, and my attitude was, I was getting everything in that I could: everything, everyone, right? Everyone was going to come see it. I could not trust the potential of this moment. Now, what is amazing, twenty years later, is all that has happened since. But I have to make you understand that on, say, November 1, 1994, I could not imagine what November 10, the day when this show opened to the public, was going to be like, because there was no context to understand it. I was just working, and the truth is I've been working ever since. That's also why I haven't had the time to have this backward glance, because there's still a whole lot of work to be done. The exhibition also took on a life of its own, a life far bigger than I would have ever imagined, in the way in which it played out not just here in New York City but also when it went to L.A. in the winter of 1995.

Copeland: Yeah, there was a huge reaction, including a voluminous body of criticism that keeps on growing. But I think so often the conversation about the show focuses on the "controversy" around it without actually thinking through the specific curatorial intelligence that was on view.

Golden: Well, the word that was used to talk about the exhibition the most was *controversial*, which used to bother me until it became a PSAT question. Yeah, I'm a PSAT question. And controversial is the answer. So here's a bit of the curatorial thinking. One of the things that was very clear early on,

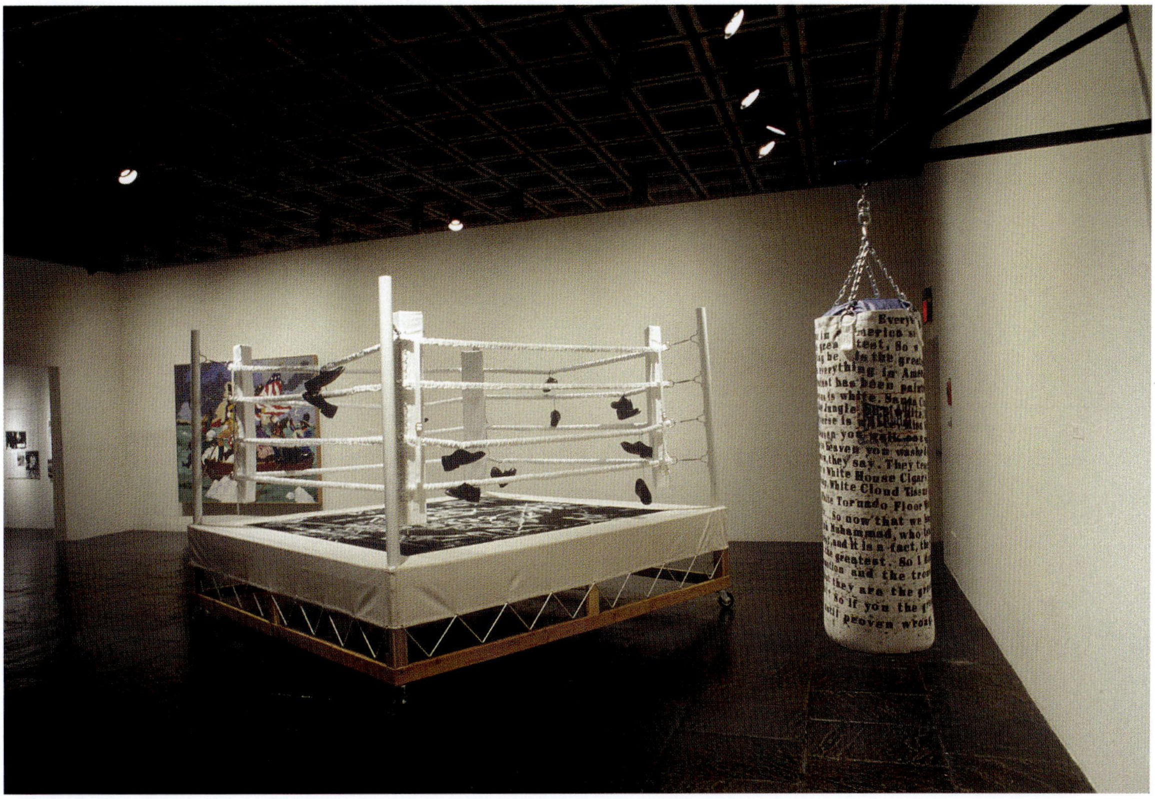

Figure 14.2
Installation view of *Black Male*. Left to right: Gary Simmons, *Step in the Arena*, 1994, Whitney Museum, 95.83.a-g, and Glenn Ligon & Byron Kim, *Rumble Young Man, Rumble (Version #1)*, 1993, paint stick, canvas punching bag, and metal. Whitney Museum of American Art, N.Y. Photograph by Geoffrey Clements. Digital image © Whitney Museum of American Art / Licensed by Scala / Art Resource, NY.

when I would say to people asking, "what are you making a show about?" I would say, "A show about black masculinity in contemporary American art." And people assumed that exhibition would only include the work of black male artists—either people wanted it to be that or they assumed it was that (Fig. 14.2). So, some of the curatorial thinking right away was, could I make an exhibition about race and about identity, but through a range of artists? It was therefore critically important to me that Leon Golub stood alongside Robert Colescott; that Jeff Koons was in the exhibition alongside Lorna Simpson, Glenn Ligon, and Carrie Mae Weems; and that the exhibition looked at artists like Mel Chin or Byron Kim through the lens of how their work was involved in this conversation.

Als: This is just a footnote, but what was emotionally and aesthetically very important to me, that I saw Thelma do intuitively, was this. Here's the thing, Huey. A lot of black men are not claimed in this country. We don't have fathers. This is the assumption, right, that we don't have fathers to learn from and that we come up like mushrooms somehow and that there's no tradition for your masculinity. There's no tradition for your blackness. There's no tradition for your intellection. There's no tradition for your ability to look and talk about and articulate where you come from. So what Thelma did was choreograph the history so that people could see that there were connections and histories between not only black artists, but perforce black men, and that's, for me, the profundity of the exhibition. What she had that a lot of people didn't have was an incredible father herself. She had been fathered beautifully, and what she gave these artists, basically the younger artists, was a tradition and a father. And so when you walked into that show as a black man/boy/child, you understood that you had a tradition, and it was one of the first instances in a cultural context where you actually saw that you belonged to someplace, and that's really important to say. Now the amusing part is how Thelma made me work. She did something that was quite extraordinary in terms of the rigor of the book. Artists and academics are not used to being edited. And I edited people. She gave me the permission, as a thinker, to say, "This can be better." She was making a visual tradition, that then was an emotional and intellectual tradition, but she also made a language tradition in the book. There had to be a book that was a memory of this, that was solid, the thing that people refer to. So that was another way in which she protected me and took care of me and the writers: by allowing me to be rigorous with them.

Copeland: It's been really striking for me, in looking back over some of the criticism, how there's this persistent anxiety on the part of black male critics with a range of ideological positions, from those who are, like, the positive-image police to people who seem to be going into the show and expecting themselves to appear.[2] And I think, Hilton, what you're saying is actually such an interesting, productive counterpoint to that. Because it's not about the show offering a kind of mirror or an image of oneself but about it providing a context and tradition to understand not only how one, as a black male, might be visually produced but also the many ways that one can work with and through that kind of visual production.

Als: I had the pleasure of teaching at Smith, Thelma's alma mater. I would always tell the students at the beginning of each semester, "Please, cherish this place. You're in the majority. Being in the majority makes you feel better. No one will care when you go out into the world, but you will know that you were in the majority of something." I can spot a Smith woman a mile away. They walk into that room and that's their room. What *Black Male* did was it put it in the majority. Regardless of color of the artists, the subject was the majority.

Golden: You know, I decided I wanted to be a curator when I was fifteen years old. It was my junior year in high school, and I didn't just say I wanted to be a curator. I said I wanted to be a curator at the Whitney Museum. Okay? Very specific. And those high school years in the '80s—going to the Whitney, seeing those exhibitions, seeing those biennials—formed my sense of what I wanted to be as a curator. So, when thinking about making the exhibition, I was not just thinking about the art and the artist, but I really was invested in audience. I was invested in an audience that was me; the me that thought about the museum as a space that was filled with wonder and inspiration, that I then had the opportunity to work in. When I think back to that moment, the opening of *Black Male*, literally that night; Hilton, do you remember that night? I can think of few other moments where I felt a shift in the culture. It felt almost like it began to position what this future might be, what it might look like, what it might feel like. The party after *Black Male* still remains the best party I ever went to in my life.

Als: Huey, it really was something where you are in a room and you can feel levitation happening. I want to say that, and I want to switch gears slightly and talk about black femaleness. One day, I was going to meet a great friend of mine and I left the Whitney. Walking from the Whitney to Second Street or Eighty-sixth Street up Madison Avenue, I found myself crying, weeping, and when I got to my friend he said, "What's wrong with you?" And I said, "In all my life, I've never seen a black woman take space like this and not worry about it." I have never seen a black woman take the arena and walk around the arena and make it her own, and that's another part of this very emotional, for me, occurrence in the world. David Ross gave her this space, and she took it. I had never seen that in my life. So there you go.

Golden: Here's what it was, though. The Whitney had this really important history. The Whitney had a history with African American artists. The Whitney through its early days in the Studio Club but all the way to the '60s was an institution that had to reckon with larger cultural conversations. I spent hours in the Whitney library in those years reading—in the archive—the volumes of correspondence that went on as the Whitney curators of that era, the late '60s into the '70s, reckoned with the changes in the world that required thinking; I also saw their answers to those questions in the many exhibitions that happened at the Whitney in the late '60s and the early '70s. You know, Jacob Lawrence's exhibition; I used to look at the press photos from that opening, again a moment when that space was so beautifully occupied by this vision.[3] I really felt like what I was doing was actually just giving light to the possibility that had already been created in the institution and then, quite possibly, that would continue to be. It didn't feel—and it still doesn't—it didn't feel singular at all. It felt like it was part of this greater history, and I felt very privileged in that moment that it could so wholly come from my ideas.

Als: No, no, no, there was nothing self-conscious about it at all. You were just doing it, and I was observing you do it. That's what I'm saying. But I have a question for you, Thelma. I only knew a few of the artists personally, so what was the response of the other artists when artists saw themselves in this context? Do you remember having conversations with some artists?

Golden: What I remember is that almost all of the conversations with artists in the exhibition usually began with their sense of surprise, while actively wanting to be a coconspirator with me in what this exhibition could be. And that's what was so amazing about it—that every single artist, every conversation about people's individual contribution of work, also took into account what was the great responsibility we all felt to what the dialogue around this exhibition would be, and that was fantastic. From a curatorial perspective, I can't think of any other project I've made that had that sense of collectivity to it, because I don't think any of us knew what that moment was going to be. That was exciting but also incredibly instructive to me. It really defined the way in which I understood I would have to be a curator moving forward.

Copeland: All that is so rich, and I think it really helps expand—in many ways, explode—the understanding we have of the show and its context. There's a sense in which, because of the timing of the show in L.A. as O.J. was happening, those became the optics: a kind of overdetermined conversation. But people have been able to take up *Black Male* and use it in a variety of ways. I think, as Hilton mentioned, the exhibition was an important model of a black woman taking space but also, I think, of a powerful feminist curatorial vision, which we see throughout your work. And in thinking about that, Hilton, I wonder if there's a way in which this sort of conversation around the show, and working on it, started to inform what you were doing in *The Women*?[4]

Als: Wow, that's a very interesting question. Thelma more than implied that it was okay to get yours—she was there when I got the review of *The Women*. And Huey was there. He was just starting to intern at the Whitney, and it came through the fax machine, and Thelma just beamed because she was reading it as it was coming through, and she was beaming because she knew that it was a very complicated thing for me to step up to myself. I think it was by example that *Black Male* influenced *The Women*, showing that you could do it. You could make the book. You could make the exhibition. You could make the catalog. It was do-it-yourself with other people, if that makes any sense at all. I just wanted to read, Huey, this little paragraph from the catalog because it really does apply to what I've been saying about the interlocked-ness of Thelma and black masculinity. This is Greg Tate, and his essay begins:

> So your soul sister, the curator, invites you to write an essay on Black Male genius and like a fool you take up the invitation, knowing it's a fool's mission on a par with trying to explain wave particle theory to a medieval alchemist, or more pointedly, like trying to explain swing to the severely unswung, funk to the arid or mad flavor to the undeaf, dumb, and bland. Writer and performer Gil Scott-Heron once identified himself as a bluesologist, a person involved with the "science of how things feel." G. W. Hegel could imagine nothing like the blues or Scott-Heron when he wrote the "Phenomenology of Mind," but he and Scott-Heron are brothers of the same mind when it comes to empirical wisdom. In black culture, as the scribe Bunny Wailer once put it, he who feels it knows it.[5]

So, in other words, there was no language. There was no economy of means to describe this. And I think, to me, Greg's essay was the hallmark of the catalog because of the piece's beautiful articulation about the struggle to say, "I don't know how to say this, but I'm saying it."

Copeland: In trying to find a way toward a conclusion, Thelma, I'm wondering if you could speak about the way in which *Black Male* became a crucible and launching pad and how your curatorial vision shifted in relationship to that moment.

Golden: Well, I say it over and over because I have to keep saying it to myself; remember this was the first fully formed exhibition I made as a curator. And so, in a way, it actually freed me. I often said if *Black Male* is the only show I ever made I would still feel I had made a curatorial contribution. And that's just because it did have this life that was so much bigger than the one I imagined for it, but that came very quickly with it. Because it happened that way, I was the controversial curator. That does give you a lot of freedom. It also created, for me, the opportunity to look at many things without them having to be determined, right? I created an incredible amount of freedom for myself, and that was amazing. Though what is perhaps most important to me about what *Black Male* created really is embodied, Huey, in you. Huey was an intern at the Whitney Museum in 1995. The reality was that when Huey applied to be an intern, he wrote his little cover letter and spoke about the impact of *Black Male*, both based on the fact that he was clearly brilliant and based on my ego. I just thought, well, hire him. Huey then came and was my intern and engaged deeply, because in those days—pre–cell phone, pre-email—my whole life was conducted on the phone. So, in those days, when the phone would ring and it was Hilton or Glenn or Lorna, the person who picked up the phone was Huey. It was very clear to all of us in that moment: you were seeing yourself as part of the dialogue that we had been a part of. And the thing I think of as the greatest gift of *Black Male* is that it did create this space that I see all of you—you and many of you who are sitting here tonight—occupying now with so much fierce courageous intellectual energy. That more than anything fills me with a great sense of both pride and gratitude, that I had the opportunity to be able, in a small way, to make that space which has become so much bigger, so much bigger because of all of you. That's what it's about.

Copeland: Well, now you're going to make me cry. I think this is the moment that we open it up to questions from the audience.

Notes

On December 14, 2014, I interviewed the curator Thelma Golden and the writer Hilton Als for "Looking Back at *Black Male*," a public program sponsored by the Whitney Museum of American Art Education Department to mark the twentieth anniversary of the exhibition's original run (November 10, 1994–March 5, 1995): https://www.youtube.com/watch?v=q9gQdRIKuhw. In this excerpt, which has been footnoted and edited by Lauren Taylor with input from the speakers, we refer to cultural events that framed the exhibition such as the automotive police pursuit and eventual arrest of the African American former football star O. J. Simpson on suspicion of murder on June 17, 1994. We also make frequent reference to the groundbreaking catalog that accompanied the exhibition, *Black Male: Representations of Masculinity in Contemporary Art* (Whitney Museum of American Art; distributed by Harry N. Abrams, 1994).

1 See, for example, Hilton Als, "Jean-Michel Basquiat, 1960–88," *Village Voice*, August 30, 1988, https://www.villagevoice.com/jean-michel-basquiat-1960-88/.

2 For the strongest and most compelling critique in this vein, see Okwui Enwezor, "Whose Body? 'Black Male: Representations of Masculinity in Contemporary American Art,'" *Third Text* 31, vol. 9 (1995): 67–70.

3 See Milton W. Brown, *Jacob Lawrence* (Whitney Museum of American Art, 1974).

4 Hilton Als, *The Women* (Noonday Press, 1996).

5 Greg Tate, "'He is truly free who is free from the need to be free': A Survey and Consideration of Black Male Genius," in *Black Male: Representations of Masculinity in Contemporary Art*, 111.

15

MAKING BLACK FEMINIST ART HISTORIES

Over the past decade, I have had the pleasure of discussing Renée Ater's 2003 article on Meta Warrick Fuller's *Ethiopia Awakening* in classes focused on twentieth-century sculpture, histories of modernism, and African American cultural politics [see Fig. 20.11 on p. 279].[1] Such range underlines the expansive address of the artist's work as well as the scholar's vital framing of it: in homing in on *Ethiopia Awakening*, the signature sculpture of a long-neglected black female artist, Ater's text subtly challenges art historical discourse while holding out a productive model of it, one that confronts rather than suppresses the importance of race and gender in the making of modern American culture.

Fuller's *Ethiopia Awakening* is a painted plaster depicting a standing woman in Egyptian-inspired attire—complete with mummy wrappings—who appears to be emerging from a deep sleep. The significance of this iconography has not been lost on other scholars of African American art who have recognized the work, albeit glancingly, as a signal achievement of the Harlem Renaissance that offers an innovative instantiation of black international consciousness (29n3).[2] Ater's article builds on, deepens, and corrects these earlier readings by nuancing our understanding of Fuller's particular brand of cultural nationalism, providing a robust sense of the historical context that informed it, and detailing, for the first time, how the sculpture was activated in a number of pageants and performances as a model and surrogate for the black female body (25–28).

As such, "Making History" deftly combines close attention to the formal dynamics of the sculpture with meticulous archival research (13, 18). Just as important, Fuller's work, as narrated by Ater—in her essay, subsequent book, and the dissertation from which both texts emerged—opens onto much-needed conversations about black feminist aesthetics and the centrality of African diasporic female bodies to avant-garde innovation.

This article first appeared in *American Art*, 30th Anniversary Issue: 30 Invited Authors Celebrate 30 Years, 31, no. 2 (Summer 2017): 27-29. https://doi.org/10.1086/694053.

For, as I have argued elsewhere—licensed, in part, by Ater's research—Western modernism has time and again taken up black female bodies as avatars of radical difference, enabling artists on all sides of the color line to push against the limits of representation, whether Édouard Manet in *Olympia* (1863) or Cindy Sherman in her *Bus Riders* (1976).[3] Fuller's practice can be understood both to sit within and to contest this tradition, especially if we follow Ater's lead across her writing as she unravels the sculpture's relationship to other sights and scenarios.

To wit: whereas in *Ethiopia* the remarkable boundness of the work seems intended to protect the figure from the violence of an objectifying gaze, in an earlier piece, Fuller confronted and thematized the actual violence to which black women have historically been subjected. The sculpture in question is *In Memory of Mary Turner: A Silent Protest Against Mob Violence* (Fig. 15.1), and any attempt to come to grips with it must turn to Ater's earlier scholarship. As she explains in her 2000 dissertation, the subtitle of the sculpture refers to the New York "Negro Silent Protest Parade," organized by the National Association for the Advancement of Colored People (NAACP) in July 1917 in recognition of the spate of murders that had taken tens of black lives in Waco, Memphis, and St. Louis in the previous year. Collapsing time and space, Fuller took the parade as a guide for her homage to the work's eponymous martyr, a tenant farmer who dared to speak out after her husband was lynched by a mob in Georgia on May 19, 1918. In retribution, Turner, then eight months pregnant, was hung from a tree, burned, and disemboweled before her body was riddled with bullets. In her sculptural response—the earliest known American artwork to depict a lynched black woman—Fuller at once refuses and registers this horrendous violence, rendering a female figure who holds her absent child in her arms, her dress giving way to the tortured hands and faces that rise like flames around the sculpture's base.[4]

Fuller never exhibited the sculpture but kept it above her desk. The small plaster sketch served, then, as a memento and a memorial but was also, I think, imagined as a monument: the work's patina of bronze paint suggests as much, and its downturned face would have offered a fitting shelter and destination for those marchers in the NAACP parade. In her 2011 book, *Remaking Race and History*, Ater argues that the artist "transformed" this work "into a positive pan-Africanist statement" with *Ethiopia*.[5] Taken together, the pair of sculptures—one miniature, private, and engulfed in flames; the other life-size, public, and swathed in bandages—outline a black feminist method that aims to both register and disrupt the violence enacted on black women in life and in representation.

Like Fuller's work on the black female figure, Ater's approach has unfolded in time, leading to the ambitious agenda for black and women's art history spelled out in *Remaking Race*.[6] Throughout her scholarship, she emphasizes the performative interventions that activated and inspired

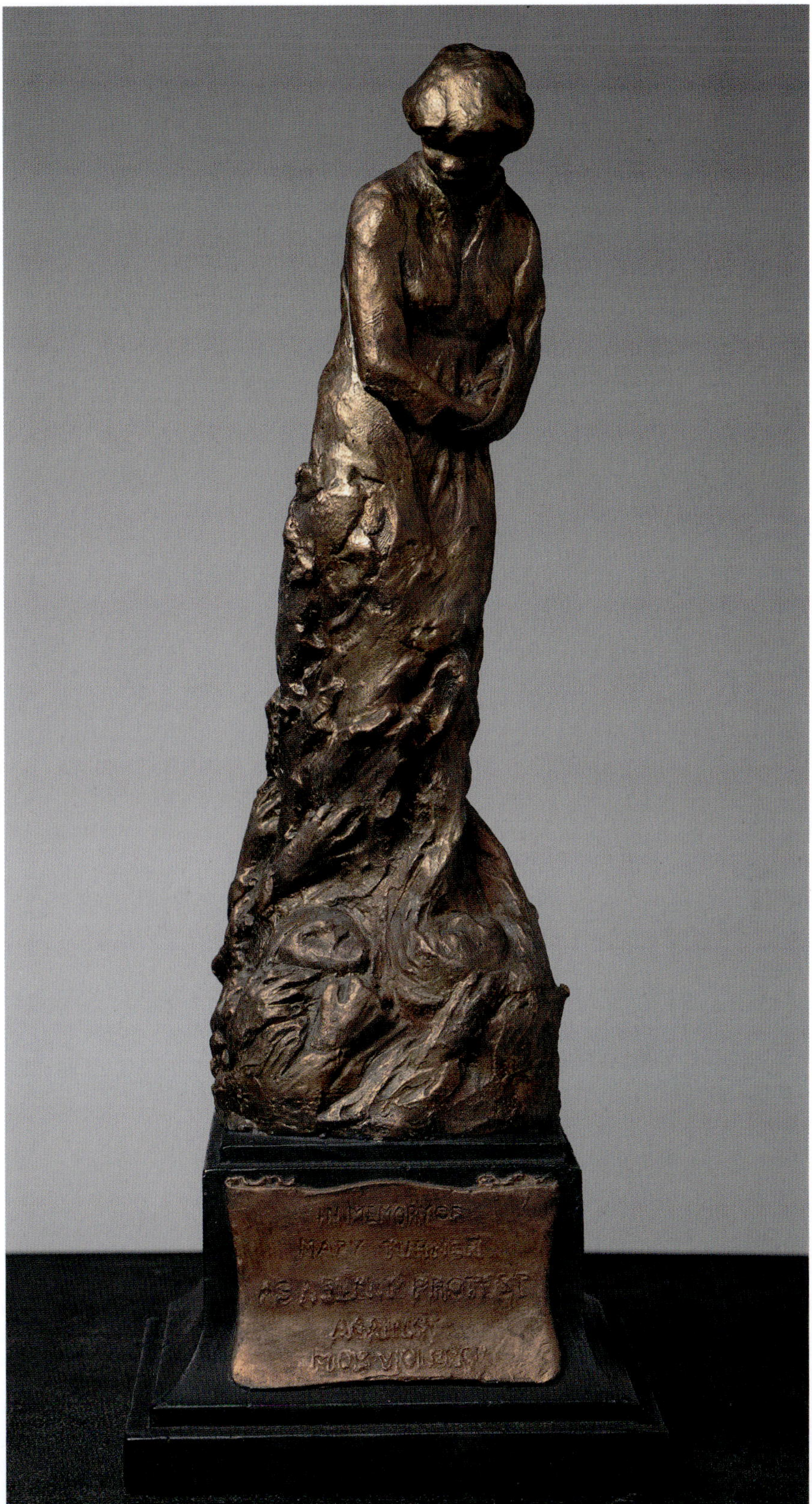

Figure 15.1

Meta Vaux Warrick Fuller, *In Memory of Mary Turner: A Silent Protest Against Mob Violence*, 1919. Painted plaster. Museum of African American History, Boston | Nantucket.

Fuller's art: the pageants and protests come alive on the page, allowing us to consider them as aesthetic interventions in their own right. "Making History" can thus be seen as one moment in an art historical trajectory that asks us not only to take black women's art seriously but also to pay heed to what Hannah Feldman calls "image tactics," those means employed by marginalized subjects to make themselves visible within the public sphere.[7] What Ater's work suggests is that in time and with effort, "American art" itself can be transformed if the fullness of black women's lives and cultural practices are placed at the fore.

Notes

1 Renée Ater, "Making History: Meta Warrick Fuller's *Ethiopia*," *American Art* 17, no. 3 (Fall 2003): 12-31; hereafter cited in the text in parentheses.

2 Ater cites the following precedents to her study: David Driskell, "The Flowering of the Harlem Renaissance: The Art of Aaron Douglas, Meta Warrick Fuller, Palmer Hayden, and William H. Johnson," in *Harlem Renaissance: Art of Black America* (Studio Museum in Harlem and Harry N. Abrams, 1987), 108; Judith Wilson, "Hagar's Daughters: Social History, Cultural Heritage, and Afro-U.S. Women's Art," in *Bearing Witness: Contemporary Works by African American Women Artists* (Spelman College and Rizzoli International, 1996), 106; and Richard J. Powell, "Re/Birth of Nation," in *Rhapsodies in Black: Art of the Harlem Renaissance* (Hayward Gallery and Institute of International Visual Arts, 1997), 18.

3 Huey Copeland, "In the Wake of the Negress," in *Modern Women: Women Artists at the Museum of Modern Art*, ed. Cornelia Butler and Alexandra Schwartz (Museum of Modern Art, 2010), 480-97 [reprinted in this volume, 265-85]. For a related argument, see Griselda Pollock, *Differencing the Canon: Feminist Desire and the Writing of Art's Histories* (Routledge, 1999).

4 Ater devotes a chapter to the work in her "Race, Gender, and Nation: Rethinking the Sculpture of Meta Warrick Fuller" (PhD diss., University of Maryland, 2000), 125-55.

5 Renée Ater, *Remaking Race and History: The Sculpture of Meta Warrick Fuller* (University of California Press, 2011), 33.

6 Ater, *Remaking Race and History*, 1-7.

7 I borrow the notion of image tactics from Hannah Feldman, "'The Eye of History': Photojournalism, Protest, and the *Manifestation* of 17 October 1961," in *From a Nation Torn: Decolonizing Art and Representation in France, 1945-1962* (Duke University Press, 2014), 159-99.

16

PAINTING AFTER ALL

A Conversation with Mark Bradford

Since the beginning of the twenty-first century, Mark Bradford has emerged on the global stage as one of the most visible and successful painters of his generation thanks to his trademark canvases built of multilayered paper—often sourced from posters and billboards in South Central Los Angeles—that suggest the historical, the cartographic, and the architectural while remaining resolutely abstract. At the same time that he has been credited with a vital reanimation of painting, earning him honors such as a 2009 MacArthur Foundation "Genius" Fellowship, Bradford has continued to work in a range of media, including video, installation, and sculpture, all of which reflect his long-standing interest in simultaneously building bridges between and deconstructing notions of the common and the cultured. Recently, he has embarked on an ambitious new project, the Art+Practice Foundation, which aims to forward that same imperative in the social sphere, providing a space where international artists and local youth in foster care might exchange ideas about contemporary culture (Fig. 16.1). On January 14, 2014, I spoke with Bradford at his former studio in Leimert Park, a 10,000-square-foot space that will be the hub of the Art and Practice cultural complex. Our conversation explored many aspects of his capacious art, life, and work, though we consistently returned to his investment in painting and the worlds it makes possible.

Copeland: I've often been struck by the richness and allusiveness of your titles: *Niagara*, *James Brown Is Dead*, and one of my recent favorites, *With That Ass, They Won't Look at Your Eyes*.[1] The affective resonance of such names can be poignant and punning, bearing an oblique or a direct relation to the objects themselves. I wonder how you arrive at these titles, as well as how you imagine them relating to the material construction of the works? In other words, how do you think about your objects and their names being read together and the kind of cross-references they create, particu-

This article first appeared in *Callaloo* 37, no. 4 (Fall 2014): 814-26.

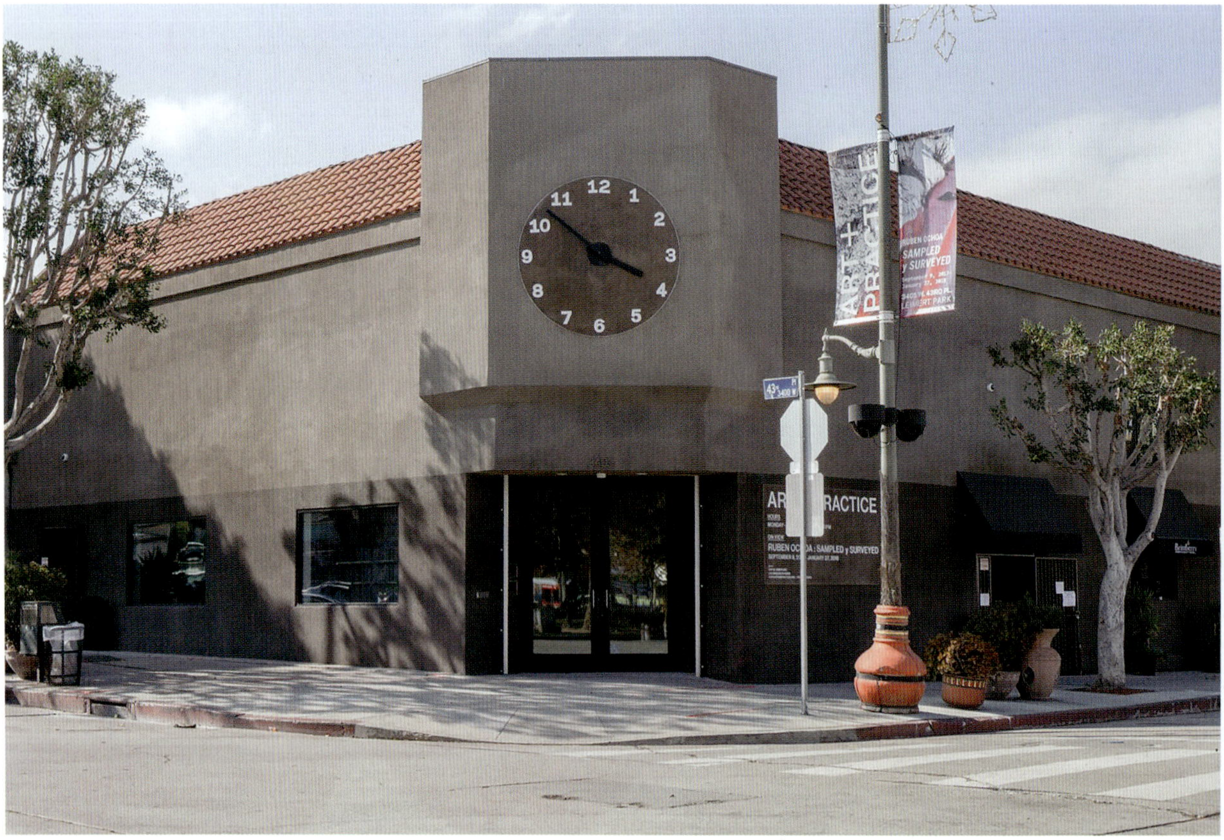

Figure 16.1
Art+Practice Foundation, exterior views, 2020. © Mark Bradford. Courtesy the artist and Hauser & Wirth.

larly given that the titles often evoke black history and its imbrication with modern art and culture?

Bradford: When I first started making work, I never thought much about titles, especially being a painter. I did notice how an artist like Agnes Martin would make very minimal paintings with very strong feminist titles, allowing her to redirect the gaze from modernism as such to social relationships. But that kind of move really was only in the back of my head; early on, most of my titles came from popular culture or music, particularly hip-hop. Eventually, I started rethinking hip-hop, especially those strands of it that I felt held very unhealthy attitudes toward the black female body, since I didn't know if I wanted to be part of that discourse. Nowadays, the way that I usually work is that I come up with an idea and then begin to research. For instance, I'm working on a suite of paintings for an upcoming show all based around Gustave Caillebotte's *The Floor*

Scrapers, so I went on Amazon and got a lot of art history books and texts on that artist and that period. I find that usually when I'm reading at night and I'm working during the day, there will be texts that jump out at me and I can extrapolate something from the text that then becomes a title. There's also an emotional relationship to the work and to the text that I'm reading, so through the naming and the form of the works—I use paper instead of just old paint—I want the viewer to think more broadly, to think about the social implications of the material, and maybe the social implications of the titles.

Copeland: What a fascinating way to describe the process, since it suggests that the titles—like the materials you use in the work—are found objects, always sourced from elsewhere.

Bradford: Yes. I always go to history. I'm comfortable there and I've always been a reader. My imagination opens up through reading because you have to create all of these visual images in your brain.

Copeland: That comment definitely helps bring out the multisensory experience of engaging your works; the paintings are so tactile and so bodily, involving various senses in their address to and conscription of the viewer. One of the things that you noted earlier, which is suggested by the title *James Brown Is Dead*, is that music is a literal and metaphorical touchstone for your practice [see Fig. 7.3 on p. 100]. In other interviews, you've said that your work has its own particular tone, and, I think, its own particular rhythm: each work—*Los Moscos* comes first to mind—seems to possess a kind of propulsive energy that slows down or speeds up as the eye moves over it [see Fig. 7.1 on p. 98].[2] With all of that in mind, could you say more about how music matters to and informs your practice, especially the tone that it establishes in relationship to a viewer?

Bradford: I seem to toggle between arriving at abstraction through structure—pictorial or architectural or topographical or cartographic—and between arriving at abstraction through process. I would say that the process-based abstraction is probably much more aggressive, much more demanding, while the structural abstraction has a different tone to it, almost like Philip Glass. I need both. On the one hand, there's Miles Davis's deconstructed jazz, which slows down and takes apart, very architectural. On the other, there's civil rights music or rap, like early Biggie Smalls and Tupac, that has a raw in-your-face insistence. I go between the two tones.

Copeland: I think one can feel that in the work, how that tension gives the paintings their energy and rhythm. I also think it's quite compelling how you describe the relationships between the various modes, since so often when we try to think about abstract visual forms and abstract musical forms together, the conversation tends to lapse into loose associations. In your practice, however, there seems to be an actual thinking through musicality and gesture as operations.

Bradford: Yeah, there's definitely a thinking through of musicality and of structure—not of the music itself, but of its appearance when written down on a sheet, looked through as text. I think about music a lot, because it is the predominant way in which we, as black people, have been allowed to express ourselves in this country. It's like when people ask me, "Are you religious?" and I say, "Well, I don't have to *be* religious. If you're black, you're born into religion similar to how if you're Hispanic, you're born into Catholicism." It's in the fiber and the tone of your people, so you don't have to be religious to be religious, and you don't have to be musical to be musical; it's an available form that there are lots of access points into, a historical precedent that I like to dip into.

Copeland: Yes! That resonates beautifully with Michelle Wallace's essay "Modernism, Postmodernism, and the Problem of the Visual in Afro-American Culture," where she argues that black folks have received recognition for achievement in music, dance, and literature, while the visual remains, in her words, "a negative scene of instruction."[3] The way that your work is able to draw on those other cultural resources thus also becomes a way of reframing the visual as a scene of instruction. This brings me back to my question about the kind of engagement that your paintings solicit, since in their very facture, they offer the possibility of a different kind of seeing, one that might be aligned with black feminist, queer, and antiracist critiques, despite the fact that the works themselves could never be reduced to any single mode of thinking, especially since they so often refuse to figure the socially marked body. To put it otherwise, your work seems to stage an experience of vision that is at odds not only with the way in which racialized or gendered perception often works, but that is also actively invested in expanding the visual to embrace the tactile and the sonic.[4]

Bradford: Sure, that all factors in. I've actually always gravitated toward black feminism; I'm sure my mother was a feminist. Also, I was made hyper-aware of my own physicality from an early age as I'm of unusual height. So I'll do a piece, like *Pinocchio Is on Fire*, where I give you a voice, I give you the tactile, but I don't give you the body (Fig. 16.2).[5] In the paintings, it's the same thing: there's a strong physicality, a sense of labor, but no figuration; I leave traces of the body, but the body is not there. That's a conscious political choice. I have done a few works that I put my body in, but it is only to critique the actions of the gaze on that body. I think one of

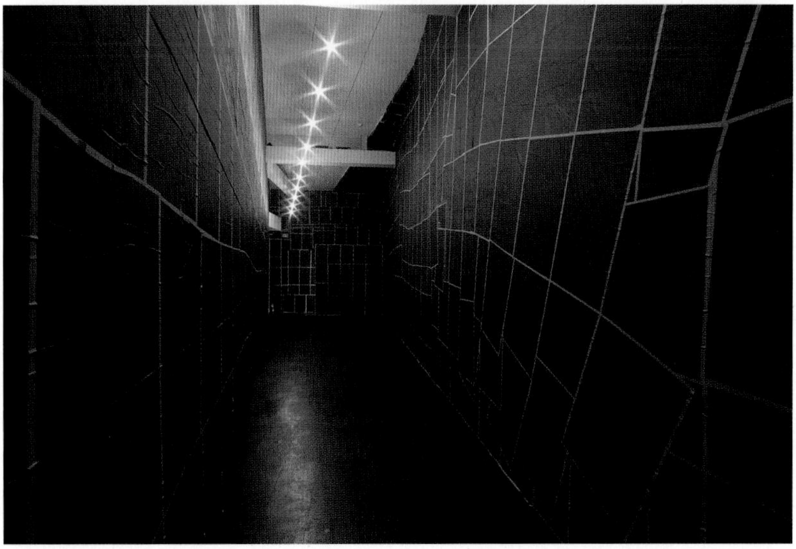

Figure 16.2
Mark Bradford, *Pinocchio Is on Fire*, 2010. Mixed media installation, dimensions variable. Installation view, Wexner Center for the Arts, Columbus, Ohio, 2010.

the most political things is to engage what I call "figurative narrative" and then to completely abstract it.[6]

Copeland: Can you say more on that score?

Bradford: I'm aware that I'm black. I'm aware that I'm 6'8". And I'm aware that I mine the territory of South Central Los Angeles, which means that I gather my material from outside of the studio. Those are all really figurative things that have been sold to the market, and people think they know what each of those terms means. I love to abstract them as a way of pushing back, of demanding freedom and play within a very closed system.

Copeland: That's helpful, especially in terms of thinking further about the ethical imperatives that animate your work. For instance, your references to black feminism and to your mother put me in mind of Hortense Spillers's essay "Mama's Baby, Papa's Maybe," where she says that "the black American male embodies the *only* American community of males which has had the specific occasion to learn *who* the female is within itself. . . . It is the heritage of the *mother* that the African-American male must regain as an aspect of his own personhood—the power of 'yes' to the 'female' within."[7] That statement opens onto one place from which the ethics of your painting might be said to emerge, but Spillers also allows us to think about the ways in which your work across a whole range of platforms critically explores the flows between and within discrepant economies, communities, and positions. Throughout your practice, you seem to take pains not to fetishize alterity, but to engage others as equal partners in a mutually beneficial exchange.

Bradford: Well, I've always thought that the most courage you could have is to simply live a life based on what really turns you on. You know, I've always hated those TV shows where they redesign your house, because they take out all of the furniture and the memories of those people and say, "Oh, no. You're doing it wrong." And they might have done everything wrong: a cheetah couch might not go with a shag throw. Then the producers come in and formalize the decor, they make it "perfect" so that it all goes together, it all makes sense. But I never like things that are tidy and that make sense. I'm okay with things being a little messy around the edges; neither I nor my career would ever be on a makeover show, because I like the cheetah couch with the shag throw and the fur coat and the chandelier. I'm not about forcing equivalences and I don't need linear histories, connections, or practices. With my painting and the ideas I've developed around it, I've always just pushed forward. Abstraction gave me a space to do that, to speak out the side of my neck, to practice a form of indirect speaking. At the same time, I wanted to use humble materials like paper but to elevate those materials to the same height as painting, since collage is always considered a lesser art in the history of modernism. I just really thought that I could put all of those things together and push them forward as a transparent investigation of myself and of my process, which gave me the freedom to dismantle normative archetypal narratives and hierarchies within both modernism and black culture. Now, it's okay to deconstruct modernism, but when you deconstruct your own folks' assumptions about culture and community, that can be a little difficult. Kara Walker had that problem: people are fine with you wanting to blow up the White House, but they never want you to talk about blowing up the Black House. And I thought, we should blow up the black house too!

Copeland: It's interesting that you make a connection with Walker in this context, since "talking out the side of your neck" resonates with her notion of "the sidelong glance" as a critical way of reframing art and culture on all sides of the color line.[8]

Bradford: Yes, it's about having the right to mumble something that you're not quite sure of. I need to have a platform to do that; abstraction allows me to stumble around and say, "Well, I think," "I'm not sure," "I might," or "Maybe," even as the works I'm putting out feel much more sure, more "front door." Personally, I've never felt comfortable going in the front door; I've always liked side doors, windows, back doors, like sneaking into the back of a club—that also gave me some freedom. As time went on, I just started to think more locally about these questions of engagement and autonomy, to push the sort of plurality that my painting demands of modernism within my neighborhood as well. That's how I developed the Foundation, which is based in contemporary art and—the "and" is what makes the relationship—social service, in this case, working with foster kids. The fit between contemporary art and social service is messy and not linear; I put them together because I want them to be together and because they need each other. The art world is quite beautiful: we have lots of money, lots of resources, lots of lots of, and a lot of times we don't look beyond it, we can become too ivory-towered and too insular. And we do have a lot of pretty buildings and galas and exhibitions; foster kids don't. They're located, in a sense, in the most nonbeautiful sight of imagination you can imagine. So, I thought, "Oh, nobody is going to tell them they can't participate in the beautiful! They can have entrée if they choose, they can walk across the bridge that the Foundation provides if they want to." When Obama said, "Yes, We Can," I took that on many levels, both locally and personally. When someone tells me I can't do something, I usually think, "Oh yeah, I can." The Foundation is more of a collective expression of that ethos: "Yes, we can do this. There can be a relationship between social service and artistic practice." I think that the contemporary art world has the best ideas and the most interesting thinkers, so some of the social service side can benefit from our ideas. And I think that the contemporary art world, when it can look outside of itself, can benefit from the social service model. So instead of building MFA programs in socially engaged practice, you could just go work at the Department of Social Services. That's social practice right there; you can do both. I've always had that attitude. When I was living in a boardinghouse, more traditional voices in the mainstream of black society said, "You know, that's wrong. You're not going to make it." And I said, "Oh yeah, I'll make it." When I started going to school, getting bullied for being small and creative and a sissy, they said, "You're not going to make it." And I said, "Oh yeah, I'll make it." When the 1980s came along—I was seventeen or eighteen—they said, "You know, AIDS is going to kill you." And I said, "Oh no, I think I'll be all right. I'll make it." When I went to art school much too late and they said, "Well, you're a little older and you *might* be able to teach," I said, "I'll be okay." When my career did what it did, they said, "Well, you know, now you're a certain type of artist." And I said, "No, no, I'll be okay. I can do it." The Foundation basically reflects that same attitude that I've had since I was eleven: I've never believed the people who told me what they thought I could or couldn't do.

Copeland: So one of the imperatives of Art+Practice as space and a platform is not only to revitalize its particular neighborhood but also to instill a mutually felt and discovered sense of "Yes, We Can" in both foster kids and museum directors?

Bradford: Yes. I don't believe that a billionaire collector is inherently evil and I don't believe that a foster kid is inherently not going to appreciate access to culture. I just don't believe the contemporary art world belongs to the few. When I was at CalArts, this great school—private, very expensive—I was fascinated by what I was learning and reading. I'd never heard of bell hooks. I'd never heard of Michele Wallace. I'd never heard of Coco Fusco, Homi Bhabha, and so many other writers. And I remember thinking every day about my friend Yasmin at the shop: if Yasmin knew what a black feminist was, she would know what she is. So much of what I was learning at CalArts really applied to what we were talking about at this women's beauty shop. I would take my course readings, print them up, and give them to the ladies at the salon. We'd have these really great discussions about the texts: "Oh honey, I heard that, that's me!" And I always thought, what if the strong women that I was reading and that I admire so much in the art world could access some of the hair-burning, churchgoing ladies? What would that be? There are so many strong women that are feminists for one reason or another, but who don't know the word *feminist* or where it comes from, but who have demanded life on their own terms. They just didn't have access to the discourse, and it's the possibility of those conversations once they have access that is exciting to me. The Foundation will sponsor a lecture series to enable just those sorts of contemporary conversations—not dumbed down, just contemporary—which I know will be amazing because I've lived it. I put myself through school working in a beauty shop, but folks there knew where I was going, they knew what I was reading, they were helping me get through my courses, and they understood exactly what it was about. I made it very transparent: I'd put my theory in my bag and head to CalArts; then I'd come back and put the theory under the shelf so we could discuss those texts as easily as we talked about "The Real Housewives."

Copeland: So again, there's an interest in refusing certain kinds of categorical boundaries or distinctions?

Bradford: Absolutely. I've done it my whole life. I've just never been interested in the word *no*. It's too short. It doesn't really have any flair to it. "Yes" sounds much better. Have you ever heard anybody having an orgasm saying, "No, no, no"? They say "Yes! Yes! Yes!"

Copeland: Right! And perhaps this sense of the affirmative also speaks to where you're coming from historically? I think, for instance, about earlier artists, say, a Robert Colescott, who was also about the "yes": he could have history painting and caricature at the same moment, he could occupy all of these different poles simultaneously. Greg Tate has argued that the work of Colescott and his cohorts in what he calls the "freaky-deke" generation—practitioners like David Hammons and Toni Morrison—opened up the possibility of the "yes" for so many of us who came after.[9]

Bradford: All people I respect. I also think of Julie Dash's film *Daughters of the Dust* (1991), her kind of postmodern abstracted social realism, or of the kind of social fantasy you see in Gabriel García Márquez's novel *One Hundred Years of Solitude* (1967). Both are works that abstract the narrative and then mix it in a way that's very complex. I'm complex because I've led a very complex life, but I'm not real complicated.

Copeland: But even as your practice embraces the "and," you maintain a distinction between the studio practice and the work of the Foundation, which raises two questions. First, why establish that separation? Second, why do you think at this moment, we see you, Theaster Gates, and Rick Lowe all developing socially oriented enterprises that are very much invested in some notion of community?

Bradford: If you look at the multiculturalism of the 1980s, that's when a renewed idea of investing in community really started. But I feel like it was a very static notion of community, in part because it was probably the first time that the larger art world was starting to think outside of itself. In multicultural discourse, community felt very stereotyped, reduced to generalities, painted in very broad brush strokes. The idea of community—black community, Hispanic community, Asian community, what have you—was racialized and essentialized in ways that made it very romantic and that flattened everything out. I think now it's sort of "post-community," like "post-black," which is, you know, still black.[10] There is still community, but we're remapping it and rethinking it by moving past easy equations, by inserting other narratives and other voices into the conversation. Community at this moment feels much more reflective of rhythms and pluralities within and between constituencies. We can think about the same site in a multiplicity of ways, instead of in a linear, flattened down, romantic, or racialized way that always harkens back to somewhere, since I don't even know where we'd harken back to!

Copeland: That way of thinking about community speaks well, I think, to the reality of black lives lived now, which are so often dispersed for any number of reasons. For one, there is no longer necessarily an old home to go back to, if there ever was. And in the US context, blackness continues to shift because of immigration from Africa and the Caribbean, so we have to have an even more expanded, complex notion of what encompasses blackness given historical and recent trends in diasporic movement. But I think your notion of community also resonates with the polemic of Saidiya Hartman's book *Lose Your Mother*, which refuses the fantasy of a return to some shared root and instead emphasizes forging community with those like-minded people who are in the same structural situation you find yourself in.[11]

Bradford: Sure, but it's also about embodying the contemporary: the conversations and the politics of your time, the ethics that you live by, your whole political, social, cultural, and racial situation. Now, I love to read biographies of artists. At the same time, I'll read a political autobiography from the period or I'll research what was happening politically. The artistic, the social, the political, and the personal all make contemporary life. Communities right now should be involved in a conversation about their time and the ideas of their time. People say, "Oh, I don't understand contemporary art." I say, "Well you do! You understand the world you live in—that's all contemporary art is." So for me, I don't think it's that different: I never left this "community," so I was never trying to recover something. I am simply adding another conversation, another idea, another point of view. I don't think you have to get rid of other voices to be heard.

Copeland: Right. So maybe we can turn now to the first part of the question: though there might be a similar ambition that animates your Foundation and Lowe's work and Gates's, they are strikingly different models. Gates's social outreach, for instance, is very much integrated into his practice, creating what he calls a "circular ecosystem," while for you they remain separate.[12]

Bradford: Yeah, I have an old school studio practice that is very much about working and playing in private, which I love. It's my go-to place to wander through my own learnings and leanings and imaginings. It's a very private space. What I bring out of that space and show to the public is something different. I think there's part of me that's very hermetic, almost reclusive, it's the part of me that's probably shy. What I mean by that is when you're in your studio and you're working out ideas, you're always in a very vulnerable state. I don't really want the public to see that. Every time I finish a work, I always think that's the last work that I'll make and that I'll probably never do it again. I never think the opposite. I always think, "I just can't," until I come the next day and the painting still happens to be there. I can't imagine mixing the vulnerable state of the studio with the work of the Foundation, which is so public and so out there, it would just be too much. Separating the two gives me a balance. There's a public structure and then there's a private structure, but I couldn't have built the public structure without the things that I make in the private structure.[13]

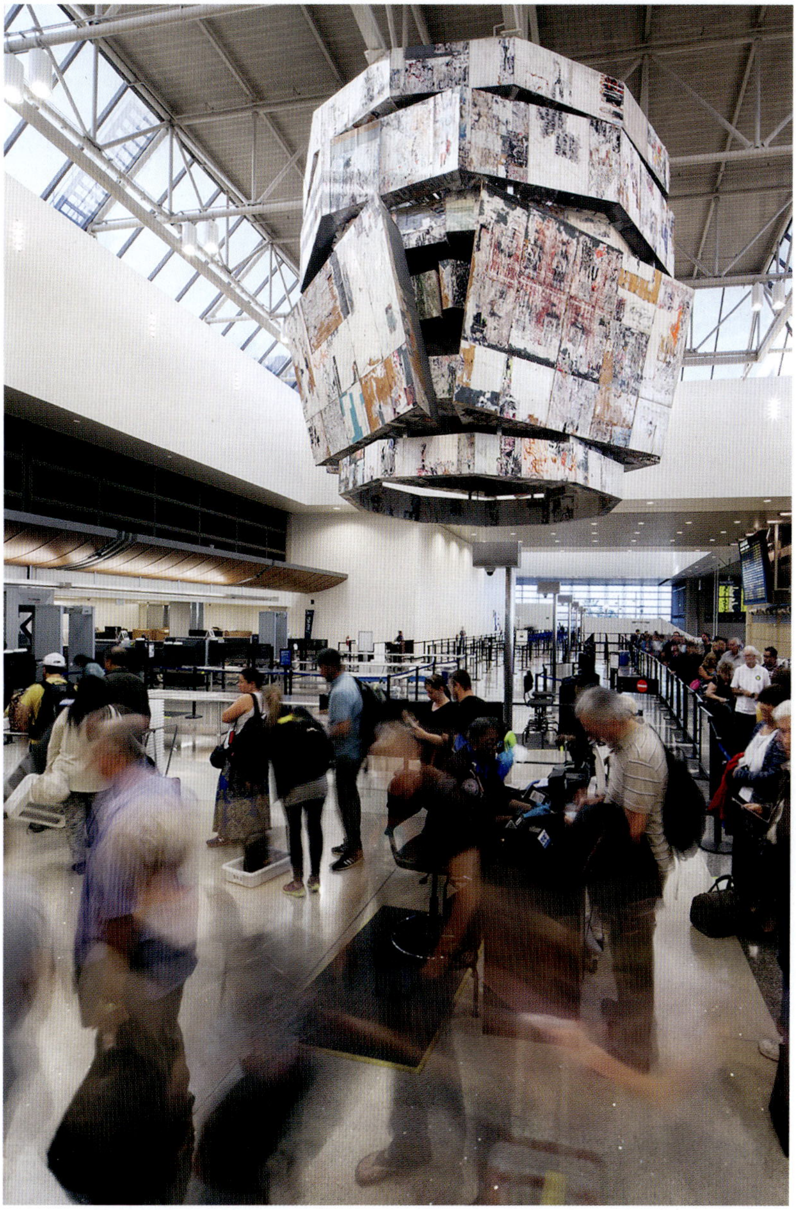

Figure 16.3
Mark Bradford, *Bell Tower*, 2014. Mixed media, 792.5 × 914.4 cm / 312 × 360 in. Installation view, Tom Bradley International Terminal, Los Angeles International Airport, Los Angeles, CA, 2014. © Mark Bradford. Courtesy the artist and Hauser & Wirth.

Copeland: Which brings us to the private work that you've been doing recently that is designed to be public, like the *Bell Tower*, which will be in the International Terminal at LAX (Fig. 16.3). How do you feel about making that kind of work that is intended for general consumption?

Bradford: Oh, anxious! I mean, I'm going to put it up and run! And every time I walk through the airport I'm going to pretend it's not mine. When I did *Mithra* in New Orleans, I started building it out in the public [see Fig.

7.9 on p. 108]. Before the form started taking shape, it was probably easier to hide, but once it was built—this one-hundred-foot ark—I thought, "Oh, this is going to be a little too public." I wanted to leave it there and go home, because I felt so vulnerable. I guess I like doing the work, but I don't like the attention that the work gets. I think that's across the board with me.

Copeland: Because you're not interested in that type of spectacularity?

Bradford: No! I'm 6′8″, for God's sake, I have born-in spectacularity! I could loan people some.

Copeland: That is too funny and again so helpful in thinking about your practice, particularly its tone and address to a public, on the one hand, and the desire you have personally for a certain kind of concealment and opacity, on the other. But I also appreciate the way you talk about the process of working in the studio since it provides a model for us as viewers: just as you're working from piece to piece to work out certain problems, as spectators, we have to try to track or reconstruct that process when viewing the canvases. It's what the work demands. But one of the things that I find most troubling about much of the discourse around your work—or around that of any number of artists—is that a common sense starts to settle in about what the work is doing that pretends it can speak to every single work when each painting is a particular effort that comes from those searching moments of uncertainty and failure and vulnerability in the studio. So I wonder, what is your dream for the viewer's engagement from work to work? And how do we hold onto material specificity within artistic discourse more broadly?

Bradford: Painting dies every three years or so only to be resurrected. But we have not really critiqued the materials that we use to engage it. Ninety-five percent of the people who paint use oils or paints from a tube. They buy it from an art store, they buy canvas from an art store, they buy frames from an art store. But painting now is a deconstructed site of materiality and, thankfully, there are a few new artists who are using nonpainting materials to paint. How do you come to that? I've often wondered how and why I came to use paper. I knew that I didn't want to use the traditional materials because I did not want to dislodge a social conversation. Adding a political title wouldn't have worked for who I was in the world that I was living in; that just didn't feel like enough. So I gravitated to the idea of paper, but I came to it in a very strange way because I never saw paper as paper. I always saw it as frozen pigment. I mean, a stack of blue paper is simply pigment that's been isolated, because it had to be liquid at some point. I thought, "Oh, well I just need to release it. I just need to wet this paper so the color is freed." So the first thing that I was very much interested in was actually interrogating the materials that we use, our language of engagement before anything else. In my case, I had to soften the paper so I could use it, so immediately all the paper went into water. And I didn't always use paper from the streets. I used store-bought paper that was big blanks of colors—blues, reds, and yellows. I was always curious why people never saw it that way. They were always looking at the utilitarian value of the material; it was a piece of paper that you write on or that you cut up to make a heart. I always saw the diamond in the rough. So again, it goes back to seeing something in something that's "regular," even with the foster kids, just believing that there's something there besides what people say is there.

Copeland: So it's a kind of painting that starts from a Duchampian place by approaching the tube of paint as a readymade.[14] But instead of going to the actual tube of paint, you turn to the readymade stack of paper, in which pigment is embedded. The material is very much of the everyday and not rooted in a specialist idiom. I think what that does is not so much to revivify the corpse of painting yet again, but to propose a counterfactual history of the medium.[15]

Bradford: Right. I just got the turquoise from a different place. I squeezed it out of a piece of paper, and you went to the art store. I thought, "Where does the pigment belong in a piece of paper?" Does it belong to the art or to the common? It's both, whereas there's nothing common about a tube of paint: it belongs only to the cultured, it only walks down the runway. But I saw the color of paper everywhere, and I was always aware that it was pigment or dye. The first paper I used was white tissue paper that I burned on the edges because I needed a visual marker. After that, I went right to colored paper. If you wet it long enough, the fibers will become very loose and the paper becomes more translucent so it's able to have the bleeds that oil paint has and the luminosities and everything else. This process was very organic, it wasn't a strategy, and it really wasn't an art. It just came about by that day-to-day process of wondering, "How am I going to make a painting?" Now I always use wet paper; it's never dry. It's usually left overnight to soak, two days, three days. If I forget about it, all the paper will just sink to the bottom and all the pigments will rise to the top. Sometimes I just scoop up all the pigment and make work out of that, or I shake the paper in the water until all of the color separates. And then I'm holding pigment. I'm holding color in my hand that belongs to a very different history than the paper. You know, I can remember as a kid loving to tie-dye. I would take the white T-shirts and dunk 'em in dye, which I used to love to do. Later at the shop, I would take color that comes in a bottle and put it on women's hair—I was a really good colorist—but there's nothing high culture about it, it doesn't belong to the art world, whereas when you go to an art store, history just meets you at the door. That history is so cultured, so cultivated, and I found a bridge to the common. When I struggle too much, sometimes the painting falls too much on the side of the everyday, and I can't lift the color out enough. Other times I lift too much of the color up and the painting goes too much towards art. I need that tension between art and the everyday so that the paintings hold: not too street, not too processed.

Copeland: You are always searching for the "and."

Bradford: Yeah, but I push it every time. I would rather have a spectacular failure than a mediocre success.

Notes

This text would not be possible in its present form without the generosity of Mark Bradford and his studio, in particular, Lisa Wedgeworth and Sean Boyle, to whom I extend my sincerest gratitude. Thanks must also go to Max Allison, Bryan Barcena, Imani Jacqueline Brown, Thomas J. Lax, Ylva Rouse, and Claire Tancons for their kind assistance with the image program.

1 Bradford's deployment of the title *Niagara* is particularly telling in its layering of affects and references. To make the video—whose title recalls a 1953 film featuring a sashaying Marilyn Monroe—the artist filmed a black man with a fierce swish as he walked down the streets of South Central, suggesting a queer sensibility that energizes urban space with both sexuality and danger. A clip of *Niagara* can be found online at https://www.youtube.com/watch?v=rl6dlbl6iH0, starting at the 0:37 second mark. A video documenting the installation of *With That Ass, They Won't Look at Your Eyes* can be found online at http://vimeo.com/53892337.

2 I refer to Bradford's comments about tone made to MoCATV in the context of discussing his collaboration with the dancer Benjamin Millepied: see MoCATV. "*Framework*: A Collaborative Performance by L.A. Dance Project/Benjamin Millepied and Los Angeles Artist Mark Bradford," http://www.youtube.com/watch?v=BdwCrCh6H9I. My subsequent language references Steven Nelson, "Mark Bradford's Allegorical Impulse," in *Mark Bradford* (Sikkema Jenkins & Co., 2006), n.p.; Huey Copeland, "A Range of Convergences," *Parkett* 89 (2011): 152-69 [reprinted in this volume, 97-110].

3 Michele Wallace, "Modernism, Postmodernism, and the Problem of the Visual in Afro-American Culture," in *Out There: Marginalization and Contemporary Cultures*, ed. Russell Ferguson et al. (MIT Press, 1990), 41.

4 My thinking here on the sonic and the haptic as alternative modes of black subjectivation is indebted to the groundbreaking work of Fred Moten, *In the Break: The Aesthetics of the Black Radical Tradition* (University of Minnesota Press, 2003); and Alexander Weheliye, "'I Am I Be': The Subject of Sonic Afro-Modernity," *boundary 2* 30, no. 2 (Summer 2003): 97-114.

5 In this installation at the ICA Boston, Bradford lined a passageway with blacked-out paper and filled it with the sounds of a recording by the jazz legend Nancy Wilson.

6 In its refusal of the body, Bradford's work can be seen to extend the writing of artist-critics such as Coco Fusco and Renée Green, a practice that I have aimed to track as a critical strategy. On these scores, see, respectively, Renée Green, "'Give Me Body': Freaky Fun, Biopolitics, and Contact Zones," in *Other Planes of There: Selected Writings of Renée Green* (Duke University Press, 2014), 197-209; Coco Fusco, "The Bodies That Were Not Ours: Black Performers, Black Performance," *Nka: Journal of Contemporary African Art*, no. 5 (Fall 1996): 28-33; Huey Copeland, *Bound to Appear: Art, Slavery, and the Site of Blackness in Multicultural America* (University of Chicago Press, 2013).

7 Hortense J. Spillers, "Mama's Baby, Papa's Maybe: An American Grammar Book," *Diacritics* 17, no. 2 (Summer 1987): 80; emphasis original.

8 Walker describes "the sidelong glance" as her "answer to the male gaze. It's the little look and it's full of suspicion, potential ill-will, or desire." Kara Walker, quoted in Jerry Saltz, "Kara Walker: Ill-Will and Desire," *Flash Art* 29, no. 191 (November-December 1996): 82. For an extended meditation on this concept and its significance for African diasporic cultural practice more broadly, see Krista Thompson, "A Sidelong Glance: The Practice of African Diaspora Art History in the United States," Centennial Essay, *Art Journal* 70, no. 3 (Fall 2011): 6-31.

9 Greg Tate, "The Return of the Black Aesthetic: Cult-Nats Meet Freaky-Deke," in *Flyboy in the Buttermilk: Essays on Contemporary America* (Simon and Schuster, 1992), 198-210. For a related inquiry, see Huey Copeland, "Truth to Power," *Artforum* 48, no. 2 (October 2009): 59-60.

10 For the key formulation of post-black, which refers to the sensibility of a generation of "artists who were adamant about not being labeled as 'black' artists, though their work was steeped, in fact deeply interested, in redefining complex notions of blackness," see Thelma Golden, "Introduction: Post . . . ," in *Freestyle*, exh. cat. (Studio Museum in Harlem, 2001), 14.

11 Saidiya Hartman, *Lose Your Mother: A Journey Along the Atlantic Slave Route* (Farrar, Straus & Giroux, 2007).

12 For a critical discussion of Gates's "circular ecosystem," see Huey Copeland, "Dark Mirrors: Theaster Gates and *Ebony*," *Artforum* 52, no. 2 (October 2013), 226-27 [reprinted in this volume, 149-62].

13 Bradford's comments here resonate well with the discussion of the studio as both a site of engagement and a place of safety for post-World War II artists in Anne M. Wagner, *A House Divided: American Art Since 1955* (University of California Press, 2011).

14 Here I reference the artist Marcel Duchamp's emphasis on the always already constructed character of artistic materials. For one analysis, see Thierry de Duve, "The Readymade and the Tube of Paint," *Artforum* 24, no. 9 (May 1986): 110-21.

15 For a useful discussion of the rhetorics of death and revivification that have surrounded painting, particularly since the 1980s, see Frazer Ward, "Undead Painting: Life after Life in the 1980s," in *This Will Have Been: Art, Love, and Politics in the 1980s*, ed. Helen Molesworth (Yale University Press, 2012).

17

NOAH PURIFOY

Los Angeles County Museum of Art

Junk Dada, the Los Angeles County Museum of Art's (LACMA's) recent survey of the work of Noah Purifoy, could hardly have felt timelier—or more belated. On the one hand, the elegantly installed show, curated by Franklin Sirmans and Yael Lipschutz, has arrived during a moment of renewed art world attention to African American elder statesmen, from Ed Clark to Stanley Whitney; it also contributes to recent efforts to rethink the racial politics of assemblage in the context of the Southern California scene, as emblematized by Kellie Jones's important 2011 exhibition, *Now Dig This! Art and Black Los Angeles 1960–1980*. On the other hand, Purifoy, who died in 2004, more than thirty years after his first appearance at LACMA, was critically and financially undervalued by the artistic mainstream for much of his career, despite his pioneering work in urban and rural settings with the found object, installation, and social practice—models of engagement that have proved influential for artists ranging from Mark Bradford to Andrea Zittel. And yet such discrepancy seems fitting if no less poignant, given how productively Purifoy challenged understandings of the object's temporal unfolding and how deftly he negotiated the impositions of what the cultural theorist Michael Hanchard has called "racial time": "the inequalities of temporality that result from power relations between racially dominant and subordinate groups" within Western civilization.[1]

Born into the segregated world of Snow Hill, Alabama, in 1917 and brought up in Birmingham, Purifoy attended the State Teachers College and became an instructor of industrial arts before enlisting in the navy. He served in the South Pacific as a Seabee from 1942 to 1945 and upon his return to the United States attended Atlanta University, earning his master's in social services administration in 1948. Two years later, after a brief stint in Cleveland, he arrived in Los Angeles, where he would become the first full-time African American student to graduate from the Chouinard

This review first appeared in *Artforum* 54, no. 2 (October 2015): 308-11.

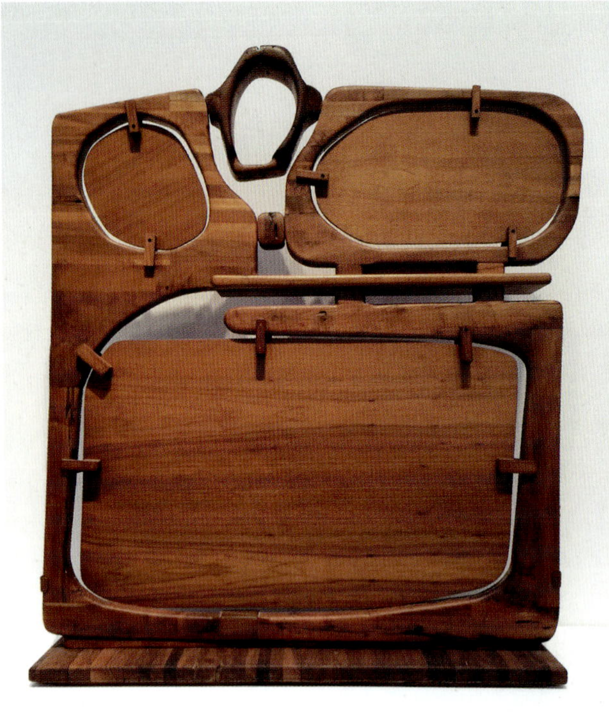

Figure 17.1
Noah Purifoy, *Untitled (Bed Headboard)*, 1958. Wood, 62 × 72 × 3 in. Courtesy Noah Purifoy Foundation © 2026.

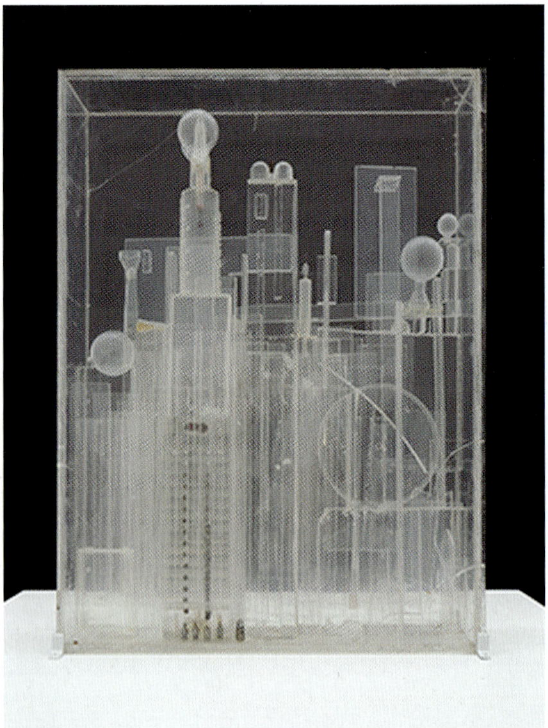

Figure 17.2
Noah Purifoy, *The City at Night*, 1966. Plexiglas, 24¾ × 18½ × 4½ in. Courtesy Noah Purifoy Foundation © 2026.

Art Institute (now CalArts). Like many American artists invested in questions of the everyday in the wake of World War II—Robert Rauschenberg and Andy Warhol come foremost to mind—Purifoy was a commercial artist, designer, and window dresser at the outset of his career. At LACMA, the artist's better-known experiments with the lives of form are provocatively reframed by revelatory works from this early period, including a beautifully hewn midcentury modern wooden headboard from 1958 and a captivating Plexiglas cityscape (*The City at Night*, 1966) that recalls Joseph Cornell's boxes while also looking toward John McCracken's Finish Fetish (Figs. 17.1, 17.2).

By the mid-'60s, Purifoy's experiments in melding the aesthetic, the social, and the environmental were already well under way. In 1964, he cofounded the Watts Towers Arts Center, aiming to deploy the assemblage aesthetic of tower architect, Simon Rodia, as a mode of social transformation and progressive pedagogy in the context of an impoverished African American community. In response to the 1965 uprising against police violence that notoriously scarred the neighborhood and set the tone for civil unrest in the decades to come, Purifoy worked with an interracial cast of artists to mount the traveling 1966 exhibition, *66 Signs of Neon*, comprising works made almost entirely from the flotsam left in the wake of the area's destruction. A brace of pieces from that exhibition was presented near the entrance to *Junk Dada*—an untitled Judson Powell sculpture and *Race Baby*, 1966, a collage by Ruth Saturensky (a.k.a. Charu Colorado), both of which rely on retooled images of black youth, were particular standouts—while archival materials pertaining to the organization of *66 Signs* appeared in a darkened gallery near the heart of the show.

Like its most relevant predecessor—Lizzetta LeFalle-Collins's exhibition, *Noah Purifoy: Outside and in the Open*, mounted at the California African American Museum in 1997—*Junk Dada* gave pride of place to pieces that the artist executed in Joshua Tree, California. In part due to a dearth of investment in his work and a waning faith in the efficacy of social policy, Purifoy relocated to Joshua Tree in 1989 and spent the remainder of his life there, creating more than one hundred works on ten acres of land. This sprawling concatenation of objects, known collectively as the Joshua Tree Outdoor Museum, highlights the ways in which Purifoy's working procedures at once rhyme with and deform the ecologies and genealogies of modern art, culture, and consumption in the American West. Again comprising discarded materials—now solicited from his neighbors rather than pulled from the streets—Purifoy's desert assemblages variously take the form of environments, installations, stand-alone works, and even a gallery, each type resonating with earlier avant-garde aesthetic tacks—particularly the readymade and *Merzbau*-style construction—as well as with the region's aesthetic vernaculars. Assemblages such as *Bowling Balls III* (1994), with its column of multicolored spheres held in place by two curved concrete L's, intersect with the SoCal mode of DIY decoration that Reyner Banham referred to as "plaster-gnomery,"[2] though in Purifoy's case, the kitsch factor has been leached away by the ingenuity of his compositions and the corrosive forces of the desert (Fig. 17.3).

As has often been noted, Purifoy's work in Joshua Tree places him in conversation with the Southwest outdoor interventions of Nancy Holt, Michael Heizer, and Robert Smithson, whose practices spatially extended the Minimal sculptor Robert Morris's imperative to consider "space, light, and the viewer's field of vision" as constitutive of the artistic experience.[3] While large-scale canonical Earthworks, such as Smithson's *Spiral Jetty* (1970), often privilege machine-assisted construction and organic materials like rocks, soil, salt, and water, Purifoy's art—replete with the detritus of mass and industrial production—is smaller in scale and marked by the bodily efforts of the artist and his collaborators. In one sense, this distinction is superficial: the temporal oscillation between geologic and anthropocentric time, so famously elaborated by Smithson, subtly underpins Purifoy's art as well.[4] The beams and bowling balls and other bits of "junk" that provide the raw materials of his work bespeak culture and its quick

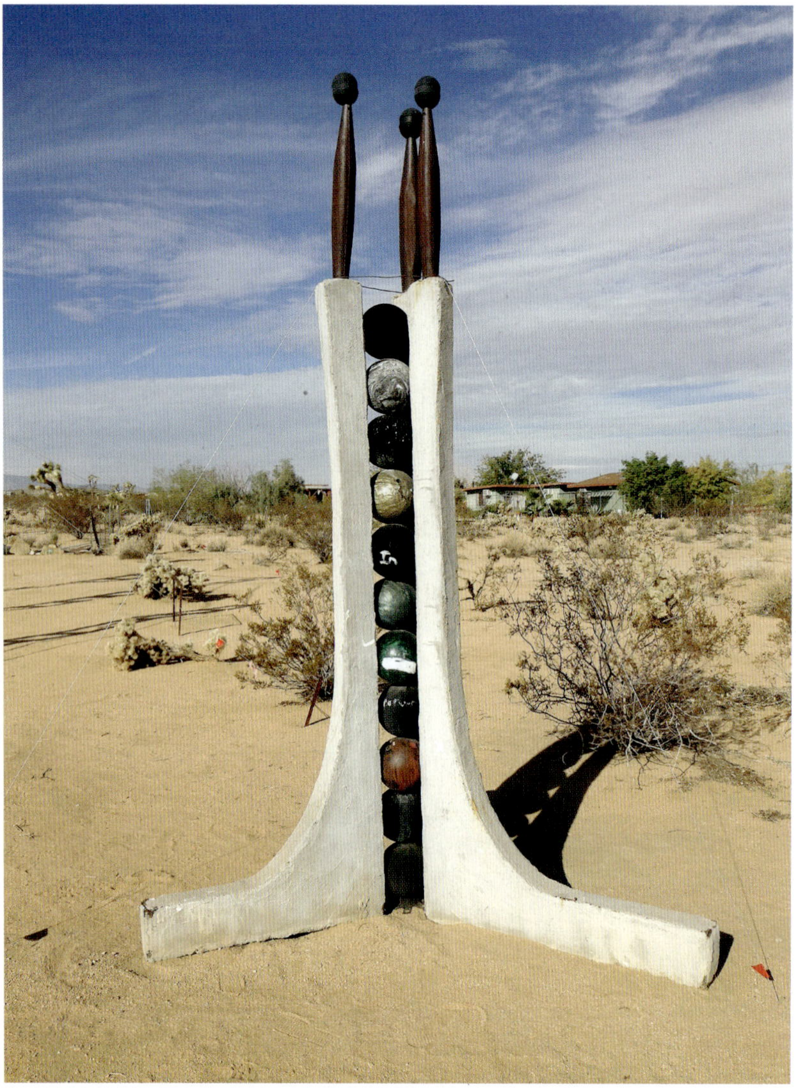

Figure 17.3
Noah Purifoy, *Bowling Ball Sculpture I*, 1994. Assemblage; 126 × 82 × 82 in. Courtesy Noah Purifoy Foundation © 2026.

cycles, but Purifoy was also conscious of the longer, planetary temporalities that were operating on and refashioning his objects. In fact, without the intervention of the caretakers now employed by the foundation that runs the Outdoor Museum, Purifoy's Joshua Tree works—like much of his now-lost '60s and '70s production—would resume their individual (and perhaps eons-long) courses of decay within the world; as the artist once put it, "I don't do maintenance. I do artwork. If it wants to deteriorate, I find some kind of gratification in watching nature participate in the creative process."[5]

In this statement, Purifoy suggests a conceptualization of the entropic that is matched by the visual flux of the desert site, which constantly shifts in relation to the viewer's expectations, the surrounding works on display, and the atmospheric conditions governing the area at any given moment. But if Smithson's entropy—aimed at leveling human temporalities and hierarchies—ultimately looks toward the heat death of history, beyond which there is only stasis, then Purifoy's entropy is one in which such endings are proliferating points of departure: the racial uprising, the social emergency, the ongoing disaster of Western conquest and civilization are terminal cataclysms that are always arriving. Viewed in this light, his assemblages can be seen as articulations of the *now*, which the Black literary scholar Michelle M. Wright has linked to the concept of a generative entropy. Calling the now an "immanent immediacy," she writes, "The present is a point on a timeline; *now* is a dispersed field of events. . . . Spacetime does not move forward. If anything, it moves outward: The universe is expanding. Entropy is not just destruction and collapse; it is a tree growing . . . and the particles that comprise all matter growing less tightly bound, looser, more chaotic."[6]

In Purifoy's art, the lived, expansive trajectories of materials; the effects of nature; embodied sensation; and the evidence of artistic labor emerge together within a singular spatiotemporal structure that is the now. As such, his "handcrafted" aesthetic is not the least bit quaint: the roughhewn quality of Purifoy's signature assemblages abets a kind of sensorial recalibration toward the object's temporality, making, and authorship. Whereas hyper-refined sculpture—Jeff Koons's metallic balloon animals, for example—hold out a homogeneous perfection that seems to collapse the time, labor, and agencies involved in their fabrication into a gleaming instantaneous *present*, Purifoy's assemblages render apparent their mixed construction by both the artist and any number of unseen forces in and over time, holding out ensemblic manifestations of the *now*. This is the time claimed by the work and, by implication, offered to anyone who may view it—or better, to any*thing* that participates in its transformations, especially at the Outdoor Museum, the most immersive and most open environment in which to take in Purifoy's art.

Of course, many of the desert works are quite capable of holding their own when removed from that setting and situated within the white cube. Indeed, Sirmans and Lipschutz's installation enabled a focused reconsideration of Purifoy's complex relationship to modernist sculpture and its institutional aftermaths at LACMA and beyond (Fig. 17.4): Joshua Tree's *Offshore Drilling* (2000), for instance, seen here in the left foreground, calls forth both the abstractions of Anthony Caro and the assemblages of Jessica Stockholder, underlining Purifoy's uncanny ability to at once collapse and recast the individual grammars, overarching narrative drive,

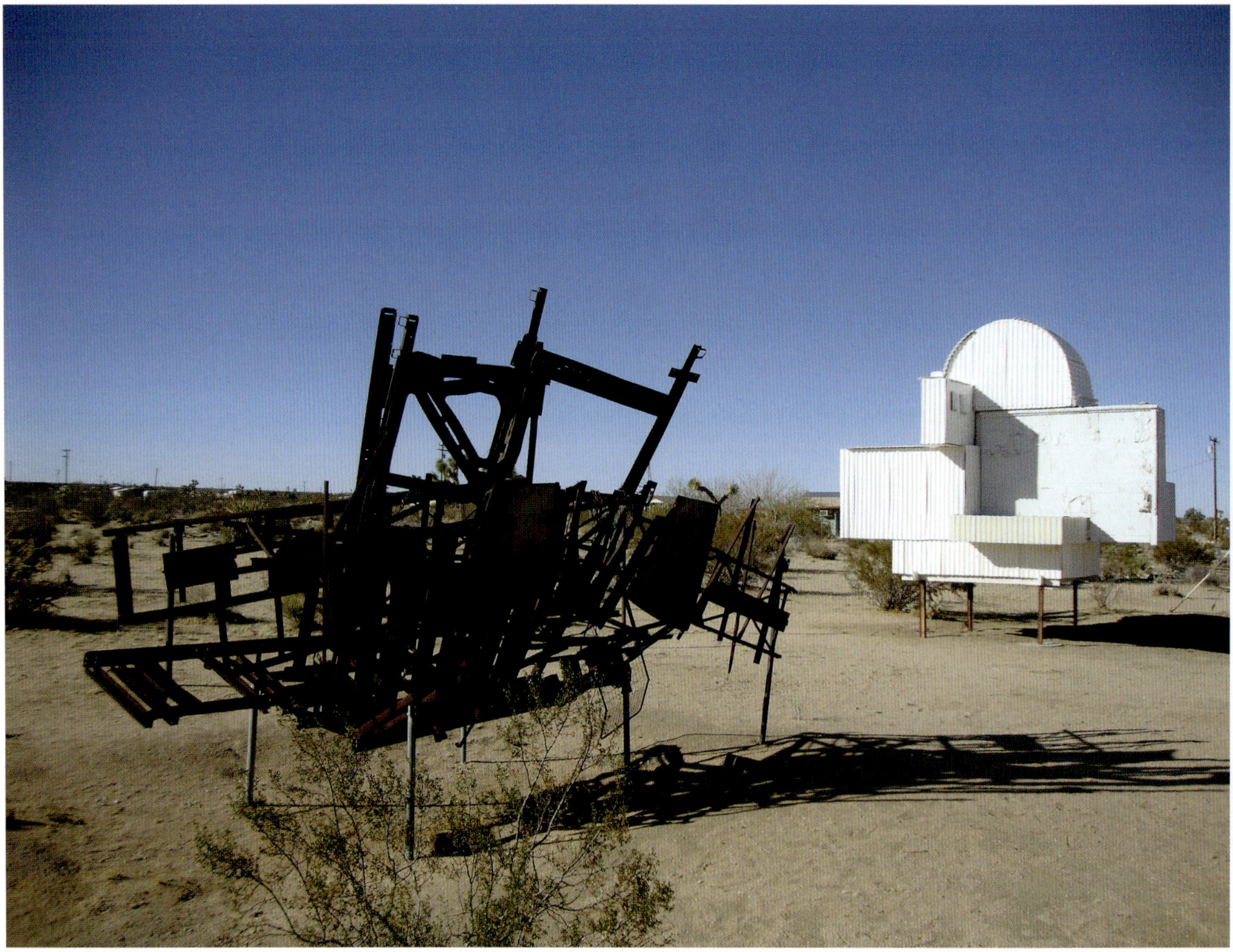

Figure 17.4
Noah Purifoy, *Offshore Drilling*, 1995, and *Ode to Frank Gehry*, 2000. Assemblage construction, 190 × 192 × 144 in. Courtesy Noah Purifoy Foundation © 2026.

and medium specificity of "advanced" formal languages. Two of the desert sculptures, including the curving white volumes of *Ode to Frank Gehry* (2000)—situated to the right of *Offshore Drilling* in Joshua Tree—were placed outside on LACMA's campus, cannily situated to play off the Renzo Piano–designed Resnick Pavilion and appropriately spaced between the large-scale permanent interventions of Heizer and the sculptor Chris Burden, whose comparatively high production values might otherwise risk reducing Purifoy's art to something less than the sum of its idiosyncratic parts. However, when shown inside the museum's galleries, the desert works were shorn of relational context and instead presented as monadic forms (Fig. 17.5): assemblages such as *No Contest (Bicycles)* (1991)—a ram-

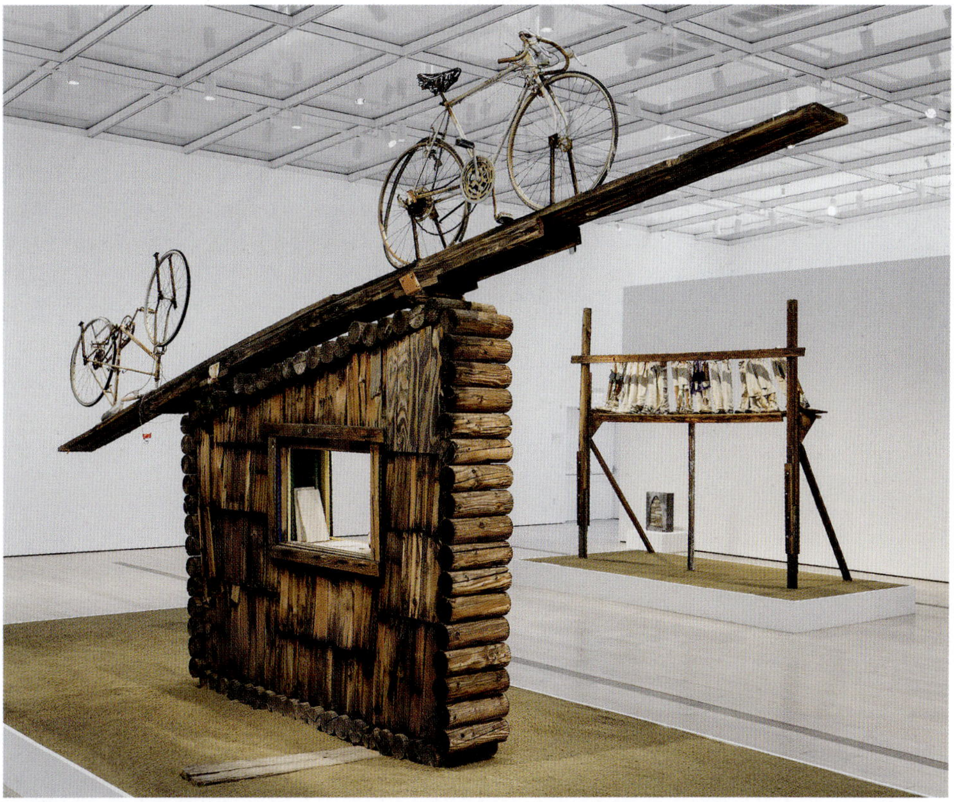

Figure 17.5
Noah Purifoy, *No Contest*, 1991. Assemblage construction, 168 × 252 × 24 in. Installation photograph, *Noah Purifoy: Junk Dada* at the Los Angeles County Museum of Art, Sunday, June 7, 2015–Sunday, September 27, 2015 BCAM 3; reopens October 10, 2015–January 3, 2016 in BCAM 3 East. Courtesy Noah Purifoy Foundation © 2026. Photo © Museum Associates/LACMA.

shackle structure with rusty bikes perched atop a seesaw-like plank—were placed on white platforms filled with sand and thus separated both from the viewer's interaction with them and from one another, in a departure from the experience of the scale, sound, and movement of the works in Joshua Tree.

While this presentational strategy had its benefits, highlighting the formal ingenuity of Purifoy's plays on color, composition, and the painterly across bodies of work grouped together in separate galleries, it also prioritized one side of his dialectical engagement with the autonomous art object. Throughout his oeuvre, Purifoy worked with the wall and the frame as sites of articulation and disruption, whether in the talismanic *Pressure* (1966), with its crushed metal container protruding from a duotone abstract grid (Fig. 17.6), or in the devastating bait-and-switch that is *Strange Fruit* (2002), whose title echoes Billie Holiday's mournful homage to lynching victims

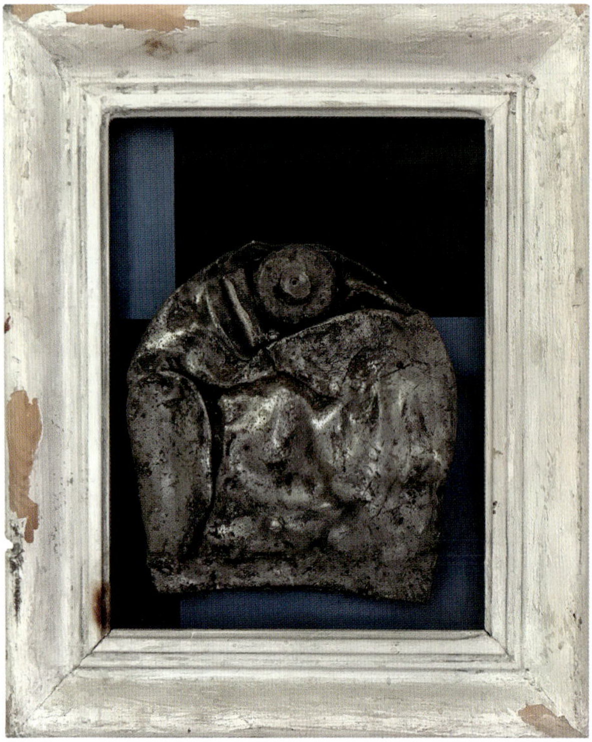

Figure 17.6
Noah Purifoy, *Pressure*, 1966. Mixed media; 17 × 14 in. Courtesy Noah Purifoy Foundation © 2026.

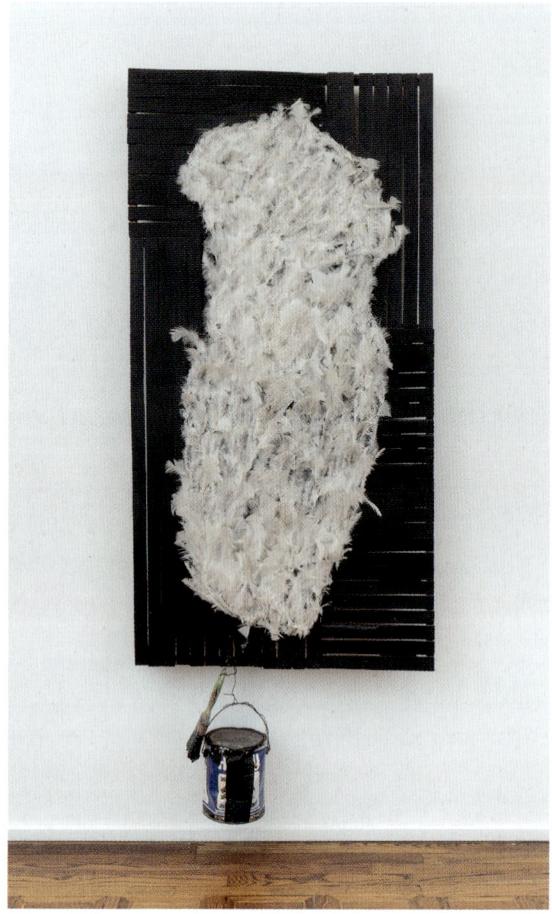

Figure 17.7
Noah Purifoy, *Strange Fruit*, 2002. Mixed media assemblage with feathers, acrylic, wood, paint can, and brush; 74 × 31½ × 6½ in. Courtesy Noah Purifoy Foundation © 2026.

even as the work itself seems to have been literally tarred and feathered, complete with a can and brush hanging from the bottom edge (Fig. 17.7). These examples underline that the artist aimed not so much to consolidate the integrity of the frame but to explore its inescapable permeability or fungibility, like the most adept sculptural precursors of institutional critique cited by the art historian Benjamin H. D. Buchloh.[7]

Like the practices of his unlikely fellow travelers, such as Hans Haacke, and his clear successors, such as Theaster Gates, Purifoy's wide-ranging activities with and beyond the object pose a formidable challenge to the protocols of museum preservation and display, particularly to a monographically framed exhibition. Although the show's richly illustrated catalog—which does not, unfortunately, reproduce all of the works included in the exhibition—provides a useful chronology of the artist's life and a compelling set of critical frames for thinking about his work, the exhibition only gestures toward, rather than stages, his complex entanglements with history, social work, activism, and arts programming as exemplified by his tenure on the California Arts Council from 1976 to 1987. By effectively sequestering the pertinent "documentary" materials within that darkened central gallery (alongside the artist's writings, a wall-size photograph of the aftermath of the Watts Riots, and installation shots of Purifoy's 1971 Brockman Gallery installation, *Niggers Ain't Gonna Never Be Nothing—All They Want to Do Is Drink and Fuck*, a scathing indictment of the racist discourses and practices that [re-]create black urban poverty), *Junk Dada* missed an opportunity to model how a pointedly multivalent cultural practice might be staged within the museum and thereby put pressure on those hard-and-fast divisions that continue to subtend the institutional policing of what counts as aesthetic experience.

Thanks to this contextual restraint, however, the exhibition did provide a much-needed opportunity to home in on the formal logic of Purifoy's work and to consider how it offers an alternate ending to the history of modernist sculpture. In his hands, this narrative does not "conclude," as Buchloh argued, with the late '70s installations of Michael Asher within institutional spaces[8] but is instead dispersed, cast out into the desert along with the artist himself, to a place where three-dimensional forms can test their mettle against the detritus of American culture from which they emerge—and which they are destined to once again become—as well as against nature itself. This is not, however, a naturalized nature. As his very materials—for example, the American flag, itself an abstract representation of colonial territory, draping part of *Aurora Borealis* (1995), an open structure that activates the shifting light conditions of the Mojave—constantly remind us, Purifoy was often in dialogue with the "nature" that human institutions everywhere travesty and reshape (Fig. 17.8). As Andrea Fraser would observe the year after Purifoy's death, such institutions are wherever art is. Purifoy's physically and politically open museum, then, literally and figuratively models the movement that Fraser advocates from a "critique of institutions to an institution of critique," holding up a discrepant mirror to all manner of hegemonic practices that still fail to give people of color sufficient airtime.[9]

With this in mind, it is all the easier to see the political implications of another key aspect of Purifoy's oeuvre: in his work and accountings of it, process is paramount, emphasizing his art's formal and conceptual affinity with Native American and African diasporic modes of ritual and making do, in which the object is a participant in a process rather than an end in itself. To frame the issue in other ontological and epistemological terms, his work can be understood as what the theorist Karen Barad would call a performative configuring and reconfiguring of the material world that is always

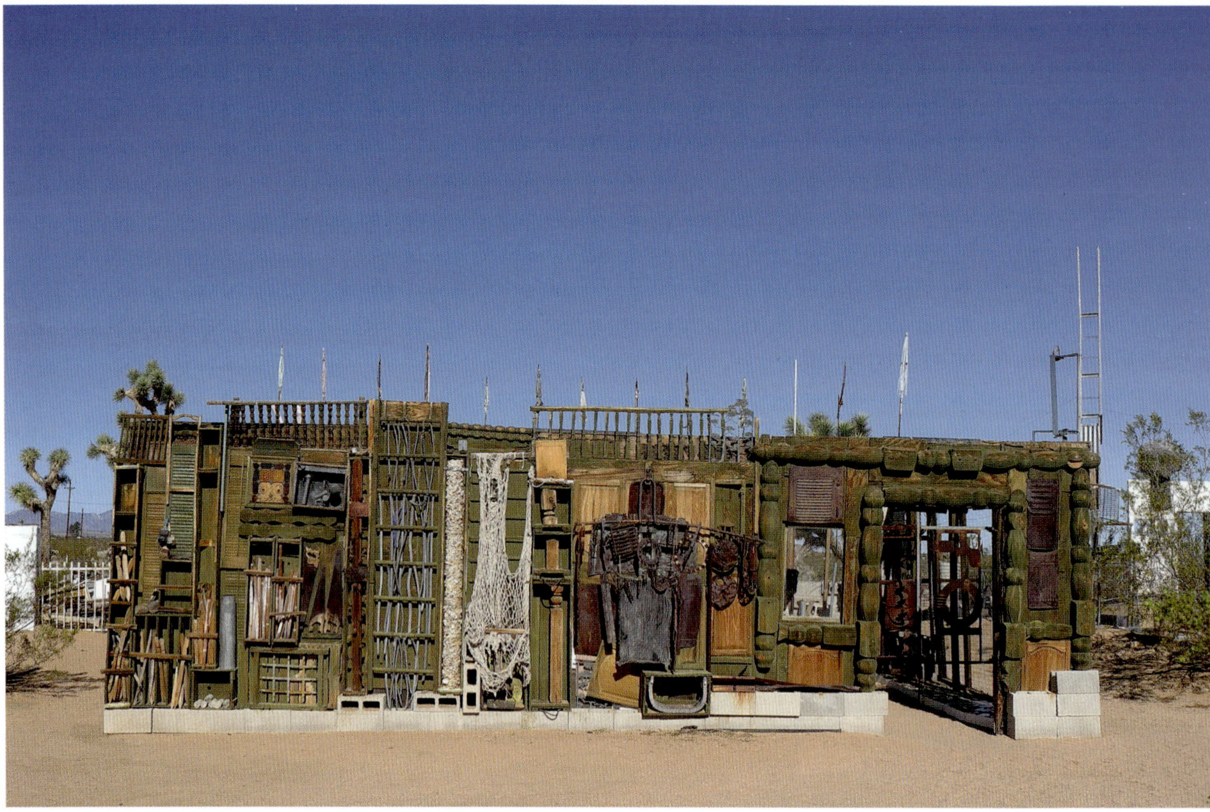

Figure 17.8
Noah Purifoy, *Aurora Borealis*, 1999-2000. Assemblage construction.
Courtesy Noah Purifoy Foundation © 2026.

open to ongoing processes of transformation, whether or not they are witnessed by human subjects.[10] In this way, Purifoy's practice suggests a remapping of the history of late twentieth-century art that prioritizes endless material promiscuity and temporal flux as opposed to high modernist purity, an approach animating recent curatorial and art historical rescriptings of both modern and American art. Of course, this approach rhymes with Rauschenberg's embrace of radical material contingency and immanence, in which the work is not merely subject to the human, but open to the fundamentally decentered, aleatory landing of "lights, shadows, and particles."[11] Yet Purifoy understands that the ceaseless reconfiguration of the material world is also always a politics of things taken and given away, things exchanged and ruined or stolen, and that these histories of circulation, of things in time, are inseparable from the things themselves. While *Junk Dada* did not quite materialize these lessons, it still brilliantly demonstrated the many beginnings that Purifoy's work continues to offer us now that its time has again arrived.

Notes

1 Michael Hanchard, "Afro-Modernity: Temporality, Politics, and the African Diaspora," *Public Culture* 11, no. 1 (1999): 253.

2 Reyner Banham, *Los Angeles: The Architecture of Four Ecologies* (Penguin Books, 1976), 114.

3 Robert Morris, "Notes on Sculpture II," *Artforum* 5, no. 2 (1966); repr. in Gregory Battock, ed., *Minimal Art: A Critical Anthology* (University of California Press, 1995), 232.

4 Robert Smithson and Jack D. Flam, *Robert Smithson, the Collected Writings* (University of California Press, 1996).

5 Noah Purifoy, quoted in C. Ian White, "On Noah Purifoy," in *Noah Purifoy: Junk Dada* (Delmonico Books, 2015), 105.

6 Michelle M. Wright, "Forces to Be Reckoned With: Michelle M. Wright on the Physics of Black Art," *Artforum* 53, no. 10 (Summer 2015): 155-56.

7 Benjamin H. D. Buchloh, "Michael Asher and the Conclusion of Modernist Sculpture," *Art Institute of Chicago Museum Studies* 10 (1983): 277-95.

8 Buchloh, "Michael Asher and the Conclusion of Modernist Sculpture."

9 Andrea Fraser, "From the Critique of Institutions to an Institution of Critique," *Artforum* 44, no. 1 (2005): 278.

10 Karen Barad, *Meeting the Universe Halfway: Quantum Physics and the Entanglement of Matter and Meaning* (Duke University Press, 2007), 139.

11 John Cage, "On Robert Rauschenberg, Artist, and His Work," in *Silence: Lectures and Writings* (Wesleyan University Press, 1961), 102.

18

SOLAR ETHICS

In the following pages, I want to return to and so differently inflect some of my persistent interests in questions regarding race, time, signification, and critical artistic practice in the United States. In so doing, I hope to reflect on the ways that art can model forms of ethical engagement with the historical production of blackness and the material world in our digitally driven, neoliberal capitalist, post-black present. The locus of my inquiry is the force field that has gathered around the musician, poet, composer, prophet, and philosopher Sun Ra, who has become increasingly central to a range of cultural producers since his death in 1993, particularly those associated with Afrofuturism. Now, as George Lewis and other scholarly luminaries of advanced music will tell you, that is not a term Sun Ra would have been likely to use. "Afrofuturism" was first popularized by Euro-American critic Mark Dery in his 1993 intervention, "Black to the Future."[1] The term has been subsequently taken up and reconfigured in a range of venues, whether the 2013 Studio Museum in Harlem exhibition, *The Shadows Took Shape*, or Alondra Nelson's 2002 pioneering special issue of *Social Text*, which looked back to Dery in broadly defining Afrofuturism as "'African American voices' with 'other stories to tell about culture, technology, and things to come.'"[2]

This is an apt enough definition, though my approach will be a bit more pointed in its attempt to understand how Ra's thinking manifests across the visual field. His continuing appeal derives, in no small part, from his self-styling not as a mere earthbound jazz pianist but as a cosmic being hailing from Saturn by way of ancient Egypt. While commentators have made much of Ra's brilliant troping on black alienation, especially his embrace of outer space, equally important to his cultural project was a rethinking of time and its materialization. For my part, I want to consider aspects of Ra's self-styling, poetics, and positions, as well as their implications for a selection of contemporary artists working and exhibiting in the American context who identify with his utopian aspirations and who have taken up the challenge thrown down by his life and work: Glenn Ligon, Mai-Thu Perret, Cauleen Smith, Edgar Arceneaux, and Rashid Johnson.

Let me be clear, then: this is not an essay *about* Sun Ra and I am no musicologist. What I ultimately hope to suggest is that Ra's figure and philosophy, as variously formed and deformed by contemporary artists, point us toward approaches to history that take seriously both the recursiveness and simultaneity of time as it unfolds within, beyond, and across the larger black world. In one sense, my thinking jives with the recent efforts of art historians, such as the modern Americanist Richard Meyer and the early modern Europeanists Christopher Wood and Alexander Nagel, to underline the plural temporality of the work of art, which the latter scholars describe as "a message whose sender and destination are constantly shifting."[3] Ra not only understood this fact, but actively *incarnated* it, modeling an ethics and producing a persona that remixed historical, vernacular, theoretical, and mystical citations drawn from various traditions. In so doing, he provided, in his words, an "*alter* destiny," a new set of possibilities for contemporary artists who, in looking to his practice, have been able to recognize their own proximity to ostensibly distant historical modes, figures, and subjects.[4] To make these claims stick, I first want to say a few words about Ra's biography and then explore why cultural practitioners have variously turned to him before lighting on the contributions of Ligon, Perret, Smith, Arceneaux, and Johnson.

Some words on Ra: Born into the crushing segregation of Birmingham, Alabama, as Herman Poole Blount around 1914, he moved to Chicago in 1946 where he would become Sun Ra. Such a transformation makes a certain sort of absurdist sense. For in physically moving north and in retroactively moving his birthplace, Ra mitigated the conceptual reach if not the felt impositions of racial time in the articulation of his own subjective horizons.[5] As both an Egyptian god and an alien being, Ra temporally constructed himself in relationship both to a fantasized black past located elsewhere and to an outer space necessarily defined as else when. Of course, the Chicago where Ra arrived was no racial utopia, but it was there that he lived until 1961, and where he founded his band, the Arkestra, as well as the record company El Saturn with Alton Abraham. At the same time, he rubbed shoulders with the heady mix of black religious, political, and eschatological sects, from the Black Hebrews to the Nation of Islam, that made Chicago's Washington Park such a vibrant intellectual playground. Ra went on to live in New York, before settling in Philadelphia in 1968, which would provide the base for his jaunts to Europe, California, and even to Heliopolis in Egypt itself. In 1971, for instance, he taught a course at the

University of California, Berkeley, "The Black Man in the Cosmos," whose reading list included everything from *The Tibetan Book of the Dead* to the Theosophist writings of Madame Blavatsky.

For cultural practitioners of numerous stripes, Ra's openness to such a diversity of sources in his poetry, philosophy, visual conceits, and far-out mythmaking have arguably been just as important as his pioneering musicianship, which was also ahead of its time, particularly, as the literary critic Aldon Nielsen has shown, thanks to its unprecedented "transmutations of the vocabularies of the big band."[6] Ra often took the same musical motifs and obsessively reiterated and recombined them, so that a single recording of his signature song, "Space Is the Place," might feature several riffs on its refrain in styles ranging from orchestral swing to free jazz. And if the sonic allows us to dig how Ra's permutational aesthetics unfold in time, then it is to the visual that we must look to begin thinking how he has come to occupy space.

In John Coney's 1972 film, *Space Is the Place*, Ra, playing himself, returns to earth in a music-powered spaceship to save black people from the forces of governmental, corporate, and criminal oppression (Fig. 18.1). At one point in the eighty-two-minute narrative, Ra provides a profound (and profoundly good-humored) meditation on the exigencies of black life at a community center in Oakland, combining a fabulous visual presence with a brilliant political philosophy that animates his plain talk to the youth whom he aims to save, recruit, and "enlight" about their mythic unreality, their total lack of ontological resistance in the eyes of the modern world.[7] While *Space Is the Place* has had an outsize impact on Ra's reception, the film is, to be sure, only the tip of the iceberg in terms of both his cultural production and its pervasive effects. Ra's visual self-articulation was promiscuous and peculiar, licensing the interstellar turns of the recording artists P-Funk, Dr. Octagon, and "Archandroid" Janelle Monae, as well as inspiring legions of practitioners from across the globe: French Lili Reynaud Dewar, Austrian Karl Heinz Jeron, Kenyan Wangechi Mutu, and the South African Tracey Rose. This list could easily go on; for the moment, it is sufficient to highlight just one example: a collage by the art band Destroy All Monsters in which Ra figures in a pantheon of Detroit heroes, considerably less slick, perhaps, than Monae's self-portraiture, though no less heartfelt as homage (fig. 18.2).

Yet Ra's continuing appeal as an inspiration and icon cannot be chalked up entirely either to his outlandish persona or to his music's discordant pleasures. Rather, it is part and parcel, I would contend, of his embrace of material and temporal impossibilities in the service of an ethical project. As he famously put it in a 1986 interview with John Corbett, "My business is changing the planet. . . . My job is to change five billion people to something else. Totally impossible. . . . [I]t can't be done but I have to do it."[8]

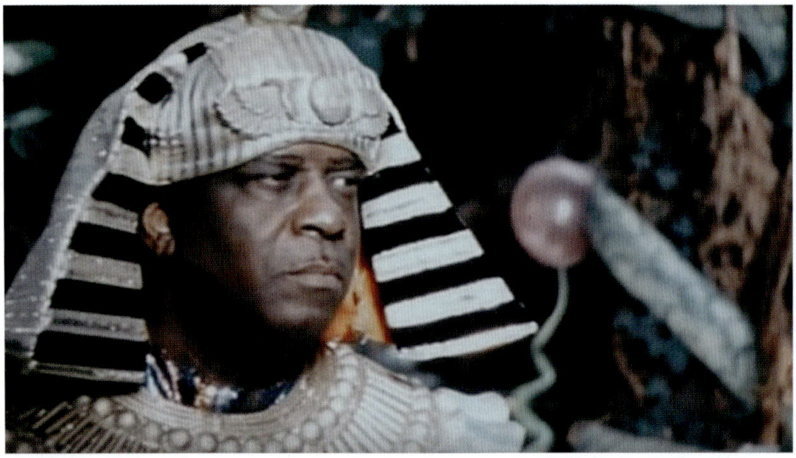

Figure 18.1
John Coney, *Space is the Place*, still, 1972.

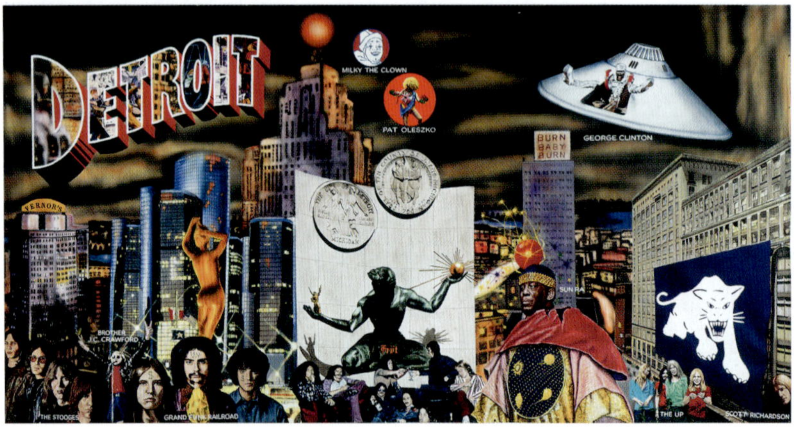

Figure 18.2
Mike Kelley and Destroy All Monsters Collective (Jim Shaw, Cary Loren), *Greetings from Detroit*, from *Strange Fruit: Rock Apocrypha* (detail), 2000. Acrylic on canvas, 120 × 228 in. © Mike Kelley Foundation for the Arts. All Rights Reserved / VAGA at ARS, NY. © Jim Shaw. © Cary Loren. Courtesy of Mike Kelley Foundation for the Arts.

Ra imagined his work as effectively interminable, an ambition that obeys neither the logic of Western linear time nor the means, whether temporal appropriation or millenarian anticipation, which political theorist Michael Hanchard cites as key strategies of African diasporic resistance.[9] Refusing to align himself neatly with earthbound politics or potentialities, Ra insisted on wedding contraries that hold out a range of models for differently imagining the unfolding of blackened existence.

To begin illuminating that imagination, we might take heed of what Ligon wrote about Ra and his onetime collaborator David Hammons, a black trickster equally out of step: "Not being from here is a movement toward placelessness, toward the utopic, *and* a deep critique of American society. Their genius was to employ a postmodern concern with the emptying of the self as a critical strategy, one that might have particular resonance with a people historically positioned at the margin of what was considered human."[10] It is this sense of Ra's ability to index and open onto a range of dreams, aspirations, and constructions for subjects on all sides of the color line despite and because of the apparently timeless and mythic quality of black dereliction that, I've come to think, makes him such a useful site for modeling the im/possibilities of counterhegemonic articulation within artistic practice *now*.[11]

Consider, in this light, the Swiss-born artist Mai-Thu Perret's 2006 *Banner for Sun Ra*, a black pennant with silver lamé geometric cutouts (Fig. 18.3). In its material form and institutional placement—usually hung high from the ceiling—the work echoes the *Space Poems* of Renée Green, each printed with phrases that recall many of her most vital inspirations and interlocutors, Ra included. The visual logic of Perret's piece, however, seizes upon a different vocabulary, even as it makes explicit an engagement with Ra only hinted at by her exhibition, *And Every Woman Will Be a Walking Synthesis of the Universe*, also mounted in 2006, at the Renaissance Society of Chicago (Fig. 18.4). There she executed a mammoth teapot-cum-spaceship, whose title, *Little Planetary Harmony*, was inspired by a Sun Ra track. Perret is perhaps best known, however, for her work's consistent engagement with European modernisms, from the German-born Josef Albers's abstract paintings to the letters of the Russian constructivist Aleksandr Rodchenko. All of these were elements in her Renaissance Society show, itself yet another iteration of Perret's ongoing project, *The Crystal Frontier*, which, through texts, exhibitions, and objects produced over the past dozen years, offers glimpses into the life of a fictional women's commune somewhere in the southwestern United States, sometime in the early twentieth century. Each iteration of the project revises and constructs its history in relation to the time of its arrival, so that when invited to participate in the 2004 international fair Art Basel for the first time Perret presented a rabbit hutch filled with live animals that reflected the commune's need—and her own—to "go to market."

To be sure, Perret is but one of many artists working today whose practice plumbs the archive of art history and attributes her objects to made-up characters, very much in line with a rage, starting in the early aughts, for art that embraces utopian and collective aesthetics. The problems inherent in this mode of making abound: it often risks reiterating earlier practices as mere fashion, so that past aspirations are cynically recycled not to activate

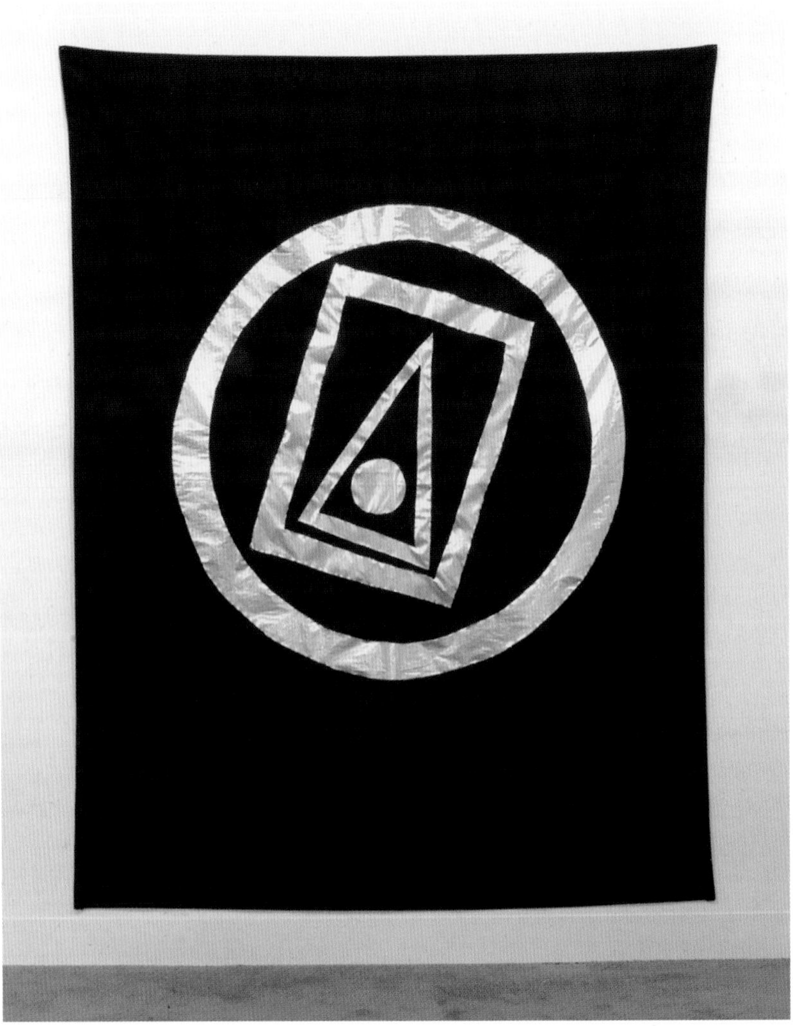

Figure 18.3
Mai-Thu Perret, *Banner for Sun Ra*, 2007. Fabric, 72 × 56 in.

their possibilities in and as the now but to add more resonant historical and interpretive cues to the work that increase its value and its ability to hook into well-trafficked circuits of meaning within the international biennial circuit. As the critic Lane Relyea has importantly argued, such artworks often mimic rather than expose the logic of capital, which increasingly prioritizes not single objects or subjects but the flows of the exhibitionary system itself.[12]

Perversely enough, in certain European quarters, Ra has become an icon of those contemporary modes of production and subjectivation that prize individual choice and personal customization in the name of a "freedom"

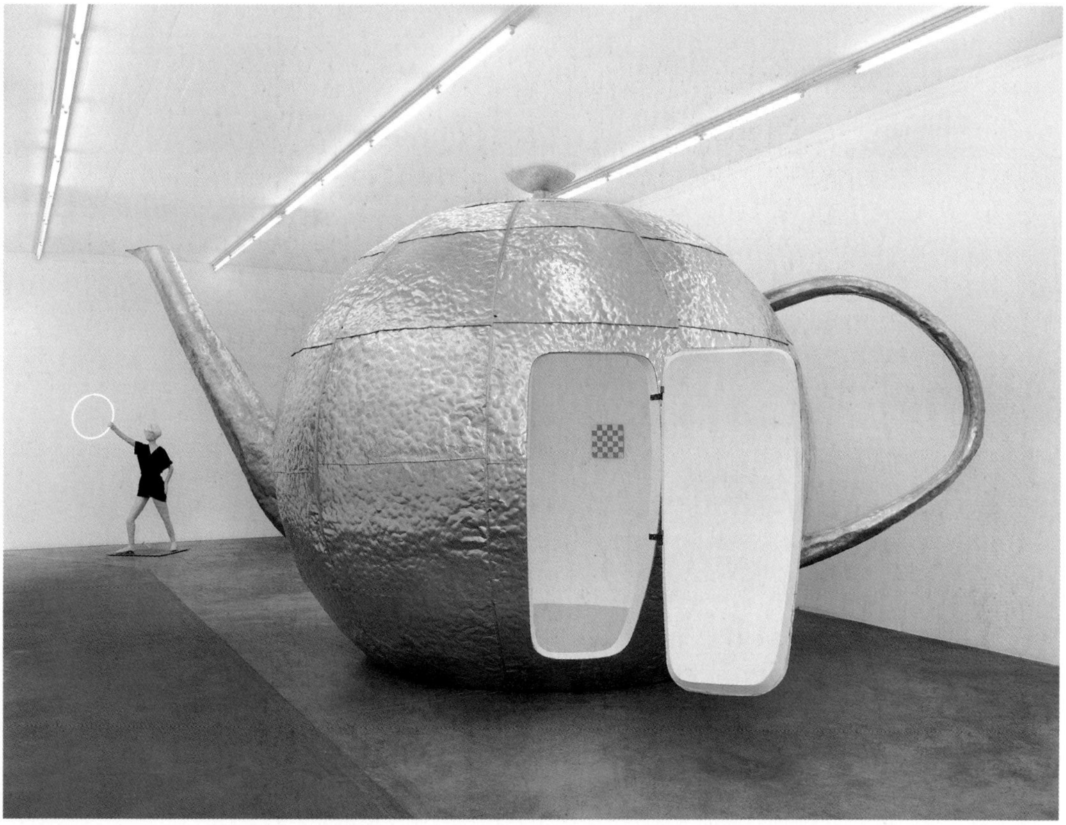

Figure 18.4
Mai-Thu Perret, *Little Planetary Harmony*, 2006. Wood slices, hammered aluminum, aluminum colored acrylic paint, foam, plaster, 353 × 665.5 × 365.7 cm. © Mai-Thu Perret courtesy the artist and David Kordansky Gallery. Photo: Annik Wetter Photographie.

that is, in fact, an intensification of those historical processes, exemplified by transatlantic slavery, aimed at the total colonization and commoditization of the human sensorium. To take Ra in that direction is to reduce his ethical project to an eccentric personal cosmology, a series of apolitical plays on an almost arbitrary set of historically deracinated signifiers, as opposed to a tactical recalibration of the system of signification itself with all the precarity such a gambit entails. A similar ambition, I think, percolates within Perret's practice. For unlike others working in speculative terrain, her art time and again emphasizes the lapses of history by looking precisely to those utopias that failed, to those trajectories that faltered, to those networks that could not sufficiently extend into the world and thereby transform it. In making a flag *for* Sun Ra, Perret does not blindly pledge allegiance *to* him—if anything the work more closely resembles an intergalactic death shroud than a rallying banner—but instead considers what his temporal distancing and arrival makes available.

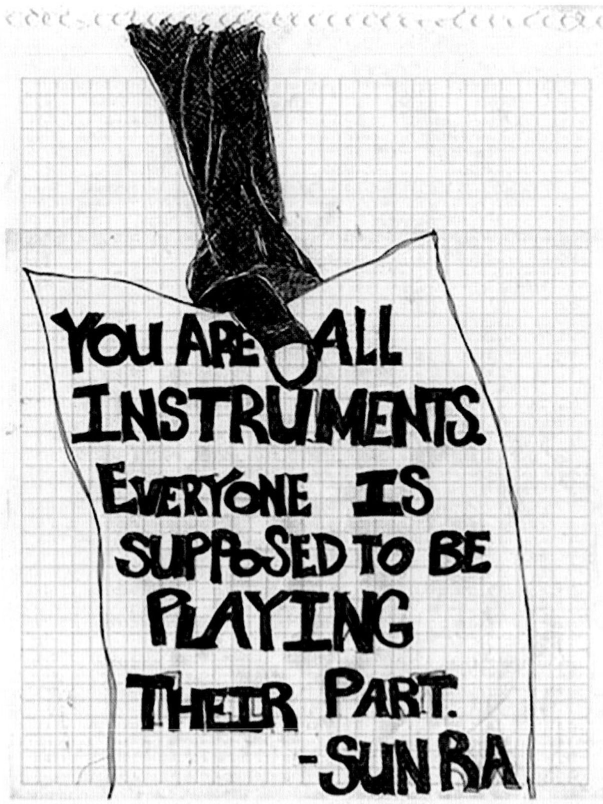

Figure 18.5
Cauleen Smith, *Journeyman*, 2008. Courtesy of the artist.

Perret's muted ambivalence toward Ra is inversely mirrored by the critical celebration of the American filmmaker Cauleen Smith, who revels in the possibilities without losing sight of the failures (Fig. 18.5). Perhaps more than any other practitioner that I know of, she has effectively apprenticed herself to the jazzman: Smith moved from San Diego to Chicago in search of Ra in 2008, and upon her arrival in the city, she immersed herself deeply in his archives at the University of Chicago, at the Experimental Station, and in various private collections. One of the results of that labor was her 2012 exhibition, *Journeyman*, at the not-for-profit space threewalls that featured a stage for performances, materials from Ra's library, and her own drawings that appropriate his words, as well as a double album containing fragments pulled from archival tapes of the musician's recording sessions.

Her most spectacular plays on Ra's legacy, however, have been her orchestrations of flash mobs throughout the city. In these works, Smith's collaborators, the Rich South High School Marching Band, suddenly appear as the Solar Flare Arkestra and play fifteen- to twenty-minute performances of Sun Ra tunes, usually "Space Is the Place" (Fig. 18.6). As a firsthand witness to one such manifestation in Chicago's Chinatown, I found

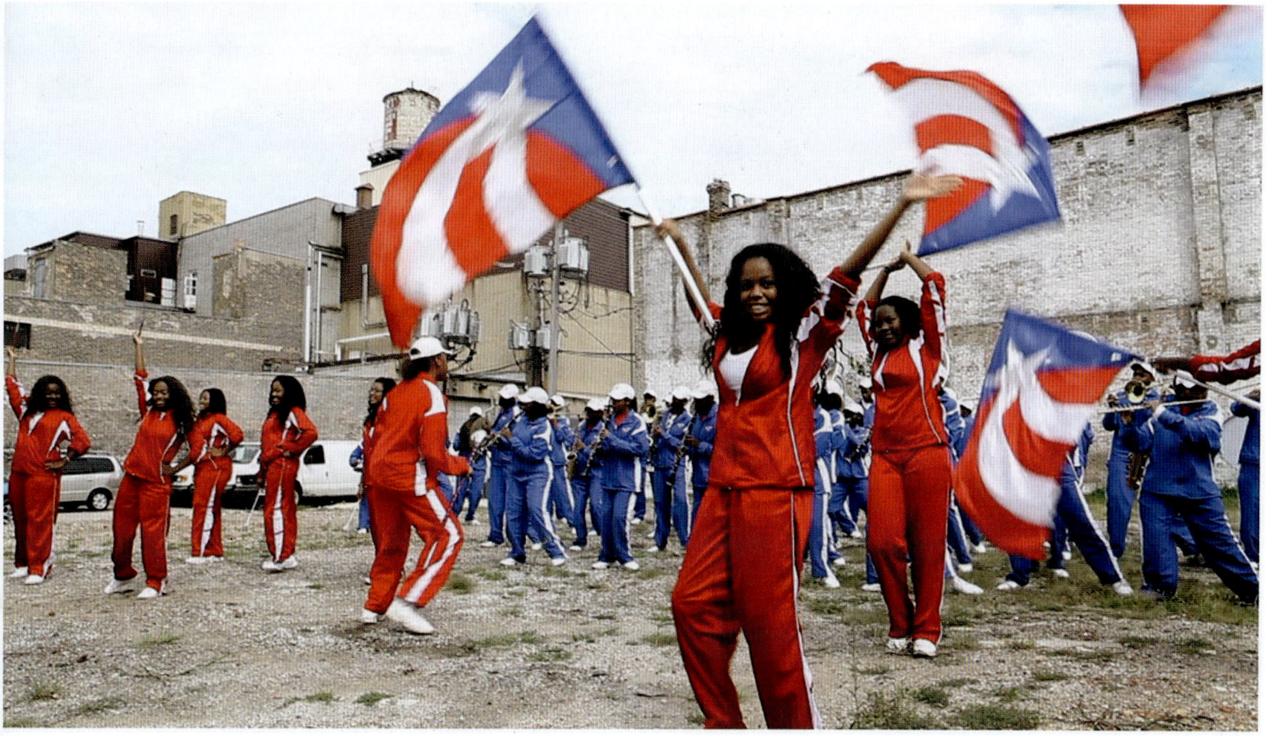

Figure 18.6
Cauleen Smith, *Solar Flare Arkestra*, 2011.

the parade absolutely thrilling to watch and continue to be moved even by the grainy footage of it featured on YouTube, a democratic platform that allows the artist to make her work available to a wider set of audiences than the prophet could have likely ever imagined.[13] And as Smith has noted, her performances—joyful, disruptive, collective—stand apart from Ra's actual reported leadership style, which, to hear some folks tell it, might be described as a brand of messianic and largely benevolent despotism intended to ensure his band members' ascetic devotion to the musical spheres.

What connects such artists to Ra's legacy, in other words, is not an attempt to reproduce his forms or structures but an investment in thinking about and modeling change despite its impossibility, perhaps not offering revolution but at least a measure of interpretive freedom. As Meyer might put it, theirs is a dialectical view of history that emphasizes that the contemporary is "a *relational* condition."[14] Simply having the "right" references to establish connections to either past masters or freshly recovered antecedents is not enough: what must be plumbed in order to arrive at a critical practice is the temporal logic driving these connections. I think this matters deeply for contemporary art in part due to the "return," with a vengeance, of the 1960s and 1970s in artistic discourse, at times, as the curator James Meyer has shown, simply to add a veneer of criticality to otherwise "problematic" works that invoke past radicalisms only, it would seem, to hollow them out.[15]

One of the more telling examples is, to my mind, the art of Kelley Walker. In a work such as *Black Star Press* of 2006, he travesties the always already fraught appearance of blackness in the visual field by appropriating an image of African American protest, rotating it 90 degrees, blowing it up to billboard size, and smearing it with white pigment and dark chocolate. In so doing, Walker not only inserts himself into a long line of Western history painting that takes racialized antagonism as its subject—think back to Édouard Manet's renditions of the execution of the Mexican emperor Maximilian of the late 1860s or to Andy Warhol's *Race Riots* made just under a hundred years later—but he also materializes our distance from and fetishistic relationship to narratives of black progress given their seeming repetitiveness and ubiquity.

As Ligon has perceptively written elsewhere, Walker's "Negro Problem" and the failure of writers to critically address it, is very much our own: in troping the logic of racial dispossession, Walker's practice cannily brings forth art history's supporting role in what I have come to call the social reproduction of white supremacy.[16] Walker's work thus productively symptomatizes the ongoing march of racial time, its looks and logic in the present, and the inequalities on which it depends. The visibility and profitability of such work, as well as our failure to engage the racial imaginary that constitutes it, raise key questions: To whom does "black" history belong? Is this history safely dead, available for appropriation without consequence, or is it always emerging into an interminable now? How do we reckon with, understand, and make ethical claims on the past to revivify them in the present? What is the logic behind such connections, and what are the criteria for evaluating them?

For Ra, that logic was arrived at through temporal, formal, musical, and—most saliently for us—linguistic permutation, the ways that words might be altered to arrive at different orders of meaning buried within them. The name of his band, the "Arkestra," was, for instance, inspired by what happens to the word *orchestra* when an Alabaman says it, much like his nickname "Sonny" led him to the Sun and eventually to the Egyptian sun god Ra. As the African diasporic scholar Brent Hayes Edwards has shown, such wordplay is part and parcel of Sun Ra's practice.[17] Take the short Ra poem, "Words and the Impossible," followed by Edwards's helpful gloss of it:

> The elasticity of words
> The phonetic-dimension of words

The multi-self of words
Is energy for thought—If it is a reality.
        The idea that words
Can form themselves into the impossible
Then the way to the impossible
Is through words.
        The fate of humanity is determined
        By the word they so or approve
        Because they reap what they so
        Even if it is the fruit of their lies

Of particular note here is how Ra has written *so*—"s-o"—where we would expect "s-o-w," *sow*. In Edwards's account, such shifts emphasize Ra's obsession with "the *multi-self of words, the phonetic-dimension of words* in action: an impossible grammar, an impossible or *immeasurable* equation between grapheme [the written word] and phoneme [the spoken utterance]. The mark on the page doesn't equal what we *hear*, and the practice of the impossible occurs in the interstices of that discrepancy."[18]

Particularly illustrative of this kind of phonetic transmutation is Ra's treatment of the word *enlightment*, which has been brilliantly parsed by the writer Terri Kapsalis, a key figure alongside the gallerist John Corbett and the curator Anthony Elms in the prophet's critical and archival resuscitation.[19] "Enlightment" is the name of a tune that Ra cowrote in 1959. The title was recorded both on that first album and in notes from Ra's hand, but in subsequent reissues, an *en* is interjected so that it becomes "Enlightenment." As Kapsalis suggests, "'enlight' and 'enlighten' share a number of meanings ('to shed upon, to illuminate'), but 'enlight' offers the additional meanings of 'to kindle' and 'to cause to shine.'"[20] Thus, in her accounting, Ra forwards the fiery truth of enlightment, which is both literally and figuratively a deconstruction of "Enlightenment" aims and ambitions, an attempt to blaze like the sun rather than just see its light.

Extending Edwards's and Kapsalis's thinking, I would contend that these kinds of transformations in language and in art not only shatter presumptions to universality in their emphasis on local accents and accentuations but also build the deformations of translation into the words and works themselves, which become records of an ongoing transfer rather than stilled concatenations of references. To my mind, this approach to the production of meaning resonates not only with Euro-American poststructuralist conceptions, such as the psychoanalyst Jacques Lacan's materialism of the signifier, but also with African diasporic writers', such as Nathaniel Mackey's emphasis on "discrepant engagement."[21] Rather than simply laud "the relational," then, Ra encourages us to think about how an artwork's permutation of its source opens onto a different history of

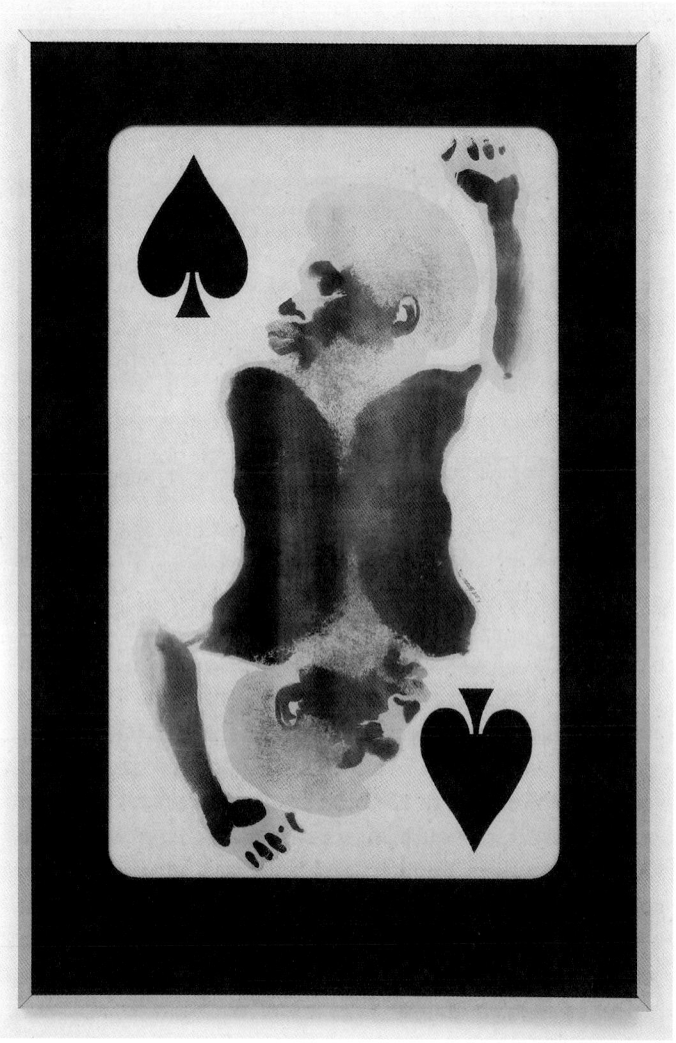

Figure 18.7
David Hammons, *Spade (Power for the Spade)*, 1969. © 2024 David Hammons / Artists Rights Society (ARS), New York.

its material and so establishes a new framework for approaching the construction of histories too often prized apart through the logics of racialized exclusion.

All of which begins to describe what might be called a solar ethics. Ra's fellow traveler Hammons, is, of course, a grand master of such tactics, modeled, for example, in his *Spade* (*Power for the Spade*) of 1969 (Fig. 18.7), which combines two referents for the titular word—the playing card symbol and the black male body—by pressing both on a singular surface so that a term of racist derogation and Black Power's response to it can be seen as

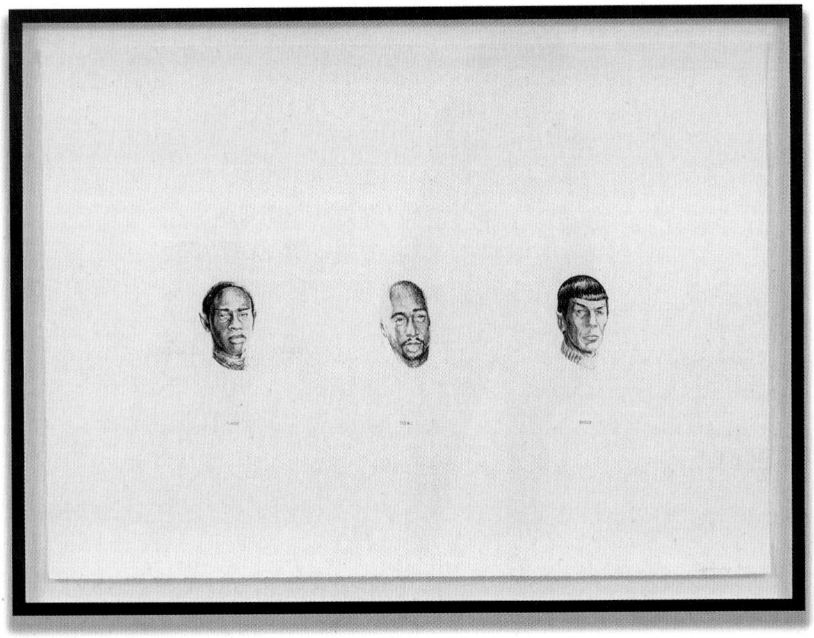

Figure 18.8
Edgar Arceneaux, *Tuvok, Tupac, Spock,* 2004. Lithograph on paper, 40 × 50 in. (101.6 × 127 cm). Edition of 20. Courtesy of the artist and Vielmetter Los Angeles.

effects of the same epistemic formation. Subsequent artists have further accentuated the importance of language to such punning plays in the visual field. Perret, for one, titled her ponderous teacup *Little Planetary Harmony*, which is how her Francophone ears heard Sun Ra's pronunciation of his title *Interplanetary Harmony*: thanks to a difference in accent, a straightforward declaration describing the unified movement of heavenly bodies becomes an indictment of the modern global political order.

The American-born L.A.-based artist Edgar Arceneaux has explicitly put such discrepancies to work in his hilarious print, *Tuvok, Tupac, Spock*, of 2006, which encompasses the Vulcan character of *Star Trek* fame, his black televisual inheritor on *Voyager*, and the slain rap star (Fig. 18.8). Two terms of that title, Spock and Tuvok, share a connection as products of the same science fictional universe, but a whole other world is opened up simply through the transformation of a single phoneme—from "vok" to "pok"—and through their triple presentation not as figures in a genealogy but as arriving all at once. In 2004, Arceneaux would build an entire exhibition around this conceit titled *Borrowed Sun* that produced Ra, the American conceptual artist Sol Lewitt, and the Earth's sun as permutations of each other merely inflected across different space-time coordinates and sprawled throughout the space of the exhibition in the form of drawings, sculptures, and projections and their intercourse. In so doing, Arceneaux

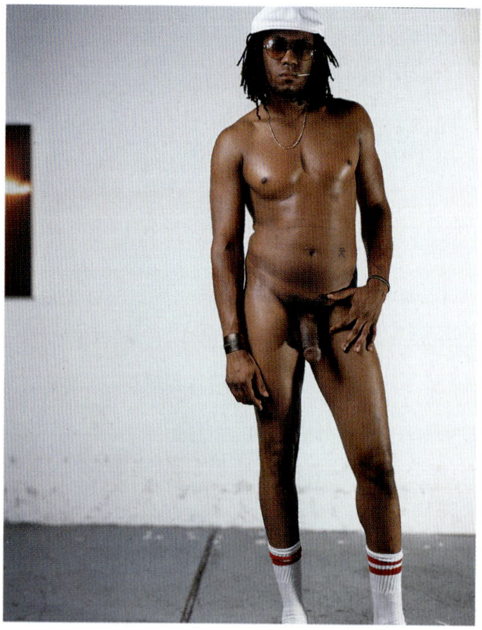

Figure 18.9
Rashid Johnson, *Self Portrait in Homage to Barkley Hendricks*, 2005. Lambda print, 188 × 142 cm / 74 × 55⅞ in. © Rashid Johnson. Courtesy the artist and Hauser & Wirth.

underlines that these figures belong together, even as he rings different changes on them and so intimates an expansive sense of how Ra might be engaged: not merely through visual references to him or other Afrofuturist icons, but by taking on the attitudes, principles, and *operations* that animate his work. It is in this direction that I now turn.

In particular, I look to Rashid Johnson—an artist based in New York and born just outside of Chicago—whose practice is also touched by Ra's influence, as evidenced by works and titles such as *Cosmic Slop*, *Space Is the Place*, and *Death by Black Hole*. Johnson's art refers wildly, no question, but it can also be taken as permutational in its approach to previous artistic antecedents. Take his *Self-Portrait in Homage to Barkley Hendricks* of 2005 (Fig. 18.9). To read this work correctly, we have to stick with the weirdness of the gesture—why suit yourself up as a naked black man in a painting from the late '70s and take a picture of yourself doing it?—and we must attend to the original work's richly discursive past. Johnson bases his confrontational image on Hendricks's 1977 painting, *Brilliantly Endowed (Self-Portrait)* [see Fig. 6.5 on p. 88], whose title is taken from an assessment of his painterly skill by the critic Hilton Kramer, who surely did not realize the Freudian slip he was making or how the artist would make it over into form when he called Hendricks "brilliantly endowed."[22]

Johnson's aim, I think, is not merely to update the slyly accommodating "fuck you" of Hendricks's painterly gesture within photographic presentation, a sexy "selfie" gone art world big-format picture. More important, the work articulates both historical novelty and structural continuity: both Hendricks and Johnson understand how, in the wake of the Black Power and black nationalist movements, the African American male body differently came to signify as a hot property, a development moored within an old logic of commoditization that finds its roots in transatlantic slavery. In his more resonant pieces Johnson differently negotiates the ways in which meaning, racial and otherwise, is generated by specific visual phenomena that consistently gesture elsewhere for their charge. This dependence and divergence emerge most forcefully when looking across Johnson's oeuvre, but they also come into focus within individual pieces. For example, in *Sweet Sweet Runner* of 2010, a middle-aged black man makes his way through New York's Central Park while the main theme to Melvin Van Peebles's blaxploitation classic, *Sweet Sweetback's Baadasssss Song* of 1971 plays in the background, registering the distance, however tenuous, that separates the DVD's bespectacled jogger from the film's fugitive hustler.

Cast in this light, Johnson's work, as seen through Ra's lens, opens onto larger cultural economies, indexing the schizophrenic attitudes toward race that have come to characterize the era of the post-black by an artist once dubbed as its prince.[23] As *its* very linguistic structure implies, post-black is still deeply entangled with the phantoms that everywhere proceed the dark subject, thereby arguably marking not so much an emergent racial paradigm as it freshly reveals the radical simultaneity of both "new" and "old" structures of racialization whose varying effects include the election of President Obama *and* the murder of black men such as Michael Brown, Eric Garner, and Freddie Gray at the hands of the police. This list, as we know all too well, goes on with no end in sight, underlining the centrality of spectacular antiblackness to Western civilization's libidinal circuitry, material overabundance, and conceptions of the human, all of which Ra aimed to leave behind.

So. What I have been arguing is that Ra's understanding of time and space puts pressure on our chronologically oriented modes of teaching, writing, and historicizing, asking that we be attentive to the *longue durée* of seemingly divergent epistemes and technologies, including our own. Indeed, it may be tempting to argue that our ability to sense such contiguities is a special province of our own moment, an age of compressed space and time, emblematized by the emergence of the internet's algorithmic gathering and leveling of cultural production, which, as the critic Tim Griffin has argued, seem to present deep informational fields but in fact function through the elimination of data.[24] And it is worth noting that the greatest uptick in interest in Ra's work in the art world seems to have occurred not during his life or at the moment of his death but in the early 2000s when the logic of Googlemind had already begun to clutch us in its grip.

Yet Ra, I think, fantasizes an imagined space outside of history and outside of that overdetermined network, a collective realm that remains fugitive today. For his genius was, in a sense, to inhabit rather than merely

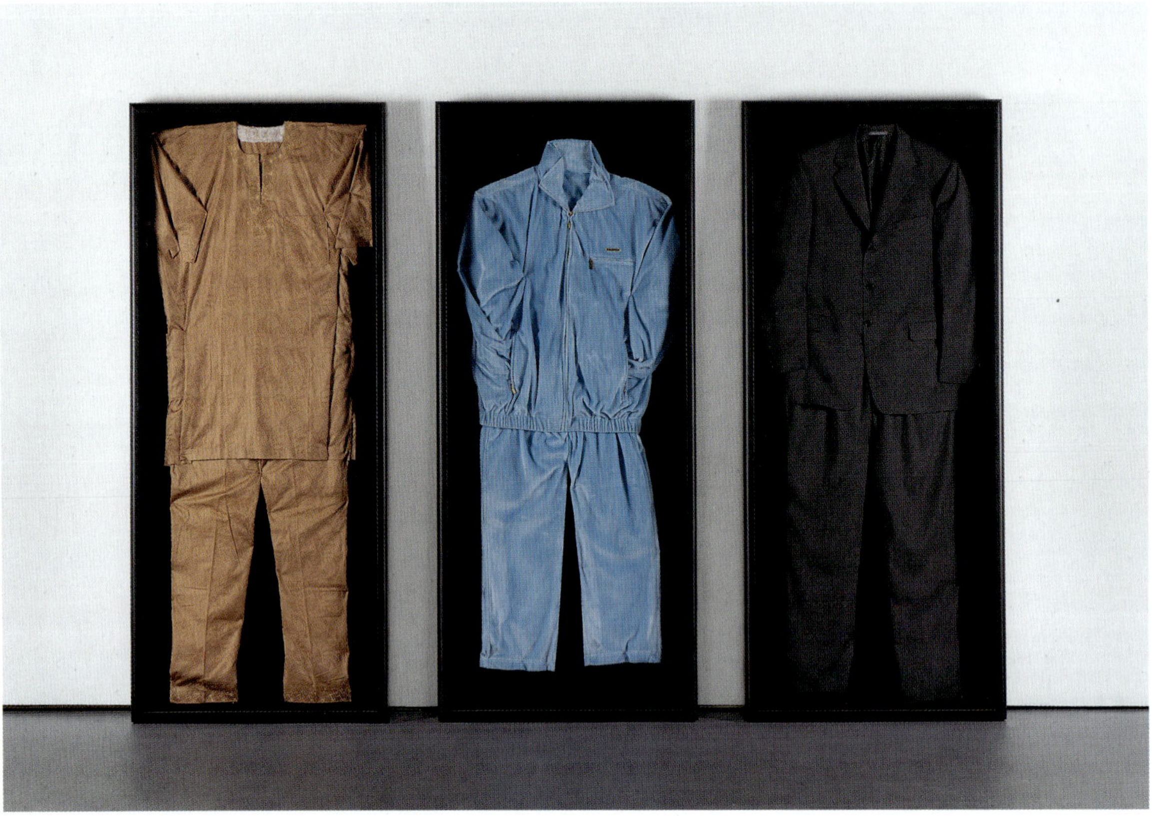

Figure 18.10
Rashid Johnson, *The Evolution of the Negro Political Costume*, 2004. Mixed media, Each: 74 × 32 × 4 in. (188 × 81.3 × 10.2 cm). Brooklyn Museum, Gift of Lawrence Calcagno, Mrs. John Colt, Mr. and Mrs. Allan D. Emil, Dr. and Mrs. Milton H. Schlesinger, and Mr. and Mrs. Harry L. Tepper, by exchange, 2005.58a-c. © Rashid Johnson (Photo: Brooklyn Museum).

gesture toward what Michelle M. Wright has called "the physics of blackness," which demands a reckoning with the relativity of temporal markers and each viewer's cultural assumptions.[25] According to Wright, most of us have not understood the radical impact of Albert Einstein's theories of general relativity, which blew apart the notion put forward by Newtonian physics that time is a fixed constant that always moves linearly and in one direction.[26] This notion of time undergirds not only Enlightenment philosophy but also narratives of black progress that take their measure from the epochal event of the transatlantic slave trade, which, as Ra knew so well, is less an event than a catastrophe that is always arriving. If we follow this lead, which allows us to appreciate how time slows down or speeds up depending on our subjective positioning, then a different view of identity comes into focus, one that is not tied to an ever upward telos but that

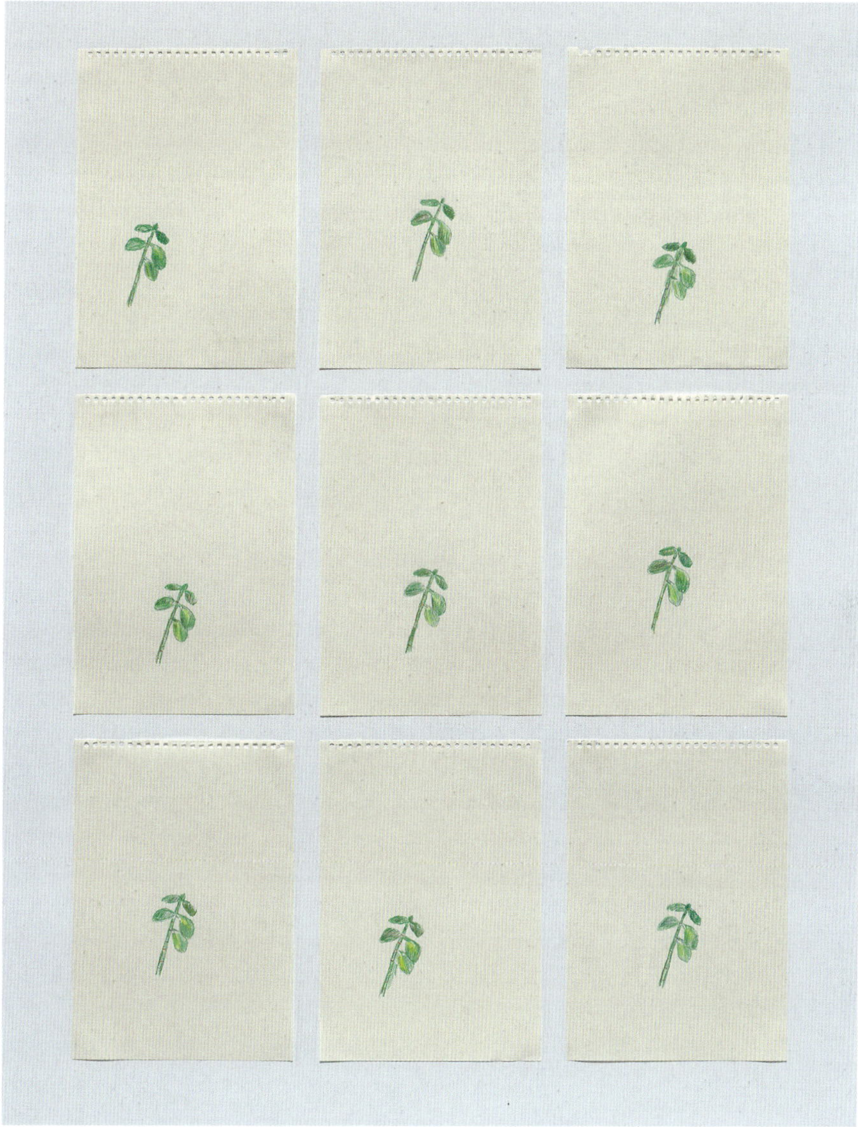

Figure 18.11
Glenn Ligon, *After Glenn (Plant Drawing)*, 2003. Colored pencil on paper; grid of 9 drawings, Each: 11.75 × 8.25 in. (29.8 × 20.9 cm). Photographer credit: Ronald Amstutz. © Glenn Ligon; courtesy of the artist, Hauser & Wirth, and Thomas Dane Gallery.

underlines the radical disjunction between space-times as they are lived, felt, and practiced in a world structured by racial time.[27]

We also each prioritize different blacknesses and different histories, as suggested by the varying affective charges of the suits Johnson assembled in his lightly satirical *Evolution of the Negro Political Costume*, which features clothes modeled after those worn by the most visible African American male politicians of the past three decades: Jesse Jackson's dashiki, Al Sharpton's once-ubiquitous tracksuit, and Obama's inaugural outfit (Fig. 18.10). Just as our attitude to such dubious icons shifts and morphs, so does our relation to blackness and the economies stemming from it that everywhere shape "a cultural unconscious in which the individual effects of racialization assume a shifting texture despite the unyielding ruthlessness of their overarching logic"[28]: we are always ahead of and behind these works, which, in Johnson's case, accounts for their funky blend of the nostalgic and the futuristic all at once.

What we see in his practice and in so many others inspired by Ra is an attempt to disturb the inequities of the present in order to grant us a past and a future that might yet belong to us all. Like Ra, Johnson misdirects in order to remain open to the strangeness and contingency of black being and for meaning itself, constantly gesturing to an outside to secure some way of being otherwise that allows not only artworks, but each of us to be materially rather than just virtually connected. Indeed, in the catalog accompanying her 2015 exhibition, *The Freedom Principle*, organized around the Ra-influenced Association for the Advancement of Creative Musicians, the curator Naomi Beckwith argues that contemporary practitioners' returns to the 1960s can be alternatively understood as a "form of social identification" that aims to rethink "the relationship between the artist and the public sphere."[29] As we have seen, the uses to which contemporary artists have put Ra's lessons in retooling such connections vary widely: I, and perhaps the man himself, would give pride of place to those practices that tend-toward-blackness in the senses of leaning into and caring for the abject, the marginal, the forgotten, all those beings constitutively darkened by their absenting from history if not from our memories.[30]

I want to close by looking to one more piece, fittingly by Ligon, as his writing and this work, *After Glenn (Plant Drawing)*, begin to suggest what a solar ethics might imply in the artistic and social fields when understood as a tactical operation independent of a particular visual referent (Fig. 18.11). Here, the artist presents us with a rendition of a jade plant, a self-portrait by other means, which he made at the tender age of ten and returned to in 2003 with the aid of a paper conservator who began to restore the substrate from which the jade emerges, a reparative operation that is extended a bit more each time the work is shown, as if the drawing were aging in reverse. In this piece, the institution of art is charged with an impossible undoing of time whose greatest promise might unfold outside of the museum's walls through a tending to the life of the world and its denizens with a care that, if Sun Ra is to be believed, is always on the horizon.

Notes

This text is derived from a lecture last delivered November 2018 at L'École des hautes études en sciences sociales (EHESS) in Paris, but it represents more than a decade of conversations. I thank Anne Lafont for the opportunity to present at EHESS; my colleagues Nana Adusei-Poku, Sampada Aranke, Graham Bader, Naomi Beckwith, Hannah Feldman, T. Jean Lax, Amy Mooney, Lane Relyea, and Krista Thompson for their thoughts on previous drafts; audiences at the Core Program, the Guggenheim Museum, Ox-Bow, the San Francisco Art Institute, and WORM Instituut voor Avantgardistiche Recreatie for their helpful comments; and, above all, my erstwhile Chicago comrades John Corbett, Anthony Elms, and Terri Kapsalis for turning me toward the Sun in undertaking the 2006 exhibition, *Interstellar Low Ways*, with Elms at the Hyde Park Art Center.

1 Mark Dery, "Black to the Future: Interviews with Samuel R. Delany, Greg Tate, and Tricia Rose," *South Atlantic Quarterly* 92, no. 4 (Fall 1993): 735-78.

2 Mark Dery, "Black to the Future," 738, quoted in Alondra Nelson, "Introduction: Future Texts," *Social Text* 71, vol. 20, no. 2 (Summer 2002): 9; *The Shadows Took Shape*, ed. Naima J. Keith and Zoé Whitley (Studio Museum in Harlem, 2013).

3 Alexander Nagel and Christopher S. Wood, *Anachronic Renaissance* (Zone Books, 2010), 9.

4 *Space Is the Place*, DVD, directed by John Coney, written by Sun Ra and Joshua Smith, produced by Jim Newman, performed by Sun Ra (1974; Plexifilm, 2003).

5 On racial time, see Michael Hanchard, "Afro-Modernity: Temporality, Politics, and the African Diaspora," *Public Culture* 11, no. 1 (1999): 253.

6 Aldon Lynn Nielsen, *Black Chant: Languages of African-American Postmodernism* (Cambridge University Press, 1997), 114-5.

7 Coney, *Space Is the Place*.

8 Sun Ra, quoted in John Corbett, "Sun Ra: Gravity and Levity," in *Extended Play: Sounding Off from John Cage to Dr. Funkenstein* (Duke University Press, 1994), 313.

9 Hanchard, "Afro-Modernity."

10 Glenn Ligon, "Black Light: David Hammons and the Poetics of Emptiness," *Artforum International* 43, no. 1 (September 2004): 249; emphasis original.

11 On this score, see Michelle M. Wright, "Forces to Be Reckoned With: Michelle M. Wright on the Physics of Black Art," *Artforum International* 53, no. 10 (Summer 2015): 156.

12 See Lane Relyea, "Your Art World: Or, The Limits of Connectivity," *Afterall: A Journal of Art, Context and Enquiry* 14 (Autumn-Winter 2006), 3-8.

13 Cauleen Smith, "Solar Flare Arkestral Marching Band #1," May 12, 2011, https://www.youtube.com/watch?v=WvcXwtqQ5ME.

14 Richard Meyer, *What Was Contemporary Art?* (MIT Press, 2013), 16; my emphasis.

15 James Meyer, *The Art of Return: The Sixties and Contemporary Culture* (University of Chicago Press, 2019).

16 See Glenn Ligon, "Kelley Walker's Negro Problem," *Parkett* 87 (2010): 79-81; Huey Copeland, "Unfinished Business as Usual: African American

Artists, New York Museums, and the 1990s," in *Come as You Are: Art of the 1990s*, ed. Alexandra Schwartz (University of California Press and Montclair Art Museum, 2014), 32 [reprinted in this volume, 175-85].

17 See Brent Hayes Edwards, "The Race for Space: Sun Ra's Poetry," in *Sun Ra: The Immeasurable Equation* (Books on Demand, 2006), 29-55.

18 Edwards, "The Race for Space," 35 (emphases original).

19 Terri Kapsalis, "Enlightment," in *Traveling the Spaceways: Sun Ra, the Astro Black, and Other Solar Myths*, ed. John Corbett, Anthony Elms, and Terri Kapsalis (WhiteWalls, 2010).

20 Kapsalis, "Enlightment," 67.

21 Jacques Lacan, *Seminar of Jacques Lacan: Book III, The Psychoses, 1955-1956* (W. W. Norton, 1997) 289; Nathaniel Mackey, *Discrepant Engagement: Dissonance, Cross-Culturality, and Experimental Writing* (Cambridge University Press, 1993).

22 Hilton Kramer, "Art: To the Last Detail," *New York Times*, June 17, 1977. See Huey Copeland, "Figures and Grounds: The Art of Barkley L. Hendricks," *Artforum* 47, no. 8 (April 2009): 142-49 [reprinted in this volume, 83-96].

23 See Rachel Furnari and David Mark Wise, "The Five Year Plan: Breakout Artists 2004-2007: Where Are They Now?," *Newcity Art: Reviews: Profiles and News about Art in Chicago*, April 24, 2008; Thelma Golden, "Introduction: Post . . . ," in *Freestyle*, exh. cat. (Studio Museum in Harlem, 2001), 14.

24 Tim Griffin, "Compression," *October* 135 (Winter 2011): 3-20.

25 Michelle M. Wright, *Physics of Blackness: Beyond the Middle Passage Epistemology* (University of Minnesota Press, 2015).

26 Wright, *Physics of Blackness*, 15.

27 Wright, "Forces to Be Reckoned With," 156.

28 I here recast lines first published in Huey Copeland, "The Blackness of Blackness," *Artforum* 47, no. 2 (October 2008): 154 [reprinted in this volume, 73-80].

29 Naomi Beckwith and Dieter Roelstraete, *The Freedom Principle: Experiments in Art and Music, 1965 to Now* (University of Chicago Press and Museum of Contemporary Art, 2015), 41.

30 For more on this score, see Huey Copeland, "Tending-toward-Blackness," *October* 156 (Spring 2016): 141-44.

19

RED, BLACK, AND BLUE

The National Museum of African American History and Culture and the National Museum of the American Indian, with Frank B. Wilderson III

Nearly one year ago today, the National Museum of African American History and Culture (NMAAHC) opened to popular excitement and critical acclaim, joining the National Museum of the American Indian (NMAI), inaugurated in 2004, as one of the only racially specific institutions on the National Mall in Washington, DC. Both museums, especially when considered against the dearth of official engagements with black and Native histories, offer vivid testimony to the artifacts, cultures, and struggles of the peoples on which they focus. Yet their presence also raises vital questions about such national projects—who, ultimately, are they "for," given what they are museums "of"?—in an era that has witnessed the rise of Black Lives Matter in response to police violence and ongoing contestations over Native sovereignty and environmental justice at Standing Rock. To take stock of these tensions, the art historian and Artforum *contributing editor Huey Copeland joined the theorist Frank B. Wilderson III—author of the influential* Red, White & Black: Cinema and the Structure of U.S. Antagonisms*—in a candid conversation about the structural logics shaping both museums, in which these scholars at once echo and extend their long-standing dialogue about radical approaches to contemporary culture.*[1]

Huey Copeland: These two museums are prominently placed on the Mall, among the other museums representing national culture, and much has been made of the "inclusiveness" of those gestures. The National Museum of African American History and Culture, for starters, enacts a particular spatial intervention, whose semiotics aren't subtle: as many have noted, it's a big, beautiful brown thing interrupting a series of white-marble buildings. The National Museum of the American Indian, on the other hand, doesn't offer much chromatic contrast. But the undulating lines, unlike the rectilinear structures of most other buildings on the Mall, are almost aerodynamic, so your gaze travels over the surface and keeps on going (Figs. 19.1, 19.2).

This conversation first appeared in *Artforum* 56, no. 1 (September 2017): 252-61.

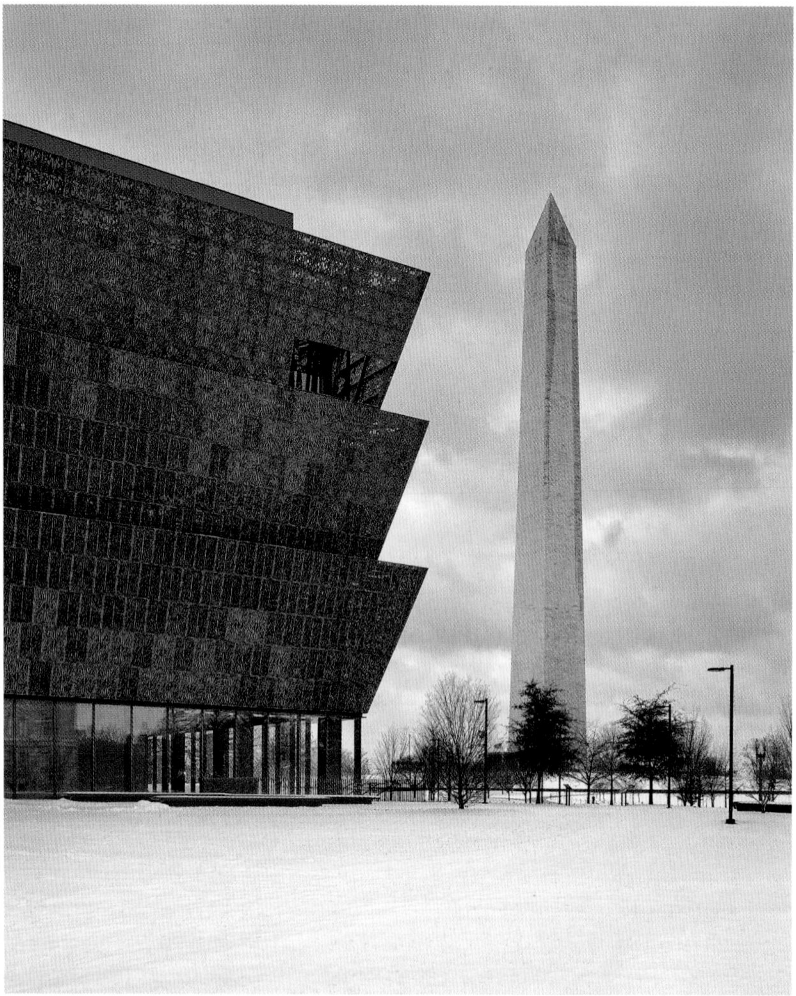

Figure 19.1
Adjaye Associates, Smithsonian National Museum of African American History and Culture, 2016.

Inside, the spatial logics of each institution are even more divergent, and I think these differences speak volumes about the questions you and I are engaging today. What's striking when you go into the NMAI is that if you start at the top floor, there is a wonderful multiplicity of pathways before you. The institution really tries to represent a wide, if not exhaustive, range of tribal identities and histories that then come together when you get to the current exhibition about treaties with the US government [*Nation to Nation: Treaties Between the United States and American Indian Nations*]. There's a respect for these tribes and their many internal distinctions as peoples, who each have a relationship, a claim, to a particular land. In fact, one of the first things you see when you enter the building is

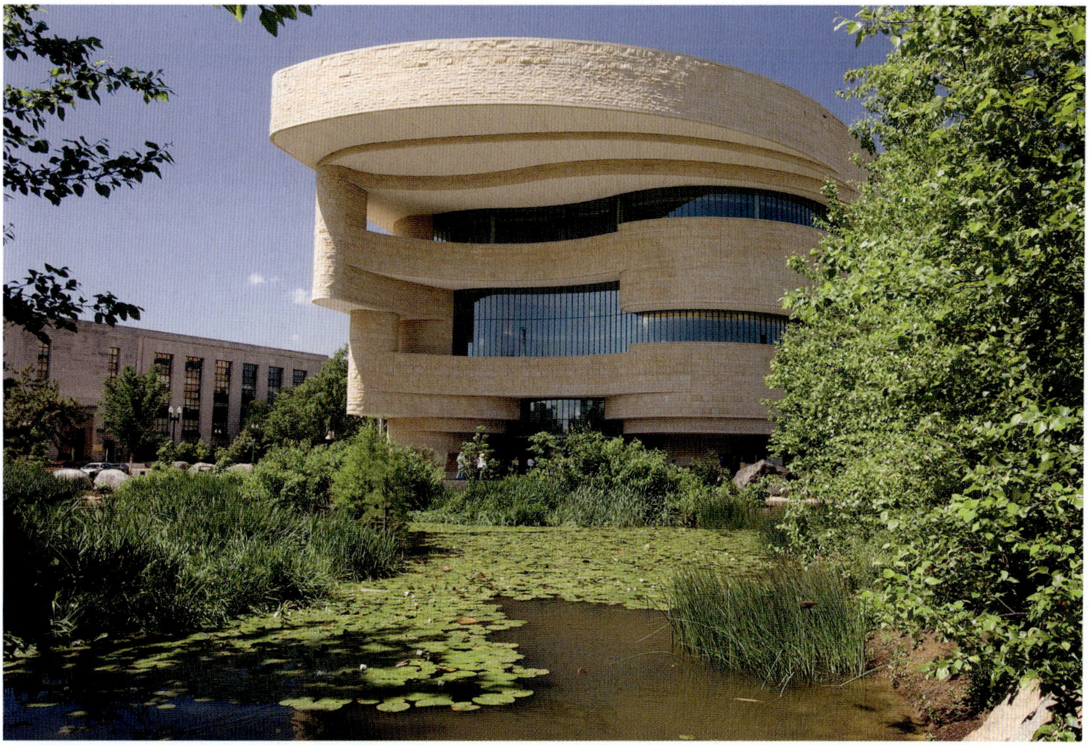

Figure 19.2
Douglas Cardinal and GQBC Architects, National Museum of the American Indian, Smithsonian Institution.

a sign reading WELCOME TO NATIVE AMERICA. That is, of course, a kind of fiction, but it's about claiming the space of this museum as a land that belongs to peoples who have a right to it and a right to be recognized as such, even if the exercise of those rights is more limited beyond the museum's walls.

Now, the NMAAHC's logic of display is, more or less, about a voyage toward personhood and "culture"—or the ruse of that narrative. You start in the basement with slavery and you move upward from there in a path that spirals up to Oprah and Obama. So it's a teleological movement—from slavery to personhood to presidency—that is effectively cleaved from actual history. This narrative allows you to blithely think that a certain kind of historical project has been achieved, when the black body continues to be anything but a person, continues to be this thing that can be murdered, violated, appropriated, reified, and repurposed for any reason whatsoever[2]. And that logic—perhaps more subconsciously than anything else—continues to inform the displays in the "Community" and "Culture" galleries, which are, in one sense, completely about the commodification of black bodies: whether in the sports section, where you have gleaming

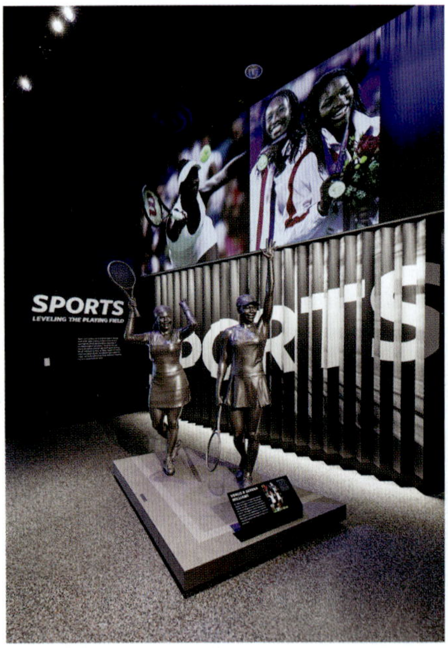

Figure 19.3
Statues of Venus and Serena Williams in *Sports: Leveling the Playing Field*, NMAAHC, 2012-16.

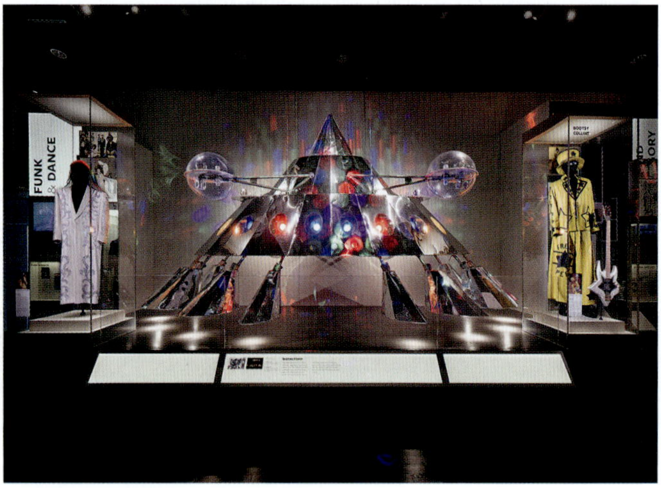

Figure 19.4
Parliament-Funkadelic's Mothership in *Musical Crossroads*, NMAAHC, 2012-2016.

silver statues of the Williams sisters and the space feels like a Foot Locker, or the music section, which took me back to the days of the Sam Goody record store (but where, amazingly, the museum has given P-Funk's Mothership pride of place) (Figs. 19.3, 19.4). In both instances, you're engaging with these incredible artifacts and histories, but in galleries that resemble tricked-out spaces of consumption that package blackness in forms that we're already comfortable consuming under the guise of expressions of personal or collective achievement, as opposed to revealing that such expressions are always tied to a broader logic of commodification that would deny both black personhood and collectivity altogether.

What do these differences mean now, and what are we to make of these particular institutions devoted to American Indian and African American history and culture in relation to the ongoing project of settler colonialism—in which foreigners variously invade, conquer, and subjugate indigenous lands and populations so that they might be remade in an imperial image? What are the ramifications not only for the reproduction of the American nation-state but also for a larger global order whose power relations are equally structured by the logic of antiblackness?

Frank Wilderson: That's the big question, and the important one. The NMAAHC reminds me of growing up in the '60s and '70s when blaxploitation came up. You knew that it was blaxploitation, that it was an exploitation of the most racist stereotypes, but just seeing black characters on the screen was so joyful that you went to every single movie.

Copeland: [Laughter.] Even if you were depicted as a pimp or a prostitute in every scene!

Wilderson: Exactly. The words to the song "Superfly" made no difference. Superfly's "hustle was wrong," as Curtis Mayfield sang, but it didn't matter.[3] We let ourselves be deluded into conceiving of blaxploitation as genuine recognition and incorporation, since we hadn't had that for so long in film. Now, I don't want to demonize the NMAAHC in the way that one might demonize blaxploitation. On the other hand, I do want to say that it's interesting that on day one, there's a five-block-long line of people waiting to get in, and the majority are black. The audience was not diverse. And yet when the museum's leadership, the director and architects, talk about its inspiration and its mission, inclusiveness is the buzzword that is constantly invoked.[4]

Copeland: Especially with the liberal narratives of progress that surround the NMAAHC.

Wilderson: There's an expectation that the NMAAHC is going to start a national conversation about race or be a major contributor to one. The other expectation is that, yes, the museum is about blacks, but it's really for everyone. This is really different from the NMAI, which is about Native people and for Native people, as well as everyone else. A sign saying WELCOME TO BLACK AMERICA at the entrance of the NMAAHC would be a scandal. But WELCOME TO NATIVE AMERICA is not a (mainstream) scandal. You cannot be black, Frantz Fanon reminds us, with impunity.[5]

So the narratives of racial "inclusion" and black social "progress" that the NMAAHC deploys are symptoms of what Jared Sexton calls "the anxiety of antagonism": there's always an anxiety about whether there's a place for blacks and the kind of poison pill that we represent in the national psyche.[6] Because unlike the Native American, the black American's (or the slave's) paradigm of subjugation is total—it's the usurpation of subjectivity that is at the core of black subjugation rather than the usurpation of land (for the Indian) or labor power (for the worker). For the slave, there is no surplus value to be restored to the time of labor. And no treaties between blacks and the government are in Washington waiting to be signed or ratified. Unlike the settler in the Native American political imagination, there is no place like Europe to which blacks or slaves can send our antagonists back. Humanity itself is the antagonist of the slave. That's a much more systemic problem. Which is why I call blackness a poison pill. What do you do with a group of people against whom the whole world is at war? Mainstream institutions of representation, no matter how liberal, aren't willing to wallow in this contradiction. So the museum suddenly has to do two things. It has to elaborate and illustrate and represent black achievements. But it's also got to make the rest of the world feel safe. And yet, in fact, these are distinctly different projects.

Copeland: Yes!

Wilderson: To take a line out of your book *Bound to Appear*: "While these interventions reflect a dramatic social and political sea change on the level of representation—emblematized by the U.S. Senate's woefully belated June 18, 2009, apology for slavery—the lasting import of rhetorical returns to the 'peculiar institution' remains to be seen: revolution on the ground, let alone reparation to the national fabric, has never seemed less tenable."[7]

I think that's incredibly relevant, because here we have this $540 million museum with $270 million coming from the state, $21 million coming from Oprah, and more from other private sources. This is a dramatic change at the level of representation. But the fact that "reparation to the national fabric has never seemed less tenable" is the real context of the NMAAHC's emergence.[8]

Copeland: Still, when I went to the museum, I was amazed at the sense of a space of black gathering and engagement, where all kinds of real talk—articulations that might be at cross-purposes with the stated ambitions of the museum—could take place. Let alone the wonder of seeing all those black folks together. The possibility of a kind of alternative gathering, of what Fred Moten and Stefano Harney have so brilliantly theorized as an "undercommons," was there.[9] This struck me, too, because the first time I went to the museum, I waited in line for day-of tickets—I didn't get in—and the conversations taking place with other folks queuing up, with the vendors hawking Michelle Obama tote bags, were energizing and sobering and revelatory in ways that I couldn't have anticipated.

So for me, the spectacle of all of us coming together around this space was just as interesting as what the museum was offering up—particularly knowing that that audience itself had the possibility to do something else with its collectivity, something that the museum might not countenance or even imagine. It's those kinds of gatherings or spaces that are actually incredibly important and valuable. Because of course we know that, structurally and historically, the place of blacks is no place, right? So with these crowds and this moment—this pause—there is a site of gathering where we can make a place of and for blackness, of and for our relationships to one another, of and for the kinds of possibility that might emerge elsewhere.

Wilderson: To even see the shell of accommodation of different constituents, of engagements—that means something different happened in the space that day. It's encouraging that you had that experience.

And, of course, I know the kind of narrative that circles around this period from 2003, when George W. Bush signs the legislation for the museum's creation, until 2016, when Barack Obama says on opening day, "We're not a burden on America, or a stain on America, or an object of pity or charity for America."[10] I understand you can't actually do anything with big dollars without that kind of packaging, in which the history of African Americans is made palatable, unthreatening, and a conduit for "inclusion."

But it's my job and your job as critical theorists to join in with the black joy but also to be the skeptics.

Copeland: Agreed—and if I could backtrack a little: I don't think your blaxploitation comparison demonizes the NMAAHC. I think it's brilliant and useful, because it points to the question, Who is speaking, and for what?, which we as skeptics always need to ask. In that regard, and I don't want to overstate the difference, maybe the NMAI broaches these issues more self-reflexively—a bit more skeptically—than the NMAAHC because of its particular history. Both at the NMAI and in the discourse that has emerged around it, there is a consistent engagement with the complexities of questions like: What does it mean to put forward a Native museology? How do you build a museum that is not always already part of a colonial project? And how do you imagine this institution as one that can make space for and entertain something radically decolonial, that has an antagonistic relationship to the nation-state?[11] If the real potential of these museums is as spaces for the activation of alternative kinds of knowledge, ontology, and community—and for the kinds of speaking, the kinds of conversation, that can transpire in such spaces—then I think you see this more strongly worked through at the NMAI, where there are rooms that seem visibly off-limits to non-Native visitors, since they are earmarked for indigenous-community gatherings. There is an intimation of spaces for autonomy and contestation, for which the museum becomes a platform.

At the NMAAHC, by contrast, while there are institutional frames for black engagement, it's harder to find places where the "speaker" is not an archetypal liberal (though I don't mean to demonize those either) who steadfastly pretends that if we can just get inclusive enough, such questions will answer themselves or won't even need to be asked. I think the liberal rhetoric that you hear from the lead architect, David Adjaye, is one that has to speak not only to a certain kind of accommodationist nationalist narrative—accompanied by a belief that all differences can eventually be incorporated into a seamless fabric—but also to corporate interests.[12] And that means, echoing Sexton's anxiety of antagonism, that the rhetoric of both of these institutions necessarily trades in a certain refusal, an antagonism to historical fact. So at the NMAI, even if in some respects the presentation is less accommodationist, the museum, as critics like Sonya Atalay and Jennifer A. Shannon have argued, still trades in the language of "conflict" as opposed to "genocide."[13] And the NMAAHC talks about the "uneven" history of black people in America, as opposed to the rapacious, ongoing extraction of value from black bodies.

Such antiantagonistic language allows the museums to bring a national project in line with the corporate interests that want to continue the extraction of value from black bodies and Native lands. Even when you see the contemporaneity of these processes, you cannot ignore the branding: at the NMAAHC, there's the Oprah Winfrey Theater, and the NMAI is partly sponsored by the Harrah's Foundation, of casino fame. These are the economic possibilities that the institutions respectively pose as open to these populations, giving evidence of models of black success or corporate collaboration with Native communities as ways forward. The question is, then, are these merely representational bandages that cover over the ongoing reproduction of the economies of power and extraction of which slavery and genocide are only the most extreme instantiations?

Because even at the moment that these economies and histories are somehow supposed to be reckoned with, they risk being all the more firmly suppressed. One of the first things you see in the NMAAHC, for instance, is a wall label that says, "Objects define a museum." And I thought, "Really?!" What does it mean, given the history of black people as objects of property themselves, to say that material remains define a museum, especially since so much of black culture—to say nothing of black peoples—is literally and figuratively lost? How might we think about those terms differently, in working toward a radical museology that reckons with, rather than sidesteps, the imbrication of museum cultures in the maintenance and reproduction of antiblack ideologies?

Now, the NMAI is trying to create narratives that are hemispheric and tribal—reaching across North and South, East and West—as opposed to national. The museum resists the nation-state as a frame, even though that's ultimately the container the institution is in. And it gestures toward a larger diasporic economy—about the movement and exchange of indigenous peoples—that also characterizes how the NMAAHC has aimed to address the ways in which blackness is produced and circulated globally. But at the end of the day, those possibilities aren't fully explored in order to think about what this kind of black institution would have to be to generate narratives that go against the status quo and that, at least potentially, have politically liberatory effects—because the museum would have to be radically, deeply other to itself in order to do so.

Wilderson: It couldn't get funded if it were radically, deeply other to itself.

Copeland: [Laughter.] Right?! And as scholars like LeRonn P. Brooks have shown, the very contested histories of the NMAAHC, of how it came to be, are themselves accounts of how structural racism continues to unfold and reproduce itself.[14]

But within the museum, aside from a few vitrines at the outset, there isn't a unified effort to tell us how the objects and materials at the NMAAHC have arrived there, whether through theft or donation or other forms of "acquisition." While there are many opportunities to mark these larger social processes in relationship to objects, those systemic inequities and structures of violence are not consistently staged or taken up, because to do so would be to confront people with the persistence of those structures in the present—as opposed to safely sealing them within a container that is now consumable as "history," which, strangely enough in a black museum, is spatially bifurcated from "culture."

Wilderson: Consumable history to be consumed as spectacle, at that. But you also have something else at the NMAI, which could start creating alternate spaces, rooms that are off-limits to nonmembers, so to speak. The sense that these are people, and that there are going to be spaces for them as a people, is a major part of the libidinal economy, which is constantly being repressed or disavowed in putatively black spaces where the project pretends to be a celebration of black personhood.

In other words, the NMAAHC functions at the level of spectacle; the NMAI functions via articulation, through exchanges and transfers and treaties, even if those articulations end up in conflict and genocide. Articulation does not happen between masters and slaves. But articulation is the essential modality of the settler-Native conflict.

Copeland: Yes.

Wilderson: I'm not saying, "Hey, recognize me as a person"—I don't think that's actually possible. I think that personhood can only be coherent because blackness exists as a foil to that coherence.

I think that from birth to death, we go through a kind of madness that is different for all kinds of black people. But we go through life knowing there's no place in which our blackness belongs. "Black America," even as a metaphor, is a contradiction in terms. Lincoln said this when he wanted freed slaves to colonize Central America and Liberia.[15] What we need in a black museum is the space to talk about that dynamic: the comprehensive psychic and material isolation we've been subjected to even in stories and exhibitions about our struggles! Instead, we have the extremely violent hydraulics of our history disavowed and repressed in the NMAAHC. So when Adjaye says, "For me, it has always been about creating a museum that has a specific narrative alongside a universal message," well, boom, there we are: dead in the water![16] And we didn't even have to get on Lincoln's boat to Belize.

It's unfortunate that we're having this conversation after the fact, that we don't have a room in "our" museum to talk about these issues, let alone produce a conceptual framework. This is precisely the crowding-out scenario that I call anger management. It's part of a disciplinary project of structural racism, and sometimes it appears in blackface.

For example, I'm thinking of that teleological movement, of the NMAAHC trajectory you brilliantly outlined at the beginning: from slavery up to personhood and Obama. This is a telos of progress that the facts don't support. I would hope for a place where we could confront the enigma of blackness, could actually critique telos itself. Then, instead of succumbing to the anxiety of antagonism and using blacks to represent the same human capacity from which we're barred, *ab initio*, we could think, collectively, about what is ignored when a timeline of progress is imposed on a group of sentient beings whose temporal capacity is not recognized or incorporated in the collective unconscious of the world. The world doesn't recognize the time of black dispossession; the world doesn't accept that blackness possessed a prior plenitude (a state of being a human subject) before slaves were made of us. Whereas a prior plenitude for Native Americans (land, custom, culture, and, above all, sovereignty) is something both genociders and the indigenous genocided can agree on.

Black dispossession is a snarl, because the libidinal economy doesn't have the means to know it, since its victim is the thing against which humans define themselves and not, like the Indian, a degraded form of humanity that is human nonetheless. But it is also because of the terror of looking the absence of subjectivity in the face, as opposed to the dispossession of aspects of subjectivity. The latter, the history of Native peoples, is a form of narrative plenitude; the arrival of the colonizer is the dispossession of this prior plenitude. The return of Turtle Island to its rightful occupants would be the third movement in that narrative progression—the restoration of plenitude.

What is not being considered is the idea, which you and I and others have written about, that blackness does not have a prior plenitude that can be disimbricated from slavery, in the way that indigeneity has a prior plenitude that can, in fact, be disimbricated from colonialism. And yet we don't have space in our museum for that to find expression in words and images. It's the dilemma, or the trauma, of the kind of structural violence that doesn't have a prior plenitude that occupies the psyche of every single black person moving through that museum—but they've got to put that trauma on lockdown to engage the museum. Or, as you've said, they have to find a trickster or counter way of engaging it—to use masks, in the way that black people would mask voodoo deities with Roman Catholic saints.[17]

Copeland: I love that. I think one of the many aspects of the NMAAHC that speaks to this problem—to this desire for a respectable teleological narrative—and to questions of perpetuity and recursiveness is the way in which there's no comprehensive framing of black desire and black perversity, let alone LGBTQI questions, within the museum. It's, "Oh, here's James Baldwin, here's Bayard Rustin, here's Audre Lorde, they were important (and gay)," as opposed to thinking about what it would mean to foreground the importance of LGBTQI subjects and subject positions to black freedoms and struggles; or thinking about the ways in which the victimization of that population continues to elucidate the ongoing threat to black bodies from all kinds of violence—structural, medical, you name it. But to confront black desire would demand an understanding of blackness itself as something that's necessarily perverse, that enables the contestation of any institutional or categorical imperative, and that, as Cedric Robinson so famously noted, is part and parcel of a thoroughgoing critique of Western civilization.[18] We have to put pressure on all forms of representation and whom we think we are in fact representing, or think can be represented, in a given frame. And that would mean challenging linear narratives of progress and respectability and instead conceiving of a black or queer approach to the unfolding of history from the bottom up.

Wilderson: It's building on the idea that blackness can be nothing but queerness. In other words, the heteronormative stability of filiation is linked to the limitless and unnamable sexual violence we have been subjected to since day one (389,000 slaves were bred like cattle into four million slaves in less than two generations), which makes any pretense of a heteronormative blackness untenable and unethical.

Copeland: Then what do we do with this museum? What would it mean to imagine alternative spaces or modes of thinking both within and beyond the museum?

Wilderson: That's heavy. What do you think?

Copeland: I think that for a number of folks associated with an Afropessimist or black radical position, it is nearly impossible to represent, say, slavery in ways that fundamentally differ from the tropes we've already got. So what would it mean to create spaces that are not beholden to the work of narrative, explanation, cultural justification, or black respectability? Spaces where we can plot the possibilities of the truly revolutionary and the radically decolonial?

Wilderson: That would be a very vibrant space for black people and a very dangerous space for everyone else. [Laughter.]

If we actually had that kind of sanctioned space, it would mean that everyone else would have to acknowledge that the regime of violence that saturates blackness does not have a corollary or cannot be reconciled with the regime of violence that saturates Native American history. And then they have to go one step further and say that the telos of "We shall overcome," which many black people live by, has to recognize that the narrative form that allows other oppressed groups' struggle stories to be told is dependent on the fact that blackness cannot tell that struggle story: because, again, there is no prior plenitude that precedes our struggle, unlike with the semiotics of colonial struggle and violence. In part, because colonial violence has characteristics that are adjacent to other forms of violence. Colonial violence is adjacent to the violence of capitalism in the same way that the word *cat* acquires meaning because of its adjacency to *tiger* and *leopard*.

But the ultimate meaning of colonial violence is not found in what's adjacent to it but in what it is not. Its opposition is to the regime of violence that subjugates blackness, and this is what Orlando Patterson articulates in *Slavery and Social Death*, where he says that every structure of domination needs an ocean of violence to get it kick-started.[19] It takes an ocean of violence over two hundred years to convert people into workers, to discipline them into temporalities that are new and more constricting—and to have them imagine their lives within those constraints: urbanization, mechanization, factories. It takes an ocean of violence to produce the position of the "Indian." Once the system of domination is set up, then the violence goes into remission and only rears its ugly head again when the people who have assumed their positions start to rebel against the hegemonic constraints.

But, Patterson says, slavery operates according to a completely different logic of violence. It takes an ocean of violence to produce a slave, singular or plural, but that violence never goes into remission. The prehistory of violence that establishes slavery is also the ongoing, concurrent history of slavery once it is established.[20] And that blows your mind. What it means is that you can't make sense out of police killings the way a proletarian or a Native person can. The murder of black people has to be explained less through Marx and more through the work of a Sexton or a David Marriott or a Saidiya Hartman on libidinal economy.[21] Because what the murders of black folks do is produce community for people who aren't black; it's a mode of pleasure and an anchor for coherence. One can look at the regime of violence that subjugates blacks and say, "If I am submitted to that kind of violence, it really won't be that kind of violence because it will come with a reason, whereas for blacks, it is always prelogical." Baldwin, as he's nearing death, says it all in *The Evidence of Things Not Seen*: murdering our children is what it means to be a nation.[22] Few of us, during our so-called productive years, are able to be that honest; we keep looking for a telos, we keep trying to shield ourselves from genealogical isolation by drawing analogies between our suffering and that of, say, Native peoples—knowing, if only in our preconscious, that our regimes of violence are not alike.

Copeland: It's worth remembering that while there's a lot of time, money, labor, and attention invested in these particular buildings—these monuments, these physical, material manifestations—such formations are always haunted by theft and death. (And the ongoing threats of both, which the recent discoveries of nooses left in the NMAAHC have soberly underlined.)[23] But it is heartening, in a way, that even as it forwards a particular vision of black experience that inspires both racial hate and celebration, the NMAAHC has still become a gathering place and a spur for alternative readings. And the museum has arrived at almost the same time as the emergence of new forms in politics, like Black Lives Matter, and art, like Theaster Gates and Eliza Myrie's Black Artists Retreat, both of which are precisely about creating spaces of quasi-autonomy where black folks can talk real to one another without the explicit imposition of some kind of respectability for an outside audience, where the plotting of new possibilities can unfold.[24] So perhaps the most interesting places to look, aesthetically and politically, are these more ephemeral formations of people—which are just as materially rich as museums of things—because they are premised on the desires of actual, living, breathing black bodies, as opposed to our inevitable fate as the corpses on which institutions, regardless of their color, continue to be built.

Notes

1 Frank B. Wilderson III, *Red, White & Black: Cinema and the Structure of U.S. Antagonisms* (Duke University Press, 2010).

2 My language here is meant to recall Wilderson's in Frank B. Wilderson III, "The Position of the Unthought: An Interview with Saidiya V. Hartman," *Qui Parle* 13, no. 2 (Spring-Summer 2003): 189-90, in which he describes the enslaved as that "body you can do what you want with."

3 Curtis Mayfield, "Superfly" (Curtom Records, 1972).

4 See, on this score, Lonnie G. Bunch III, "The National Museum of African American History and Culture: The Vision," *Journal of Museum Education* 42, no. 1 (2017): 8-12.

5 Frantz Fanon, "The Fact of Blackness," in *Black Skin, White Masks*, trans. Charles Lam Markmann (Grove Press, 1967), 109-41.

6 Jared Sexton, "Afro-Pessimism: The Unclear Word," *Rhizomes* 29 (2016), http://www.rhizomes.net/issue29/sexton.html.

7 Huey Copeland, *Bound to Appear: Art, Slavery, and the Site of Blackness in Multicultural America* (University of Chicago Press, 2013), 204.

8 On this score, see Calvin Tomkins, "A Sense of Place," *New Yorker*, September 23, 2013, 76.

9 Stefano Harney and Fred Moten, *The Undercommons: Fugitive Planning* *and Black Study* (Minor Compositions, 2013).

10 See, respectively, "The National Museum of African American History and Culture Act," Public Law 108-84, December 16, 2003; Barack Obama, "A Richer Story of Who We Are," Address Delivered at the Dedication of the National Museum of African American History and Culture, National Mall, Washington, DC, September 24, 2016, in *Vital Speeches of the Day*, November 2016, 346.

11 Here consider the rich special issues, "The National Museum of the American Indian" and "Decolonizing Archaeology," published by *American Indian Quarterly*: respectively, 29, no. 3-4 (Summer-Autumn 2005); and 30, no. 3-4 (Summer-Autumn 2006).

12 See the architect's comments in Charles Rowell, "Designing a Nation's Museum: An Interview with David Adjaye," *Callaloo* 38, no. 4 (2015): 762-70.

13 Sonya Atalay, "No Sense of the Struggle: Creating a Context for Survivance at the NMAI," *American Indian Quarterly* 30, no. 3-4 (Summer-Autumn 2006): 597-618; Jennifer A. Shannon, *Our Lives: Collaboration, Native Voice, and the Making of the National Museum of the American Indian* (School for Advanced Research Press, 2014).

14 LeRonn P. Brooks, "Past/Present/Future: Memory, Legislation, and the National Museum of African American History and Culture," *Callaloo* 38, no. 4 (2015): 711-28.

15 For a comprehensive overview of Lincoln's views on slavery and black colonization, see Phillipp W. Magness and Sebastian N. Page, *Colonization After Emancipation: Lincoln and the Movement for Black Resettlement* (University of Missouri Press, 2011).

16 See Adjaye, quoted in Rowell, "Designing a Nation's Museum," 764.

17 For a comprehensive accounting of Caribbean masking practices, see Gerard Aching, *Masking and Power: Carnival and Popular Culture in the Caribbean* (University of Minnesota Press, 2002).

18 Cedric J. Robinson, "Capitalism, Marxism, and the Black Radical Tradition: An Interview by Chuck Morse," *Perspectives on Anarchist Theory* 3, no. 1 (1999): 1, 6-8.

19 Orlando Patterson, *Slavery and Social Death: A Comparative Study* (Harvard University Press, 1982).

20 Patterson, *Slavery and Social Death*.

21 David Marriott, *On Black Men* (Columbia University Press, 2000); Saidiya Hartman, *Scenes of Subjection: Terror, Slavery, and Self-Making in Nineteenth-Century America* (Oxford University Press, 1997).

22 James Baldwin, *The Evidence of Things Not Seen*, 1st ed. (Holt Rinehart and Winston, 1985).

23 See Lorraine Boissoneault, "Noose Found in National Museum of African American History and Culture," May 31, 2017, https://www.smithsonian-mag.com/smithsonian-institution/noose-found-national-museum-african-american-history-and-culture-180963519/.

24 For vital overviews of both developments, see Keeanga-Yamahtta Taylor, *From #BlackLivesMatter to Black Liberation* (Haymarket Books, 2016); Theaster Gates, *Black Artists Retreat: Reflections on Convening* (Black Madonna Press, 2018).

PART IV

ART HISTORY AFTER INTER-SECTIONALITY

20

IN THE WAKE OF THE NEGRESS

Nineteen ninety was a watershed year for Lorna Simpson. The artist's trademark photographs of black female figures paired with evocative texts were featured in exhibitions from Long Beach, California, to Venice, Italy. In New York, she was simultaneously positioned on the encroaching margins and at the contested center of artistic discourse. Her work was included in *The Decade Show: Frameworks of Identity in the 1980s*, an exhibition jointly presented by the Museum of Contemporary Hispanic Art, the New Museum, and the Studio Museum in Harlem that became a touchstone of multicultural critique; at the same time her show at the Museum of Modern Art (MoMA)—the twenty-third in the Projects series devoted to living artists—became the first solo exhibition by an African American woman in the institution's sixty-year history.[1]

Blindness in the face of racially and sexually marked subjects is arguably endemic to Western culture. Yet more than a belated victory for colored girls everywhere, Simpson's MoMA exhibition can be seen as one of the signal moments of black feminine rupture, revelation, and misrecognition, which, for good or ill, have shaped the Museum's accounting of modern art. In this essay, I examine a few of those moments in order to articulate how "the black woman"—as absence and presence, artist and model, agitator and adherent, fiction and fact—matters to and puts pressure on MoMA's guiding assumptions and collecting practices, which have become paradigms of hegemonic modernism. In so doing, I conceive of the Museum and other cultural institutions, broadly construed, as contested sites in black women's struggles to represent themselves and to articulate

This essay was originally published in *Modern Women: Women Artists at the Museum of Modern Art*, ed. Cornelia Butler and Alexandra Schwartz (Museum of Modern Art, 2010), 480-97. It was initially spurred, however, by an invitation from Bridget Cooks to speak at the conference "Extended Provocations: New Lectures in Dialogue with the Pioneering Scholarship of Judith Wilson," which took place at the University of California, Irvine, in October 2007.

critical practices that describe modernity's terrain with an alternative set of aesthetic imperatives and political cartographies.[2] Taken together, the works by and about black women in the Museum's holdings constitute a necessarily incomplete archive that allows us to reconsider not only the lives and strategies of individual artists but also the circumstances in which African diasporic female identity, visibility, and history have been produced and transformed.[3]

Carrie Mae Weems's landmark *From Here I Saw What Happened and I Cried* (Fig. 20.1) offers an incisive meditation on just those circumstances, particularly the ways in which visual technologies have been mobilized to render black subjects transparent to a racializing gaze. This multipart work was commissioned by the J. Paul Getty Museum as a response to *Hidden Witness*, a 1995 exhibition of mid-nineteenth-century photographs of black men and women.[4] Weems selected reproduced, enlarged, and tinted red thirty-two images, each of which she placed under a glass plate etched with affectively charged phrases: "scientific profile," "mammie, mama, mother," "playmate to the patriarch." This far-reaching pictorial inventory is bracketed on either end with an indigo-tinted reproduction of Paul Poirier's 1925 photograph of Nobosodrou, one of many Mangbetu women whose distinctive busts have been reproduced on everything from Belgian stamps to Central African sculpture. Here, the artist inscribed an image of a singular woman with text that serves to mourn and witness the pernicious economies of classification and exchange that have determined the historicity of blackness in the visual field.[5]

From Here I Saw What Happened and I Cried was presented to MoMA, in 1997, as a gift on behalf of the Friends of Education, a Museum affiliate group founded, in 1993, by the lawyer and banker Akosua Barthwell Evans to "foster a greater appreciation of art created by African Americans and to encourage African American participation and membership in MoMA."[6] Like Simpson's and Weems's work, Evans's advocacy reflects a remapping of social and sexual privilege in the late 1980s and early 1990s that transformed the cultural landscape as well as the relationship of black women to the Museum. MoMA has historically emphasized the individual author, medium specificity, and a formalist conception of quality, often denuding even the most politically astute art of its social context and downplaying artists' ambitions for social change in favor of a modernist narrative based on stylistic progression.[7] As a result, it has effectively reiterated the storied disjuncture between dominant teleological constructions of history and the fragmented, horizontal configuration of black memory, which is pieced together at the margins.[8]

For the black feminist artists, scholars, and advocates who emerged in the age of multiculturalism, MoMA's conceptions of the past and of the art object were inadequate to address the visual position of a Nobosodrou, let alone the historical re-vision of a Weems, whose work signifies on domi-

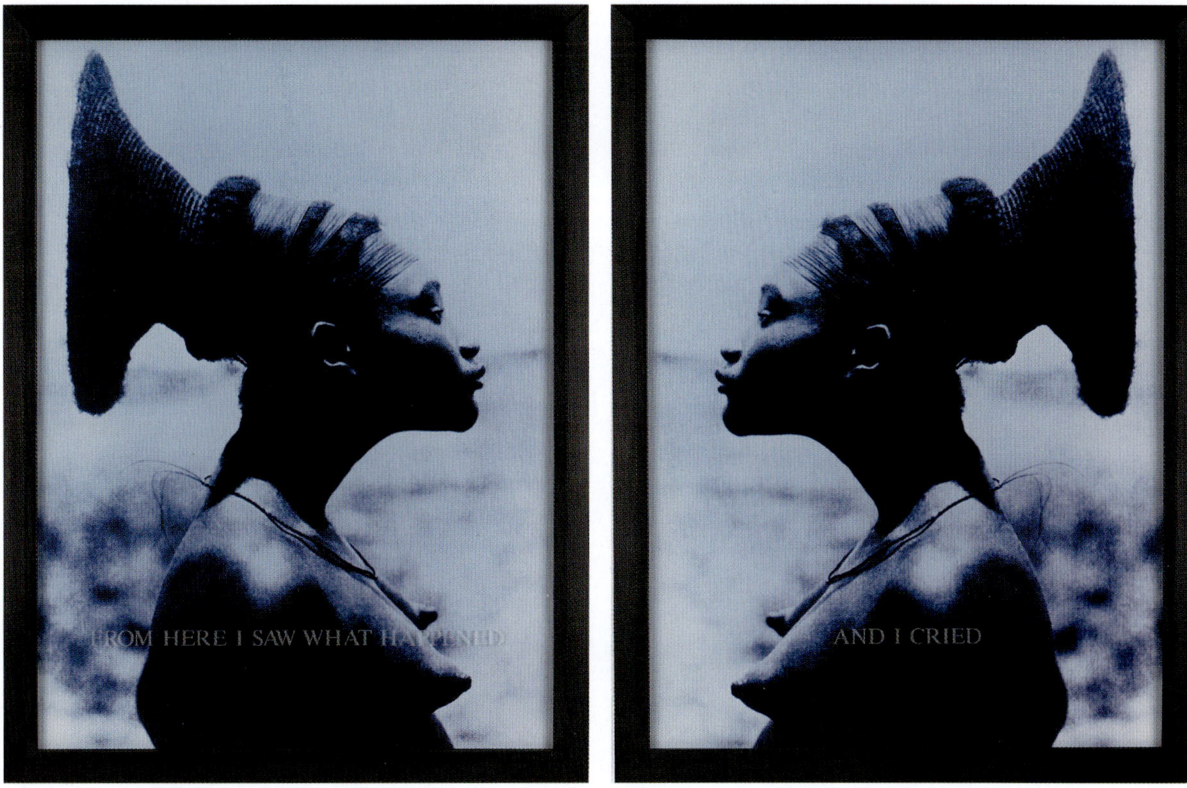

Figure 20.1

Carrie Mae Weems, *From Here I Saw What Happened and I Cried (diptych)*, 1995–96. C-print with sandblasted text, 40 × 30 in. (101.6 × 76.2 cm), 42⅝ × 32⅝ × 1¼ in. (108.3 × 82.9 × 3.2 cm) framed, each. © Carrie Mae Weems. Courtesy of the artist and Gladstone Gallery, New York; Fraenkel Gallery, San Francisco; and Galerie Barbara Thumm, Berlin.

nant representations of the black, the feminine, the photographic, and the modern all at once.[9] Cultural practitioners such as Frieda High Tesfagiorgis, Lorraine O'Grady, Gilane Tawadros, and Michele Wallace have argued that we must reckon with the multiple sites and symbols through which African diasporic women's history has been routed, not only to reclaim black female subjectivity from the clutches of stereotype, but also to comprehend the practices of violence and visualization, which, in shaping raced and gendered bodies, have determined the contours of modernist practice.[10]

Western phantasms of difference doubled—blackness and femaleness untethered from the particularity of any given subject—arguably take their measure from *la négresse*, that foundational figure of black femininity first named in seventeenth-century France, who has come to epitomize unalloyed darkness and sexuality.[11] To be sure, "Negress" is an absurd and

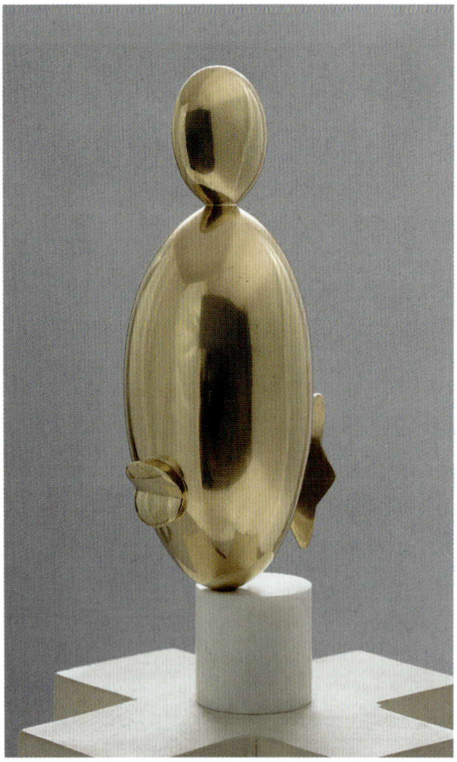

Figure 20.2
Constantin Brancusi, *Blonde Negress, II*, 1933. Bronze, on four-part pedestal of marble, limestone, and two wood sections, overall, 71¼ × 14¼ × 14 ½ in. The Museum of Modern Art; The Philip L. Goodwin Collection. (97.1958.a-e vw2). Digital Image © The Museum of Modern Art/Licensed by SCALA / Art Resource, NY.

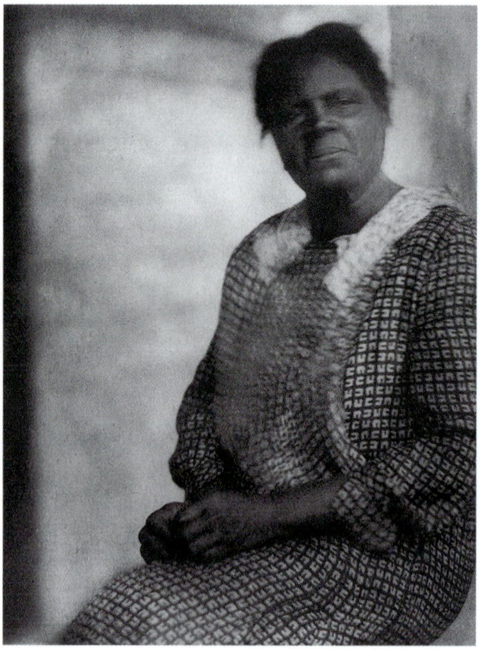

Figure 20.3
Doris Ulmann, *Untitled*, 1929-31. Photogravure, 8⅜ × 6 5/16 in. (21.3 × 16.0 cm). The Museum of Modern Art; gift of Blanchette Hooker Rockefeller. Digital Image © The Museum of Modern Art/Licensed by SCALA / Art Resource, NY.

excessive appellation. Yet that is precisely why the term so effectively sums up what the literary critic Hortense J. Spillers has called the "signifying property *plus*" of the black female body, which is everywhere marked by the trauma of colonial enterprise, the dislocations of transatlantic slavery, and the logic of international capital as mere flesh and recalcitrant thing.[12] Whether on the auction block or in the museum, the Negress casts a shadow over the black woman that has consistently overdetermined the conditions of her appearance.

MoMA's collection tells the tale. Consider the Romanian-born sculptor Constantin Brancusi's *Blonde Negress, II* (Fig. 20.2), a bronze made in Paris whose interest evolves from the apparent contradiction of an Africanized subject rendered as a golden piscine abstraction, at once primitive and futuristic. Look to one of Doris Ulmann's numerous black-and-white

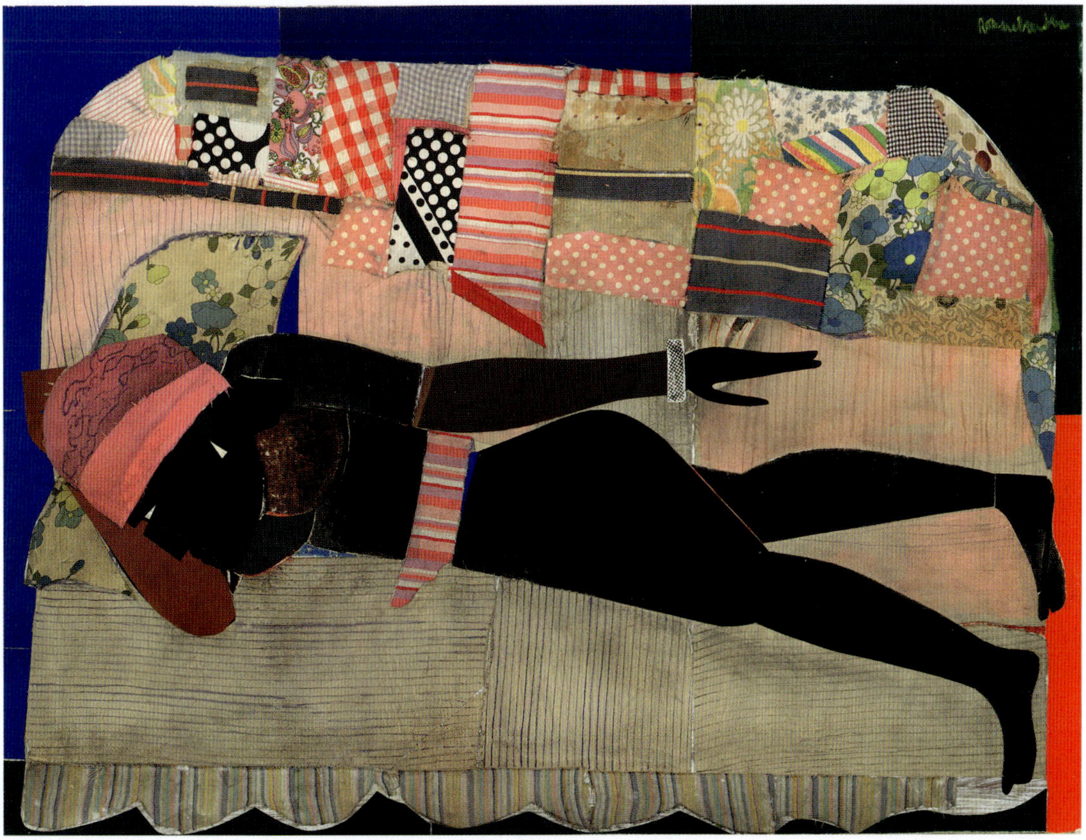

Figure 20.4
Romare Bearden, *Patchwork Quilt*, 1970. Cut-and-pasted cloth and paper with synthetic polymer paint on composition board, 35¾ × 47⅞ in. (90.9 × 121.6 cm). The Museum of Modern Art; Blanchette Hooker Rockefeller Fund. © 2024 Romare Bearden Foundation / Licensed by VAGA at Artists Rights Society (ARS), NY. Digital Image © The Museum of Modern Art/Licensed by SCALA / Art Resource, NY.

photographs depicting an aged woman pausing in her work (1925–34) (Fig. 20.3), an image that seems intent on fixing an idealized vision of black labor in the American South before it is lost to modernity. Recall too how in Romare Bearden's 1970 collage, *Patchwork Quilt* (Fig. 20.4), an Egyptian goddess turned down-home odalisque precariously perches on a couch that is equally suggestive of African American fabric traditions and the nearly monochromatic canvases of Agnes Martin. Contemplate the weirdly proportioned creature—half animal, half woman—who stares out from George Overbury "Pop" Hart's *Nude Negress, Souvenir of the Tropics* (1922) (Fig. 20.5), a rebarbative little print given to the Museum in 1940 by one of its founders, Abby Aldrich Rockefeller.[13] Finally, think back to Pablo Picasso's *Les Demoiselles d'Avignon* (1907) [see Fig. 22.4 on p. 319], that scandalously disjointed conjunction of Africanness and the feminine, which

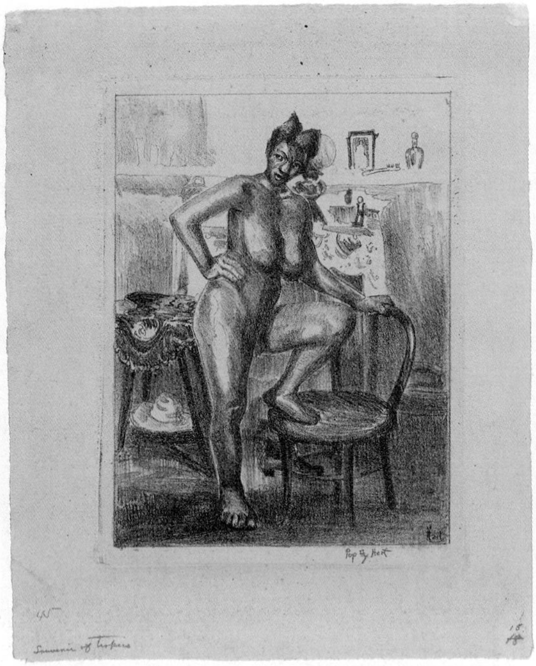

Figure 20.5
George Overbury "Pop" Hart, *Nude Negress, Souvenir of the Tropics*, 1922. Lithograph. The Museum of Modern Art; gift of Abby Aldrich Rockefeller. Digital Image © The Museum of Modern Art/Licensed by SCALA / Art Resource, NY.

famously served the artist as a talisman of sexual aggressivity and MoMA as an epochal marker of what founding director, Alfred H. Barr Jr., identified as "a new period in the history of modern art."[14] Despite the varying racial, national, and sexual identities of their makers and the divergent ontological assumptions that govern them, all of these works attest to the black woman's historical availability and transnational presence as Negress, an indispensable vehicle that both grounds the Museum's accounting of itself and allows for the grounding of modern artistic practices.

The work of Kara Walker offers the most recent and well-known example of what it might mean for a black woman to take on and take up that vehicle for her own purposes. It has been reviled for its perceived infliction of further injury to the black female body as well as for its runaway success among white critics, collectors, and institutions; in fact, her 1994 New York debut, *Gone: An Historical Romance of a Civil War as It Occurred Between the Dusky Thighs of One Negress and Her Heart* (Fig. 20.6), was acquired by MoMA in 2007. In this work, as elsewhere in her oeuvre, the artist uses black construction paper cut into silhouettes and affixed to white walls to outline a panoramic landscape, "an inner plantation," populated by figures that make reference to and quickly depart from those conjured up in classic narratives of the antebellum South, such as Margaret Mitchell's *Gone with the Wind* (1937).[15] Exploiting the medium's defined edges and amorphous centers, Walker carves out grotesque figurations meant to physically and psychically unmoor the viewer's sense of place and racial identity,

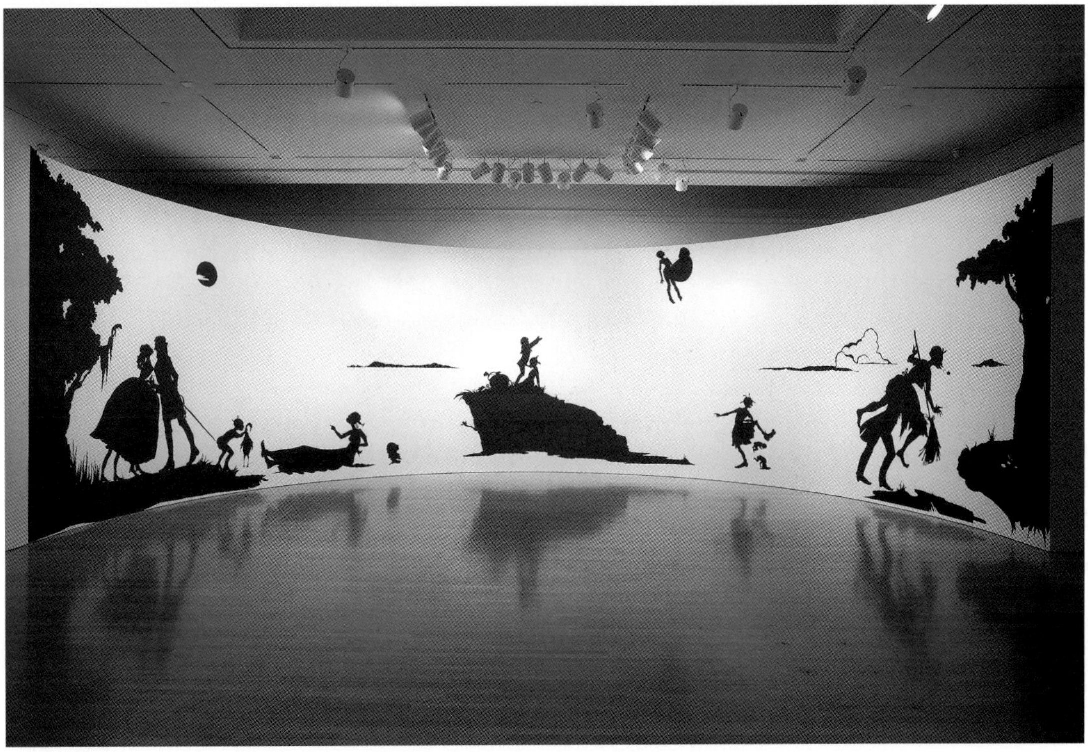

Figure 20.6
Kara Walker, *Gone: An Historical Romance of a Civil War as It Occurred Between the Dusky Thighs of One Negress and Her Heart*, 1994. Cut paper on wall, 13 × 50 ft. (396.2 × 1524 cm). Installation view: *Kara Walker: My Complement, My Enemy, My Oppressor, My Love*. Hammer Museum, Los Angeles, 2008. Photo: Joshua White. © Kara Walker, courtesy of Sikkema Jenkins & Co. and Sprüth Magers. Gift of The Speyer Family Foundation in honor of Marie-Josée Kravi.

everywhere confronting audiences with the phantasm of the Negress given precise optical form.[16]

The logic at work in these tableaux is not merely one of primitivist reversal, carnivalesque refiguration, or subjective exorcism. Rather, in Walker's practice, as in so many others that recruit the Negress, there is the mark of a determinative unconscious rooted in modernity's most extreme modes of symbolic and physical violence that have taken the black female body as a primary locus. As the critic T. Denean Sharpley-Whiting has written, to be a black woman is to be "a body trapped in an image of itself," to be "imprisoned in an essence . . . created from without."[17] Not unlike her precursors, from the nineteenth-century sculptor Edmonia Lewis to the jazz-era sensation Josephine Baker, Walker has made her name in reckoning with rather than running from the Negress: the figure that underlines the recursiveness and ubiquity of Western culture's profoundest misrecognitions of the Other as well as the expansive capacities of countervailing raced, sexed, and gendered performances of self.[18]

A figure, a tactic, a subject, a structural position, and a means of mark making, the Negress stands at the boundary of hegemonic and resistive discourses within and beyond the walls of the Museum. For modern artists, to grasp for the Negress, to conjure her into being, is to collapse a limit, to bring the world unbearably close, to perform a sort of alchemy that transmutes subjects into objects and back again. Such transformations are made possible by the flows of bodies and images that have produced black women as fungible property, yet allow also an oppositional approach to the figuration of African diasporic femininity and the aesthetic terms in which it is couched. In light of this economy, it is possible to imagine an alternative history of the Museum and its modernisms that centers on the work of African American women practitioners while also bringing forth the specific forms of affiliation, patterns of subjugation, and corollary modes of image making that differentially produce black subjects in the wake of the Negress.

The faded career of Thelma Johnson Streat—likely the first black woman to have work collected by the Museum—provides one kind of object lesson. A dancer, folklorist, and painter born in Yakima, Washington, circa 1912, Streat was a woman of African and Native American descent who lived and worked in recognized hubs of modern artistic production: Paris, New York, Chicago, San Francisco. Her peripatetic existence can be viewed as a product both of the policing of space that necessarily impinged on black subjects in segregated America and of a desire to engage with alternative cultural formations. Streat spent time in Hawaii, British Columbia, and Ireland, where she made portraits of locals and collected material that would eventually be incorporated into her performances and paintings such as *Rabbit Man* (Fig. 20.7), a gouache that suggests the range of influences, from Squamish to Kota, that informed her lushly colored and hieratic work.[19]

Streat might be thought of as taking up the same primitivist dictionary used by her white male contemporaries, such as Adolph Gottlieb, but for the cross-purpose of enacting a cultural reparation meant to situate her heritages within their rightful historic and ritual contexts.[20] There were, of course, consequences in doing so: the press labeled her the "colored girl" painter, and European audiences feted her as "a charming Negro." These designations attest to the specters that accrued to the artist's person and practice if not to their ambivalent effect.[21] While she often remains a marginal figure in accounts of black women's art, Streat's self-primitivizing self-promotion, so redolent of the Negress, made her work visible, legible, and laudable to modernist luminaries such as Barr, who was responsible for the acquisition of *Rabbit Man* in 1942.[22]

MoMA's investment in Streat and other African American artists was, however, inconsistent, even during the institution's early, more experimental years. The writer Russell Lynes recounted that in the 1930s and

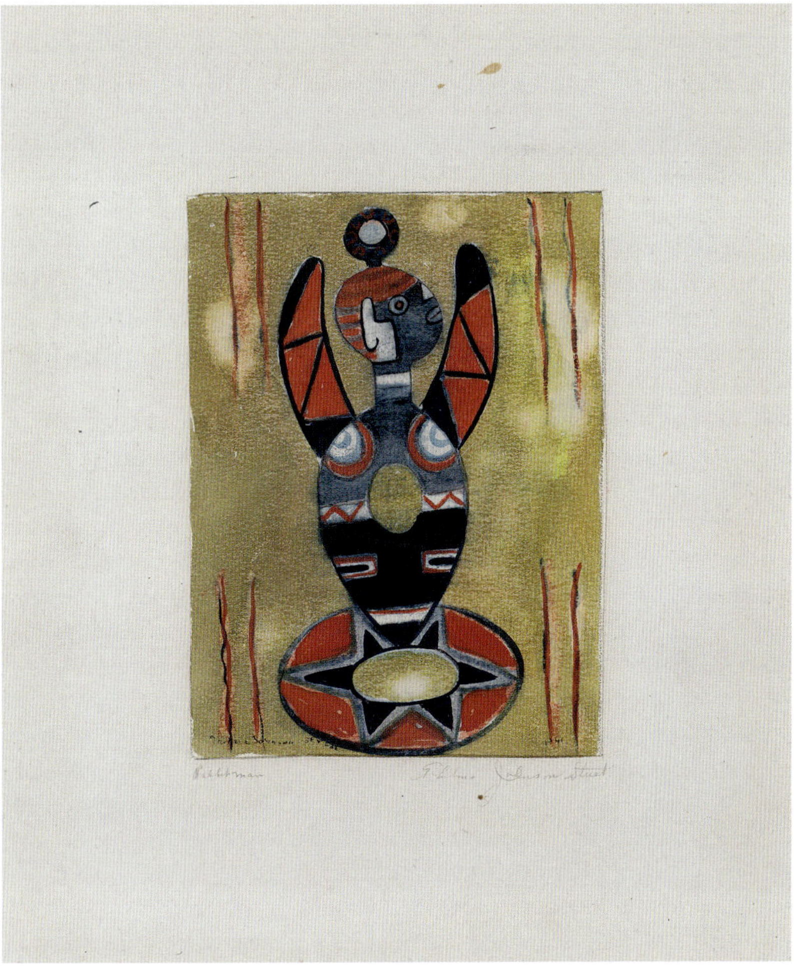

Figure 20.7
Thelma Johnson Streat, *Rabbit Man*, 1941. Gouache on cardboard, 6⅝ × 4⅞ in. Purchase. (216.1942). The Museum of Modern Art. © Thelma Johnson Streat. Digital Image © The Museum of Modern Art/Licensed by SCALA / Art Resource, NY.

1940s the museum "had lived on purposeful improvisation," exhibiting an incredible range of material, from industrially designed objects to popular film to children's drawings.[23] The aim of the institution's founders was to educate the New York public in the aesthetic appraisal of modern production, with a particular view to illuminating the prehistory of European and American pictorial innovation.[24] Accordingly, its early exhibitions featuring black art, such as *Ancestral Sources of Modern Painting* of 1941, emphasized African sculpture, highlighted American folk traditions, and occasionally gave pride of place to the work of an African American master such as Jacob Lawrence.[25] If these shows often reproduced the kind of primitivist logic that positioned African diasporic art as ancillary to mainstream modernism, then the Museum's collecting practices came to enshrine that marginalization by focusing on, in Barr's words, "the best works by the best artists," or "pioneer" objects that occasioned a shift within a narrowly defined aesthetic field.[26]

By the late 1960s the Museum had become the face of the establishment, its "masterpieces" increasingly displayed according to white-cube gallery conventions, its linear account of modern art effectively naturalized, its ideal viewer imagined as a universal subject.[27] Such tendencies, however, threw the Museum's ties to the military-industrial complex and its elision of nonwhite, nonmale, living, and American artists into sharp relief.[28] As such, MoMA, like other museums across the city, became a key site of ideological conflict in the ensuing decades of social crisis, a time that saw increased attempts to dismantle hegemonic culture and to redefine figures of visible difference, blackness foremost among them.[29]

Artists inspired by the civil rights and black nationalist movements worked to establish alternative museum sites in African American communities, such as the Studio Museum in Harlem, even as they clamored against the treatment of African Americans within mainstream institutions.[30] Perhaps the most signal of these came in April 1969: members of the Art Workers Coalition (AWC) protested the exclusion of black artists from MoMA's memorial exhibition in honor of Martin Luther King Jr., occasioning a series of extended dialogues between artists and Museum staff.[31] In this brief moment of opening, it appeared that MoMA might be transformed into a space of black radical imagining and connection between diasporic cultures. Numerous ideas were put forward, even if only fleetingly entertained: a study center devoted to black and Puerto Rican culture; the decentralization of the collection, which would be placed at the behest of community groups throughout the city; and additional exhibition opportunities for women artists and artists of color.[32]

Almost from its inception the AWC had lobbied for the inclusion of underrepresented groups in the Museum, but more often than not the demands of each faction were articulated separately. Consequently, the black and women artists' movements came to parallel rather than inform each other, emphasizing the specificity of their respective identities and the different wells of experience from which they drew.[33] In some cases it appeared that these positions could not be occupied at the same time: although the women's AWC group, Women Artists in Revolution, advocated for people of color, according to its thinking, the black woman was colored second and female first, "since this involved a more profound discrimination."[34] African American women were thus produced as the sum of two differences rather than as individuals with their own ends and histories, but artists would soon emerge whose work and activism would challenge both the movements and the museum.

Few figures reflected these tensions more acutely than Faith Ringgold, who played a central role in the AWC's negotiations for black representation while also contesting the sexism of the African American artists' group Spiral and the exclusionary practices of the white-male-dominated group Art Strike Against Racism, War, and Oppression. In 1970 Ringgold's quest for a space for black feminists led her to organize Women Students and Artists for Black Art Liberation (WSABAL) with, among others, her daughter, Michele Wallace, and eventually to shift the address, form, and structure of her own work.[35] Trained in figurative and abstract oil painting, Ringgold embarked on *The Slave Rape* series in 1973 (Fig. 20.8), a group of acrylic works executed on fabric sewn by the artist's mother, the fashion designer Willi Posey. This series marked Ringgold's turn to a collaborative textile-based practice that materially and pictorially illustrated the folk traditions and historical experiences of black diasporic women.

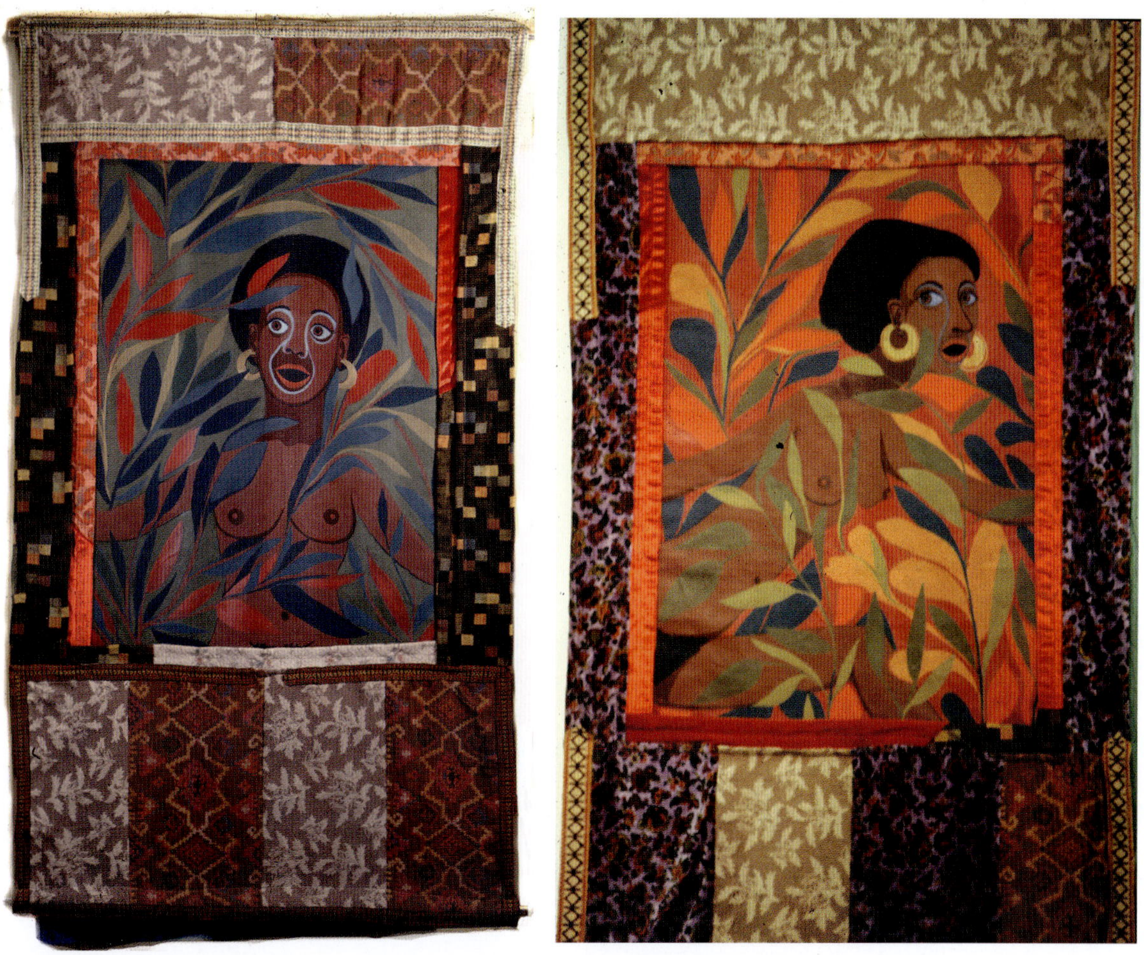

Figure 20.8

Faith Ringgold, *Slave Rape Series #1: Fear Will Make You Weak*. Oil on canvas, 86 × 48 in. *Slave Rape Series #2: Run You Might Get Away*. Oil on canvas, 87 × 48 in., 1972.

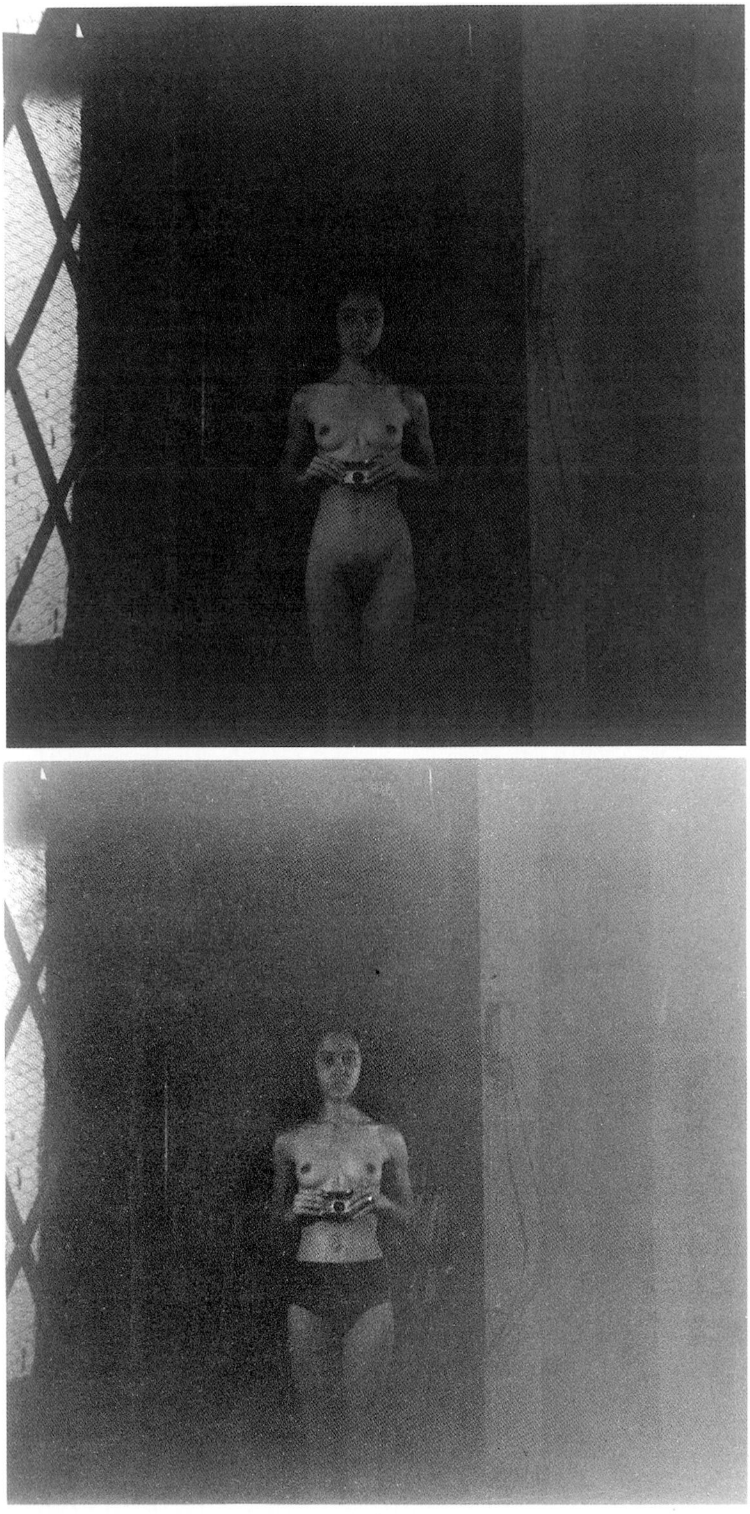

Figure 20.9

Adrian Piper, *Food for the Spirit*, 1971. Fourteen silver gelatin prints (reprinted 1997). 14.81 × 14.5 in. (37.7 × 37 cm). Detail: photographs #3 (*top*) and #4 (*bottom*) of 14. Collection of the Museum of Modern Art, New York. © Adrian Piper Research Archive Foundation.

As the artist Lorraine O'Grady has observed, the 1970s marked a key stage in black female "auto-expression," when practitioners of very different aesthetic means and political sensibilities availed themselves of visual terms that both moved out of the shadow of the Negress and subverted the biases of the Museum.[36] The early work of Adrian Piper provides a case in point. The artist was represented in *Information*, MoMA's landmark 1970 exhibition of Conceptual art, by a typewritten page that revealed nothing about her race or gender.[37] In a series of nude and seminude photographs taken in a mirror one year later (Fig. 20.9), Piper faced the visual facts of her difference, which had contributed both to her marginalization in the art world and to her increasingly radical stance toward its institutions.[38] The story of Howardena Pindell is equally telling. A curator in MoMA's Department of Prints and Illustrated Books for twelve years, Pindell grew weary of the "casual racism" and the "double-speak" around quality that alienated her from her own work and precluded black artists from being visible within the Museum.[39] After a personal crisis in 1979, she left her post, began teaching, and began a series of pieces that mobilized her previous abstract visual vocabulary toward autobiographical ends and that eventually explored affinities with African practices of textural adornment (Fig. 20.10).[40]

As artists and activists, these women and their cohorts did bring about immediate change. Thanks to the platform laid out by WSABAL and pro-

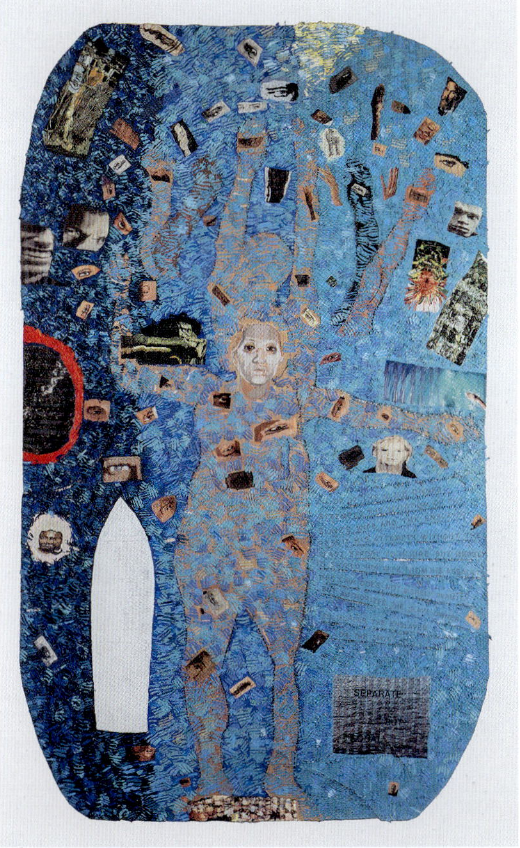

Figure 20.10
Howardena Pindell, *Autobiography: Water/Ancestors/Middle Passage/Family Ghosts*, 1988. Acrylic and mixed media on canvas, 118 × 71 in. (299.8 × 180.4 cm). Wadsworth Atheneum Museum of Art, Hartford, CT. The Ella Gallup Sumner and Mary Catlin Sumner Collection Fund, 1989.17. Photo: Allen Phillips/Wadsworth Atheneum.

tests organized by Ad Hoc Women Artists, for example, black women were included in the 1970 Whitney Biennial.[41] Just as important, their writings created the discursive backdrop against which the work of subsequent practitioners could be seen while emphasizing those persistent realities that, to paraphrase Piper, triply negate black women artists, that give rise to what Pindell calls "art world racism," and that continue the career of the Negress.[42] As Wallace has argued, the incommensurable status of black women as the other of the other, both invisible and ubiquitous, means that their art has been inextricably linked to the modern, yet left out of established art historical narratives and museum collections.[43]

MoMA is no exception. To search for the black woman within its archives is to encounter a series of traces that conjure up a host of absences. There are no works by Maren Hassinger or Lois Mailou Jones or May Howard Jackson; no signs that Martha Jackson Jarvis or Senga Nengudi or Rose Piper were there; no evidence of Harriet Powers, Renée Stout, Alma Thomas, Pat Ward Williams, or even of Meta Vaux Warrick Fuller, whose life and career were "pioneering," to say the least. Born in 1877 to a middle-class black Philadelphia family and educated at the Pennsylvania Museum and School of Industrial Arts, Fuller went to Paris, where she studied until 1902, rubbing shoulders with the likes of W. E. B. Du Bois and having her work positively appraised by no less than Auguste Rodin.[44] As the art historian Judith Wilson has argued, Fuller, in her *Ethiopia Awakening* (Fig. 20.11), manifested not only an innovative approach to sculptural form but also one of the earliest artistic iterations of a feminist African diasporic consciousness. Executed following the publication of the West African writer Joseph Casely-Hayford's novel *Ethiopia Unbound* (1911) and after Emperor Menelik II successfully fended off invading Italian forces in 1896, Fuller's sculpture became a beacon of new black transnational potentialities in art and politics.[45]

Her work has also been seen as indicative of how black women's art opens onto another order of aesthetic priorities. Here is how the scholar Alain Locke began the entry on Fuller in his foundational 1936 survey, *Negro Art: Past and Present*.

> The next artistic career of note was that of a woman artist and sculptor. Sculpture has been strangely prominent in the work of Negro artists, for painting usually claims in modern times far the greater share of attention. But sculpture has been unusually popular with Negro artists, in spite of its technical difficulties and expensive processes. Certainly we have to deal with a more direct and vivid sense for form, unless we try to explain it by some doubtful carry-over of the African preference for three-dimensional form. Another odd fact, the majority of the outstanding Negro sculptors have been women.[46]

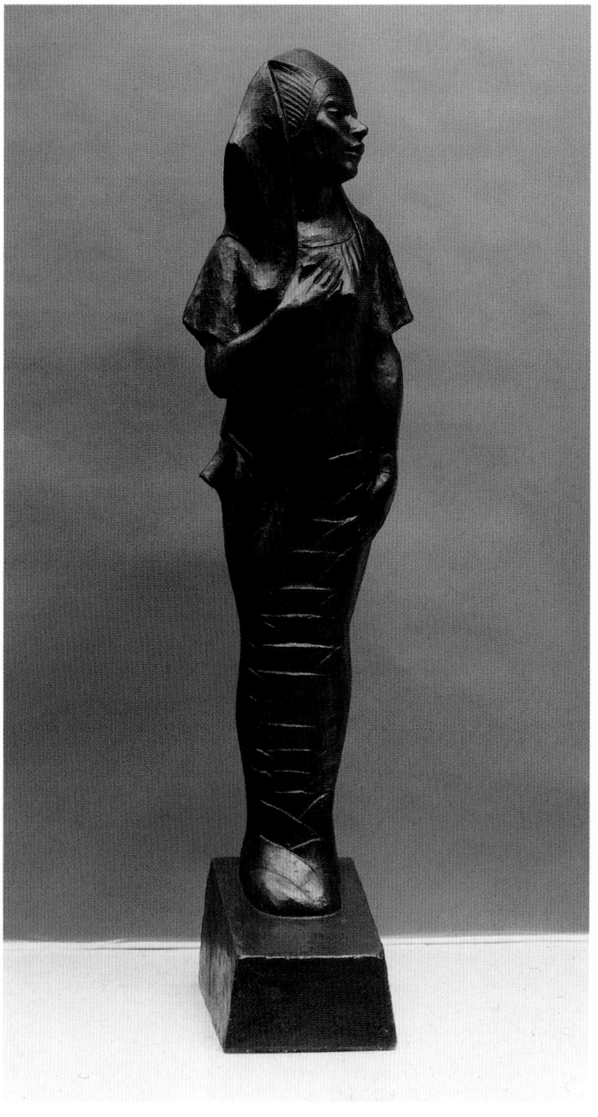

Figure 20.11
Meta Vaux Warrick Fuller, *Ethiopia Awakening*, 1921. © Art and Artifacts Division, Schomburg Center for Research in Black Culture, The New York Public Library.

The art historian Lowery Stokes Sims has argued that such a preference for the sculptural highlights the significance of "tactility as a transmitter of cultural values" within a variety of black women's creative practices—hairdressing, weaving, quilting, performing—all of which take their measure from and embrace the sensate body.[47]

Historically confronted with scopic regimes that denigrate the black female image and received canons that privilege optical perception, African diasporic women have turned to the haptic as a resource for self-fashioning and for the preservation of memories otherwise lost to history. Touch can bring the world close without presuming to master it, allowing

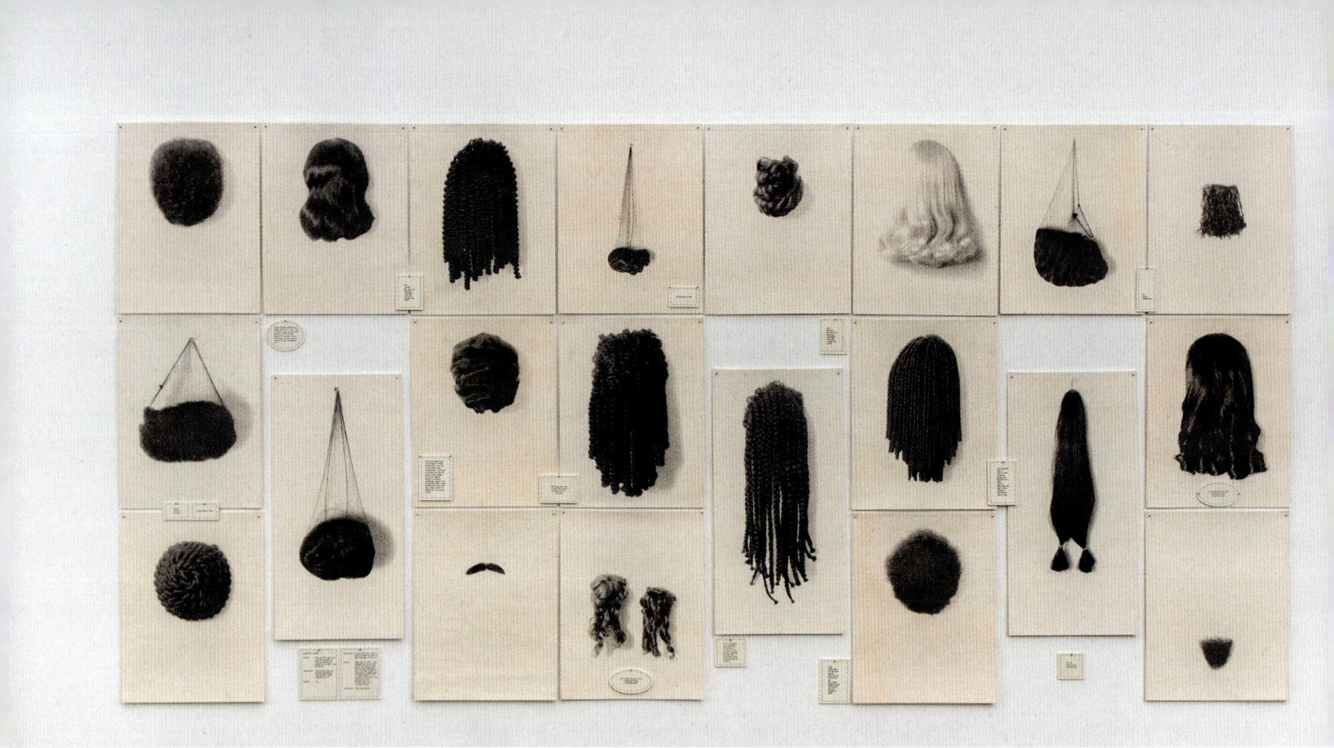

Figure 20.12
Lorna Simpson, *Wigs (Portfolio)*, 1994. Waterless lithograph on felt, 38 panels total, including 17 with text, overall: 72 × 162 in. (182.9 × 411.5 cm). © Lorna Simpson. Courtesy the artist and Hauser & Wirth. Photo: James Wang.

for a recalibration of the self and the object, the aesthetic and the vernacular, that disarticulates notions of quality, medium, and cultural hierarchy. Pindell's investment in African textiles, Ringgold's turn to quilting, even Piper's lingering photographic contact with herself—these black women's engagements with the visual constitute manifestations of a modernist sensibility predicated not on the look of racial phantasm but on the feel of the subject's psychic and corporeal position.[48]

Simpson's work illustrates how the seemingly antithetical modalities of vision and touch hold each other in productive tension (Fig. 20.12). Her multipart *Wigs* is composed of serigraphs, printed on felt, that depict hairpieces purchased in Brooklyn set alongside narrative fragments ranging from a psychoanalyst's interview with the mother of an avowed fetishist to lines lifted from William and Ellen Crafts's 1860 slave narrative, which describes how they disguised themselves in order to escape from bondage. Simpson's wigs suggest that the look of black femininity might be altered to preserve the sensate self, a combination of visual ruse and tactile identity hinted at by the richly textured surfaces on which the images are printed. In this work it is as if the conditions affecting black women can only come into view when the body and the presumptions that accompany it are absented from the field of vision.

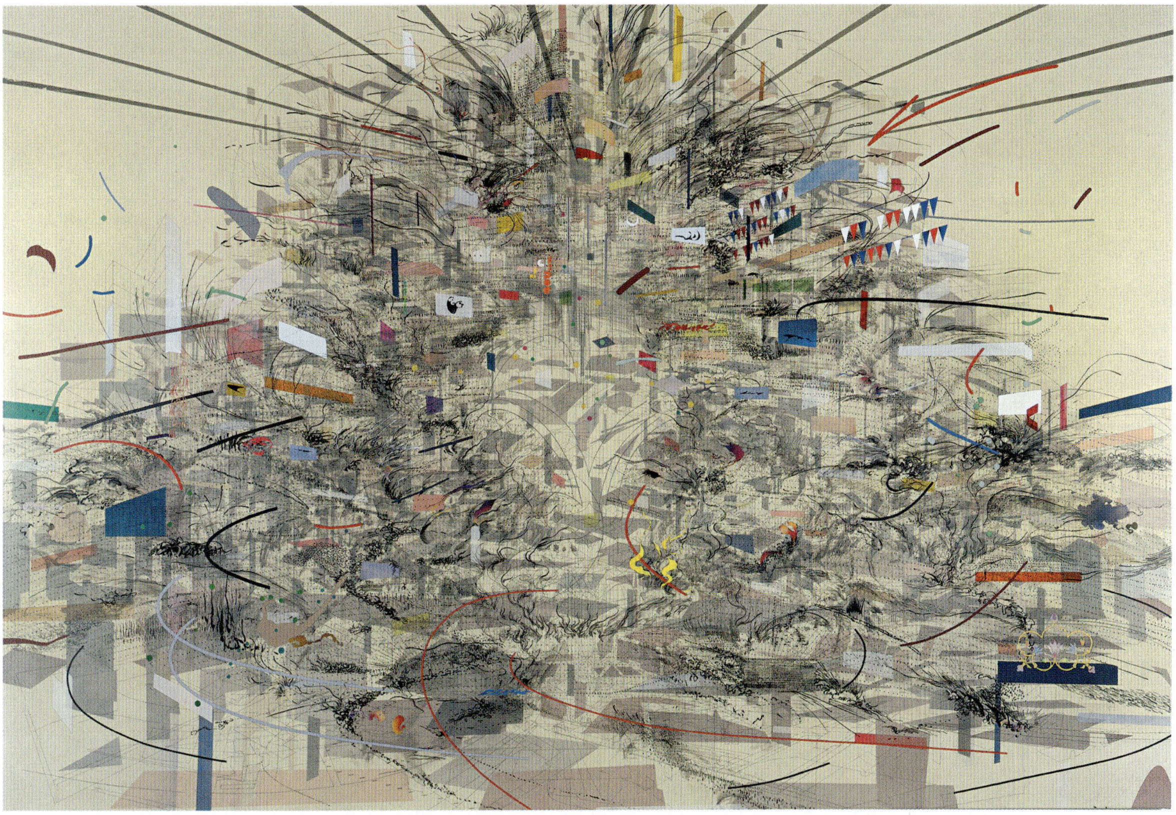

Figure 20.13
Julie Mehretu, *Empirical Construction, Istanbul*, 2003. Ink and synthetic polymer paint on canvas, 10 × 15 ft. (304.8 × 457.2 cm). The Museum of Modern Art; fund for the Twenty-First Century. © Julie Mehretu.

Much the same might be said of Julie Mehretu's *Empirical Construction, Istanbul* (2003) (Fig. 20.13), in which space is both homogenized and hopelessly undone, giving disembodied visual form to the sorts of cultural displacements that took the artist from Ethiopia to the United States and to those historical vectors that have shaped the experience of the modern subject. Both Simpson's and Mehretu's works reveal the range of possibilities available to black women artists in the present; that the pieces are found in MoMA's collection suggests the viability of their practices in the culture at large. Yet the terms of their appearance are still haunted by the specter of the Negress, a figure that makes clear how the production of the aesthetic and of the human within Western institutions remains structured by the desire to locate cultural renovation in bodily difference: whether real or virtual, the black woman in the Museum continues to tell untold stories and to give rise to an uncertain future.

Notes

1 On Simpson's discursive construction in the age of multiculturalism and its aftermath, see Huey Copeland, "'Bye, Bye Black Girl': Lorna Simpson's Figurative Retreat," *Art Journal* 64, no. 2 (Summer 2005): 62-77.

2 Katherine McKittrick conducts a related inquiry in *Demonic Grounds: Black Women and the Cartographies of Struggle* (University of Minnesota Press, 2006).

3 For a useful reckoning with the conceptualization of the African diaspora–which refers both to the forcible dispersal of black peoples from the continent and their efforts to create political and cultural community in the wake of such displacement–see Brent Hayes Edwards, "The Uses of *Diaspora*," *Social Text* 66, vol. 19, no. 1 (Spring 2001): 45-73.

4 Images in the exhibition–based on the holdings of the Getty Museum and those of the collector Jackie Napolean Wilson–are reproduced in Wilson's *Hidden Witness: African-American Images from the Dawn of Photography to the Civil War* (St. Martin's Griffin, 2002).

5 My reading of this work expands on Enid Schildkrout's in "*Les Parisiens d'Afrique*: Mangbetu Women as Works of Art," in *Black Womanhood: Images, Icons, and Ideologies of the African Body*, exh. cat., ed. Barbara Thompson (Hood Museum of Art, Dartmouth College; and University of Washington Press, 2008), 71-93.

6 The Friends of Education, http://www.moma.org/support/support_themuseum/affiliate_groups/index.

7 My account of the Museum's practices draws on Douglas Crimp, "The Art of Exhibition," in *On the Museum's Ruins* (MIT Press, 1993), 262-71.

8 On this disjuncture, see Michael Hanchard, "Black Memory versus State Memory: Notes Toward a Method," *Small Axe: A Caribbean Journal of Criticism 12, no. 2* (June 2008): 45-62.

9 Here I use "signify" in the sense elaborated by Henry Louis Gates Jr., who traces the term's history as a form of troping and ironic reversal in black expressive cultures in "The Blackness of Blackness: A Critique of the Sign and the Signifying Monkey," in *Figures in Black: Words, Signs, and the "Racial" Self* (Oxford University Press, 1987), 235-76.

10 Frieda High W. Tesfagiorgis, "In Search of a Discourse and Critique/s That Center the Art of Black Women Artists," in *Theorizing Black Feminisms: The Visionary Pragmatism of Black Women*, ed. Stanlie M. James and Abena P. A. Busia (London: Routledge, 1993), 228-65; Lorraine O'Grady, "Olympia's Maid: Reclaiming Black Female Subjectivity," *Afterimage* 20 (Summer 1992): 14-15, 23; Gilane Tawadros, "Beyond the Boundary: The Work of Three Black Women Artists in Britain," *Third Text* 3, no. 8-9 (Autumn-Winter 1989): 121-50; Michele Wallace, "Modernism, Postmodernism, and the Problem of the Visual in Afro-American Culture," in *Out There: Marginalization and Contemporary Cultures*, ed. Russell Ferguson et al. (MIT Press, 1990), 39-50.

11 T. Denean Sharpley-Whiting offers an invaluable gloss on the meaning of the Negress in *Black Venus: Sexualized Savages, Primal Fears, and Primitive Narratives in French* (Duke University Press, 1999), 56. The *Oxford English Dictionary* offers a thorough account of the etymology of "Negress."

12 Hortense J. Spillers, "Mama's Baby, Papa's Maybe: An American Grammar Book" (1987), in *Black, White, and in Color: Essays on American Literature and Culture* (University of Chicago Press, 2003), 203.

13 On Abby Aldrich Rockefeller's collection, its importance for the Museum, and her investment in George Overbury "Pop" Hart, see Sybil Gordon Kantor, *Alfred H. Barr, Jr. and the Intellectual Origins of the Museum of Modern Art* (MIT Press, 2002), 191–95.

14 Alfred H. Barr Jr., *Picasso: Forty Years of His Art* (Museum of Modern Art, 1939), 60.

15 Kara Walker, quoted in Jerry Saltz, "Ill-Will and Desire," *Flash Art* (November-December 1996): 84.

16 I have relied on Darby English's thoroughgoing account of Walker's practice in *How to See a Work of Art in Total Darkness* (MIT Press, 2007), 110–12.

17 Sharpley-Whiting, *Black Venus*, 10.

18 My theorization of the Negress is indebted to Hilton Als's memoir, *The Women*, which tells the stories of black gay men and women, most notably the author's mother, whose "remarkable way[s] of being" constitute their "Negressity." Hilton Als, *The Women* (Noonday Press, 1996), 19.

19 On Thelma Johnson Streat's life and work, see Lizetta LeFalle-Collins, "Streat, Thelma Johnson," in *St. James Guide to Black Artists*, ed. Thomas Riggs (St. James Press, 1997), 512-13; Judith Wilson, "How the Invisible Woman Got Herself on the Cultural Map: Black Women Artists in California," in *Art/Women/California, 1950-2000: Parallels and Intersections*, ed. Diana Burgess Fuller and Daniela Salvioni (University of California Press and San Jose Museum of Art, 2002), 201-16; Ann Gibson, "Two Worlds: African-American Abstraction in New York at Mid-Century," in *The Search for Freedom: African American Abstract Painting, 1945-1975*, exh. cat. (Kenkeleba Gallery, 1991), 11–54.

20 I borrow the notion of a "dictionary of 'primitivist' styles" from Ann Gibson, *Abstract Expressionism: Other Politics* (Yale University Press, 1997), 160; and that of "ethnocultural redemption and retrieval" from Wilson, "How the Invisible Women Got Herself on the Cultural Map," 207.

21 In characterizing Thelma Johnson Streat's discursive production, I have drawn on clippings included in the Museum of Modern Art Archives, Painting and Sculpture Artist File I. 315: "Colored Girl to Exhibit Paintings," *Oregon Journal*, September 19, 1934, C3, 5; and "The News That's Going Around," *Irish Press*, May 6, 1950.

22 The MoMA file on Streat contains lists of the artist's notices, critics, and collectors that she produced herself and submitted to the Museum. Between 1947 and 1953, Streat also wrote several letters to Barr and to the curator Dorothy Miller that reveal her consistent desire to show at the Museum.

23 Russell Lynes, *Good Old Modern: The Museum of Modern Art* (Atheneum, 1973), 212.

24 Alfred H. Barr Jr., "A New Art Museum" (1929), in *Defining Modern Art: Selected Writings of Alfred H. Barr, Jr.*, ed. Irving Sandler and Amy Newman (Harry N. Abrams, 1986), 71.

25 For a working draft of the museum's exhibition history, see http://www.moma.org/research/archives/exhibhistory.html; on Barr's various engage-

ments with black diasporic culture, see the Alfred H. Barr Papers, Museum of Modern Art Archives.

26 Barr, quoted in Kantor, *Alfred H. Barr, Jr. and the Intellectual Origins of the Museum of Modern Art*, 369.

27 Mary Anne Staniszewski, *The Power of Display: A History of Exhibition Installations at the Museum of Modern Art* (MIT Press, 1998), 110-11.

28 Lucy Lippard, "Dreams, Demands, and Desires: The Black, Antiwar, and Women's Movements," in *Tradition and Conflict: Images of a Turbulent Decade, 1963-73*, exh. cat., ed. Mary Schmidt Campbell (Studio Museum in Harlem, 1985), 78.

29 For a brilliant gloss on the multiple valences of the black sign in the 1960s and 1970s, see Kobena Mercer, "Tropes of the Grotesque in the Black Avant-Garde," in *Pop Art and Vernacular Cultures*, ed. Kobena Mercer (MIT Press and Iniva, 2007), 147.

30 For useful surveys of black art and activism, see Campbell, *Tradition and Conflict*, 45-68; as well as Mary Ellen Shannon, "A Question of Relevancy: New York Museums and the Black Arts Movement, 1968-1971," in *New Thoughts on the Black Arts Movement*, ed. Lisa Gail Collins and Margo Natalie Crawford (Rutgers University Press, 2006), 92-116.

31 Lippard, "Dreams, Demands, and Desires," 78.

32 "The Demands of the Art Workers Coalition," May 6, 1970, Museum of Modern Art Archives, John B. Hightower Papers, III.1.8; and "Byers Committee Report to Trustees," February 1971, Hightower Papers, I.9.70.

33 Lisa Gail Collins, "The Art of Transformation: Parallels in the Black Arts and Feminist Art Movements," in Collins and Crawford, *New Thoughts on the Black Arts Movement*, 274.

34 Betsy Jones, "Report on Meeting with the Women's Committee of the AWC," n.d., p. 2, Museum of Modern Art Archives, John B. Hightower Papers, III.1.11.a.

35 Faith Ringgold reflects on this moment in *We Flew Over the Bridge: The Memoirs of Faith Ringgold* (Little, Brown, 1995), 143-216.

36 O'Grady, "Olympia's Maid," 23.

37 Adrian Piper, "Three Models of Art Production Systems," in *Information*, ed. Kynaston McShine (Museum of Modern Art, 1970), 111.

38 Adrian Piper, "Introduction: Some Very forward Remarks," in *Out of Order, Out of Sight*, vol. 2, *Selected Writings in Art Criticism, 1967-1992* (MIT Press, 1996), xxx-xxxiii.

39 Howardena Pindell, "Art World Racism: A Documentation, 1980-1988," 1988, in *The Heart of the Question: The Writings and Art of Howardena Pindell* (Midmarch Arts Press, 1997), 7, 17.

40 On autobiography and adornment in Pindell's practice, see "Autobiography: In Her Own Image" (1988); "Free White and 21" (1992); "The Aesthetics of Texture in African Adornment" (1984), in Pindell, *The Heart of the Question*, 72-73, 65-69, and 84-86, respectively.

41 Michele Wallace, "Reading 1968: The Great American Whitewash" (1988), in *Invisibility Blues: From Pop to Theory* (Verso, 1990), 196.

42 Adrian Piper, "The Triple Negation of Colored Women Artists" (1990), in *Out of Order, Out of Sight*, 161-73; Pindell, "Art World Racism," 3-19.

43 Wallace, "Variations on Negation and the Heresy of Black Feminist Creativity," in *Invisibility Blues*, 218.

44 See Renée Ater, "Making History: Meta Vaux Warrick Fuller's *Ethiopia*," *American Art* 17, no. 3 (Fall 2003): 14.

45 Judith Wilson, "Hagar's Daughters: Social History, Cultural Heritage, and Afro-U.S. Women's Art," in *Bearing Witness: Contemporary Works by African American Women Artists*, exh. cat. (Rizzoli International, 1996), 95–112.

46 Alain Locke, *Negro Art Past and Present* (Associates in Negro Folk Education, 1936), 27–28.

47 Lowery Stokes Sims, "African American Women Artists: Into the Twentieth-First Century," in *Bearing Witness*, 85.

48 This paragraph expands my thinking on the subject's visual and sensual predication in Copeland, "'Bye, Bye Black Girl,'" 74–75, in light of Tesfagiorgis's and Sims's thinking about the disruptive and healing forces of black women's vernacular traditions. See Tesfagiorgis, "In Search of a Discourse," 232; Sims, "African American Women Artists," 86.

21

FLOW AND ARREST

We start with a story. In 2002, while researching the dissertation from which my first book, *Bound to Appear: Art, Slavery, and the Site of Blackness in Multicultural America*, would emerge, I had the opportunity to pose for the artist Lorna Simpson. Her practice had already become a locus of my thinking about aesthetics, slavery, and the aporias of representation, so I eagerly agreed to serve as her model. With characteristic economy, Simpson made good use of the photographs resulting from our session, eventually deploying them in a range of artworks that together comprise her 2002–3 exhibition *Cameos and Appearances*. Yet however reproduced, framed, or occluded, those initial Polaroid images are also documents of an encounter in which the "art historian" became the "subject" of "his artist's" "objective" gaze, leaving each of the quoted words estranged from itself and underlining an entanglement in the artistic procedures that I set out to describe.[1]

Estranged and entangled: these terms begin to articulate not only the queer experience of belatedly gazing at myself through Simpson's lens but also that of reading the critical engagements with *Bound to Appear* commissioned by *Small Axe* and penned by two black literary scholars, Stephen Best and Hortense Spillers, whose work has long mattered to my own. Like Simpson's photographs, my book bears the name of a single author, but it is necessarily a collaborative affair: every writer will admit—at least in his acknowledgments if not through his method—that his work is a condensation of social, conceptual, and material relations that encompass an array of attitudes, objects, practices, and interlocutors. The present company is no exception. Best, whom I first encountered while a graduate student at

This article first appeared in *Small Axe: A Caribbean Journal of Criticism* 19, no. 3 (48) (November 2015): 205–24, as the third entry of the "Book Discussion" devoted to *Bound to Appear* that also featured Hortense J. Spillers, "Art Talk and the Uses of History," and Stephen Best, "Come and Gone," 175–85 and 186–204, respectively.

Berkeley, makes brief but vital appearances in the book's first chapter on Fred Wilson and the third on Glenn Ligon, whose art provides the opening frame for his remarks here. The field-turning scholarship of Spillers, whom I met only recently, has been an invaluable touchstone for my thinking and that of countless others with an investment in black thought and liberation. Unsurprisingly, then, the means of argumentation and modes of address that these two writers adopt in reading *Bound to Appear* refract not only their own intellectual commitments and personal dispositions but also those of the book itself.[2]

Spillers's and Best's divergent responses make for a generative pairing that reveals the dynamic tensions within black cultural discourse today and that begins to suggest the flows and arrests that animate the book. In attempting to move away from the models of "historical ontology" that, by his lights, undergird *Bound to Appear* as well as his own previous scholarship, Best offers a white queer understanding of radicalism meant to intervene both within African American studies broadly construed and within the increasingly trafficked discourse on contemporary black abstraction, particularly in relation to the work of Mark Bradford.[3] As a result, Best focuses less on what *Bound to Appear* specifically enacts and more on what its contentions and silences might otherwise enable; by contrast, Spillers offers an immanent critique that reads the text closely, innovatively, inimitably. In so doing, she brings out the urgency of *Bound to Appear*'s approach to the visual and presciently suggests how its claims might extend the material scope and intellectual preoccupations of African diasporic artistic discourse. Both writers have my thanks; in the pages that follow, I address individual comments by each before closing with a meditation on the implications of Spillers's thinking for my current scholarship.

Ultimately, to consider these texts together is to be challenged and gratified by my work's positioning as a spur for black thought, a revelatory scrim for various writers' projections onto, investments in, and desires for critical work at the intersection of art history and black studies. It is also to reckon with the book's errors and omissions while appreciating its achievements as an intellectual intervention and a professional milestone, without which I could hardly occupy the positions I am now privileged to hold. Even more important, reading Spillers's and Best's accounts is an occasion to think further about what a black radical art history might be both methodologically and conceptually, especially as my own thinking has evolved in the years since *Bound to Appear*'s completion in 2012.[4] In responding to these particular essays and to the critical field that has begun to emerge around the book, I aim to shed fresh light on its operative assumptions and to position it amid the personal, intellectual, and professional networks from which it emerged.[5] For this rare opportunity and for his tremendous patience, I thank *Small Axe* editor, David Scott, who, in soliciting my response, has returned me to the primal scene of my intellectual formation—with all the pleasure and difficulty that entails—and enabled me to rethink *Bound to Appear* from an estranged distance now that the book has properly begun its life in the world of which it was always a part.

First Things

Thanks to Spillers's inquisitive engagement with and brilliant riffs on *Bound to Appear*'s primary works, a detailed reiteration of each of the book's chapters seems redundant here. I do want, however, to articulate the text's key claims as a way of spelling out why, in fact, it came to appear. For the sake of the uninitiated reader, let us begin with the dust jacket, the site where an authorial framing of the book comes to an end and the reader's encounter with it begins.

> At the close of the twentieth century, an appreciable number of black artists began to figure prominently in the mainstream American art world for the first time. Thanks to the social advances of the civil rights movement and the rise of multiculturalism, African American artists in the late 1980s and early '90s enjoyed unprecedented access to established institutions of publicity and display. Yet in this moment of ostensible freedom, black cultural practitioners found themselves turning to the history of slavery.
>
> *Bound to Appear* focuses on four of these artists—Renée Green, Glenn Ligon, Lorna Simpson, and Fred Wilson—who have helped shape the field of American art over the past two decades, in part, through large-scale installations that radically departed from prior conventions for representing the enslaved. Huey Copeland shows that their projects draw on strategies associated with minimalism, conceptualism, and institutional critique to position the slave as a vexed figure—both subject and object, property and person. At the same time, these artists pointedly engage the visual logic of race within modernity and the challenges negotiated by black subjects in the present. As such, Copeland argues, their work reframes strategies of representation and rethinks how blackness might be imagined and felt long after the end of the "peculiar institution."

These lines are, of course, meant to produce a particular audience for *Bound to Appear* and to solicit its purchase with the promise of the new, as emphasized by that opening sentence's final words, "for the first time." Whatever its promotional value, the rhetoric of "firstness" does offer a starting point from which to elaborate the book's innovations in relation to the various fields within art history that it means to engage and contest, particularly as these concerns are not exhausted by Spillers's and Best's essays.

A few things ought to be said right off the bat: *Bound to Appear* is the first historically oriented study to consider the four artists in question as a group and to recognize the thematic links between and formal convergences in their postminimal practices of the early 1990s. The book joins a small number of volumes focused on the art of that decade, which has become a burgeoning site of study and recollection in cultural discourse in the United States and abroad.[6] What's more, *Bound to Appear* is the first scholarly monograph to home in intensively on contemporary approaches to slavery in the visual field, examining a quartet of temporary installations—Wilson's *Mining the Museum* (1992); Simpson's *Five Rooms* (1991), executed in collaboration with the vocalist Alva Rogers; Green's *Mise-en-Scène* (1991); and Ligon's *To Disembark* (1993)—that are distinguished by their visual recalcitrance, spatial dispersion, use of recorded sound, and archival engagements (Fig. 21.1).

Rather than depict heroic actors or sympathetic victims, as had many previous painted and sculpted reckonings with the slave past, these artists deployed an array of everyday materials—Wilson, a set of shackles (among numerous other things); Simpson, jars of rice; Ligon, shipping crates; and Green, printed fabric—that were to meant conjure the economies in which the enslaved were enmeshed and to function as active participants in the multisensory ensemble comprising each installation. Unlike their artistic contemporaries, who were equally invested in figuring slavery at the same historical juncture, each of the artists examined in *Bound to Appear* drew on visual as well as sonic cues to stage an immersive bodily encounter with things—either objects touched by the enslaved or surrogates for them that brought home the captive's fraught ontological status, from the nineteenth-century earthenware jug made by one Melinda and featured in *Mining the Museum* to the scenes of bondage visualized in eighteenth-century engravings and subsequently translated into Green's own version of *toile indienne*.

Bound to Appear argues that by mapping the material worlds of transatlantic slavery, these projects avoid the trap of foisting an imagined subjectivity on the enslaved, instead producing forms of "antiportraiture"—a term borrowed from the critic Lauri Firstenburg—that demonstrate how captive bodies were literally and figuratively woven into the texture of everyday life and consumption within capitalist culture.[7] The installations thereby variously reveal how structural dynamics undergirding slavery and resistance to it—redress (*Mining the Museum*), objecthood (*Five Rooms*), fugitivity (*To Disembark*), and diaspora (*Mise-en-Scène*)—continue to inform the production of black bodies as fungible properties despite the apparent successes of the civil rights and multicultural move-

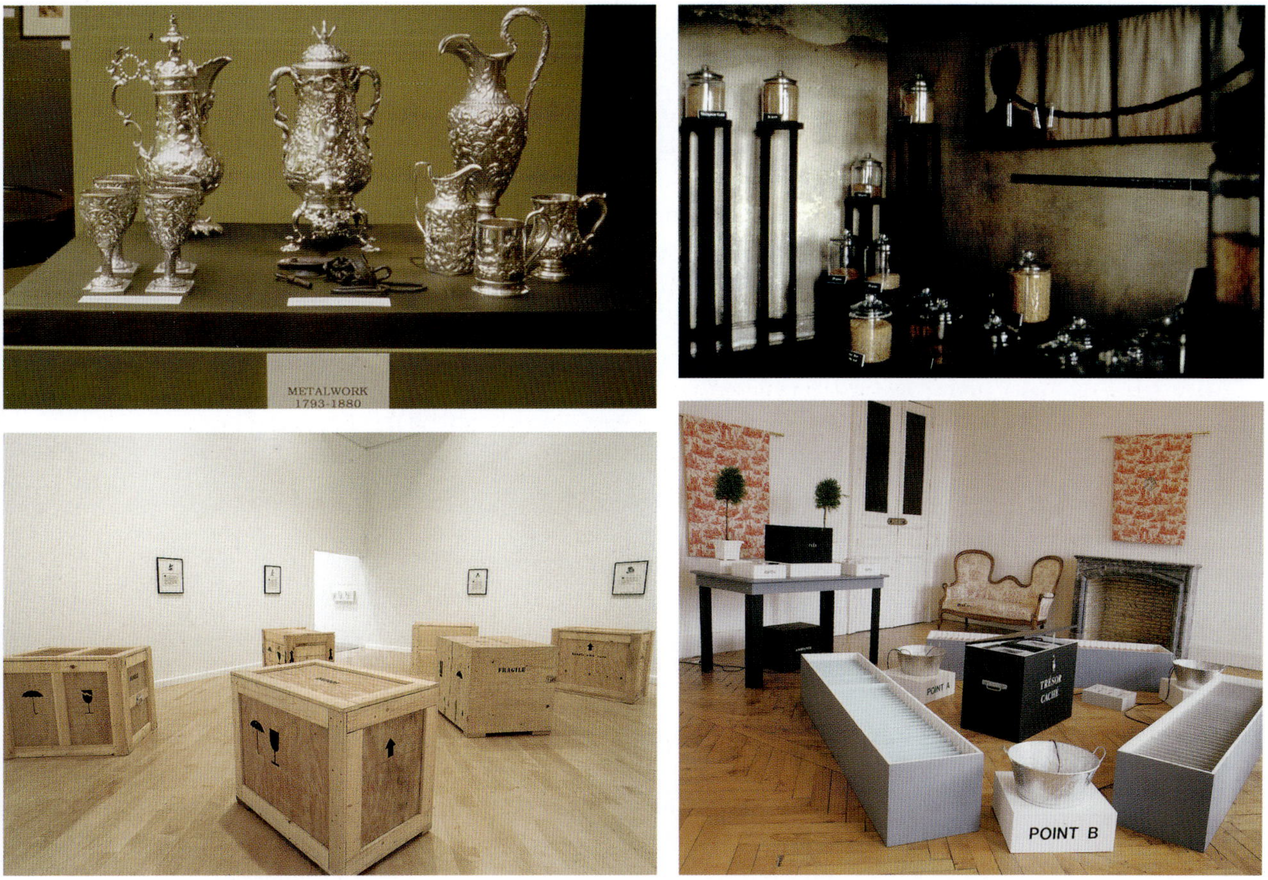

Figure 21.1

Clockwise from upper left: Fred Wilson, *Metalwork, 1793-1880* from *Mining the Museum: An Installation by Fred Wilson*, The Contemporary and Maryland Historical Society, Baltimore, April 4, 1992-February 28, 1993. © Fred Wilson, courtesy Pace Gallery; Lorna Simpson and Alva Rogers, *Five Rooms*, detail, 1991. Glass jars, rice, water, plastic engraved plaques, gelatin silver and Polaroid prints, audio. Installation in collaboration with Alva Rogers, Dependency Governor Thomas Bennett House, Charleston, North Carolina. Installation dimensions variable. © Lorna Simpson. Courtesy the artist and Hauser & Wirth; Renée Green, *Mise-en-Scène*, 1991. Mixed media, dimensions variable. Frac des Pays de la Loire. Image: Bernard Renoux. Courtesy of the artist and Free Agent Media; Glenn Ligon, *Untitled (To Disembark)*, detail, 1993. Nine wood crates with synthetic polymer, acrylic paint, and nine audio recordings, 31.25 × 38.25 × 25.25 in. (79.4 × 97.2 × 64.1 cm). © Glenn Ligon.

ments, whose rhetorics are often haunted by older and far from liberatory assumptions.

As stated in the book's introduction, "The primary impact [of these installations] is *not* of a replaying of the trauma of slavery, which would imply that repressed horrors have somehow been recovered or bubbled up from a temporal interregnum" (9; my emphasis). Indeed, what must be stressed, particularly in light of Best's misreading, is that these projects and *Bound to Appear*'s framing of them are not primarily intended to act as historical recoveries that enable or even accede to what he terms the logics of "witnessing," "mutuality," or "compassionate resuscitation."[8] Rather, the improbable forms of these works and the surrogates for captive bodies that they held out are meant to underline the difficulty of establishing any relation to the past, to the other, even to the "self"; what would it mean to "identify" with a glass container of rice or a shipping crate? These facts begin to account for the overall tone of the installations: melancholic, as Best points out,[9] but also absurdist, given the enormity of the task at hand. In other words, *Bound to Appear* proceeds from the works' assumption that slavery is structurally constitutive of Western art and culture, regardless of its visual, social, or political acknowledgment within hegemonic discourses.

This assumption also speaks to the historical interest and formal difficulty of the installations, which, in refusing the visual clichés associated with slavery, point out the inadequacy of any representational framework to figure captive subjects, whose ghosts are everywhere present—in the halls of the Hirshhorn Museum where Ligon first installed *To Disembark* and in the actual slave quarters that Simpson and Rogers occupied in making *Five Rooms*. Indeed, all four of the works' material complexity, brief exhibition periods, and emphasis on corporeal engagement pose considerable challenges to retrospective narration even with the best of documentation. Accordingly, *Bound to Appear* features a robust image program—thanks to a Creative Capital/Andy Warhol Foundation Arts Writers Grant—that reproduces many pieces by these artists for the first time in order to restore unacknowledged aspects of their practices to the field and to provide illustrated guides to installations usually known through the same handful of photographs.

In its ambition to make these works freshly available for reference, engagement, and critique, the book proceeds in full knowledge of the archival and discursive forgetting that too frequently attends African American art.[10] And at stake is not just the writing—or even the "righting"—of the recent art historical past. In the book's interpretation of them, the shared visual strategies and temporal arrival of *Mining the Museum*, *Five Rooms*, *To Disembark*, and *Mise-en-Scène* continue to matter deeply for imagining the possibilities of critical artistic practice. These works instance and engender a brief interval when four like-minded practitioners pointedly defied the demands for recognizable imagery and recognizable difference imposed on them as black artists in the context of a multicultural art world hungry for easily registered and consumed iterations of alterity. Of course, as the book's conclusion spells out, the approaches that these artists developed for figuring the enslaved in the early 1990s were in many ways transitional within their oeuvres and certainly not the only means available for addressing the slave past, as evidenced by the silhouettes of Kara Walker (197–206). What they model, then, and what the book describes is the search for critical modes of representation in a moment when the black figure, as pictured in American art and culture—remember Willie Horton, Rodney King, and O. J. Simpson—seemed to be more overdetermined than ever, reduced to either victim or menace.[11]

By bracketing the image, Wilson's, Simpson's, Ligon's, and Green's "circumlocutive" interventions—to borrow a word from Spillers[12]—rerouted the visual logic of identification on which political and communal claims are often based, instead offering a peculiar brand of poststructuralist realism that brought to light the ongoing effects of slavery as well as the barriers posed time and again to the political recognition of black subjects, to say nothing of the social will required to bring about some semblance of racial justice.[13] As Spillers reminds us at the outset of her essay, the recent high-profile murders of several unarmed black men by white police officers, especially those that were digitally recorded, underline both how little and how much the "truth" of the image matters to the social and legal reproduction of white supremacy.[14] Then as now, the works gathered together in *Bound to Appear* hold out means through which to explore this quandary and, as Spillers suggests, to "recalibrate" our response both to the "emergency" at hand as well as to its "emergence" from the economies of seeing and not seeing brought to bear within transatlantic slavery.[15]

In Search of a Method

Back in 1998, these concerns certainly were not on the tip of my tongue, but I had already begun groping toward them in an undergraduate thesis on contemporary black queer artists.[16] Though support for my project was strong, I was nagged by suspicions that my intellectual interests were inappropriate as the objects of further study or as the basis for a successful career in art history. One adviser rather offhandedly put it to me like this: leave behind all that "my-fabulous-black-body stuff of the last five minutes" and do the "sensible" thing, which, to his mind, meant enrolling in graduate school out west to write a dissertation on nineteenth-century French painting with an éminence grise. My father, ever the pragmatist, concurred with this plan, though for very different reasons: art history was already enough of a gamble for a black gay man, so why redouble the opportunities for the expression of the homophobic and antiblack sentiments that would surely be leveled not only against me, but now also against my work? In those moments, I experienced the visual as freighted with the "image anxiety" and the "outcry" against it that Spillers identifies as vital to "the African American critical posture."[17] My mentor's and my father's comments served to bring into focus my own anxieties in the face of the discipline's unstated presuppositions: namely, that the work of contemporary African American artists could not support the kinds of rigorous inquiry that is the hallmark of the most innovative scholarship in the field and that visual technologies of race are ancillary to the discipline, its key sites of interrogation, and the signal achievements art history takes as its objects.[18]

As my sister-girl Krista Thompson has noted, the suppression of race, slavery, and the contributions of African diasporic peoples has long been central to the operations of artistic discourse, whether in the writing of the late nineteenth-century British aesthete John Ruskin or those of the mid-twentieth-century American critic Clement Greenberg.[19] We hardly need look back so far to see how elisions of blackness and of black artists manifest themselves in the literature. Take one example drawn from my undergraduate reading, Thomas Crow's 1996 book, *The Rise of the Sixties: American and European Art in the Era of Dissent*. Despite its titular emphasis on dissent, in Crow's accounting, racial movements and counterhegemonic visual cultures are mostly ignored or briefly invoked as fodder for white artists such as Andy Warhol. The lone African American practitioner whose work is illustrated in Crow's book, Betye Saar, is mentioned not so much because of her work's visual acuity but because it exists at all, providing evidence that even that most often and easily excluded of figures, the "colored woman artist," received a measure of presence, visibility, and opportunity thanks to the era's upheavals.[20] While *The Rise of the Sixties* is now more than a decade old—and, admittedly, an easy target—it nonetheless exemplifies how art history continues to sidestep questions of race and their complex entanglement with the constitution of the visual field.[21]

Since the publication of Crow's book and my own moment of paterno-pedagogical misfire, a veritable cadre of artists and art historians invested in black art and culture has emerged, shifts that reflect what Spillers identifies as "the quiet revolution . . . in American higher education," which enabled a refashioning of "notions of tradition, of canonical significance," and the accommodation of "new knowledges."[22] It is in this milieu, often associated with market and institutional drives toward "diversity," that *Bound to Appear* took shape and with which it took issue: despite the openings that it effected, American multicultural discourse in the visual arts tended to analogize identarian positions rather than to think structurally about how the economies of racialization differentially position black subjects in relationship to power.

It was a desire to think in these terms that, in part, drove my decision to head west after all in search of that éminence, T. J. Clark, and to write a dissertation in dialogue with his pioneering approach to the social history of art, which emphasizes the importance of cultural context in interpreting singular objects and enables a range of productive deformations as to what that context might mean and how it might matter. In the hands of my primary adviser, Anne M. Wagner, questions of identarian position could be productively explored in relation to the work of art, the positioning of the artist, and the discursive construction of both: hers was a feminist method that could be extended and retooled in efforts to work through modern and contemporary art's deep imbrication with the historicity of blackness and to engage African American artists as sophisticated makers of forms inflected by but not overdetermined by their identities.[23]

Like its author, *Bound to Appear* benefited much from these lessons. In narrating the installations, the book aims to give each project its proper due and to enable a thinking of all four comparatively—their facture, ambitions, afterlives, and address—without prizing one over another or failing to reckon with the limitations that differently impinged on their making and reception. While the first half of the project emphasizes the negotiation of constraint and the second half the quest for a semblance of freedom, each chapter attempts to understand how one artist came to slavery as an aesthetic locus as well as the social, discursive, and historical conditions that enabled her or him to take up and participate within a larger discourse on the recrudescence of the "peculiar institution" in American cultural life since the 1960s. To do so, *Bound to Appear* in fact moves in the "centrifugal" fashion that Best advocates,[24] casting a multilayered network of contexts and constituencies around each installation, from renewed interest in slavery's narratives on the part of scholars, writers, and the general public to increased attention to the history of the black subject's scripting within Western narratives of art and representation. There are necessarily risks entailed in such a writerly tack, particularly of closing the gap between historicization and interpretation, but this approach is uniquely equipped to foreground the imbrication of blackness and the visual, the material and the discursive, the aesthetic and the ideological, the work and the world, particularly in the face of cultural protocols that would prize them apart.[25]

In this sense, *Bound to Appear*'s methods also quietly reflect the transformation of advanced artistic discourses since the 1960s, when the divisions between art, art history, and criticism truly began to fray, a blurring of boundaries that Green's work as writer, artist, and organizer compellingly models.[26] Accordingly, the book takes its formal and methodological cues from the works that it engages, which also define many of its structures and structuring conceits. Each chapter, for instance, is divided into roughly the same number of sections as the installation that it treats by a marker—stars, numbers, quotations, or titles—meant to alternatively stage the work's unfolding. In this way, the book manifests a nuanced mode of art writing—the slow-witted might even call it sly—that enters into the creative field engendered by its signal works: *Bound to Appear* is also, as Spillers suggests, an "act of revision and correction in light of Western legacies of modern art forms . . . in relationship to . . . specific cultural imperatives," always already caught up in, if estranged from, the installations' modes of signification.[27] While these moves are embedded in the book itself, they are not necessarily announced as a result of its author's need to demonstrate both discursive "mastery" over a field and to write "objectively" about artists who had become friends and interlocutors as well as "subjects" of inquiry. In the end, it was my father, in a righting of his own, who most clearly brought home the fundamental link between *Bound to Appear*'s structure and my own experience in a series of sticky note responses he penned after reading the book: "*Un*site of blackness seems to be the discovery that you so eloquently unsited in this magnificent art form. . . . It is amazing to envision how you and your mother arrive at your black consciousness in diverse means."

Few responses could be more gratifying or on point. My father's emphasis on the book as an *art form* resonates with the commentaries here in suggesting an approach to contemporary art, only intimated by the book, in which the situatedness of one's own knowledge of the artworks and artists in question might lead both to a creative scripting and—to repurpose a phrase of Spillers's—to a "liberatory aim . . . in the very unknowing," without sacrificing an ideal of "objectivity."[28] In deploying that last word, I have in mind not its classical meaning but its reframing through the lens of Niels Bohr's philosophy-physics in the work of the feminist theorist Karen Barad. She is intent on undoing distinctions between the observer and the observed, the discursive and the material, the temporal and the spatial, the epistemological and the ontological, underlining that our apparatuses determine not only what we "know" but also what at any given moment can be said to *be*. This approach, which is anticipated by and resonates with those of African diasporic theorists such as Édouard Glissant, Michel-Rolph Trouillot, and David Scott, "refuses the representationalist fixation on words and things and the problematic nature of their relationship, advocating instead a *relationality between specific material (re)configurings of the world through which boundaries, properties, and meanings are differently enacted (i.e., discursive practices, in my posthumanist sense) and specific material phenomena* (i.e., differentiating patterns of mattering)."[29]

Viewed in this light, *Bound to Appear* can be considered an apparatus necessarily inseparable from its "objects," one that puts pressure on the categories of person and thing in order to move toward an expanded conception of materiality, blackness, and representation that can encompass the whole of the universe in its unfolding. While the book does not arrive at this end, crucial to it and to Barad's work is an emphasis on those facts and forces that are part and parcel of material phenomena but that are constitutively excluded from the processes of measurement and narration—still present, still felt, even if unaccounted for and unseen.

Blackness as Model

My thinking in this vein, like Barad's, would be hard to imagine without the work of black and postcolonial theorists, who were intent on understanding the complexity, depth, and political import of expressive cultures constitutively marginalized by hegemonic discourses. In attempting to do so, such thinkers—here Henry Louis Gates Jr., Houston Baker, and Spillers herself come first to mind—turned away from essentializing and reductively formal modes of interpretation and, like so many American academics of their generation, instead embraced poststructuralist theory, which emphasized the contingency and constructedness, the fundamental undecidability of the signifier. Yet more than merely exulting in the multiplicity of the racial mark, African American poststructuralist thinkers posited blackness itself as both the prime figure of and ground for the aporias of Western knowledge. The conjunction of racial and sexual difference might then be understood as structured by what Spillers, in her seminal 1987 essay "Mama's Baby, Papa's Maybe: An American Grammar Book," called "a signifying property *plus*," which emerges from the black female body's central position within the economies of colonial enterprise, the dislocations of war, and the logic of transatlantic slavery that transmutes subjects into objects and back again.[30]

This thinking in its turn draws inspiration from the writings of Frantz Fanon, especially his essay "The Fact of Blackness"; much the same can be said of *Bound to Appear*.[31] Thanks to Fanon's example, blackness has become a lens through which to approach race and the construction of the modern world, most saliently for me as modeled by Saidiya Hartman. In fact, it was in the context of Hartman's 1999 graduate seminar Histories of Slavery that my dissertation began to crystallize and in dialogue with her first book that it began to take shape. In *Scenes of Subjection: Terror, Slavery, and Self-Making in Nineteenth-Century America*, Hartman examines the everyday scenes of violence and suffering that have constituted the enjoyments of whiteness since the nineteenth century, posing a crucial challenge to discourses on the visual that has yet to be systematically answered, even as her critique has been rigorously extended in the work of scholars such as my comrades-in-arms Jared Sexton and Frank Wilderson, "who have taught me more than I can say about the blackness of things" (xiii).[32]

By Best's lights, *Bound to Appear* can be situated alongside Hartman's volume because of its exploration of the "afterlife of slavery" through the lens of "historical ontology."[33] Although I am honored to be included in this company, I do think it is important to bring out the difference of my project as an art historical study from that of Hartman's *Scenes of Subjection*, which peels back from the spectacle of black suffering, refusing to reproduce the formerly enslaved Frederick Douglass's infamous account of his aunt Hester's beating in the 1845 *Narrative of the Life*. *Bound to Appear* does not perform a similar gesture, given its investment in what remains of the visual, but instead explores the artistic strategies of Hartman's generational cohorts: Wilson, Simpson, Ligon, and Green produce absence as well as presence, enacting what Spillers aptly identifies as "the paradox of the negative" by which referents are engendered through their very cancellation.[34] In its emphasis on considering modes of refusal as themselves assertions, the book owes just as much to the work of Fred Moten, who, in his introduction to *In the Break: The Aesthetics of the Black Radical Tradition*, takes Hartman's resistance as a fulcrum with which to plumb the rich veins opened up by practices of foreclosure and negation within African diasporic culture, enabling a rethinking of Western art, culture, objecthood, and materiality in light of the constructive and corrosive touch of blackness.[35]

For Moten, blackness is "that dangerous constitutive supplement," whose trace subtends the visual field and whose denigration gives shape to the human.[36] Or as *Bound to Appear*'s introduction puts it:

> Blackness functions, then, as both a free-floating trace unmoored from individual subjects and as a concrete index of power relations that reveals the deep structure of modernity's modes of visualization, the despotism on which they rely, and the ways that they might be contested in the present. At once abstract and bodily, literal and metaphorical, the ultimate sign of aesthetic negation and the prime marker of the socially negated, blackness marks those historical forces that continue to differentially engender subjects and objects in the modern world, everywhere shaping a cultural unconscious in which the individual effects of racialization assume a shifting texture despite the unyielding ruthlessness of their overarching logic. (11)

Here blackness becomes a site that artists on both sides of the color line—Pablo Picasso, Cindy Sherman, Kara Walker—have occupied in grounding their formal innovations. This approach provides means through which to take hold of the present by elaborating the racialized regimes that continue to shape art, politics, being, and the very structure of our imaginary. And it is this imbrication that spurred the book's framing of Wilson's, Simpson's, Ligon's, and Green's art in relation to a black radical tradition as named if not solely articulated by Cedric Robinson in his *Black Marxism: The Making of the Black Radical Tradition*.[37]

As Best notes, to take up Robinson's volume in relationship to the work of thriving contemporary African American artists is to extend and "twist" the senior scholar's critical framework, especially given its interest in those historical acts of inward-directed violence whose aim was less rebellion than the preservation of autonomy.[38] In *Bound to Appear*, the black radical tradition emerges as the site of a primary process—always entangled with the means of its own making—that encompasses the aesthetic and the political, the material and the discursive, the avowed and the excluded, Robinson and Moten, the political collective and the individual scholar, conjoinings that arrive only in and through each other. Even if we accept the relatively straight and narrow—yet perversely prescriptive—terms in which Best frames Robinson's argument, the works that the book examines at length square well with an anti-individualist account of black radicalism aimed at securing ontological totality. Look back to the wooden museum crates that dominate Ligon's *To Disembark*, each installed with speakers playing a variety of musical tracks and inspired by Henry "Box" Brown's escape from slavery by shipping himself to freedom and Philadelphia in 1849. Are not these works, these conflations of captives with their containers, records of a violence undertaken by bodies against themselves to preserve a collectivity, producing a noisy negative sociality that at once seduces and repels the viewer, filling her ears and institutional space with KRS-One's "Sound of da Police" and other ballads of black emergency?

In moving toward his account of what he terms "black ascesis," that "long genealogy of sustained and practiced antipathy to appearance in the black tradition," Best selectively lights upon several quasi-abstract canvases by Mark Bradford composed of tattered billboards, posters, and advertisements pilfered from the streets of South Central Los Angeles and subjected to further ripping and abrasion in the artist's studio. For Best, these works record acts of antisocial inscription, visual immurement, and actual violence that connect them both to a black radical tradition and to queer practices aimed at reconceptualizing the grounds of the social "through the performance of antirelationality."[39] Despite its tendency to flatten out the immense formal, thematic, and material diversity of Bradford's practice, there is much to appreciate in Best's interpretation of his art.[40] Such a reading, however, might be more convincingly undertaken by thinking Bradford's work in relation to the black queer and feminist traditions that the artist has claimed as his own and that, strangely, have no bearing in Best's account.[41] For as Spillers and so many others have shown, queering, with all the sense of failure and incompletion that it entails, is part and parcel of the operations of blackness, allowing Moten, for instance, to see how the late abstractions of Piet Mondrian index an engagement with African diasporic culture not through its literal enfolding or material enactment but through the paintings' openness to and infection by black sound.[42]

The difference here is more than rhetorical. While Best seems at pains to escape from blackness as a "historical ontology," what animates *Bound to Appear* is an engagement with black political ontology—grounded, in Wilderson's words, in "accumulation and fungibility as a grammar of suffering"—which demands a radical disruption of the touchstones and categorical divisions of Western art, culture, and theory.[43] Thus, each of the book's chapters deploys an approach to the object—Marxist, psychoanalytic, literary, anthropological, or aesthetic—to at once seize upon its insights and reveal its limitations: none of these frameworks can fully account for the particularity of embodied black experience or even the viewer's encounters with the book's prime installations. As Spillers so provocatively notes, these works unfolded within the institutional frame the better to make the institution seem "quite beside itself," to queer it, to *un*site it, to momentarily open a space for the reimagining of relations between persons and things only perceptible through a black apparatus.[44] Rather than rely on any single fantasy of "form" or naively subscribe to a singular "theory," *Bound to Appear* moves promiscuously among them to demonstrate how blackness deforms and so recasts all that it touches: if black studies is, as Robinson once averred, "the critique of Western civilization," then there is perhaps no better place from which to articulate this tactical undoing than art history, a discipline long dedicated to the celebration of masterpieces no matter the bodies crushed beneath their weight.[45]

Seeing Beyond Sight

What, then, is *Bound to Appear*? At its best, the book strives toward a transdisciplinary encounter between art history and black studies, between the difficulty of figuring slavery in the present and the disruption of the aesthetic undertaken by artists since the 1960s: African American writer Toni Morrison meets European American artist Robert Morris, each differently aiming to travesty that taken to be constitutive of representation.[46] While Best clearly understands the installations' debt to and difference from Morrison's writing, particularly in *Beloved*, what he does not countenance, and what the book is at pains to illuminate, are the ways the artworks' staging of the black body's "appearance-in-disappearance" brings them into a discrepant historical and conceptual relation with the most radical gestures of twentieth-century artistic practice, which has time and again figured its advances into the visual field through techniques of aesthetic withdrawal, misdirection, and impoverishment.[47]

In bringing together such ostensibly distant histories, strategies, and thinkers, at times too seamlessly, *Bound to Appear* not only foregrounds the importance of enslaved bodies to modern constructions of materiality but also emphasizes the strategies that black subjects have deployed in contesting their depictions within the visual field, which might be read—to borrow a phrase from the art historian Griselda Pollock—as "avant-garde gambits" in their own right.[48] In this vein, I think first and foremost of Harriet Jacobs, the author of the 1861 slave narrative, *Incidents in the Life of a Slave Girl*, who appears throughout the artistic practices discussed in the book, thanks to her brilliant mode of escape from the sexual and physical abuse of her master by imprisoning herself in a garret hardly larger than a coffin for nearly seven years while using letters to project apparitions of herself up and down the Eastern Seaboard. Produced as a readymade, fantasized as a part-object, and forced to bodily enact her own "social death," Jacobs faced, and developed means of resistance to, conditions whose structures anticipate much of what we take for granted as modernist aesthetic innovation.[49] Viewed in this light, the most vaunted achievements of the twentieth-century avant-garde, from Marcel Duchamp's 1917 *Fountain* [see Fig. 22.1 on p. 315] to Morris's 1961 *Box for Standing*, cannot help but read as aestheticized rehashings of Jacobs's survival tactics, now enacted with uncanny objects in the gallery rather than on fleshly things on the plantation.[50]

In engaging such narratives, *Bound to Appear* aims to reorient genealogies of modern and contemporary art and to underline the complex imbrication of beauty and terror, enabling a complication not only of African diasporic cultural production but also of the Western object world, which becomes constitutively darkened.[51] However, blackness is not imposed as the final word on the installations in question; rather, it opens up the works' dialogical construction and complex material entanglement.[52] Accordingly, the book weds close looking and social engagement to make clear how the very process of vision itself is deformed by race and racial will. As the book's introduction makes clear, this is an ethical as well as a methodological intervention.

> The modes and methods of art history matter to the project of African diaspora studies because they emphasize the merits of looking with sustained attention to objects in all of their multiplicity. Conversely, such an approach ought to matter deeply to black subjects, who have been at once produced as things and denuded of complexity, a depth and differentiation that the procedures of artistic discourse might freshly give us to see.[53]

While the book's reliance on black poststructuralist theory is certainly novel within the field, the attempt to bring varying interpretive approaches to bear on a single artwork has been vital in art history for some time; in many ways, the formalist/historical divide that Best aims to reinstantiate has been of waning importance in the discipline at least since the mid-1990s.[54] Now, in the wake of black visual, cultural, and postcolonial studies, in the midst of object-oriented ontologies, and with the triumph of the so-called performative turn, we have the opportunity to reimagine what the visual and the aesthetic are in ways that speak to the contemporary art world's preoccupations—performance art, social practice, ecological intervention—and to reframe them in relationship to more expansive aesthetic models deriving from outside of the canonical Western tradition.[55]

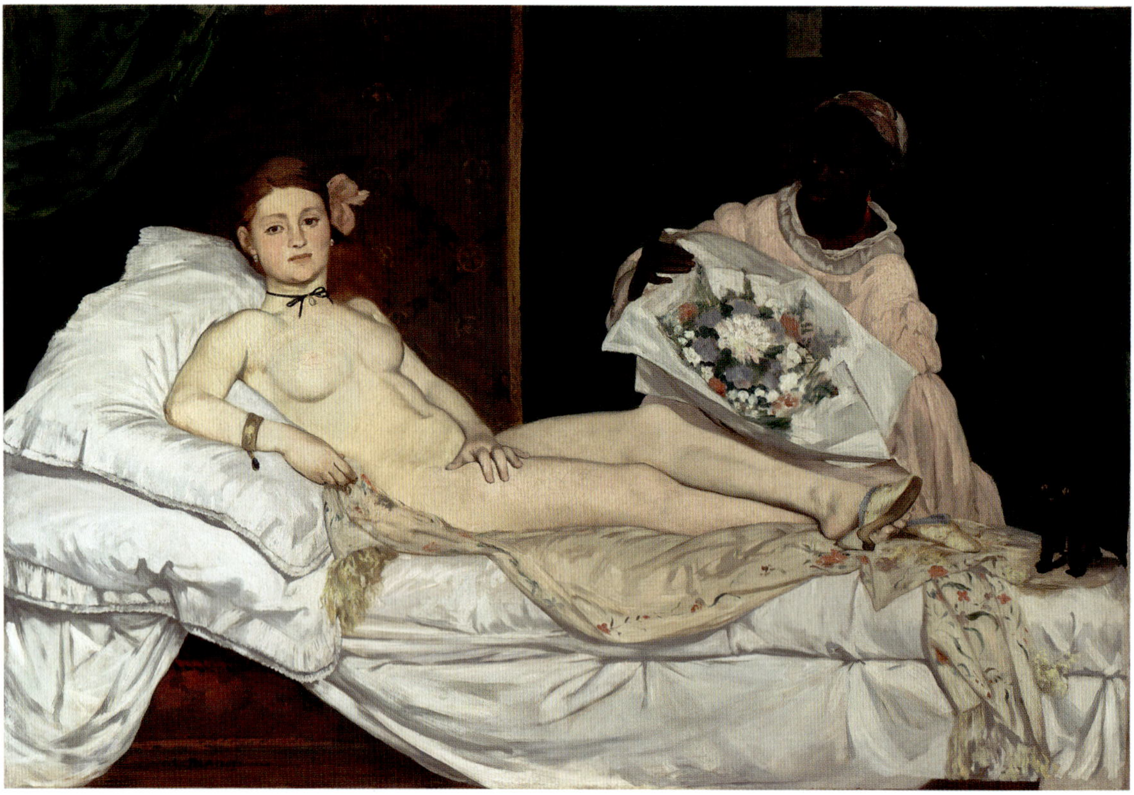

Figure 21.2
Édouard Manet, *Olympia*, 1863. Oil on canvas, 130.5 × 190.0 cm. RF644. Photo: Patrice Schmidt. Musée d'Orsay. © RMN-Grand Palais / Art Resource, NY.

Despite her stated remove from such disciplinary debates, Spillers, I think, fully appreciates this fact, as well as *Bound to Appear*'s attempt to transform art history by taking slavery as a site that is both too far and too close, creating "a distance on the one hand . . . but not enough of a distance, on the other," that at once directs and disallows our seeing.[56]

Perhaps no better example comes than in Spillers's meditation on the white female figure who sat reading on a chaise longue while decked out in pajamas made of Green's signature toile as part of the artist's 1994 exhibition, *Taste Venue*. My reading of this fabric, itself inextricably caught up in the history of the transatlantic slave trade, put Spillers in mind of Édouard Manet's *Olympia* (Fig. 21.2): if, as I argue, "Green's choice and repeated use of toile reveal how every mode of capitalism . . . is haunted by the body of the slave, who incarnates the changing form of the commodity" (192), then might we not, Spillers proposes, draw a connection between the two reclining women, the French painter's prostitute and the installation artist's model, both engaged in the traffic of immaterial value and propped up by the apparition of blackness?[57] With uncanny prescience, Spillers's question anticipates both the directions of my own work and of art histories to come, which rethink Manet's canvas in light of contemporary practices in order to bring out the ways that the social deforms form and the formal nurtures fantasies of the social.[58] Contrary to Best's presumptions, such a protocol of reading does not rely on a causal relationship between formal appearance and social acknowledgment but seeks to understand how the logic of recognition can foreclose the seeing of what so abundantly appears.

To wit, in reviewing his previous treatment of *Olympia*, in many ways the authoritative account of the painting, my erstwhile mentor T. J. Clark lamented how "the snake of ideology" prevented him from seeing the canvas's black maid as a full participant in the scene despite the fact that she occupies half of the composition, instead reducing her to another of the white woman's attributes as did initial critics of the work, often with the dismissive mantra, "the Negress, the bouquet, the cat."[59] Clark's overlooking underlines how the black figure becomes the ground of both further forgetting and productive contestation. My own return to the painting—so central to my earliest art history lessons—has come in light of works by the Kenyan-born, New York–based artist Wangechi Mutu, best known for ferocious collages such as *A'gave you*, which conjoin blackness, the feminine, the animal, and the machinic into singular figures that suggest the entire world stuffed inside the African female body and tortuously turned inside out (Fig. 21.3). As such, Mutu's art might be said to challenge what Mel Y. Chen, following linguistic theory, calls the "animacy hierarchy, which conceptually arranges human life, disabled life, animal life, plant life, and forms of non-living material in orders of value and priority."[60]

So reframed, Manet's painting and the responses that it spurred take on a different cast. For although the black maid, Laure, has been discursively produced as stilled, partial, and deeply conventional, her coupling alongside those other creatures suggests that what was at stake in the work's initial reception was, in no small measure, the very definition of what counts as being alive, human or otherwise. We might recall the critic Félix Jahyer's observation that in order to see *Olympia* as installed at the 1865 Salon, "you need the eyes of a lynx"; or the caption that accompanied the cartoonist Bertall's caricature of the painting in which he declared that the work itself is "the bouquet of the Exposition"; or the writer Théophile Thoré's oft-noted charge that the strange disordering of categories in Manet's painting was testament to his "pantheism."[61] Unlike its inspiration, Titian's *Venus of Urbino* (1538), where the figure's attributes recede into the background, offering little resistance to a viewer's delectation in the female from, *Olympia* presses its human, plant, and animal others onto the same plane. This is the success and the scandal of the picture so exacerbated in the caricatures of it and in critics' likening of the white woman and her cohorts to ink, dirt, apes, and India rubber, an undoing of the order of things and the genres of art that represent them.

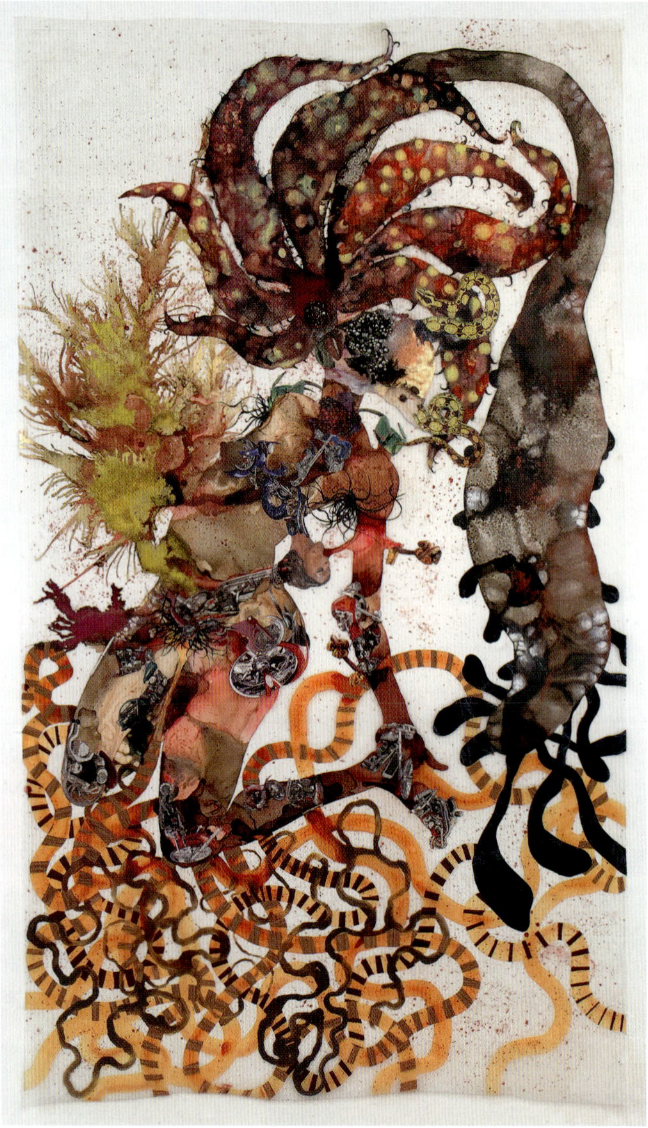

Figure 21.3
Wangechi Mutu, *A'gave you*, 2008. Mixed media collage on mylar, 93 × 54 in. (236.22 × 137.16 cm). Courtesy of the artist and Vielmetter Los Angeles. Photo credit: Robert Wedemeyer.

Olympia thus represents what Chen might call a mode of "queer animacy" whose conjoining of forms of life, which threaten to leak out of the canvas and transform the viewer, is a kind of "improper affiliation."[62] It is such modes of impropriety, I would argue, that Laure signals, that Mutu embraces, and that blackness at once marks, enacts, and makes visible, allowing it to serve as the grounds for an ontology, an ethics, a method, a "critical posture" of "philosophical 'disobedience,'" to quote Spillers, in relation both to disciplinary protocols and to modes of visual arrangement.[63] Blackness holds out the possibility of the ongoing disarticulation and reconstruction of art history so that the discipline might allow us to think the ties linking Laure and Harriet even as they come in and out of view. *Bound to Appear* aims to move us one small step in that direction, toward an art history beside itself: the journey has already begun, but if experience has taught me anything, there is never flow without arrest.

Notes

1 I here revisit thematics first explored in Huey Copeland, "Outtakes," *Art Journal* 67, no. 4 (2008): 20-32 [reprinted in this volume, 57-72].

2 Huey Copeland, *Bound to Appear: Art, Slavery, and the Site of Blackness in Multicultural America* (University of Chicago Press, 2013), 3; hereafter cited in the text in parentheses.

3 For one measure of this discursive shift in regard to race and abstraction, compare Dawoud Bey, "The Ironies of Diversity, or The Disappearing Black Artist," www.artnet.com/magazine/features/bey/bey4-8-04.asp, with Adrienne Edwards, "Blackness in Abstraction," *Art in America*, January 2015, 62-69.

4 In this sense, the present essay functions as the conceptual pendant to Huey Copeland, "Feasting on Scraps," *Small Axe: A Caribbean Journal of Criticism*, no. 38 (July 2012): 198-212.

5 For an exemplary account of the book's aims and ambitions, see Kim Bobier's review in *Nka: Journal of Contemporary African Art* 34 (Spring 2014): 116-18.

6 Recent exhibitions in this vein include *NYC 1993: Experimental Jet Set, Trash, and No Star* at the New Museum (2013) and *Come as You Are: Art of the 1990s* at the Montclair Art Museum (2015). For two contrasting reckonings with the art of the decade, see Nicolas Bourriaud, *Relational Aesthetics*, trans. Simon Pleasance and Fronza Woods, with the participation of Mathieu Copeland (Les presses du réel, 2002); Jennifer A. González, *Subject to Display: Reframing Race in Contemporary Installation Art* (MIT Press, 2008).

7 On the dangers of identification in the context of enslavement, see Saidiya V. Hartman, *Scenes of Subjection: Terror, Slavery, and Self-Making in Nineteenth-Century America* (Oxford University Press, 1997). On the antiportrait, see Lauri Firstenberg, "Autonomy and the Archive in America: Reexamining the Intersection of Photography and Stereotype," in *Only Skin Deep: Changing Visions of the American Self*, ed. Coco Fusco and Brian Wallis (International Center for Photography and Harry N. Abrams, 2003), 317-19.

8 Best, "Come and Gone," 193.

9 Best, "Come and Gone," 189-90.

10 For a useful elaboration of this problem, see Sharon F. Patton, "Bibliographic Essay," in *African-American Art* (Oxford University Press, 1998), 283-99.

11 This retreat from the figure in the late 1980s and early 1990s is not limited to artists of a single generation or mode of making, as demonstrated by the trajectory of the painter Barkley Hendricks. See Huey Copeland, "Figures and Grounds: The Art of Barkley L. Hendricks," *Artforum* 46, no. 8

(April 2008): 149 [reprinted in this volume, 83-96]. For accountings of the crises around the visual production of black, particularly male, subjectivity in the early 1990s, see Elizabeth Alexander, "'Can you be black and look at this?': Reading the Rodney King Video(s)," in *Black Male: Representations of Masculinity in Contemporary American Art*, exh. cat. (Whitney Museum of American Art and Harry N. Abrams, 1994), 91-110; Robert Gooding-Williams, ed., *Reading Rodney King, Reading Urban Uprising* (Routledge, 1993); Kobena Mercer, "Black Masculinity and the Sexual Politics of Race," in *Welcome to the Jungle: New Positions in Black Cultural Studies* (Routledge, 1994), 130-70.

12 Spillers, "Art Talk," 179.

13 On this score, see Huey Copeland and Krista Thompson, "Perpetual Returns: New World Slavery and the Matter of the Visual," *Representations* 113 (Winter 2011): 1-15.

14 Spillers, "Art Talk," 175 n. 1. On "the social reproduction of white supremacy," in the context of the 1990s New York art world, see Huey Copeland, "Unfinished Business as Usual: African American Artists, New York Museums, and the 1990s," in *Come as You Are: Art of the 1990s*, ed. Alexandra Schwartz (University of California Press and Montclair Art Museum, 2014), 32 [reprinted in this volume, 175-85].

15 Spillers, "Art Talk," 185.

16 Huey Copeland, "Darrel Ellis, Lyle Ashton Harris, and Glenn Ligon: New Conceptions of the Black Male Body in American Art" (BA honors thesis, University of Michigan, 1998).

17 For an expanded accounting of the "African American critical posture," see Hortense J. Spillers, "Introduction: Peter's Pans: Eating in the Diaspora," in *Black, White, and Color: Essays on American Literature and Culture* (University of Chicago Press, 2003), 5.

18 See Wallace, "Modernism."

19 Krista Thompson, "A Sidelong Glance: The Practice of African Diaspora Art History in the United States," *Art Journal* 70, no. 3 (2011): 23.

20 Here I mean to invoke Adrian Piper, "The Triple Negation of Colored Women Artists," in *Out of Order, Out of Sight*, vol. 2, *Selected Writings in Art Criticism, 1967-1992* (MIT Press, 1996), 161-73.

21 Thomas Crow, *The Rise of the Sixties: American and European Art in the Era of Dissent* (New York: Harry N. Abrams, 1996). Ironically, Crow's text echoes–though does not engage with–the groundbreaking Mary Schmidt Campbell, ed., *Tradition and Conflict: Images of a Turbulent Decade, 1963-1973* (Studio Museum in Harlem, 1985). Such suppressions of race continue to mar even the most compelling engagements with art of the 1960s and 1970s as evidenced by Julia Bryan-Wilson, *Art Workers: Radical Practice in the Vietnam War Era* (University of California Press, 2009); Alex Potts, *Experiments in Modern Realism: World Making, Politics, and the Everyday in Postwar European and American Art* (Yale University Press, 2013).

22 Spillers, "Art Talk," 175. Here I have in mind the work of Renée Ater, John Bowles, Kirsten P. Buick, Anne Anlin Cheng, Romi Crawford, Kellie Jones, Amy Mooney, Kym Pinder, Richard A. Powell, Leigh Raiford, and Shawn Michelle Smith, in addition to the scholars cited elsewhere in these notes. For a useful gloss of the emergence of a critical mass of black artists and art historians in the 1990s, see Lisa Gail Collins, "A Visual Paradox: Art and Aesthetics in African American Thought," in *The Art of History: African*

American Women Artists Engage the Past (Rutgers University Press, 2002), 1-10.

23 See Anne M. Wagner, *Three Artists (Three Women): Modernism in the Art of Hesse, Krasner, and O'Keeffe* (University of California Press, 1998). For another example of how Wagner's work on gender might be taken up in addressing questions of race, see Darby English, *How to See a Work of Art in Total Darkness* (MIT Press, 2007), 20-21.

24 Best, "Come and Gone," 193.

25 For a cogent critique of *Bound to Appear* on just these grounds, see Rachel Haidu, "Striking the Ground," *Oxford Art Journal* 37, no. 2 (2014): 218.

26 The possible examples are many, but here I have in mind the artistic/academic collective Our Literal Speed, as well as the writing of Rosalind Krauss, in particular, her "Poststructuralism and the 'Paraliterary,'" *October* 13 (Summer 1980): 36-40; and *The Optical Unconscious* (MIT Press, 1993).

27 Spillers, "Art Talk," 176. For a fine meditation that takes the book's writing seriously, see Levi Prombaum's review in *Immediations: The Research Journal of the Courtauld Institute of Art*, no. 3 (2014): 138-41.

28 Spillers, "Art Talk," 185. For an exemplary recent work undertaken in this mode, see Nana Adusei-Poku, "'Rooted In but Not Limited By': Re-iterations of Post-Black Art" (PhD diss., Humboldt Universität zu Berlin, 2015).

29 Karen Barad, *Meeting the Universe Halfway: Quantum Physics and the Entanglement of Matter and Meaning* (Durham, NC: Duke University Press, 2007), 136; emphasis in original. It is worth noting that throughout her book, Barad aims to debunk the lay epistemological understanding of Heisenbergian uncertainty on which Best relies in favor of Bohr's emphasis on ontological indeterminacy. See Best, "Come and Gone," 194-95.

30 Hortense J. Spillers, "Mama's Baby, Papa's Maybe: An American Grammar Book," in *Black, White, and Color*, 203, emphasis in original. My extension of Spillers's thinking here draws on lines first published in Huey Copeland, "In the Wake of the Negress," in *Modern Women: Women Artists at the Museum of Modern Art*, ed. Cornelia Butler and Alexandra Schwartz (Museum of Modern Art, 2010), 484 [reprinted in this volume, 265-85].

31 Frantz Fanon, *Black Skin, White Masks*, trans. Charles Lam Markmann (Grove Press, 1967).

32 See Hartman, *Scenes of Subjection*, as well as Frank B. Wilderson III, "The Position of the Unthought: An Interview with Saidiya V. Hartman," *Qui Parle* 13, no. 2 (Spring-Summer 2003): 183-201; Jared Sexton, *Amalgamation Schemes: Antiblackness and the Critique of Multiracialism* (University of Minnesota Press, 2008); Frank B. Wilderson III, *Red, White & Black: Cinema and the Structure of U.S. Antagonisms* (Duke University Press, 2010).

33 Best, "Come and Gone," 189-91.

34 Spillers, "Art Talk," 184.

35 Fred Moten, *In the Break: The Aesthetics of the Black Radical Tradition* (University of Minnesota Press, 2003).

36 Fred Moten, "The Case of Blackness," *Criticism* 50, no. 2 (2008): 202.

37 Cedric Robinson, *Black Marxism: The Making of the Black Radical Tradition* (1983; repr. University of North Carolina Press, 2000).

38 Best, "Come and Gone," 196.

39 Best, "Come and Gone," 194, 200.

40 For alternative accountings of Bradford's art that rhyme with yet ulti-

mately depart from Best's, see Huey Copeland, "A Range of Convergences," *Parkett* 89 (2011): 152-59 [reprinted in this volume, 97-110]; Steven Nelson, "Mark Bradford's Allegorical Impulse," in *Mark Bradford: Merchant Posters* (Sikkema Jenkins, 2006), 8-13.

41 For the relevant comments by the artist, see Huey Copeland, "Painting after All: A Conversation with Mark Bradford," *Callaloo* 37, no. 4 (2014): 817 [reprinted in this volume, 201-15], which might be productively considered in relationship to Roderick A. Ferguson, *Aberrations in Black: Toward a Queer of Color Critique* (University of Minnesota Press, 2004); and Robert F. Reid-Pharr, *Black Gay Man: Essays* (New York University Press, 2001).

42 See Spillers, "Mama's Baby, Papa's Maybe"; Moten, "Case of Blackness."

43 Best, "Come and Gone," 190-91; Wilderson, *Red, White & Black*, 55.

44 Spillers, "Art Talk," 181.

45 Cedric J. Robinson, "Capitalism, Marxism, and the Black Radical Tradition: An Interview by Chuck Morse," *Perspectives on Anarchist Theory* 3, no. 1 (1999), quoted in Fred Moten, "Black Op," *PMLA* 123, no. 5 (2008): 1743.

46 I borrow the notion of the travestying or negation of form and its constitutive importance to the modernist tradition from T. J. Clark, "Clement Greenberg's Theory of Art," in *Pollock and After: The Critical Debate*, ed. Francis Frascina (London: Routledge, 2000), 78.

47 Best, "Come and Gone," 189-94.

48 See Griselda Pollock, *Avant-Garde Gambits 1888-1893: Gender and the Color of Art History* (Thames and Hudson, 1993).

49 I borrow the quoted phrase from Orlando Patterson, *Slavery and Social Death: A Comparative Study* (Harvard University Press, 1982).

50 For a related treatment of Jacobs's ruses, see Fred Moten, "Taste Dissonance Flavor Escape: Preface for a Solo by Miles Davis," *Women and Performance* 17, no. 2 (2007): 217-26.

51 On the blackening of the object world, see the most incisive commentary on the book to date: Sampada Aranke, "Objects Made Black," *Art Journal* 73, no. 3 (2014): 86-88.

52 For a sustained consideration of these questions, see Kobena Mercer, "Art History and the Dialogics of Diaspora," *Small Axe: A Caribbean Journal of Criticism*, no. 38 (July 2012): 213-27.

53 Copeland, *Bound to Appear*, 19-20.

54 On this score, I think, in particular, of the art historian James Meyer's accounting of his own approach: "In combining aspects of formal, structuralist, and social art historical analysis, this book reflects what I hold to be a larger tendency of current scholarship to integrate these methodologies as the divide between these interpretive camps, which once seemed so salient, has diminished of late. . . . No doubt, it is the nature of such debates to remain unsettled and to return." See James Meyer, *Minimalism: Art and Polemics in the Sixties* (Yale University Press, 2001), 9.

55 One example in this vein is the exhibition *En Mas': Carnival and Performance Art of the Caribbean at the Contemporary Arts Center New Orleans* (2015).

56 Spillers, "Art Talk," 178.

57 Spillers, "Art Talk," 180-81.

58 Here I have in mind a recent tour-de-force reinterpretation of Manet's picture, which carefully reconstructs the histories of racial labor in nineteenth-century France. See Darcy Grimaldo Grigsby, "Still Thinking about Olympia's Maid," *Art Bulletin* 97, no. 4 (Fall 2015): 430-51. In the reading of *Olympia* that follows, and throughout this section of the essay, I draw from my current book project, "In the Shadow of the Negress: A Brief History of Modern Artistic Practice," whose key contentions are outlined in Copeland, "In the Wake of the Negress," 480–97.

59 T. J. Clark, Preface to *The Painting of Modern Life: Paris in the Art of Manet and His Followers*, rev. ed. (Princeton University Press, 1999), xxvii; Félix Deriège, "Salon de 1865," *Le Siècle*, June 2, 1865, quoted and translated in Clark, *Painting of Modern Life*, 98.

60 Mel Y. Chen, *Animacies: Biopolitics, Racial Mattering, and Queer Affect* (Duke University Press, 2012), 13; emphasis in original.

61 Félix Jahyer, *Etude sur Les Beaux Arts, Salon de 1865* (1865), 283; and Bertall, *Manette, ou La Femme de l'ébéniste, par Manet, Le Journal Amusant*, May 27 1865; quoted and translated in Clark, *Painting of Modern Life*, 85 and 97, respectively. See also Théophile Thoré, *Salons de W. Burger, 1861 à 1868* (1870), 2:532.

62 Chen, *Animacies*, 98, 104.

63 Spillers, "Peter's Pans," 5.

22

ALREADYMADE

Black Visual Thought, Duchamp's *Fountain*, and the Ends of White Art History, Circa 2020

There is no document of civilization which is not at the same time a document of barbarism. And just as such a document is not free of barbarism, barbarism taints also the manner in which it was transmitted from one owner to another. A historical materialist therefore dissociates himself from it as far as possible. He regards it as his task to brush history against the grain.
Walter Benjamin, "Theses on the Philosophy of History," 1940[1]

In 2013 I coined the term "alreadymade" in discussing Lorna Simpson's installation with Alva Rogers, *Five Rooms* (1991), in which the products of slave labor such as Carolina gold rice sat in jars on stools, serving as figural surrogates for captive female bodies [see Fig. 21.1 on p. 291]. In that chapter of my book *Bound to Appear*, I argued that for the artist, "blackness is 'alreadymade,' capable of being evoked with the lightest of touches."[2] While that brief reference to Simpson and other black conceptualists' engagements with the readymade tradition—particularly as inaugurated by the white European artist Marcel Duchamp—was relatively underdeveloped in *Bound to Appear*, in her review of the book Sampada Aranke cogently argued:

> As *alreadymade*, blackness is a historical object/subject/feeling/being that reaches far before the 1913 call to see commodities in other lights, stagings, and presentations. The weight of Duchamp's heavy-handedness and the color of his epidermis—both epistemologically referenced in Simpson's work with or without the figure and always through the opacity of slaves who jumped overboard to escape the "peculiar institution"—each is colored, each is lighted, each is marked, is alreadymade by blackness.[3]

With Aranke's comments at hand, we can now begin.

Portions of this chapter were published in a different form in Susanne Pfeffer, ed., *Marcel Duchamp* (Museum für Moderne Kunst, 2026).

The premise from which this essay departs can be stated simply enough: to belatedly revisit the readymades of Marcel Duchamp through the lens of blackness circa 2020 from a US perspective is not only to see his work and its structural presumptions as if for the first time but also to confront head-on the logics that continue to make art history and the broader world of which it is part prime sites for the "social reproduction of white supremacy." By that I mean, "the activities and attitudes, behaviors and emotions, responsibilities and relationships directly involved in the maintenance of the racially based political regimes that emerged post-fifteenth-century."[4] For me, a black intellectual accustomed to living in a culture "in which," as Saidiya Hartman once put it, "your consciousness is at war with the given," this claim is almost a commonplace barely in need of qualifying.[5] Within "mainstream" discourses, however, such an argument can prove explosive, especially to those at a remove from contemporaneous debates in the humanities and invested in the institution of hegemonic modernism, so a few more words are in order to more fully situate these remarks as well as my own critical posture.

Here is the backstory: I began writing this essay while a professor at the Center for Advanced Study in Visual Art at Washington, DC's National Gallery of Art, located on the ancestral lands of the Nacotchtank, Piscataway, and Pamunkey peoples; from my office in the Center, I had an unobstructed view of the US Capitol, that symbol of freedom built by the labor of enslaved black artisans. I recite these facts not just to acknowledge them or even to lambaste the repressions, hypocrisies, and untruths with which they are usually met, but to articulate the continuously structuring historical conditions that undergird our presence on these lands as well as my own approach to the unfolding of the aesthetic. Rather than place faith in the redemptive power of art, I hope, as the philosopher Walter Benjamin famously did, to push history against the grain in exploring one link between "barbarism" and "civilization," in this case, between the enslavement of blackened things and the appropriation of black cultures, the denigration of African lives and the production of Western cultural property. In so doing, I depart from prior scholarship on Duchamp, which, like much art history, tends to be highly hagiographic and unconsciously overidentified with the artist's supposed genius. Instead, I want to provincialize, deterritorialize, alternatively emplot, and effectively recalibrate our understanding of Duchamp's tactics in light of the horizons opened up by black studies, the oldest of the new interdisciplinary formations whose world-making and world-breaking ramifications for thought have, for the most part, gone unexamined art historically.

As the critic Michele Wallace importantly remarked in 1990, the visual has long served as a "negative scene of instruction" for black folks, who have been ceaselessly caricatured within Western discourses at the same time that their indispensable contributions to modern artistic practice have been travestied, minimized, and suppressed when not entirely erased.[6] To be sure, this is no longer the whole story: these days there is a critical mass of African American art historians and curators, just as black artists across the globe have enjoyed increasing market attention, facts impossible for anyone in the art and academic worlds to ignore. Yet, some thirty years on from Wallace's diagnosis—and even further from the 1960s cataclysms that would integrate higher education, birth Black Studies programs, and eventually transform departments like English—"mainstream," or better, *white*, art history, perhaps more than any other discipline within the humanities, continues to dodge the significance of blackness to all facets of Western culture since the advent of transatlantic slavery even when they so forthrightly appear as to seem unavoidable. For, even at its most politically astute, white art history in the West—a discipline often said to be predicated on "close looking"—tends to selectively blind itself to art *and* history when its ideological coherence is threatened and its presumed whiteness marked, passively aligning with those very modes of social control that it elsewhere seeks to expose and critique. To better understand how white art history's antiblack ideology is both maintained and dissimulated these days—particularly in the study of Duchamp—it is useful to examine how the discipline, in reproducing itself professionally and discursively, has lately managed the pressures brought to bear by questions of race on both sides of the black Atlantic.[7]

In the wake of the United States' reckoning with the realities of antiblack violence, which reached a horrific apogee of sorts with the May 25, 2020, video-recorded murder of George Floyd, an unprecedented number of North American art history departments sought to address their own complicity in the social reproduction of such violence by attempting to hire someone—preferably of African descent—to teach something, *anything*, Black.[8] The job postings themselves, often issuing from departments that have never hired, let alone tenured, a single black person, make it plain: despite the warnings to the contrary so well-articulated by the African diasporic art historian Krista Thompson ten years prior, the most egregious, and so instructive, advertisements still seek applicants to teach "African and/or African Diaspora and/or African American art," which not only suggests that these different areas are fundamentally interchangeable, but that they are barely worthy of being thought of as specific fields of inquiry (even more telling are the email solicitations whose headers express an interest in "African" while the advertisements themselves seek "African Diaspora"). Such a lack of precision is particularly galling in the context of a discipline whose tremendous overspecialization in the past several decades has set its subfields adrift from each other and frequently hived it off from conversations in the humanities writ large.[9] The goal of the 2020 as well as subsequent hires, it seems, was to secure black representation as a kind of alibi or coverage so that blackness itself might remain unthought.[10]

C. Riley Snorton and Hentyle Yapp have succinctly described the assumptions behind such tokenizing moves in the introduction to *Saturation*, their critical reader on the visual production of race and value within global capitalism.

> The popular logic goes that if only the right representative from a group or a larger plurality of embodied difference were present, then institutions like the museum and the university would be absolved from historic forms of exclusion. However, we know this to not be true, *even* with the slow and growing presence of people of color. Further, institutions profit from increased representation. Even if they answer calls for more visibility, they do so without a fundamental reordering of protocols or a dynamic redistribution of resources.[11]

The recent African/Diaspora searches, by extension, regardless of their particular intentions, all in some measure aim to answer the ongoing question of racial injustice by presenting a freshly procured negro, or negro specialist ("negrologist"?) whose presence is meant to imply that some measure of justice has already been achieved. Here I use the anachronistic term "negro" quite purposefully, for it, I think—more than any iteration of "black" or "African"—is the subconscious presumptive category with which the field continues to operate.

All of which is to say that white art history, despite its relative openness to social historical, feminist, queer, postcolonial, and structuralist approaches, remains caught up within an Enlightenment ideology in which the negro, regardless of the form she takes, represents, following the theorist Sylvia Wynter, "the nadir of Man."[12] In her remarkable 2020 book, *Becoming Human*, Zakiyyah Iman Jackson draws on the work of Wynter and other black radical thinkers to show how the negro has been constructed as, in the words of the Afro-pessimist Frank Wilderson, "a body that you can do what you want with."[13] Jackson argues that this praxis of "plasticity" "seeks to define the essence of a black(ened) thing as infinitely mutable, in antiblack, often paradoxical, sexuating terms as a means of hierarchically delineating sex/gender, reproduction, and states of being more generally," all while "'probing the limits up to which it is possible to discipline [a] body without extinguishing the life within.'"[14] It is *this* ideology and its practice, refined and extended by thinkers from Kant to Lévi-Strauss, that both haunt and structure white art history's means of racial segregation and taxonomic classification today, just as they did over one hundred years ago when Duchamp began producing his readymades.[15]

Despite the voluminousness of Duchamp historiography, it is only recently

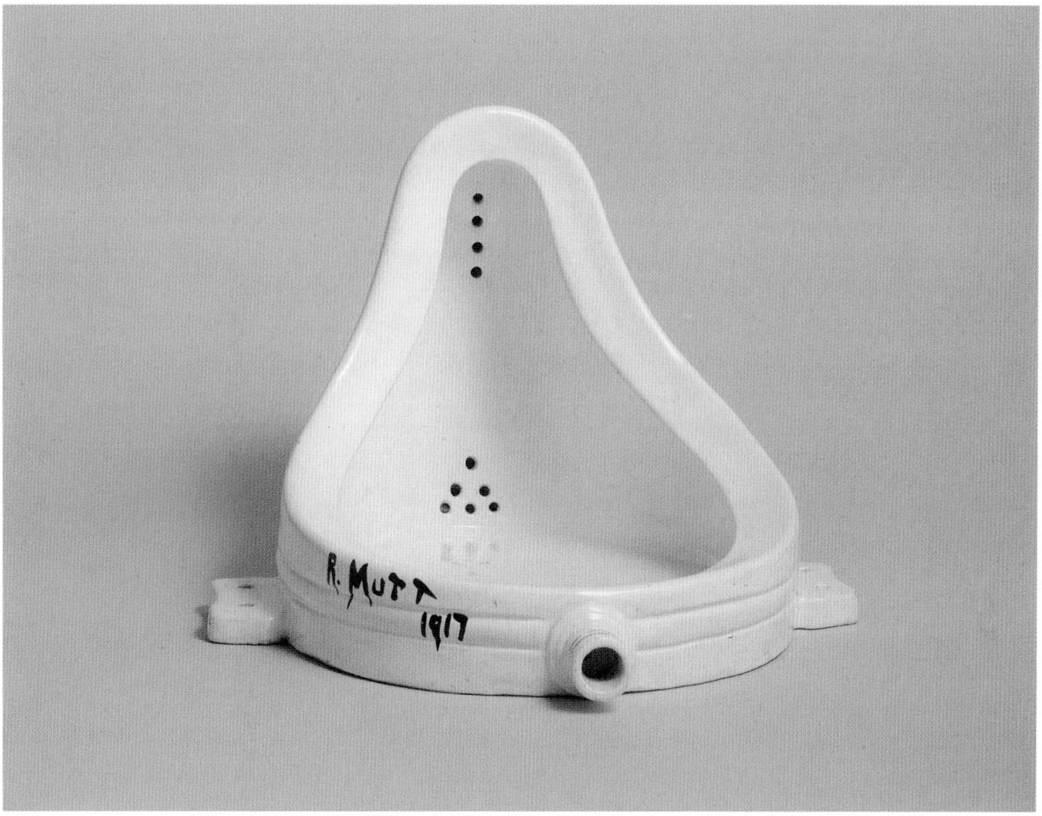

Figure 22.1
Marcel Duchamp, *Fountain*, 1917. © Association Marcel Duchamp / ADAGP, Paris / Artists Rights Society (ARS), New York 2024. Photo: Jerry L. Thompson / Art Resource, NY.

that modernist art historians have taken seriously the artist's formative "emersion in a culture saturated by primitivism."[16] I take that phrase from a 2020 article published in *Art History*, the discipline's flagship journal in the United Kingdom, in which Thomas Folland convincingly argues that the readymades, which Duchamp produced by the elective ontological translation of mass-manufactured commodities into works of art, serve to echo the transformation of stolen African ritual artifacts into objects of aesthetic delectation: both are governed by "the *idea* of African art as entertained by the West."[17] Folland tracks how Duchamp's readymades and their visual production in the United States, most of all, that of *Fountain* (1917) (Fig. 22.1)—a urinal turned sculpture that secured the artist's critical legacy by successfully scandalizing its first white bourgeois viewers—allegorize the ways that such transmogrification is accomplished by deploying the same processes of spatial rotation and photographic sacralization applied to "Negro art."[18] For, despite their radical differences, both African artifacts and Duchamp's commodity fetishes conceal even as

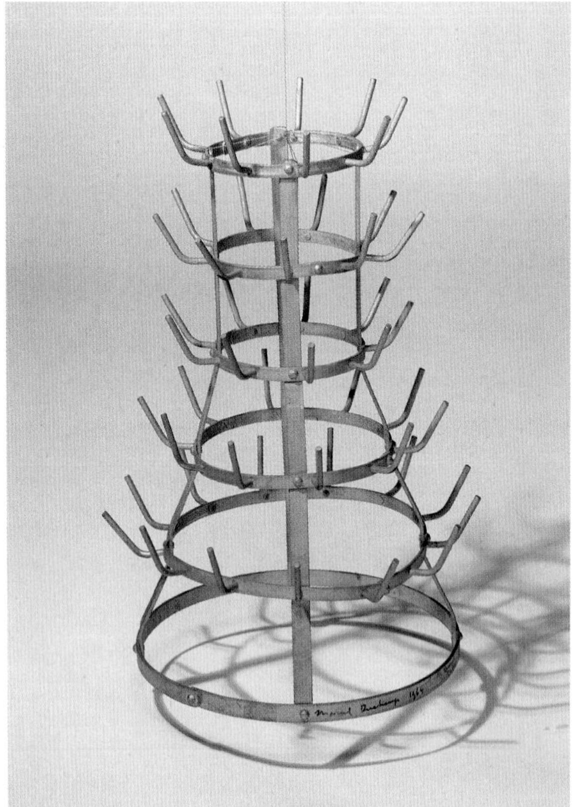

Figure 22.2
Marcel Duchamp, *Bottle Rack*, 1914. Galvanized metal, 64 × 24 cm. Musée National d'Art Moderne, Centre Georges Pompidou, AM 1986-288. © Association Marcel Duchamp / ADAGP, Paris / Artists Rights Society (ARS), New York 2024. Digital Image © CNAC/MNAM, Dist. RMN-Grand Palais / Art Resource, NY.

they gesture toward the relations of exploitation on which their being present for us as disturbatory art depend.

Folland's vital interventions, however, are limited by his inability or refusal to engage with primitivism and industrial capitalism's structural and historical conditions of possibility, namely, colonialism, conquest, and slavery. Such *pre*conditions necessitate a black radical recoding of the artist's work and its circumstances of production, what Rizvana Bradley would call its anteaesthetics, those suppressed re/productions of black (fem) flesh that both haunt and undergird the modern West's metaphysics of form, medium, and aisthesis itself.[19] In her 1977 book chapter "Forms of Readymade," the art historian Rosalind Krauss provides the necessary context. She explains how Duchamp's turn to his signature mode, as well as the related rotorelief, was inspired by witnessing a staging of Raymond Roussel's 1910 novel, *Impressions of Africa*. Neither the play nor the novel, composed of a series of spectacles, has much narrative coherence; what matters is the overall mise-en-scène and what unfolds within it: European scientists and circus performers shipwrecked in Africa have organized a festival to celebrate the investiture of their hosting king. Rather than make art themselves, they produce primitive machines, each more fantastical than the next, that churn out paintings, music, sculptures, even a thinking machine styled as a statue of Kant.[20]

Krauss argues that for Duchamp, alienated by his own efforts in painting, *Impressions d'Afrique* offered a model of automated artistic production in which the presumed psychological, material, and affective ties between the maker and the resulting work are severed, licensing him to select a commercially produced bottle rack as one of his first two readymades in 1914 (Fig. 22.2). This the art historians certainly get right.[21] But what they elide and Jackson helps us comprehend is that Duchamp's and Roussel's object choices, while certainly motivated in their respective cases, are foundationally enabled by an embrace of the very arbitrariness that has historically been viewed as that which consigns the negro to a near-bestial state. Indeed, for Western philosophers, none more than Hegel, Africans' seeming worship of randomly chosen natural objects was concrete evidence of their animality: blacks had no cognizance of history, "eternal law or providence," which meant that they had no access to the concepts of ethics and morality that define the European rational subject.[22] Thus, with *Fountain*, Duchamp did not merely allegorize, but he *performed* a Western fantasy of the fetishistic blackened persona let loose in the metropole; like Constantin Brancusi's, his brand of technological primitivism not only highlighted white culture's hypocrisies and reversals but also signified on the antiblackness of its means of aesthetic appraisal.[23]

This interpretation is furthered by the artist's chosen pseudonym—initially intended to be used by his *female* friend who would submit the porcelain for exhibition—that Duchamp eventually affixed to the work as her/his "signature":[24] the letters "R. Mutt," scrawled on the urinal like a graffito, bring to mind a mixed breed dog, so that the work flirts with those associations of animality, impurity, and sex/gender fluidity that also inform Western ideations of black being. With the 1920 invention of his Jewish female alter ego, Rrose Sélavy—a homophonic French name usually translated as "eros, that's life,"—the artist, famously captured in character by Man Ray, further played on discourses of androgyny and what today we might call gender queering and transness (Fig. 22.3). As Snorton has shown, however, all of these frameworks tend to presume a normative whiteness, although Sélavy's ethnic/racial/religious difference is one that, in the European context, could be variously construed as total or invisible, even, as Duchamp might say, as *inframince*, a barely perceptible "thin-ness."[25] In this way, the artist conceptually embraced and physically identified himself with all of the ethnic, sexual, and gender diversity that might thrive within "white" corporeality, a fantasy of being that only maintains its coherence through the negation of blackness.

Now, both Duchamp and Sélavy remained muted on their relationship to race, African art, and black culture, but for more than one practitioner of African American descent, well versed in the shadow play of white projec-

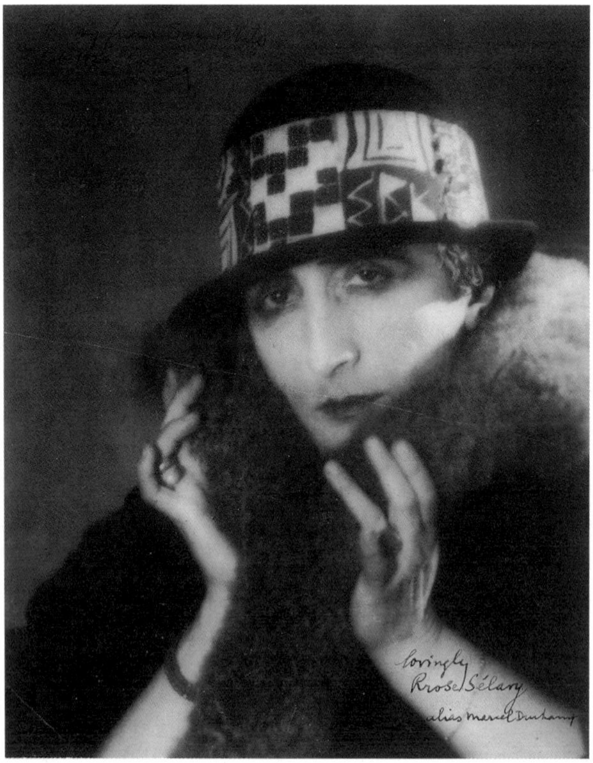

Figure 22.3
Man Ray, *Marcel Duchamp as Rrose Sélavy*, ca. 1920. Gelatin silver print, $8\frac{1}{2} \times 6\frac{13}{16}$ in. (21.6 × 17.3 cm). Philadelphia Museum of Art; The Samuel S. White 3rd and Vera White Collection, 1957.

tions and black refusals that have shaped the modern world, the ties have long been apparent.[26] Here is what the video collagist Arthur Jafa opined nearly twenty years ago in a collection edited by the late great Greg Tate.

> Duchamp was initially as content as Picasso, and others, to explore the space/time implications of African artifacts. But, inevitably, Duchamp, smarter than anyone else around, became deeply interested in how African artifacts *behaved* rather than simply how they looked (their gaze). Duchamp peeped that these artifacts were, in fact, not art but instruments whose functionality had been arrested, and that much of their power was derived from their radically alienated, and de facto transgressive, relationship to the context in which they found themselves. Consequently, Duchamp's urinal was engendered by his desire to model a work after the contextual dissonance provoked by the placement of these (black) artifacts in (white) museums. And it's no accident that Duchamp chose the urinal, a white artifact which contains and channels dark matter, or shit, the stuff of black being. Surrealism can be understood as an investigation of the psychic frisson produced by the juxtaposition of incongruent objects (a cow and an ironing board), the paradigmatic example being the "the black body in white space."[27]

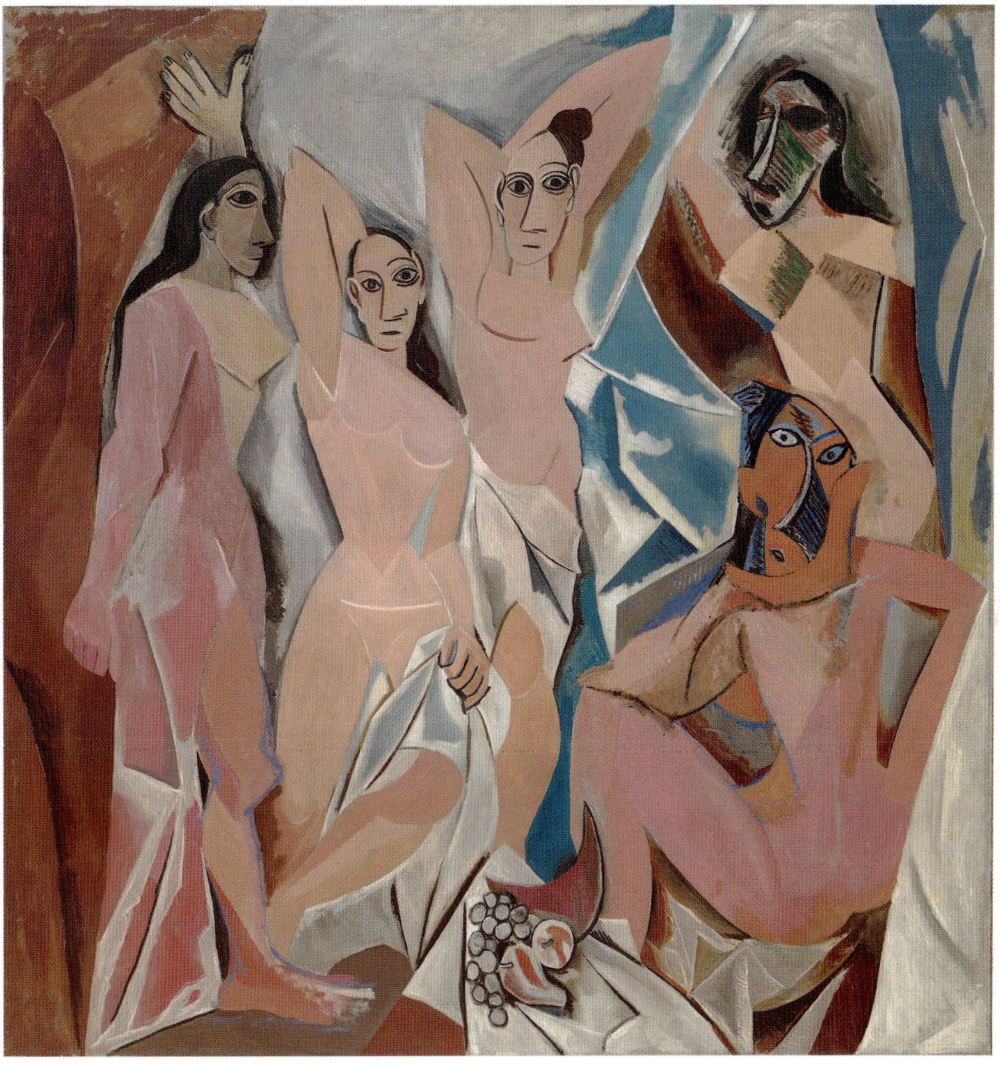

Figure 22.4
Pablo Picasso, *Les Demoiselles d'Avignon*, 1907. Oil on canvas, 8 ft. × 7 ft. 8 in. (243.9 × 233.7 cm). The Museum of Modern Art; acquired through the Lillie P. Bliss Bequest. © 2024 Estate of Pablo Picasso / Artists Rights Society (ARS), New York. Digital Image © The Museum of Modern Art/Licensed by SCALA / Art Resource, NY.

With *Fountain*, in other words, Duchamp/Sélavy aimed to produce the same sort of scandal Picasso had engendered with *Les Demoiselles d'Avignon* (1907) (Fig. 22.4), not through that picture's figurative conjoining of "African" and "female" signifiers, but through relying on the plasticity of blackness. On the one hand, Jafa's reading cannily reproduces the kind of semiotic sliding that blackness is and enables, moving seamlessly from the *Fountain*, a repository for standing urination, to the toilet and its darker

Fountain by R. Mutt

Photograph by Alfred Stieglitz

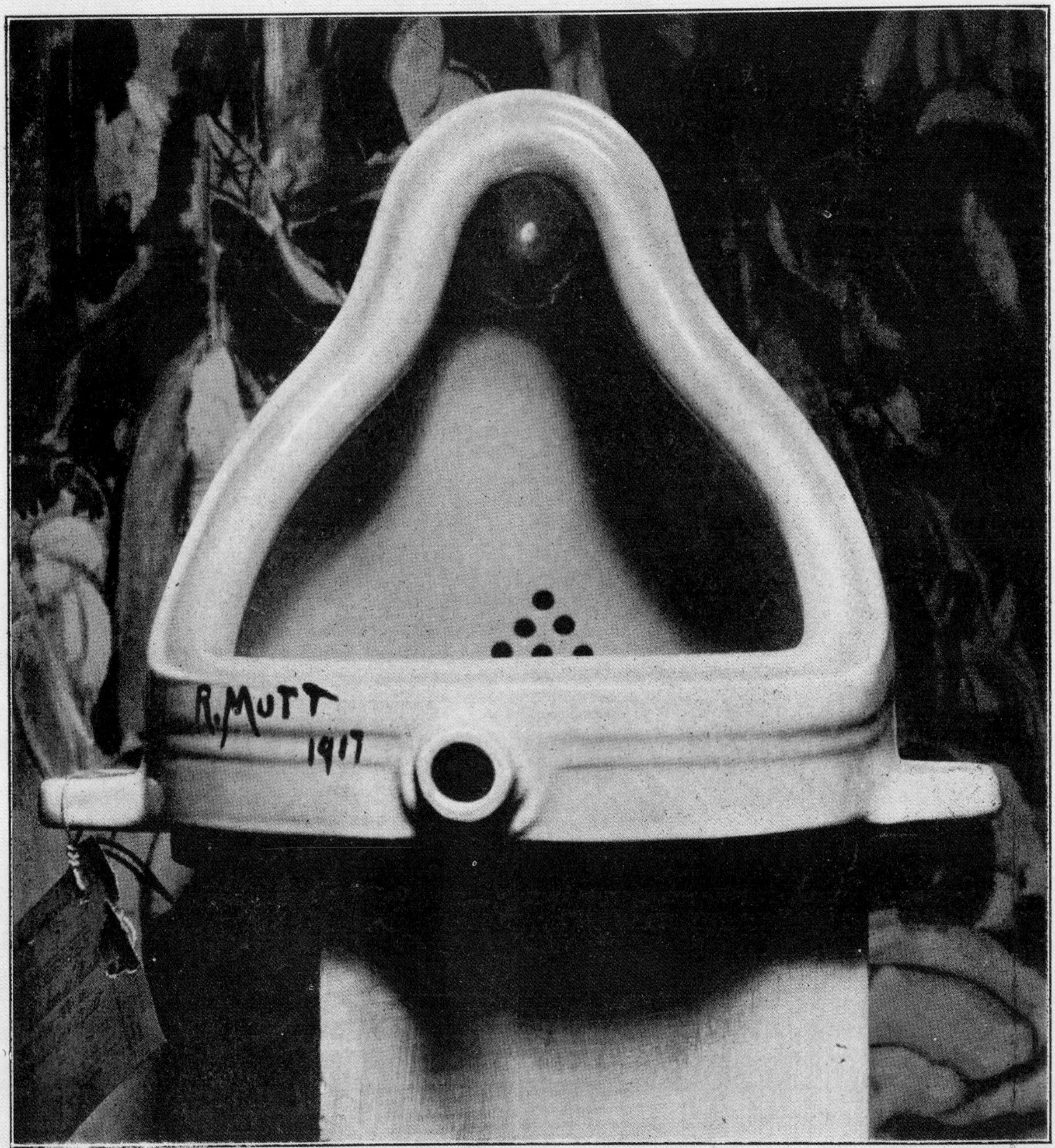

THE EXHIBIT REFUSED BY THE INDEPENDENTS

associations, in which bodily waste becomes conflated with racial ontology. On the other hand, his analysis calls attention to the way that *Fountain* was literally darkened in the American photographer Alfred Stieglitz's iconic photograph of it, again reorienting the urinal, now as a feminized form that has called forth art historical associations ranging from a silhouette of the Buddha to the human uterus flipped upside down (Fig. 22.5).[28]

This abstract blackening and thereby sexuating of *Fountain* photographically makes sense, particularly in light of the American wonders that Duchamp encountered, all at once, upon his emigration to New York: indoor plumbing, Negro art, and available black bodies just beyond a color line that he could easily, *legitimately*, transgress.[29] Unlike those in Europe, intellectual property laws in the United States actively took their measure from the figure of the fugitive slave, the commodity who had stolen himself: in the 1857 Dred Scott decision—and later in those regarding image, voice, persona, and other "reproducible" forms of self—the prerogatives of the owner would reign supreme. Consequently, "black personae" in America were legally constructed, according to the literary critic Stephen Best, as "presumptively translations; presumptively repetitions; presumptively mechanical reproductions."[30] Duchamp leaned into this plasticity metaphorically as well as materially, eventually producing more than a dozen *Fountains* after the lost original that vary significantly in size, shape, media, and facture, a diaspora of readymades if you will, that pointedly echoes, even in radically departing from, the fates of stolen African beings in the Americas.[31] In fact, I would argue that the eventual acceptance of Duchamp's object choices would license all manner of practitioners across the globe to deploy the power of the arbitrary, now legitimated as part and parcel of the artist's right to the world rather than denigrated as evidence of a fetishistic relation to the natural. In other words, the material promiscuity of "global modern and contemporary art," has, since the early twentieth century, been structurally enabled even as it is everywhere haunted by the plasticity of blackness.

Meanwhile, artists back in Europe, like Brancusi with his *Blonde Negress* of 1925 [see Fig. 20.2 on p. 268], continued suturing preestablished "negro" and "feminine" forms together to evoke the specter of *la négresse*, that mythical female figure of unalloyed difference and sexuality that has haunted the West for centuries and has been foundational to so many of its most renowned aesthetic ruses, from the nineteenth-century paintings of Frenchman Edouard Manet to the twenty-first century collages of Kenyan Wangechi Mutu.[32] Duchamp's and Stieglitz's photographic coproduction of *Fountain* proleptically one-ups these efforts in further dispersing the signifiers of marked identity across the visual field. They are nonetheless held together, I would argue, by the cipher of the black maternal, that repressed matrix of

Figure 22.5
Alfred Stieglitz, *Fountain by R. Mutt*, 1917 as it appears in *The Blind Man* 1 (1917). Periodical with paper covers. Sheet (each) 11 × 8 in. (27.9 × 20.3 cm). The Louise and Walter Arensberg Collection, 1950. (1950-134-1053), Philadelphia Museum of Art. Photo: The Philadelphia Museum of Art / Art Resource, NY.

modern capital itself whose reproductive capacities are travestied so that they may be more fully denied in order, as the artist and critic Lorraine O'Grady avers, to "stabilize the West's construct of the female body."[33]

What I am arguing is that in evoking only to detain the specter of the blackened maternal—perhaps the trickster's greatest joke of all—Duchamp secured his position within the pantheon of modern art, knowing full well, thanks to Picasso's example, that such a figure's actual representation would have immediately delimited his provocation's reach. For a cautionary tale that suggests both the art and social worlds' aversion to such direct imaging, just recall Jacob Epstein's *Genesis* of 1931, a critically reviled Africanized pregnant female rendered in stone, that, for all its forthrightness about the body, also ultimately forgoes the representation of genitalia to instead foreground the fullness of the womb (Fig. 22.6).[34] As Hartman teaches us, "The reproduction of human property and the social relations of racial slavery were predicated upon the belly. Plainly put, subjection was anchored in black women's reproductive capacities. The captive female body . . . 'locates precisely a moment of converging political and social vectors that mark the flesh as a prime commodity of exchange.'"[35]

Fred Moten has further articulated the intimate relation between black female bodies and the commodity form in critically revisiting and revising Karl Marx's foundational disquisition on the production of value within capitalist economies, "The Fetishism of the Commodity and Its Secret." The relevant passage begins by considering the ontological status of a wooden table and ultimately leads to the counterfactual proposition, "If the table could speak, it would say," so as to perform the very process of fetishization through which capital imbues the commodity with a seeming liveliness that effectively conceals the lives of those dispossessed by its production.[36] For Moten, reading Marx with and against Frederick Douglass's accounting of his aunt Hester's torture by their slave master, certain commodities—in particular enslaved women—did, in fact, speak, and sigh, and shriek: "The sound—the inspirited materiality—of that speech constitutes a kind of temporal warp that disrupts and augments not only Marx but the mode of subjectivity that the ultimate object of his critique, capital, both allows and disallows."[37]

Far from white art historical, Moten's writing instances a critical orientation toward the sensible rooted in the production of black flesh—suspended between sexes and genders, animate and inanimate, person and thing, subject and object, animal and machine, agent and material, human and non—that underlines the porousness of ontological categories as well as the brittleness of Western culture's epistemological foundations, which time and again place the black female body as limit and exemplar, whether captives in the slave ship hold, specimens on the examining table, or magnetized targets of state violence in the streets.[38]

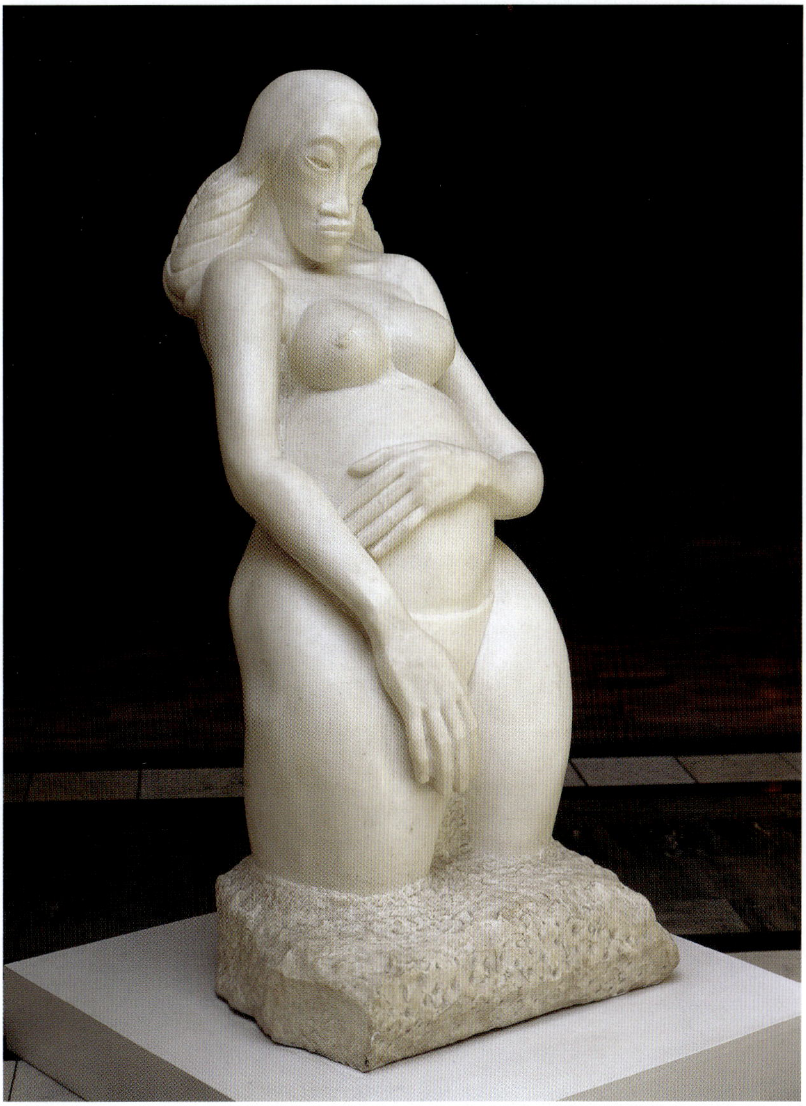

Figure 22.6
Jacob Epstein, *Genesis*, 1932. © The estate of Sir Jacob Epstein / Tate Images. Photo: The University of Manchester Whitworth Art Gallery/ Bridgeman Images.

This approach, what I have called a "tending-toward-blackness—a leaning into and caring for," animates a range of artistic, social, political, and theoretical practices aimed at establishing an ethical posture toward black subjects and those related forms of being that have been positioned at the margins of thought and perception yet are necessarily co-constitutive of them.[39] If, in the words of the latest rallying cry, "Black Lives Matter," then we must recalibrate our modes of reading, thinking, and acting in order to pay heed to the political ontology of race and to the mattering of blackness itself.[40]

From this perspective, to echo Aranke, long before Duchamp entered the picture, blackness was alreadymade thanks to its historical production as the prime model of "plasticity." Jackson further describes it as a mode of transmogrification whereby the fleshy being of blackness is experimented with

> as if it were infinitely malleable lexical and biological matter, such that blackness is produced as sub/super/human at once, a form where form shall not hold: potentially "everything and nothing" at the register of ontology. It is perhaps prior scholarship's interpretation of this tradition as "denied humanity" that has facilitated a call for greater inclusion, as a corrective to what it deems is a historical exclusion of blackness. One consequence of this orientation is that many scholars have essentially ignored alternative conceptions of being and the nonhuman that have been produced by blackened people.[41]

Their bodies everywhere infected by the animal, the machine, and the commodity before they can even know themselves, black visual thinkers have offered their own solutions to and plays on the problem of being alreadymade, despite art history's inconsistency in recognizing let alone grappling with such alternative knowledges and their implications.[42]

We needn't look too far afield to make the case. In announcing the journal *Art History*'s new direction in 2018, its editor, Dorothy Price, reflected on the British academy's lack of response to calls, some thirty years earlier, for the field to "put black women's creativity at its centre."[43] As if to put paid to this contention, the November 2020 cover of the journal—presumably chosen in response to the protests that erupted globally following Floyd's murder—featured Betye Saar's 1972 assemblage, *I've Got Rhythm*, a devastating riposte to Man Ray's *Indestructible Object (Object to Be Destroyed)* of 1923 (Figs. 22.7, 22.8). Saar's revision, among other moves, replaces the white photo-printed paper eye glued to the metronome with a beaded skeletal corpse so that it is the tortured black body's capture by the racist gaze that at once keeps the clock ticking and undoes its meaning given the transhistorical dereliction of African captives before, during, and after the imposition of standard time. It is surprising, then, that Saar's prescient work and her searing critique of the readymade tradition receive no further mention in the issue, illustrating how, as the art historian Sarah Lewis has argued, the work of black artists tends to be "over-exhibited and under-theorized."[44]

Thus, it is not an article on Saar but a review of Kellie Jones's 2017 book on African American assemblage artists in Los Angeles that at once serves as the alibi for representing black women's work on the cover, while

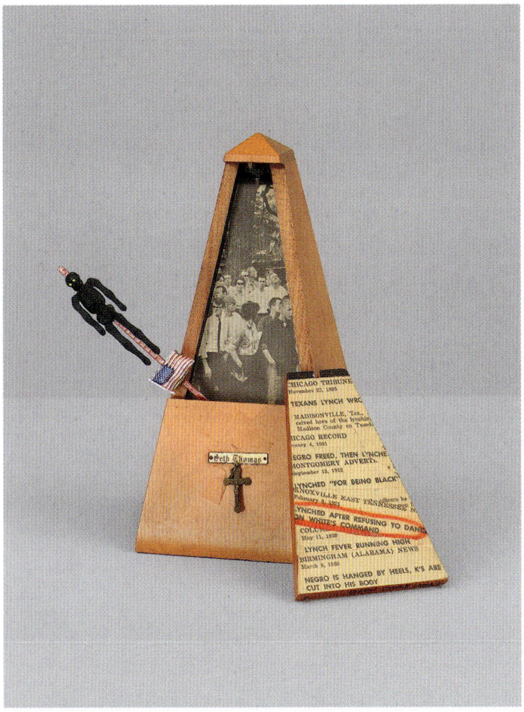

Figure 22.7

Betye Saar, *I've Got Rhythm*, 1972. Mechanical metronome with wood case, plastic toy, American flag pin, paint, and paper collage. Overall: 8 9⁄16 × 4 7⁄16 × 4 7⁄16 in. (21.7 × 11.3 × 11.3 cm). Whitney Museum of American Art, New York; purchase, with funds from the Painting and Sculpture Committee. Inv.:99.87.a-b. © Betye Saar. Courtesy of the artist and Roberts Projects, Los Angeles, California.

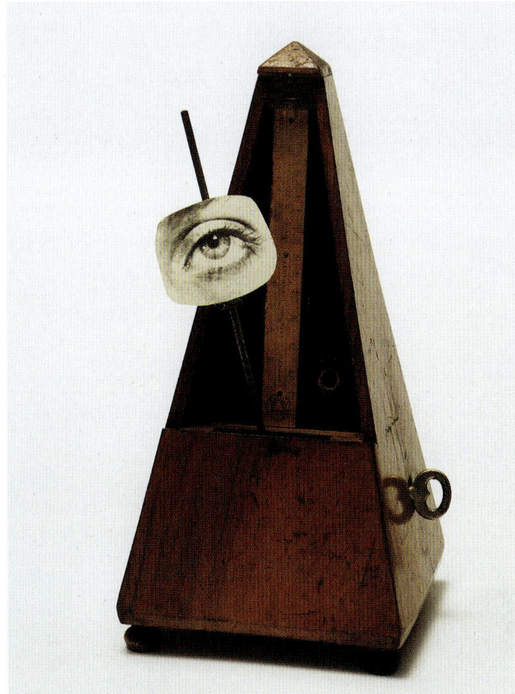

Figure 22.8

Man Ray, *Indestructible Object (Object to Be Destroyed)*, 1964 (replica of 1923 original). Metronome with cutout photograph of eye on pendulum, 8 7⁄8 × 4 3⁄8 × 4 5⁄8 in. (22.5 × 11 × 11.6 cm). The Museum of Modern Art; James Thrall Soby Fund. © Man Ray 2015 Trust / Artists Rights Society (ARS), NY / ADAGP, Paris 2024. Digital Image © The Museum of Modern Art/Licensed by SCALA / Art Resource, NY.

their thought is further denigrated in the journal's pages. The reviewer notes that "Jones does not deconstruct the category of race or pursue what we lately in academe seek as 'intersectional.'"[45] I here want to call your attention to the author's placement of "intersectional" in literal scare quotes with nary a footnote, highlighting the disconnect, the deep time lag, between white art historical common sense and black intellectual praxis: the scholar Kimberlé Crenshaw first coined the term "intersectionality" *in the late 1980s* in order to recover and respond to the structurally neglected efforts and experiences of black women, an approach that has proved influential for almost every mode of critical analysis within the humanities and social sciences since, with, as we know, some notable exceptions.[46]

Yet as Saar's work makes clear, black artists have simultaneously taken the commodity form into alternative directions eminently worthy of our attention due to their disturbatory effects on the canon. In fact, as the art

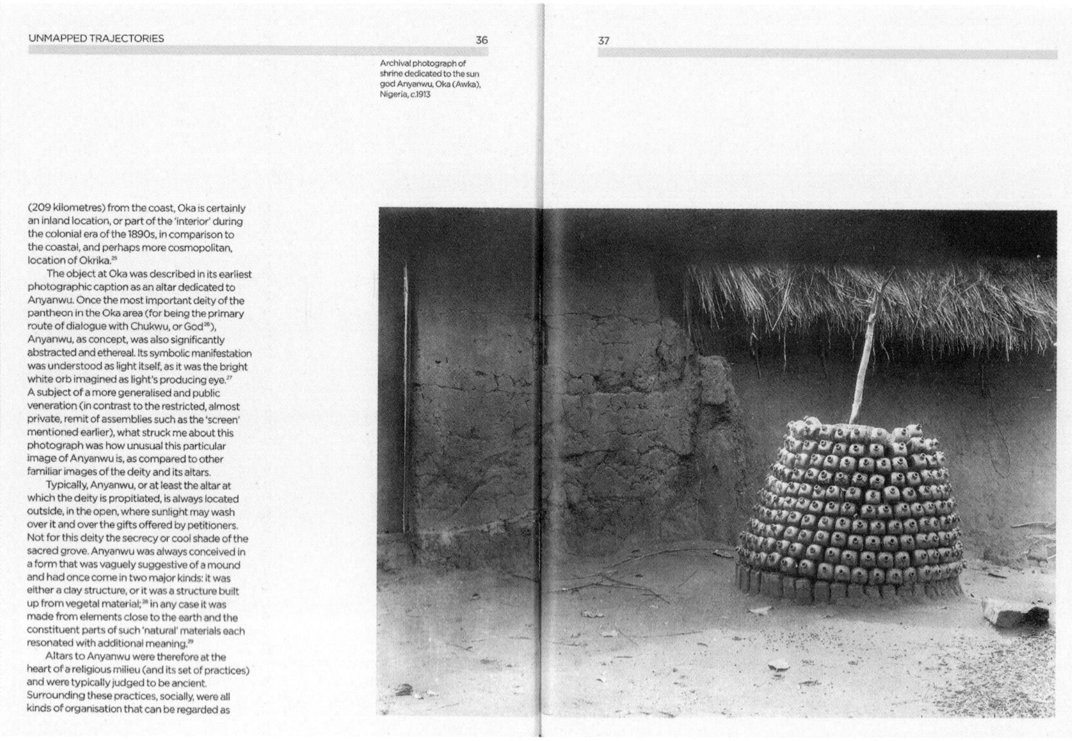

UNMAPPED TRAJECTORIES 36

37

Archival photograph of shrine dedicated to the sun god Anyanwu, Oka (Awka), Nigeria, c.1913

(209 kilometres) from the coast, Oka is certainly an inland location, or part of the 'interior' during the colonial era of the 1890s, in comparison to the coastal, and perhaps more cosmopolitan, location of Okrika.[25]

The object at Oka was described in its earliest photographic caption as an altar dedicated to Anyanwu. Once the most important deity of the pantheon in the Oka area (for being the primary route of dialogue with Chukwu, or God[26]), Anyanwu, as concept, was also significantly abstracted and ethereal. Its symbolic manifestation was understood as light itself, as it was the bright white orb imagined as light's producing eye.[27] A subject of a more generalised and public veneration (in contrast to the restricted, almost private, remit of assemblies such as the 'screen' mentioned earlier), what struck me about this photograph was how unusual this particular image of Anyanwu is, as compared to other familiar images of the deity and its altars.

Typically, Anyanwu, or at least the altar at which the deity is propitiated, is always located outside, in the open, where sunlight may wash over it and over the gifts offered by petitioners. Not for this deity the secrecy or cool shade of the sacred grove. Anyanwu was always conceived in a form that was vaguely suggestive of a mound and had once come in two major kinds: it was either a clay structure, or it was a structure built up from vegetal material;[28] in any case it was made from elements close to the earth and the constituent parts of such 'natural' materials each resonated with additional meaning.[29]

Altars to Anyanwu were therefore at the heart of a religious milieu (and its set of practices) and were typically judged to be ancient. Surrounding these practices, socially, were all kinds of organisation that can be regarded as

Figure 22.9

Shrine to Anyanwu, Oka, Nigeria, 1913, as it appears in Ikem Stanley Okoye, "Unmapped Trajectories: Early Sculpture and Architecture of a 'Nigerian' Modernity," in *Exiles, Diasporas, Strangers*, ed. Kobena Mercer (Cambridge, MA: MIT Press; London: Institute of International Visual Arts, 2008), 36–37.

historian Ikem Okoye has demonstrated, one year *before* Duchamp conceived of the readymade and around the same time he produced his first assemblage, *Bicycle Wheel* (1913), an unnamed team of practitioners in Oka, Nigeria, would also draw on mass-produced wares—this time used green Dutch gin bottles—to construct a shrine to the god Anyanwu in a radical formal departure from any prior known altar to the deity (Fig. 22.9). The choice of bottles was by no means accidental and not because of its anticipatory rhyming with Duchamp's rack: as Okoye notes, gin had been the preferred libation to the ancestors for over two hundred years, and the green glass, with its "vegetal" coloring and "scintillating" refraction of light, made for a fitting means of honoring a god most closely associated with the sun.[47]

This tradition would be taken up and extended across the American South in the form of funerary and celebratory bottle trees made by the descendants of enslaved Africans. Several decades later, the African American artist David Hammons produced an untitled spiraling circular sculp-

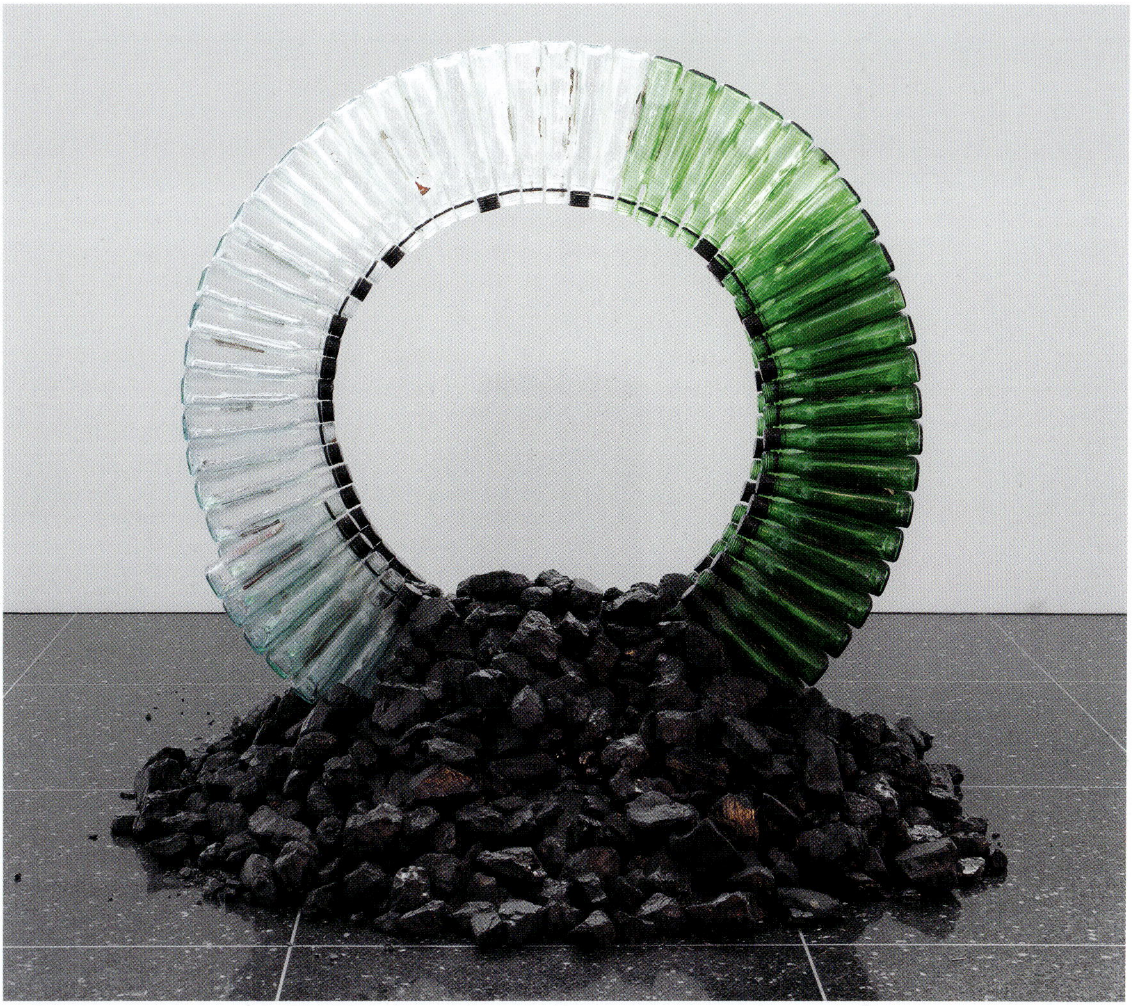

Figure 22.10
David Hammons, *Night Train*, 1992. Glass, silicone glue, and coal; 42 × 42 × 30 in. (106.7 × 106.7 × 76.2 cm), depth and width variable. The Museum of Modern Art; gift of the Hudgins Family in memory of Lawrence D. "Butch" Morris. © 2024 David Hammons / Artists Rights Society (ARS), New York. Digital Image © The Museum of Modern Art/Licensed by SCALA / Art Resource, NY.

ture constructed out of clear and green bottles of Night Train and Thunderbird, inexpensive alcohols often associated with black indigent men in New York (Fig. 22.10). In these cases of African/diasporic innovation, manufactured objects are darkened not so much through the machinations of plasticity as through the inspiriting breath of the black folks who handled them before each object assumed its place in an aesthetic ensemble materially redolent of and entangled with their presences.[48] As instances of black visual thought—both anti- (as in "against") and ante- (as in "anterior" or "before") readymades, to follow Bradley's lead—these works do not solicit us to wonder about bottle racks belonging or not within the museum; instead, they call us to consider the production, circulation, and embodied use of things by black people who have time and again been conflated with them.

Not content with such oblique engagements with Duchamp, Hammons, for his part, also eventually signified on his predecessor's most notorious readymade with this 2004 installation, *Toilet Trees*, urinals, ostensibly available for use, tied, as their name spells out, to arboreal supports. Whereas Duchamp's homophonic doubling in "Eros c'est la vie" and other instances aimed to expand chains of signification beyond their textual referents, Hammons's work presents us with a slightly twisted, nearly tautological loop—toilet trees could, in this case, be considered a form of toiletry—which emphasizes our bodily relationship to, counterfactual understanding of, and material-discursive engagement with the works in question. Each of Hammons's works, I want to say, enables a reframing of art's histories attuned to the ways that blackness, labor, and the body are suppressed yet constitutive of our understandings of the aesthetic and that on which it relies, turning us to other scenes, ecologies, and logics that might register multiple entanglements and realities.

Such holistic scenes of instruction can only emerge from thinking Western art's characteristic forms alongside centuries of black visual intelligence that stems from an ongoing intimate proximity with other forms of devalued being, humanity, animality, and objecthood, the strange inheritance of what the novelist Ishmael Reed called "comrade[s] of the inanimate."[49] White art history now, though usually a methodological step behind, may well be poised to contend with the implications that W. E. B. Du Bois's "problem of the color line" sharply brought into focus more than a century ago but only if it can actually confront the structuring effects of blackness that the discipline so often aims to avoid, embracing the "negro" already within as much as chasing us Africans on (and off) the market. In and of themselves, the current gestures toward "inclusion"—most often programs, fellowships, and other short-term modes of performative investment—usually function as defensive postures.

When institutions do attempt to make permanent hires, the positions either implicitly or explicitly come with strings attached, as laid bare by the following advertisement, which appeared on the US art historians' professional website on February 16, 2022. It read, in part:

> The Department of Art History at Hudson University invites applications for an Assistant Professor to teach African American Art, African Diasporic Art, and African Art, covering every geographic location and

every period of time since the dawn of humankind. Knowledge of Latin American, Caribbean, and Indigenous art histories would be a plus. All of these fields would complement and constructively contrast with our department faculty members' narrow, long-canonized specializations. . . . The candidate should expect a large course load and high volume of service assignments, but this will definitely not impede progress toward promotion. Other forms of labor not counted by the University will include training faculty and the administration in all matters related to race and racism, mentoring students of color traumatized by their experiences at the University, and authoring weekly public statements attesting to the department's long unrealized commitments to diversity and equity. . . . Please send CV and cover letter to magicalnegrosearch@gmail.com by the April 1st deadline.

For many, the posting registered as authentic—despite it being for a salary "less than you deserve" at an institution of higher learning that only exists in the *Law & Order* TV universe—right up until they read the "magicalnegrosearch" email address. Like the 2001 artistic intervention in which Mendi + Keith Obadike offered Keith's blackness for sale on eBay [see Fig. 13.5 on p. 182], the academic ad parodically reveals the unconscious bias percolating beneath the face of white liberalism. It also underlines how racialized labor is fundamentally devalued even as it is everywhere put to work in maintaining a status quo predicated on the plasticity of blackness, which again becomes both a site of active unknowing and a transactional quantum that further abets the extraction and circulation of value for white ends.

The relative homogeneity of white art history's audiences, categories, demographics, institutions, and intellectual genealogies only serves to reinforce the fact that the field is *necessarily* shot through with the antiblackness constitutive of the Western "civilization" whose masterpieces it was designed to uphold. This, of course, is what Cedric Robinson's *Black Marxism* so magisterially demonstrated back in 1983: "As an enduring principle of European social order, the effects of racialism were bound to appear in the social expression of every strata of every European society no matter the structures upon which they were formed. None were immune."[50] Rather than ancillary to art history, black radical study—ethical heir to the legacies of critical historical and poststructuralist praxis in the humanities—provides, I would contend, the most vital means today for undoing Western hegemony and envisioning futures that disrupt the racialized, cisgendered, heteropatriarchal violence on which it depends.

To my mind, the longer black visual thought goes pointedly ignored, instrumentally engaged, or epistemically erased in art history, the more the discipline's validity as an intellectual enterprise is cast in doubt. This is especially true today as the leading humanistic institutions in the United

States move to align their funding priorities with the aims of social justice and as the most trenchant and influential modes of visual analysis increasingly drift away from the discipline and toward Africana, cultural, literary, performance, and visual studies; and to art-making itself, sites in which black thinkers have been given some pride of place.[51] Whether white art history as practiced today will survive another hundred years is an open question, but the alreadymade, with or without Duchamp, will still matter as it continues to pose recursive questions of ontology that go straight to the heart of the modern world, the black presence within it, and our means of narration for confronting both.

Notes

In returning to and expanding on the notion of the alreadymade, I have been fortunate to benefit from the research assistance of Miriam Said and Lauren Taylor at the Center for Advanced Study for the Visual Arts, as well as from the conceptual engagement of Sampada Aranke, Leah Dickerman, David Joselit, Saidiya Hartman, Steven Nelson, Bibiana K. Obler, and Krista Thompson; as ever, they have my thanks. This essay was commissioned by Susanne Pfeffer for the catalog meant to accompany her 2022 Duchamp retrospective at the Museum für Moderne Kunst, Frankfurt. I dedicate it to the memory of the cultural critic Greg Tate whose music, writing, and generative way of being black in the world continue to inspire us all.

1 Walter Benjamin, "Theses on the Philosophy of History," in *Illuminations*, ed. Hannah Arendt, trans. Harry Zohn (Shocken Books, 1968), 256-57.

2 Huey Copeland, "Lorna Simpson's Figurative Transitions," in *Bound to Appear: Art, Slavery, and the Site of Blackness in Multicultural America* (University of Chicago Press, 2013), 99.

3 Sampada Aranke, "Objects Made Black," *Art Journal* 73, no. 3 (Fall 2014): 87; emphasis in original.

4 For more on this phrase, see Huey Copeland, "Unfinished Business as Usual: Black Artists, New York Institutions, and the 1990s," in *Come as You Are: Art of the 1990s*, ed. Alexandra Schwartz (University of California Press and Montclair Art Museum, 2014), 32 [reprinted in this volume, 175-85].

5 Saidiya Hartman, quoted in Frank B. Wilderson III, "The Position of the Unthought: An Interview with Saidiya V. Hartman," *Qui Parle* 13, no. 2 (Spring-Summer 2003): 196.

6 Michele Wallace, "Modernism, Postmodernism, and the Problem of the Visual in Afro-American Culture," in *Out There: Marginalization and Contemporary Cultures*, ed. Russell Ferguson et al. (MIT Press, 1990), 41. For a related discussion of white art history's suppression of blackness and slavery to the literal footnotes of the discipline that featured in one of the two flagship publications of the College Art Association, see Krista Thompson, "A Sidelong Glance: The Practice of African Diaspora Art History in the United States," Centennial Essay, *Art Journal* 70, no. 3 (Fall 2011): 22-23.

7 For a recent and far-reaching white art historical revision of Manet's picture in this vein, see Darcy Grimaldo Grigsby, "Still Thinking about

Olympia's Maid," *Art Bulletin* 97, no. 4 (Fall 2015): 430–51; for an incisive black radical critique of her and Clark's approaches, see Athi Mongezeleli Joja, "About Race: A Critical Appraisal of the Concept of Cultural Work," in *Mintirho Ya Vulavula: Arts, National Identities and Democracy*, ed. Innocentia J. Mhlambi and Snaidle Ngidi (Mapungubwe Institute for Strategic Reflection, 2021), 137–40. My own reading is offered in Huey Copeland, "Flow and Arrest," *Small Axe: A Caribbean Journal of Criticism* 19, no. 3 (48) (November 2015): 223–24 [reprinted in this volume, 287–309].

8 It is worth noting that Canadian law, unlike that in the United States, allows universities to stipulate that a position is specifically earmarked for individuals of African descent.

9 Thompson, "A Sidelong Glance," 7.

10 Here I refer to and rely on Wilderson, "The Position of the Unthought," 184–85.

11 C. Riley Snorton and Hentyle Yapp, "'Sensuous Contemplation': Thinking Race at Its Saturation Points," in *Saturation: Race, Art, and the Circulation of Value* (MIT Press, 2020), 1–2; emphasis in original.

12 Zakkiyah Iman Jackson, *Becoming Human: Matter and Meaning in an Antiblack World* (New York University Press, 2020), 20.

13 Wilderson, "The Position of the Unthought," 188–89.

14 Jackson, *Becoming Human*, 11, 10. The quoted phrase derives from Stephanie E. Smallwood, *Saltwater Slavery: A Middle Passage from Africa to American Diaspora* (Harvard University Press, 2007), 36.

15 Jackson, *Becoming Human*, 11, 10.

16 Thomas Folland, "Readymade Primitivism: Marcel Duchamp, Dada, and African Art," *Art History* 43, no. 4 (September 2020): 806. For a key anticipatory anthropological account, see Sally Price, *Primitive Art in Civilized Places* (University of Chicago Press, 1989).

17 Folland, "Readymade Primitivism," 806; emphasis in original.

18 Folland, "Readymade Primitivism," 812.

19 Rizvana Bradley, *Anteaesthetics: Black Aesthesis and the Critique of Form* (Stanford University Press, 2023).

20 Rosalind E. Krauss, *Passages in Modern Sculpture* (MIT Press, 1977), 69–81.

21 Krauss, *Passages in Modern Sculpture*.

22 Jackson, *Becoming Human*, 30.

23 I derive the term "technological primitivism" from Anne M. Wagner, who advised the UC Berkeley dissertation that formed the basis for *Bound to Appear* as well as my 2001 master's thesis, "Brancusi's *Girls*: Repairing the Subject of Modern Sculpture."

24 On this point, see Richard Meyer, "'Big, Middle-Class Modernism,'" *October* 131 (Winter 2010): 80.

25 C. Riley Snorton, *Black on Both Sides: A Racial History of Trans Identity* (University of Minnesota Press, 2017); I also owe a note of thanks to Leah Dickerman for providing an incisive framework through which to consider Duchamp's gender- and ethnic-drags.

26 For a central theorization of how the psychodynamics of race inform American culture, see Toni Morrison, *Playing in the Dark: Whiteness and the Literary Imagination* (Vintage, 1993).

27 Arthur Jafa, "My Black Death," in *Everything But the Burden: What White People Are Taking from Black Culture*, ed. Greg Tate (Broadway Books, 2003), 247; emphasis in original. For a thoroughgoing account of *Fountain*'s making and its critical reception, see William A. Camfield, *Marcel Duchamp/Fountain* (Houston Fine Art Press, 1989).

28 On the Buddha and the female body, see, respectively, Meyer, "'Big, Middle-Class Modernism,'" 84-85; Krauss, *Passages in Modern Sculpture*, 79.

29 Folland, "Readymade Primitivism," 807; for the prime white art historical accounting of *Fountain*'s Americanness, see Wanda Corn, *The Great American Thing: Modern Art and National Identity, 1915-1935* (University of California Press, 1999), 43-89.

30 Stephen Best, *The Fugitive's Properties: Law and the Poetics of Possession* (University of Chicago Press, 2004), 98.

31 William A. Camfield, "Typology–*Fountain*," in *Marcel Duchamp/Fountain*, 162-65. For a contrasting African/Diasporic perspective on confronting object loss–specifically, the reconstruction of a Nigerian shrine after its plundering by European colonialists–see the artist Tiona Nekkia McClodden's *I prayed to the wrong god for you* (2019).

32 On *la négresse* as constitutive fiction of Western art, see Huey Copeland, "In the Wake of the Negress," in *Modern Women: Women Artists at the Museum of Modern Art*, ed. Cornelia Butler and Alexandra Schwartz (Museum of Modern Art, 2010), 480-97 [reprinted in this volume, 265-85].

33 Lorraine O'Grady, "Olympia's Maid: Reclaiming Black Female Subjectivity," *Afterimage* 20 (Summer 1992): 14.

34 Anne M. Wagner, "(De)Generation," in *Mother Stone: The Vitality of Modern British Sculpture* (Yale University Press, 2005), 193-243.

35 Saidiya Hartman, "The Belly of the World: A Note on Black Women's Labors," *Souls* 18, no. 1 (January-March 2016): 168; the internally quoted phrase derives from Hortense J. Spillers, "Mama's Baby, Papa's Maybe: An American Grammar Book," *Diacritics* 17, no. 2 (Summer 1987): 65-81, 75.

36 Karl Marx, "The Fetishism of the Commodity and Its Secret," in *Capital: A Critique of Political Economy, Volume I* (1867), trans. Ben Fowkes (Penguin Books, 1990), 176. My thoughts on the fetish are informed, as ever, by William Pietz, "The Problem of the Fetish, I," *Res* 9 (Spring 1985): 5-17.

37 Fred Moten, *In the Break: The Aesthetics of the Black Radical Tradition* (University of Minnesota Press, 2003), 11.

38 In addition to Moten's work and that of other scholars cited in this essay, I here mean to conjure an even further range of raced materialisms and racialized material practices from the advent of transatlantic slavery to the present: on hierarchies of animation, see Mel Y. Chen, *Animacies: Biopolitics, Racial Mattering, and Queer Affect* (Duke University Press, 2012); on the human in and as machine, see Donna Haraway, "A Manifesto for Cyborgs: Science, Technology, and Socialist Feminism in the 1980s" in *The Haraway Reader* (Routledge, 2003), 5-45; on being in the slave ship hold, see Omise'eke Natasha Tinsley, "Black Atlantic, Queer Atlantic: Queer Imaginings of the Middle Passage," *GLQ* 14, no. 2-3 (2008): 191-215; on the black female body as a site of scientific production, see Rebecca Skloot, *The Immortal Life of Henrietta Lacks* (Broadway Paperbacks, 2010); and on the black body's vulnerability to state violence, see Steve Martinot and Jared Sexton, "The Avant-Garde of White Supremacy," *Social Identities* 9, no. 2 (2003): 169-81; as well as John Marquez, "The Black Mohicans: Representations of Everyday Violence in Postracial Urban America," *American Studies Quarterly* 64, no. 3 (2012): 625-51.

39 "Tending-toward-blackness" is "meant to rhyme with Martin Heidegger's notion of 'being-toward-death'–the subject's existential ownership of his own demise–particularly as recast in light of the dynamics of slavery

in Abdul R. JanMohamed, *The Death-Bound Subject: Richard Wright's Archaeology of Death* (Durham: Duke University Press, 2005), 15." See Huey Copeland, *Bound to Appear: Art, Slavery, and the Site of Blackness in Multicultural America* (University of Chicago Press, 2013), 92, 218n88.

40 For the most trenchant account of how the positionality of the Slave disrupts questions of politics and ontology, see Frank B. Wilderson III, *Red, White & Black: Cinema and the Structure of U.S. Antagonisms* (Duke University Press, 2010). The foregoing paragraph recasts lines first published in Huey Copeland, "Tending-Toward-Blackness," *October* 156 (Spring 2016): 142-43.

41 Jackson, *Becoming Human*, 3.

42 For a compelling example in this vein, see Anne Anlin Cheng, *Second Skin: Josephine Baker and the Modern Surface* (Oxford University Press, 2011); for a related line of inquiry focused on the singing crates featured in Glenn Ligon's installation *To Disembark* (1993), see Copeland, *Bound to Appear*, 141-50.

43 Dorothy Price, "Editorial," *Art History* 41, no. 1 (February 2018): 9.

44 Folasade Ologundudu, "Art Historian Sarah Lewis on Why Black Artists Have Been 'Over-Exhibited and Under-Theorized'," *Artnet*, February 27, 2021, https://news.artnet.com/art-world/sarah-lewis-1946964.

45 Miguel de Baca, "A Field Made Visible: New Directions in African-American Contemporary Art History," *Art History* 43, no. 5 (November 2020): 1078-85.

46 See Kimberlé Williams Crenshaw, "Demarginalizing the Intersection of Race and Sex: A Black Feminist Critique of Antidiscrimination Doctrine, Feminist Theory, and Antiracist Politics," *University of Chicago Legal Forum* 1 (1989): 139-67; Kimberlé Williams Crenshaw, "Mapping the Margins: Intersectionality, Identity, and Violence Against Women of Color," *Stanford Law Review* 43, no. 6 (July 1991): 1241-1300; Leslie McCall, "Toward a Field of Intersectionality Studies: Theory, Applications, and Praxis," *Signs: Journal of Women in Culture and Society* 38, no. 4 (2013): 85-810; Jennifer C. Nash, "Intersectionality and Its Discontents," *American Quarterly* 69, no. 1 (March 2017): 117-29.

47 Ikem Stanley Okoye, "Unmapped Trajectories: Early Sculpture and Architecture of a 'Nigerian' Modernity," in *Exiles, Diasporas, Strangers*, ed. Kobena Mercer (MIT Press and Institute of International Visual Arts, 2008), 37-39.

48 On black vernacular traditions, see John Michael Vlach, *The Afro-American Tradition in Decorative Arts* (University of Georgia Press, 1990); on Hammons's approach to the found object, especially African masks, see Claire Tancons, "An Elective Affinity: David Hammons's *Hidden from View* and *Made in the People's Republic of Harlem*," *Third Text* 19, no. 2 (March 2005): 169-75.

49 Ishmael Reed, *Flight to Canada* (Scribner, 1976), 64.

50 Cedric Robinson, *Black Marxism: The Making of the Black Radical Tradition* (1983; repr., University of North Carolina Press, 2000), 28.

51 Think, for instance, of how Darren Walker and Elizabeth Alexander have recently restructured the Ford and Mellon Foundations, respectively, to focus on racial equity or of how the black visual thinkers Hartman (2019), Moten (2020), and Nicole Fleetwood (2021) have each received MacArthur Foundation "Genius" Fellowships.

Figure 23.1

Howardena Pindell, *Untitled #20 (Dutch Wives Circled and Squared)*, 1978. Courtesy the artist and Garth Greenan Gallery, New York / Collection of Museum of Contemporary Art, Chicago, Gift of Albert A. Robin by exchange.

23

NECESSARY ABSTRACTIONS, OR, HOW TO LOOK AT ART AS A BLACK FEMINIST

I

In this essay, I consider the art historical implications of a methodological centering of black women in the making of the modern world, particularly for our understanding of twentieth-century painterly abstraction in the United States. Ultimately, I will turn to the "errant forms" of Howardena Pindell and the curator Naomi Beckwith's brilliant framing of works such as *Untitled #20 (Dutch Wives Circled and Squared)* of 1978, a sprawling canvas covered, like much of the elder African American artist's output from that era, with thousands of tiny hole punches (Fig. 23.1).[1] However, in order to provide a historical and theoretical frame for approaching her art and those of her contemporaries now just receiving their critical and commercial dues, I first want to lay out, in some detail, both the proclivities and the blind spots of the broader American artistic field and their implications for black women practitioners.

To do so, it is useful to revisit a few of the key contentions that have guided my thinking about the vexed intersection of race and gender, Western "fine art" and black radical aesthetics today.[2] Over the past twenty years, those of us working in North America and Western Europe have witnessed an explosion of market, exhibitionary, and critical interest in the modes of black abstraction, such as Pindell's, that emerged in the 1960s and 1970s. Of course, folks in the black US art world and its institutions have been advocating for abstract work by African Americans for decades, arguably none more than the Studio Museum in Harlem, whose inaugural exhibition in 1968 featured the light sculptures of Tom Lloyd, and which has gone on to consistently mount solo exhibitions of major African American abstractionists, Pindell included. The inimitable art historian and curator Kellie Jones would revisit these legacies in her important 2006 show, *Energy/Experimentation: Black Artists and Abstraction, 1964–1980*, which, in its turn, looked back to April Kingsley's pioneering 1980 exhibition, *Afro-American*

This article first appeared in *Africanidades* 2, no. 2 (Special Issue, "Beyond the Black Atlantic, Its Visual Arts," March 2023): 124-39.

Abstraction, at New York's P.S.1. Yet crucial as these interventions have been in raising the profiles of black abstract artists, they have tended—as Jones's title "Black Artists" and "Abstraction" suggests—to see black artistry and abstraction as terms in need of conjoining rather than of always already belonging together.

From one perspective, this makes a certain cultural sense: as the literary critic Philip Brian Harper reminds us in his book *Abstractionist Aesthetics: Artistic Form and Social Critique in African American Culture*, within certain circles, the black US tradition is one that, as the poet June Jordan noted in 1985, "abhors all abstraction."[3] For is not a form of abstraction key to those very processes of racialization and stereotyping—think Sambos, Mammies, and all their outrageous progeny—that have tended to render the visual what the black feminist critic Michele Wallace famously called "a negative scene of instruction," in which black folks are ceaselessly caricatured within the visual field at the same time that their contributions to modern artistic practice are rendered effectively invisible?[4] Such processes have also, I think, profoundly affected the cultural fates of black women, as the opening gambit of the theorist Hortense Spillers's influential essay "Mama's Baby, Papa's Maybe" begins to make clear.

> Let's face it. I am a marked woman, but not everybody knows my name. "Peaches" and "Brown Sugar," "Sapphire" and "Earth Mother," "Aunty," "Granny," God's "Holy Fool," a "Miss Ebony First," or "Black Woman at the Podium": I describe a locus of confounded identities, a meeting ground of investments and privations in the national treasury of rhetorical wealth. My country needs me, and if I were not here, I would have to be invented.[5]

"The black woman," in other words, is culturally imagined and violently produced as a kind of *necessary abstraction*, without, however, being attributed capacities for abstract thought and mark making despite the overwhelming evidence provided by her very survival, thereby crystallizing the seeming misfit between the racial and the nonobjective.

Confronted with this impasse, writers aiming to think black being *and* abstraction have often resorted to approaches that seek out African diasporic referents buried within abstract visual languages, compare abstract painting to jazz in order to license its unfurling, or throw their hands up altogether in relying on the identity of the maker to solve the problem. Recently, Whitney Museum curator, Adrienne Edwards, has done vital work to address this problem by exploring the relation between chromatic and racial blackness in twentieth-century abstraction by artists on all sides of the color line.[6] But how do we develop a language, a critical framework, for thinking the multifariously hued abstract work of black artists, male and female, that honors, to paraphrase the art historian Rosalind Krauss, these practitioners' careful work on the signifier?[7] How might we imagine the potentiality of abstraction as a site of political possibility for imagining the world otherwise, especially given that figurative work seems to more directly address the unfolding of black life?

II

Answering such questions is, in fact, the ostensible aim of the critic Darby English's *1971: A Year in the Life of Color*.[8] His book, it must be said, owes much to a 2004 article by the photographer Dawoud Bey that demonstrated how mainstream aesthetic discourse has come to appreciate black artists as signs *of* diversity while suppressing the diversity *of their practices*, with particularly deleterious consequences for work and thought on abstraction. For Bey, these consequences were, in fact, emblematized by the case of Pindell, whose scathing performance video *Free, White and 21* of 1980 was critically lauded yet whose earlier works like *Dutch Wives* were effectively forgotten for decades [see Fig. 9.7 on p. 120].[9] English's critical project ends up being quite different but nonetheless instructive as it trades in a vulgar formalism of the sort in which the Yale-educated Pindell was trained and which still shapes many approaches to abstract art.[10] I thus want to spend a few moments laying out his argument before articulating my own, which both gives us other objects to see and, more fundamentally, I hope, furthers an understanding of what it might mean to look as a black feminist from a US perspective.

In one sense, *1971* is a welcome and much-needed addition to the burgeoning art historical literature on African American art of the 1960s and 1970s, a discourse that has tended to focus on conceptual practice, performance, printmaking, and figurative painting, often with a political bent. Yet English's aim is not merely to recover color field painting; he holds out this art, perhaps above all, that of Peter Bradley and of his inspiration, the white artist Jules Olitski, as offering alternatives to the black nationalisms that, to English's mind, both saturated the cultural field and delimited imaginings of aesthetic and political possibility. As he put it, "By mobilizing modernism as a politics, these figures (and the experiments they factored into) illuminated the crisis of artistic freedom precipitated by the black liberation movement."[11] However, in order to critically advocate for the specialness of abstract art by black practitioners, English feels compelled not only to summarily dismiss his scholarly antecedents, from Jones to Ann Eden Gibson, who, by his lights, "appropriate abstract art to a racialist cause," but also to cherry-pick words and phrases from black artists, theorists, and art historians that suit his argument despite his warning to avoid "selective quotation" when engaging contemporaneous white critics.[12]

Most illustrative in this regard is English's treatment of the legendary American modernist critic Clement Greenberg, who worked alongside Bradley and an interracial cast of abstract artists to produce the DeLuxe Show in Houston, the subject of English's third chapter. While Greenberg never, to my knowledge, said a kind word in print about the work of an African American artist, he maintained friendly "relationships" with a number of black practitioners, including the Guyanese British painter Frank Bowling. In fact, Greenberg's letters to Bowling were published not so long ago by the curator Okwui Enwezor, and they vividly illustrate the complex logics of racialization at work in the critic's mind and in the culture at large, all which English is at pains to suppress.

Take this missive that Greenberg sent from Zimbabwe (then Rhodesia) on December 10, 1975:

> That racist business. You too run over at the mouth. . . . Some people think I'm anti-Irish or anti-Anglo-Saxon or anti-Gentile or even anti-Jewish, not to mention being a male chauvinist. So I'm anti-black too. Well, I do delight in ethnic, racial, & sexual distinctions. Among them are the different smells: do you realize that Germans smell different from English, & Italians from French, & that they all smell different from Jews? And that Zulus smell different from blacks over here? It's not just w. respect to body odor but also breath. Also, domestic interiors smell different, as I'm sure you know, & it's always along ethnic or racial lines.[13]

This is an incredibly strange passage that is obviously worthy of further analysis; here I want to call your attention to Greenberg's complex olfactory schema, which has all the trappings of a racist taxonomy of aesthetic discrimination. But smell, for Greenberg, is less "an index of character" than of cultural positioning within the socioeconomic field that then opens onto various subjective horizons of possibility, as well as onto questions about the relation between the various senses in any act of aesthetic appraisal, despite his public privileging of the optical above all in engaging works of art.[14]

Our eventual turn to Pindell will occasion an undoing of such racio-aesthetic schemas. Here I simply want to note how English keeps his distance from such productive complications, especially those stemming from the dynamics of gender, to say nothing of modeling an intersectional approach to the manifestation of those dynamics in the aesthetic and cultural fields.[15] Thus, unsurprisingly, his narrative does not consider the ways that African diasporic women's cultural practices may inform, intersect with, or intervene in what he construes as the modernist tradition: while Alma Thomas is spared a few lines, English barely engages the work of black women abstract artists such as Pindell and Barbara Chase-Riboud. It must be said, however, that English is not alone in this regard; indeed, his oversight is symptomatic: in the historical recovery of black abstract artists, it is men and their formal innovations—Jack Whitten was painting with a squeegee years before Gerhard Richter, *Artforum* reminds us!—that have garnered the lion's share of interest both from critics and the market, since their practices can often be more easily mobilized to justify rather than challenge the modernist canon.[16]

Now, thankfully, further work is being done to unearth, celebrate, and reframe the work of black women abstract artists. One exhibition mounted in 2018 is particularly worthy of note: *Magnetic Fields: Expanding American Abstraction, 1960s to Today*, curated by Erin Dziedzic and Melissa Messina for the Kemper Museum of Contemporary Art in Kansas City, a revelatory display of work by twenty-one black women abstractionists, many of whom were being shown in a museum context for the very first time despite having active careers since the 1960s. These artists included figures such as Mildred Thompson, whose white-on-white relief constructions of found wood beg to be considered both in their own right and in relation to the white monochromes of the late Robert Ryman, as well as to the black-on-black sculptural assemblages of the white artist Louise Nevelson.[17]

This and other intergenerational exhibitions are welcome interventions, to be sure: they not only continue Gibson's work of righting the historical record in her 1997 book, *Abstract Expressionism: Other Politics*, but also expand what might be found at the intersection of blackness, the feminine, and the aesthetic.[18] As such, the catalog accompanying *Magnetic Fields* tends to focus on historical overviews and biographical accountings, as is perhaps befitting a discourse still in various minds about itself; as Brent Hayes Edwards argued about the black anthologies of the 1930s that crisscrossed the Atlantic, such initiatives serve not so much to confirm as to found the traditions they ostensibly document, with all the risks of exclusion and simplification such a process entails.[19] Consider the curator Valerie Cassel Oliver's essay in the *Magnetic Fields* catalog, which argues that black women abstract artists "have eschewed figuration to construct new visual languages around corporeal representation" aimed at "reconstitut[ing] the whole of blackness."[20] These lines are wonderfully suggestive, and we shall return to them as well in order to explore how Cassel Oliver's conceptual framework might be further operationalized as black feminist praxis.

III

With this mapping of the discursive terrain in view, we have now arrived at the heart of the matter: What would it mean to develop a black feminist materialist approach to late twentieth-century American abstraction—regardless of the identity of its maker—that pays heed to, indeed, takes it stance *from*, an understanding of the political, ontological, and visual predication of African diasporic women in the modern world? Can we develop criteria of aesthetic evaluation based not on the achievements of an inherently racist, sexist, homophobic and patriarchal canon but instead stemming from the assumption that—given the necessary imbrication of the formal and the social, the artwork and the world—the historical positionality of black women is uniquely situated to open onto the most radical of political and aesthetic commitments, whatever form that they might take?

In cobbling together my own framework of analysis, which I am calling, for lack of a better phrase, black feminist materialist, I have found it useful to revise my own previous engagements with certain theoretical, artistic, and discursive touchstones, particularly those held out by African diasporic women's various forms of cultural practice. As perhaps goes without saying, in the history of the modern world, roughly from the fifteenth century to the present, no figure or site has been so constitutively and consistently excluded from the scope of the human and the universal than the black woman, whose unassimilability as an intellecting subject within the Western socius has rendered her, to repurpose a phrase from Slavoj Žižek, "*a universal singularity*," that one who is always already consigned to the out-outside.[21]

Of course, this presumption was already articulated in the Combahee River Collective's "Black Feminist Statement" back in 1977.

> We are not just trying to fight on one front or even two, but instead to address a whole range of oppressions. We do not have racial, sexual, heterosexual, or class privilege to rely upon, nor do we have even the minimal access to resources and power that groups who possess any of these types of privilege may have. . . . We might use our position at the bottom, however, to make a clear leap into revolutionary action. If black women were free, it would mean that everyone else would have to be free since our oppression would necessitate the destruction of all the systems of oppression.[22]

This freedom, of course, must be arrived at materially and discursively both in the art world and beyond given that the black female body has long functioned as the locus of what Spillers calls "a signifying property *plus*" within Western culture since the advent of transatlantic slavery.[23] Her flesh everywhere riven, the fruits of her womb stolen, and her being reduced to a species of property, the female slave has been produced historically as a talking commodity whose shrieks of pain articulate the bases of modern capital, yet whose speech is rarely countenanced or heard.[24]

What's more, as the literary scholar Tracy Sharpley-Whiting argues, "the black woman" remains subjected to optical regimes that would empty her of particularity and imprison her within an image conjured up by someone else and imposed from without.[25] It is no wonder, then, that black women cultural practitioners have time and again aimed both to expand our conceptualization of the visual and to play off other senses of it—the haptic, the sonic, and, yes, even the olfactory, Clem!—in order to carve out spaces for some provisional autonomy given that the whole of the material world is potentially posed against them.[26] Such an understanding is central to Beckwith's essay in the magisterial retrospective catalog she coedited with Cassel Oliver.

> Visuality is obscured or deprivileged in Pindell's practice in order to foreground a somatic, or bodily, register for a work of art. . . . [W]e are challenged to think about a racial arena whose first terms are not about *seeing* the black body, but rather about *feeling it out*. If from the late 1960s (when Pindell started her professional career) through to the present, a scopic mode of social and political engagement set the terms for thinking about bodies, then we should take a retrospective look at Pindell's oeuvre to see how her work, which deprivileges the very system of seeing, disrupts our models of how seeing, knowledge, and power operate.[27]

Inimitably put. But Beckwith's approach has a much a longer history whose implications for our looking at modern and contemporary art we ought to further consider.

Just think back, as I have often done, to the ruse invented by an enslaved Harriet Jacobs and detailed in her astonishing narrative, *Incidents in the Life of a Slave Girl*: while hiding in her grandmother's attic for *seven* years, just a stone's throw away from her erstwhile master's house, Jacobs nonetheless was able to send out letters, in her own hand, that were then ferried to locations across the Eastern Seaboard and mailed back to her grandmother where she knew her old master would intercept them. In so doing, she produced an illusion of herself elsewhere as a mobile free agent to preserve her bodily autonomy even though constrained in a space hardly larger than a coffin, a paradigmatic example of using a visual conceit to hold onto the actual self. As I argue in "Flow and Arrest,"

> Produced as a readymade, fantasized as a part-object, and forced to bodily enact her own "social death," Jacobs faced, and developed means of resistance to, conditions whose structures anticipate much of what we take for granted as modernist aesthetic innovation. Viewed in this light, the most vaunted achievements of the twentieth-century Euro-American avant-garde, from Marcel Duchamp's 1917 *Fountain* to Robert Morris's 1961 *Box for Standing*, cannot help but read as aestheticized rehashings of Jacobs's survival tactics, now enacted with uncanny objects in the gallery rather than upon fleshly things on the plantation.[28]

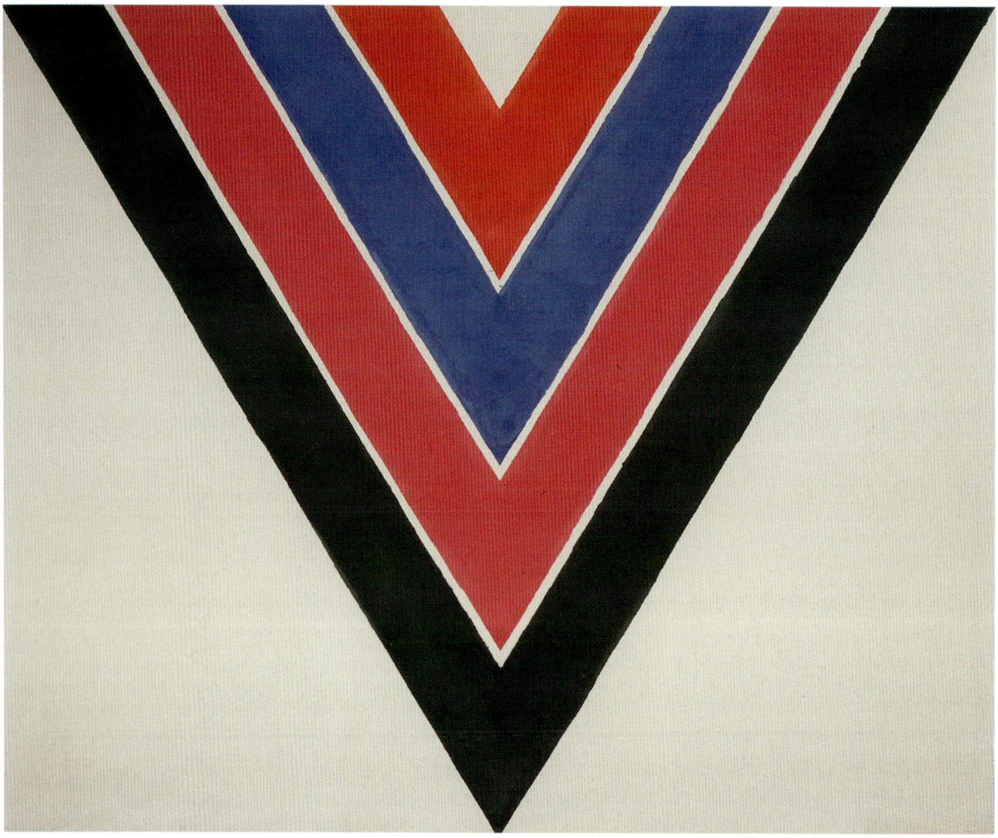

Figure 23.2
Kenneth Noland, *Shoot*, 1964. Acrylic on canvas, 103¾ × 126¾ in. (263.5 × 321.9 cm). Smithsonian American Art Museum; purchase from the Vincent Melzac Collection through the Smithsonian Institution Collections Acquisition Program (1980.5.8). © 2024 The Kenneth Noland Foundation / Licensed by VAGA at Artists Rights Society (ARS), NY. Photo: Smithsonian American Art Museum, Washington, DC / Art Resource, NY.

With Jacobs in mind and as model, we can now begin testing how these precepts might be put into practice in relation to specific works emerging from the United States in the '60s and '70s that aimed to turn vision against itself, to disrupt the kinds of despotic scopic energies directed at black female bodies.

The New York art world of that moment was witnessing what, to many, seemed to be the last gasps of late modernist abstraction, emblematized by the work of Olitski, Helen Frankenthaler, Frank Stella, and Kenneth Noland (Fig. 23.2). Their work was advanced by Greenberg and his acolyte Michael Fried as a mode of Kantian immanent critique that saw the development of each medium, whether painting or poetry, as dependent on its practitioners' ability to entrench themselves ever deeper in their area of competence and to excise all features not ontologically central to their chosen form. Thus, as we know too well, painting needed to be flat, nonillusionistic, purely optical, its fullness and extent everywhere present, almost as if graspable within a single instant of perception.[29] Few artists better exemplify this mode of painting than Noland, whose work the critic Leo Steinberg saw as possessing a "one-shot" efficiency aimed at a maximum speed of visual communication that he aligned with "design technology."[30]

The mode of looking initially solicited by Noland's work, I want to say, is that produced and abetted by capital—advertising, logos, branding—but rooted, perhaps, in the viewing of black bodies as commodities trapped in the carapace of an invented racial blackness, an abstraction that prevented them from being seen as individuals if at all. Taken together, what the rather idiosyncratic pairing of Sharpley-Whiting and Steinberg helps us understand is that the modes of looking that reduce a particular subject to a "black woman" and that allow for the apprehension of Noland's painting are undergirded by the same perceptual episteme and the same habits of looking. Vision is never neutral: it is necessarily overdetermined by the logics of race and gender. It is a sort of implicitly biased "quick-seeing," I would argue, that a black feminist materialist optics often aims to travesty, since every work of art is a proposition—not only about what it is to see and be seen, but also about *how* we should look at that which appears before us both within and beyond the frame.

IV

With *this* said, let's now look differently at Pindell, Olitski, and their contemporaries. Like English in at least this respect, in thinking the senior white artist's achievement I find myself indebted to the early work of Krauss, before *October*, the poststructuralist turn, and her necessary repudiation of Greenberg. In her catalog essay for a 1968 Jules Olitski retrospective, she declared that his art questions the frontality of Western painting and as such must be seen obliquely, requiring the viewer to navigate it temporally and spatially. In a painting like *High A Yellow* (1967) (Fig. 23.3), for instance, the edges of the canvas declare themselves emphatically in order to delineate drawing from painting and to construct separate registers of seeing, the one immediate and cognitive, the other occurring only with focused looking. In a closely related picture, *Magic Number* (1967), the clear-cut margins induct us into the center of the painting by bringing our eyes and our bodies to its sides so that we can look across the surface and begin to understand its confounding logic: what appears to be a solid yellow field when viewed frontally is seen to be impregnated with green at an angle, as if the color were casting a shadow of itself.[31]

Figure 23.3

Jules Olitski, *High A Yellow*, 1967. Acrylic and vinyl paint on canvas. Overall: 89½ × 150 in. (227.3 × 381 cm). Whitney Museum of American Art; purchase, with funds from the Friends of the Whitney Museum of American Art. Inv. N.: 68.3 © 2024 Jules Olitski Art Foundation / Licensed by VAGA at Artists Rights Society (ARS), NY. Digital image © Whitney Museum of American Art / Licensed by Scala / Art Resource, NY.

What Krauss gives us to see in Olitski, in other words, is no less than a painting both deeply corporeal and cunningly anamorphic. In this accounting, his work's demand for oblique and bodily response, rather than mere optical/frontal attention, offers a compelling visual experience that for a moment might allow us to step outside our world of instant communication, racial, gendered, or otherwise. In fact, the critical tide that would eventually damn Olitski to obscurity for decades was at least on one occasion openly articulated in ethnicizing and feminizing terms of taste. Here is one of the conservative critic Hilton Kramer's 1973 dismissals of the artist:

> The paintings to be sure, abound in pretty colors—the colors of sherbet and Indian saris and romantic sunsets—and thus have at times a certain decorative appeal. But it is the appeal of something superficial, something merely pretty. Beyond the prettiness of the color, one feels only the cold decisions and the mechanical calculations of an artist working to fulfill a narrow historical formula.[32]

Olitski thus risked his work being seen as only decorative because it was at odds with the presumptions of the tradition that he was seen to extend; or, as Kramer's criticism implies, in following Greenberg's avant-gardist prescriptions so closely, Olitski had ended up, ironically, falling into an aesthetic of kitsch.[33]

Black artists working at the same moment, however, would explicitly draw on other histories, encounters, and experiences that would enable them to disrupt quick-seeing in forwarding black feminist materialist practices that variously trafficked in: mainstream modernisms, the exigencies of life lived black in the United States, and, most important for my argument, African American women's traditions. In particular, I have in mind the stunning quilts, some still surviving from the 1920s, made by the community of women artists working for generations in Gee's Bend, Alabama, such as those of Martha Jane Pettway, whose daughter Joanna, also a quilter, describes the interleaving of life and work from which these world-making objects emerged.

> We were kind of a big family—seven sisters and five brothers. Back then we cut dresses to make quilts. Go to the field, pick cotton. Go to the gin, wrap it up, put the padding on the quilt. We just enjoyed it. This time of year, the cotton opens up. We pick cotton and go to quilting, after you finish with the cotton, you go back to quilting. All the time, something to do all the time. It isn't like it used to be. Used to have fun taking quilts from one house to the other one. Get out quilts down here, go up there, then go up that one. Quilt so many in a day. We're just sitting down thinking back about old times—how they do and what they do. And looking for days to come.[34]

Cast in this light, the quilts come to us as vital modes of individuals' creative autonomy and as material evidence of how black women collectively aimed to disrupt the imposition of what the political theorist Michael Hanchard defines as "racial time," in order to tend-toward-blackness, in the senses of both leaning into and caring for black beings.[35]

Most saliently, we might also see these quilts as ambitious modernist articulations, not only because they are made from scraps reconfigured into new patterns, but also because the very form of sociality that produced them represents a critical response, a haptic bulwark of safety, against both the cold nights and the terrors of modernity, which have time and again taken black flesh as its prime targets. These works are *necessary abstractions*, indeed, even if not "proper" ones: their hard-won aesthetic and material intelligence confound the West's production of the black woman and so enable a radical reconsideration of artistic modernism as such. A proposition, then: If, as the social historian of art T. J. Clark argues, modernism goes with socialism, because the latter "occupies the

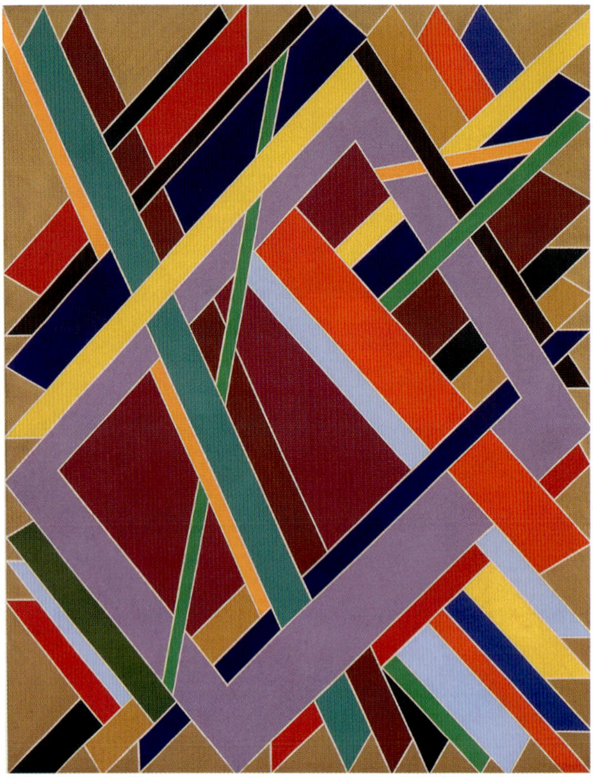

Figure 23.4
William T. Williams, *Trane*, 1969. Acrylic on canvas, 108 × 84 in. (274.3 × 213.4 cm), The Studio Museum in Harlem; gift of Charles Cowles, New York. © William T. Williams; Courtesy of Michael Rosenfeld Gallery LLC, New York, NY. Photo: Marc Bernie.

real ground on which modernity could be described and opposed," then it is black women's resistive struggles that might be placed at the heart of the modernist enterprise since they, as the sisters of Combahee remind us, have had to oppose the constitution of the world tout court without even a proper politics to call their own.[36]

Indeed, the exigencies of this battle echo both formally and materially in subsequent artists' engagements with quilting and its structures. Doubtless, the most well-known example in this genealogy is Faith Ringgold's *Slave Rape* series, a group of figurative acrylic works begun in 1973 and sewn on fabric quilted by the artist's mother, the fashion designer Willi Posey [see Fig. 20.8 on p. 275]. Yet, if we pursue the nonobjective, we could look to a trio of male artists working around the same time. William T. Williams offers us a surface engagement that takes up the patterns of quilt making and transforms them into a kind of hard-edged abstraction quite legible to a Fried and his fans (Fig. 23.4). Sam Gilliam's flirtation with quilting is also relevant if not so immediately apparent, leading him to twist and bend canvas as fabric, producing part-paintings/part-sculptures that, like the works of Eva Hesse, demand a slowed down corporeal time. Of African American male artists, Al Loving's engagement with quilting is perhaps deepest: he started his public career with hard-

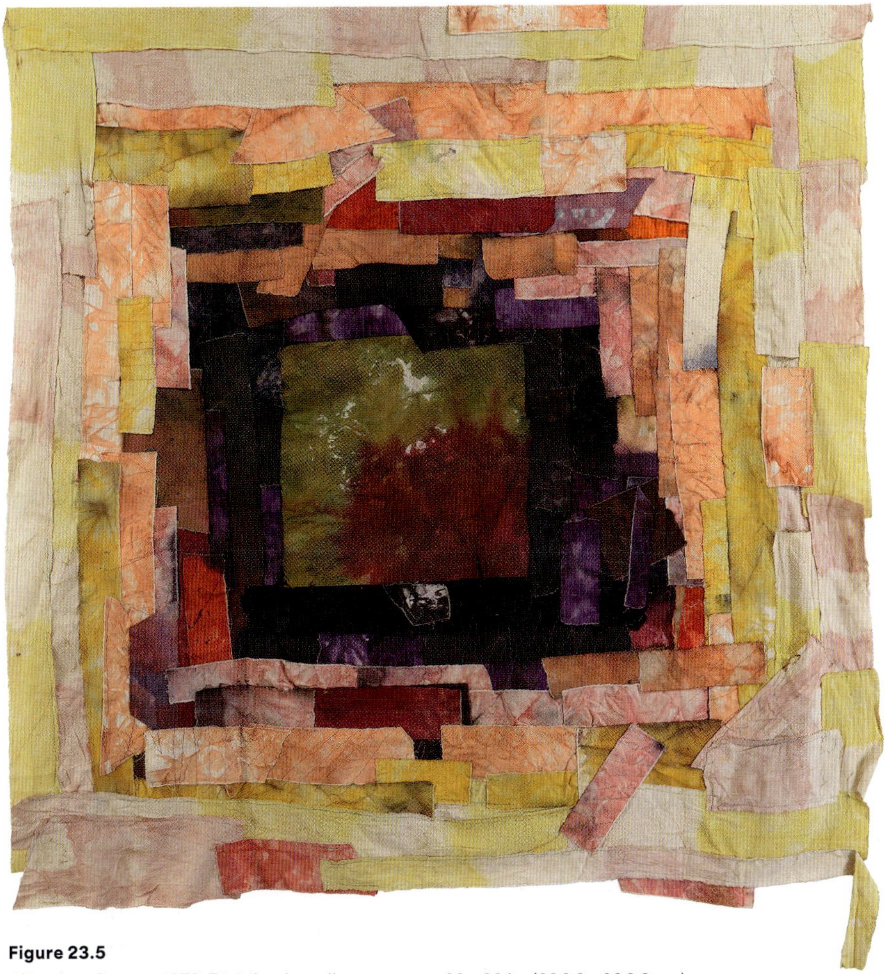

Figure 23.5

Al Loving, *Square*, 1973-74. Mixed media on canvas, 93 × 93 in. (236.2 × 236.2 cm).

edged efforts but, directly influenced by textile traditions, shifted to making works literally woven from the shreds of his own previous canvases, as if to eviscerate the very mode that brought him fame and to align himself with a black feminist material ethos (Fig. 23.5).

Just as these male practitioners give us much to see and feel, I think the operative coordinates of black women's feminist materialism are productively charted by Fred Moten in his *In the Break: The Aesthetics of the Black Radical Tradition*. Building on the work of Spillers and Saidiya Hartman, he roots that tradition in the experiences of enslaved women, so key to racial slavery and the "advances" that it made possible. For Moten, these women not only literally embody Marx's counterfactual notion in *Capital* of "if the commodity could speak . . . ," but their resistance to becoming objects also shapes every form of black radical practice. In particular, he

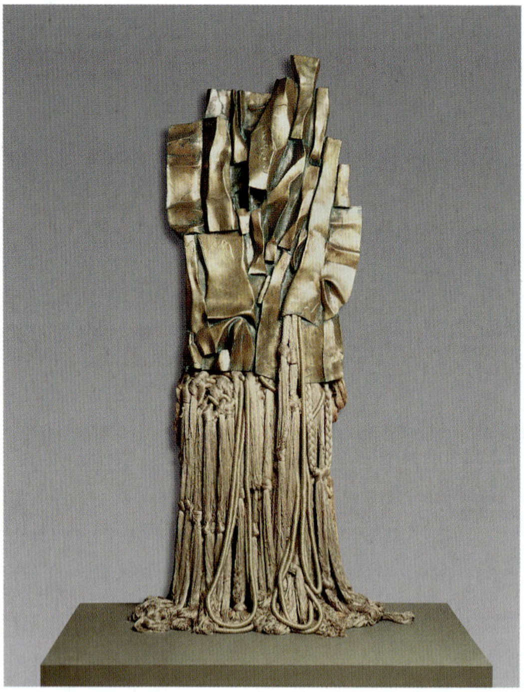

Figure 23.6
Barbara Chase-Riboud, *Malcolm × #3*, 1969. Polished cast bronze with spun artificial silk and mercerized Egyptian cotton, 8 ft. 6½ in. × 3 ft. 1 in. × 2 ft. 8 in. (260.4 × 94 × 81.3 cm). Philadelphia Museum of Art. 125th Anniversary Acquisition. Purchased with funds contributed by Regina and Ragan A. Henry, and with funds raised in honor of the 125th Anniversary of the Museum and in celebration of African American art, 2001. © Barbara Chase-Riboud.

lights upon Adrian Piper's *Untitled Performance at Max's Kansas City* (1970), in which the artist—with eyes blindfolded, hands covered, mouth closed, and nostrils pinched—aimed to produce herself as an object in an unwitting echo of the female slave's ontological status. What Piper's performance demands, for Moten, is precisely *not* the presumptions of formalist modernist criticism that posit the object as an autonomous form open to quick-seeing, but rather that emphasize the "holosensual, invaginatively ensemblic internal differentiation of the object."[37]

The phrase bears repeating: "holosensual, invaginatively ensemblic internal differentiation of the object." Which is to say, I think, that the work of art, not unlike the human body, is imagined to recruit all of the senses, to be a conjoining of disparate parts that fold in on themselves to produce a richly differentiated internal structure that demands a *feeling out*, to recall Beckwith, beyond the surface, the threshold at which a mere seeing of "the black woman" would stop and from which *deep* looking can truly begin. Moten's phrase speaks beautifully, I think, to a whole range of works, including Pindell's, but perhaps most directly to the relief sculptures of Chase-Riboud, particularly her now twenty-piece series, begun in 1968, in homage to Malcolm X (Fig. 23.6). These works suggest a logic of invagination, of a woven and worked object folding into itself, but now activated to provide testament to the internal complexities of the great black nationalist leader, often imagined as an icon of black masculinism but whom, as we know now, was more than a little queer and much more complex in his vexed positions than he is often given credit for.[38]

While Pindell's work of the 1980s would later explicitly turn to African and diasporic modes of production, her early work also manifests, I think, a black feminist materialist approach in its very facture and production.[39] Her paintings are made up of quilted squares, each covered with those tiny hole punches that are meticulously glued to canvas, creating a multiplicity of views that cannot be held all at once. What's more, Pindell occasionally sprinkled her canvases with glitter and sprayed them with perfume, creating a richly olfactory experience that not only cross wired the senses to expand what it means to look, but that also brought the base world of smells into the elevated realm of painting, which becomes a surrogate and emblem for the being of blackness in the social world.

Pindell's choice to use those hole punches, however, is perhaps the most telling: she settled on the circular form while working as a curator in the Prints and Drawings Department at New York's Museum of Modern Art between 1977 and 1980 as the requisite office supplies were easily available. This material choice was actually inspired by the artist's memories of traveling with her family in the segregated South: glasses to be used by black people were marked on their bottoms with red circles so that they would never touch white lips.[40] Pindell thus takes a basic form that has been coded as racist, materially rediscovers it in her alienating workplace, and then makes it over into a building block for a mode of abstraction that both refutes the kind of seeing required of segregationist logic and provides a means of reinvestment in her own life and practice.

Pindell's work, in other words, like each of the "late modernist" practices we have considered, differentially aims to *détourne* vision, to direct us back to the past of modern art and civil conflict, and to bring the black woman into the picture without her having to be there yet again as a site of surveillance and extraction. For is not any evocation of "the black woman" a necessary abstraction that can only asymptotically address the complexities of African diasporic women's lived experiences? Taken together, these works, following Cassel Oliver, point us to the whole of blackness without, however, hoping to contain them all.

Notes

This essay is drawn from a keynote lecture delivered in March 2019 at Dakar's Musée Théodore Monod d'Art africain as part of the "Anthropology and Contemporary Visual Arts from the Black Atlantic" seminar series spearheaded by Christoph Singler. In revising the text for publication, I have benefited from the commentary of audiences at the Musée, Harvard University, Michigan State University, the University of Pennsylvania, and Wesleyan University. For their invaluable insights on earlier drafts, I thank T. J. Clark, with whom I first thought about Olitski, Sampada Aranke, Janet Dees, Hannah Feldman, Amy Mooney, and Krista Thompson. Thanks also to Lauren Taylor and Darlene Jackson for their invaluable assistance in assembling and executing the image program.

1 Naomi Beckwith, "Body Optics, or Howardena Pindell's Ways of Seeing," in *Howardena Pindell: What Remains to Be Seen*, ed. Naomi Beckwith and Valerie Cassel Oliver (Museum of Contemporary Art Chicago, 2018), 90.

2 The next few pages replay Huey Copeland, "One-Dimensional Abstraction: Darby English, *1971: A Year in the Life of Color* (Chicago: University of Chicago Press, 2016)," *Art Journal* 78, no. 2 (Summer 2019): 116–18.

3 June Jordan, "Nobody Mean More to Me Than You and the Future Life of Willie Jordan," in *On Call: Political Essays* (South End, 1985), 129, quoted in Philip Brian Harper, *Abstractionist Aesthetics: Artistic Form and Social Critique in African American Culture* (New York University Press, 2015), 69.

4 Michele Wallace, "Modernism, Postmodernism, and the Problem of the Visual in Afro-American Culture," in *Out There: Marginalization and Contemporary Cultures*, ed. Russell Ferguson et al. (MIT Press, 1990), 41.

5 Hortense J. Spillers, "Mama's Baby, Papa's Maybe: An American Grammar Book," *Diacritics* 17, no. 2 (Summer 1987): 65.

6 Adrienne Edwards, *Blackness in Abstraction* (Pace Gallery, 2016).

7 Rosalind Krauss, quoted in Hal Foster, Rosalind Krauss, Silvia Kolbowski, Miwon Kwon, and Benjamin Buchloh, "The Politics of the Signifier: A Conversation on the Whitney Biennial," *October* 66 (Fall 1993): 9.

8 English, *1971: A Year in the Life of Color.*

9 Dawoud Bey, "Ironies of Diversity, or The Disappearing Black Artist," 2004, artnet.com, http://www.artnet.com/magazine/features/bey/bey4-8-04.asp.

10 English's critical approach to the narration of black abstraction in *1971* is presaged by his "Review: Kobena Mercer, ed., *Discrepant Abstraction*," *caa.reviews*, October 7, 2008, http://www.caareviews.org/reviews/1171#.XFm1_C2ZPOQ. He makes clear his debt to Bey in "Darby English and David Breslin on *1971: A Year in the Life of Color*," January 9, 2017, https://whitney.org/WatchAndListen/516?series=45.

11 English, *1971*, 27.

12 English, *1971*, 13, 7. See Ann Eden Gibson, *The Search for Freedom: African American Abstract Painting, 1945–1975* (Kenkeleba Gallery, 1991).

13 "Letter from Clement Greenberg to Frank Bowling, December 10, 1975," in *Frank Bowling: Mappa Mundi*, ed. Okwui Enwezor (Haus der Kunst and Prestel Verlag, 2017), 232–33.

14 See Clement Greenberg, "Modernist Painting" (1960), in *Clement Greenberg: The Collected Essays and Criticism*, vol. 4, *Modernism with a Vengeance, 1957–1969*," ed. John O'Brian (University of Chicago Press, 1986), 85–94.

15 On intersectionality, a critical approach developed by the legal scholar Kimberlé Crenshaw in the late 1980s that centers black women given their structural positionality, see Leslie McCall, "Toward a Field of Intersectionality Studies: Theory, Application, and Praxis," *Signs: Journal of Women in Culture and Society* 38, no. 4 (2013): 785–510.

16 Michelle Kuo, "Artist's Portfolio: Jack Whitten," *Artforum*, February 2012, https://www.artforum.com/print/201202/artist-s-portfolio-jack-whitten-30076.

17 Erin Dzeidzic and Melissa Messina, eds., *Magnetic Fields: Expanding Abstraction, 1960s to Today* (Kemper Museum of Contemporary Art, 2017).

18 Ann Eden Gibson, *Abstract Expressionism: Other Politics* (Yale University Press, 1997).

19 Brent Hayes Edwards, *The Practice of Diaspora: Literature, Translation, and the Rise of Black Internationalism* (Harvard University Press, 2009), 44.

20 Valerie Cassel Oliver, "Kindred: Materializing Representation in the Abstract," in Dzeidzic and Messina, *Magnetic Fields*, 50.

21 Here I follow James Bliss, "Hope Against Hope: Queer Negativity, Black Feminist Theorizing, and Reproduction Without Futurity," *Mosaic* 48, no. 1 (March 2015): 89, emphasis in original; the quoted phrase derives from Slavoj Žižek, *In Defense of Lost Causes* (Verso, 2008), 17.

22 The Combahee River Collective, "A Black Feminist Statement" (1977), in *All the Women Are White, All the Blacks Are Men, But Some of Us Are Brave: Black Women's Studies*, ed. Gloria T. Hull, Patricia Bell Scott, and Barbara Smith (Feminist Press, 1982), 18.

23 Spillers, 65; emphasis in original.

24 This line is culled from Huey Copeland, "Feasting on Scraps," *Small Axe: A Caribbean Journal of Criticism*, no. 38 (July 2012): 210; its approach to the speech of the commodity is informed by Fred Moten, "Resistance of the Object: Aunt Hester's Scream," in *In the Break: The Aesthetics of the Black Radical Tradition* (University of Minnesota Press, 2003), 1–24.

25 T. Denean Sharpley-Whiting, *Black Venus: Sexualized Savages, Primal Fears, and Primitive Narratives in French* (Duke University Press, 1999), 10.

26 For further elaboration on this score, see Huey Copeland, "In the Wake of the Negress," in *Modern Women: Women Artists at the Museum of Modern Art*, ed. Cornelia Butler and Alexandra Schwartz (Museum of Modern Art, 2010), 480–97 [reprinted in this volume, 265–85].

27 Beckwith, "Body Optics," 90; emphasis in original.

28 Huey Copeland, "Flow and Arrest," *Small Axe: A Caribbean Journal of Criticism* 19 no. 3 (48) (November 2015): 220 [reprinted in this volume, 287-309].

29 Greenberg, "Modernist Painting"; Michael Fried, "Art and Objecthood" (1967), in *Minimal Art: A Critical Anthology*, ed. Gregory Battcock (E. P. Dutton & Co., 1968), 116–47.

30 Leo Steinberg, *Other Criteria: Confrontations with Twentieth-Century Art* (Oxford University Press, 1975), 79.

31 Rosalind Krauss, *Jules Olitski: Recent Paintings* (Institute of Contemporary Art, University of Pennsylvania, 1968), n.p.

32 Hilton Kramer, "Jules Olitski: A Sectarian Scenario," *New York Times*, September 16, 1973, 25, https://www.nytimes.com/1973/09/16/archives/jules-olitski-a-sectarian-scenario.html.

33 On the presumed foundational antagonism between the two terms, see Clement Greenberg, "Avant-Garde and Kitsch," in *Art and Culture: Critical Essays* (Beacon Press, 1961), 3–22; as well as their vital recasting in T. J. Clark, "Clement Greenberg's Theory of Art," *Critical Inquiry* 9, no. 1 (September 1982): 139–56.

34 Joanna Pettway, https://www.soulsgrowndeep.org/artist/joanna-pettway.

35 "Racial time is defined as the inequalities of temporality that result from power relations between racially dominant and subordinate groups." See Michael Hanchard, "Afro-Modernity: Temporality, Politics, and the African

Diaspora," *Public Culture* 11, no. 1 (January 1999): 220; Huey Copeland, "Tending-Toward-Blackness," *October* 156 (Spring 2016): 141–44.

36 T. J. Clark, Introduction to *Farewell to an Idea: Episodes from a History of Modernism* (Yale University Press, 1999), 7.

37 Fred Moten, "Resistance of the Object: Adrian Piper's Theatricality," in *In the Break*, 235.

38 See Manning Marable, *Malcolm X: A Life of Reinvention* (Penguin, 2011).

39 See, for example, Howardena Pindell, "The Aesthetics of Texture in African Adornment," in *The Heart of the Question: The Writings and Paintings of Howardena Pindell* (Midmarch Arts Press, 1997), 84–86.

40 Sarah Cowan, "Clearly Seen: A Chronology," in Pindell, *Howardena Pindell*, 33.

24

"I AM A MAN" AND THE WRITING OF AFROTROPIC ART HISTORIES

In the pages that follow, I want to think critically, visually, and self-reflexively with you about the modes of writing that certain strands of African American cultural production, it seems to me, at once demand and enable. What I hope to stage is one approach to art historical writing that aims to make vivid the constitutive entanglements in life and research that produce artworks, subjects, and political possibilities in what Saidiya Hartman has called the "afterlife of slavery."[1] To do so, I engage a chain of works: Glenn Ligon's *Condition Report* of 2000 (Fig. 24.1); the piece to which the *Report* refers, his *Untitled (I Am a Man)* painting of 1988 [see Fig. 2.2 on p. 29], one of Ligon's earliest published works to focus so intently on language; and, of course, the sign itself, captured most memorably in the African American photographer Ernest Withers's image of striking Memphis sanitation workers taken on March 29, 1968, outside of Clayborn Temple [see Fig. 2.1 on p. 28].

Forming an unforgettable frieze, the men and their posters, which obscure the faces of all but those of the protesters in the very front, are several rows deep in a line that stretches the width of the frame, bracketed above by sky, building, and trees and anchored below by the street on which they gather. As Ligon tells it, he first saw one of the placards depicted in this now-iconic image of the US civil rights movement when he visited the offices of New York congressman Chuck Rangel in the late 1970s, only to return to the sign time and again in his practice.[2] Much the same can be said of my own relationship to the artist and this work, with and about which I have been writing, wrestling, and thinking for more than twenty-five years. Indeed, the various connections that link me to Ligon and his practice are notable insofar as they serve to illustrate how his art has served as a model of thinking and being that at once accommodates and enables various modes of engagement between subjects, objects, dis-

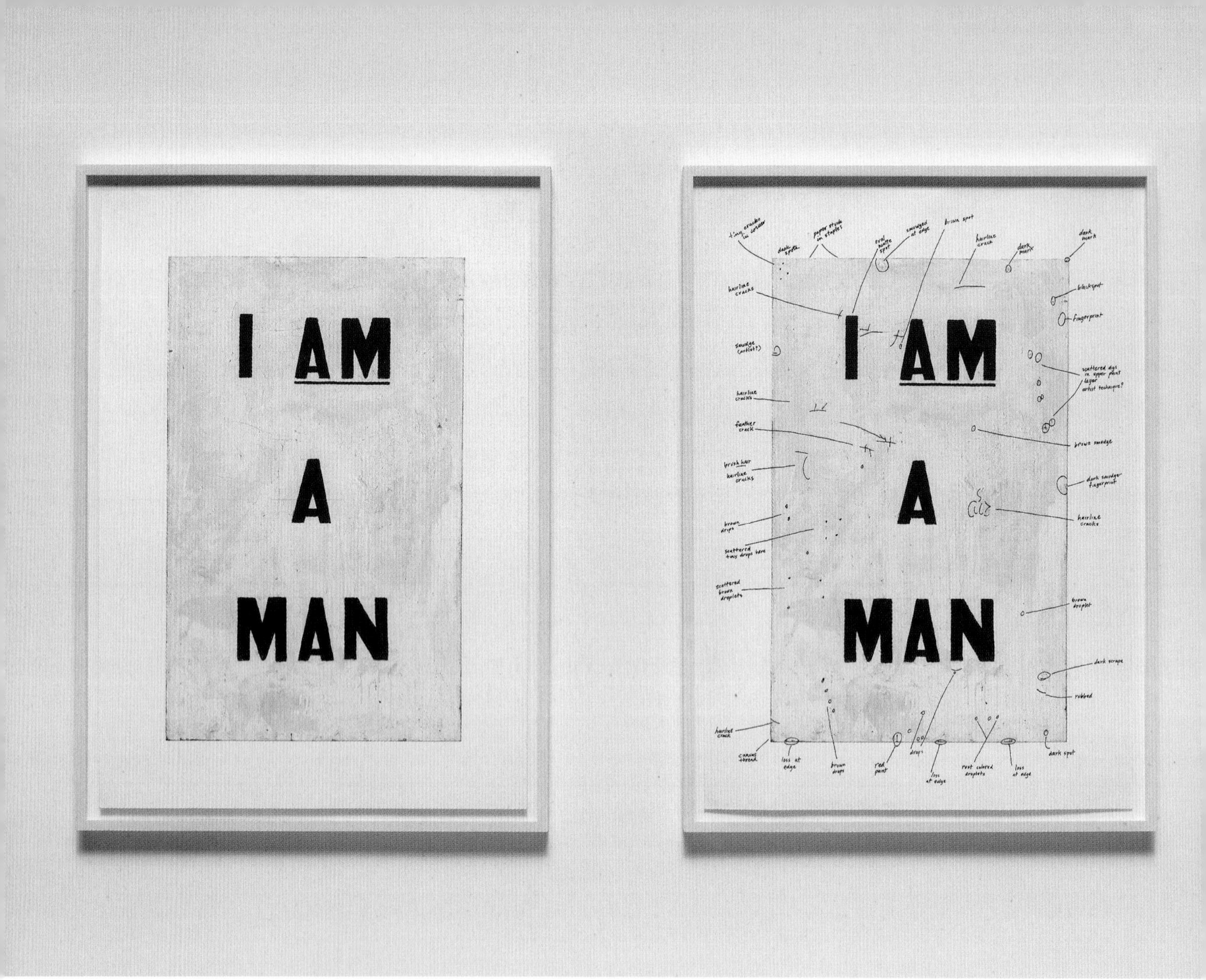

Figure 24.1

Glenn Ligon, *Condition Report*, 2000. Iris print and iris print with serigraph; diptych, each 32 × 22¾ in. (81.3 × 57.8 cm); edition of 20 and 7 Aps. Photographer credit: Ronald Amstutz. © Glenn Ligon; Courtesy of the artist, Hauser & Wirth, and Thomas Dane Gallery.

courses, and the worlds encompassing them.

Take three possible points along my own continuum. A poster of Withers's image, a gift from my father on the publication of my first book—in which Ligon plays a starring role—still hangs in my office.[3] The artist's *Condition Report* took pride of place in *Encore*, a 2007 exhibition on returns of the 1960s in contemporary art that I co-curated at Chicago's gallery 40000 with my colleague Hannah Feldman. And a gift from Glenn, the slyly erotic *Coming and Going* of 1996, now resides at home alongside an oblique portrait by the Canadian video artist Steve Reinke (Fig. 24.2). In Ligon's silkscreen diptych, presented to me the year of its execution and just a few

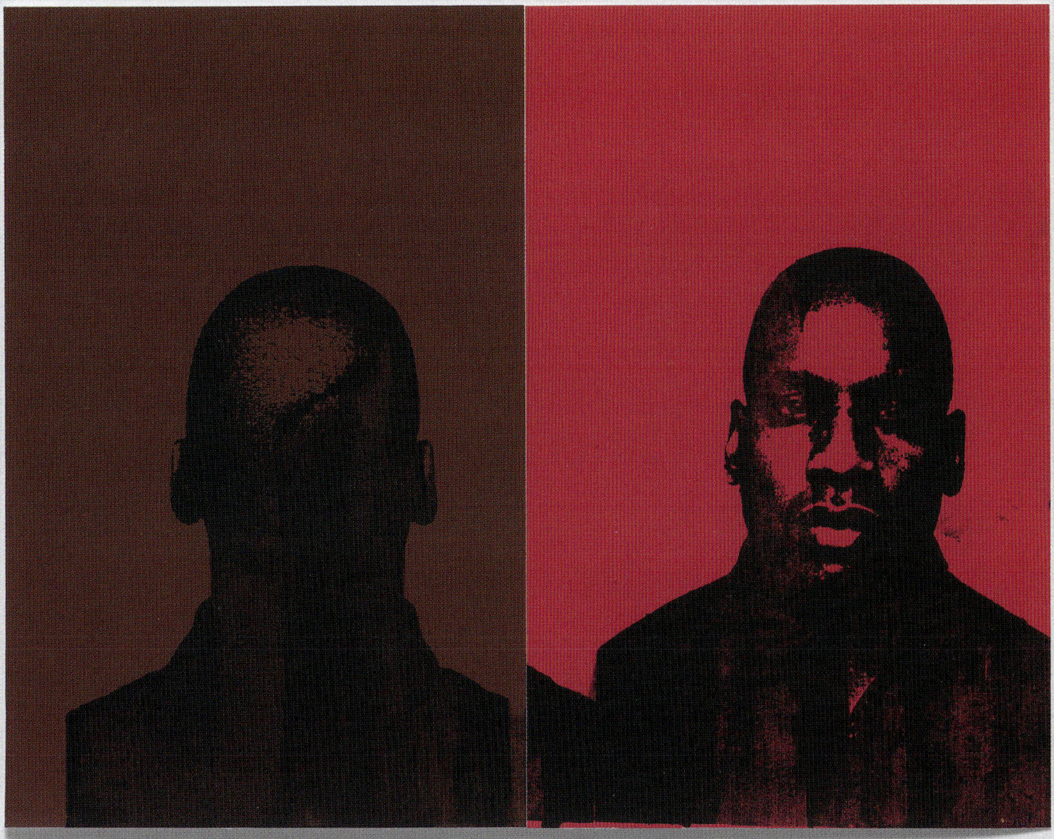

Figure 24.2
Glenn Ligon, *Coming and Going*, 1996. Two sheets of silkscreen on color aid paper mounted on card, 11½ × 12 in. (29 × 30.5 cm). Photography credit: Ronald Amstutz. © Glenn Ligon; Courtesy of the artist, Hauser & Wirth, and Thomas Dane Gallery.

days before I returned to college in Ann Arbor after a summer interning in New York City, the artist gives two images of himself, each perfectly scaled for a passport photograph: on the left, the back of his head is rendered in black against a sumptuous brown field; on the right, his darkly inked visage stares out from a hot pink ground. Here front and back appear together, a doubling that likewise pairs absence and presence, refusal and return, type and portrait, departure and arrival, sex and death, all simultaneously coming into and going out of view.

I offer such testimony in order to underline not only how Ligon's art often functions *en abîme*, continually recalling and remediating its various referents, but to illuminate how his works can operate as spurs to any number of analytic modes, affective registers, networked histories, and personal encounters, those ephemeral experiences and states of mind that all too often fall out of "proper" art historical narration but that can be vital to critically exploring the grounds *and* limits of our scholarly approaches. Such concerns have long animated my praxis and my attempt to model an approach to art writing and to humanistic inquiry broadly construed that both takes seriously the pressures African/diasporic cultures put on disciplinary conventions and acknowledges my own imbrication in the production of disciplinary knowledge.

The art history I am after, then, is black, queer, feminist, situated, and material. As such, it is generatively discrepant in the poet Nathaniel Mackey's sense of a practice that "in the interest of opening presumably closed orders of identity and signification, accent[s] fissure, fracture, incongruity, the rickety imperfect fit between word and world."[4] In this instance, I take inspiration from the critic Kobena Mercer's writing on Robert Mapplethorpe's photographs of black men: his two essays, subsequently grouped together under the title, "Reading Racial Fetishism," record contrasting takes on the artist at two very different yet proximate historical moments. Mercer revised his scathing 1986 feminist critique of Mapplethorpe's white male gaze just three years later, in the context of the US "culture wars," both to distinguish his critical voice from those of bigoted conservatives and to think more seriously about his own implication as a desiring gay male subject in the actual and imagined queer networks that the photographs document and produce.[5] My aim here, however, is not so much to repudiate my own previous readings as to hold them in tension and, in so doing, to articulate the shifting contexts and conditions that have informed my various engagements with Ligon and his work as well as its ostensible sources. This approach, if not its autoethnographic expansion, is anticipated art historically by Reva Wolf's *Andy Warhol, Poetry, and Gossip in the 1960s*, which explores how works of art serve as means of explicit and illicit communication with varying valences for differently positioned individuals and publics in mid- to late twentieth-century American culture.[6]

With that interpretive horizon in view, I now want to begin contextualizing Ligon's work in fairly conventional terms, if only to eventually turn them out. For starters, *Condition Report* can be understood as an instance of the ways that artists continue to historically extend and affectively refashion procedures associated with the aesthetic tendencies of appropriation and institutional critique, the twin subjects of the 2014 exhibition *Take It or Leave It: Institution, Image, Ideology*, which was curated by Johanna Burton and Anne Ellegood for the Hammer Museum in Los Angeles. Leaving aside canonical white male figures such as Michael Asher, the curators instead foregrounded the pioneering efforts of gay artists like Ligon and white feminist practitioners such as Dara Birnbaum, whose *PM Magazine* of 1982 graced the cover of the catalog. Through such moves, Burton and Ellegood aimed to suggest that the most trenchant modes of conceptual practice are anything but dry, didactic, or exclusively white male enterprises whose implications stop short of the museum's entrance.[7]

Ellegood's invitation to speak briefly at the symposium, "Acts of Politics and Becoming," which marked the closing of *Take It or Leave It*, spurred my return to Ligon's *Report*, which, in its way, also insists on the belonging together of appropriation and institutional critique. The work mimes the museum's protocols for evaluating the material status of art objects by turning them on one of the artist's own paintings, which he has gifted to Washington, DC's National Gallery of Art. Yet like much of Ligon's practice, the twenty iterations of the *Condition Report* also intimate a kind of extensibility into the social field, creating links between art institutions, black subjects, and the varying sociopolitical conditions inflecting each at a given moment.

For now, let us attend a bit more closely to the thing itself, comprising two framed prints, each about 81 by 58 centimeters. The form on which the work relies, the museum condition report, is a vital administrative tool used in tracking and recording objects, whether in storage or on loan for traveling exhibitions. For example, the second page of the condition report on *Condition Report* completed by the staff at the Hammer Museum notes, among other things, that the left panel has an "accretion on plexi" (Fig. 24.3). Since the days of Dorothy Dudley—the first registrar at the Museum of Modern Art, New York—the condition report has become a somewhat standardized form, with a complex lexicon of its own undergirded by a shared set of techniques for the handling, storage, and physical assessment of artwork. But we should remember that storage and display conditions vary from one institution to another, as do the looking habits of their staffs, discrepancies that are exacerbated by the different technologies of reproduction in Ligon's work.[8] His prints index these contingencies, building them into the very structure of the piece, since there is damage—say, the "rubbed" area noted on the right—that is obscured by the very mark pointing toward it and that would otherwise seem invisible when seen in reproduction.

These formal choices and the piece itself, so the story goes, began with a conversation: Ligon asked a conservator friend to make a condition report on his aging *Untitled* (*I Am a Man*) canvas, which has always had a weathered look, thanks, in part, to the artist's decision to layer the visibly white oil painted surface over an earlier black quasi-abstract floral painting—revealed through x-ray technology by the Gallery's conservators—before finally applying the letters in black enamel. *Condition Report* extends and hyperbolizes this process of imagistic mediation: both prints stem from color Xeroxes that were then digitally scanned and printed using the Iris process, which has fallen out of favor as it does not possess the same archi-

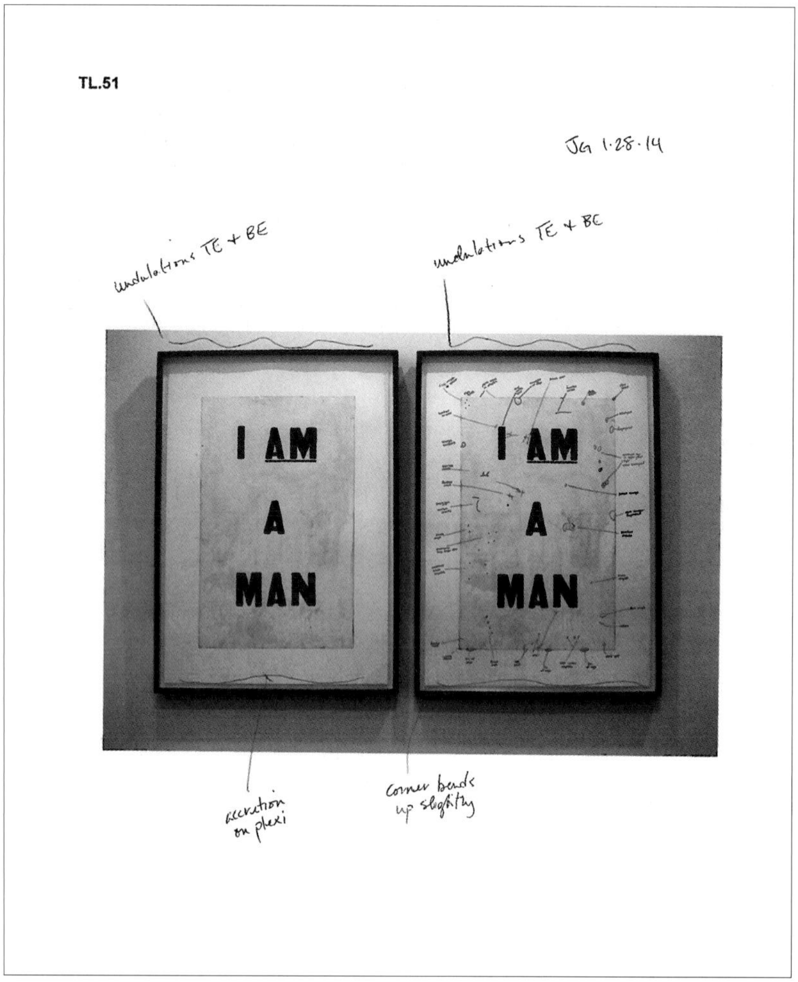

Figure 24.3
Hammer Museum Condition Report, 2014. © Hammer Museum.

val stability as more recent technologies. The portion of the diptych that bears the conservator's commentary has been additionally silkscreened with the notations we see—all those dark or brown spots, smudges, scrapes, and droplets—that cannot help but bring up a metaphorics of race and class given the source of the work. We would be wise to note, however, that each of these annotative processes, in focusing on the frontal surface of the image, leaves out—indeed, becomes a surrogate for—the materiality of the painting itself, which is nothing if not a particular, contingent, and surprisingly colorful object, especially if seen from its jury-rigged back (Fig. 24.4).

All of this makes a certain sense given the surrogative logic that animates so much of Ligon's practice. As the art historian Richard Meyer

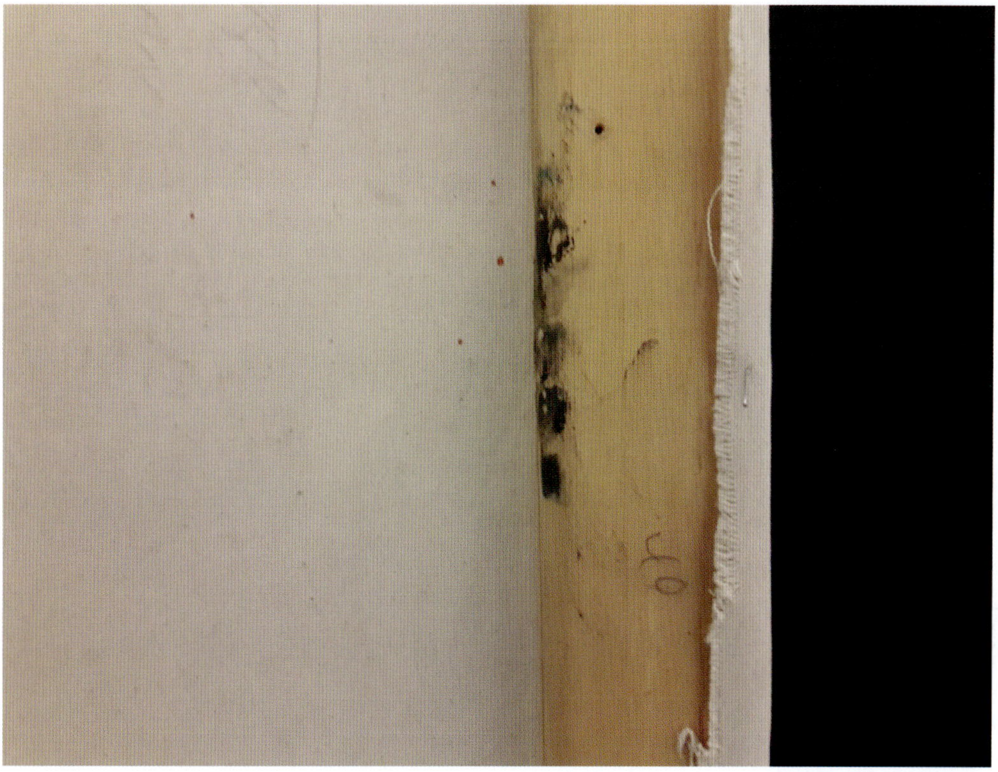

Figure 24.4
Glenn Ligon, *Untitled (I Am a Man)*, detail, 1988. Photography by the author.

reminds us, because of the numerous levels of representation at play in the *Report*, the artist might be said to simultaneously court and detain the direct conflation of black bodies, dark marks, and artistic objects.[9] In the 2005 catalog essay, "Untitled (Jackpot!)," my very first stab at the genre, I argued that Ligon's appropriation of the sanitation workers' sign is meant to further emphasize the doubt created by the assertion itself. Here is what I wrote:

> When he turned to Withers's iconic image exactly twenty years after it was taken, artist Glenn Ligon chose as his subject the sign. . . . In this revision, Ligon has subtly altered the Memphis poster's line breaks ["I AM / A MAN"], so rather than reading as a compact two-tiered mass that proposes an indisputable link between subject and object—"I" and "MAN"—in this untitled work, that lonesome central "A" becomes the thread that holds the sentence and the composition together ["I AM / A / MAN"]. It is as if in momentarily staving off the final word, the artist wants to emphasize that manhood, whatever it might be, is necessarily unstable and never assured.[10]

Ligon's apparent queering of the poster, created in the thick of the AIDS crisis, I argued, put pressure on ideas of who might be included within the scope of the sign's assertion in the present. In returning to Ligon's painting more than a decade later, the "alteration" of the poster has turned me back to the place and time of its earliest manifestations and thus to other histories, archives, and subjects rarely given pride of place within art historical accountings, including my own.

The historical record is illuminating. The majority of the I AM A MAN posters—two batches of around 500 each—were produced by the Memphis outfit Wimmer Brothers Fine Printing and Lithography at the behest of their comrades in the local union. However, according to the organizer James Epps, another 300 to 400 posters were made in the Clayborn Temple print shop under the direction of the minister Malcolm Blackburn, the Reverend James Lawson, and union executive, William Lucy. The uncertainty surrounding the poster's production is amplified further when one seeks to understand who, in fact, came up with the "I Am a Man" slogan. One story—now partially legitimated by the plaque in front of the home of the sanitation worker Joe Warren—is that the idea was generated by Warren and Blackburn there on site. But where did the phrase come from? Some commentators argue that it was meant to recall musical tracks, from Muddy Waters's "Mannish Boy" to Bo Diddley's even more proximate, "I'm a Man," both songs released in 1955, the year that the Chicago native Emmett Till was gruesomely murdered while visiting relatives in Mississippi. Others claim that the phrase was a reference to a speech made by Lawson, while Warren himself claims to have written a poem containing the declaration, "I am a man," in the early 1950s.[11] With so many of the original actors now passed on, deciding on which narrative to believe seems arbitrary at best if not altogether beside the point: taken together, these various claims manifest "a collective intelligence," to borrow the scholar Cedric Robinson's phrase, that underlines a multivocal demand for the recognition of black "manhood," locally and nationally, by folks both renowned and unsung in the face of a virulently racist political and visual culture.[12] Memphis was, after all, a city that still looked back nostalgically to the days of the plantation, leading to the erection of a monument to Jefferson Davis in Confederate Square in *1964*, the year the Civil Rights Act was made law.

On the fateful day in March 1968 when the protesters gathered before the temple, the signs they held up functioned apotropaically, which is to say, as a means of warding off scopic and physical violence. And to be sure, means of defense were needed. The workers had gathered yet again to protest segregation, low wages, and obscene mistreatment, emblematized by the city sanitation department's callous reaction to the deaths of Echol Cole and Robert Walker, who were crushed by a malfunctioning garbage truck the previous month. In fact, the I AM MAN posters would be attached to heavy sticks so that they might serve to protect the folks brandishing them should the National Guard renew its attacks; and while the signs obscured many of the faces of those that carried them, in retrospect, this too was a useful move.[13] As was revealed by *The New York Times* in 2010, Withers, who took this image and so many other celebrated depictions of the civil rights movement, was employed as an informant by the FBI to keep tabs on figures such as Martin Luther King Jr., who was assassinated in Memphis not long after the I AM A MAN photograph was taken.[14]

Despite its newly vexed status, the image remains a stunning record of solidarity and visual dissent, a literal enactment of what the psychoanalyst Jacques Lacan called the subject's "fading" before the signifier. In his accounting, becoming human means acceding to language's role as a mediator between one's being and the world; to be a man is to fade before the linguistic sign "man."[15] Thus, in placing the placards before themselves, the marchers do not merely accede to language; they perform their own canny and poignant act of critical aesthetic practice. On the one hand, I would contend, their statement recasts the interrogative, "Am I not a Man and a Brother?," placed in the mouths of slaves by eighteenth-century abolitionists and later taken up by Ligon himself in an untitled 1989 drawing; on the other, their gesture rhymes with those of cultural practitioners of various stripes who would use language to obfuscate the ruses of phantasmatic projection and so question the visual processes through which difference is produced, managed, and delineated in the United States.

Of course, the protesters' declaration and Ligon's citation of it are imbricated in broader economies of resistance and self-making, especially those employed by African diasporic cultural practitioners since the 1960s. These tactics demonstrate particular densities in relation to certain visual formations, from the cult of Anastácia in Brazil, which developed in the 1970s around a nineteenth-century lithograph of an enslaved woman, to the famous 1967 photograph composed by Eldridge Cleaver of an armed and enthroned Huey Newton, which has inspired countless followers to have themselves pictured in that ubiquitous wicker chair. It is just such resonant images that my colleague Krista Thompson and I have come to term "afrotropes," which we define as visual forms that recur across time and space in the African diaspora, influencing how black subjects imagine themselves and negotiate technologies of visual transmission. Whereas Krista's work on the afrotropic returns of Ivanhoe Martin, the Jamaican outlaw who inspired the 1972 cult film *The Harder They Come*, entails negotiating archival absence, the "I AM A MAN" sign means working through a kind of material excess. These two kinds of polarity—between the "South" and the "North," the centrifugal and the centripetal—should not, however, be thought of as a pair of binary oppositions; rather, they lay out the endpoints of the spectra that afrotropes shuttle between, through, and within as they complete their circuits in and out of a contingent visibility. As con-

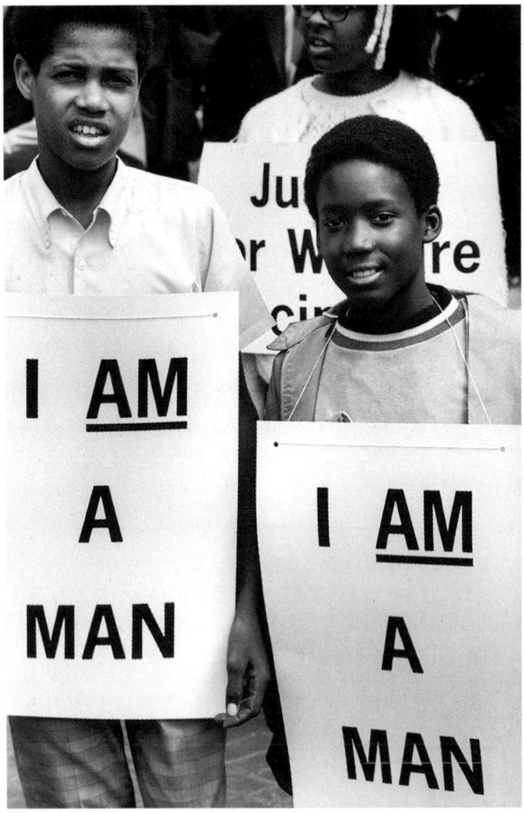

Figure 24.5
Flip Schulke, *Boys Carrying Signs at King Speech*, 1968. Photo by © Flip Schulke/CORBIS/Corbis via Getty Images.

cept and operation, the afrotrope underlines the importance of collaboration in the emergence of alternative knowledges.[16]

With these insights at hand, let us now return to the poster so as to reconfigure our approach to its temporal unfolding, material transmutation, and historical resonance in order to better understand the broader cultural field that it engenders. Check out this black-and-white picture that the photojournalist Flip Schulke took in March 1968, (Fig. 24.5). The image depicts two boys of African descent: one holds a copy of the sign in his hands before him; the other smiles brightly, the poster hanging by a string around his neck. Their placards are printed in a different font from that pictured in Withers's image but with *precisely* the same line breaks that appear on Ligon's canvas ("I AM / A / MAN"). What this photograph suggests is that the origin and form of the sign have, from almost the very first, been multiple, shifting, and collectively authored. Pace Ligon's recollection in 2006, which licensed my initial interpretation, Withers's photograph may not have been his only encounter with the sign and its fellows.[17]

In other words, my long-standing relationship with Glenn and my faith in the memory of the author prevented me from reckoning with what the scholar Christina Knight has aptly termed the "shiftiness"—archival, physical, and hermeneutic—of Ligon's art and its ostensible referents.[18] Such indeterminacy is borne out by the differing accounts Ligon has offered over the years regarding his first encounter with the sign, but despite the mercurial nature of personal memory, the fact remains that he lighted upon a far less iconic iteration of the sign's layout that was also in circulation back in '68.[19] At the same time, my bias toward the work of art over its "inspiration" led me and so many others to approach the sign as stilled material available for appropriation. Rather than merely a source for the artist, a *Venus of Urbino* for our Manet, we ought to consider the poster as itself a complex aesthetic operation always in motion whose histories continue to evolve and cannot be taken for granted.

In returning to the sign afrotropically, I have increasingly come to think about the visual cultures of the strike itself and what Feldman has productively called, with a nod to Michel de Certeau, "image tactics," in writing about the Algerian community's October 17, 1961, *manifestation* on the streets of Paris in the face of a colonially imposed curfew.[20] While Withers's photograph in Memphis presents us with a single posed instant, the strike was, of course, a series of tactical interventions that unfolded over the course of weeks across the city of which there is far less consistent and iconic visual documentation. There were marches, boycotts, sit-ins, a mock funeral for democracy held in city hall, a gospel singing marathon, and wonderfully insolent acts. My favorite was the passing of garbage cans—cheekily labeled with the last name of the city's intransigent white mayor, Henry Loeb—so that funds could be gathered to support the protesters and their families. All told, the sanitation workers' walkout lasted more than sixty-three days; its solidarity was constantly under pressure, and its members were under threat from white civic leaders, the mainstream press, and their agencies.[21] In fact, on the day Withers took his picture, rumors spread that a black female high school student, who had ditched to demonstrate, had been murdered by the police, spurring an uprising that broke out amid the peaceful protest. Martin Luther King Jr., who was leading the march, was, for the first time in his career, unable to quell the crowd's anger or their destruction of private property, which gave Mayor Loeb all the reason he needed to dispatch the National Guard and place the city under martial law. The garbage, meanwhile, kept piling up.

Thankfully for us, many of the Memphis protesters' shifting visual interventions over time are chronicled in *At the River I Stand*, an hour-long 1993 documentary by David Appleby, Allison Graham, and Steven Ross that narrates the strike using archival footage of key players and events as well as interviews with survivors like Reverend Lawson. *At the River I Stand* documents a whole host of hand-stenciled signs that articulate alternative declarations, dreams, and demands. "KEEP YOUR / MONEY / IN YOUR / POCKET," for instance, was the slogan chosen for a boycott of downtown stores designed to intensify pressure on the city's powers that be and to stoke the engagement of the black community after several other tactics had failed to bring the city's mayor to the collective bargaining table (Fig. 24.6). More provocative were the signs reading, "Watts Waited Too Late, Too," a reference to the riots of 1965 that ravaged the eponymous black Los Angeles neighborhood and made international headlines.

Yet the film too eventually homes in on the iconic poster, which is introduced with a voice-over whose rhetoric is clearly intended to telegraph the image's legendary status: "One day," recounts the narrator, "a new sign appeared on the picket line . . ." This focus on the sign parallels the film's increasing focus on King, foreshadowing his Messianic death and relegating the prime organizers of the strike to the sidelines of the overarching narrative. *At the River I Stand* not only renders the poster as a kind of analogue for King's presence but also deploys it as an index of the various stages of the strike and of its shifting economies of symbolic valuation. On the one hand, the signs ironically became trash themselves, props abandoned in the street as the National Guard bore down and the city erupted in flames (Fig. 24.7); on the other, they functioned as icons to be re-presented and re-membered photographically in the context of the nearly silent march of April 8 in the wake of King's death that betokened the end of the strike and a modicum of success for the sanitation workers' efforts, leading to the recognition of their union and increased wages.

What the film underlines, I want to argue, is that the aesthetic operations and effects on which Ligon's works rely are part and parcel of the sign's conditions of possibility from the very first, dynamics that come even more sharply into focus in exploring the Memphis Search for Meaning Committee (MSMC), Archives at the University of Memphis Special Collections, my primary access point for materials documenting the strike. This set of materials, collected and organized by the activist intellectuals David Yellin and Carol Lynn Yellin while the strike was unfolding, serves as the key archival source both for the film and for the 1985 book of the same title by Joan Beifuss on which the filmmakers drew.[22] Despite its inherent limitations, the Yellins' archive also provides fascinating evidence of how the signs were reinscribed for various purposes that exceeded their original functions and take us in other directions. The verso of one poster even read, "Restroom Downstairs," pointing to the utilitarian lives that the majority of the signs lived.[23]

On the back of another placard from the archives, this one made for the 1969 march commemorating Martin Luther King Jr.'s assassination the previous year, the simple conjoining of two male names, "Ted & Ralph," suggests a homosocial bond, a queering of the record—a coming and going, we might say—whose particulars are lost to history, yet returns us to both personal memory and archival fact (Fig. 24.8). Manhood, particularly within the framework of black intra-racial politics, was already at issue. Ligon has most recently stated that in "queering" the sign, he aimed

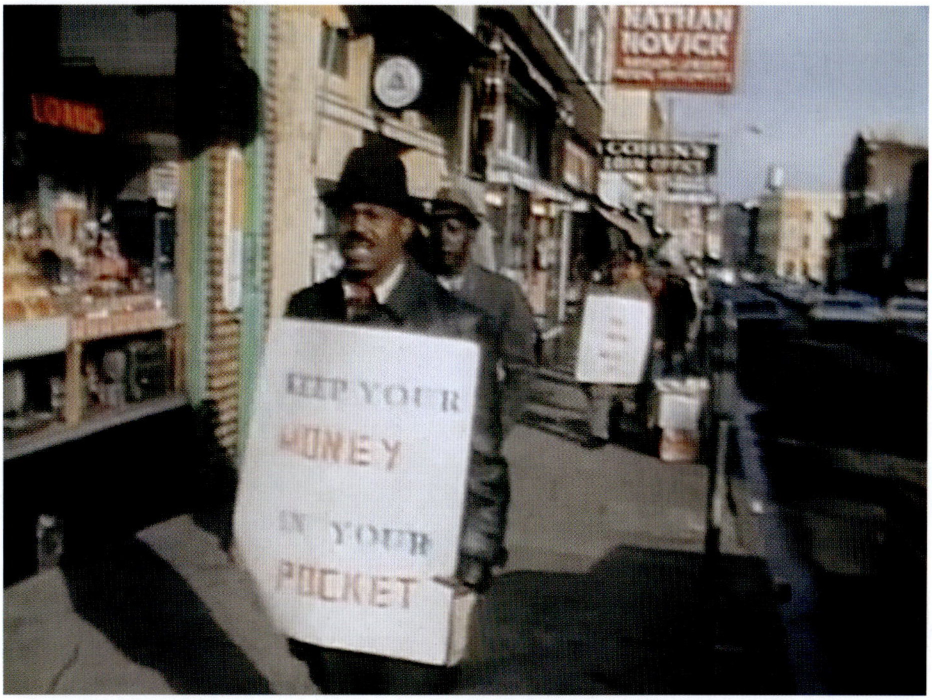

Figure 24.6
David Appleby, Allison Graham, and Steven Ross, *At the River I Stand*, still, 1993.

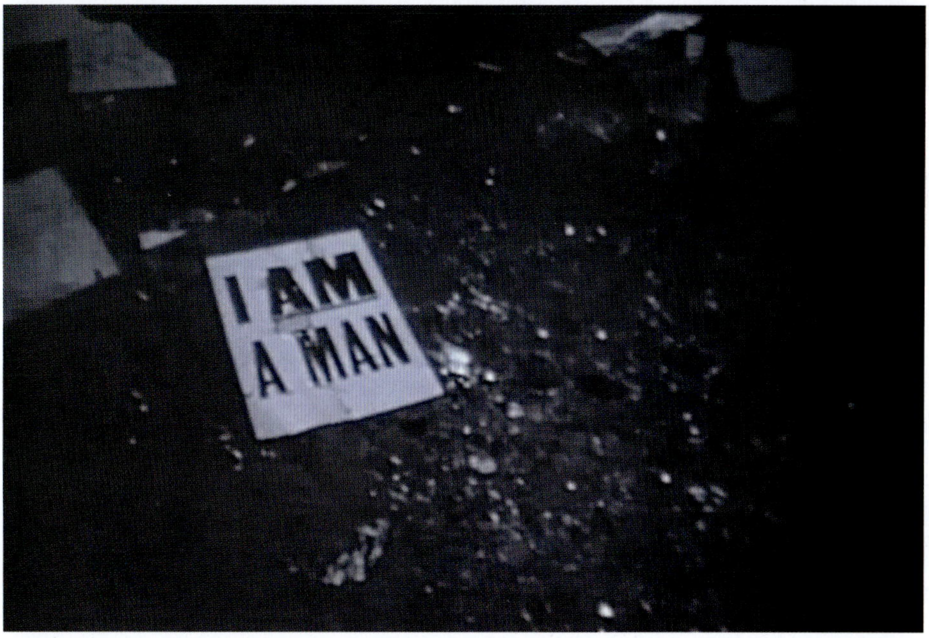

Figure 24.7
David Appleby, Allison Graham, and Steven Ross, *At the River I Stand*, still, 1993.

to bring a measure of sidelong visibility to black gay civil rights leaders such as James Baldwin and Bayard Rustin, who was by King's side on the ground in Memphis.[24] As the film's archival footage shows, for more militant protesters in '68, like Coby Smith's Black Power Invaders, none of these men was quite masculinist enough, their nonviolent tactics seen as far less effective than the threat of armed defense.

These conflicts are only asymptotically indexed by the poster. However, both the Memphis collections and Beifuss's book capture glimpses of the placard's entanglement with personal lives and histories to an unusual degree. The MSMC Archives, for instance, possess a sign that was carried by the sanitation worker Ed Gillis with whom Beifuss conducted an hour-long interview, enabling the ongoing transmission of histories in and through the body as well as on the page. Born in Savannah, Tennessee, Gillis was nearly seventy years old when he marched with the other strikers, variously carrying placards labeled "BOYCOTT" and "I AM A MAN." Over the course of his life, Gillis worked on farms, boats, and the railroad before joining the Memphis Public Works department. As he put it to Beifuss, "I joined Mr. T. O. Jones and the union in 1966 'cause we wasn't getting justice. A lot of the men were scared to join and a lot o' them wouldn't join. . . . But we had to get better satisfaction."[25]

Gillis's narrative is undeniably affecting, and I could not help myself from materializing a felt sense of historical connection to him when I visited the archives initially. In fact, I was able to hang Gillis's actual sign around my neck and, with the help of a local archivist, captured an impromptu self-portrait on my cell phone that I promptly sent along to my father. He responded with some riffs of his own on the poster via text, my favorite one—"I AM / A / HUE-MAN"—playing on both of our first names and resonating with any number of Afrocentric attempts to redefine the human in language that centers both the hue of black skin and black culture's persistent critique of Western notions of hu-manity. These connections and admissions underline the various engagements, whether in person, in the archive, or digitally mediated, that continue to shape the poster and thereby encourage an expansive approach to its art historical narration intended to reckon with the performative and networked character of black cultural production wherever it might appear.

Another photograph appeared online about a decade ago.[26] It depicted Thomas Beard, founder and director of New York's Light Industry, a venue for film, video, and electronic art. While the ostensible subject of the image is not uninteresting, my curiosity was primarily stoked by seeing a small scaled-down version of Ligon's *Untitled (I Am a Man)* painting just to the left of his head (Fig. 24.9). As soon as I noticed the piece, I reached out to my colleague Steve Reinke—my ex-boyfriend, the author of that other portrait in my living room and a friend of Beard's—who put me in touch with the curator. According to Beard, the photograph, a cal-

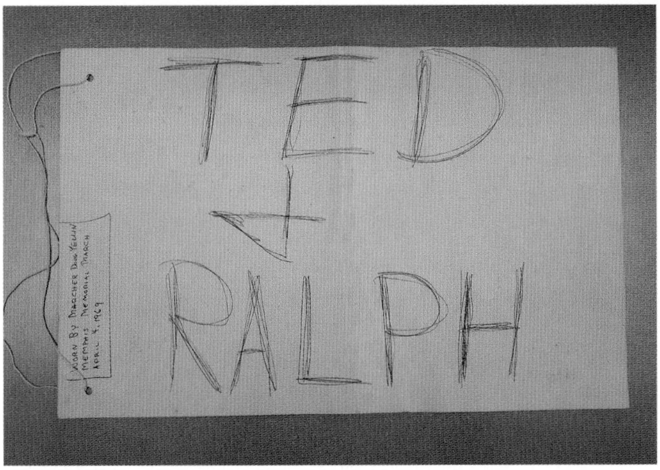

Figure 24.8
I AM A MAN poster, verso, 1968. Memphis Search for Meaning Committee Records, MSS.178, Container 52, Folder 6, Special Collections Department, University of Memphis Libraries. Photography by the author.

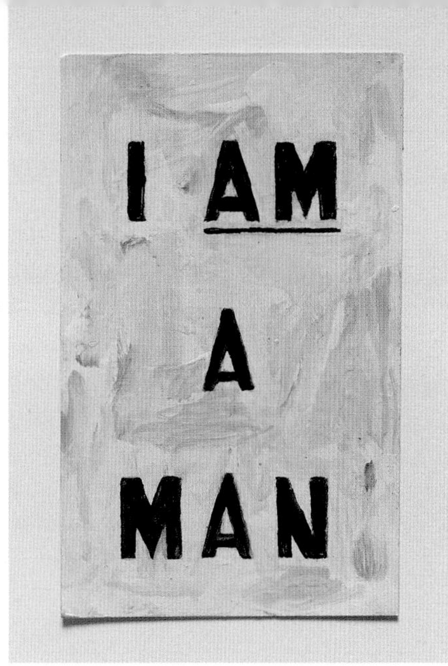

Figure 24.9
Glenn Ligon, *Untitled*, 1988. Oil and enamel on paper, 8 × 5 in. (20.3 × 12.7 cm). Photography credit: Ronald Amstutz. © Glenn Ligon; Courtesy of the artist, Hauser & Wirth, New York, and Thomas Dane Gallery, London.

culated self-presentation for those in the know, was taken sometime in 2011 in the apartment of his friend and former teacher, the cultural critic Wayne Koestenbaum, who intended to use the snapshot as the basis for a painting.[27] Glenn agreed to introduce us via email, and Koestenbaum not only entertained my many questions but also sent me a few quick and dirty snaps of the work's recto and verso, which contains an inscription by the artist offering "this small imitation" to his friend and critic "as a gift with no particular occasion attached to it."[28]

Painted on board in acrylic just months after the "original" breakthrough work in oil, Koestenbaum's iteration of Ligon's *Untitled (I Am a Man)*—to my knowledge, never before mentioned, let alone reproduced in accounts of either the artist's career or the poster's—provides another opportunity to reframe the sign and its painted incarnation. Not only is the second version smaller, more postcard-like, and chromatically murkier than the first, but it also seems more rather than less gesturally expressive. Koestenbaum might even say swishy: in general, he averred during our conversation, when he engages Ligon's art, it becomes *gayer*.[29] This contention also begins to describe the complex ontological status of Koestenbaum's piece, which is at once a painting, a sign, an original, a copy, a miniature, a commodity, a collectible, a gift, and a souvenir. As Beard reminded me during our conversation, the work of the literary theorist Susan Stewart is helpful in this regard: Ligon's initial imitation of his own "I AM A MAN" painting can be seen as "a reduction in physical dimensions corresponding to an increase in significance, and as an interiorization of the exterior [that] . . . encapsulates the time of production."[30]

Such multiplicity testifies to the poster's—and the afrotrope's—functioning as both a didactic declaration and a site of dialogic engagement, in this case, articulating the links between "public" and "private" performances of self within gay networks and knowledge economies. My own privileged position within these circuits has made my research possible even as it further conditions our understanding of "I AM A MAN," which continues to be haunted by its queer pasts as well as its black futures. Perhaps unsurprisingly, given its visual punch and poignant declaration, which has made it an icon among graphic designers, the sign was taken up and appropriated for a variety of ends almost from the very first. Here I think of just four different versions of the many created in the first five years after the poster's appearance that can be found in the MSMC Archives: a photograph in which the Memphis labor leader Leamon Hood writes the phrase on a chalkboard; a union poster commemorating the strike that keeps the slogan but puts the focus on the actors; a version made in Atlanta for a similar protest that takes a slight typographic turn; and a bright red iteration copied after those made for the summer 1968 Poor People's March in Washington, DC, that was produced for profit by an outfit in San Francisco to appeal to its liberal customer base.[31] Conditions reporting, if you will, but not yet entirely accounted for given the poster's higher and even more highly commoditized profile in contemporary art and popular culture.

These days, the sign continues to undergo permutations, which have only increased in Memphis and elsewhere since the fiftieth anniversary of King's assassination in 2018 and, to be sure, with the rise of the internet, whether translated into Arabic and printed on a sign held up in Benghazi during the Arab Spring or visually checked by the rapper Jidenna in his 2015 video, *Classic Man*, shot by the artist Arthur Jafa.[32] These and any number of other deployments speak to the posters' currency in multiple senses, especially their increasing value and visibility as prized collectibles: in 2010, one of the "original" signs fetched more than $30,000 at a New York auction, at which news the lithographer Fred Wimmer could not but help lament that his studio no longer owns a single one of the posters that he helped produce, reiterating the storied logic through which signs of black bodies become sources of a pecuniary circuitry that ultimately leaves laboring subjects out of the loop.[32] Not unrelatedly, while the National Civil Rights Museum in Memphis, built around the Lorraine Motel where King was assassinated, makes frequent and anachronistic use of the *red* version of the sign first produced for the DC march in its displays and its gift shops, it owns no original posters either (Fig. 24.10).

In the American fine-art context, it is Ligon's afrotroping that has arguably sparked further engagements with the poster that continue to expand its subjective reach and its cultural capital. In 2008, Hank Willis Thomas

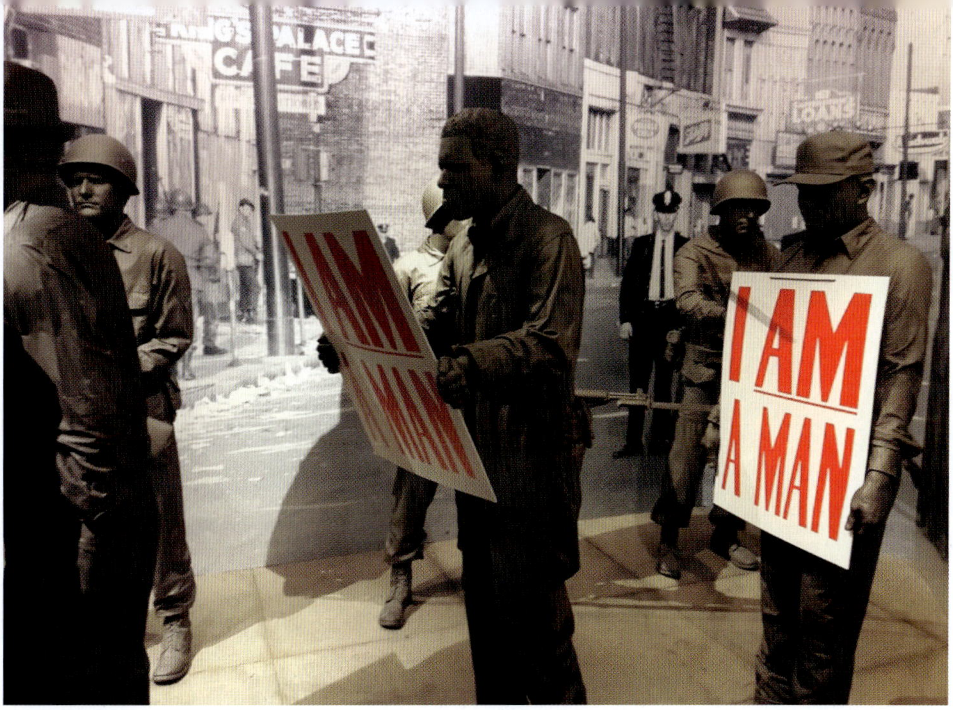

Figure 24.10
Installation View, National Civil Rights Museum, 2016. Photography by the author.

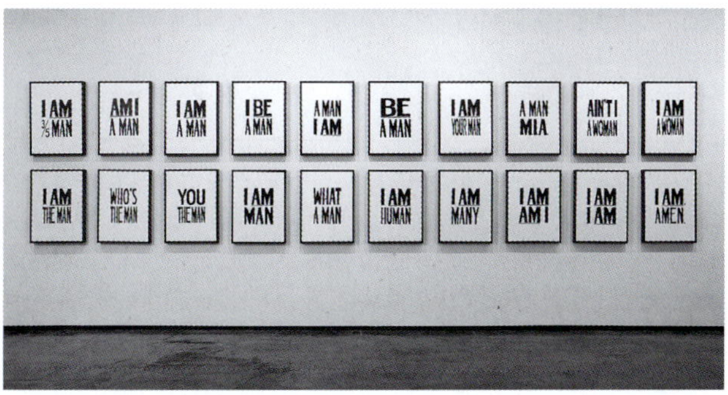

Figure 24.11
Hank Willis Thomas, *I AM A MAN*, 2009. Liquitex on canvas, 55 ½ × 228 × 2¼ in. installed, 25⅜ × 19¼ × 2¾ in. per panel. © Hank Willis Thomas. Courtesy of the artist and Jack Shainman Gallery, New York.

hired a sign painter to produce twenty canvases, each of which offers a different riff on the poster, together providing a historical traipse through the fraught construction of black subjectivities in the United States (Fig. 24.11). In 2009, Dred Scott would altogether negate the declaration in his New York street performance, which was intended to highlight both the ontological absence that is black manhood in the eyes of the state and the ongoing dereliction of black being. Shortly before, in 2005, Sharon Hayes had walked the streets of New York with her version of the sign as part of *In the Near Future*, a series of performative interventions recorded photographically and included in a slide installation that are meant to reiterate and hold onto the possibilities of public speech (Fig. 24.12).

Hayes's work is deeply instructive, in part, because it highlights questions of race as well as gender. The Yellins were a white couple, and the

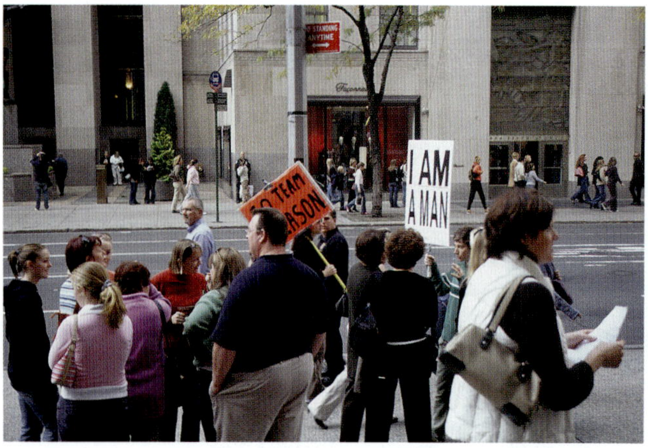

Figure 24.12a
Sharon Hayes, *In the Near Future*, detail, 2009. 35 mm multiple-slide-projection installation, 13 projections. Projection dimensions variable. Courtesy of the artist.

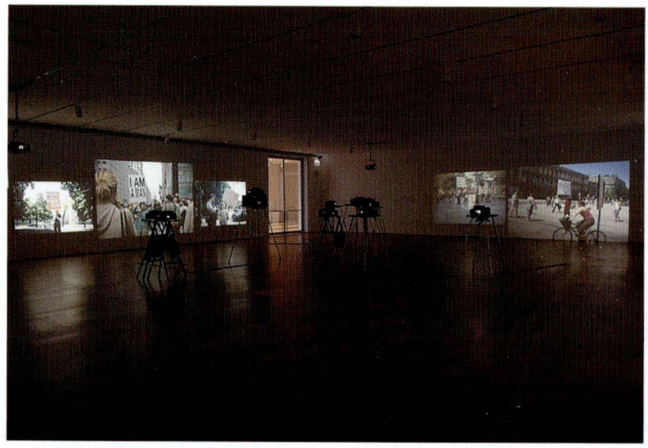

Figure 24.12b
Installation view of *In the Near Future*, Art Institute of Chicago, November 10, 2011–March 11, 2012. Courtesy of the artist.

film *At the River I Stand* records a few seemingly Euro-American men and women on the picket lines. More glaring is the film, the book, and the Memphis archive's slighting of the vital contributions of black women, both to the lives of the sign and to the success of the strike. In the Memphis archives, little heed is paid to the work of the organizer Maxine Smith, to the complex role of Gwen Aswumb, the only (white) woman on the city council, let alone to the sole woman on the left in Withers's iconic photograph, who inducts us into the scene and whom my colleague and former student Nana Adusei-Poku has, with a fair amount of sleuthing, tentatively identified as the activist and public school teacher Ann Hall Weathers.[33] Consider, finally, one woman's handmade transformation of the poster; in most reproductions of this photograph, her addition of "wo" before "MAN" is hard to see but nonetheless captured, as if to proleptically telegraph black women's fading within initial histories of the strike for decades. However, in recent prints by the original photographer Builder Levy, her words, visage, and intentions make a clear visual claim both to the past and on our present (Fig. 24.13).

There has been a shift in the historiography and the commemoration of the strike since 2005, in part due to Steve Estes's book, *I Am a Man: Race, Manhood, and the Civil Rights Movement*, which was published that same year. Moving beyond the Memphis archives to those stored at the Ralph Bunche Oral History Project in Washington, DC, Estes freshly brings into view the contributions not only of Smith, but of Fannie Lou Hamer, Hazel McGhee, and Cornelia Crenshaw, who founded the Concerned Citizens group that passed around those Loeb-labeled trash bags, made sandwiches, and both materially and emotionally supported the strikers and their families.[34] There

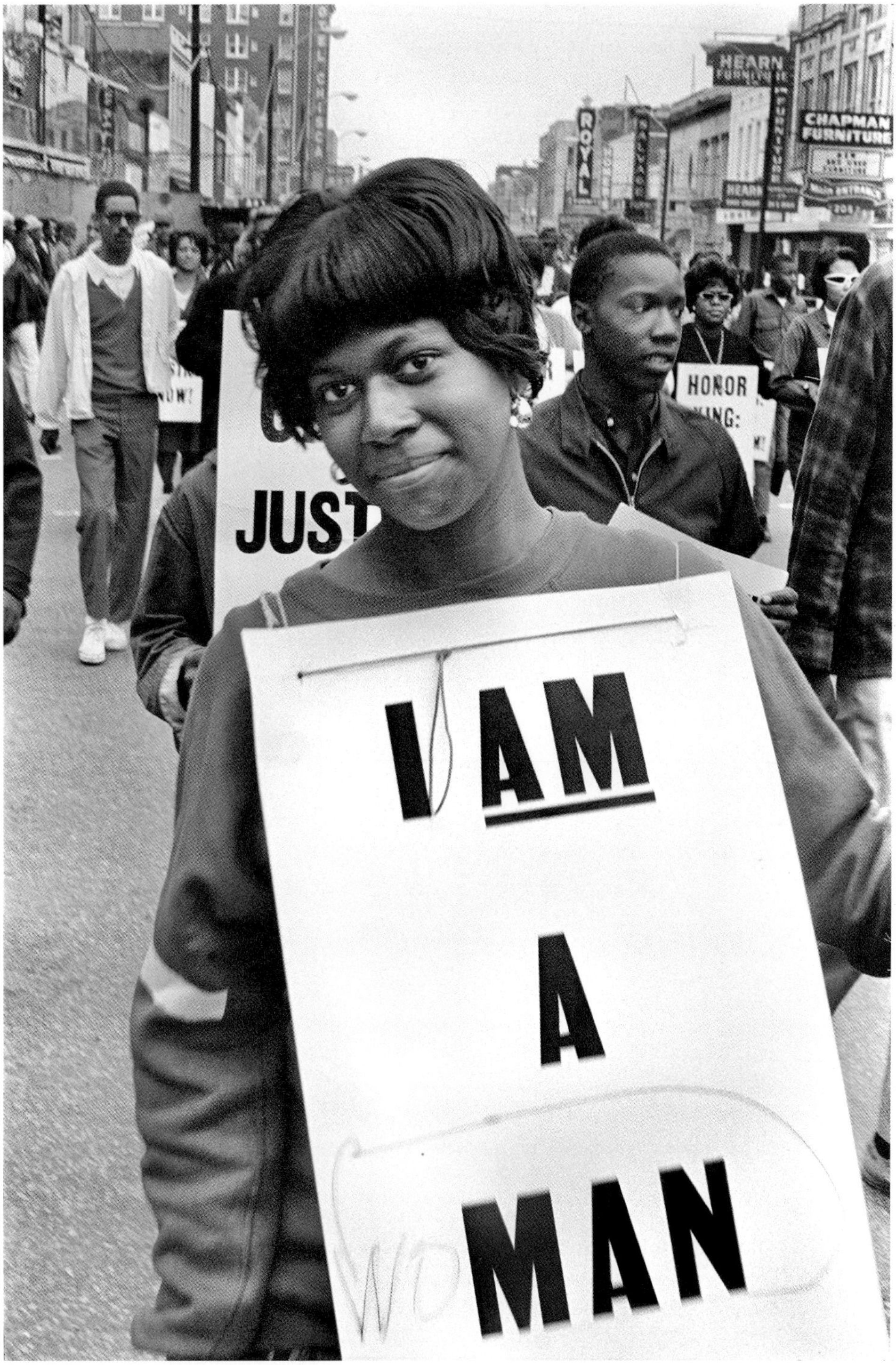

Figure 24.13

Builder Levy, *Photography of Unidentified Female Protester*, April 8, 1968. Gold toned silver and photographic gelatin on photographic paper, image: $12\frac{15}{16} \times 8\frac{5}{8}$ in. (32.9 × 21.9 cm); sheet: $13\frac{15}{16} \times 10\frac{7}{8}$ in. (35.4 × 27.6 cm). Collection of the Smithsonian National Museum of African American History and Culture; gift of Arnika Dawkins and the Arnika Dawkins Gallery, 2017.43.2. © Builder Levy.

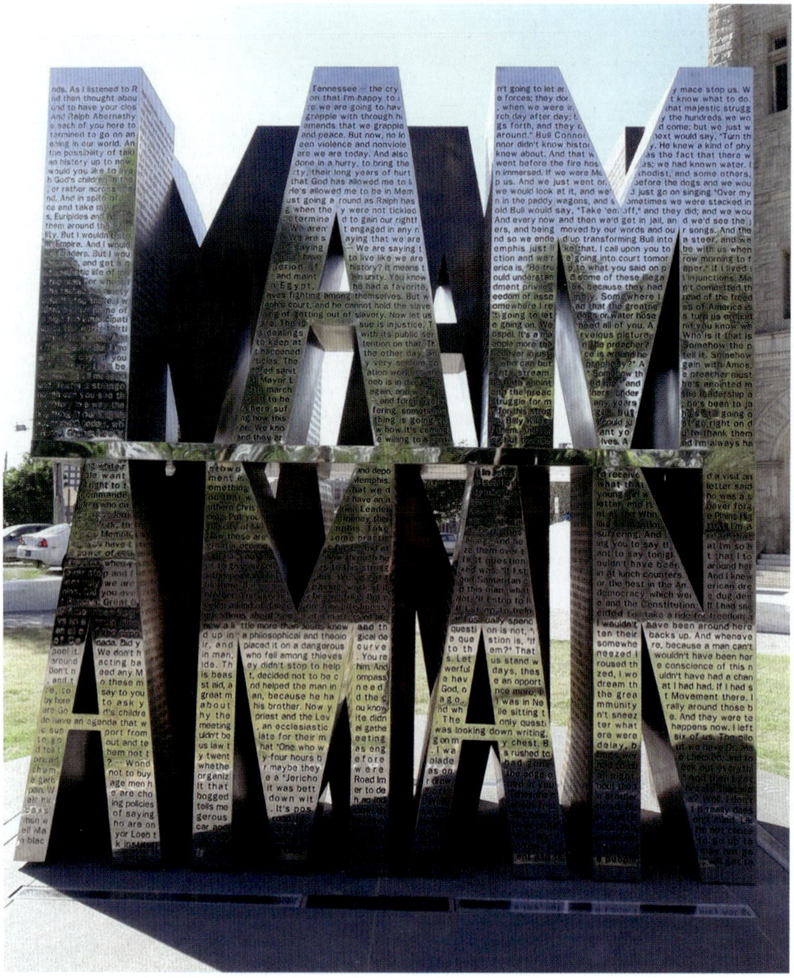

Figure 24.14
I AM A MAN monument, Memphis, Tennessee, 2018.

is now an elementary school named after Crenshaw, and her, McGhee's, and Smith's words are permanently inscribed in the walls of the plaza completed to celebrate the fiftieth anniversary of the strike, though it too ultimately takes its main sculptural form from the sign, which is perforated with words from King's famous "I've Been to the Mountaintop" speech, delivered shortly before his assassination (Fig. 24.14).

Ligon's *Condition Report* comes to us as a work entangled in these histories, though perhaps the most salient aspect of the artist's work with the sign, which, to my knowledge, has gone completely unremarked, is what his and the camera's eyes consistently leave out (Fig. 24.15): that is, the colophon at the bottom of the poster, which, instead of being the creation of a lone painter in his studio, insists on the sign's belonging to a vexed history

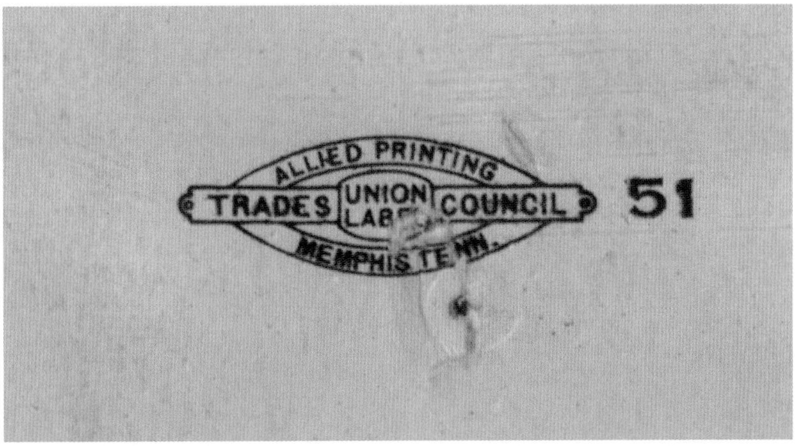

Figure 24.15
I AM A MAN poster, detail, 1968.

of labor, unionization, and collective action in the streets on the part of subjects who made a claim for rights in order to preserve black being in the only terms, those of "manhood," that might be heard and in some measure respected. And it is other images, histories, and subjects, other gestures of refusal and celebration made, as Hartman might say, by "colored girls assembled in a riotous manner," to which we must attend if we are to continue rethinking and expanding the aesthetic beyond the purview of Western art history (Fig. 24.16).[35]

For its part, the *Report* insistently symptomatizes its own moment of arrival: unstilled, in process, and on the move, the work can be considered what the art historian David Joselit would call a "transitive" object, "defined by [its] circulation from place to place and [its] subsequent translation into new contexts."[36] At the Hammer, the *Report* hung between a Rirkrit Tiravanija *Demonstration Drawing* focused on the Rodney King uprising and Nayland Blake's *Dual Restraint* of 1990, a curatorial move intended to bring out and crosswire various histories of resistance to institutionalized racial violence. However, the risk of such an approach and of the work itself, as intimated by the displacement of women's and workers' narratives in *At the River I Stand*, is that the *Report* comes to reproduce discursive and economic divides, standing in for and covering over the material specificity of its referent. In bringing together the disparate iterations of the sign, we can not only expand art history's brief but also measure the distance between material permutation and on-the-ground conditions in real time? This is what it means to attune ourselves afrotropically, to those sights and sensibilities on the edges of the given. I think doing so means looking forward and back, through and beyond, toward imaging a collective politics of the present.

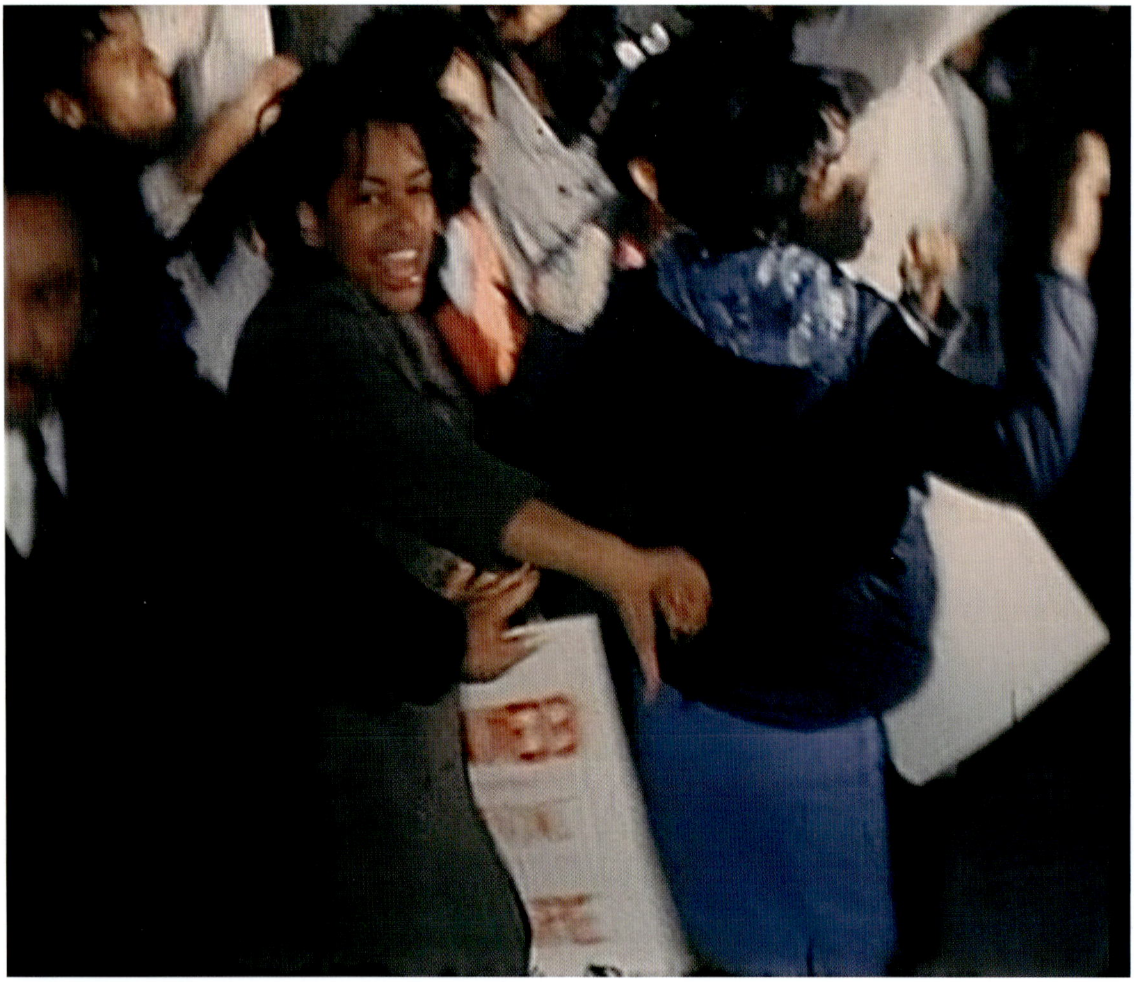

Figure 24.16
David Appleby, Allison Graham, and Steven Ross, *At the River I Stand*, still, 1993.

Notes

This article emerged from a talk first delivered in May 2014 at the "Acts of Politics and Becoming" symposium organized by Rhea Anastas and Anne Ellegoode at the Hammer Museum, https://www.youtube.com/watch?v=SIsPb5Xwcy4. In the intervening years, my research and thinking have been encouraged by the comments of Sampada Aranke, Gwendolyn DuBois Shaw, Hannah Feldman, Sharon Hayes, David Kim, Amy Mooney, Michael W. Phillips, and Krista Thompson, as well as by audiences at Carnegie Mellon University, L'Institut national de l'histoire de l'art, Johns Hopkins University, Musée du quai Branly, Princeton University, Stanford University, the University of Pennsylvania, and the University of the Western Cape; they all have my thanks. I owe special notes of appreciation to Gerald Chaudron and his team at the University of Memphis and to the artists engaged in these pages, above all, Glenn Ligon, whose work continues to set me flowing.

1 Saidiya Hartman, *Lose Your Mother: A Journey Along the Atlantic Slave Route* (Farrar, Straus & Giroux, 2008).

2 Scott Rothkopf, *Glenn Ligon: AMERICA* (Whitney Museum of American Art and Yale University Press, 2011), 19.

3 See Huey Copeland, *Bound to Appear: Art, Slavery. and the Site of Blackness in Multicultural America* (University of Chicago Press, 2013).

4 Nathaniel Mackey, *Discrepant Engagement: Dissonance, Cross-Culturality, and Experimental Writing* (Cambridge University Press, 1993), 7.

5 Kobena Mercer, "Reading Racial Fetishism: The Photographs of Robert Mapplethorpe," in *Welcome to the Jungle: New Positions in Black Cultural Studies* (Routledge, 1999), 171-219.

6 Reva Wolf, *Andy Warhol, Poetry, and Gossip in the 1960s* (University of Chicago Press, 1997). My "autoethnographic expansion" has been guided by the methodology of E. Patrick Johnson, *Appropriating Blackness: Performance and the Politics of Authenticity* (Duke University Press, 2003).

7 Johanna Burton and Anne Ellegood, eds., *Take It or Leave It: Institution, Image, Ideology* (Prestel, 2014).

8 On Dudley, see Joe Hannan, "Safeguarding Modern Art," *MoMA* 4, no. 6 (July-August 2001): 34-35; on museum conservation practices more broadly, see Nathan Stolow, "Conservation Policy and the Exhibition of Museum Collections," *Journal of the American Institute for Conservation* 16, no. 2 (February 1977): 12-20.

9 Richard Meyer, "Light It Up, Or How Glenn Ligon Got Over," *Artforum* 44, no. 9 (May 2006), https://www.artforum.com/features/light-it-up-or-how-glenn-ligon-got-over-173983/.

10 Huey Copeland, "Untitled (Jackpot!)," in *Glenn Ligon: Some Changes*, exh. cat. (Power Plant, 2005), 123 [reprinted in this volume, 27-40].

11 Steve Estes, *I Am a Man! Race, Manhood, and the Civil Rights Movement* (University of North Carolina Press, 2005), 136.

12 Cedric Robinson, *Black Marxism: The Making of the Black Radical Tradition* (1983; University of North Carolina Press, 2000), xxx.

13 Richard Lentz, *Symbols, the News Magazines, and Martin Luther King* (Louisiana State University Press, 1990), 273.

14 Robbie Brown, "Civil Rights Photographer Unmasked as Informer," *New York Times*, September 13, 2010, https://www.nytimes.com/2010/09/14/us/14photographer.html.

15 On fading or aphanisis, see Jonathan Scott Lee, *Jacques Lacan* (University of Massachusetts Press, 1991).

16 See Huey Copeland and Krista Thompson, "Afrotropes: A User's Guide," *Art Journal* 76, no. 3 (Fall 2017): 7–9; Leah Dickerman, David Joselit, and Mignon Nixon, "Afrotropes: A Conversation with Huey Copeland and Krista Thompson," *October* 162 (Fall 2017): 3–18.

17 See Copeland, "Untitled (Jackpot!)," 144n9.

18 Christina Knight, "Performing Passage: Contemporary Artists Stage the Slave Trade" (PhD diss., Harvard University, 2013), 147.

19 Bordowitz, *Untitled (I Am a Man)*, 82.

20 Hannah Feldman, "'The Eye of History': Photojournalism, Protest, and the *Manifestation* of 17 October 1961," in *From a Nation Torn: Decolonizing Art and Representation in France, 1945–1962* (Duke University Press, 2014), 159–99.

21 Laurie B. Green, "Challenging the Civil Rights Narrative: Women, Gender, and the 'Politics of Protection,'" in *Civil Rights History from the Ground Up: Local Struggles, A National Movement*, ed. Emily Crosby (University of Georgia Press, 2011), 52–79.

22 Joan Beifuss, *At the River I Stand: Memphis, the 1968 Strike, and Martin Luther King* (St. Luke's Press, 1990).

23 Memphis Search for Meaning Committee Records, MSS.178, Container 9, Folder 69, Preservation and Special Collections Department, University Libraries, University of Memphis.

24 Gregg Bordowitz, *Glenn Ligon: Untitled (I Am a Man)* (Afterall, Central Saint Martins, University of the Arts, 2018), 38.

25 Beifuss, *At the River I Stand*, 12.

26 Nicholas Kemp, "Thomas Beard Joins the Film Society as Programmer at Large," *FilmInc Daily*, December 9, 2015, https://www.filmlinc.org/daily/thomas-beard-joins-the-film-society-as-programmer-at-large/.

27 Thomas Beard, in conversation with the author, November 13, 2016.

28 Wayne Koestenbaum, in conversation with the author, January 19, 2017.

29 Wayne Koestenbaum, "Color Me Glenn," in *Glenn Ligon: Some Changes*, 93–97.

30 Susan Stewart, *On Longing: Narratives of the Miniature, the Gigantic, the Souvenir, the Collection* (Duke University Press, 1992), 143.

31 Memphis Search for Meaning Committee Records, MSS.178, Container 52, Folder 6, Preservation and Special Collections Department, University Libraries, University of Memphis.

32 Thomas L. Friedman, "'I Am a Man,'" *New York Times*, May 14, 2011, https://www.nytimes.com/2010/09/14/us/14photographer.html.

33 Michael Lollar, "'I Am a Man' Poster Nets $34,000," *Commercial Appeal*, February 26, 2010, https://www.pressreader.com/usa/the-commercial-appeal/20100226/281638186363960.

34 Nana Adusei-Poku, *Taking Stakes in the Unknown: Tracing Post-Black Art* (Transcript Verlag, 2021), 54.

35 Estes, *I Am a Man!*, 135; Green, "Challenging the Civil Rights Narrative," 76.

36 Saidiya Hartman, "The Anarchy of Colored Girls Assembled in a Riotous Manner," *South Atlantic Quarterly* 117, no. 3 (July 2018): 465–90.

37 David Joselit, "Painting Beside Itself," *October* 130 (Fall 2009): 128.

25

TAKING CARE

Huey Copeland and Allison Glenn on *Promise, Witness, Remembrance,* Introduction by Huey Copeland

Over the past year, American museums have been forced to consider how they might address antiblack violence and center marginalized voices, especially when their collecting, exhibitionary, and outreach practices have historically abetted rather than challenged the social reproduction of white supremacy. While any number of institutions have made statements or proposed changes, the exhibition Promise, Witness, Remembrance *at the Speed Art Museum in Louisville, Kentucky—organized in honor of Breonna Taylor, whose murder at the hands of Louisville police on March 13, 2020, eventually spurred nationwide protests—offers a timely, local, and pointed curatorial response to some of the most pressing questions facing cultural institutions today. To better understand how museums might reframe notions of audience, value, and the politics of belonging from an intersectional perspective,* Artforum *invited contributing editor Huey Copeland and the exhibition's curator, Allison Glenn, to speak about the show's emergence and ambitions a few weeks before its June 6 closing.*

Huey Copeland: Allison, I thought I'd start by asking how you came to organize this exhibition: In what ways did the process of making it demand a rethinking of your approach to curatorial practice and your understanding of the roles museums can play within contemporary cultural discourse?

Allison Glenn: This is a really great question. I was invited by the director of the Speed Museum, Stephen Reily, who sent me an email outlining the project as he saw it, and letting me know that if I took this on, I'd be working closely with [Breonna Taylor's mother] Tamika Palmer as a key stakeholder. That made it clear to me that the museum's priorities were in line. I had a few meetings with Stephen and the team at the Speed, and it became clear very quickly that the museum had a lot of ambition for the project.

This interview first appeared in *Artforum* 59, no. 8 (Summer 2021): 186–91.

An exhibition is one moment, it's temporal, and it cannot hold everything. So I wanted to align with Tamika Palmer and understand what she thought the exhibition could do, what it could mean for her and her daughter's legacy. And Ms. Palmer is very clear. She is very generous. She is very kind, and she is very clear on what she wants. I developed the exhibition's three sections from a text message she sent me. She didn't say, "Promise, witness, remembrance," but I inferred those terms from her message, and they became the title of the exhibition and the curatorial framework.

At the same time, I began building a national panel of advisers. I knew I needed a kind of cabinet of people I could trust, who I could be vulnerable with, who could point out blind spots, and who knew me and my practice. I was very sensitive to the fact that I don't live in Louisville. I'm not from Louisville. And I wanted to create this framework of solidarity. The national panel was a way of saying, "We, on a national level, stand in solidarity with you." I respect the city and what it's gone through so much that I'm not going to show up as just me. I'm going to stand in concert with a group of people that have dealt with these issues before. I invited the artists Theaster Gates and Hank Willis Thomas, as well as La Keisha Leek, whose cousin is Trayvon [Martin]. We had worked together on some projects in Chicago when La Keisha was working through her understanding of Trayvon's murder and how to respond to it. And then I asked a friend in town, Raymond Green, whose cousin is Alton Sterling, to join. And it just kept building.

So I had a combination of artists who had responded to the intersecting pandemics of gun violence and police brutality and private citizens who lost loved ones to those epidemics. Arguably George Zimmerman is an extension of the state. So that is state-sanctioned violence against Black people. And I wanted an art historian who has a history with critical race studies and art of the global south.

Copeland: So that's how Allison Young came on.

Glenn: Yes.

Copeland: It's interesting to hear how the project unfolded, and revelatory in terms of thinking about what the key components of this kind of exhibition are. One being: There has to be institutional will from the get-go. And then there has to be a real understanding and engagement with the communities and the people impacted by the events or issues the show explores. I really loved the way you insist not only on your alignment in solidarity with Ms. Palmer, and this community of activists and thinkers, but also the way you emphasize producing another kind of collective through this advisory panel that is brought into conversation with other kinds of discursive networks and groups that you're building on the ground. So in many ways, *Promise, Witness, Remembrance* seems to model, in both form and content, a Black feminist ethos of care in cultural production. I wonder if you would situate this show within that tradition?

Glenn: Absolutely. It's important to note that the entire exhibition was led by black women: me, the Speed's community engagement strategist Toya Northington, Tamika Palmer, her lawyer, Lonita Baker. Amy Sherald has been a very important force. The co-acquisition of her portrait of Breonna Taylor by the Speed and the Smithsonian will have a positive impact on the Louisville community (Fig. 25.1). And of course Breonna Taylor herself is at the center of this conversation. And the Louisville protests were led by Black women.

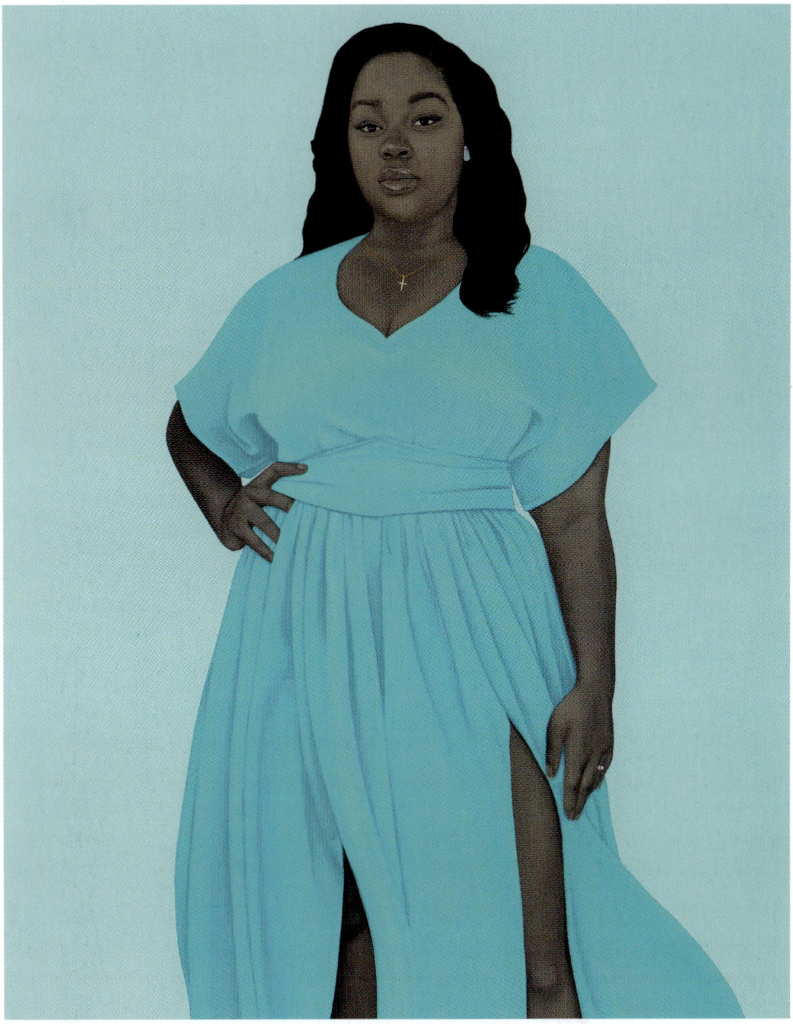

Figure 25.1
Amy Sherald, *Breonna Taylor*, 2020. Oil on linen, 137.16 × 109.22 × 6.35 cm / 54 × 43 × 2½ in. Speed Museum and Smithsonian National Museum of African American History and Culture. © Amy Sherald. Courtesy the artist and Hauser & Wirth. Photo: Joseph Hyde.

There is definitely a culture of care. The reason we worked so closely with the Louisville steering committee, and the national panel, and Ms. Palmer is that there's too much at stake. There were too many ways to get it wrong, and we needed to get it right. And I would say that situating it within this larger framework is a radical act of decentering that not only decenters the institution but also decenters my voice. So through this act of creating community, of calling people in, you in fact center them. A great example of this is deinstalling the Dutch and Flemish collection, the collection the museum is known for internationally. There was one artist on the Louisville steering committee who is probably of my mother's generation. And she said she used to go to the Speed Museum in the original building, before they built the contemporary wing. She said she never saw art by people who look like her, that she didn't feel that work by people who look like her or of people who look like her was valuable, because it wasn't in the space. That's the impact of decentering (Fig. 25.2).

Another example is, when I presented the proposal to Tamika Palmer for consideration, I told her I knew that we needed to include a timeline of her daughter's life to tie the exhibition together. And I said, "I'm not the person to write it," and she said, "Oh, I'll write it" (Fig. 25.3). She wrote a text on the walls of the gallery in which Amy Sherald's portrait is installed and therefore became the authorial and the authoritative voice in that space. During the installation, there were discussions regarding whether or not we should include a label to contextualize the tone of the timeline, as the institutional voice is very different than a mother's voice about her daughter's life. There were good points for and against didactics. I felt strongly that we did need to put up a label to tell people why we've given space to Tamika Palmer. That is not decentering. Decentering is giving the space. The team ultimately understood the importance and impact and agreed.

Copeland: I think it's so important that the decentering also enables a shifting of how we understand economies of value, particularly in the context of the museum. And I think in making this kind of collective—that is democratized, that is led by Black women and that gives Black women priority in terms of their position in relationship to Breonna and this history and this moment—it really starts to question how we think about the processes of valuation and devaluation that the museum represents and how we can disrupt those by doing this work of decentering. That also involves the centering of different kinds of voices. I love that the show includes this range of contributors, from local activists to internationally renowned artists. And of course, Ms. Palmer. There's also this huge variety of contemporary visual modes, from street photography to abstract painting. So I wonder, how did your ambitions for the show shape the selection of works?

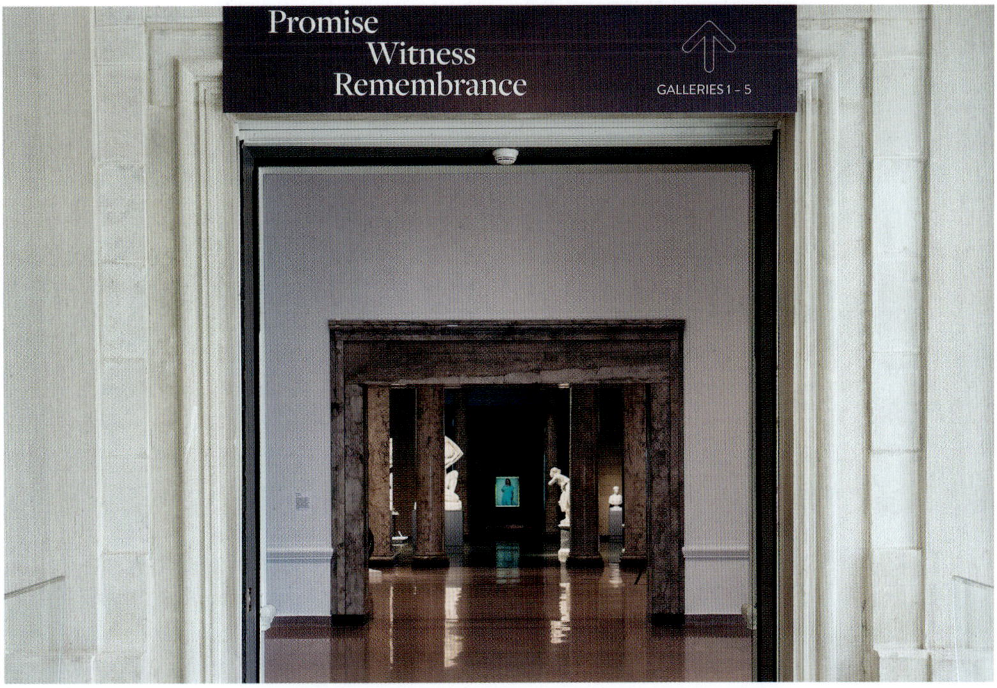

Figure 25.2
Promise, Witness, Remembrance, installation view at Speed Art Museum, 2021. © Bill Roughen. Courtesy of Speed Art Museum.

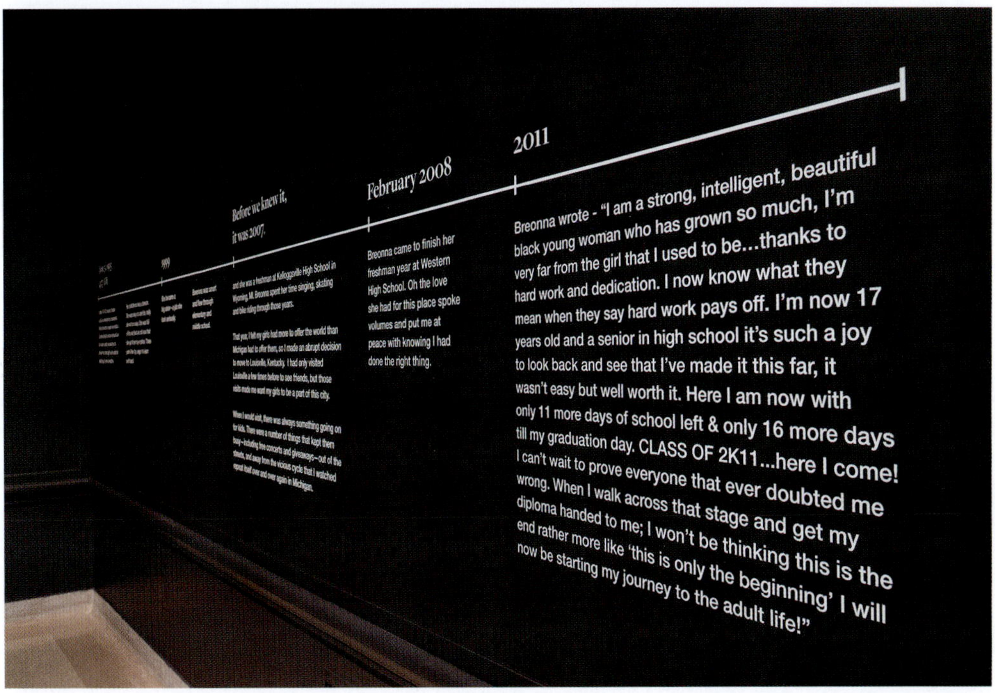

Figure 25.3
Promise, Witness, Remembrance, installation view at Speed Art Museum, 2021. © Bill Roughen. Courtesy of Speed Art Museum.

Glenn: At first I wanted to take up space—I knew I was interested in works that had a sense of scale. We were dealing with 22-foot ceilings, terrazzo floors, marble doorways, these kind of regal spaces. And I wanted to think about what it might be to occupy that space physically with, for example, Terry Adkins's sculpture *Muffled Drums* (from *Darkwater* [2003]). I also knew that many people who saw the show would be visiting the museum for the first time. And it would be people who probably didn't feel very welcome in institutionalized spaces. If you're not going to those spaces regularly, you're going to feel uncomfortable because they're not legible. They're in fact quite illegible and inaccessible. I want you to feel that you know where you're going and that if you get lost, you'll have an anchor. That's what led to the decision to hang the portrait of Breonna so that it's directly in your line of sight when you enter the museum. Although it's the first thing you see when you enter the exhibition space, it's part of the show's closing section, "Remembrance," which memorializes those lost to police brutality and gun violence.

But let me back up a little bit and talk about the "Promise" section. What I wanted to do there was provide a framework through which to understand the rest of the exhibition. That section is meant to drive home the truth we all know—that the United States was founded on horrible inequities, and the inefficacies of our system are inherently indebted to that founding.

I wanted to borrow from these tropes of nationalism, because I think we're in a moment where we're dealing with a lot of tropes of nationalism and of democracy, yet still living in a space that does not feel democratic. And then the decision to also have framing devices. There are works by Hank Willis Thomas in both the "Promise" section (where we installed *15,433* and *19,281*, two flags whose stars represent those killed by gun violence in America in 2019 and 2020, respectively) and in the "Remembrance" section (which includes his neon sculpture *Remember Me* [2014]). So that's how "Promise" unfolded.

Artists help us understand the contemporary moment. In the "Witness" section, you'll see a mixture of works that are timely yet enduring. We're in the midst of a global pandemic. Breonna Taylor's family has not gotten the justice they seek. This section was also an opportunity to present the work that had happened during the protest, which was really important to Ms. Palmer. These galleries include artworks that respond to this moment, as well as other moments of conflict, change, and unrest in the twentieth and twenty-first centuries.

The steering committee built this incredible spreadsheet of photographers who had been at the protest. I chose five for inclusion in the show. Breonna Taylor's story includes all of these people around it, and I wanted to honor those people, including the many that were lost to gun violence, such as Tyler Gerth, one of the five photographers. He was shot and killed at the protest. The show was the first posthumous exhibition of his work. I worked with his sisters to select the images. Jon Cherry, a local photographer, had a portrait in the show of Travis Nagdy, a young man who found his voice in the movement. He was meeting with elected officials and had found his path. And he was shot and killed in an unrelated incident. Of course, I wanted to include a Black woman photographer. T. A. Yero took some very powerful photographs (Fig. 25.4).

I hung the photographs in a linear way to create this tight timeline. The first is from what would have been Breonna's twenty-seventh birthday. The last was the portrait of Travis Nagdy. And it's on the same plane as the portrait of Breonna. So you look in the second gallery, and you see Travis, and you see Breonna kind of in the distance. It was very intentional to pair those two portraits. I also chose to hang them tight and horizontal knowing that *Muffled Drums* was going to have such height. I wanted to have the horizontal timeline of photographs intersect with it. *Muffled Drums* commemorates [W. E. B.] Du Bois organizing one of the first Black-led protests for Black lives.

Copeland: The silent protest parade in 1917.

Glenn: Exactly. He organized it with the NAACP. I wanted to create a historical framework of a century of protest for Black lives and to highlight the impact of these protests nationally and globally.

Copeland: In the context of this national, global quote-unquote reckoning, which has brought such scrutiny to modern culture's ongoing expropriation and waste of Black lives in these spectacular ways, many institutions are finding themselves at a crossroads. Some are planning exhibitions like *Promise, Witness, Remembrance*. Of course, those shows and the decolonial gestures they stand for are temporary, even though what this kind of exhibition does is open a radically new, expansive framework for museums to understand what they do. And I guess part of the question is: How does that then become something that is institutionalized as part of the museum's identity and your understanding of your own curatorial practice?

Glenn: Great question. I mean, I realized that this project reaffirmed for me that I am most successful working close to the ground with diverse publics. That's not only where my strength is; that's also where my heart is. That's where the work feels rewarding. It's challenging institutions to radically rethink the way they present ideas through exhibitions, through solo projects, through conversations, and continuing to imagine worlds where this kind of terror doesn't exist.

Copeland: Maybe we can close by discussing what your understanding of success is, because I think it's so telling and useful for thinking about what it is that we want the space of the aesthetic and the museum and the cultural to be.

Glenn: Well, when working in consultation and conversation and collaboration, often success exists outside commonly held registers. I think for any project that seeks to bring people in, there's going to be a collective imagining and redefining of what success is. For me, the most important thing, the successful moment in this exhibition, was that Tamika Palmer was pleased. She said she felt the exhibition was a blessing and that she felt peaceful walking into the space and seeing Breonna's portrait and her timeline—I'm paraphrasing her. She felt seen and she felt heard. That, to me, was the greatest success.

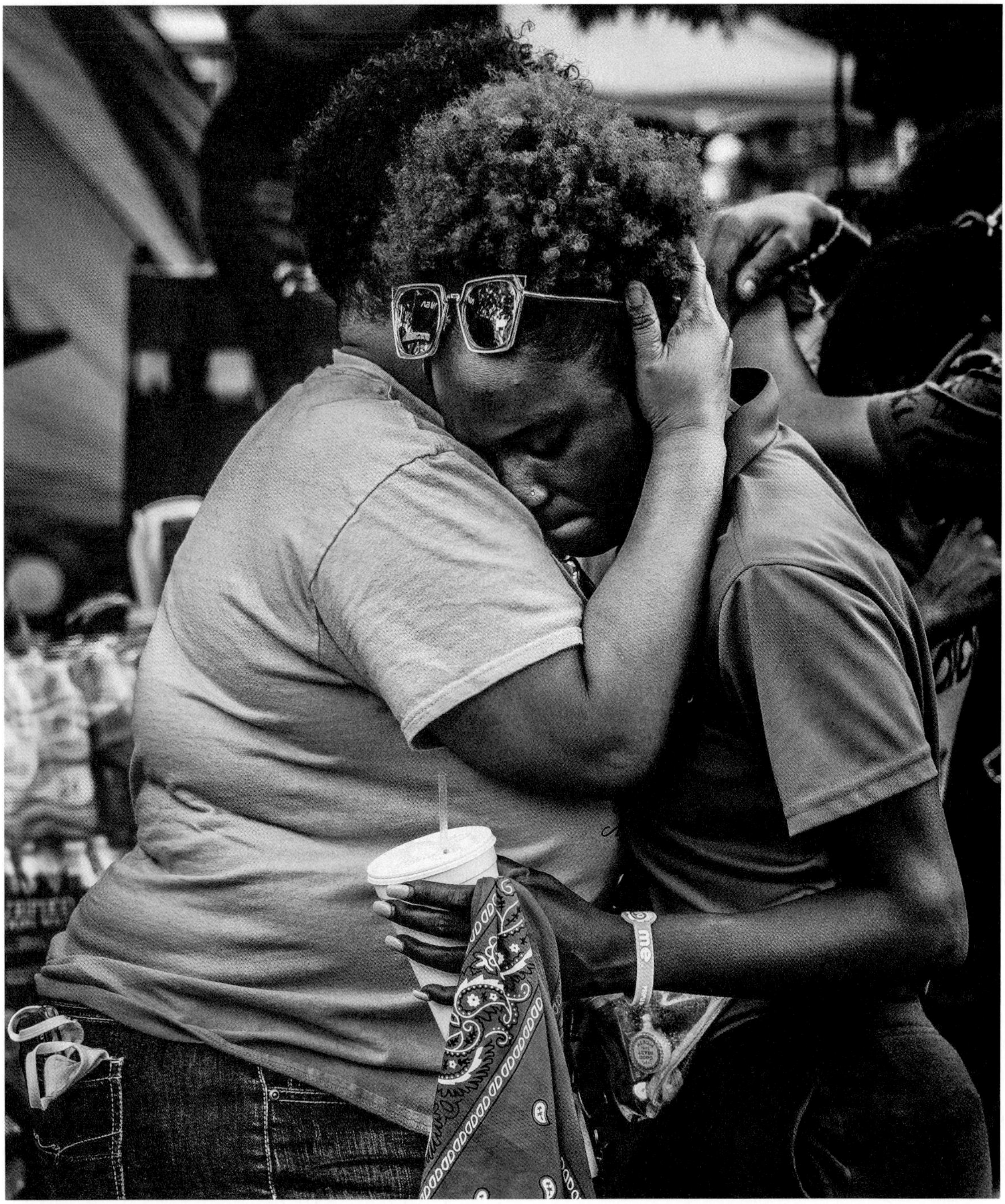

Figure 25.4

T. A. Yero, *Healing*, June 15, 2020, 7:41 p.m., Breonna Taylor Memorial at Jefferson Square Park, Louisville, KY (printed 2021). Giclée print on Hahnemuhle rag paper.

ACKNOWLEDGMENTS

I first want to thank the contemporary artists whose work appears within and animates this volume: Laylah Ali, Edgar Arceneaux, Elizabeth Axtman, Dawoud Bey, Michael Ray Charles, Barbara Chase-Riboud, Gregg Conde, Harry Gamboa Jr., Theaster Gates, Renée Green, Alicia Hall Moran, David Hammons, Thomas Allen Harris, Lyle Ashton Harris, David Hartt, Sharon Hayes, Derek Jackson, Rashid Johnson, Jason Lazarus, Builder Levy, Cary Loren, Kerry James Marshall, Paul McCarthy, Dave McKenzie, Julie Mehretu, Wangechi Mutu, Kori Newkirk, Mendi + Keith Obadike, Clifford Owens, Mai-Thu Perret, Howardena Pindell, Adrian Piper, Betye Saar, Jim Shaw, Amy Sherald, Lorna Simpson, Cauleen Smith, Mickalene Thomas, Kara Walker, Carrie Mae Weems, William T. Williams, Hank Willis Thomas, Fred Wilson and T. A. Yero. A special note of appreciation is due to my fearless artistic and intellectual collaborators—Hilton Als, Mark Bradford, Allison Glenn, Thelma Golden, Zoe Leonard, Jared Sexton, Frank B. Wilderson III, and especially Glenn Ligon—whose words, work, and wisdom have both shaped my practice and expanded my horizons.

This stellar cast of interlocutors could not have been gathered in this form without the efforts of staffs at archives, estates, foundations, galleries, licensing agencies, museums, presses, publications, and studios across the nation, all of which have my thanks. I am especially grateful for Victoria Barry at the University of Chicago Press, Sophie Jones at Art Resources, and Daniel Trujillo at Artists Rights New York, as well as for the diligent research assistance I received over the past eight years from Sarah Estrela, Richelle Kota, Tabitha Love, and Miriam Said. The volume would be unimaginable in its current form without the eagle-eyed appraisal of its earliest reader, Lauren Taylor, or the joyful persistence of its final compilers, Janina López and Emma C. Roberts, treasured colleagues at the University of Pittsburgh who have my deepest respect and appreciation. *Touched by the Mother* began under the editorial aegis of the legendary Susan Bielstein—"Just the pearls, Huey!"—and arrives in your hands thanks to the stewardship of Karen Levine, an executive editor who actually edits! The book's production and robust image program were funded by my Andrew W. Mellon Chair at the University of Pittsburgh, the University of Pennsylvania, and the 2017 Absolut Art Writing Award.

While many of these contributions open with words of gratitude, a few more are needed to honor those who mattered to the making of this book. Foremost, I thank Hortense Spillers, whose transformative praxis gives *Touched by the Mother* its title as well as its ethical orientation toward black feminist futures. Equally key have been the tireless advocacy and inimitable examples of Mary Copeland, Saidiya Hartman, and Anne M. Wagner; the treasured and trenchant engagement of my fellow travelers Sampada Aranke, Hannah Feldman, Amy Mooney, and sister-girl Krista A. Thompson; and the beloved communities of mentors, peers, and students, past and present, of which they are part. Among them are Nana Adusei-Poku, Rhea Anastas, Kader Attia, Naomi Beckwith, Daniel Birnbaum, Garrett Bradley, Rizvana Bradley, Julia Bryan-Wilson, Johanna Burton, Antawan Byrd, Tina Campt, Emma Chubb, Jasmine Cobb, John Corbett, Sharon Corwin, Romi Crawford, Janet Dees, Penelope Deutscher, Grace Deveney, Aaron Deyonker, Leah Dickerman, Claire Didier, André Dombrowski, Ryan Dohoney, Anthony Elms, Ntone Edjabe, Adrienne Edwards, Alex Fialho, Hal Foster, Chelsea Frazier, Henry Louis Gates Jr., Vanina Géré, Erin Gilbert, Faye R. Gleisser, Tim Griffin, Darcy Grimaldo Grigsby, Michael Hanchard, Jessica Horton, Arthur Jafa, Zakiyyah Iman Jackson, Steffani Jemison, Nathalie Joachim, E. Patrick Johnson, Kellie Jones, Athi Mongezeleli Joja, Terri Kapsalis, Arnold J. Kemp, David Kim, the late Koyo Kouoh, Michelle Kuo, Premesh Lalu, Anne Lafont, T. Jean Lax, Pamela M. Lee, Sarah Lewis, Sarah López, C. C. McKee, Eve Meltzer, Fred Moten, Steven Nelson, Rachel Grace Newman, Zita Nunes, Bibiana Obler, Chika Okeke-Agulu, Meg Onli, Tyrone Palmer, Richard J. Powell, Guy Ramsey, Kirk Savage, Elizabeth Schambelan, Gwendolyn DuBois Shaw, J. P. Sniadecki, Keeanga Yamahtta-Taylor, Hamza Walker, Michelle Wright, Hamed Yousefi, Elvan Zabunyan, and Mlondolozi Zondi.

I am also appreciative of the thought and consideration of audiences who offered useful feedback on the project as a whole at the Archives of American Art; the Center for Advanced Study in the Visual Arts; l'École des hautes études en sciences sociales, Paris; the Graduate Center, City University of New York; the High Museum of Art; New York University; Northwestern University; Rutgers, the State University of New Jersey; University College, London; the University of Arizona; the University of Maryland, College Park; the University of Notre Dame; and the University of Pennsylvania. A special note of thanks to my students and colleagues in History of Art and Architecture at the University of Pittsburgh, which I am honored to call my institutional home.

Even closer to heart, H. John Hair and his family have patiently supported this undertaking across four continents, three universities, two cities, and one Cora Jane Copeland Hair's singular life; Howie, I am blessed by your presence and deeply grateful for the life we have built together in the city of brotherly love. Rachel Copeland continues to be a steadfast supporter and hilarious heckler: thank you for keeping the faith and me humble, sissy. Ultimately, whatever wisdom can be gleaned from these pages was cultivated and deepened by the touch of my parents, Mary Towns and Huey G. Copeland I, whom I have been lucky to count as my kindest and most consistent reader. It is with him in mind that I dedicate this book to "Annie Mae and all her heirs."

Philadelphia

INDEX

Page numbers in italics refer to figures.